I 10 20

KT-177-201

THE ROUGH GUIDE TO
JAMAICA

This seventh edit
Lebawit Lily

C016625399

ROUGH
GUIDES

Contents

DOCTOR'S CAVE BEACH, MONTEGO BAY

Introduction to
Jamaica

Beautiful, brash Jamaica is much more than beaches and swaying palm trees. A sensual land of bright colours, soulful rhythms and unfailing creativity, the island retains an attitude – a personality – that's more resonant and distinctive than you'll find in any other Caribbean nation. There's certainly plenty of white sand and gin-clear sea to enjoy, but away from the coast are spectacular mountains and rivers, tumbling waterfalls and cactus-strewn savannah plains. This verdant natural environment forms the backdrop to a dynamic cultural history in the island's towns and cities, illustrated most vividly by the explosive reggae scene, but also in the powerful expression of its artwork and the startlingly original flavours of its national cuisine.

Jamaicans are justifiably proud of a rich musical heritage imitated the world over, as well as their incredible sporting successes on the running track and cricket pitch. This prominent and vibrant culture has left scarcely a corner of the world untouched – quite some feat, and out of all proportion to the island's relatively tiny size. In some respects it's a country with a swagger in its step, confident of its triumphs in the face of adversity, but also with a weight upon its shoulders. An unsparingly tough history has had to be reckoned with, and the country hasn't avoided familiar problems of development like dramatic wealth inequality and social tensions that occasionally spill over into localized violence and worldwide headlines. The mixture is potent, producing a people as renowned for being sharp, sassy and straight-talking as they are laidback and hip. People don't mince their words here; Jamaicans get on with life, and their directness can make them seem cantankerous, or even uncompromising or rude. Particularly around resort towns and the major attractions this can be taken to extremes at times, though the harassment of tourists that once bedevilled the island is much less noticeable these days.

REGGAE SUMFEST, MONTEGO BAY

The Jamaican authorities have spent millions making sure the island treats its tourists right, and as a foreign visitor, your chances of encountering any real trouble are minuscule. As the birthplace of the **all-inclusive** hotel, Jamaica has become well suited to tourists who want to head straight from plane to beach, never leaving their hotel compound. But to get any sense of the country at all, you'll need to do some exploring. It's undoubtedly worth it, as this is a place packed with first-class attractions and natural attributes, oozing with character. Jamaica's food and drink are one of the island's main draws, from a plate of grilled lobster served up by the sea to conch soup or jerk chicken from a roadside stall, not to mention a variety of rums and fine Blue Mountain coffee. And with a rich music scene at its clubs, sound-system parties and stageshows, if you're a reggae fan, you're in heaven.

Where to go

Most of Jamaica's tourist business is concentrated in the "big three" **resorts** of Montego Bay, Negril and Ocho Rios. A busy commercial city, **Montego Bay** has a string of hotels, bars and restaurants along its beach-lined tourist strip, and manicured golf courses and high-end all-inclusives hogging the coast to the east. West of here, its low-rise hotels slung along eleven kilometres of fantastic white sand and three

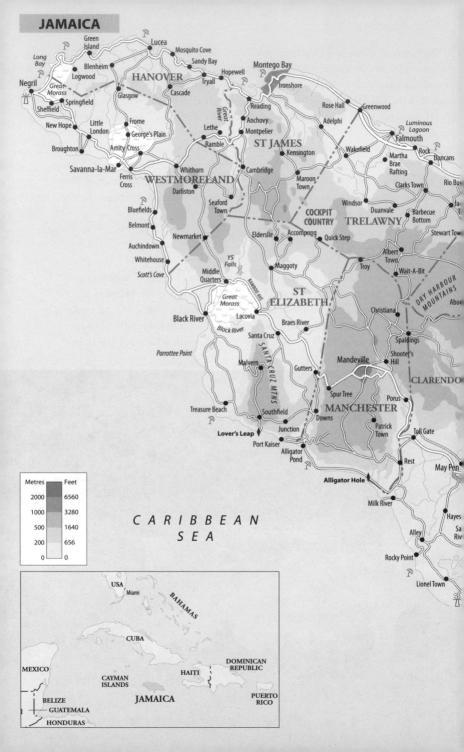

0   20
kilometres

–––– ––– Parish boundary

N

CARIBBEAN SEA

Discovery Bay
Runaway Bay
Priory
own's own
Sevilla la Nueva
St Ann's Bay
Philadelphia
Ocho Rios
Alexandria
Dunn's River Falls
Prospect Plantation
ST ANN
Nine Mile
Claremont
Albion
Golden Grove
Galina Point
Pedro
Fern Gully
Oracabessa
White River
Firefly
Cabarita Island
Moneague
Port Maria
Kellits
ST MARY
Robins Bay
Whitehall
Troja
Richmond
Annotto Bay
Linstead
Castleton
Chovey
Glengoffe
Bog Walk
Buff Bay
ST CATHERINE
Balcarres
Orange Bay
Colbeck
Hope Bay
Old Harbour
Spanish Town
ST ANDREW
PORTLAND
St. Margaret's Bay
Stony Hill
Wakefield
Somerset Falls
Freetown
Newcastle
Fruitful Vale
Rio Grande River
Port Antonio
Old Harbour Bay
BLUE MOUNTAINS
Winnifred
Port Esquivel
Portmore
Swift River
Little Goat Island
KINGSTON
Site of Nanny Town
Great Goat Island
Port Henderson
August Town
Boston Bay
HELLSHIRE HILLS
Port Royal
JOHN CROW MTNS
Long Bay
Lime Cay
Comfort Castle
Bull Bay
Ramble
Millbank
Manchioneal
Eleven Miles
Reach Falls
ST THOMAS
Hector's River
Yallahs
Wilmington
Bath
Rozelle
Golden Grove
Salt Ponds
Lyssons
Morant Bay
Retreat
Port Morant

kilometres of dramatic cliffs, **Negril** is younger, more laidback and with a long-standing reputation for hedonism and buzzing nightlife. East of MoBay, **Ocho Rios** is the smallest of the three biggies, with an attractive downtown that seamlessly brings together tourists and locals, and a vast array of easily-accessed natural attractions: beautiful Blue Hole, famous Dunn's River Falls, and the eco-smart Mystic Mountain, where there's a bobsled tour through rainforest.

In the island's east, lush, rain-fed, sleepy **Port Antonio** and a number of nearby villages provide gateways to some of the country's greatest places to get out on the water, such as the cascading **waterfalls** at Reach, swimming at the Blue Lagoon and **rafting** on the majestic Rio Grande.

The **south coast** offers different pleasures, such as gentle black sand beach action at the terminally easy-going **Treasure Beach** – the perfect base for exploring local delights like the YS waterfalls or boat safaris in search of crocodiles on the **Black River**. Set in the upper reaches of the Santa Cruz Mountains, the south's inland towns, such as **Mandeville** and **Christiana**, offer respite from the heat of the coast and an interesting insight into Jamaica away from the resorts.

Kingston is the true heart of Jamaica. A thrilling place pulsating with energy and spirit, it's not just the nation's political capital but the focus of its art, theatre and music scenes, with top-class hotels, restaurants and shopping, and legendary fried fish on offer at the fabulous **Hellshire beach**. This is the best place to experience Jamaica's electric nightlife scene; its venues and street dances are nearly always packed, the music super-loud and dancers vying with each other for the best moves and dress. A stunning backdrop to the city, the cool **Blue Mountains** are a captivating antidote, with plenty of marvellous hiking, while the nearby fishing village of **Port Royal**, once a great pirate city, provides some historic diversion.

GOING OFF THE BEATEN TRACK

Though beaches and buzzing resort areas are obvious first-timer draws, Jamaica's greatest asset is its spectacular **interior**. With everything from mist-swathed mountains to steamy rainforest, lush wetland and cane-covered agricultural plains, the Jamaican countryside is one of the most diverse in the Caribbean and is a joy to explore, as much for its scenic delights as for its profusion of one-horse towns, where you can sink a glass or two of overproof in the obligatory rum shop, enjoy late-night **sound-system parties** at fenced-off village "lawns" and get a flavour of Jamaican life that couldn't be more different to that in the resorts. And whether your goal is a swim in a waterfall or river, or a hike into the hills, the journey can be as much of a joy as the destination itself, especially if you stop off en route to sample pepper shrimp, roast yam and saltfish or jerk chicken from one of the country's innumerable roadside stalls.

When to go

Jamaica's **climate** means hot sun year-round, but the weather is at its most appealing during the peak tourist season (mid-Nov to mid-April), when rainfall is lowest and the heat is tempered by cooling trade winds. Nights can get chilly during this period, and you'll probably want to bring a sweater. Things get noticeably hotter during the summer and, particularly in September and October, the humidity can become oppressive. September is also the most threatening month of the annual hurricane season, which runs officially from June 1 to November 30.

Prices and crowds are at their highest during peak season, when the main attractions and beaches get pretty busy. Outside this period everywhere is quieter and, though the main resorts throb with life pretty much year-round and the summer school holidays see an upsurge in visitor arrivals, less popular tourist areas like Port Antonio and Treasure Beach can feel a little lifeless. The good news is that hotel prices fall by up to 40 percent, there are more bargains to be had in every field of activity and a number of **festivals** – including the massive annual Reggae Sumfest – inject some summertime zip.

AVERAGE DAILY TEMPERATURES AND MONTHLY RAINFALL

	Jan	Feb	March	April	May	June	July	Aug	Sept	Oct	Nov	Dec
TEMPERATURE												
Max/min (°F)	86/67	86/67	86/68	87/70	87/72	89/74	90/73	90/73	89/73	88/73	87/71	87/69
Max/min (°C)	30/19	30/19	30/20	31/21	31/22	32/23	32/23	32/23	32/23	31/23	31/22	31/21
RAINFALL												
inch/mm	0.9/23	0.6/15	0.9/23	1.2/30	4.0/100	3.4/86	3.4/86	3.5/89	3.8/96	7.0/178	3.0/76	1.4/36

Author picks

Authors Lily Girma and Sarah Hull share a deep love for Jamaica and its *irie* culture. The following are a few of their favourite spots on the island:

Ultimate view Jamaica is not short of fine vistas, but standing over Canoe Valley (see page 245), a lush nature preserve melding forests and mangrove swamps, offers an unparalleled coastal panorama of the island's southernmost edge.

Roadside eats Conch soup, sublime fruit, sweet potato pudding, *toto*, roast peanuts and pepper shrimp (particularly from Middle Quarters; see page 247): Jamaica is a paradise of roadside delights (see page 28).

Jamaican relaxation Azure water, fresh fish and the quirks of numerous friendly residents draw repeat visitors to Belmont (see page 227) and Bluefields (see page 226) in Westmoreland – low-key fishing villages with hillside adventures.

Must-see art gallery Kingston's National Gallery (see page 54) is a rich and provocative journey through Jamaica's history, culture and identity.

Romantic rafting The longest and best of the island's river trips is a glide through spectacular scenery aboard a bamboo raft on the Rio Grande (see page 122).

Mountain dining *FITS Café* (see page 93) uses the freshest organic products from its own farm, blending both traditional and global recipes.

Reggae vibes Showcasing the best of the island's musical talent, the stage of Rebel Salute (see page 32) is unmissable, while live tunes on Negril's beach is an equally worthy, and near-daily, experience.

Exhilarating swims Like a postcard come to life, the cascading waters of Reach Falls (see page 118) and its adjoining pools make for one of Jamaica's most beautiful dips.

> Our author recommendations don't end here. We've flagged up our favourite places – a perfectly sited hotel, an atmospheric café, a special restaurant – throughout the Guide, highlighted with the ★ symbol.

I WAYNE AT REBEL SALUTE
FRUIT STALL IN OCHO RIOS

15

things not to miss

It's not possible to see everything that Jamaica has to offer in one trip – and we don't suggest you try. What follows, in no particular order, is a selective and subjective taste of the country's highlights, including dazzling beaches, dynamic festivals and clubs, and the very best food and drink. All highlights are colour-coded by chapter and have a page reference to take you straight into the Guide, where you can find out more.

1 FIREFLY
See page 144
Left just as it was when he died, Noël Coward's former home offers a poignant insight into his life, and with a spectacular location above the St Mary coastline, Firefly has the ultimate "room with a view".

2 NIGHTLIFE
See pages 72, 177 and 214
From stageshows like Rebel Salute or Reggae Sumfest, to legendary street dances, live music and the best clubs in Kingston and Negril, Jamaica's nightlife scene is unforgettable.

3 ACKEE AND SALTFISH
See page 28
Sample the national dish, a delectable and addictive combination of salt cod and the little-known ackee fruit.

4 KINGSTON
See page 46
The cultural heart of the nation, Jamaica's atmospheric capital holds museums to Marley, galleries galore, blissful public parks and some simply brilliant bars, restaurants and clubs.

5 BEACHES
See page 201
From the north coast's strips of fine white sand – Negril (pictured) is the longest – to the wind-whipped breakers and black volcanic sand in the south, Jamaica's shoreline is immensely varied – but the Caribbean Sea is always warm and inviting.

6

7

8

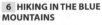

6 HIKING IN THE BLUE MOUNTAINS

See page 92

Cool, misty and fragrant with coffee and wild ginger flowers, the Blue Mountains are perfect hiking territory, the ultimate challenge being the highest point in Jamaica, Blue Mountain Peak.

7 TAKE A BOAT CRUISE

See pages 131, 174 and 207

The catamarans, sail-swathed pirate boats and souped-up pirogues that cruise Jamaica's coastline offer a wonderful perspective of the island as well as access to some of its best snorkelling spots.

8 BLUE LAGOON

See page 114

Jamaica abounds with turquoise swimming holes, but their king is undoubtedly Portland's Blue Lagoon, where deliciously cool spring water layers over salty seawater from the blue depths below.

9 PORT ROYAL

See page 77

This former pirate haunt bristles with character, and is also the jumping-off point for the clear waters of nearby Lime Cay.

10 NATIONAL GALLERY

See page 54

This Kingston institution offers the country's premier collection of work by Jamaican artists.

11 RIVER RAFTING
See page 122
A glide through the cool waters of a Jamaican river such as the Rio Grande is a beguiling way to see the countryside.

12 NEGRIL SUNSETS
See page 205
Right at the island's western tip, Negril is in pole position for the best sunset-watching in Jamaica.

13 TREASURE BEACH
See page 237
With its laidback atmosphere, Treasure Beach offers a restorative antidote to the north coast resorts.

14 COMMUNITY TOURS
See pages 25 and 251
Learn to cook classic Jamaican fare, tour an organic farm or visit a Rastafari community.

15 WATERFALLS
See pages 132, 247 and 118
Jamaica's waterfalls are a delight: clamber up Dunn's River, swing over the water at YS or enjoy a natural jacuzzi at Reach.

11

12

13

14

15

Itineraries

The following itineraries will help you get the most out of Jamaica, taking in the island's best attractions, and quite a bit of the rest as well. The island's main sights – from beautiful beaches to a Bob Marley pilgrimage – make up the Grand Tour, while Back Roads Jamaica will help you get off the beaten track. If you're after a more active holiday, the Great Outdoors covers everything from cricket and hiking to caving and mountain-biking.

THE GRAND TOUR

Jamaica's highlights can be easily seen in just seven days, though a little longer will help you get the most from each destination.

❶ **Negril** Catch live reggae on the beach, and, on an island where marijuana has spiritual significance, witness the sacred herb aspect of Rastafarian culture at Negril's annual Rootz Fest. See page 198

❷ **Appleton Estate Rum Tour** Head inland through lush fields of sugar cane to learn about – and more to the point, try – the island's favourite drink. See page 247

❸ **White River** A string of splendid natural pools – including the famous Blue Hole – offer breathtaking options for swimming (and rope-swinging). See page 134

❹ **Bob Marley Kingston pilgrimage** Find out who the man was and what inspired his iconic music at the Bob Marley Museum and Trench Town Culture Yard. See pages 60 and 64

❺ **Rio Grande rafting** Glide gently downriver through pristine countryside aboard a bamboo raft, stopping for an atmospheric lunch or rum on the riverbank. See page 122

❻ **Portland's sandy coves** Somewhat alike in appearance, Frenchman's Cove and Winnifred Beach are arguably the island's most attractive sands – but their atmospheres display two quite different Jamaicas. See page 112 and 114

BACK ROADS JAMAICA

This two-week tour takes in the less-visited south coast, off-the-beaten-track beaches, the finest mountain food and coffee, and music, architecture and horseracing around Kingston.

❶ **Bluefields Bay** This western Jamaica fishing village comes with fine white sand, hillside hikes and the mausoleum of reggae-royal Peter Tosh, an atmospheric alternative to Bob Marley's final resting place. See page 226

❷ **Accompong Town** Visit an original eighteenth-century Maroon settlement in the hills of Cockpit Country and don't miss its annual festival in January. See page 191

❸ **Treasure Beach** Tourism at its most laid back and hassle-free: chill out on the beach, eat the freshest local food, watch turtles nest in season, and grab drinks at *Pelican Bar*, on stilts out to sea. See page 237

❹ **Alligator Hole to Alligator Pond** In fact, reptiles aren't to be found along this little-populated strip of coastline; instead expect cacti-filled desert, mineral springs, manatees and excellent seafood. See page 245

❺ Caymanas Park and Hellshire Regardless of an interest in horseracing, a trip to animated Caymanas track offers riotous fun in an exquisite setting. Follow it with fried fish at Hellshire. See page 81

❻ Port Royal The former buccaneer stronghold boasts fantastic colonial architecture and is a great spot for a plate of steamfish; you can snorkel at nearby Lime Cay. See page 77

❼ Kingston Hope Botanical Gardens offers lovely respite, and there's your pick of chic restaurants and reggae parties, including under-the-radar *Dub Club* on Sunday nights. See pages 66 and 73

❽ The Blue Mountains Dramatic views, excellent hikes and fresh mountain streams await you, with the world's finest coffee and superb dining options also on offer. See page 86

❾ St Thomas Drive through the cane fields of Jamaica's least-visited parish for sunrise at Morant Point, and relax in hot mineral springs at nearby Bath. See page 100

THE GREAT OUTDOORS

You'll need ten to twelve days to make the most of this sport- and nature-infused journey across the island, encompassing hiking, caving and catching your breath over a game of cricket.

❶ Farm to Table Take a meander through the family-run agricultural wonderland that is Bluefields Organic Fruit Farm; along the paths, sample giant-sized sweetsop, star fruit, pears, honey banana and mango. See page 227

❷ Negril Located at Jamaica's western tip, this seven-mile beach offers plentiful opportunities for snorkelling, diving and jaunts on glass-bottom boats. See page 198

❸ Cockpit Country hike The wild hinterland in Jamaica's west is an extraordinary landscape of troughs and hillocks; end your tour spelunking in one of the island's largest cave systems. See page 190

❹ Glistening Waters Luminous Lagoon Take a dip in waters that literally glow turquoise – one of only four such wonders in the world. See page 184

❺ Hooves horse ride One of the best such tours, taking in tropical forest and the ruins of a Taíno village and Spanish settlement, before heading to the beach and into the water. See page 151

❻ Shaw Park Botanical Gardens Sited up in the hills, with views down to Ocho Rios, this tranquil garden cultivates an array of hibiscus, tufted "cat whiskers" and heliconia, plus a banyan tree with swing-able vines. See page 133

❼ The Blue Mountains A downhill mountain-bike tour is a great way to see this spectacular coffee- and waterfall-covered landscape. If you have time, hike up Blue Mountain Peak. See page 92

❽ Cricket at Sabina Park The West Indies revolutionized cricket in the 1980s, routing all visitors right here. Catch a game and take in the electric atmosphere, with reggae played loud and dancing in the stands. See page 33

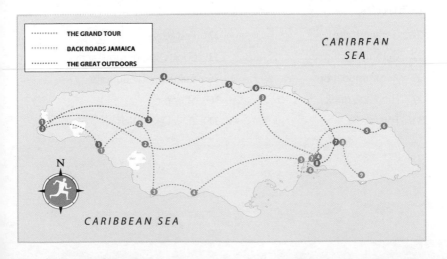

BOATS ON NEGRIL BEACH

Basics

Getting there

As one of the Caribbean's most visited islands, Jamaica is well served by direct flights from North America, the UK and other parts of Europe. Most visitors buy packages that include flight, accommodation and airport transfers, but there are plenty of good flight-only deals available. The majority of airlines fly into Montego Bay, and some also land at Kingston – more convenient if you're heading for Port Antonio or the Blue Mountains.

Airfares always depend on the **season**, with the highest prices around December to mid-January, when the weather is best, and during the summer school holidays (July to early Sept). Fares drop during the "shoulder" seasons – October, November and mid-January to April (excluding Easter) – and you'll get the best prices during the low season: May, June and mid-September to November.

Flights from the UK and Ireland

From the UK, British Airways and Virgin have direct flights to Montego Bay and Kingston from London Gatwick (9hr). Average high/low season scheduled fares are £950/600, though special deals can bring fares down to the £550 mark. Your best bet for deals with these airlines are Caribbean specialist agents such as Newmont Travel (see page 22), who often have cheaper fares than those offered by the airlines themselves.

Booking a **charter flight** can cut costs, with an average fare of around £500 and occasional deals for as low as £300; charter airlines' flight and accommodation packages also represent great savings. Charter operators currently offering flights to Montego Bay are First Choice, from Gatwick, Birmingham and Manchester; Thomas Cook from Gatwick and Manchester; and Thomson from Gatwick.

As there are no direct flights to Jamaica **from Ireland**, the easiest way to get to Jamaica is to travel to the UK and take a direct flight from there.

Flights from the US and Canada

The popularity of all-inclusive **package** holidays means that the majority of visitors fly to Jamaica with a charter airline. However, there are also plenty of daily **direct flights** from many parts of the US, and Canada is still catching up, though Sunwing recently added 100,000 seats to Jamaica for the 2017–18 season.

Flying time **from the US** varies enormously. The flight from Miami to Montego Bay only takes 1 hour 25 minutes, making the city the main US departure point to Jamaica, while from New York, flying time is 3 hours 20 minutes. **Caribbean Airlines** (Wcaribbean-airlines.com) – a Trinidad and Tobago-based airline – links Montego Bay and Kingston to New York (3hr 20min), Fort Lauderdale (1hr 43min), Toronto (4hr) and a host of other Caribbean islands. Caribbean Airlines' high- and low-season **fares** from these destinations to Montego Bay average US$500/350 (plus taxes) and there are often special deals available during the summer months.

In addition, a number of budget carriers offer very competitive fares. No-frills round-trip flights from Fort Lauderdale to Montego Bay and Kingston with Spirit (Wspirit.com) start from as little as US$99 plus taxes. JetBlue (Wjetblue.com) fly from New York to Montego Bay and Kingston from US$230 plus taxes, with connections from numerous US cities including LA, Phoenix and Chicago. A number of other US airlines also fly direct to Jamaica: American Airlines (Waa.com) from Miami to Kingston; United (Wunited.com) from Houston and New York to Montego Bay and Kingston; Delta (Wdelta.com) from Atlanta and New York to Kingston, and from Atlanta, New York, Memphis, Detroit, Washington, Minneapolis and LA to Montego Bay; and US Airways (Wusairways.com) from Boston, Charlotte and Philadelphia to Montego Bay.

From **Canada**, WestJet (Wwestjet.com) and Air Canada (Waircanada.com) have direct flights from Toronto to Kingston and Montego Bay (both around 4hr), while Sunwing (Wsunwing.com) offers vacation packages; high/low season **fares** average Can$700/500. Travelling from other parts of Canada, you'll have to fly first to either Toronto or to a regional hub in the US before taking a connecting flight to Jamaica.

A BETTER KIND OF TRAVEL

At Rough Guides we are passionately committed to travel. We believe it helps us understand the world we live in and the people we share it with – and of course tourism is vital to many developing economies. But the scale of modern tourism has also damaged some places irreparably, and climate change is accelerated by most forms of transport, especially flying. All Rough Guides' flights are carbon-offset.

Flights from Australia and New Zealand

There are **no direct flights** from Australia or New Zealand to Jamaica; the best option is to fly to the US, the UK or Europe (Italy or the Netherlands) and pick up an onward connection. The least expensive and most straightforward **route** is via Los Angeles. Expect to pay around NZ$1820 from Auckland and Aus$1920 from Sydney to reach Jamaica, with an average flying time of around 44 hours.

AGENTS AND OPERATORS

Caribbean Airlines US ☎ 1 800 920 4225, ⊕ caribbean-airlines. com. All-inclusive or package holidays. Offers occasional good specials.
Caribbean Destinations Australia ☎ 1800 354 104, ⊕ caribbeanislands.com.au. Themed holidays to Jamaica and the Caribbean based around everything from cricket to festivals.
Caribbean Journey US ☎ 1 866 828 5424, ⊕ caribbeanjourney. com. Caribbean specialists offering all-in packages, weddings and holidays.
Caribic Vacations Jamaica ☎ 876 953 9897, ⊕ caribicvacations. com. Established Jamaican destination management company, offering lodging, transport and community tours.
Caribtours UK ☎ 020 7751 0660, ⊕ caribtours.co.uk. Long-established, fairly upmarket company offering all types of trips and plenty of personalized advice.
Dragonfly Expeditions US ☎ 1 305 774 9019, ⊕ dragonflyexpeditions.com. A well-run, energetic company featuring interesting holidays in western Jamaica with an eco-tourism slant.
Newmont Travel UK ☎ 020 8920 1155, ⊕ newmont.co.uk. Caribbean flight specialist that's been around for years and offers some excellent deals; worth trying before any others.
North South Travel UK ☎ 01245 608 291, ⊕ northsouthtravel. co.uk. Friendly, competitive travel agency, offering discounted fares worldwide. Profits are used to support projects in the developing world, especially the promotion of sustainable tourism.
Sackville Travel UK ☎ 020 7326 7676, ⊕ sackvilletravel.com. Caribbean specialists offering cheap charter and scheduled fares.
See Jamaica Cheaply Jamaica ☎ 1 888 254 0637, ☎ 876 802 2023, ⊕ seejamaicacheaply.com. Jamaica-based agent representing an excellent selection of hotels and guesthouses islandwide.
Sunbird Tours UK ☎ 01767 262522, ⊕ sunbirdtours.co.uk. Birdwatching specialists offering eight-day trips to Jamaica covering all the top spots.
Thomas Cook UK ☎ 01733 224 808, ⊕ thomascook.com. Inexpensive flight and accommodation packages, with hotels in all the big resorts, and flight-only deals too.
Wings Birding Tours US ☎ 1 866 547 9868, ⊕ wingsbirds.com. Specialists in birding holidays, offering eight-day trips to Jamaica.

Getting around

Many visitors to Jamaica spend their entire holiday tanning and beachcombing, but the less sedentary will find a variety of ways to get around. Privately run minibuses provide a comprehensive and cheap – if chaotic – public transport system, while shared route taxis are great for short hops. Renting a car is the most convenient way of seeing the island, but it's expensive in comparison to the US or UK; if you just want to make the odd excursion, it is more cost-effective to hire a driver for the day.

By bus and minibus

Comprising anything from pockmarked minivans to air-conditioned, tinted-window coaches, Jamaica's fleet of privately owned buses and **minibuses** (the names are used interchangeably) are eclectic and lively (see page 24). Though minibus transport is pretty anarchic, with no timetables and regulation stopping at the red "PPV" plates that denote a vehicle is licensed for public carriage, the system does work, and is a viable option for short hops and cross-island trips. One exception to the rule is the **Knutsford Express** (☎ 971 1822, ⊕ knutsfordexpress.com), with smart, air-conditioned buses that connect Kingston, Ocho Rios, Montego Bay and Negril on the north coast and on the south coast Kingston, Mandeville, Luana, Savanna-La-Mar and Montego Bay, according to scheduled services. Kingston, meanwhile, is served by a fairly comprehensive network of government-owned buses (see page 68). Bear in mind that you may not be able to get a direct service to your destination, especially if you're travelling a fair distance – the journey from Montego Bay to Port Antonio, for example, might involve changing buses in Ochi, Port Maria and Annotto Bay. Non-stop long-distance buses do operate though, so if you're not up for an interrupted journey, ask the locals if and when direct buses leave. In general, services in major towns and cities start at around 6am and continue until 7 or 8pm, but are severely reduced on Sundays and public holidays. Note that some parts of Jamaica may have more limited public transport. **Fares** (J$50–300) are paid to a conductor after boarding, and having the right change, or at least small bills, will make your life easier.

By car

Renting a car is by far the best way of getting around and seeing the island. Though some of the roads beggar belief, Jamaica is a relatively easy country to drive in. You should avoid driving at night, however, as road visibility is reduced. Distances are relatively small, and while some locals have a kamikaze approach to driving, most are courteous. However, rental **prices** are high, averaging around US$50 per day – though rates can go as low as US$30, and you'll usually get a discount if you rent for more than a few days. Third-party insurance is normally included in the rental rate; you'll have to pay another US$12–25 per day to cover potential damage to the car. If you choose not to take this out, you're liable for every scratch on the car, whether caused by your own error or not. Websites like ⓦrentalcars.com and ⓦholidayautos.com usually offer slightly better rates than going direct to the car hire firm; expect savings around US$5–10 a day.

There are **rental companies** all over the island, from international outfits to small-scale local offices, with the best selection in Kingston, Montego Bay and Ocho Rios – we've listed the main players below, and local operators within the Guide. You'll often get a better deal by going with a local company, especially as the more premium outfits offer guaranteed roadside assistance and allow you to pick up and drop off in different major towns for no extra fee. To rent a car, you'll need a current licence from your home country or an international licence and, in theory, you'll need to have held it for at least a year. Most companies stipulate that drivers must be at least 21 years old (though some will rent only to drivers over 25). Before you set off, check the car to ensure that every dent, scratch or missing part is inventoried, and that the petrol tank is full (bear in mind that you'll have to return the vehicle with the same amount of petrol).

CAR RENTAL AGENCIES

INTERNATIONAL OPERATORS
Avis ⓦ avis.com.jm
Budget ⓦ budgetjamaica.com

JAMAICAN OPERATORS
Cavanor ⓦ cavanorautorentals.com
Fiesta ⓦ fiestacarrentals.com
Island ⓦ islandcarrentals.com

Rules of the road

Driving in Jamaica is on the **left**, and **speed limits** are 50kph in towns and on minor roads, 80kph on main roads and highways (though some stretches of the new highways have 110kph limits). The Jamaican police often set up **roadblocks** to check for illegal firearms and drugs, as well as proper licensing and registration, and do **speed checks** by way of radar gun – the safest bet is to stick to 50kph unless you see a sign indicating otherwise. Jamaican drivers

> ## HITCH-HIKING
> Many Jamaicans **hitch** rides – and will flag you down for a lift if you're driving through a rural area in a half-empty car. But very few tourists hitch-hike, and it's not something we recommend for safety reasons – if you're short of cash, stick to buses or route taxis.

have an informal system of flashing their lights to other drivers to indicate police presence ahead. If you're stopped, be polite and cooperate fully. Note that wearing **seat belts** in the front and back of cars is mandatory and driving with an unsecured child can lead to a ticket.

Unless there's been recent heavy weather, most main A-roads are in pretty good condition. The highways along the north, in particular, are pristine and a pleasure to drive, and while the south is just as scenic, it has more potholes in parts and is best taken slower (keep in mind that the south's Highway 2000, and the causeway from Kingston to Portmore have **toll fees** ranging J$160–440).

Jamaicans can be pretty cavalier behind the wheel, with many drivers (particularly those in charge of taxis or air-braked, diesel-spitting juggernauts) often dangerously macho and impatient. Always **drive defensively**; watch out for overtaking traffic coming towards you, as passing a long line of cars (even if it's impossible to see what's coming) is common practice; untethered animals also stray onto roads in country areas, so be on the lookout at all times. At night, many locals drive with undipped headlights; keeping your eyes on the left verge helps to avoid being dazzled. You should use your horn as freely as most Jamaicans do; a toot is just as likely to mean "thank you" as it is an indication of some kind of hazard or an intention to overtake (and in the case of the latter, it's always safest to slow down and let the overtaker pass you). Daredevil stunts notwithstanding, Jamaican drivers tend to be pretty courteous, often giving way at junctions and offering loud vocal suggestions as to how best to handle situations.

By taxi

Jamaican taxis vary from the gleaming white vans and fancy cars of the **Jamaican Union of Travellers Association** (JUTA; Kingston ☎ 927 4534; Montego Bay ☎ 952 0813, Negril ☎ 957 4620, Ocho Rios ☎ 974 2292; ⓦjutatoursltd.com), the official carriers, to the Japanese estate cars that are the vehicle of choice for most taxi men. Licensed taxis carry red number plates with "PP" or "PPV" on them, and there are a number unlicensed taxis that will offer their services – although hiring one (for a variety of reasons from lack of insurance to general safety) is not recommended. We've given numbers of taxi firms throughout the Guide, and while during the day, it's usually just as easy to flag a private taxi car down in the street – except in Kingston, where you have to call one instead and it can be difficult to obtain one during rush hour or rainy days – it's always safest to know who is driving you in the evening hours.

Fares are pretty reasonable in Kingston and the less touristy areas – a taxi from New Kingston to Devon House or the Bob Marley Museum will cost about US$5, from the airport to New Kingston around US$30, and US$12 for the journey from New Kingston to Stony Hill. On the north coast, prices are rather heftier – around US$50 for ten miles, and you'll always pay a little more if you take a taxi affiliated with a hotel. As taxis are unmetered, always establish a price before you get in (or over the phone if you're calling for a taxi). If you hail a vehicle on the street, the first figure may be just an opener; don't be afraid of negotiating. Note that at the time of publication, app-based taxi services such as **Uber** don't yet operate in Jamaica.

Shared taxis, or "route taxis" (see below) are used more by Jamaicans than visitors, so it's not uncommon for a driver to assume that you want to charter the whole taxi if you flag one down, in which case he'll throw the other passengers out – make it clear that this is not what you want. Prices are much closer to bus fares than to charter taxi rates; a route

taxi from Parade to New Kingston will cost approximately J$100, from Negril Beach to the West End J$120, or from Ochi to MoBay J$800.

If you don't drive – or don't want to – but still want to travel independently around the island, hiring a **local taxi driver** for a day or more is an excellent option. Rates vary widely according to distance, your bargaining skills and the number of passengers – expect to pay around US$75–180 per day. Local drivers often make good tour guides, too. We've recommended reliable drivers throughout the Guide.

Bikes and scooters

Jamaica should be much better for **cycling** than it is. Places like the Blue Mountains, perfect for biking, are not well geared towards independent cyclists, though several tour companies offer an easy, if pricey, way of seeing them on a bike (see p.25). Throughout the island, rental outlets are thin on the ground; we've listed them where they're available – Treasure Beach (see page 240) is particularly popular.

Renting a **scooter** or small motorbike is easier, and can be an exhilarating way of touring the island, though not all resorts have outlets – most are in Negril (see page 207), and Treasure Beach (see page 240). Rates are on average US$40 per day, and though in theory you'll need to show a driving licence, these are rarely asked for. Under Jamaican law, all motorcycle or scooter riders must wear helmets – you'd be a fool not to in any case. Zooming about on two wheels, though hugely enjoyable, does of course bring the

---

ROUTE TAXIS AND MINIBUSES

If you want to get a window into everyday Jamaican life away from the resorts, you should travel in a route taxi or minibus. Despite the definite downsides – drivers can show little interest in the rules of the road, and passengers are squeezed in with scant regard for comfort – they are a great way to hear local radio, listen to unguarded patois chats and possibly hold someone's baby.

Route taxis operate on short, busy set routes picking up and dropping off passengers anywhere along the way. Some are marked by the PPV number plate, but many more are not, making them difficult to identify, except by the squash of passengers and the wad of small bills in the drivers' hands. **Minibuses** have a similar system, but travel longer distances and carry a conductor who takes fares along the way. All towns have a **bus terminal** of sorts, either a proper bus station or a designated area along the main road, often near the market. Minibuses have their routes written on the front, back and sides of the vehicle and conductors shout out the destination repeatedly before departure, scouting the area for potential passengers and cramming in as many as possible. Once on the road, minibuses will also stop anywhere to pick up or drop off passengers (except in Kingston, where they're restricted to bus stops and terminals). If you want to get off before the terminus, tell the conductor and fellow passengers where you're going when you get on, or yell "one stop, driver", or something similar, when you get there.

To get on a bus or route taxi mid-route, just stand by the side of the road and flag it down (they will beep twice if they are full or otherwise unavailable); bear in mind that the earlier in the day you travel, the better – being stuck in a bursting Jamaican bus on a boiling afternoon is no picnic. If you're coming in at the start of the route, note that both taxis and minibuses only leave when full.

usual dangers; be on your guard for potholes and daft goats and dogs straying onto the tarmac.

Organized tours

There's plenty on offer if you're after an **organized tour**; most hotels have a tour desk which organize trips to well-known attractions – some of which are perennially crowded – like Rose Hall or Dunn's River Falls, or "highlight" tours of the local area, usually run by one of the "conventional" operators below. At best, they're a hassle-free and comfortable means of getting around; at worst, they barely skim the surface of the country and its culture from the shelter of an air-conditioned bus. **Prices** start from around US\$60 for a simple half-day excursion to US\$100 for full day-trips. Tours of specific sights are listed in the relevant chapters throughout the Guide.

For a more tailor-made, one-of-a-kind cultural experience – at a similar price to bus tours – book with a company not affiliated with your hotel (prices start from US\$60 for a half-day); options might include visiting a Rastafarian village, discovering a private lagoon or checking out an off-the-beaten-track rum bar. Country-style Caribbean Vacations and Tours (☎507 6326, ✉iiptcaribbean@yahoo.com), founder of community tourism in Jamaica, offers fascinating half-day trips into the rural Jamaican countryside, led by a community resident – discover lesser-known historical sights, tour an organic farm, enjoy live Jamaican Mento music and visit the neighbourhood bar, among other options. A percentage of tour proceeds go directly to the community visited, benefiting all involved.

The Jamaica Tourist Board's **Meet the People** programme introduces holidaymakers to local Jamaicans with shared interests – religion, nature, art and culture – at no charge; register in advance online (Ⓦvisitjamaica.com) or contact your local JTB branch.

TOUR OPERATORS

Barrett Adventures Rose Hall, Montego Bay ☎382 6384, Ⓦbarrettadventures.com. Customized packages to waterfalls, plantations and beaches island wide.

Caribic Vacations ☎953 9878, Ⓦcaribicvacations.com. Jamaica-based tour company that provides both typical and off-the-beaten-track trips around the island in small private cars or large buses.

Countrystyle Caribbean Vacations and Tours ☎507 6326, ✉iiptcaribbean@yahoo.com. Founder of community tourism in Jamaica and the Caribbean, offering enriching community day trips in various locations around the island, including Hanover, Negril, Mandeville and Kingston areas.

Glamour Tours ☎953 3810, Ⓦglamourdmc.com. A destination management company that offers concierge services to plan events including weddings, activities, excursions and longer itineraries.

Jamaica Cultural Enterprises Kingston ☎374 6370 or ☎540 8570, Ⓦjaculture.com. Operated by a solo entrepreneur, offering sightseeing and food tours in Kingston and surrounding areas, such as Port Royal. Can provide airport transfers.

Jamaica Tour Society Montego Bay ☎357 1225, Ⓦjamaicatoursociety.com. A boutique tour service that organizes unconventional and customized trips for the discerning traveller in search of an authentic Jamaican experience. Tours can range from a half-day up to full holiday planning.

My Jamaica Travels Kingston ☎362 9319, ✉myjamaicatravels2030@gmail.com. A collective of small and medium sized guesthouses and tour operators, offering custom itineraries for travellers with immersive Jamaican neighbourhood stays, and cultural tours.

Our Story Tours Kingston ☎377 5693, ✉ourstorytours@gmail.com. Offbeat historical tours. Emphasis is on Kingston, Spanish Town and Port Royal, but custom-designed tours are available to any part of the island. It's the only company to offer trips to see the racing at Caymanas Park.

Sun Venture 30 Balmoral Ave, Kingston 10 ☎924 4515, Ⓦsunventuretours.com. Reliable, innovative and eco-friendly scheduled and custom-designed tours – the best on the island for offbeat excursions. Mainstays include Blue Mountain and Cockpit Country hikes, bicycle tours, south coast safaris, caving and city tours.

Treasure Tours Calabash Bay, Treasure Beach ☎965 0126, Ⓦtreasuretoursjamaica.com. Small, personal tour company with eight different day tours to south coast attractions, and a popular day-long "non-tourist tour" that visits inland St Elizabeth and some of the local deserted and hidden beaches.

Your Jamaican Tour Guide Montego Bay ☎377 7634, Ⓦyourjamaicantourguide.com. A range of private tours (plus transfers) and personal guides by local Alrick Allen and his team of drivers, including activities like cooking with a Rastafarian community and going to a local bar.

Accommodation

Jamaica has a huge amount of choice when it comes to accommodation, including some of the world's finest luxury hotels, but it's extremely rare to find anywhere to stay for less than US\$50 per night in the resorts (Treasure Beach and Port Antonio being potential exceptions in the low season), and you'll usually pay quadruple that for anything approaching luxury. With the explosion of Airbnb, now widely available across the island and growing at a rapid pace, you're now more likely to snag a cosy room in a Jamaican home or an apartment in a fantastic location – with a more authentic experience to boot – without the accompanying hotel price tag.

Deals from some of these independent, Airbnb properties can also be found on additional websites

ACCOMMODATION ALTERNATIVES

Useful websites that provide alternatives to standard hotel and hostel accommodation include:

Airbnb ⓦairbnb.com. Covering a wide range of budgets, offering accommodation in anything from a private room in someone's house to an ocean-view villa.

Booking.com A mix of small to medium-sized properties, from villas to B&Bs and resorts, all competing with excellent seasonal offers.

CouchSurfing ⓦcouchsurfing.org. Best for travellers on a budget, this site connects guests with homeowners willing to (literally) allow guests to crash on their couches.

FlipKey ⓦflipkey.com. TripAdvisor's holiday rental arm, Flipkey provides candid reviews on properties that can be booked direct through the site.

Vacation Rentals by Owner (VRBO) ⓦvrbo.com. Villa rental website that often has very competitive rates due to booking directly through the property owners.

such as Booking.com, or by contacting the property directly. If you haven't booked a flight package that includes accommodation, it's worth reserving a room for your first night or two to save hassle on arrival, and to satisfy immigration requirements. Note that some guesthouses and hotels have a minimum-stay requirement – where this is the case, we have mentioned it in the text.

During the low season, rates often decrease by up to forty percent (though this is rare at the cheaper hotels), and proprietors may be more amenable to bargaining. Although the law requires prices to be quoted in Jamaican dollars, most hotels give their rates in US dollars; payment can be made in either currency.

Hotels, hostels and guesthouses

Jamaica has a handful of **youth hostels** (in Kingston, Treasure Beach and Montego Bay), which offer a combination of dorm and private rooms and basic facilities; expect to pay around US$20–30 for a dorm room, and upwards of US$40 for a private room. A step up from this are small, family-run **guesthouses**, most of which offer cheap and cheerful – but clean – fan-only rooms, with prices from US$50. Around US$150 is likely to get you a room in a small **hotel** with cable TV, a/c and on-site facilities like a pool, bar and restaurant; US$200 and upwards will see your options widen to chic, creatively-decorated boutique hotels. In Jamaica's most luxurious hotels, you can expect notable architectural design, lavish artwork in the rooms and lobby, impeccably dressed staff, excellent facilities and fabulous cuisine, with prices starting around US$250.

Camping

Camping options though limited are present on the island, including rustic mountain settings or glamping at boutique hotels – in Treasure Beach, Negril Beach, Kingston, the Blue Mountains, and Portland. Where available, we have noted the best options, including details on tent provision. Prices between US$20–30.

All-inclusives

Jamaica was the birthplace of the **all-inclusive** hotel, where a single price (expect to pay upwards of US$270/night) covers your room, all meals, drinks and watersports too. **Sandals** (ⓦsandals. com) remains the largest and best known of the all-inclusive chains, with seven in Jamaica alone, while other popular Jamaican all-inclusive resorts include the boutiquey **Couples** (ⓦcouples.com) chain and raunchy **Hedonism** (ⓦhedonism.com).

Several Spanish chains – including **Riu** (ⓦriujamaica. com), **Grand Bahia Principe** (ⓦbahia-principe. com), **Iberostar** (ⓦiberostar.com) and the **Grand**

ACCOMMODATION PRICES

The rates indicated in this guide are for the **cheapest available double or twin room during the high season** – normally mid-November to mid-April – and are inclusive of all taxes, but are liable to change. Rates are quoted per person per night based on double occupancy. Breakfast is not usually included; we've mentioned when it is, or when it's worth the additional cost. Wi-fi and a/c availability are the norm, but we've indicated where that is not the case.

Finally, note that small establishments may include a three percent surcharge for credit card use and hotels often add a **service charge** of usually ten percent, as well as a fifteen-percent **government tax** (GCT) to your bill; before you agree on anything, check whether taxes are included in quoted rates.

THE IMPACT OF ALL-INCLUSIVES

Taking up huge chunks of pristine coastline and privatizing access to large sections of the island's beautiful beaches, all-inclusives have taken a battering from critics questioning (primarily) their **environmental impact and sustainability**. This is particularly true as of late in Negril, where the three-storey beachfront limit was modified to accommodate four at Royalton Resorts in Bloody Bay, despite the area's major beach erosion dilemma. In addition, many all-inclusive resorts' hard to compete with rates make it difficult for Jamaica to escape the image of a cheap holiday destination and subsequently, and perhaps most importantly, to increase the amount of money spent and spread beyond the resort walls. Nevertheless, for better or worse, it is undeniable that these all-inclusives have become one of the country's largest employers and, as such, have come to play a vital role in the local economy.

On a side note, perhaps because of their reputation, some all-inclusives have started foundations that aim to contribute in positive ways to the local communities in which they operate. Most notable is the Sandals Foundation (ⓦ sandalsfoundation.org), which has done some incredible work across the island in the areas of sports, education and health.

Palladium Jamaica (ⓦ grandpalladiumjamaicaresort. com) – have constructed sprawling thousand-plus room properties on the north coast, offering a cheaper (prices start around US$110/night), but more generic experience. More recently, luxury all-inclusive resorts have taken a firmer hold on the north coast between Montego Bay and Negril, with the arrival of brands such as **Excellence** (ⓦ excellenceresorts.com), **Royalton** (ⓦ royaltonresorts.com), and **AM Resorts'** (ⓦ amresorts.com) trendy **Breathless** and **Zoëtry**, offering suites and penthouses with all the bells and whistles (prices start around US$367/night), and an ambiance that is a far cry from the real Jamaica.

Villas

There are hundreds of **villas** available for visitors to rent throughout Jamaica, normally by the week. Ranging from small beachside chalets to grand mansions, these are typically self-catering places, often with maid service (occasionally with a cook and a security guard), and can make a reasonably priced alternative to hotels if you are travelling as a family or in a group, as well as offering a wonderful level of privacy. Areas such as Hanover, Whitehouse, Treasure Beach, and Ocho Rios boast a multitude of spectacular villas, at affordable rates. We've listed individual properties throughout the Guide. A quick internet search will

also turn up a host of options, from VRBO and Airbnb, to specific area sites such as Treasure Tours Jamaica (ⓦ treasuretoursjamaica.com) for Treasure Beach. The Jamaica Association of Villas and Apartments (JAVA), PO Box 298, Ocho Rios (☎ 1 800 845 5276 or ☎ 1 773 463 6688, ⓦ villasinjamaica.com) may be of additional help with its select villa inventory.

Food and drink

From fiery jerk pork and chicken to inventive seafood and ubiquitous rice and peas, Jamaican cuisine is delicious and varied, and even vegetarians are fairly well catered for with the meatless offerings of Rastafarian Ital dishes. Snacking is good, too, with spicy meat, vegetable or seafood patties the staple fare, along with a vast selection of fresh fruits and vegetables. The global farm-to-table trend has taken hold in Jamaica too – local farmers stand to benefit as luxury hotels as well as small Ital cafes turn to seasonable, organic produce.

Eating out

All the resort towns, as well as cosmopolitan Kingston, have a wide variety of eating options, from posh seafood places to Italian, Indian, Japanese and Mediterranean cuisine. Elsewhere on the island, Jamaica's **restaurants** tend to be of two types: no-frills filling stations patronized mostly by locals and with a standard menu of Jamaican staples, or tourist-oriented places with more in the way of decor and a menu geared towards American and European palates. If you're after fast food, you'll find

TOP 5 BOUTIQUE HOTELS
The Caves Negril. See page 211
Goldeneye Oracabessa. See page 143
Jakes Treasure Beach. See page 241
Strawberry Hill Irish Town. See page 93
Trident Hotel Port Antonio. See page 112

TOP 5 FARM TO TABLE

Jakes Treasure Beach. See page 243
Round Hill Hopewell. See page 187
Stush in the Bush Free Hill. See page 152
Sun Valley Plantation Oracabessa.
See page 143
Zimbali Retreat and Cooking Studio
Westmoreland. See page 224

---

chains such as *Burger King, Wendy's, KFC* and *Pizza Hut* in all the larger settlements. Jamaica has the honour of being one of the few countries in which lack of demand prompted *McDonald's* to close its few local franchises, and the island is now golden arch-free. Note that a fifteen-percent service charge is often added to restaurant bills in touristy places.

Breakfast

The classic – and totally addictive – Jamaican breakfast is **ackee and saltfish**. The soft yellow flesh of the ackee fruit is sautéed with onions, sweet and hot peppers, fresh tomatoes and flaked salted cod, producing a dish similar to scrambled eggs in looks and consistency but wildly superior in taste. You'll often find it served with the leafy, spinach-like **callaloo**, boiled green bananas, fried breadfruit, and fried or boiled dumplings, or Johnny cakes (a Caribbean version of fresh baked scones). Other popular morning options include delicious and filling cornmeal, plantain, hominy corn or peanut porridge; or smoked mackerel "rundown", cooked with coconut milk, onions and seasoning. All hotels and restaurants in resorts serve more international breakfasts, from continental (rolls, jam, juice and coffee) to omelettes and American-style bacon, pancakes and scrambled eggs, as well as fresh fruit plates.

Lunch and dinner

Chicken and **fish** are the mainstays of lunch and dinner. Chicken is stewed, fried, jerked or curried, while fish can be grilled, steamed with okra and pimento, brown-stewed in a tasty tomato-based sauce or "**escovitched**" – seasoned, fried, and then doused in a spicy sauce of onions, hot scotch bonnet peppers and vinegar. Red snapper is the most common (and the tastiest) variety of fish, but you'll also be offered juicy steaks of kingfish, jackfish, tuna and dolphin (mahi-mahi, rather than the mammal).

Other staples include stewed beef, curried goat, oxtail with butterbeans and **pepperpot soup**, made from callaloo, okra and beef or pork. More

adventurous palates might fancy "**mannish water**" (goat soup that includes the testicles, considered an aphrodisiac), **cowfoot** (a gelatinous and arguably tasty stew of bovine hooves) or **fish tea**, a delicious broth of fish and veg, sold by the cup at roadside stalls. Pumpkin soup, often made with chicken stock, is also a tasty lunch filler. Another great option for a quick meal is a hunk of **jerk chicken** or **pork** (jerk fish or seafood are also widely available): spicy, marinated meat cooked slowly over an open fire and served with **festival** (a deliciously light sweet fried dumpling), roast yam or breadfruit or slices of hard-dough bread. Specialist jerk centres are scattered all over Jamaica, while **pan chicken**, seasoned in the same way as jerk but barbecued in a modified ex-oil barrel over coal rather than the traditional pimento wood, is cooked up by vendors who set up on street corners in the evenings, typically on Friday and Saturday nights.

Seafood is another Jamaican joy, with fresh **lobster** – curried or grilled with garlic butter – and **shrimp** widely available, and surprisingly inexpensive, too. Freshwater **crayfish** (known as *janga*) are pulled from rivers across Jamaica, and in Middle Quarters vendors sell bags of them, hotly peppered and ready to eat; an equally tasty alternative is janga soup. Though it's not the most visually appealing fruit of the sea, **conch** (the inhabitant of the huge pink shells sold in the resorts) is dense and delicious, cooked up into a fortifying soup or curried in silver-foil parcels at roadside stalls and served with **bammy** (a substantial bread made from cassava flour which is soaked in milk or water and then fried or steamed). **Seapuss**, also occasionally on menus, is octopus or squid.

Rice and peas (white rice cooked with coconut, spices and red kidney beans) is the accompaniment to most meals, though you'll sometimes get bammy, festival, sweet or regular **potatoes** (the latter often referred to as Irish potatoes), yam, dasheen, Johnny cakes or fried or boiled **dumplings**.

The island produces a fabulous array of fresh produce, and **vegetarians** are increasingly catered for other than just at Rastafarian **Ital** restaurants, where

---

TOP 5 ROADSIDE EATS

Fried fish Hellshire Beach. See page 82
Jerk chicken and pork Boston Bay,
Portland. See page 115
Miss Merle's Fish Joint Ocho Rios.
See page 138
Fresh fruit Coronation Market, Kingston.
See page 57
Pepper shrimp Middle Quarters, St
Elizabeth. See page 247

---

meals are meat-free and, in theory, cooked without salt. Mainstays include ackee and vegetable stews served with rice and peas; tofu, gluten and soya are cooked up in various forms as alternative sources of protein. You should usually be able to get patties filled with pulses, soya chunks and ackee. The majority of Ital restaurants are in Kingston, though there are also organic cafes and restaurants popping up in Ocho Rios, Montego Bay, Negril, Treasure Beach and Port Antonio.

Snacks

Along with jerk meat, **patties** are Jamaica's best-known snack, a flaky pastry case usually filled with highly spiced minced beef, though also available with veg, chicken, shrimp, ackee and saltfish, soya or lobster, and sold at bakeries, cafés and snack bars. Brands to look out for are Tastee and Juici Beef, though there are still independent restaurants baking their own patties, such as *Miss Sonia's* in Negril.

Other popular snacks are **bun and cheese** – a sweet currant bun sold with a hunk of processed cheese – or **meatloaf** and **callaloo loaf**, both made with bread rather than pastry. Bakeries also offer buttery folds of **coco bread** (eaten wrapped around a patty for the classic working-man's lunch), **bullas** (flat, heavy ginger cakes, improved upon in the Portland area by the creation of lighter "holey bullas"), **totos** (cakes made with freshly grated coconut, cinnamon, nutmeg and evaporated milk), rock cakes (hard coconut-filled buns) and **gizzadas** (tarts filled with shredded coconut and spiced with nutmeg and ginger). If you're lucky, you'll find **duckanoo** (also known as "blue drawers"), made from cornflour, sugar and nutmeg, wrapped in a banana leaf and steamed.

Jamaicans are enthusiastic **roadside** eaters, and you shouldn't miss out on breaking long journeys with a cup of fish tea, conch or pepperpot soup, which are all sold from steaming mobile cauldrons, or a chunk of buttered roast yam and saltfish. Peanuts and cashews are also hawked at major road junctions, sold salted or "Ital"; if he's not holding a pile of them aloft, you'll recognize a "nuts man" by the high-pitched, steam-driven whine that emanates from the pushcart roasting equipment.

Fruit and vegetables

One of the delights of touring Jamaica is stopping off at roadside stalls to try the local fruits. Bananas,

STAMINA POTIONS AND NOTIONS

Ever careful to safeguard his powerful libido, the average Jamaican man couldn't live without gallons of potions concocted to supplement the diet and ensure health and sexual stamina. With self-explanatory names such as **tan-pon-it-long** or **front-end lifter**, these vitamin and mineral-rich drinks often include peanuts, oats and **Irish moss**, a seaweed boiled and strained into a glutinous milky-white potion and which serves as the main component of the ubiquitous **magnum** (Irish moss and linseed), **strong back** (Irish moss, oats, peanuts, paw-paw, Dragon stout and a decoction of the strong-back herb) and **pep-up** (Irish moss, Dragon stout, Red Label wine and liquefied green corn). Most people have their own favourite blend with a suitably libidinous name to match.

Another popular tonic is **roots wine**, now commercially produced and sold in shops and bars islandwide – look out for Zion's Bedroom Bully, Ital Jockey and Mandingo varieties, as well as the Baba Roots brand. Roots wine is classically made by Rastafarian herbalists, however, who mix various quantities of roots and herbs such as arrowroot, chainy root, bridal wisp, strong back and occasionally ganja, boiling them with molasses or honey to make an evil-smelling brew. Most people have their own recipes, but as preparation is time-consuming, many prefer to visit their favourite "juice man", who sells old rum bottles full of the stuff in most markets.

Most recently, and rather oddly, it's the **lionfish** that has caught the attention of men trying to improve their prowess. An invasive species introduced by chance to the Caribbean waters, it has no natural predators (regionally) except humans which makes the fact that it is a voracious breeder and eater – threatening reef life – a point of serious national concern. In an effort to curb its growth rate the government set up campaigns and competitions for who can shoot the most (its poisonous barbs means it can only be killed by spear-gun).

LOBSTER AND CONCH CLOSED SEASONS

In a bid to boost decimated fish stocks, the Jamaican government has enforced **closed seasons** on lobster and conch during their reproductive cycles – August 1 to December 31 for conch, and April 1 to June 30 for lobster. It is **illegal** for restaurants to serve lobster or conch caught during these times, and while many will tell you that the stock is frozen and predates the deadline, this is obviously not always true, and you should avoid restaurants that don't comply with the law.

oranges, guavas, pineapples and paw-paws (papaya) are the most common, while **mangoes** come in all shapes and sizes (though the juicy, non-stringy Julie variety is a universal favourite). Of more unusual offerings, the suitably named **ugli fruit** looks like a disfigured grapefruit but is more tasty, while the origins and flavour of the Jamaican-bred **ortanique** are described by its hybrid name – orange, tangerine, unique. Something like a green-skinned lychee, with delicate flesh around a large pip, **guineps** (in season from July to October) have a refreshingly tart sweetness; the brown, orange-sized **naseberries** are sweeter and slightly gritty; **sweetsops**, or custard apples, look like pine cones and, as they ripen, the sections separate for eating. Other options include **soursops** (a bigger, sharper and indescribably better version of the sweetsop, often made into a juice); green or deep purple, milky-fleshed **star apples**; and the perfumed, rose-tinted flesh of **otaheite** (or "Ethiopian") **apples**, crimson-red, pear-shaped and with white, delicately perfumed and very refreshing flesh.

Ubiquitous **vegetables** include the whitish-blue **dasheen**, a slightly chewy and very delicious tuber. Of a variety of squashes, the watery **cho-cho** is the most common, and you'll also find **callaloo**, **okra**, **yams**, **cassava**, **breadfruit** and **plantains**, the latter ripened and served as a fried accompaniment to main meals.

Drinking

Jamaica's water is safe to drink, but locally bottled **spring water** is widely available and much nicer. For a tasty non-alcoholic **drink**, look no further than the roadside piles of coconuts in every town and village, often advertised with a sign saying "**ice-cold jelly**". The vendor will open one up with a few strokes from a machete, and you drink straight from the nut (with a straw if you're lucky), after which the vendor will split the shell so you can scoop out the soft flesh using a piece of the shell. **Sky juice** – shaved ice flavoured with syrup or fresh cane juice – is also popular, usually served in a plastic bag with a straw.

Elsewhere, you'll find the usual imported **sodas**, plus Jamaica's own D&G brands: Ting (a refreshing sparkling grapefruit drink), Malta (a fortifying malt drink) and throat-tingling ginger beer. Most places also sell "**box drinks**" – from additive-filled, over-sweetened peanut punch or eggnog to sweetened fruit juices. The unsweetened Tru-Juice brand comes in some interesting varieties, including West Indian cherry or June plum with ginger. **Fresh natural fruit juices** – tamarind, June plum, guava, soursop, strawberry and cucumber – are always delicious, and are available at local restaurants, while blended fruit juices are a meal in themselves; if you haven't got a sweet tooth, ask for yours to be made without syrup.

Jamaican **coffee** (see page 99) is usually excellent. Blue Mountain beans are among the best and most expensive in the world, though the other local brews, such as High Mountain, Low Mountain or Mountain Blend, are also good. Made from balls of locally grown cocoa spiced up with cinnamon and nutmeg and then boiled with water and condensed milk, **hot chocolate**, known as cocoa tea, is a traditional but rather labour-intensive breakfast drink. **Tea**, in Jamaica, can mean any hot drink, from regular, insipid Lipton's to fish tea, herbal tea or even ganja tea.

Alcohol and bars

Jamaica's national **beer** is the excellent Red Stripe, available in distinctive squat bottles and occasionally on draught; Red Stripe Light is a lower-alcohol version. Heineken is also widely available, as is locally brewed Guinness (stronger than British varieties), which competes with the sweeter Dragon as the island's stout of choice.

Wine is also widely available in restaurants and bars by the glass or bottle, though it's more expensive

SMOKING BAN

In 2014 the government of Jamaica issued a smoking ban for all public transportation, enclosed spaces (such as nightclubs and indoor restaurants), workplaces, places for collective use (such as bus stops), spaces for sports or recreational use and areas specified for children. Look for proper signage or ask for the designated smoking area before you light up your cigarette or spliff.

than locally produced drinks; super-markets sell wine at more reasonable prices. A rum-shop staple, the local Red Label wine is a pretty grim fortified tipple.

Rum is the liquor of choice (see page 248), with a huge variety at a range of prices. Rum-based **liqueurs** are the other local speciality; Sangster's make award-winning rum creams and liqueurs flavoured with orange, coffee, pimento and more, while the coffee-infused Tia Maria is quite delicious.

Jamaica's traditional rum shops are hole-in-the-wall places patronized by groups of men drinking rum, playing dominoes and gazing at the scantily clad ladies on the Red Stripe posters, but within the cities and resorts, there are hordes of drinking holes, from sports bars to English-style pubs.

The media

Jamaicans consume as much media as their North American neighbours, and like to stay on top of nationwide developments. Morning and dinner conversations often veer toward the latest runnings – from politics to sports, music, and the social issues of the day. Newspapers – in print and online – and radio remain significant sources of information and entertainment across the island.

Newspapers

Jamaica has three daily **newspapers** – the broadsheet **Daily Gleaner** (Wjamaica-gleaner.com), with solid coverage of local news and sports, the pick of the island's feature writers and good entertainment listings. It's rivalled by the **Observer** (Wjamaicaobserver.com), with a similar mix of news and features, and known for its excellent style and lifestyle coverage, including food and events. The **Star** (Wjamaica-star.com) is the island's tabloid, full of salacious tittle-tattle – the "Dear Pastor" problem page is worth a glance. Sunday brings fat weekend issues of the *Gleaner* and *Observer*.

International newspapers – the main US dailies and UK broadsheets – are sold in major pharmacies and the gift shops of the bigger hotels, usually a couple of days out of date.

Radio

Jamaica's **radio stations** are predictably awash with local music, from hyped-up dancehall to roots reggae, R&B and hip-hop. Music faces tough competition from daytime phone-in talk shows, which offer a pertinent insight into the local psyche, as well as sports coverage.

Irie FM (Wiriefm.net) is easily the most listened-to music station, with a non-stop reggae playlist and some of the island's best-known DJs. **Zip FM** (Wzipfm. net) has a slightly more eclectic mix of musical styles, from soca and Latin to techno and rock, as well as local tunes, while **Fame FM** (Wfame95fm.com) plays plenty of upfront dancehall, R&B and hip-hop. **Kool 97** (Wkool97fm.com) is another worthy choice, offering a laidback mix of music, with some excellent 1980s soul as well as reggae, soft rock and oldies. New to the scene and increasingly popular (for it's lack of talk and few ad breaks) is Fyah 105 (Wfyah105.com), which plays mostly top 40 hits. For many Jamaicans, talk shows are essential listening, with main players including **RJR** (Wrjr94fm.com) and **Power 106** (Wgo-jamaica.com/power). Note that most of the radio station websites allow you to listen live online.

RADIO STATIONS AND FREQUENCIES

KLAS 89FM
RJR 90.5/91.1/92.9/94.5/103.3FM
Fame 95FM
Roots 96.1FM (in Kingston area only)
Love 101.1FM
Hot 102 102FM
Zip FM 103 FM
Fyah 105 FM
Irie FM 107.7FM
Power 106 106.5FM
BBC World Service 104FM

Television

You'll find a **television** set in most hotel rooms, usually hooked up to the cable network with countless American-based channels as well as the two domestic channels, **TVJ** (Wtelevisionjamaica. com) and **CVM** (Wcvmtv.com), competent if rarely thrilling; look out, though, for the excellent music-based programme *Entertainment Report* on TVJ. Output is dominated by news, local sport and US re-runs. Those desperate for international sports coverage will find that most towns have one or two bars with big-screen TVs broadcasting major US sporting events – NFL and NBA games and occasionally baseball – though you won't find much from Europe other than the odd football game.

Local cable channels have mushroomed in recent years, with Hype and RETV broadcasting from dances and parties islandwide and showing local music videos on a loop. Look out also for Tempo, MTV's Caribbean music channel.

Festivals

From regional food festivals to massive music concerts, Jamaica plays host to a huge variety of annual events, with as many geared towards tourists as they are to locals. We've detailed the main and most interesting events here, but for comprehensive listings, visit the website of the JTB (Ⓦ visitjamaica.com) for details of each year's programme.

Throughout the year, the **Jamaican Cultural Development Commission** stages various events centred on traditional Jamaican song, dance and the arts, with the Festival Song Competition Finals at the Ranny Williams Entertainment Centre in Kingston being one of the highlights; see Ⓦ jcdc.gov.jm for full details.

A FESTIVAL CALENDAR

JANUARY

Accompong Maroon Festival Accompong, St Elizabeth. All-day celebration of the 1739 Maroon peace treaty, held on January 6. Food and craft stalls, drumming, traditional dancing, speeches and a sound-system dance till dawn.

Jamaica Jazz and Blues Festival Greenfield Stadium, Trelawny Ⓦ facebook.com/jamaicajazzandblues. This increasingly popular event has a fabulous setting and a big enough purse to attract some excellent international performers, from John Legend to Al Green.

Rebel Salute Grizzly's Plantation Cove, Priory, St Ann Ⓦ facebook.com/rebelsalutejamaica. Large-scale annual concert with a festival atmosphere, featuring a huge line-up of cultural artists and attracting a large rootsy crowd. Meat and alcohol are banned from the grounds (but ganja certainly isn't).

FEBRUARY

Bob Marley Birthday Week Nine Mile, St Ann; Bob Marley Museum, Kingston; Trench Town Cultural Yard , Kingston Ⓦ bobmarleyfoundation.com, Ⓦ bobmarleymuseum.com. Celebrations for the king of reggae are held on and around the anniversary of Marley's birthday on February 6, from seminars to live shows and sound-system jams.

Jamaica Carnival Kingston, Ocho Rios and Montego Bay Ⓦ bacchanaljamaica.com. Featuring dynamic performances from top artists across the Caribbean, these high energy parties see scantily clad patrons "get on bad" at parties in Mas Camp (Kingston) and across the island, of which the best is Beach Jouvert in Oracabessa. Carnival culminates in a costumed parade through the streets of Kingston in April.

Blue Mountain Music Festival St Andrew Ⓦ facebook.com/bluemountainmusicfestival.com. A two-day music festival at Holywell Recreational Park that includes opportunities to hike, practise yoga and listen to Maroon drumming. Past performers include Third World and Chronixx. Family-friendly camping available.

Jamaica Fat Tyre Festival Ocho Rios Ⓦ singletrackjamaica.com/fat-tyre-festival.com. One-of-a-kind mountain-biking festival with

unique organized rides that take participants through parts of St Mary, St Ann, up and over the Blue Mountains, and finishing in Bull Bay.

MARCH

Spring Break Negril. Although not as popular as it used to be, Negril still pulls a decent Spring Break crowd when students descend on the main resorts (particularly Negril) for a two-week orgy of beer-drinking and slapstick antics. Student ID gets discounts on hotels and events.

APRIL

Trelawny Yam Festival Albert Town, Trelawny Ⓦ stea.net. This tiny town, with a stunning setting on the outskirts of Cockpit Country, plays host to an incongruously large open-air party. As well as the prize tubers, competition categories include cooking and best-dressed goat.

Western Consciousness Savannah-la-Mar. Excellent rootsy stage show featuring the best of Jamaica's cultural artists.

Jakes Off Road Triathlon St Elizabeth Ⓦ jakeshotel.com. Jamaica's only off-road triathlon provides a unique trip through the local community by way of its three-leg course that takes participants for a swim across a beautiful sea bay, on a bike down bumpy farm lanes and finishes with a run through a quiet country town.

MAY

Calabash International Literary Festival Treasure Beach, St Elizabeth Ⓦ calabashfestival.org. Fabulous free literary festival in the laid-back surrounds off Treasure Beach, with book and poetry readings, seminars, discussions and some excellent parties too. Takes place on even years.

JUNE

Ocho Rios Jazz Festival Ocho Rios Ⓦ ochocriosjazzja.com. Jamaica's original jazz festival, attracting top performers from all over the world. Concerts take place in hotels and open spaces in Ocho Rios, with a few events in Montego Bay and Kingston.

All Jamaica Grill Off Kingston Ⓦ facebook.com/alljamaicagrilloff. A great family and food lovers' barbecue and grilling event that sees teams compete for the title of King/Queen of the Grill.

Caribbean Fashion Week Kingston Ⓦ caribbeanfashionweek.com. A week-long event that draws international attention to local and regional designers who come to present their collections.

JULY

Kingston on the Edge Kingston Ⓦ kingstonontheedge.org .This brilliant urban arts festival sees a series of events, from gallery shows to poetry readings, dance performances and concerts, staged across the capital and showcasing the work of the country's most interesting young artists and performers.

Little Ochi Seafood Carnival Alligator Pond, Manchester. Great seafood and music festival at this renowned beachside seafood joint.

Portland Jerk Festival Boston Bay, Portland Ⓦ facebook.com/originsofjerk. Celebration of Jamaica's most famous dish, with jerk everything and all the trimmings cooked up by Portland's finest on the beautiful Folly Estate amid music, kids' attractions and games.

Makka Pro Surf Contest St Thomas Ⓦ jamsurfas.webs.com/whatsnew.htm. Two days of competitive surfing by local, regional and professional surfers preceded by a week of activities such as heritage tours and a culinary festival.

Reggae Sumfest Catherine Hall Entertainment Centre, Montego Bay ⓦ reggaesumfest.com. Dubbed the greatest reggae show on earth, this massive four-night festival is the main event in the musical calendar, with sets from all the big players in the local music scene as well as international artists from Beyoncé to Ne-Yo. See page 177.

NDTC Season of Dance Kingston ⓦ ndtcjamaica.com. Two weeks of performances by the highly acclaimed National Dance Theatre Company, Jamaica's premier dance troupe.

AUGUST

International Dancehall Queen Contest Pier One, Montego Bay ⓦ internationaldancehallqueen.com. Excellent annual event in which Jamaica's most accomplished movers (as well as contestants from overseas) don sequins, fishnet and plenty of bling to vie for the coveted title of Dancehall Queen. Expect a brilliant display of all the latest dances and dancehall fashions, as well as some seriously sexy gyrating.

Dream Weekend Negril ⓦ jamaicadreamweekend.com. The "Jamaican Spring Break", held over Independence weekend, which sees thousands of well-heeled young Jamaicans descend on Negril for five days/four nights of non-stop all-inclusive parties and stageshows.

Denbigh Agricultural, Industrial and Food Show Denbigh Showground, May Pen ⓦ jas.org.jm. This annual three-day event, which is over 60 years old, aims to showcase the best of the farming sector through creative displays of farm produce and livestock by farmers from across the country.

OCTOBER

Jamaica Food & Drink Festival Kingston ⓦ jafoodanddrink.com. A week-long festival celebrating Jamaican cuisine with themed nights, including a seven-course plated, wine-paired dinner, a Meet Street food truck festival on Kingston's waterfront and brunch at the National Gallery.

NOVEMBER

Restaurant Week ⓦ facebook.com/restaurantweekjamaica A great chance to delve into the dining scene, with some of the best restaurants in Kingston, Ocho Rios and Montego Bay offering three-course set menus at significantly discounted prices.

(Biennial) National Exhibition National Gallery, Kingston ⓦ nationalgalleryofjamaica.wordpress.com. Biennial showpiece exhibition of new artists and established names.

DECEMBER

LTM National Pantomime Little Theatre, Kingston ⓦ ltmpantomime.com. Annual theatrical institution, with ribald jokes, great costumes, political commentary and traditional Jamaican song and dance.

Reggae Marathon Negril ⓦ reggaemarathon.com. Join thousands of people who come to participate in this uniquely Jamaican marathon, half marathon and 10k. Everyone receives a medal and the winners get the Bob and Rita Marley trophy.

Rastafari RootzFest Negril ⓦ rastafarirootzfest.com. A four-day festival celebrating all things ganja and Rastafari, including a Ganja Cup contest for qualifying farming participants, reggae concerts, cannabis cultivation seminars and arts and crafts vendors.

Sports and outdoor activities

As you'll quickly discover, sport is a Jamaican obsession – hardly surprising in a country that continues to produce so many world-class athletes – and you'll find newspapers and TV news awash with sports reports. Jamaica is also a great place to indulge your own sporting passion, with excellent watersports and top-class golfing in particular.

Spectator sports

Virtually every Jamaican has an opinion on **cricket**, the national game, and bringing it up in conversation is a sure-fire way to break the ice – though if you want to win friends, gloating over the recent failings of the West Indies cricket team may not be a brilliant idea. If you get the chance to catch a match, particularly a Test fixture or 20/20 game at Sabina Park, you'll find the atmosphere very Jamaican – thumping reggae between overs, vendors hawking jerk chicken and Red Stripe, and a full scale party at the Mound stand. As well as Sabina and the Greenfield Stadium in Trelawny, built for the Cricket World Cup in 2007, there are smaller venues throughout the island: Melbourne Oval in Kingston; Chedwin Park near Spanish Town; Alpart Sports Club in Nain, St Elizabeth; Jarrett Park in Montego Bay, and Kaiser sports ground in Discovery Bay, St Ann. For more on West Indies cricket, visit ⓦ windiescricket.com.

CRICKET IN KINGSTON

For a truly Caribbean sporting experience, take in one of the one-day or four-day international **cricket matches** held at Kingston's refurbished **Sabina Park** (South Camp Road; ☎ 967 0803, ⓦ windiescricket.com). While grandstand seats are available for purchase (for serious spectators), most locals tend to grab their portable lawn chairs or throw down towels on Appleton Rum Mound where for a premium price patrons can enjoy an all-inclusive bar and party-like atmosphere.

Since Jamaica's national team, the **Reggae Boyz** (Ⓦ thereggaeboyz.com), qualified for the 1998 World Cup, **football** (soccer) has become another national obsession, more popular amongst young people than cricket. Although international matches, held at the National Stadium in Kingston, are relatively rare, league games (the main one being the Wray and Nephew Premier League) attract large and passionate crowds at grounds across the island. These are well worth attending, as much for the atmosphere as for the action on the pitch – visit Ⓦ premierleaguejamaica.com for details of fixtures.

Watersports

Scuba diving and **snorkelling** are concentrated on the north coast, between Negril and Ocho Rios, where visibility is best. The state of the reefs is variable – pollution and aggressive fishing techniques have affected many areas, but there are still some gorgeous sites very close to the shore. The fish are nonetheless impressive, with multi-tudes of parrot, angel and trigger fish, as well as moray eels, turtles and evil-looking barracuda. There are a handful of wreck dives – including several plane wrecks off the coast of Negril – and good trenches, overhangs and wall dives.

The main resorts are packed with operators offering dive trips and snorkelling excursions; the most reputable are listed throughout the Guide. For beginners, the most popular options are the one-day introductory **resort courses** (US$95–120), which offer basic instruction and a short supervised shallow dive close to shore. The longer **PADI** (Professional Association of Diving Instructors) **open-water certification course** costs around US$420 and takes a few days, with practical and theoretical tests, safety training and several dives. Once you're certified, you can dive without an instructor, though you'll still need to go with a licensed operator – expect to pay US$90 for a two-tank dive, and remember to take your certifica-tion with you.

Parasailing, **jet-skiing**, **water-skiing**, **kayaking**, **glass-bottom boat rides** and **sailing** are available at all of the major resorts. You can **surf** at Boston Bay and Long Bay in Portland and Bull Bay just east of Kingston, though board rentals are scarce. **Deep-sea fishing** is best around Portland, particularly during October's Blue Marlin tournament. Fully equipped boats are available for rent in all the major resorts; though, at a starting price of US$900 a day, the pursuit of big fish doesn't come cheap.

Away from the coast, **river rafting** was first popularized in the 1950s by movie idol **Errol Flynn**, who saw that the bamboo rafts used to transport bananas along Portland's Rio Grande could be used for pleasure punting. The Rio Grande remains the most spectacular spot for an idle glide, but operators have also set up in Ocho Rios, Falmouth and Montego Bay. Costs start at around US$75 for a two-person raft, more if you need transport to and from your hotel.

River swimming is idyllic in Jamaica, particularly in the Rio Grande in Portland, the Great River in Montego Bay and the White River in Ocho Rios. Dunn's River in Ocho Rios offers the island's ultimate **waterfall climb**, but there are plenty more cascades, many untouristed. For more relaxing options, **mineral springs** and **natural spas** are Jamaica's hidden gems – locals flock to Bath in St Thomas (see page 102), Rockfort in Kingston (see page 76) and Milk River in Clarendon (see page 245) for the restorative powers of the mineral water. River rising pools, such as Roaring River in Westmoreland (see page 225) or the Blue Lagoon in Portland (see page 114), are also a delight.

Golf

Jamaica boasts no fewer than twelve **golf courses**, from the magnificent championship Tryall course near Montego Bay (see page 222) and the world-class course at Rose Hall, just east of Montego Bay (see page 173), to less testing nine-hole links in Mandeville, Kingston and Port Antonio. All are open to the public, except during tournaments. **Green fees** vary wildly from course to course, and there are additional charges for caddies, club and cart rental. For more on golf, visit Ⓦ visitjamaica.com or Ⓦ jamaicagolf.com

Hiking

Though the heat doesn't encourage strenuous exercise, **hiking** is by far the best way to get a flavour of the Jamaican countryside. The best opportunities are in the dense wildernesses of the **Blue and John Crow mountains**, where the ultimate trek is to the top of Jamaica's highest point, Blue Mountain Peak, and in **Cockpit Country**, where trails originally blazed by Maroon warriors lead deep into the Jamaican interior, though there are enjoyable minor walks elsewhere.

It is strongly recommended that you use a **guide** for all but the shortest of hikes, as it's perilously easy to get lost. Always stick to paths and trails; veering off

---

TOP 5 SWIMMING SPOTS

Doctor's Cave Montego Bay. See page 165
Irie Blue Hole Ocho Rios. See page 134
Maiden Cay Kingston. See page 79
Reach Falls Portland. See page 118
West End Negril. See page 205

THE RULES OF CRICKET

The rules of cricket are so complex that the official rulebook runs to some twenty pages. The basics, however, are by no means as Byzantine as the game's detractors make out.

There are two teams of eleven players. A team wins by scoring more runs than the other team and dismissing all the opposition – in other words, a team could score many more runs than the opposition, but still not win if the last enemy batsman doggedly stays "in" (hence ensuring a draw). The match is divided into **innings**, when one team bats and the other fields. The number of innings varies depending on the type of competition: one-day matches have one per team; test matches have two.

The aim of the fielding side is to limit the runs scored and get the batsmen "out". Two players from the batting side are on the pitch at any one time. The bowling side has a bowler, a wicket keeper and nine fielders. Two umpires, one standing behind the stumps at the bowler's end and one square on to the play, are responsible for adjudicating if a batsman is out. Each innings is divided into **overs**, consisting of six deliveries, after which the wicket keeper changes ends, the bowler is changed and the fielders move positions.

The batsmen **score runs** either by running up and down from wicket to wicket (one length equals one run), or by hitting the ball over the boundary rope, scoring four runs if it crosses the boundary having touched the ground, and six runs if it flies straight over. The main ways a batsman can be dismissed are: by being "clean bowled", where the bowler dislodges the bails of the wicket (the horizontal pieces of wood resting on top of the stumps); by being "run out", which is when one of the fielding side dislodges the bails with the ball while the batsman is running between the wickets; by being caught, which is when any of the fielding side catches the ball after the batsman has hit it and before it touches the ground; or "LBW" (leg before wicket), where the batsman blocks with his leg a delivery that would otherwise have hit his stumps.

These are the bare rudiments of a game whose beauty lies in the subtlety of its skills and tactics. The captain, for example, chooses which bowler to play and where to position his fielders to counter the strengths of the batsman, the condition of the pitch and a dozen other variables. Cricket also has a beauty in its esoteric language, used to describe such things as fielding positions ("silly mid-off", "cover point", etc) and the various types of bowling delivery ("googly", "yorker", and so on).

---

into uncharted foliage not only encourages disorientation, but can destroy plants and lead to soil erosion. Never throw rubbish when hiking; even cigarette butts should be pocketed – a carelessly discarded cigarette can easily start a massive bush fire.

Other activities

A labyrinth of **caves** networks Jamaica's limestone interior, and many have been opened up as attractions with lights and stairs, so you don't have to be an experienced spelunker to enjoy them. Serious cavers should head for Cockpit Country, where the limestone is at its thickest and many of the caves are unexplored; a guided scramble through Printed Circuit Cave is an unforgettable, bucket-list experience (see page 195). Elsewhere on the island, it's worth seeking out Roaring River Park in Westmoreland (see page 225) and Dromilly Cave in Trelawny (see page 190). Contact Sun Venture Tours or Cockpit Country Adventure Tours (see page 190) for caving trips.

Horse riding is a lovely way of exploring the island, though some stables and their mounts are rather run-down; stick to those listed in the chapters or check with the JTB. The best stables are Hooves in St Ann (see page 151), Chukka Cove in St Ann (see page 151) and Chukka Caribbean (see page 222) and the Half Moon Equestrian Centre in Montego Bay (see page 173); the latter also offers polo, dressage and horse-jumping lessons. If you're interested in watching a polo match, contact the Jamaica Polo Association (☏ 926 2916); fixtures are held throughout the year.

Cycling is surprisingly underpromoted in Jamaica. An alternative to demure processions aboard colour-coordinated resort cycles is a guided **mountain-bike tour**, available in the Blue Mountains (see page 92); more serious mountain bikers should contact the St Mary Off-Road Biking Association.

If you're after some well-regimented thrills, Chukka Caribbean (🌐 chukka.com) have the island's **soft adventure** market completely sewn up, with bases in or around the three main resorts offering everything from zip-lining "canopy tours" to river kayaking and tubing, ATV rides and dogsled tours, with sleds pulled by rehabilitated pot-hounds.

Finally, many hotels offer **tennis courts**, and for those who can't survive without their workout, plenty of resorts also provide **gyms** and **aerobics classes**.

Culture and etiquette

Take a look at a roomful of Jamaicans enjoying a night out and you might easily think this is one of the most free, open societies on the planet, what with the downright sexiness of the dancing and the frankness of the chat-up lines. But the party scene is just one aspect of Jamaican culture, and the society as a whole is actually pretty conservative. The vast majority of Jamaicans are practising Christians, far more likely to spend Sunday mornings in church than recovering from the night before.

Jamaica can be quite a paradoxical place; it's fine to turn up at a sound-system party wearing little more than a few strips of fabric, but wear your bikini anywhere away from the beach and you're likely to cause offence. Similarly, as most locals take a great deal of pride in their appearance, grubbing around in a crumpled T-shirt speckled with last night's jerk sauce is a guaranteed way not to be taken seriously. In terms of general **dress codes**, though, you'll want something smart if you plan on clubbing, and men will need long trousers if planning to dine at the better restaurants (jackets are required only at the most expensive places).

Jamaicans are refreshingly direct; your big nose or bald head will be seen as fair game for comment, and while an open invitation to bed within the first five minutes of meeting someone can be disconcerting, you at least know where you stand. At the same time, old-fashioned **manners** are maintained here; passing someone on a rural street without acknowledging them will be seen as rude, as will failing to greet a shop assistant with a "good morning/afternoon" before launching into your request. The elderly are revered in Jamaican culture, and it's usual to preface someone's name with Mr or Miss when addressing someone much older than you; kids are taught to respect their elders at all times and never answer back. Bear in mind, too, that many locals are a bit weary of serving as the "Jamaican Rasta" or "market lady" in the holiday snaps of a thousand visitors – it's polite and ethical to ask before taking someone's picture.

Women travellers

For women **travelling solo**, Jamaica can be a social jolt – just as it can be for male travellers – because of the constant male attention. In the resort areas particularly, unaccompanied women can expect to receive a barrage of attention from Jamaican men, and although some of it is from sheer curiosity, a walk down the street will have you sized up by a thousand eyes. Just as you would in any destination you're visiting, cope with your new status as a sex goddess with humility and humour; it probably has more to do with your foreign allure – or perceived economic clout – than your personal charms, and a lot of the come-ons can be extremely amusing.

As lots of women do come to Jamaica in search of romance, many locals may inevitably assume that single female travellers have come here to find a man – or several – or are open to the idea. The news that you're not will lead to being left in peace by the semi-professional **gigolos** (and full-blown male prostitutes) who work the resorts and beach areas. If you're not interested, simply decline politely, avoid idle chat and keep your distance.

LGBT travellers

Jamaica is not a gay-friendly country. Sodomy (and so-called lewd acts, taken to mean any homosexual activity) is illegal here, condemned as a sin by the church and the moral majority, and fuel for much hysterical press coverage. And while there's a sizeable gay community here, it's very much an undercover scene, with parties and events publicized by word of mouth.

But this doesn't mean that gay and lesbian travellers should avoid Jamaica – many hotels are welcoming – just avoid displaying affection in public outside of the resort or you will likely attract negative reactions, and potential downright aggression. For more information contact J-Flag, the Jamaican gay and lesbian support group (☎ 754 2130 or ☎ 379 9834, ⌨ jflag.org).

Shopping

The Jamaican souvenir industry is precisely that – many of the carvings and knick-knacks are mass-produced, with little variation from maker to maker. However, the most common products tend to be the best, and though your "lignum vitae" Lion of Judah may be a pitch-pine copy of a thousand others, quality is generally good. Haggling is a natural part

of the trade at craft markets and stalls, but not in hotel boutiques and the more expensive, air-conditioned shops.

Where to shop

Virtually every town in Jamaica has at least one **market**, most selling fruit, vegetables and other produce, and often a limited selection of crafts, too. The resorts have dedicated craft markets selling T-shirts, wooden carvings, jewellery, straw goods, hats and assorted knick-knacks, and nearby are often ubiquitous roadside **craft stalls**. Ask if there's a women's community arts and crafts shop nearby, as this is often the best place to find unique handmade items.

Specialist **souvenir stores** also have a good stock of crafts and indigenous art as well as rum and cigars, while local galleries often have paintings, sculptures and woodcarvings for sale. Both souvenir stores and galleries tend to be pricier than the markets and stalls, but the standard of merchandise is higher.

In-bond – or duty-free – shops are usually clustered together in glitzy plazas and malls, stocked with perfume, spirits, designer clothes, brand-name watches, crystal, porcelain, diamonds and gold. Savings range from twenty to forty percent, all goods must be paid for in foreign (ie US) currency, and major credit cards are usually accepted. You'll need your passport and proof of onward travel.

What to buy

There are many alternatives to "Rasta" tams (a knitted hat) with attached fake locks or bamboo shakers: a custom-designed pair of leather sandals, the ubiquitous red-gold-and-green string vests and bandanas and tassels for car mirrors are all available in market areas of most towns. T-shirts have improved immeasurably in recent years; there are still plenty of dreadful ones emblazoned with caricature Rastas

---

SHELLS AND CORAL

Especially on the north coast, you'll see **coral** (particularly black coral) and "**tortoiseshell**" products (made from the endangered hawksbill turtle) on sale, but the trade in these protected species is **illegal**. Don't buy; you're liable to serious fines if you're caught with them. Though not illegal, conch shells, too, should be avoided, as demand has eclipsed supply and conch are slowly disappearing from Jamaican waters.

---

yowling "Yeh Mon it Irie", but you can also get some fantastically stylish alternatives.

Not surprisingly, **reggae music** is big business in Jamaica, and fans will have a field day. The best record stores are in downtown Kingston (see page 74), but music shops in any major town will sell CDs and some records too. Compilation CDs are available from roadside vendors throughout Jamaica (though note these are usually illegal copies); they also sell recordings of the most recent sound-system dances.

Other good Jamaican gifts include the prettily packaged range of essential oils, soaps, candles and bodycare accessories from Blue Mountain Aromatics and Starfish Oils, all made from natural local ingredients; both are available from more upmarket gift shops.

Food and drink

For a taste of Jamaica back home, you can pick up fiery **jerk sauce** or delicious **guava jelly** at any supermarket – the main locally made brands, such as Walkers Wood, Spur Tree and Busha Brown, are substantially cheaper when purchased in non-tourist shops. **Cocoa tea** balls, used to make the local version of hot chocolate, fresh **nutmeg**, and the delectable **honey**, sold in old rum bottles at any market, will all bring your memories flooding back. At both international airports, you can buy boxes of frozen Juici Beef and Tastee patties.

Rum (see page 248) is an obligatory memento – gift shops sell cardboard "Jamaica Farewell" packages holding two or three bottles for easy transit, though these are usually cheaper in the airport departure lounge; you can also save if you buy from a wholesale liquor shop or supermarket. The Sangster's company produces excellent **liqueurs**, on sale everywhere, and the ubiquitous Tia Maria coffee liqueur is another must-have. Finally, a packet of **Blue Mountain coffee**, sold all over the island but most reasonably in situ, is an essential souvenir, by far the best brand is Old Tavern, available in more upmarket outlets, but the JABLUM brands, sold in fetching hessian pouches, are good too.

Travel essentials

Costs

Jamaica's reputation as a "luxury" destination combined with the high cost of living compared to most developing countries means that this isn't a cheap destination by any means, though there are ways to make savings if you're on a budget. Some things, like car rental and petrol (and hence taxis, too), cost more than in Europe and a lot more than in the

US, while you'll pay a fair bit extra for a drink or a meal in a tourist-oriented restaurant or bar than you will in a locals' joint. Eating at local restaurants, and taking route taxis and public transport are the main ways to keep costs down, and there are inexpensive (if rather basic) accommodation options across the island. Equally, don't be scared to negotiate on prices – particularly in taxis and at markets and roadside stalls, the first price quoted is often an opening gambit, and even hotels and guesthouses are generally fair game for a bit of bargaining, especially during low season.

In terms of daily budgets, **accommodation** is likely to be the major expense. If you're prepared to put up with extremely basic guesthouses or hotels, eat and drink in locals' restaurants and travel around by route taxi or minibuses, you should be able to get by on a daily budget of around US$40/£26/€32 a day. A step up from this – a hotel with better decor and facilities, meals in tourist restaurants and bars, and car rental – will set you back around US$230/£147/€184 a day. At the upper end of the scale, staying at the best resorts, dining at the best restaurants, and hiring a car and driver will set you back at least US$360/£230/€288 a day – though the sky is really the limit.

Crime and personal safety

Jamaica has a bad reputation for violent crime, but while the island certainly does have its problems, you're very unlikely to get mixed up in them. Keep your common sense about you, and leave the valuables at home. The resort towns are generally well policed, Jamaicans are generally a hard-working and friendly people, and the JTB are keen to stress that you are more likely to be robbed in New York than Montego Bay. Most tourists still steer clear of the capital – even rural Jamaicans are wary of going into "Town", and you'll be warned against going out of the resorts – but such trepidation is incredibly misplaced. You'll be surprised at how safe and friendly Kingston feels. Drug-related organized crime is a frightening reality, but like most destinations, it affects mostly locals and it's almost always restricted to low income areas – pockets of west Kingston and Spanish Town that you're never going to go to; elsewhere, the vast majority of visitors experience no crime or violence during their stay.

POLICE

The **emergency number** for the Jamaican **police** is ☎119. Individual police stations are detailed throughout the text.

TIPPING

No tip is necessary at any **restaurant** that imposes an automatic service charge (although obviously you can leave one if service is good); ten to fifteen percent is the norm anywhere else. Tip **taxi drivers** at your discretion; route – or shared – taxi drivers do not expect a tip. A small consideration for services rendered, from minding your car to carrying your bag to your room, is the norm for most Jamaicans, and will always be appreciated, as will leaving something for your hotel **chambermaid** at the end of your stay.

At the same time, robberies, assaults and other crimes against tourists do occur, and it's wise to apply the **precautions** you'd take in any foreign city. Don't flaunt fat rolls of bank notes, avoid walking alone late at night, don't go mad smoking ganja in the street, lock your hotel room door at night – in short, use your common sense and you'll prevent potential problems before they happen. You might also want to read the travel advice of your own government (see below).

GOVERNMENT TRAVEL ADVICE

Australian Department of Foreign Affairs Ⓦ smarttraveller. gov.au.
British Foreign & Commonwealth Office Ⓦ gov.uk/foreign-travel-advice.
Canadian Department of Foreign Affairs Ⓦ gc.ca.
Irish Department of Foreign Affairs Ⓦ dfa.ie/travel/travel-advice.
New Zealand Ministry of Foreign Affairs Ⓦ safetravel.govt.nz.
US State Department Ⓦ state.gov/travel/.

Hustling

Hustling – the hard-nosed, hard-sell pitches you'll be endlessly subjected to on the north coast (see page 168) – can be the chief irritation of time spent in Jamaica. The tourist trade has long been adversely affected by the stream of young hopefuls aggressively (or humorously) accosting foreigners in the street with offers of transport, ganja, aloe massages, hair braiding and crafts. It's wearisome, but much of what is perceived as harassment is simply an attempt to make a living in an economically deprived country, and while some locals see tourists as easy prey for exploitation, many street touts are genuine. Hustling is a game played in the true entrepreneurial Jamaican spirit; the sales pitch is finely honed and modified to match the perceived nature of the potential client, and the national aptitude for "lyrics" (artful banter designed

MARIJUANA

Tourists do come to Jamaica in search of what aficionados agree is some of the finest marijuana in the world, and certainly ganja is part and parcel of the culture here to a greater degree than in other Caribbean islands, smoked more openly and available more freely – even when it was illegal. In 2015, Jamaica's government finally **decriminalized** possession of up to two ounces of marijuana. This means you can no longer go to jail for possessing two or less ounces but you may get a J$500 ticket instead, at police discretion. Note that Jamaican ganja packs a mightier punch than anything you're likely to have experienced before. Jamaicans who've been smoking since their teens can cope with a spliff before breakfast – fresh-off-the-plane visitors probably can't.

Bear in mind, also, that despite the stereotypical view of an island populated by ganja fiends, those Jamaicans who smoke are in a minority. Today, after centuries of abuse and arrest for minimal amounts of possession, ganja's links with the **Rastafarian** religion and frequent use as a medicinal draught is respected. Rastafari can consume the herb it as part of their religion, without limits. Also exempt from prosecution are visitors and locals using the herb per a doctor's prescription. For all others, any amount over two ounces of ganja on your person – tourist or local, unless Rastafari – remains criminal and carries stiff jail penalties.

If you choose to smoke ganja, stay within the legal consumption limit and trust your instincts. You will be approached with offers; buy only from someone you feel you can trust. You should be equally wary of carrying ganja around the island; if you pass a car at the roadside flanked by a worried-looking white person and a swarm of cops, you can bet that the police are conducting one of their routine searches. Finally, do not attempt to smuggle ganja out of the country under any circumstances; however devious you think your method, customs officials have seen it before, while sophisticated scanning machines can pick up the tiniest amounts. Even carrying rolling papers can prompt protracted questioning.

to break down even the most hardened sensibility) can make encounters with street vendors an-entertaining and educative experience rather than a trial. This often depends on your attitude to the approaches, so try to respond with humour and charm rather than irritation and frustration (which, admittedly, can be difficult when the fiftieth taxi driver of the day offers his services).

Electricity

The island standard is 110 volts, with two-pin sockets, though some older hotels still use 220 volts. Take adapters for essential items – some of the upmarket hotels and guesthouses have them, but you shouldn't rely on it. Current is poor in some areas, and foreign appliances can run slowly.

Entry requirements

Visitors from North America, the UK, Australasia and South Africa do not need a visa and are allowed stays of up to six months without one. On arrival, your passport will be stamped by an immigration officer who may ask you for proof of adequate funds, where you're staying during your holiday (if you don't know yet, pick any hotel in our listings, as you may be delayed if you can't name a place) and evidence of a return or onward flight.

It's possible to apply for an **extension** for up to twelve further months. You'll need to contact the Ministry of National Security, located at the Mutual Life Building, North Tower, 2 Oxford Rd, Kingston 10 (**☎** 876 754 7422, **🌐** mns.gov.jm) or, in Montego Bay, the Immigration Office at Overton Plaza, Union St (**☎** 952 5380 1).

JAMAICAN EMBASSIES AND CONSULATES ABROAD

Note that there are no Jamaican embassies or consulates in Australia, New Zealand or South Africa.

Canada Jamaica High Commission, 275 Slater St, Suite 800, Ottawa, Ontario KIP 5II9 **☎** 613 233 9311, **🌐** jhcottawa.ca.

UK and Ireland Jamaica High Commission, 1–2 Prince Consort Rd, London SW7 2BQ **☎** 020 7823 9911, **🌐** jhcuk.org.

US Embassy of Jamaica, 1520 New Hampshire Ave NW, Washington DC 20036 **☎** 202 452 0660, **🌐** embassyofjamaica.org.

Health

Health-wise, travelling in Jamaica poses few problems. Food tends to be well and hygienically prepared and the filtered and heavily chlorinated tap water is safe to drink. Jamaica is not generally malarial and malaria prophylaxis are not considered necessary for visitors. There are occasional outbreaks of **dengue fever**, and more recently **Chickungunya**, carried by the *Aedes aegypti* mosquito, found throughout the

HEALTH AND WELLNESS TOURISM

Aside from the reggae, sun, and ganja, visitors have long flocked to Jamaica in search of a spiritual and physical recharge. While some now officially seek out medically approved amounts of marijuana, others can delight in a range of improved wellness offerings across the island, created in an effort to encourage **health and wellness tourism**.

Recently opened **Grande Spa in Montego Bay** boasts 30,000 square feet of space, with quartz spa beds, yoga and barre studio, and the Caribbean's first Himalayan salt halotherapy lounge. Reflexology, tabata, pilates and yoga are on the menu at **The Cliff Hotel in Negril**, though **Jackie's On the Reef** remains a respected, secluded wellness and spiritual escape. In the meantime, the mineral baths in Milk River and St Thomas still await promised developments.

island, which can be serious for the infirm, very young or very old. Symptoms include extreme aches and pains in the bones and joints, rashes around the torso, dizziness, headaches, fever and vomiting. There's no effective vaccination. **Zika** has also been detected in Jamaica, and though incidences dropped sharply in 2017, it's good to remain vigilant if you are trying to get pregnant. The virus is transmitted by female *Aedes aegypti* and *Aedes albopictus* mosquitoes, which tend to be active from dawn to dusk; Zika can also be transmitted sexually, through saliva, and urine. Symptoms include mild fever, muscle and joint pain, vomiting and headaches, and is often characterized by pink eye and skin rashes. There's no antiviral treatment for Zika.

To avoid being bitten by **sandflies** and **mosquitoes**, cover arms and legs at dusk and dawn, and apply lots of DEET-rich repellent. Mosquito coils are sold everywhere and can be effective, if a bit smelly, and many hotels provide plug-in anti-mossi devices, too. Of more natural alternatives, the locally produced Starfish Oil of No Mosquito is a nice citronella-based repellent. Once you've been bitten (and you will be), gently apply some antihistamine, after which you shouldn't touch the area at all. Though

OUTDOOR DANGERS

Jamaica has no poisonous snakes, but there are a few underwater hazards to be aware of. **Spiny black sea urchins** are easily missed in a bed of sea grass – if you tread on one, remove the spines immediately, soak the skin in vinegar (or urine) and see a doctor; water heated as hot as you can stand is useful for getting out the spines. Never touch **coral**; apart from the fact that contact kills the organism, coral can cut and you'll come away with a painful, slow-to-heal rash. If you do have a brush with the reefs, don't touch the affected area directly, but wash it with a diluted vinegar or ammonia solution.

hellishly tempting, scratching (or even a light investigative rub) will always lead to more irritation, bigger red marks and possibly infection.

If you're unused to it, Jamaica's **humid climate** can bring on a host of minor complaints. Open wounds take longer to heal and easily become septic: clean cuts straight away, and dress with iodine, dry antiseptic spray or powder rather than creams. Blocked sweat ducts can cause uncomfortable and unsightly **prickly heat** rashes; to treat or avoid these, wear loose cotton clothes, take frequent cool showers without soap, dust with medicated talcum powder and don't use sunscreen or moisturizer on affected areas. It's also important to remember to drink plenty of water, and always apply high factor sunscreen when outside (and, if possible, keep out of the sun between 11am and 3pm).

Jamaica has the third-highest incidence of **AIDS** in the Caribbean, with the disease being the leading cause of death for Jamaicans in their twenties. Unofficial sex tourism has long been a part of the scenery in the resorts; if you do have sex while away, always use a condom. Brand-names such as Durex are available in pharmacies and larger gas stations.

There are two, sizeable public hospitals in Kingston, while Cornwall Regional in Montego Bay is the best equipped on the north coast. Although many locals can't afford it, you are guaranteed better care, facilities and service at private hospitals or clinics in the main towns, with Hospiten Montego Bay, opened in October 2015, and St Andrew's Memorial in Kingston being two of the best. The easiest way to find a doctor in a hurry is to ask at your hotel; some have a resident nurse, and all will be able to recommend a doctor or private clinic locally. Most of these are reliable, but you'll have to fork out for the treatment and claim on your insurance (see page 41) once back home, so make sure you get receipts.

Every town has at least one **pharmacy**, with those in resort towns well stocked with expensive brand-name products; they will only issue anti-biotics with a doctor's prescription.

MEDICAL RESOURCES

Canadian Society for International Health ☎ 613 241 5785, ⓦ csih.org. Extensive list of travel health centres.

CDC ☎ 800 232 4636 ⓦ cdc.gov/travel. Official US government travel health site.

International Society for Travel Medicine US ☎ 1404 373 8282, ⓦ istm.org. Has a full list of travel health clinics.

Hospital for Tropical Diseases Travel Clinic UK ⓦ www.thehtd.org/TravelClinic.aspx

MASTA (Medical Advisory Service for Travellers Abroad) UK ⓦ masta-travel-health.com for the nearest clinic.

The Travel Doctor – TMVC ⓦ traveldoctor.com.au. Lists travel clinics in Australia, New Zealand and South Africa.

Tropical Medical Bureau Ireland ☎ 1850 487 674, ⓦ tmb.ie.

Insurance

It's always sensible to take out **travel insurance** before visiting Jamaica to cover against theft, loss and illness or injury. A typical policy will provide cover for loss of baggage, tickets and – up to a certain limit – cash or cheques, as well as cancellation or curtailment of your journey. Most exclude so-called dangerous sports unless an extra premium is paid: in Jamaica, this can mean scuba diving, windsurfing or white-water rafting, though probably not kayaking or jeep safaris. When securing baggage cover, make sure that the per-article limit will cover your camera or any other valuables. If you need to make a claim, you should keep receipts for medicines and medical treatment, and in the event of having anything

ROUGH GUIDES TRAVEL INSURANCE

Rough Guides has teamed up with **WorldNomads.com** to offer great travel insurance deals. Policies are available to residents of over 150 countries, with cover for a wide range of adventure sports, 24hr emergency assistance, high levels of medical and evacuation cover and a stream of travel safety information. Roughguides.com users can take advantage of their policies online 24/7, from anywhere in the world – even if you're already travelling. And since plans often change when you're on the road, you can extend your policy and even claim online. Roughguides.com users who buy travel insurance with WorldNomads.com can also leave a positive footprint and donate to a community development project. For more information, go to ⓦ roughguides.com/shop.

stolen, you must obtain an official statement from the police.

Internet

Internet access is available in all towns and resorts, with both dedicated cybercafés and wi-fi in many bars and restaurants. Almost all hotels have a connection, too, with terminals for guests' use and/or wi-fi, while libraries and larger post offices sometimes have free access.

Laundry

Most hotels have a **laundry service**, but check prices before handing over a huge load as charges can be per-item and not at all cheap. Many large towns have at least one public laundry (listed in the relevant chapters), which is a less expensive option.

Maps

For touring or driving around the island, the best map to get hold of is the **Shell Jamaica Road Map** (1:250,000), which is contoured and includes excellent street maps of Kingston, Montego Bay and Ocho Rios as well as Spanish Town, Mandeville and Port Antonio. It's sold in good bookshops and selected Shell petrol stations islandwide. Also useful, and a more manageable size, is the JTB road map, *Discover Jamaica*, which includes a 1:350,000 map of the entire island, a 1:34,000 map of Kingston and small maps of the other main towns. It's available from JTB offices abroad, and, in Jamaica, from the offices in Kingston and Montego Bay – you may have to pay a small fee. A useful app to download, available free of charge for smartphones, is maps.me – allowing offline access to downloaded country maps of choice.

Money

Jamaica's unit of currency is the **Jamaican dollar** (J$), divided into 100 cents. It comes in bills of J$5000, J$1000, J$500, J$100 and J$50 and coins of J$20, J$10, J$5 and J$1, plus seldom-used copper coins (in locals' stores, it's common to be given boiled sweets in lieu of small change). Note that the J$100 and $1000 bills look very similar – it's surprisingly easy to mix them up. At the time of writing, **exchange rates** were US$1=J$125, £1=J$164 and €1=J$143. Given the constant fluctuation of the Jamaican dollar, the **US dollar** has long served as an unofficial parallel currency, particularly at the north coast resorts, and prices for tourist services – hotels, car rental, sightseeing tours, etc – are usually quoted in US$. Restaurants and bars vary, with some quoting US, others Jamaican; for minor items like bus fares, short taxi rides or roadside snacks, drivers and vendors will always quote Jamaican dollars. In the resorts, US dollars are as widely accepted as Jamaican, but when paying a bill, check in advance that your change will be given in the same currency or, if in Jamaican dollars, at a decent exchange rate. It's a good idea to always carry some Jamaican dollars to pay for small things like snacks, drinks, tips and taxi fares.

Credit and debit cards

The easiest way to access funds in Jamaica is by using your ATM card; machines are widespread, at some shopping malls and petrol stations as well as banks. Note that there have been cloning issues at select ATMs in heavy tourist areas – while there are no guarantees, choose one inside a resort, or inside the bank for less probability of outside tampering. Before you leave home, check with your bank that your card is cleared to use abroad, and find out what the fees for overseas withdrawals are. Some can be quite high, so you may want to make one large withdrawal rather than several small ones. ATMs dispense local cash and, in large resorts, US dollars. Major **credit cards** – American Express, Visa, Master-Card – are widely accepted in the larger tourist hotels, but smaller hotels and restaurants may not take them.

Banks and exchange

Banking hours in Jamaica are generally Monday to Thursday 9am to 2pm and Friday 9am to 3pm or 4pm, and will often have a separate queue for foreign exchange. Given their limited hours, though, you'll probably find you make more use of **cambios**, ubiquitous in the resorts and also within many supermarkets. They usually offer a better exchange rate than the banks, particularly when the currency is fluctuating wildly, as well as opening longer hours. A firm favourite, with consistently good rates, are the islandwide branches of FX Trader, often conveniently situated within super-markets and shopping malls; you can find out the location of the nearest office by calling toll-free on ☎ 1 888 398 7233. Exchange bureaux at the main airports offer rates slightly lower than the banks, and at **hotels**, the rate is invariably

> The **area code** for Jamaica is 876. As of May 2018, a 658 area code will be added, which will also require everyone to use ten-digit dialling across the board.

significantly lower – it's only worth changing money at hotels if you have no other choice.

Opening hours and public holidays

Jamaican offices are normally open for business between 8.30am and 4.30 or 5pm Monday to Friday, often closing for an hour at lunch, while **shops** are typically open from 8am to 5pm Monday to Saturday, although **supermarkets** tend to open until 8 or 9pm, as well as on Sundays. **Museums** normally close for one day a week, either Sunday or Monday, while most other places you'll want to visit – private beaches, waterfalls, gardens, churches and so on – are generally open daily.

PUBLIC HOLIDAYS

The main **national holidays**, when virtually all shops and offices close, are as follows:

New Year's Day (January 1)
Ash Wednesday
Good Friday
Easter Monday
Labour Day (May 23)
Emancipation Day (August 1)
Independence Day (first Mon in August)
National Heroes Day (third Mon in October)
Christmas Day (December 25)
Boxing Day (December 26)

Phones

The main national telecommunications providers in Jamaica are FLOW (Ⓦ discoverflow.co/jamaica) and Digicel (Ⓦ digiceljamaica.com).

If you have a tri-band **mobile phone**, you can use it in Jamaica by way of roaming. You'll pay a lot less for local and international calls if you buy a local SIM card from any of the innumerable outlets island-wide (around US$15). You're given a local number, and you can top up your credit at shops, bars, petrol stations and restaurants islandwide.

Another cheap way to make international calls from hotel phones or private landlines is to use pre-paid WorldTalk **phonecards**, widely available from hotels, post offices, gift shops and supermarkets.

Photography

Jamaica is made for pretty pictures, though overex-posure can also be a problem: watch out for the glare from sea and sand, and try to take pictures early or late in the day when the sun is less bright. When photographing people (or their homes and

CALLING HOME FROM JAMAICA

To make an international call, dial the international access code (in Jamaica it's 011), then the destination's country code, before the rest of the number. Note that the initial zero is omitted from the area code when dialling the UK, Ireland, Australia and New Zealand from abroad.

US and Canada international access code + 1

Australia international access code + 61

New Zealand international access code + 64

UK international access code + 44

Ireland international access code + 353

South Africa international access code + 27

property), always ask permission – some like it, others don't – and anticipate a request for a donation.

Post

International mail is slow – reckon on around ten days to a fortnight for airmail to reach Europe or North America. If you're really in a hurry to send something overseas, try DHL (toll-free ☎ 1 888 225 5345 or ☎ 920 0010, ⓦ dhl.com.jm) or FedEx (toll-free ☎ 1 888 463 3339, ⓦ fedex.com/jm).

Most towns and villages have a **post office**, normally open Monday to Friday from 9am to 5pm; smaller postal agencies in rural areas keep shorter hours. Those in large towns have **poste restante** facilities: mail is held for about a month, and you'll need your passport or other identification to collect it. **Stamps** are sold at post offices and in many hotels. It costs J$60 to mail a postcard to anywhere in the world; rates for international letters are J$60–100. Rates for parcels are available online at ⓦ jamaicapost.gov.jm.

Time

Jamaica is on Eastern Standard Time and does not adjust for Daylight Saving Time. Accordingly, it's on the same time as New York (one hour behind from spring to autumn) and five hours behind London (six hours from spring to autumn).

Tourist information

Though Jamaica spends a great deal on lavish advertising campaigns, the **Jamaica Tourist Board** (JTB) isn't a user-friendly source of information on the island. Offices in Jamaica – in Montego Bay, Kingston and Port Antonio (see pages 173, 68 and 108 respec-

tively) – aren't really geared up to deal with enquiries from visitors, though they can answer basic questions. The **internet** is a far better source of information; start off at the JTB's website, ⓦ visitjamaica.com, which has a regularly updated calendar of events, plus accommodation, resort and attraction listings and hoards of local information. Other good general sites include ⓦ jamaicans.com, a huge site with everything from language and culture to cookery and tourist info, plus busy message boards; and ⓦ go-jamaica.com "Jamaica's portal to the world" that lists everything from career opportunities to online dating, events and links to news.

Jamaica has no entertainment listings' magazine, so to find out what's going on, you have to rely on the **radio** (particularly Irie FM; see page 134), **newspapers** (see page 31) and – the usual way of announcing -forthcoming events – **flyers** and **banners** posted up all around the towns. There are also a host of websites dedicated to entertainment listings; try ⓦ cometojamaica.com, ⓦ partyhaad. com, ⓦ yardflex.com, ⓦ keepitjiggy.com and ⓦ digjamaica.com.

Travellers with disabilities

Large- to medium-sized hotels, and most of the big all-inclusive chains, have ramps or lifts on their properties, though Jamaica isn't particularly geared toward people with disabilities – expect accessibility to be a recurrent problem. However, though facilities are poor, you'll find that most people are quick to help out should you have mobility issues. The Combined Disabilities Association of Jamaica, 18 Ripon Rd, Kingston (☎ 929 1177) may be able to help with further advice.

Travelling with children

Pellucid seas, gently shelving beaches, no serious health risks and an indulgent attitude towards kids make Jamaica an ideal destination if you're travelling with children. Though some larger hotels (the *Sandals* chain in particular) operate under a couples-only policy, most welcome families, and some all-inclusive properties are specially geared for families, with extensive facilities, daily events and personal nannies: best are the *Beaches* resorts in Negril, Boscobel and Sandy Bay (ⓦ beaches.com), *Hilton Rose Hall* (ⓦ rosehallresort.com) in Montego Bay, the *Royalton* (ⓦ royaltonresorts.com) in Falmouth and Negril and the *Franklyn D. Resort* in Runaway Bay (ⓦ fdrholidays. com). There are also many hotels with kids' clubs that offer parents an afternoon off. Equally, it's usually easy to arrange babysitting through your hotel.

Kingston and around

DEVON HOUSE, KINGSTON

1 Kingston and around

Overwhelming and fascinating in equal measure, Kingston is quite unlike anywhere else in the Caribbean. Overhung by the magnificent Blue Mountains to the north and lapped by a huge natural harbour to the south, the city holds as many pockets of opulence as it does zinc-fenced ghettos, and its wide boulevards see top-of-the-range SUVs fighting for space with pushcarts and the odd goat. Nonetheless, in the 1950s, Ian Fleming called Kingston a "tough city", and that still holds true today. Jamaica's capital is rough and ready, a little uncompromising, but always exciting – and though its troubled reputation means that few tourists visit, Kingston is infinitely more absorbing than any of the resorts and bursting with culture.

With some 700,000 residents (22 percent of the island's total population), Kingston seethes with life, noise and activity, the glitzy malls of uptown and the faded, rough charm of downtown revealing a side of Jamaica that couldn't be more different to the north coast. As well as being the seat of government and the island's administrative centre, Kingston is Jamaica's cultural and historical heart, the city that spawned Bob Marley, Buju Banton, Beenie Man and countless other reggae stars, and the place where Marcus Garvey first preached his tenets of black empowerment. And, with a plethora of theatres and galleries, it's one of the best places on the island to fully appreciate the country's home-grown art, theatre and dance scenes.

If you do decide to visit – and it's well worth the effort for anyone with even a passing interest in Jamaican culture – you'll find that not only is it easy to steer clear of trouble, but that there's none of the persistent **harassment** that bedevils parts of the north coast. In comparison to Ochi or Negril, the capital feels refreshingly real, with most Kingstonians far more interested in going about their business than trifling with a tourist. That's not to say that city dwellers are unfriendly; in fact, it's far easier to strike up a decent conversation here than in more conventional tourist honeypots, where every interaction can seem like a precursor to a sales pitch. The pulsating, live-for-today vitality of the place, combined with the urbane outlook of its citizens, injects a shot of adrenalin that often proves addictive, and the exuberant atmosphere is tempered by a cool elegance and a strong sense of national history. If you follow the herd and avoid the capital, you'll have missed one of Jamaica's undoubted highlights.

Brief history

Though the Spanish first settled in Jamaica in 1510, replaced by British colonists in 1655, there was little development in present-day Kingston until 1692. The area held just a small pig-rearing village, glamorously known as Colonel Beeston's Hog Crawle, and a handful of fishing shacks. All of the action was across the harbour on the island of Port Royal, then Jamaica's second city (after Spanish Town) and home to most of

TUFF GONG RECORDING STUDIOS, KINGSTON

Highlights

❶ National Gallery A wealth of works from Jamaica's most important artists, from Edna Manley to Kapo. See page 54

❷ Bob Marley pilgrimage Tour the Trench Town Culture Yard, where Marley grew up; the museum in his former home; and, the family's Tuff Gong Recording Studios. See pages 60 and 61

❸ Sports events Music, flowing Red Stripe and plenty of crowd participation are fine accompaniments to seeing a football match at the National Stadium, some cricket at Sabina Park or the horseracing at Caymanas. See pages 61, 68 and 81

❹ Gastronomy Indulge in the best dining scene in Jamaica, from local restaurants to farm to table gourmet dining, wine and cheese shops, and an annual Jamaica Food & Drink Festival. See page 70

❺ Nightlife Fancy cocktails at the *Regency Bar*, reggae jams at the *Dub Club*, weekly street dances and all night clubbing: the capital's nightlife scene is legendary. See page 72

❻ Port Royal and Lime Cay Peppered with eighteenth-century military buildings, this former pirate stronghold is an atmospheric place for a plate of fresh seafood or an island hop to Lime Cay. See page 77

HIGHLIGHTS ARE MARKED ON THE MAPS ON PAGES 48 AND 50

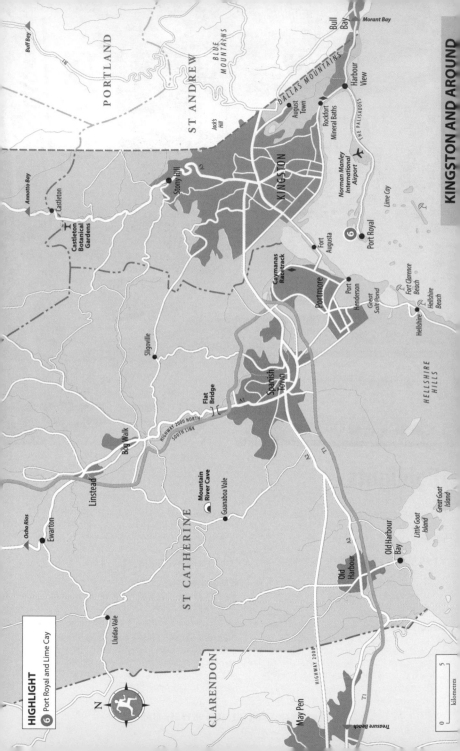

HIGHLIGHT

6 Port Royal and Lime Cay

N

0   5
kilometres

PORTLAND

ST ANDREW

Buff Bay

BLUE MOUNTAINS

Morant Bay

Bull Bay

DALLAS MOUNTAINS

Jack's Hill

August Town

Rockfort Mineral Baths

Harbour View

THE PALISADOES

KINGSTON

Stony Hill

Annotto Bay

Castleton

Castleton Botanical Gardens

Fort Augusta

Norman Manley International Airport

Lime Cay

6 Port Royal

Caymanas Racetrack

Portmore

Port Henderson

Great Salt Pond

Fort Clarence Beach

Hellshire

Hellshire Beach

Sligoville

Spanish Town

HELLSHIRE HILLS

Flat Bridge

A1

HIGHWAY 2000 NORTH

SOUTH LINK

Bog Walk

Linstead

Mountain River Cave

Guanaboa Vale

A2

T1

ST CATHERINE

Ewarton

Ocho Rios

Great Goat Island

Little Goat Island

Old Harbour

Old Harbour Bay

A2

Lluidas Vale

CLARENDON

HIGHWAY 2000

T1

May Pen

Treasure Beach

EXPLORING KINGSTON

Kingston's main sights are divided between the area known as "downtown", which stretches north from the waterfront to the busy traffic junction of Cross Roads, and "uptown", spreading up into the ritzy suburbs of Jack's Hill and Cherry Gardens at the base of the mountains with the division lying roughly at Half Way Tree. It'll take you a couple of days to check out the main sights downtown, and about the same amount of time to catch those uptown. **Downtown** is the city's industrial centre, its factories and all-important port providing most of the city's blue-collar employment; the law firms, stock exchange and the Bank of Jamaica are also prominent features. **Uptown** is different, and you may be surprised at how attractive and easy-going it feels, as suited businessmen and office workers go about their daily routines. Most of Kingston's hotels, restaurants, clubs and shopping centres are here, and it's where you'll spend most of your time.

Finding your way around Kingston is pretty straightforward. Downtown uses a grid system, while uptown is defined by a handful of major roads. You'll quickly get used to the main landmarks, and as a reliable fallback, the mountains to the northeast and the high-rises of New Kingston serve as good compass references should you lose your way, while locals are invariably helpful with directions.

the country's leading lights. In 1692, however, a violent **earthquake** devastated Port Royal; several thousand people died instantly and the rest went scurrying for a more hospitable place to live. The Hog Crawle was the obvious choice – on the mainland but beside the harbour – and the former citizens of Port Royal promptly snapped up two hundred acres of land there.

Within a few months of the earthquake, the plans for the new town had been drawn up. Newborn Kingston was named in honour of William of Orange, king of England from 1689 to 1702, and the town was laid out beside the water to take advantage of the existing **sea trade**. The road plan mostly followed a grid system (which remains largely intact today) with the big central square of the **Parade** left open in the heart of town.

Kingston develops

By the early eighteenth century, Kingston had become a **major port** for the transshipment of English goods and African slaves to the Spanish colonies of South America. Merchants, traders and brokers made rapid fortunes and began to build themselves ostentatious homes, while fresh waves of **immigrants** piled into the booming city – some from Europe, some from other Caribbean islands, some from other parts of Jamaica, all in search of opportunity.

With its swelling population and rising wealth, the city soon began to challenge for the role of the **nation's capital**, though the authorities in Spanish Town – comfortably ensconced in their grand Georgian buildings – proved stubborn in handing over the title to their upstart neighbour. By 1872, when Kingston finally became Jamaica's capital city, many wealthy families were already moving beyond the original town boundaries to the more genteel areas that today comprise **uptown** Kingston. Meanwhile, the less affluent huddled downtown and in the **shanty towns** that began to spring up on the outskirts of old Kingston, particularly west of the city, their ranks swollen by a tide of former slaves hoping to find prosperity beyond the sugar estates.

The twentieth century

Jamaica's turn-of-the-century boom, engineered by tourism and agriculture, largely bypassed Kingston's poor and helped to reinforce the divide between uptown and downtown. While the rich got richer and sequestered themselves in the new suburbs uptown, the **downtown** area continued to deteriorate. Those who could afford to do so continued to move out, leaving behind an increasingly destitute

1

KINGSTON

HIGHLIGHTS

1 National Gallery
2 Bob Marley pilgrimage
3 Sports events
4 Gastronomy
5 Nightlife

BLUE MOUNTAINS

GORDON TOWN

GORDON TOWN ROAD

Newcastle & Buff Bay

B1

Mavis Bank

N

SKYLINE DRIVE

JACK'S HILL ROAD

Stony Hill, Castleton Botanical Gardens & Annotto Bay

BARBICAN ROAD

CONSTANT SPRING

CHERRY GARDENS

JACK'S HILL

HOPE PASTURES

Hope Botanical Gardens

OLD HOPE ROAD

PAPINE

UTech Campus

University of the West Indies

AUGUST TOWN

WINDWARD ROAD

Norman Manley International Airport, Port Royal & Morant Bay

MONA

MONA ROAD

DALLAS MOUNTAINS

BEVERLY HILLS

MOUNTAIN VIEW AVENUE

National Stadium

3

WELLINGTON DRIVE

LIGUANEA

Bob Marley Museum

OLD HOPE ROAD

TRAFALGAR ROAD

4

OXFORD ROAD

NEW KINGSTON

HALF WAY

TREE RD

VINEYARD TOWN

CAMP ROAD

ALLMAN TOWN

SOUTH CAMP ROAD

RAE TOWN

WINDWARD ROAD

CONSTANT SPRING ROAD

HAVENDALE

SEE "UPTOWN KINGSTON" MAP

WATERLOO RD

Devon House

5

A3

DUNROBIN AVENUE

MOLYNES ROAD

HALF WAY TREE

LYNDHURST ROAD

SLIPE ROAD

A4

TRENCH TOWN

2

Trench Town Culture Yard

HARBOUR STREET

SEE "DOWNTOWN KINGSTON" MAP

1

RED HILLS

RED HILLS ROAD

FOREST HILLS

RED HILLS ROAD

MOLYNES ROAD

WALTHAM PARK

HAGLEY PARK ROAD

MAXFIELD AVENUE

TIVOLI GARDENS

Tuff Gong

Tinson Pen Airport

WASHINGTON BOULEVARD

PATRICK CITY

WASHINGTON GARDENS

SPANISH TOWN ROAD

SEAVIEW GARDENS

MARCUS GARVEY DRIVE

Kingston Harbour

SIX MILES

A1

CAYMANAS PARK RACE TRACK

PASSAGE FORT DRIVE

PORTMORE PARKWAY

DAWKINS DRIVE

CAUSEWAY

AUGUSTA DRIVE

GREATER PORTMORE

Port Henderson, Hellshire & Great Salt Pond

Spanish Town

May Pen

0   1   2
kilometres

population that proved fertile recruitment ground for the **Rastafari** movement during the 1920s and 1930s.

There were major **riots** during the 1930s, with the city feeling the knock-on effects of an islandwide economic crisis sparked by the plunging price of key crops like bananas and sugar on world markets. The riots led to the development of local trade unions and political parties during the 1940s; these organizations spoke for the workers and the dispossessed, but improvements in working conditions and the physical infrastructure were slow in coming. Finally, in the 1960s, the city authorities began to show some interest in reversing the decay. Efforts were made to give the old downtown area a face-lift; redevelopment of the waterfront resulted in a much-needed expansion of the city's **port facility** (still a vital part of the city's commerce today) and a smartening-up of the harbour area with the introduction of shops, offices and even the island's major art gallery.

A mini-**tourist boom** was sparked by the new-look Kingston (and by the growing popularity of Jamaican music abroad), with cruise ships arriving to inject a fresh air of hope into the city. Sadly, the optimism proved short-lived. For the people of downtown Kingston, the redevelopment of downtown was only cosmetic. Crime – an inevitable feature in the crowded ghettos – was getting out of control, sponsored by politicians who distributed weapons and patronage to their supporters. At election time (particularly in 1976 and 1980), hundreds of people were killed in bloody campaigns, many of them innocent bystanders. Tourists ran for cover, heading for the new beach resorts on the island's north coast, and the city sank into a quagmire of unemployment, poverty and crime (see page 59).

Kingston today

Today, Kingston remains a divided city. The wealthy have moved further and further into the suburbs, coming in to work in the downtown business district or the smart uptown area of New Kingston but rarely venturing downtown after dark; meanwhile, the ghettos remain firmly under the control of gangs, led by infamous characters euphemistically referred to as "area leaders". Rays of hope are slowly breaking through the tough facade of downtown, with a cautious optimism suggesting that the status quo might be beginning to change.

SAFETY AND HARASSMENT

The **pestering** of tourists, irritatingly widespread on the north coast, is refreshingly uncommon in Kingston. Nevertheless, Kingston's crime statistics are undeniably ugly and, as with any big city, there are some places that you should steer clear of. There is serious poverty in the eastern and western residential areas of downtown Kingston (see page 59) – these ghettos are not places for casual sightseeing and, with the exception of visiting the Trench Town Culture Yard (see page 60) for example, there is no reason to venture into them. If you are unlucky enough to be the victim of an attempted robbery, do not, under any circumstances, resist your assailant – hand over whatever they're asking for, and get away as quickly as possible.

The more central part of **downtown**, covered in this guide, has its share of impoverished enclaves, and violence occasionally spills over from the surrounding ghettos to the core commercial streets described in this book, but if you use your common sense and don't flash cash, jewellery or fancy cameras, you're unlikely to have any problems during the day. However, once the area's office workers have departed – around 5.30pm – there is little reason to linger.

During the day, the **uptown** area feels fine, particularly once you're familiar with the main roads. At night, you're best off getting a taxi if you're travelling any distance. If you're driving late at night, be aware that some local drivers may not stop at traffic lights to prevent potential robberies; whether or not you choose to follow suit, it's wise to slow down and look each way at junctions even when you have a green light.

1 Downtown

Flattened by an earthquake in 1907, **downtown Kingston** has lost most of its grand eighteenth-century architecture, and much of what remains is slowly crumbling into dereliction. Nevertheless, numerous historic buildings can still be found along Rum Lane, Water Lane and King Street, and if you peer into the most unlikely yards you can often find evidence of the intricate structures that used to proliferate here, with their fancy ironwork, marble floors, red-brick facades and wrap-around verandas. In recent years, government tax incentives have been created to encourage redevelopment of the area, although it is alleged that much of downtown has since been bought up by speculators, and the only evident development spawned from these incentives was the building of telecom giant Digicel's flagship headquarters on the waterfront; their foundation also spent US$1 million restoring the famous Coronation Market to its former glory (see page 57).

Though many locals still hesitate to walk the downtown streets, you'll find that exploring on foot is not only the best way to get the full flavour of the area but also feels surprisingly **safe**. The usual common-sense rules apply, of course (see page 51), but unless the violence that occasionally breaks out in the surrounding ghettos spills over into downtown's central commercial streets, there's no reason to expect any problems.

The waterfront

The chief beneficiary of the city council's 1960s bid to beautify elements of downtown, the **waterfront** saw its historic buildings swept away and replaced by spanking new high-rises – icons of the era. Today, these modern monuments define the eastern end of the waterfront's main strip, **Ocean Boulevard**. Much of Kingston's economic strength still derives from its impressively huge natural **harbour** – the seventh largest in the world. Once grimly polluted, there are now concerted government efforts to clean up the waterfront and revitalize it. With the pending opening of new restaurants – currently under construction – along the wind-whipped **waterfront**, its wide grassy boulevard, pelicans and people, benches and concrete piers, will become an even better place and a good spot to start a tour of the downtown area.

Negro Aroused Statue

Junction of King St and Ocean Blvd

The striking reproduction of the sculpture **Negro Aroused** is not to be missed; the bronze sculpture is by the late Edna Manley, one of Jamaica's leading artists and wife and mother, respectively, of former Prime Ministers Norman Manley and Michael Manley. One of the icons of twentieth-century Jamaican art, it captures the incipient labour movement and the spirit of unrest of the 1930s, and is dedicated to the workers of Jamaica (though you wouldn't know it, as the title plaque is long gone).

Money Museum

Nethersole Place • Mon–Fri 10am–4pm • Free • ☎ 922 0750, ⊛ boj.org.jm

Located in the high-rise headquarters of the Bank of Jamaica, the small **Money Museum** is a surprisingly absorbing, if compact, exhibition on the country's currency. The well-labelled collection takes you through a history of money, from barley grains, cowrie shells and Taino beads to notes and coins, including the "anchors" and "Christian quatties" first issued by the British in Jamaica. It's worth calling ahead to arrange a (free) guided tour with one of the very informative curators.

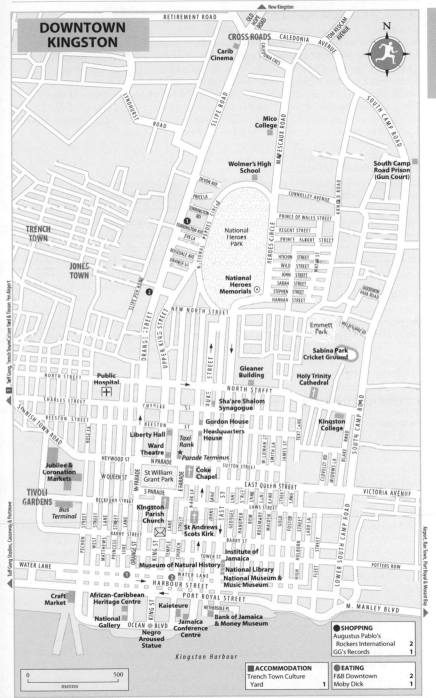

DOWNTOWN KINGSTON

1

New Kingston

RETIREMENT ROAD

OLD HOPE ROAD

CROSS ROADS   CALEDONIA   AVENUE

TOM REDCAM AVENUE

N

Carib Cinema

CALEDONIA CRES

Mico College

SLIPE ROAD

MINESCAUX ROAD

SOUTH CAMP ROAD

Wolmer's High School

DEVON AVE

CONNOLLEY AVENUE

ARNOLD ROAD

South Camp Road Prison (Gun Court)

PRICE LA

TORRINGTON RD

TORRINGTON AVE

EVE LA

ROSEDALE AVE

ORANGE LI

NATIONAL HEROES CIRCLE

National Heroes Park

PRINCE OF WALES STREET

REGENT STREET

PRINCE ALBERT   STREET

HTICHIN   STREET

WAY ST

WILD   STREET

JOHN   STREET

SARAH   STREET

STEPHEN   STREET

HANNAH   STREET

GOODWIN PARK ROAD

HEROES CIRCLE

National Heroes Memorials ⊙

TRENCH TOWN

JONES TOWN

SLIPER ROAD

NEW NORTH STREET

Emmett Park

MELROWNE AV

ORANGE STREET

UPPER KING STREET

STREET

Gleaner Building

Sabina Park Cricket Ground

Holy Trinity Cathedral

Public Hospital H

NORTH STREET

NORTH STREET

SOUTH CAMP ROAD

CHARLES STREET

CHARLES   ST

DUKE   STREET

Sha'are Shalom Synagogue

SPANISH TOWN ROAD

BEESTON STREET

ROSE LA

BEESTON   ST

Gordon House

Headquarters House

Kingston College

Liberty Hall

Ward Theatre

HEYWOOD ST

N PARADE

Taxi Rank ★

Parade Terminus

WLDMAN ST

SMITH LA

JAMES ST

TEXT LANE

BLAKE ROAD

Jubilee & Coronation Markets

W QUEEN ST

St William Grant Park

SUTTON STREET

Coke Chapel

EAST QUEEN STREET

CLOVELLY RD

WIDOWS' LA

TIVOLI GARDENS

S PARADE

PARK LA

Kingston Parish Church

BECKFORD STREET

St Andrews Scots Kirk

DANE ST

GEORGES ST

HANOVER ST

RUM LANE

ROSEMARY LANE

MAIDEN LANE

GOLD STREET

FOSTER STREET

LADD LA

VICTORIA AVENUE

SOUTH CAMP ROAD

Bus Terminal

PECHON STREET

WEST STREET

MATHEWS LANE

PRINCESS STREET

LUKE LANE

ORANGE ST

KING ST

TEMPLE LANE

CHURCH ST

BARRY STREET

BARRY ST

LAWS STREET

HOLBORN STREET

HIGH STREET

FLEET STREET

LOWER SOUTH CAMP ROAD

POTTERS ROW

WATER LANE

TOWER ST

Museum of Natural History

Institute of Jamaica

WATER LANE

National Library

HARBOUR STREET

National Museum & Music Museum

PORT ROYAL STREET

M. MANLEY BLVD

Craft Market

African-Caribbean Heritage Centre

Kaieteure

NETHERSOLE PL

Bank of Jamaica & Money Museum

National Gallery

OCEAN BLVD

Negro Aroused Statue

Jamaica Conference Centre

Kingston Harbour

Tuff Gong, Trench Town, Cane Yard & Tinson 'en Airport ◄ **T1**

Tuff Gong Studios, Causeway & Portmore ◄

Airport, Rae Town, Port Royal & Morant Bay ►

0 — 500
metres

1

Jamaica Conference Centre

14-20 Port Royal St • Mon–Fri 9am–4pm • ☎ 922 9160, ⓦ jamaicaconference.com

Built in 1981 to host meetings of the United Nations' International Seabed Authority, the enormous **Jamaica Conference Centre** boasts an impressive lofty design with an abundant use of glass and local crafts, providing a poignant glimpse of a time when downtown Kingston looked forward to a heady future at the centre of a vibrant Caribbean economic community. Upstairs, look out for a huge rendition of the Jamaican coat of arms, wrought out of metal and forming the end to one of the building's corridors, with a lovely view stretching down to the sea visible between the figures. You should also be able to get a free tour (ask at reception).

The National Gallery

12 Ocean Blvd, but entered around the corner on Orange St • Tues–Thurs 10am–4.30pm, Fri 10am–4pm, Sat 10am–3pm, last Sun of month 11am–4pm • J$400 • Guided tours J$3000, call in advance to arrange • ☎ 922 1561, ⓦ natgalja.org.jm

The pleasantly air-conditioned **National Gallery** – opened in 1974 – is one of the highlights of a visit to Kingston. The permanent collection here is superb, ranging from delicate woodcarvings to flamboyant religious paintings, while the temporary exhibitions (up to four annually), including the Biennial (see page 33), showcase the best of contemporary Jamaican art from the new vanguard of Jamaican painters, sculptors and mixed-media artists. **Guided tours** of the gallery are well worth taking, providing essential background to, and interpretation of, the works on show, and can be tailored to personal tastes.

The permanent collection consists of ten chronological galleries housed on the first floor, representing the Jamaican School, 1922 to the present. Dominating the earlier rooms are works by artists deemed to have been the forerunners of the art movement in Jamaica, including Edna Manley, John Dunkley, Albert Huie and David Pottinger. Later galleries feature the prolific work of Carl Abrahams and show a move towards abstraction which was capped by Colin Garland and David Boxer (a longtime curator of the gallery). Realism returned later with Barrington Watson, Kay Brown and Dawn Scott, whose *A Cultural Object* is a particularly unique and powerful re-creation of a Kingston ghetto and not to be missed. Look out for colourful, spiritual works by Everald Brown, Karl Parboosingh, Gloria Escoffery and Ralph Campbell. There is also an entire room that houses the Larry Wirth Collection of African-style sculpture and paintings by Revivalist Shepherd Mallica "Kapo" Reynolds, as well as a slew of beautiful wood sculptures.

Institute of Jamaica

IOJ 10–16 East St • Mon–Thurs 8.30am–5pm, Fri 8.30am–4pm, Sat 10am–3pm • J$400 • ☎ 922 0620, ⓦ instituteofjamaica.org.jm • **National Library** 12 East St • Mon–Thurs 9am–5pm, Fri 9am–4pm • ☎ 967 2494, ⓦ nlj.gov.jm

Founded in 1879 by the then Governor Sir Anthony Musgrave "for the encouragement of literature, science and art in Jamaica", the **Institute of Jamaica** has responsibility for eight organizations, including its neighbouring buildings – the Natural History Museum, the National Library, the National Museum and the Music Museum (access to all of which are included in the entrance fee) – and, elsewhere in downtown, Liberty Hall (see page 56), the National Gallery (see page 54) and the African-Caribbean Institute of Jamaica/Jamaica Memory Bank. The **National Library** is an incredible resource for anyone wanting to research all things Jamaican.

The museums

Natural History Museum ⓦ nhmj-ioj.org.jm • **National Museum** ⓦ museums-ioj.org.jm • **Music Museum** ⓦ jamm-ioj.org.jm

The **Natural History Museum**'s main exhibition consists of a collection of musty cabinets filled with dust-gathering stuffed birds, and displays explaining the origins of the country's most important "economic plants" – sugar cane, bananas, coconuts and

JAMAICAN ART

Although the Tainos left paintings on cave walls and visiting British artists captured the colonial era on canvas, **Jamaican art** really only came into its own in the twentieth century. The island's modern art movement was led by **Edna Manley** (1900–87), an English sculptor who had married prime-minister-to-be Norman Manley and moved to Jamaica in 1921, and whose arresting work has come to be seen as a turning point in Jamaican art. In 1939, she led a group of artists who stormed the annual meeting at the Institute of Jamaica to demand an end to the domination of Anglophile attitudes to art, and the replacement of the colonial portraits that hung in the galleries with works by local artists. Though more symbolic than revolutionary, their gesture did galvanize Jamaican painters and sculptors, and Manley's classes at the **Jamaica School of Art** (now the Edna Manley College of the Visual and Performing Arts), which she co-founded, helped give direction to a new wave of local artists.

There were two distinct artistic styles in the work of this new crop of Jamaican artists. Most studied in England at one time or another and followed a classical European approach. **Albert Huie** (1920–2010) and **Barrington Watson** (1931–2016) used natural forms and landscapes as reference points, incorporating the lives of black Jamaicans into their work for the first time, while **Gloria Escoffery** (1923–2002) played with abstract themes, depicting a range of subjects, from quiet pastoral scenes to the traditional Saturday market.

The paintings of the self-taught artists, known as "**Intuitives**", were perhaps more distinctive. The prodigious **John Dunkley** (1891–1947) made his name by covering every inch of his Kingston barber shop with pictures of trees, vines and flowers; his later paintings (now much sought after) continued his obsession with dark, brooding scenes from nature. Many intuitive artists focused their work around religious imagery. **Mallica "Kapo" Reynolds** (1911–89), the shepherd (head) of a Revivalist group in Kingston, became the first self-taught Jamaican painter to be fully accepted by local and foreign audiences, and is still seen as the island's foremost intuitive sculptor and painter. Other artists such as **Albert Artwell** (born 1942) and **Everald Brown** (1917–2002) – a priest in the Ethiopian Coptic Church – concentrate on Rasta beliefs.

In the 1960s and 1970s, Jamaican art became more experimental, most noticeably in the surrealism represented by the work of **David Boxer** (born 1946) and Australian-born **Colin Garland** (1935–2007). Today, Jamaica's art scene continues its diversity. At the bottom end, it's dominated by the huge carving and painting industry that has grown up around mass tourism, and although much of it is relentlessly mediocre, there is some decent art at the craft markets in Kingston and across the north coast, and in Kingston's clutch of galleries. The establishment of the **National Gallery** in 1974 gave the art scene an important institutional infrastructure, and the regular exhibits of Jamaican art continue to encourage the development of young painters and sculptors, as witnessed by the proliferation of studios and galleries islandwide. You can also see the best of contemporary Jamaican art during the annual **Kingston on the Edge** arts festival (see page 32).

---

pineapples – almost all imported from areas of Asia during the early years of Spanish and British colonialism, and now widely grown for export. The museum was being refurbished at the time of writing and only a small temporary but colourful exhibition of the endemic butterflies of Jamaica was available for viewing.

Only temporary exhibitions are held at the **National Museum** and the **Music Museum**, both of which are more modern than their natural history counterpart; although displays are always clearly labelled, guided tours (free) are available and worth asking from. Previous exhibitions have included ones on the cover album art of Jamaican records and the evolution of Rastafari in Jamaica.

The Parade

A large square left open by the original city planners, the **Parade** was used as a parade ground by British troops during the eighteenth century. Today, it's one of the busiest parts of town, serving as downtown's transport hub. In the middle of the Parade is

1

St William Grant Park, originally Victoria Park but renamed in 1977 for the (often overlooked) 1938 labour leader William Grant. Rather fierce statues of political rivals Norman Manley and Bustamante guard the park's north and south entrances, while Queen Victoria – the one-time "Supreme Lady of Jamaica" – stands to the east, looking a little lost among all the mayhem.

Ward Theatre
North Parade • ☎ 922 0453, ⓦ wardtheatrefoundation.com

Looking like an elaborately iced birthday cake, the once elegant **Ward Theatre** occupies a site with a long theatrical tradition. It is reckoned that public performances have been staged here since at least the mid-eighteenth century and probably earlier. The present building, bestowed on the city by one-time Custos and rum baron Colonel Charles Ward, dates from 1911; sadly, it's showing its age these days and was, at time of writing, closed for performances as it awaits completion of a much-anticipated renovation. It's slated to reopen sometime in 2018.

Coke Methodist Church
East Parade • Service Sun 9.30am • Free • ☎ 922 2224 • Guided tours available, call in advance to arrange

The large red-brick Methodist church dates from 1840 when it was erected over the remains of a smaller eighteenth-century chapel. Damaged in the 1907 earthquake, it was redesigned in the neo-Gothic style, with greater structural support provided by filling in features like the underground tunnel that allowed slaves to worship. Named after Dr Thomas Coke, founder of the Methodist mission to the West Indies, the church was declared a national monument in 2002.

Kingston Parish Church
70b King St • Services Sun 6.30am & 8.30am • Free • ☎ 922 6888 • Guided tours available, call in advance to arrange

The **Kingston Parish Church** was first built in 1699, although little of the present structure predates the 1907 earthquake. Airy and spacious, the church is used for important state funerals and such, although the regular congregation has dwindled to almost nothing due to migration out of the downtown area.

King Street

King Street, striking north and south from the centre of the Parade, was once downtown's grandest thoroughfare and the heart of the island's financial district. Some illustrious structures still remain – look out for the courthouse and the GPO buildings, south of the Parade near the junction with Tower Street – and though the usual melee of fast-food restaurants, haberdasheries and general stores vastly outnumber the banks and government buildings these days, the street remains an absorbing place for a wander.

Liberty Hall
76 King St • J$400 • **Museum** Mon–Thurs 10am–4pm, Fri 10am–3.30pm • ☎ 948 8639, ⓦ libertyhall-ioj.org.jm

Set back from King Street in a tree-shaded yard stands **Liberty Hall**, site of the Kingston headquarters of **Marcus Garvey**'s Universal Negro Improvement Association, or **UNIA** (see page 150). Over a thousand Liberty Halls were established by the UNIA worldwide, and this one, first opened in 1923, was a hotbed of activity in Garvey's heyday, serving both as a community resource – with a laundry, canteen, job centre and cooperative bank – and as social club-cum-meeting place for UNIA members and associated organizations; it was from here in 1927, following his deportation from the US, that Garvey addressed a huge crowd of supporters. After Garvey's departure for England in 1935, however, the building was used variously as an entertainment and sports centre before falling into disrepair. It was acquired by the Jamaica National

Heritage Trust in 1987, and restored and reopened in 2003; today, as in Garvey's time, it serves as a community resource, with a reference library and a multimedia centre offering low-cost computing courses. It runs educational outreach programmes for local children, including a summer arts course, as evidenced by the lovely mosaic on the exterior walls and the murals around the top-floor Great Hall.

Also on site is an engaging **museum**, with interactive touch-screens, a collection of UNIA-related memorabilia, a small theatre screening films on Garvey and pan-Africanism and, of course, a shop. The building is also used for regular concerts, poetry performances and lectures.

Coronation Market

Pechon St • Mon–Sat 7am till late

Jamaica's oldest and largest market, **Coronation Market**, is also its busiest, especially on Saturday (market day) when all eight hundred booths are occupied by vendors with produce from across the island. Though not a traditional tourist spot, and backing on the occasionally volatile community of Tivoli Gardens, the market is a complete sensory experience, offering a unique insight into one of the island's economic streams, and a great opportunity to people-watch while sampling local fruits and snacks. It's best visited with someone who knows their way around, as it can be hard to navigate the throngs of people.

Headquarters House

79 Duke St • Mon–Fri 8.30am–4.30pm • Free • ☎ 922 1287, ⓦ jnht.com • Guided tours available, call in advance to arrange

Currently home to the head office of the Jamaica National Heritage Trust, **Headquarters House** was built in 1755 by Thomas Hibbert, a wealthy merchant from Lancashire who had come to exploit the rich trading opportunities Kingston afforded. After Hibbert's death, the building served as the city's military headquarters (hence the name) until Jamaica's legislative assembly moved in full time and operated there between 1872 and 1960. The house remains a good example of what life was like for a merchant in Kingston's mercantile heyday and although the building now houses the JNHT offices, the staff are happy to let visitors wander around.

Gordon House

81 Duke St • ☎ 922 0200, ⓦ japarliament.gov.jm

Named after National Hero, George William Gordon (see page 58), **Gordon House** has been the home of the Jamaican Parliament since 1960. Today the House of Representatives meets here most Tuesdays at 2pm (and at the same time on Wednesdays and Thursdays if there is sufficient business), while the Senate sits in the chamber on Fridays at 11am. At these times, surrounding streets are sometimes cordoned off. Entrance to the public gallery is free, and when the chamber is empty you can ask the marshal to show you round.

Sha'are Shalom Synagogue

92 Duke St Museum • Mon–Thurs 10am–4pm • Suggested donation US$5 • ☎ 922 5931, ⓦ ucija.org

Jamaica's only Jewish synagogue, the **Sha'are Shalom Synagogue** was built after the 1907 earthquake that destroyed the original two synagogues – the Ashkenhazi and the Sephardic. The building, with its mahogany staircase and gallery, is worth a visit if you're passing and has a regular schedule of services which you can find out about on their website. Although usually kept locked, a quick call ahead might afford you a guided tour that features a short and engaging film about the history of Jews in Jamaica.

1

> ### JAMAICA'S NATIONAL HEROES
>
> Since independence, the Jamaican parliament has elevated seven of the island's greatest people to the status of **National Hero**, all of whom carry the title "The Right Excellent". As yet, none of the Heroes hail from the worlds of sport or music, but it is widely anticipated that Bob Marley will be next to join the pantheon. Michael Manley, who died in 1997, is another popular candidate. The present National Heroes are:
>
> **Paul Bogle** (unknown–1865). Baptist preacher who led the 1865 Morant Bay Rebellion and was executed for his participation.
>
> **Alexander Bustamante** (1884–1977). Labour leader, founder of the Jamaica Labour Party and first prime minister of the independent country from 1962 to 1967.
>
> **Marcus Garvey** (1887–1940). Founder of the Universal Negro Improvement Association and widely viewed as the father of the black power movement.
>
> **George William Gordon** (1820–65). "Free coloured" leader of Jamaica's nationalist movement after slavery, executed by the British for his part in the Morant Bay Rebellion.
>
> **Norman Manley** (1893–1969). Lawyer, founder of the People's National Party and leader of Jamaica's movement for independence.
>
> **Nanny** (birth and death dates unknown). Legendary eighteenth-century female leader of the Windward Maroons in their battles with the English.
>
> **Sam Sharpe** (1801–32). Baptist preacher executed after leading the 1831 slave rebellion in Jamaica's western parishes.

National Heroes Park

National Heroes Circle

The largest open space in Kingston at almost 20 hectares, **National Heroes Park** is, thanks to renovations and landscaping, showing more signs of its former glory than ever before. Once home to the city's racecourse, it now boasts a small playground, several large stretches of grass, used for spontaneous games of football, and beautiful clusters of tropical flowers that soften the concrete-heavy surroundings, creating an oasis among the chaos of downtown. The highlight of the park is the monument to Jamaica's **National Heroes** (see above) some of whom are interred here. The area is still patrolled by gun-toting soldiers and guarded by two JDF sentries sweltering in full ceremonial uniform (there's a foot-stomping changing of the guard each hour).

Adjacent to the monument is a bust of **Antonio Maceo** and a statue of **Simón Bolívar**, independence leaders in Cuba and Venezuela respectively, and inspirational to Jamaica's early nationalists. Bolivar was exiled to Jamaica for a year in 1815 following his unsuccessful revolt against Spanish rule in Venezuela. While living in a boarding house on the corner of Princess and Tower streets, he survived an assassination attempt by the Spanish and penned his "Letter from Jamaica", in which he laid out the reasoning behind his struggle for South American liberation.

Alpha Institute

26 South Camp Rd • Tours Mon–Thurs 9am–4pm • Suggested donation US$15 • ☎ 928 1345, ⊛ alphaboysschool.org

Formerly called the Alpha Boys' School, the 137-year old **Alpha Institute** has turned young men from inner city communities into musical stars over the century – its most notable graduates being the Skatalites, accredited for giving birth to the sound of ska music in the early 1960s. The school has recently evolved in its curriculum thanks to the opening of a Sean Paul Music Technology Centre, where hundreds of youths can earn certificates in their chosen musical vocation. The three-year music programme admits students with experience in basic instrument playing, and provides training in trades such as mixing, radio broadcasting, and disc jockeying, while learning from experienced entrepreneurs. Call at least 24 hours in advance to arrange an hour-long campus tour to see where past Jamaican artists perfected their craft, and listen to tomorrow's future stars.

Trench Town

Eulogized in Marley and the Wailers' *Trench Town Rock, No Woman, No Cry* and *Natty Dread*, **Trench Town** – one of the government social housing communities of West Kingston – has earned the title of the birthplace of reggae and popular Jamaican urban culture. This was the first Kingston home of Bob Marley, who earned his nickname – the "Tuff Gong" – on the community's football fields after his mother relocated to the capital when he was a small boy and moved into a government-built house at 19 Second Street. In Trench Town Bob Marley found a community rich in music, religion, nationalism and sports. Though the area's "**government yards**", built in the colonial 1940s, were conceived as part of a planned community and were seen as desirable places to live when Mother Booker (Marley's mum) moved there in 1956, the political violence of Jamaica in the 1970s soon took its toll. Trench Town today is as infamous for garrison politics and gang feuds as it is for having spawned some of the biggest

KINGSTON'S GHETTOS

Taking up huge swathes of downtown, Kingston's **ghetto communities** are the country's urban nightmare. Bob Marley sang fondly of growing up in the "government yards in Trench Town", but the contemporary reality is a huge underclass confined to crowded, makeshift homes enclosed by rusting, graffiti-daubed zinc, their communities bearing suitably conflicted names, from Dunkirk and Jungle to Tel Aviv and Zimbabwe.

In the city's early years, downtown was a popular residential zone – well laid out and central. Trench Town's government yards were planned communities that proudly boasted all the modern conveniences and for a time (despite their cramped nature) provided a desirable place to live for Jamaica's working class. Before long, however, the combination of a high influx of rural job seekers, a soaring rate of unemployment and a lack of housing made downtown a grim place to live. Criminal elements were quick to take advantage of these conditions, recruiting and arming gang members from the ranks of the poor. The crime problem was exacerbated in the **1970s** as politicians provided guns and favours for their supporters, asking them to intimidate – at the very least – opponents or drive them out of their "**garrisons**" or constituencies. The "PNP zone" or "JLP enter at your own risk" graffiti that you'll still see plastered over downtown walls stand testament to the strong political allegiances of the communities, many of which remain divided along political lines.

While political violence still flares up at election times and army-enforced night-time curfews are sometimes in effect for months on end, the people of the ghettos of West Kingston have largely washed their hands of a political class that seems to have done them no long-term favours despite the years of promises. Instead, many now give their allegiance to high-profile "**area leaders**" or "**dons**", who earn the favour of their communities as much as by staging free "fun days" for local people and doling out school books and cash to the needy as they do by "keeping the peace" through sheer fire-power and their publicly declared truces with rival areas. Over the years, various government-established anti-crime initiatives have led to several high-profile arrests – most notably that of Christopher "Dudus" Coke in 2010, a drug lord and leader of the violent Shower Posse gang which had controlled Western Kingston since the 1980s. But with continued profits from drug trafficking and protection rackets said to be worth millions, the government faces a seemingly insurmountable task of ever truly ridding the ghettos of dons and their gangs. These days it's money, not party politics, that rules.

If you're considering a visit to Trench Town, it's worth considering a tour (see page 60). Keep an ear out for reports of trouble in the area, don't carry too much money with you, and it's a good idea to start early, to avoid being here after dark. But you'll be fine if you come for the night-time concert that's staged here around the time of Bob Marley's birthday – and there's something very special about, in the words of Bob Marley himself, "grooving in Kingston 12".

For more on the capital's ghettos, Laurie Gunst's book *Born Fi Dead*, David Howard's *Kingston* and Orlando Patterson's powerful novel *Children of Sisyphus* provide an interesting insiders' view of life here. For a cinematic perspective, check out *Third World Cop*, while Perry Henzell's seminal *The Harder They Come*, though released in the early 1970s, still has much relevance today.

1

names in the rock steady and reggae pantheon, including the Wailers, Joe Higgs, Delroy Wilson, Alton Ellis, Ernie Ranglin, Dean Fraser and the Abyssinians. Also from here are numerous Jamaican notables, from Labour leader and Garveyite St William Grant to the late Rastafarian elder Mortimer Planno, and famous sports personalities such as cricketer Collie Smith and footballer Carl Brown. Trench Town is also home to two top Premier Club League football teams, Boys Town and Arnette Gardens.

Though Trench Town remains one of Kingston's poorest areas, the picture isn't entirely bleak. Over recent decades, enterprising members of this tight-knit community have clubbed together to find ways in which to regenerate their area using their heritage and cultural status for economic development. The first initiative was the establishment, in 1993, of the **Trench Town Reading Centre** on First Street (ⓦtrenchtownreadingcentre.com), a library and resource centre with a mission to arm local people with information rather than weapons. By 1996, the aim had widened, and the **Trench Town Development Association** was formed to address the pressing issues of sanitation, security, housing, health and employment.

Trench Town Culture Yard

6 & 8 Lower First St • Daily 6am–6pm • US$12 • ☎ 859 6741

The **Trench Town Culture Yard** (TTCY) is set in the government yard where Bob Marley sought refuge after returning from living in the US, and where he was taught to play the guitar by his mentor, community elder Vincent "Tarta" Ford, who himself wrote *No Woman, No Cry* here. Shaded from the street by a lush canopy of mango-tree leaves, it's also where Peter Tosh, Bunny Wailer and Bob formed the Wailers and wrote the *Catch a Fire* LP. The museum is a work in progress; its galleries have greatly improved and the overall restoration of the buildings has been successful, the experience and presentation commendable, and it was declared a National Heritage Site by the Government of Jamaica in 2007. It's also possible to stay here (see page 70).

The collection

The tour of the museum's collection begins in one of the property's restored residential buildings. These well-designed buildings are oriented around the yard's central open-air courtyard, where residents would have washed clothes, gardened and socialized; the rusting remains of Marley's powder-blue VW van sit in a corner, while around the back is Jah Bobby's original, colourful and rather odd statue of Marley with his preferred guitar and football, which formerly graced the front yard of the Hope Road museum (see page 64). Sensitively refurbished and retaining many original features and fittings, from "Tarta" Ford's graffitied bedroom walls to the single bed on which Bob and Rita slept, the rooms also hold one of Tarta's and Marley's first acoustic guitars and a selection of Adrian Boot's beautiful photographs of the man himself taken during his time in the yard. Tours end at the *Casbah Bar* at the front of the property which, together with the shady veranda outside, provides a lovely space to kick back and reflect on the life and work of a man whose music and message has achieved such long-standing and universal appeal.

ARRIVAL AND TOURS   TRENCH TOWN

While your safety is assured in and around the Culture Yard (there's a community-based vested interest in ensuring the success of the project, after all), wider Trench Town itself remains a volatile place (see page 59).

By taxi Entering the area by taxi (versus walking, bus or otherwise) is recommended. On Time Taxi (see page 68) will happily take you there – from New Kingston it will cost you J$800 one-way, from Ocean Blvd J$600; they will wait (at an additional fee) or come back for you as requested.
Tours The Trench Town Culture Yard (see above) offers a number of tours of Trench Town and the surrounding area, from simple visits to the Culture Yard (US$12) to ones that also take in more of the area, including Bob Marley's childhood home and the former home of Delroy Wilson (US$30); night tours to street dances and bars are also available, from US$5.

Tuff Gong Recording Studios

220 Marcus Garvey Drive • Mon–Sat 9am–4pm • Tour 55min • US$20; combo ticket with Bob Marley Museum US$40 • ☏ 923 9383, ⓦ tuffgong.com • A route taxi will cost J$100 from the waterfront to Three Miles and nearby Marcus Garvey Drive

If you're a Bob Marley devotee, you might want to head to Marcus Garvey Drive, a battered but wide thoroughfare lined with warehouses and factories. The state-of-the-art **Tuff Gong Recording Studios**, established by Bob Marley, is now one of Kingston's premier recording studios, as well as one of its biggest CD pressing plants. It's a commercial venture rather than a tourist sight, but you can **tour** the facility to see the self-same mixing board used on Wailers' classics such as *Stir It Up*, *Concrete Jungle* and *No Woman, No Cry*. If the studios are in use, you may not get access to all areas – it's up to whoever's recording. While not wildly exciting, it's a nice stop for Marley disciples, with a gift shop for that essential CD, LP or T-shirt.

Uptown

The phrase "uptown Kingston" is used as a catch-all for areas of the city north of Cross Roads, including the business and commercial centres of **Half Way Tree** and **New Kingston** as well as residential areas like **Hope Pastures Mona** and **Beverly Hills**.

The National Stadium

Independence Park, Arthur Wint Drive, east of New Kingston • ☏ 926 1514 • For schedules and ticket information visit ⓦ jff.live, ⓦ facebook.com/jamaicanationalstadium • Bus #83 runs here regularly from New Kingston (till 11pm; J$120)

The forty-thousand-capacity **National Stadium** was built to coincide with Jamaica's independence celebrations in 1962; the first event here was the raising of the new nation's black, green and gold flag, and the 1966 Commonwealth Games were held here. The stadium hosts most of Jamaica's premier sporting events; the facilities for athletics, swimming, netball, basketball and cycling are first-rate, but the centrepiece is the football pitch and athletics track – home to the national football team, fondly known as the Reggae Boyz, and Jamaica's track and field superstars – surrounded by towering aisles of bleachers and overlooked by arc lights. Just inside the railings by the car park is a statue of Jamaican athlete Herb McKenley coming off the starting blocks; at the 1952 Helsinki Olympics, McKinley became the first man in the world to run in the 200-, 400- and 800-metre races.

JAMAICA'S TRACK AND FIELD SUCCESS

Although historically famous for its contribution to West Indies cricket, Jamaica's outstanding achievements in the area of track and field continue to propel the island nation into the limelight of the sporting world. Its record of achievement, remarkable for such a small country with limited resources, began in 1948 when the island, still a British colony, entered its first Olympics and has included the successes of medallists such as Arthur Wint, Herb McKenley, Don Quarrie and Merlene Ottie. In more recent years, team Jamaica, spearheaded by the likes of **Usain "Lightning" Bolt** and team members Asafa Powell, Yohan Blake, Michael Frater, Nestor Carter, Shelly-Ann Fraser-Pryce, Melaine Walker and Veronica Campbell-Brown, have broken records and created history in the Beijing (2008), London (2012) and Rio (2016) Olympics.

Despite their base in Jamaica, it is rare to see the country's star athletes in action on their home turf. A great way to see Jamaica's rising stars, however, is to catch the annual **Inter-Secondary Boys and Girls Championship**, otherwise known as Champs. This four-day event (usually held the week before Easter) at the National Stadium sees the very best high-school athletes competing against each other; it is here that university coaches and sporting companies – such as Puma and Adidas – come in search of the sporting stars of the next generation.

1

▲ ❶ 🚊 Stony Hill & North Coast

UPTOWN KINGSTON

0   500
metres

N

■ DRINKING & NIGHTLIFE

Club Privilege	12
Countryside Club	8
CRU	7
Cuddy'z	11
Dub Club	1
Fiction	3
Jojo's Jerk Pit	6
Mas Camp	10
Red Bones Blues Café	9
Regency Bar	4
Ribbiz UltraLounge	2
Waterfalls	5

● EATING

Café Blue	7
Cannonball Café	1
Chez Maria	15
Chilitos	6
Deli Works	7
Dragon Court	13
Earl's Juice Garden	22
East	4
Fromage Gourmet	16
I-Scream	17
Jojo's Jerk Pit	14
Juici Patties	8
Opa	11
Pita Grill	10
Red Bones Blues Café	19
The Steakhouse at the Verandah	18
Tamarind	9
Tastee	20
Tea Tree Creperie	12
The Terrace at Liguanea Club	21
Tracks and Records	5
Triple Tz	2
Uncorked	3

ALLERDYCE

The Barbican Center

BARBICAN

King's House

Bob Marley Museum

Sovereign Centre

Jamaica House

Devon House

Vale Royal

BEVERLY HILLS

HWT Terminus

St Andrews Parish Church

HALF WAY TREE

CAMPERDOWN

Peter Tosh Museum

0   100
metres

NEW KINGSTON

Central Stage Theatre

New Kingston Shopping Centre

Putt n Play

Emancipation Park

Bob Marley Statue

National Arena

National Stadium

Little Theatre & Little Little Theatre

Parish Library

Carib Cinema

CROSS ROADS

● SHOPPING

Carby's Souvenir and Craft Village	6
Craft Cottage	5
Derrick Harriot's One Stop	6
HiQo Art Gallery	3
Island Art	2
Music Mart	4
My Jamaica	2
Starfish	7
Tads International	1

■ ACCOMMODATION

Alhambra Inn	8
Altamont Court	9
Courtleigh	12
Eden Gardens Wellness Resort and Spa	5
Hotel Four Seasons	7
Inn at 6	2
Jamaica Pegasus	11
Liguanea Club	10
Neita's Nest	1
Reggae Hostel	4
Spanish Court Hotel	6
Terra Nova	3

▼ Downtown   Port Royal & St Thomas ▼

Half Way Tree

Before it got swallowed up by the expanding city, **Half Way Tree**, west of New Kingston, was a tiny village and the capital of the parish of St Andrew. Its central plaza – today a busy shopping area and one of Kingston's key road intersections – once provided a resting place for farmers travelling into the city's markets. The eponymous cotton tree under which they sheltered is long gone, and a clock tower now stands in its place, a 1913 memorial to British King Edward VII. With nose-to-back traffic sweltering under the sun, vendors hawking iced water and newspapers at the traffic lights, and queues of hungry workers standing in line at the pretty-pink *Tastee Patties* outlet, Half Way Tree today is about as far away from a resting place as it's possible to imagine.

St Andrew's Parish Church

Hagley Park Rd · Services Sun 6.30am, 8am, 10.30am & 6pm; Tues & Fri 9am; Wed 6.30am · ☎ 968 9366, ⓦ standrewparishchurch.com

Founded in 1664, **St Andrew's Parish Church** remains one of the oldest churches in Jamaica and perhaps for that reason stands oddly marooned between the streams of traffic and city life. Though largely submerged by the modern buildings that have arisen around it, this is still a tranquil and gently alluring edifice; despite being in its fourth incarnation, the church features some of the oldest and most beautiful monuments and memorials (including stained-glass windows) of any church on the island.

New Kingston

The heart of uptown is the high-rise district of **New Kingston**, contained in an eccentric triangle bounded by Trafalgar Road, Old Hope Road and Half Way Tree Road. The chances are that you'll stay and do much of your eating and drinking in or around this area, some of the interesting sights are within walking distance, the rest are a short bus or taxi ride away. Although there are only a couple of places of note in New Kingston itself, the Peter Tosh Museum and the peaceful and attractively landscaped Emancipation Park, with its striking bronze statues and fountain, are both definitely worth a visit, as is the Liguanea Club, for a cool drink on the airy veranda.

The Peter Tosh Museum

38a Trafalgar Rd · Mon–Fri 9.30am–6pm, Sat 10am–6pm · US$20 · ☎ 960 0049, ⓦ petertosh.com/museum

Peter Tosh fans might rejoice at the sight of the new **Peter Tosh Museum** opened in the heart of New Kingston in late 2016, despite a hefty price for a small and sparse display occupying a single floor. The museum walls recount the trajectory of Tosh's life and contribution to Jamaica's music scene with a combination of text and a few photographs, starting with his youth, and continuing through his time with the Wailers until his murder in 1987. On display are a few memorabilia, including his original M16 guitar, and golden microphones that Mick Jagger gifted Tosh. You can skip the audio room where a rotating Tosh concert playlist runs on Youtube, and instead watch a brief documentary on Tosh's life as told by the people who were closest to him and his music.

Emancipation Park

Corner of Oxford Rd and Knutsford Blvd · Mon–Fri 5am–11pm, Sat & Sun 5am–midnight · Free · ☎ 926 6312, ⓦ emancipationpark.org.jm

Opened in 2002 as a memorial to the 1838 cessation of slavery in Jamaica, **Emancipation Park** has become the preferred oasis for people seeking respite from the hustle and bustle of the surrounding city. A manicured and well-maintained space, with more concrete than grass, the park features a well-used jogging track and an amphitheatre/stage that frequently hosts free concerts. Make a beeline for the stunning **Redemption Song** by local sculptor Laura Facey-Cooper, a majestic study of a Jamaican couple facing each other and looking skywards; their ample breasts and genitals inevitably caused outrage when the sculpture was first installed in 2003. Though the park is a nice spot to take a breather during the day, it comes into its own at night, when couples canoodle and families turn

1

out to promenade and gaze at the central "sky cascade" fountain, its ever-changing jets of water lit by coloured lights to delightful effect.

Liguanea Club
Knutsford Blvd • ☎ 926 8144, ⓦ theliguaneaclub.com

Established in 1910, the **Liguanea Club** still retains its old colonial buildings as well as lots of lovely tennis courts (available for rent). In theory the club is open to members only, but it's easily accessible if you're passing, and also offers accommodation (see page 70) and a good restaurant (see page 72) on a light and breezy outdoor patio shaded by mango trees. The building served as the fictional Queens Club, where James Bond took cocktails on the veranda with Professor Dent in the classic movie *Dr No*.

Devon House
26 Hope Rd, vehicular entrance on Waterloo Rd • Tours by appointment • US$10 • ☎ 929 6602, ⓦ facebook.com/devonhousejamaica

Tall iron railings overhung by towering trees mark the grassy complex ranged around **Devon House**, built in 1881 by Jamaica's first black millionaire and still one of the city's grandest buildings. Rumour has it that nearby Lady Musgrave Road, which circuitously bypasses Devon House, was built at the request of the wife of Anthony Musgrave, Jamaica's governor from 1874 to 1883, so that she could get to King's House without having to pass such a fine house owned by a black Jamaican.

Born in Kingston in 1820, building contractor **George Stiebel** made his fortune mining gold in Venezuela, returning home in 1873 to snap up 99 properties throughout Jamaica (ownership of a hundred was prohibited by law). Among these was Devon Pen, where he built the house that was his Kingston home until he died in 1896. Bought by the Jamaican government in 1967, and first used to house the National Gallery before it moved to its present downtown location, the house has gradually been furnished with West Indian and European antiques as well as more modern Jamaican reproductions.

The grounds
The landscaped grounds of Devon House make a fine place for a leisurely stroll, with plenty of breezy benches and shady spots to while away the midday heat. You've a good chance of running into one of the numerous wedding parties who come here for their photos (regular tourists may only use smartphones to take images on site). Most visitors, though, make straight for the former stables, which now house a handful of gift shops stocking a good range of rather expensive ephemera, as well as a smattering of cafés, restaurants and the ever-popular I-Scream ice-cream shop (see page 71).

The Bob Marley Museum
56 Hope Rd • Mon–Sat 9.30am–5pm (last tour 4pm) • US$25; combo ticket with Tuff Gong US$40 • ☎ 630 1588, ⓦ bobmarleymuseum.com

For reggae fans, the **Bob Marley Museum** is the whole point of a visit to Kingston and, even if you're not a serious devotee, it's well worth an hour of your time – though don't expect a Disney-type theme-park ambience. Hidden from the street by a red-, gold- and green-painted wall and marked by fluttering Rasta banners, this beautiful colonial-era wooden building was Marley's Kingston home from 1975 until his death from cancer in 1981, and was designated a National Heritage site in 2006. It's been kept much as it looked when he lived here, and is a gentle monument to Jamaica's greatest musical legend. The hour-long **tour** starts as soon as you pass through the gates (no photography, filming or taping is allowed inside the house), with the guide pointing out photographs of the singer and his family mounted on the walls, a battered jeep formerly owned by Marley, and Pierre Rouzier's fine sculpture of the man himself. You're then led around the back of the house to the room where Marley was almost

1

assassinated during the 1976 election campaign. Blown-up newspaper reports from the time cover the walls, with space left for the bullet holes that riddle the brickwork. After the shooting, Marley left Jamaica for a two-year exile in Britain.

The house

Inside, the house is decorated with gold and platinum discs depicting sales of the albums *Exodus* (1977), *Uprising* (1980) and *Legend* (1984), as well as the covers of all of his LPs, a commemoration of Marley's induction into the Rock and Roll Hall of Fame in 2003, his Grammy Lifetime Achievement Award, posthumously presented in 2001, and his Order of Merit from the Jamaican government. Upstairs, there is a re-creation of Wail 'n' Soul, Marley's tiny, shack-like Trench Town record shop, where he once hung out with band members Peter Tosh and Bunny Wailer, while the walls of another room are entirely covered with yellowing newspaper articles from home and abroad, which make fascinating reading. There's also a chart of all the cities the Wailers played in worldwide – prominence is given to shows in Africa, particularly the independence celebrations in Zimbabwe in 1980, but the band clearly worked hard, notching up performances in places as far-flung as the Mediterranean party island of Ibiza. You can peek into Marley's bedroom and kitchen, the latter complete with the blender in which he made his natural juices.

The tour ends behind the house in the air-conditioned movie theatre that once housed Marley's Tuff Gong recording studio. There's moving footage of the "One Love" concert held during the bloody election year of 1980, at which Marley brought together rival party leaders Michael Manley and Edward Seaga, and interviews with the great man cut together with appropriate music videos – the return to Africa and *Exodus*, celebration of "herb" and *Easy Skanking*.

King's House

Hope Rd • Mon–Fri 9am–2pm • Free tours arranged in advance • ☎ 927 6424, ⓦ kingshouse.gov.jm

The official home of Jamaica's Governor-General – a representative of the Queen of England – **King's House** is one of the most iconic residences in the city. A mile-long driveway leads to the three-storey white building, rebuilt after the original residence suffered in the 1907 earthquake. Notable features include the vast gardens with plants from around the world, the ballroom where ceremonial events are held, with walls showcasing portraits of past governors and visiting royals, and a drawing room with hurricane globe chandeliers adorned in gold leaves. The annual National Heroes Day ceremony is held at King's House. Tours must be arranged and approved in advance.

Hope Botanical Gardens

Old Hope Rd • Daily 6am–7pm • Free • ☎ 927 1257

In the early days of English settlement in Jamaica, Major Richard Hope, an officer with the invading British forces of Penn and Venables, set up a thriving sugar estate on the sprawling plains at the foothills of Kingston, with a stone aqueduct (parts of which can still be seen today) bringing water down from the Hope River. In 1881 the government acquired two hundred acres of land from the Hope Estate and laid out the **Hope Botanical Gardens** in much the same form as you see them today. The gardens are a lovely escape from the clamour of the city and a popular venue for weekend strolls, picnics and get-togethers. There are huge lawns, bougainvillea walks, a lily-smothered pond and a dizzying variety of unusual trees, including a great collection of palms.

Kingston Zoo

Adjacent to Hope Gardens • Mon–Fri 10am–5pm, Sat & Sun 10am–5.30pm • J$1500 • ☎ 927 1085, ⓦ hopezookingston.com

This is a small but attractive **zoo**, with crocodiles, monkeys, mongooses, tapirs, peccaries, snakes and tropical birds. Huge improvements have been made in recent years to its design and infrastructure, breathing a whole new life into the facility. There are several new animals – including deer, a bobcat and a lion, plus a small petting zoo (call ahead to arrange a visit) and a budgie feeding area where (for an additional J$100) visitors can feed the birds from the palm of their hands.

University of the West Indies

Mona Rd • ☎ 927 1660, ⦿ mona.uwi.edu
The extensive campus of the **University of the West Indies**, usually just called UWI, was first established here in 1948, as a College of the University of London, and achieved full university status in 1962. With sister campuses in Trinidad and Barbados, UWI accepts students from all over the Caribbean. Look out for sections of the 1758 **Paine-Mona Aqueduct**, which once sluiced water from the Hope River in the Blue Mountain foothills to a sugar-processing works that was part of the old Mona, Hope and Papine estates.

The university's Jamaican-Georgian **chapel**, has an interesting history. Built in 1799, the building was originally a warehouse on a Trelawney sugar estate, but was brought here and rebuilt brick by brick in 1955 at the suggestion of a former UWI chancellor. You can see the name of its former owner, one Edward Morant Gale, esquire, inscribed along the northern outer wall. If you're in Kingston around the February 6 anniversary of Bob Marley's birthday, try to attend the annual Marley lecture presented here by the university's Reggae Studies unit; past speakers have included Finance Minister Omar Davies discoursing on Peter Tosh, and there's usually a reggae performance afterwards; details can be found on the university website.

ARRIVAL AND DEPARTURE

BY PLANE

All international and some domestic flights land at Norman Manley International Airport (NMIA; ☎ 924 8452-6 or ☎ 1 888 AIRPORT, ⦿ nmia.aero) on the Palisadoes – a strip of land that juts out into the Caribbean Sea southeast of the city. There's a currency exchange desk just past Immigration, and a number of car rental firms have desks alongside the arrivals area (see page 68); others will meet you there on request. City bus #98 runs from just outside the arrivals area to the Parade downtown roughly every half-hour (J$100), with the last service leaving the airport at 10.57pm. However, unless you're familiar with Kingston, you're far better off opting for a cab – the fare for the twenty- to thirty-minute journey to New Kingston is US$35 in a JUTA taxi; there are always drivers outside the airport to meet flights.

Airlines Aerogaviota, NMIA (☎ 924 8092); Air Canada, NMIA (☎ 1 800 677 2485); American Airlines, Barbican Centre, 29 East Kings House Rd (☎ 1 800 744 0006); British Airways, NMIA (☎ 1 800 247 9297); Caribbean Airlines, 7 Trafalgar Rd (☎ 1 800 744 2225); Cayman Airways, 31 Upper Waterloo Rd (☎ 926 1762 or ☎ 1 800 422 9626); Copa Airlines, 68 St Lucia Ave (☎ 968 5330 or ☎ 1 800 234 2672); Delta, NMIA (☎ 1 800 221 1212); Insel Air, 31 Upper Waterloo Rd (☎ 924 8092); interCaribbean Airways, NMIA (☎ 1 800 572 7628); JetBlue, NMIA (☎ 1 924 8937 or ☎ 800 963 3014); WestJet (☎ 1 888 937 8538).

BY BUS

Most of the buses into Kingston pull in at the swarming terminal at the junction of Beckford and Pechon streets, just west of the crowded Parade, though some terminate at the safer and more convenient Half Way Tree. If you have a lot of luggage, you're best off hopping straight into a taxi from the busy rank on Parade, but if you want to use public transport, local bus #76 runs from nearby Duke Street to New Kingston and Liguanea; from Half Way Tree buses #70 and #75 run to Liguanea and Papine.

BY CAR

If you're arriving by car, there are four main entry points to the city, all fairly well signposted to New Kingston on "follow the hummingbird" markers, though you're best off getting a handle on your route rather than relying on these.

From the east This is where you'll be coming from if you drive in from the airport – the signposts direct you into New Kingston via the heart of downtown, along South Camp Road; this isn't the most direct route, but it avoids Mountain View Avenue, which runs through some occasionally volatile areas.

From the north coast Most visitors come in from the north coast on the busy A3 road, which runs straight through the northern suburb of Stony Hill onto Constant Spring Road from which you can turn left onto Hope Road or head onto Half Way Tree Road. Also from the north coast, the more winding but scenic B3 from Buff Bay through the Blue Mountains

1

will eventually bring you out at Papine, northeast of town; following the main Hope Road due west, and turning left at Trafalgar Road, takes you into New Kingston. The road has undergone substantial reconstruction (due to landslides and erosion in recent years) and although considered passable by some, the drive is not one for the fainthearted.

From the southwest Coming from the southwest, either off the toll road or Mandela Highway from Spanish Town,

the road is elevated just past the Ferry Police station at Six Miles on Kingston's western edge; take the left fork for New Kingston, carrying straight along on Washington Boulevard and Dunrobin Avenue. The latter ends at a T-junction with Constant Spring Road; turn right, and either carry on to Half Way Tree, or take the first left once over the bridge to Waterloo Road, from where you can cross over Hope Road onto Trafalgar Road and the heart of New Kingston.

GETTING AROUND

The heat and the distances between places mean you're not going to want to do a lot of walking, though the downtown sights are fairly easy to navigate on foot. It's not advisable to walk the streets at night in any part of the city; most Kingstonians don't.

BY TAXI

Taxis are the best way of getting around the city and are reasonably cheap; a ride from New Kingston to downtown costs around J$500. Bear in mind that cabs don't carry meters and you'll need to fix a price before you get in. It's standard practice to phone for a taxi, particularly at night, and you are better off having a couple of personal drivers as taxi services are notoriously difficult to reach on the phone during rush hour or when it rains. Taxis are not flagged down on the main streets unless they are route taxis (see page 24); look out for red "PP" or "PPV" plates. Your best bet to find a private taxi is to head to one of the major hotels. In addition to JUTA taxis (☏ 927 4534), other decent companies include El Shaddai (☏ 618 2005) and On Time Taxi (☏ 926 3866).

BY BUS

Operated by the government-run Jamaica Urban Transit Company (JUTC), Kingston's buses are a viable option for visitors. Smart and clean "bendy" buses cover all the main routes; all have numbers displayed, along with their destination, at the front. The best way to ensure you get to your destination is to ask – most bus users seem to have an exhaustive knowledge of schedules and services. Alternatively for routes, fares and general information, call ☏ 1 888 588 2287 (toll-free) or ☏ 749 3192; there's also a full list of routes online at ⊕ jutc.com. Any journey in and

around the city will cost J$120; the main bus terminals are at Parade and Half Way Tree.

BY CAR

Though traffic jams are a real problem, particularly around the morning and evening rush hours (roughly 7.30–9.30am & 4–6.30pm), when traffic slows to a crawl along all the main roads, renting a car is the best way to explore Kingston – if you plan on spending more than a couple of days in the capital, it'll work out cheaper to drive yourself than to keep forking out for taxis. A car of your own also makes it a lot easier to check out Kingston's nightlife (it's not advisable to walk from venue to venue). Rental is usually cheaper in Kingston than at the resorts.

Car rental companies Avis, Norman Manley Airport (☏ 924 8293) and 1 Merrick Ave (☏ 926 8021); Budget, Norman Manley Airport (☏ 924 8762) and 53 South Camp Rd (☏ 759 1793); Econocars, 11 Lady Musgrave Rd (☏ 927 9989); Hertz, Norman Manley Airport (☏ 924 8028); Island, Norman Manley Airport (☏ 924 8075) and 17 Antigua Ave (☏ 925 5875).

BY ORGANIZED TOUR

City tours (see page 69) can be an excellent way to negotiate the main sights efficiently and check out the capital's nightlife.

INFORMATION AND ACTIVITIES

Tourist information The main office of the Jamaica Tourist Board (Mon–Fri 8.30am–4.30pm; ☏ 929 9200) is right in the heart of New Kingston at 64 Knutsford Blvd. Staff can provide basic information, but the office is not really geared up to assist visitors. There's a smaller, more

tourist-oriented booth at Norman Manley Airport.

Spectator sports Tickets for games at the National Stadium (see page 61) or at Sabina Park (see page 33) can be obtained at the respective venues' ticket booths. Purchase them at least a day ahead to ensure seating.

ACCOMMODATION

Most of Kingston's **hotels** and **guesthouses** are in and around the small uptown district of **New Kingston**, convenient for sightseeing and close to most of the restaurants, theatres, cinemas and clubs. Only a few of the city's accommodation options cater specifically to the tourist trade, relying instead on a steady stream of Jamaican and international business visitors, though finding a room here is rarely a problem. Unless otherwise stated, all rooms have air conditioning, cable TV, wi-fi and phone and include breakfast as part of their rates.

TOURS FROM KINGSTON

All of the places around Kingston can be explored on an **organized tour** from the city. You shouldn't need a tour to see Port Royal, which is small, safe and relaxed enough to wander around alone, as well as being a straightforward bus or taxi ride from the city, if more time consuming. But a tour is not a bad option for Spanish Town, which is a bit awkward to get to and, with its ongoing violent outbursts, better navigated with someone who knows where they're going. Generally, you'll get a fuller perspective on all the sights by engaging the services of a tour company, many of which offer individualized, small-scale jaunts.

TOUR COMPANIES

Beat'n'Track Music Tours ☎ 395 8959, ✉ driakeeys@ yahoo.ie. For the lowdown on the Kingston music scene, or just to see the capital from a local's perspective, look no further than tour operator Andrea Lewis who conducts excellent trips. A typical itinerary might have you checking out the record stores of Orange Street, visiting recording studios, jamming with local musicians or hanging out with reggae stars. Other options include the Trench Town Culture Yard, Port Royal, Hellshire, Cane River and surfing at Bull Bay. Tours cost US$200/person for transport and guide (meals and entry fees are extra). Night tours US$150.

Jamaica Cultural Enterprises ☎ 540 8570, ⓦ ja culture.com. With a weekly schedule of organized culture trips – from a Kingston city tour to a rum, music, or food tour – JCE has earned a reputation for providing

excursions that are geared to both Jamaicans and tourists alike. Tours start at US$60–85/person; airport transfers are also available.

Our Story Tours ☎ 377 5693, ✉ ourstorytours@ gmail.com. Brilliant for historical perspectives, offering custom-designed tours of Kingston, Spanish Town and Port Royal, Caymanas Park for horseracing, and other destinations across the island. Rates negotiable.

Sun Venture 30 Balmoral Ave ☎ 924 4515, ⓦ sun venturetours.com. Another good Kingston-based option which offers interesting, professional day long city tours of the more conventional sights – the National Gallery, Bob Marley Museum, Devon House, as well as Tuff Gong Recording Studios and out to Port Royal – for US$115/person (four-person minimum). Sun Venture is also your best choice if heading into the Blue Mountains.

Alhambra Inn 1 Tucker Ave ☎ 978 9072, ✉ alhambra inn@cwjamaica.com; map p.62. Set on a quiet cul-de-sac in a residential neighbourhood, this small quirky hotel (with a pool and outdoor restaurant/pub) is the perfect place to stay if you want to catch a game or event at the National Stadium/Mas Camp – a five-minute walk down the road – though it's otherwise a bit out of the way. There's a plethora of great Jamaican antiques (some of which are for sale) strewn throughout the lobby and garden areas. US$110

Altamont Court 1 Altamont Terrace ☎ 929 4490, ⓦ altamontcourt.com; map p.62. By far Kingston's best mid-range option, *Altamont* is arranged around a flower-filled courtyard. The comfortable, modern rooms boast pleasant decor with all the usual amenities, plus a full breakfast, a swimming pool, sun deck, jacuzzi and a good restaurant and bar. US$180

Courtleigh 85 Knutsford Blvd ☎ 936 3570, ⓦ court leigh.com; map p.62. Typical business hotel good for short stays, with a tasteful lobby, 24-hour business centre, good restaurant, and bar, pool and gym. Each of the rooms has a balcony, includes breakfast, and there is a coin-operated laundry facility. US$259

Eden Gardens Wellness Resort and Spa 39 Lady Musgrave Rd ☎ 927 3485, ⓦ edengardenswellness. com; map p.62. Branded as a wellness retreat, *Eden*

Gardens also offers eighteen modern suites in a relaxing garden setting just outside the main New Kingston area. The property features a spa, gym, juice bar and three restaurants with wholesome and tasty vegan (one of the only places in the city) and vegetarian options. US$160

Hotel Four Seasons 18 Ruthven Rd ☎ 929 7655, ⓦ hotelfourseasonsjam.com; map p.62. A sound choice in a quiet area, but near New Kingston, with two pools, plus a restaurant and bar. The ground-floor rooms have walk-in showers, while higher floors have balconies with partial views of the mountains. A number of rooms can be linked, making it a popular choice with groups and families. US$150

★ **Inn at 6** 6 Chester Ave ☎ 381 5124, ⓦ facebook.com/ innat6; map p.62. This cosy villa turned guesthouse, run by a friendly Jamaican couple, sits on a quiet residential street in the upscale Barbican neighbourhood, one of the safest in the capital, and at a convenient walking distance from shopping plazas, restaurants – including *Uncorked* (see page 72) – and sights. Three contemporary rooms and one deluxe suite hug a manicured back garden and terrace, and boast all the key amenities, including spacious baths, mini-fridge, and flatscreen TV. A fully equipped central kitchen is shared, as well as multiple recreational rooms. Breakfasts are included. US$65, suite US$140

Jamaica Pegasus 81 Knutsford Blvd ☎ 926 3691, ⓦ jamaicapegasus.com; map p.62. Despite its

1970s exterior, this business-oriented behemoth has a modern interior feel. The rooms and suites – all of which have balconies – are updated with American-chic decor. In addition to pristine facilities – including two pools, tennis courts and a jogging trail – there are four restaurants (including one 24-hour café), two bars and a gaming room. US$296

Liguanea Club Knutsford Blvd ☎ 926 8144, ⊛ the liguaneaclub.com; map p.62. Although primarily a members-only tennis and squash club, this old colonial New Kingston landmark (see page 64) also offers comfortable accommodation in the heart of the city. Ask for one of the rooms in the main building, with their restored wooden floors, cheerful spreads in tropical prints and mini balconies that overlook the central garden area. A particularly great choice if travelling on your own as the buzz of people in the public areas gives a feeling of community. US$140

Neita's Nest Stony Hill, St Andrew ☎ 469 3005, ⊛ neitasnest.com; map p.62. Cosy private home tucked into the mountains above Kingston, which offers a friendly, local bed-and-breakfast experience. There are three rooms for rent with private (across the hall) bathrooms, communal living and dining areas, and a breezy veranda with beautiful forested valley views, where a full breakfast is served. A good distance from New Kingston, this peaceful, quiet spot is also popular with birdwatchers. US$170

Reggae Hostel 8 Burlington Ave ☎ 968 1694, ⊛ reggae hostel.com; map p.62. The city's first hostel, offers (a few) private rooms but mostly basic rooms with bunk beds (sleeping between four and eight) and shared bathrooms, breakfast included. In keeping with its name, the communal

area pipes reggae day in and out, complimenting the continuous buzz of this busy commercial area (just south of Half Way Tree). There's a useful "concierge" service that can book excursions, guides and taxis, and a small bar area in the back where films are shown and guests mingle. With a "no guest will be turned away" credo, camping in the back yard is also available (for US$15) if the hostel is full. Dorms US$19, doubles US$66

Spanish Court Hotel 1 St Lucia Ave ☎ 926 0000, ⊛ spanishcourthotel.com; map p.62. This trendy hotel, in a great, central New Kingston location, offers sleek modern rooms in a contemporary, boutique setting. There's a rooftop infinity pool and most of the rooms feature panoramic views of the mountains. US$228

★ **Terra Nova** 17 Waterloo Rd ☎ 926 2211, ⊛ terra novajamaica.com; map p.62. Once home to one of Jamaica's wealthiest families, *Terra Nova* is the top choice of visitors making any kind of prolonged holiday in Kingston. A smart hideaway substantially set back from the road amid generously landscaped gardens, this mid-sized hotel features a small pool, gym, charming terrace restaurant, formal dining room, gaming lounge and, at time of writing, Kingston's trendiest lounge. Rooms combine the best of old-world colonial charm and new-world luxury with their sophisticated (but unpretentious) gold and black decor and mod cons. US$289

Trench Town Culture Yard 6 & 8 Lower First St ☎ 859 6741; map p.53. It's possible to stay in the very basic one-room cottage at the back of the Culture Yard (see page 60) – for more information, contact the TTCY; note that prices rise significantly during special events. US$50

EATING

After the sun goes down and the heat lifts, the Kingston area is hard to beat for **eating**. Particularly uptown – which is where you'll want to be in the evenings – you'll find a wider choice of **restaurants** than anywhere else in Jamaica and an excellent standard of food. Most places offer variations on traditional Jamaican fare, from tiny jerk bars to exquisite local seafood establishments, but there's also good Chinese, Japanese, Indian, Italian and Middle Eastern cuisine, as well as a good spread of vegetarian restaurants.

CAFÉS AND SNACK OUTLETS

★ **Café Blue** Sovereign Center, Hope Rd ☎ 978 7790; map p.62. Clean, bright café serving delicious Blue Mountain coffee and great light snacks. Perfect for breakfast as well as a light lunch, with a nice selection of omelettes, bagels and pastries and coffee beverages. Try their extraordinarily caloric mochaccino (J$500) or a smoked marlin bagel (J$800). Mon–Thurs 7am–7pm, Sat 7am–9pm, Sun 9am–3pm.

Cannonball Café 29 East Kings House Rd ☎ 946 0983; map p.62. With its three great locations (Manor Park and New Kingston being the others), *Cannonball* has garnered a well-deserved reputation of not just being a convenient spot to have a good coffee and tap into their free wi-fi but also for tasty sandwiches (from J$640), soups (J$450) and meals

such as quiche and salad (J$900). There's a great bulletin board at this location to find out what's happening locally. Mon–Fri 7am–7pm, Sat 8.30am–7pm, Sun 9am–5pm.

Deli Works Sovereign Centre, Hope Rd ☎ 927 4706; map p.62. Reliable canteen-style diner (menu changes daily) that's an affordable lunch or breakfast spot, serving local dishes alongside options like veggie or meat lasagne (J$550), Chinese roasted chicken (J$800) and lots of salads. Mon–Sat 11.30am–8.30pm, Sun 9am–6pm.

Earl's Juice Garden 28 Haining Rd ☎ 893 7151; map p.62. Simple spot tucked away on a backstreet in New Kingston, serving delicious freshly pressed juices, smoothies and shakes as well as light lunches including veggie patties (J$120) and stews (J$400). Mon–Fri 7am–6pm, Sat 8am–4pm.

F&B Downtown Swiss Stores, 107 Harbour St ☎922 1109; map p.53. Despite humble beginnings, *F&B Downtown* has become the most upmarket lunch spot south of New Kingston. Rub shoulders with locals at communal bistro tables or sit in small quiet alcoves while you enjoy a glass of wine (J$580) and dishes like jerk sausage pomodoro (J$900) or teriyaki chicken salad (J$900), and finish lunch off with an espresso (J$300) or tub of Haagen Daz (J$350). Mon–Fri 8am–5pm.

I-Scream Devon House, Barbican Rd ☎929 7028; map p.62. This island-famous ice-cream shop serves up delicious island flavours including heavenly home made soursop, rum and raisin, and coffee and Guinness. Located within the grounds of the beautiful Devon House (see page 64) and recently relocated into a new building nearly five times larger than its previous location, it's a great place to grab a scoop and enjoy the outdoor veranda setting. Mon–Thurs noon–10pm, Fri–Sun noon–11pm.

Juici Patties Shop 24, Lane Plaza, Hope Rd ☎970 4092; map p.62. Aside from patties – beef, soy, shrimp, veggie, chicken and cheese – *Juici* does a great Jamaican breakfast (from J$130) popular with locals checking in or out of an early shift. Try the thick and creamy cornmeal porridge or the ackee and saltfish, which includes ample servings of "food" (yam and dumplings). Mon–Thurs 6am–7pm, Fri & Sat 6am–8pm, Sun 7am–4pm.

Moby Dick 3 Orange St ☎922 4468; map p.53. No frills downtown "institution" that serves tasty cookshop-style lunches to local residents and business people alike. Cheap and cheerful, the simple menu includes fried chicken (J$600), curried goat (J$600) and sweet and sour chicken (J$670). Mon–Fri 10.30am–4pm.

Pita Grill 20 Barbican Rd ☎960 4571, ⓦpitagrill jamaica.com; map p.62. Bright, modern café with a canteen-like feel and outdoor seating. Try their tasty sliders (Philly cheese steak J$450) and sandwiches (chicken club J$1250), or the simple Lebanese dishes, which include a falafel platter (J$1395). Popular with the late-night, after-party crowd. Daily 24hr.

Tastee 11 Knutsford Blvd ☎929 0019; map p.62. Before *Juici Patties* (see above) there was *Tastee*'s patties (since 1966). *Tastee* has always been known for their delicious flaky-crust patties (from J$130) and sugary jellied pastries (J$115 for a Danish roll) – great to grab on the go – but these days it also serves hearty Jamaican cookshop food for lunch, including oxtail (J$600), and breakfast, such as mackerel rundown (salted mackerel cooked in coconut milk; J$300). Mon–Sat 7am–9pm, Sun 7am–5pm.

Tea Tree Creperie 8 Hillcrest Ave ☎927 8733, ⓦtea treecreperie.com; map p.62. Though the deliciously decadent crepes – savoury and sweet – and loose-leaf teas are the main draw, they also serve up a delicious frozen mint lemonade (J$300), milkshakes, great salads and desserts. Try the decadent apple crisp crepe (J$1350).

RESTAURANTS

Chez Maria 80 Lady Musgrave Rd ☎927 8078, ⓦchezmaria.webs.com; map p.62. A lovely outdoor setting, with tables scattered around a garden; tasty Italian and Lebanese food is on offer, from hummus (J$800) and kebabs (from J$1550) to bruschetta (J$680) and pizza (from J$1150), and of course pasta – try the lobster spaghetti with garlic, olives and chilli (J$1900). Mon–Sat 11.30am–3pm & 6–10pm, Sun noon–9pm

Chilitos 88 Hope Rd ☎634 6243, ⓦfacebook.com/chilitosjamexican; map p.62. Find all of your Mexican favourites here, plus a handful of Jamaican fillings to choose for your tacos and burritos, including jerk (J$1000), and ackee and plantain (J$900). Mon–Thurs 11am–10pm, Fri & Sat 11am–11pm.

Dragon Court 6 South Ave ☎920 8506; map p.62. One of the best of the many Chinese restaurants in Kingston, *Dragon Court* serves a huge variety of tasty dishes. All the expected items are here (sweet and sour pork J$1200; vegetable lo mein J$1294) but it's their traditional Sunday Dim Sum that really draws a crowd, offering delights like steamed shrimp dumplings (J$460) and spare ribs (J$400). Reservations recommended. Daily 11.30am–9.30pm.

East The Marketplace 67 Constant Spring Rd ☎960 3962; map p.62. Friendly sushi bar and restaurant run by some of the first Japanese chefs to arrive on the island, offering great lunch specials and sushi/sashimi combos. Lunch mains include shrimp tempura (J$1224) and chicken teriyaki (J$1107) – prices include rice, salad and soup – while a sushi lunch will set you back J$1340. Tues–Sun noon–10pm.

Fromage Gourmet 8 Hillcrest Ave ☎622 9856, ⓦface book.com/fromagegourmetmarket; map p.62. Serving rich and hearty dishes such as panini Jamaique (jerk pork, guava glaze and Monterey Jack cheese in a panini, J$874) and a goat's cheese and chive scramble (J$950), this little French-themed bistro is a Sunday brunch favourite. Mon–Sat 8am–10pm, Sun 8am–4pm.

Jojo's Jerk Pit 12 Waterloo Rd ☎906 1509, ⓦjojos jerkpit.com; map p.62. This casual uptown rum bar (seats are converted rum barrels) and restaurant brings together Kingstonians of all walks of life for its delicious jerk and theme nights. Enjoy spicy, pimento-wood jerked chicken and pork (served under a mango tree) with a side of roasted breadfruit, hard-dough bread or *tostones* (flattened, salted and fried green plantains) for J$700. Mon–Sat 11am–11pm.

Opa 26 Hope Rd, Devon House ☎631 2000, ⓦopa jamaica.com; map p.62. Tastefully designed and meticulously managed by Grecian-born Alexx Antaeus Opa celebrates the delicious traditional Greek food of his homeland in an intimate yet friendly setting. Try the tangy tzatziki (J$775) or filling moussaka (J$1975), alongside one of the many wines on offer. Mon–Sat 5pm–midnight.

Red Bones Blues Café 1 Argyle Rd ☎978 6091 or ☎978 8262, ⓦredbonesbluescafe.com; map p.62. Stylish, upmarket restaurant-cum-music venue with a distinguished but laidback atmosphere, and tables in a pretty dining room or outdoor courtyard setting. The imaginative and delicious food has a contemporary flavour, from herb-crusted snapper (J$2550) to ackee, callaloo and feta pasta (J$1750), and the kitchen takes last orders at a satisfyingly late 11pm. Mon–Fri 11am–11pm, Sat 6–11pm.

The Steakhouse at the Verandah 67 Constant Spring Rd, Devon House ☎616 8833; map p.62. The latest addition to the city's growing food scene, delivers on its farm to table promise with organic home grown, locally aged meats, such as ribeye, or bone-in fillet (J$2000), served with coconut callaloo and jerk truffle butter, among other surprising creations. There are also chicken dishes and vegetarian options. Reservations required. Mon–Thurs noon–9.30pm, Fri & Sat noon–10.30pm.

Tamarind 18–22 Barbican Rd ☎977 0695, ⓦtamarind indiancuisine.com; map p.62. Typical but decent tasty Indian dishes (they also have a good Asian-fusion menu) served family-style in a small, modern setting. Try the chicken tikka masala (J$1095), methi malai mutter (J$1095) or channa masala (J$895). Reservations recommended at weekends. Mon–Sat 11.30am–10pm, Sun 1pm–9.30pm.

The Terrace at Liguanea Club Knutsford Blvd ☎926 8144, ⓦtheliguaneaclub.com; map p.62. Casual and convenient, *The Terrace* is a great, central spot to grab lunch in New Kingston. With seating on the breezy veranda or under the shady mango trees, you can enjoy affordable light lunches such as a chicken club sandwich (J$975) or a more filling bean- and gravy-rich oxtail for J$1150. Dinner is also available, with the menu boasting the likes of shrimp ceviche (J$1010), and lobster thermidor (J$2600) Mon–Sat noon–9pm, Sun 7am–3pm.

Tracks and Records 67 Constant Spring Rd ☎906 3903, ⓦtracksandrecords.com; map p.62. The premier location for Usain Bolt fans in Kingston, this massive sports bar and restaurant features 45 flatscreens showing various sporting events on demand. The informal Jamaican menu includes Appleton barbecue wings (J$700) and pulled jerk chicken wraps (J$1000). Daily 11.30am–midnight.

★ **Triple T'z** 1 Annette Crescent ☎969 1345, ⓦtriple tseatery.com; map p.62. Two trees punctuate the dining room at this colourful restaurant, winner of a 2017 Observer Food award for its ultra-Jamaican menu including legendary oxtail (J$1200), barbecued pork chops (J$1600), whole fish (J$2000) and vegetarian options. To top it off are freshly squeezed fruit juices served in carafes (J$400), recycled decor including wash basins turned lamps – and a mix of traditional chairs and sofas. Mon–Thurs 8am–9pm, Fri–Sun 8am–10pm.

★ **Uncorked** 29 Barbican Rd ☎632 5500; ⓦuncorked jamaica.com; map p.62. This gourmet wine and cheese market and bistro recently expanded its offerings to keep up with its popularity among the city's hip and professional crowd, serving tapas-style starters such as stuffed peppers (J$650), as well as gourmet paninis (J$750), delicious burgers (J$1750) and salads (J$900), paired on request with their great selection of wines – though cocktails are also available. Popular for light casual lunches and after-work drinks and bites. Mon–Wed 10am–10pm, Thurs–Sat 10am–11.30pm.

DRINKING AND NIGHTLIFE

For an overall idea of **what's on**, it's a good idea to check the entertainment sections of the *Gleaner* and *Observer* on a Friday, and keep an eye and an ear out for press and radio ads throughout the week.

BARS

Kingston has legions of great places for a drink, from sophisticated hangouts with a long wine list to buzzy bars crowded with the capital's bright young things. When choosing a bar, bear in mind that you'll rarely want to walk between places at night, and taxis are the best way of getting around.

CRU 71 Lady Musgrave Rd ☎579 9362, ⓦfacebook. com/crubbarandkitchen; map p.62. Sophisticated rooftop lounge with panoramic mountain views; guests can hang out at the bar or chill out with table service in one of the many seating areas (wine from J$800, beer J$300). Happy hour Tues–Fri 5–7pm. Tues–Fri 4.30pm–1.30am, Sat 7pm–2am.

Cuddy'z Shop 4–6 New Kingston Shopping Centre ☎920 8019, ⓦcuddyzsportsbar.com; map p.62. Operated by cricketing legend Courtney Walsh, who often passes through to the delight of patrons, this well-equipped, high-tech sports bar is a lively place for a drink (beer J$3000) or to catch a baseball, cricket or football game. Mon–Thurs 11am–midnight, Fri & Sat 11am–1am, Sun 10am–1am.

Jojo's Jerk Pit 12 Waterloo Rd ☎906 1509, ⓦjojosjerk pit.com; map p.62. Uptown rum bar that has popular theme nights including I Hate Monday on Monday, Karaoke Thursday and Live Music Tuesday and Saturday. It's most atmospheric after dark with twinkling lights strung up in the outdoor area. Mon–Sat 11am till late.

Regency Bar Terra Nova All-Suite Hotel, 17 Waterloo Rd ☎ 926 2211, ⓦ terranovajamaica.com; map p.62. With its gold and black decor, private booths and collection of premium and vintage wines and champagnes displayed in an eye-catching vault, *Regency* sets the stage for Kignston's most upmarket night out, almost guaranteeing that you get a glimpse of the who's who of Kingston's social scene. Serving top-shelf liquors straight up or in fancy cocktails (lychee martini J$700), you can choose to be inside with the DJ and main bar, or outside in a cool tropical setting for a quieter drink. Daily 10.30am till late.

Ribbiz UltraLounge 29 East Kings House Rd ☎ 410 7637, ⓦ facebook.com/ribbiz; map p.62. Mid-sized sports bar with less of an emphasis on sports and more on people-watching and drinking (beer J$250), attracting a young professional crowd. There's always a good DJ and bar snacks are available. There's generally no cover charge but on some theme nights (usually Mon, Thurs, Fri and Sat), when there are all you can drink specials, the door may charge up to J$1000. Daily noon–4am.

CLUBS

Kingston's club scene ranges from jam packed, a/c indoor venues with big-name DJs, state-of-the-art equipment and the latest tunes to small, dark, oldies' clubs for the more mature dancers. Anticipate cover charges of between US$5 and US$10 – more if there's a live performance or a big-name sound system; the *Gleaner* advertises regular ladies' nights, when women get in free. As you'll find islandwide, nothing much happens before midnight except on Friday, when after-work jams pull an early evening crowd. Security at most of the clubs is tight, and you'll often be searched on your way in.

Club Privilege 14–16 Trinidad Terrace ☎ 754 8561, ⓦ clubprivilegejm.com; map p.62. Modern, medium-sized club pulling in a young, trendy crowd (including on occasion Usain Bolt and Sean Paul) with its champagne bar, table service and spacious dancefloor. Open only twice a week. Friday's "Uber" theme night tends to be the most popular night, featuring popular local DJs spinning house, dance and the latest dancehall. Fri & Sat 10pm–4am.

★ **Fiction** 67 Constant Spring Rd ☎ 631 8038; map p.62. Large indoor club with two bars, private booths

and great music, plus regular theme nights. Thurs–Sat 9pm till late.

Waterfalls 9 Mona Plaza, Liguanea ☎ 977 0652; map p.62. Great Thursday nights with Merritone playing on the turntables. Much older crowd but nice vibes. Thurs 9pm–4am.

LIVE MUSIC

Live music in the capital is less predictable, but almost always more interesting, than the anaesthetized reggae dished up for tourists on the north coast. Regular shows are held at *Red Bones* and *Countryside* as well as, occasionally, Mas Camp, although most of the live music parties here happen during Carnival.

Countryside Club 7 Derrymore Rd ☎ 920 6645; map p.62. Frequently featuring live reggae music, this great venue, with its palm trees, open courtyard setting and fretworked buildings, offers an oasis in the middle of the city – it's also a nice place to grab a bite to eat. Admission varies, usually from around J$500. Wed & Thurs 4–10pm, Fri 5pm–2am, Sat 5pm–midnight.

Dub Club 7b Skyline Drive ☎ 815 1184, ⓦ facebook. com/officialkingstondubclub; map p.62. Local and international DJs take their turns spinning the best roots, rock, reggae and dub in an open-air venue on a mountain ridge above Kingston. Authentic and full of vibes, the weekly Sunday session draws a mix of trendy locals, expats, aspiring musicians and reggaephiles of all ages who come as much for the music as they do for the cooler climate and spectacular views of the city by night. Sun 8pm–2am.

Mas Camp Stadium North ☎ 754 5396; map p.62. Kingston's largest open-air venue for concerts gets its name from being the hub for Jamaica's annual carnival. Every weekend and some week nights leading up to parade day there are live music events featuring regional and local artists. Prices vary according to concert; check press for details. 9pm till late.

Red Bones Blues Café 1 Argyle Rd ☎ 978 8262 or ☎ 978 6091; map p.62. The most consistent place to hear live music, with everything from alternative reggae to blues and jazz, *Red Bones* also has a lively bar scene that draws in a mixed crowd of expats and well-heeled locals. Mon–Fri 11am till late, Sat 6pm till late.

ENTERTAINMENT

Next to nightlife, **theatre** is Kingston's strongest cultural suit. The performance scene is limited but buoyant, with a small core of first-rate writers, directors and actors – including Oliver Samuels and David Heron – producing work of a high standard. Most of the plays are sprinkled with Jamaican patois, but you'll still get the gist. Comedies (particularly sexual romps and political satire) are popular, and the normally excellent annual **pantomime** – a musical with a message, totally different from the English variety – is a major event, running from December to April at the **Little Theatre** (see page 74). For details of performances, check the *Gleaner* or *Observer* newspapers, particularly the Friday entertainment sections. Many of these venues also stage dance performances featuring the acclaimed National Dance Theatre Company or L'Acadco; check the press to see what's on.

1

STREET DANCES

Held on street corners, in town squares, local rum shops or empty car parks across the island, **street dances** make up an important part of modern Jamaican culture. Drive anywhere across the island and you are bound to see a brightly decorated sign tacked to a lamp-post or hear a local "**town crier**" (a car with massive speakers attached to its roof) blaring news of a neighbourhood street dance. Raw, earthy and intensely atmospheric, these (typically free) dances attract huge crowds who dress to impress and come to hear a local sound system spin reggae, dancehall, oldies and other popular hits. In Kingston these street dances are immensely popular with dancehall and reggae aficionados who come to hear the island's best selectors as well as rub shoulders with the big names in the dancehall fraternity – from dancers who come to "bring out" their latest move to Jamaica's best-known DJs, who might take to the mic for an impromptu performance.

Your **security** at a street dance is pretty much guaranteed – anyone foolish enough to ruin everyone's fun by starting trouble or attempting a robbery will inevitably be swiftly dealt with by irate locals. Nonetheless, it's obviously sensible to keep your wits about you, leave your valuables at home and, if possible, go with a local escort. Similarly, avoid street dances if there's been recent trouble in any of the areas – just ask around.

Parties come and go, and every town and village in every parish have their own events (both weekly and occasional) but at the time of writing, the main jams in Kingston were: Early Monday at Savannah Plaza (Constant Spring Road); Cadillac Saturday at Limelight (Half Way Tree); Dubwise on Wednesday (no fixed location, check ⓦ facebook.com/dubwisejamaica); and Rae Town Old Hits Sunday. Weddy Wednesdays, staged at Stone Love's headquarters on Burlington Avenue, is the only regular uptown street dance; the action doesn't start until the small hours of Wednesday morning, though, and there's not much point turning up before 1am.

Center Stage Theatre 18 Dominica Drive ☎ 968 7529. Once the concession area of the drive-in cinema (where it's located), Center Stage is the most consistently active of the local playhouses. Crowds pack in tightly here on the ground or mezzanine floor to watch these (typically) lewd comedies in broad patois. Although light-hearted and reflective of one current social issue or the other, their adult content is generally not suitable for children.

Little Theatre & Little Little Theatre 4 Arthur Wint Drive ☎ 926 6129, ⓦ ltmpantomime.com. Large, airy and prominent theatre, and its smaller sister facility behind, the Little Theatre and Little Little Theatre have been home to the Jamaican Pantomime, the Jamaica Folk Singers and the National Dance Theatre Company since the 1960s when they were founded.

Phillip Sherlock Centre for the Creative Arts 1 Sherlock Drive ☎ 927 1456 or ☎ 977 9770, ⓦ facebook. com/PSCCA. Small arts centre located at the University of the West Indies that often puts on original student productions, dance recitals and, once a year (around December), a children's musical.

SHOPPING

As you'd expect, reggae fans are in shopping heaven in Kingston with downtown's Orange Street having some of the last remaining record shops and pressing plants on the island. Art and crafts also make great souvenirs, with more authentic pieces available here than on the north coast.

MUSIC SHOPS

Augustus Pablo's Rockers International 135 Orange St ☎ 365 6179, ⓦ facebook.com/rockersinternational; map p.53. Although slightly remodelled in recent years, Rockers International remains largely in its vintage state and is a great throwback to Orange Street's heyday as the "Hollywood" of Kingston. It carries an extensive stock of vinyl ska, rock steady, dub and reggae classics. Mon–Sat 10am–5pm.

Derrick Harriot's One Stop 25 Constant Spring Rd ☎ 586 8066; map p.62. Record shop of the legendary reggae producer – good for old and new reggae, LPs and 45s. Mon–

Fri 10am–6.30pm, Sat 10am–7pm.

GG's Records 1 Torrington Rd, cnr of Orange St and Parade ☎ 922 7518 or ☎ 948 9419, ✉ ggrangling@ hotmail.com; map p.53. Great for vinyl, as well as CDs, GG's is particularly well stocked, and is as vibrant and loud as its location. Hardcore fans might be interested in having a chat with the GG himself who is one of the last remaining veterans of the industry and is happy to give a personal tour of the studio and pressing plant if he's available. Mon–Sat 8.30am–5pm.

Music Mart 8 South Ave ☎ 926 4687, ⓦ musicmartjm. com; map p.62. Leading seller of music equipment on the island, it also has a good selection of local and international CDs. Mon–Thurs 9.30am–5pm, Fri & Sat 9.30am–6pm.

Tads International Shop 21, 78 3/4 Hagley Park Rd ☎ 929 2563, ☻ tadsrecord.com; map p.62. Extensive catalogue of music – from oldies to contemporary, and mostly CDs – as well as DVDs of stageshows, interviews and Jamaican movies. Mon–Fri 9am–5pm.

ARTS AND CRAFTS

HiQo Art Gallery 24 Waterloo Rd ☎ 926 4183, ☻ facebook.com/hiqoartgalleryjamaica; map p.62. Centrally-located, family-run framing shop that also sells contemporary and traditional paintings, sculptures and carvings. The small gallery upstairs sometimes has shows. Very knowledgeable staff. Mon–Fri 9.30am–5pm, Sat 9.30–4pm.

Island Art 20 Barbican Rd ☎ 977 0318, ☻ facebook.com/islandartandframing; map p.62. Chock a block shop and framing centre filled with contemporary art, furniture (local and imported), sculpture and prints in an uptown location. Mon–Sat 10am–6pm.

GIFTS AND SOUVENIRS

Carby's Souvenir and Craft Village Twin Gates Plaza, Constant Spring Rd ☎ 926 4065; map p.62. This is the place where all Jamaica supporters gear up for big sporting events, selling (national) yellow and green shirts, plus novelty shot glasses, key rings and the Jamaican flag. Mon–Fri 9.30am–6.30pm, Sat 9.30am–7.30pm.

Craft Cottage Village Plaza, Constant Spring Rd ☎ 926 0719, ☻ facebook.com/craft-cottage-jamaica; map p.62. For years this has been the place locals go to buy all-Jamaican gifts – from sauces to sweets, posters to CDs – for family and friends overseas. Mon–Thurs 9.30am–5.30pm, Fri & Sat 9.30am–6pm.

My Jamaica Liguanea Plaza, Old Hope Rd ☎ 977 2805, ☻ facebook.com/myjamaicastore; map p.62. Nice boutique-style store offering a wide selection of stylish Jamaican T-shirts, clothing, bags, crafts and jewellery. Mon–Sat 10am–7pm, Sun 10am–5pm.

Starfish Devon House ☎ 906 8045; map p.62. Small shop selling locally made candles, incense and oils. Mon–Fri 10.30am–6.30pm, Sat 10.30am–7.30pm.

DIRECTORY

Ambulances For a public ambulance, call ☎ 110 or St John's Ambulance on ☎ 926 7656; for a private ambulance, call Ambucare on ☎ 978 2327 or ☎ 978 6021.

Doctors and dentists For doctors, try Dr Suzanne Minott-Arscott, Unit 1, Seymour Park (☎ 946 3896) or Dr Richard Gomes, Unit 28, 21 Kingsway (☎ 926 7161). Reliable dentists include the Oxford Dental Centre, 22g Old Hope Rd (☎ 926 7311) or Dr Ingrid Matthis, 5 Arden Rd (☎ 631 4943).

Embassies British High Commission, 28 Trafalgar Rd (☎ 936 0700); Canadian High Commission, 3 West Kings House Rd (☎ 926 1500); US Embassy, 142 Old Hope Rd (☎ 702 6000).

Hospitals Kingston's best public hospital is the University Hospital at Mona (☎ 927 1621); otherwise there's the Kingston Public Hospital downtown on North Street (☎ 922 0210. Private hospitals with 24hr A&E services include Medical Associates, 18 Tangerine Place (☎ 926 1400) and Nuttall Memorial, 6 Caledonia Ave (☎ 926 2139).

Internet St Andrew Parish Library, 2 Tom Redcam Drive (☎ 926 3310; Mon–Fri 9am–5pm; free); Inc Ltd, Liguanea Post Office Mall, 115 Hope Rd (☎ 978 1007; Mon–Fri 8.30am–7pm, Sat 9.30am–6pm, J$150/15min); YIOR Computer Solutions, 12 Melmac Ave (☎ 906 7913; Mon–Wed 8.30am–6pm, Thurs & Fri 8.30am–5pm; J$150/hr).

Money and exchange Uptown banks with ATMs include: Citibank, 63 Knutsford Blvd; National Commercial Bank, 1–7 Knutsford Blvd; RBTT, Sovereign Centre, 106 Hope Rd; ScotiaBank, 2 Knutsford Blvd. You'll get better rates at FX Trader, 2–6 Trafford Place.

FESTIVALS

If you're in Kingston between January and April, you can take in Jamaica's **Carnival**. Adopted from the Trinidadian event, Carnival is on a smaller scale here and focused more on all-inclusive parties and outdoor street jams, though it does culminate with an early-hours Jouvert (a body-paint-spattered street parade) and a traditional-style costume parade through New Kingston. Though there's plenty of soca, dancehall is inevitably a big part of Carnival here, and you'll see lots of DJs and bands (including local stalwarts Byron Lee and the Dragonaires) as well as big stars from Trinidad and the Eastern Caribbean – such as Alison Hinds, Machel Montano and Bunji Garlin. Events are widely publicized on the radio and in the press, and you can also contact the JTB (☎ 929 9200) or visit ☻ bacchanaljamaica.com. Another worthwhile event to plan your trips around is the Jamaica **Food & Drink Festival** (see page 33), a popular week-long celebration in October featuring Jamaican chefs and cuisine; themed nights include a Meet Street food truck evening on the waterfront, and Vintage, a seven-course wine-paired dinner created by an international chef on a hilltop mansion terrace overlooking Kingston's city lights.

1

GAMING

In line with the growing popularity of **gaming lounges** throughout Jamaica, Kingston features several places where you can hit the slots or electronic roulette machine. Even if you don't want to gamble, all venues offer room to lounge and sip a cocktail or order something from the bar menu and are great options for a late, late night drink.

Acropolis Gaming Lounge 29 East Kings House Rd ☎ 978 1299, ⓦ facebookacropolisgaminglounge. Busy, upbeat gaming lounge attracting a young professional crowd for a game or two as they pass through on their way to the adjoining sports bar. Minimum bet US$10. Mon–Thurs, Fri & Sat 11am–4am, Sun noon–3am.

Monte Carlo Terra Nova All-Suite Hotel, 17 Waterloo Rd ☎ 926 2211, ⓦ terranovajamaica. com. Offering a more premium experience than other stand-alone lounges in the city, this hotel gaming lounge serves top-shelf liquor and snacks from the nicely appointed bar area – which means even if you aren't playing, it's a nice place to grab a late night drink. Minimum bet J$2000. Mon–Thurs & Sun 11am–4am, Fri & Sat 11am–6am.

Pharmacies There are pharmacies at most of the shopping malls. Late-opening options are Monarch, Sovereign Centre (Mon–Fri 8am–10pm, Sat 9am–10pm, Sun 9am–8pm), York Pharmacy at the Half Way Tree junction (daily 8am–11pm) and Discount Pharmacy, Liguanea and Manor Park (8am–11pm).

Police The main station is at East Queen St (☎ 922 0308). Stations uptown include Matilda's Corner, Old Hope Rd (☎ 926 6517). In an emergency, call ☎ 119.

Post offices The GPO is at 13 King St downtown, and there are post offices in the Liguanea Post Mall, 115 Hope Rd, and at the airport.

East of Kingston

The main route east out of the city, Windward Road follows the coastline out of Kingston, scything through an industrial zone of oil tanks and a cement works that towers over the ruined defensive bastion of Fort Rock, now the **Rockfort Mineral Baths**. If the scenery looks familiar, you may be recalling the classic scene in the **James Bond** movie *Dr No*, in which Bond leaves Norman Manley Airport in a nifty red Sunbeam Alpine. A kilometre or so further on, turning right at the roundabout takes you onto the **Palisadoes**, a narrow sixteen-kilometre spit of land that leads out past the international airport to the ancient city of **Port Royal**, from where it's a short hop to the tiny island of **Lime Cay**.

Rockfort Mineral Baths

Rockfort, 9km southeast of Kingston • Tues–Fri 8am–3pm, Sat & Sun 7am–5pm • J$450 • ☎ 938 5055 • Buses #99, #98, #97 run regularly from the Parade

Huddled below the immense Carib Cement works and suffering somewhat from a surfeit of dust, **Rockfort Mineral Baths** offers one of the few public swimming pools in the Kingston area. This was the site of the British Fort Rock, first strengthened against a threatened French invasion in 1694 and remanned in 1865 amid fears that the Morant Bay Rebellion further east might spread to Kingston. Today, the baths sit in a neat modern facility and offer a chance to enjoy some laidback pampering. Fed by a spring high in the hills that appeared following the 1907 earthquake, the mineral spas are all fitted with jacuzzis, and you're allowed to wallow in them for up to 45 minutes. The mineral water is moderately radioactive; it's claimed that the radioactivity helps to infuse the therapeutic minerals into the body. Therapeutic massage is available using natural essential oils, and there's a canteen serving Jamaican food.

Port Royal and around

PORT ROYAL, a short drive from downtown Kingston, once captured the spirit of early colonial adventure. For several decades in the late seventeenth century, Port Royal was a riotous town – the notorious haunt of cut-throats and buccaneers, and condemned by the church as the "the wickedest city in the world". Little of that past remains, and it's now a pleasant and hospitable little town, home to the base of the Jamaica Defence Force Coastguard and a small fishing and tourism industry. Most people who visit come for the seafood at famous *Gloria's* (see page 80), while others use the area as a launch pad for day-trips to nearby Lime Cay (see page 79), a small sandy spot that offers lovely swimming and snorkelling.

1

Brief history

In 1655, when the English sailed into what is now Kingston harbour, they passed a cay known as "cayo de carena", as it was where the Spanish careened their vessels to clean and caulk them. Having captured Spanish Town, the invaders set about fortifying this point, eventually building five separate **forts** to defend the inner harbour (the world's seventh largest) and the town, soon to be called Port Royal, that grew up within. Over the next fifteen years, Port Royal grew through trade and was enriched by the booty of the **buccaneers** armed with royal commissions. It was recognized that its location at the entrance to the harbour of what became Jamaica's capital city, Kingston, needed to be strengthened, and several fortifications were built in the tumultuous period between 1655 and 1692, the year of the catastrophic **earthquake**, which swallowed two-thirds of the landmass. Port Royal never recovered its mercantile prominence, although it remained the western Caribbean headquarters of the Royal Navy for two centuries.

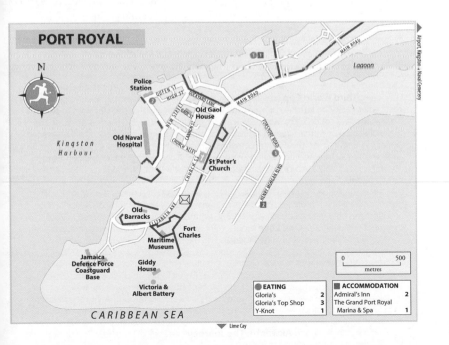

● EATING		■ ACCOMMODATION	
Gloria's	2	Admiral's Inn	2
Gloria's Top Shop	3	The Grand Port Royal	
Y-Knot	1	Marina & Spa	1

1

St Peter's Church

Church St; ask for Yvette (who "always sits under the tree across from the doors") to let you in

Built in 1725 on the site of a church lost in the earthquake, **St Peter's Church** contains several examples of fine commemorative art and a beautiful eighteenth-century organ loft. Ask to see the exquisite communion plate said to be a gift of Sir Henry Morgan. More interesting though are the ancient tombs in the small and rambling graveyard, particularly that of the Frenchman **Lewis Galdy**. Swallowed by the earthquake in 1692, he was seconds later spat out into the sea by an eruption, from where, amazingly, he scrambled to safety and lived until 1739.

JAMAICA ON FILM

From *Dr No* to *The Blue Lagoon*, with *Club Paradise* and *The Mighty Quinn* in between, Hollywood has long used Jamaica as a tropical backdrop against which tales of international adventure and romance are set. Dig a bit deeper, though, and you'll find a solid tradition of Jamaican film-making. The island's best-known and best-loved movie is Perry Henzell's **The Harder They Come**, which tells the story of Ivan (played by Jimmy Cliff) as he strives to make a better life for himself in Kingston. Pulling no punches in its gritty depiction of life in 1970s Jamaica, it offers a unique window into the life of the "sufferer", and has rightly become a cult classic. Equally realistic but with a dollop of humour, **Smile Orange** (1974) features Ringo, a head waiter in a resort hotel, played by Carl Bradshaw, who uses all his guile and wit on tourists to overcome the harsh economic realities of contemporary Jamaica. Unsurprisingly, it still has plenty of relevance today, and is well worth seeking out despite the often poor audio quality.

The man who brought Bob Marley to the attention of the world, Jamaican impresario Chris Blackwell, also had a hand in classic Jamaican films. As well as acting as location scout on *Dr No* in 1962 and releasing the soundtrack of *The Harder They Come* on his Island label, he established Island Pictures in 1982 with the production of **Countryman**, a gorgeous tale woven around a scheme operated by corrupt government officials to discredit their opposition through the framing of two innocent American tourists as CIA gunrunners, and with a killer soundtrack to boot. Island were also behind **The Lunatic**, adapted by Jamaican author Anthony Winkler from his novel. An engaging, achingly funny mixture of burlesque humour, folklore and satirical comment on the sexual tourism prevalent in Jamaica, it stars Paul Campbell as the insane Aloysius. Campbell also starred in both **Dancehall Queen** (1997) and **Third World Cop** (1999), which together defined modern Jamaican cinema. The former tracks the fortunes of Marcia (played by Audrey Reid) as she struggles to support her family by way of being crowned Dancehall Queen; its underlying themes of incest and the exploitation of women generated plenty of controversy in Jamaica, and it still makes for a gripping watch. *Third World Cop*, meanwhile, takes the stock characters, action sequences and narrative cliché associated with the modern Hollywood action thriller and fleshes them out with distinctively Jamaican motivations and language, with Campbell playing the truly sinister baddie, Capone.

A Jamaican take on the classic gangster movie, **Shottas** (2002) mines the same vein of violence, albeit much more graphically, with Kymani Marley and DJ Spragga Benz playing two Kingston boys who take their life of crime from Jamaica to the US. Released in 2005, the sweet and delightful **One Love** represents a departure from the action genre; producer Sheelagh Farrell deliberately avoided focusing on the drugs-and-guns Jamaica, instead choosing to concentrate on the social tensions created when a pastor's daughter falls controversially in love with a Rasta musician. Other recent films include *Ghetta Life* from veteran director (of *Third World Cop* and *Dancehall Queen* fame) Chris Browne, and *Better Mus Come* from emerging film-maker Storm Saulter, both of which revisit the theme of bridging the great divide of warring ghettos and political strife through self-empowerment and star-crossed romance. More recent releases are **Marley** (2012), a poignant and moving documentary examining the life of the reggae legend through the people and events that affected him the most, and **Akwantu: The Journey** (2012) by director Roy T. Anderson, with a fascinating look at the Maroons of Jamaica.

Fort Charles

Church St • Daily 9am–5pm • US$10 • ☎ 967 8438

Fascinating **Fort Charles** was originally known as Fort Cromwell (but renamed after King Charles II was restored to the British throne in 1660). The present fort looks much as it did in 1692, except that then it was bordered by the sea on three sides. Clearly identified is Nelson's Quarterdeck, where the hero of the Battle of Trafalgar, Horatio Nelson, served as a young lieutenant in the English navy. There are two small **museums** containing artefacts recovered from the sunken city. The two structures that now stand between the fort and the water both date from the 1880s. The squat, rectangular **Giddy House**, an ammunition store, partially sank in 1907, while the circular bunker beside it was the **Victoria and Albert Battery**, an emplacement for a nineteenth-century supergun that was fired only once. The 1907 earthquake dropped the gun turret several metres into the earth, while the storeroom somehow remained intact but tilted, making walking across it without slipping over a challenge.

The Old Gaol

Gaol St

Once a seventeenth-century prison, the **Old Gaol** is a sturdy example of shipwrights' work – it has survived fourteen hurricanes, six earthquakes and two disastrous fires in the area.

The Old Naval Hospital

Old Naval Hospital New St

Behind the old garrison wall, at the end of Gaol Street and the beginning of New Street you'll find the decaying red bricks of the **Old Naval Hospital**. Built by the Bowling Ironworks in Bradford, England, the two-storey iron prefab, shipped over and erected here in 1819, remains the oldest prefabricated structure in the New World. Unfortunately it has been closed since it was damaged by Hurricane Gilbert in 1988.

The Naval Cemetery

Port Royal Rd

The **Naval Cemetery** – slightly out of town on the road back to Kingston – has its entrance marked by an anchor-shaped memorial to the crew of HMS *Goshawk*, who drowned when their vessel sank in Port Royal harbour, and marks the final resting place of many of Port Royal's long-forgotten sailors. Buccaneer-turned-enforcer Henry Morgan (see page 80) was buried here too, but the earthquake tipped his body into the sea, along with a large part of the old graveyard.

Lime Cay and around

Boats run regularly from Port Royal (J$1500/person), boats from *Y-Knot* (see page 80) tend to be better maintained and carry life jackets, but you can also ask one of the fishermen on (the sea side of) Queen St just up from *Gloria's* who might offer a cheaper rate but come at more of a gamble in terms of safety; arrange pick-up time at drop-off to avoid paying twice

Just fifteen minutes from Port Royal, **Lime Cay** is a tiny uninhabited island with white sand, blue water and easy snorkelling. It was here that Ivanhoe ("Rhygin") Martin – the cop-killing gangster and folk hero immortalized in the classic Jamaican movie *The Harder They Come* – met his demise in 1948. Though you'll often find the beach deserted on weekdays (bring your own refreshments), it's a very different story at the weekends, when hordes of Kingstonians descend to display their latest designer swimwear and relax with friends, and music blares from the stalls selling cooked meals and cold beers.

Other cays

If you desperately want your own private island, ask to be dropped at **Maiden Cay**, a tiny, shadeless sandspit, or **Twin Cays**, shadier but with poorer swimming than at Lime Cay. En route to any of these, you'll pass the once heavily armed **Gun Cay**, still bearing

1

PIRATES AND BUCCANEERS

To assist with the defence of their new Caribbean colonies, English, French and Dutch governors turned to the **buccaneers**, who were more than willing to plunder Spain's towns in the Caribbean and Gulf of Mexico. The earliest buccaneers were a ragged assortment of deserters, fugitives and even runaway slaves who banded together on the island of Tortuga on the Atlantic coast of present-day Haiti. They lived by hunting wild pigs and cattle (brought to the island by European settlers), smoking their meat on a wooden frame over a pit known as a *boucan* (hence the name *boucaniers*). When the game became scarce they took to the open sea to prey on shipping, especially Spanish.

As their numbers and their skills increased, the buccaneers became a serious fighting force under resourceful leaders like **Henry Morgan**, who had arrived with the English army. Morgan's successful sack of the city of Panama with three thousand men in 1671 coincided with the conclusion of a peace treaty between England and Spain. After a brief incarceration in the Tower of London to appease the Spanish, Morgan returned to Jamaica as Lieutenant Governor with a mandate to eradicate what was now deemed piracy.

Reminders of the era of piracy at Port Royal include Gallows Point at the end of the promontory and, offshore, Rackham's Cay where "**Calico Jack**" **Rackham**, after being executed, was squeezed into a cage and hung in the air as a warning to others. His two accomplices, Anne Bonney and Mary Read, escaped punishment by declaring themselves pregnant.

evidence of its eighteenth-century fortification by the British, and the fast-disappearing **Rackham's Cay**, a visible victim of beach erosion.

ARRIVAL AND DEPARTURE
PORT ROYAL AND AROUND

By bus Bus #98 (J$100) leaves every 30min (on weekdays, less regularly on the weekend) from Parade in downtown Kingston and travels via the airport.

By taxi A taxi will set you back around US$35 in each direction.

ACCOMMODATION

★ **Admiral's Inn** Henry Morgan Blvd ☎ 353 4202; map p.77. This family-run place in the housing scheme at the very end of Henry Morgan Blvd has clean, en-suite rooms with a/c, fridge and microwave; there's a pretty garden out back, with a gazebo and a bar. The owners can organize transfers, boat trips and other excursions. __US$60__

The Grand Port Royal Marina & Spa 1 Port Royal ☎ 833 6321, ⓦ grandportroyal.com; map p.77. Formerly *Morgan's Harbour Hotel* and immortalized in *Dr No*, this rebranded and renovated hotel boasts elegant rooms, some of which benefit from ocean-front balconies, plus a pool, restaurant and bar. Rates include breakfast. __US$102__

EATING

You can buy fried fish from stalls in the main square; on Friday evenings, make a beeline for the curried crab and conch soup sold at the *Martin's Sweetness* cart here– it's delicious and usually runs out around 7pm. On Fridays, speakers are stacked up in the main square for an outdoor party; a friendly crowd piles down from Kingston, and it's a great opportunity to enjoy a very easy-going Jamaican street dance.

★ **Gloria's** 1 High St ☎ 967 8066; map p.77. The most popular seafood restaurant in town with seating both in roadside tents and (preferably) upstairs on a breezy dining veranda overlooking the harbour and city. *Gloria's* is as famous for its fried fish (J$1200), as for the shrimp in garlic sauce (J$1500) and lobster curry (J$1450). It's a good idea to place your order and book a table in advance, otherwise the wait (especially on the weekends) can be lengthy. *Gloria's Top Shop* (15 Foreshore Rd; ☎ 967 8220; same hours; map p.77) is an offshoot of the original restaurant and can be equally

busy. Mon–Thurs & Sun 10.30am–11pm, Fri & Sat 10.30am–1am.

★ **Y-Knot** Port Royal Main Rd (before Grand Port Royal Hotel) ☎ 967 8448 or ☎ 304 8141; map p.77. Set around a large wooden deck over the water adjacent to *Grand Port Royal Hotel*, *Y-Knot* is another excellent spot for a drink and something to eat. Most Kingstonians take their Lime Cay boats from here (see page 79), and it's a busy scene at the weekends, with sand-dusted cay visitors piling off the boats and heading straight to the bar for a cool drink or the grill for jerk chicken (J$500). Mon–Sat 9am–7pm.

Portmore and the Hellshire Hills

1

Southwest of Kingston, off Marcus Garvey Drive, a **causeway** connects the city to the bland but booming dormitory town of **Portmore**. Below Portmore, the road cuts across the eastern fringe of the **Hellshire Hills** and down to Hellshire's white-sand **beaches**. Covered in low, dense scrub and towering cacti, the arid Hellshire Hills extend for around 160 square kilometres west of Kingston. From Port Henderson, the signposted road to the Hellshire beaches runs under the flanks of the Hellshire Hills, passing a huge scar in the mountainside gouged out to provide marl for the construction of Portmore's homes. Just before the quarry stands an abandoned high-rise building, formerly the *Forum Hotel*, built by the government in an unsuccessful attempt to entice tourists to the area. Past here, the road hits the coast again beside the **Great Salt Pond**. An old Taíno fishing spot, the pond is a site of ecological significance that continues to be polluted by excesses from Portmore's woefully inadequate sewerage system.

Portmore and around

Home to an estimated 200,000 people (and built to accommodate far fewer, as the recent strain on the sewerage system illustrates), **PORTMORE** itself has nothing much of interest save its **racecourse** and a few shopping malls. But **Port Henderson**, a brief detour away, has a handful of colonial-era relics and fine views across Kingston harbour.

Caymanas Park

Caymanas Blvd • Price dependent on seating area, expect to spend around J$500 for admission • ☎ 988 2524 • ⓦ caymanasracetrack.com

In its heyday **Caymanas Park Racetrack** was one of the best racetracks in the Caribbean, with its gorgeous backdrop of the Blue Mountains and Kingston shimmering across the harbour. Now under the ownership of the government, the course and facilities are in decline, showing years of wear and tear without any real indication or inclination from the government of future improvement. Still, it has the potential to be a great day out and shouldn't be overlooked, if only for the commentary and cursing from racegoers making for a colourful scene, though it's best visited with a tour guide (see page 69). You can sit either in the air-conditioned North Stand or, for a lot less, in the Grand Stand or outdoor bleachers, a more raucous affair with plenty of catcalls and shrieks of encouragement from the punters. Race meetings are held most Wednesdays and Saturdays (call ahead to check).

Fort Clarence beach

Hellshire Main Rd, south of Portmore • Mon–Fri 10am–5pm, Sat & Sun 8am–7pm • J$500

Owned by the Urban Development Company (UDC), **Fort Clarence beach** is often used as a venue for dancehall stageshows and pay parties, but it's also the preferred choice for Kingstonians seeking a less harassing, slightly more upscale venue to have a beach day (rather than Hellshire Beach). It's a decent place for a swim, with clean changing rooms and toilets and a bar/restaurant where you can order up delicious fried fish. Busy particularly on the weekends and especially (almost to the point of avoiding) on public holidays. Lifeguards are on duty during opening hours.

Hellshire beach

Adjacent to Fort Clarence beach • Free

Much more atmospheric than its just-across-the-reef counterpart, **Hellshire beach** has been a day-trip destination for Kingstonians since as far back as anyone can remember. With its maze of zinc shacks, salty fishermen, hustlers, higglers, herds of roaming goats and piping hot white sand, guests come here as much for the sights, sounds and sea as

1

they do for the famous Hellshire fried fish, best eaten with festival and vinegary home-made escovitch sauce, which is utterly delicious. Bring towels to spread on the beach or get there early enough to nab one of the wooden loungers set up under the shady eaves of the area's multiple **fish joints** – delightfully ramshackle and wholeheartedly Jamaican affairs which compete to sell the freshest fish, lobster and festival. Hellshire is buzzing at the weekends, with sound systems (particularly on a Sunday) and a party atmosphere. Also present at the weekends are **watersports operators** touting jet skis and snorkelling equipment, while horses (wearing fetching eye-gear to protect against flying sand grains) parade up and down giving children rides. If parking, be aware of hustlers offering to "watch your car" – in itself not a bad idea although you should never leave any valuables in sight – with the unspoken understanding that when you leave you'll provide a small tip (at your discretion) for the service.

ARRIVAL AND DEPARTURE

PORTMORE AND THE HELLSHIRE HILLS

By bus Any bus from Parade can take you to central Portmore (Portmore Mall; roughly every 15min). To get to Greater Portmore (also frequent), take bus #17, #18 or #20.

Bus #1 runs direct to Hellshire (every 2hr) from Parade.
By taxi A taxi from New Kingston will cost approximately US$75 for two people, one way.

EATING

★ Prendy's on the Beach Hellshire ☎859 7926, ⓦfacebook.com/PrendysOTB. The best cookshop on the beach, *Prendy's* is directly in front of you as you follow the sandy main road into Hellshire. As well as fried fish, they serve a divine version of steamed fish, cooked in a thick

pumpkin soup with potatoes, vegetables and bammy for J$1200. For a nice Sunday vibe, check out their free, family-oriented, day-time oldies party on the beach. Mon–Wed 9am–9pm, Thurs 9am–10pm, Fri & Sat 8am–11pm, Sun 7am–midnight.

Spanish Town

SPANISH TOWN, which was called St Jago de la Vega when it was founded by the Spanish in 1534, remained the island's capital under the English until 1872. It sits nineteen kilometres west of Kingston and these days contains only vestigial traces of its former glory. The town itself lies west of the Rio Cobre, with Burke Road, the main highway from Kingston, running across its southern end, fifteen minutes' walk from the central square. Once here, the main sights can easily be explored on foot, as the city is still laid out on its original neat grid system. Although it has its volatile hotspots, and attracts few tourists, it's still worth a half-day visit, preferably however with a tour guide (see page 69).

When leaving Spanish Town, it's possible to pass the old **Iron Bridge** that spans the Rio Cobre on the eastern end of town, just up the road from the Prison Oval on Burke Road. No longer in use for vehicular traffic, the bridge was cast in England by British engineer Thomas Wilson at a cost of £4,000 and erected after the prefabricated parts were shipped to Jamaica in 1802. At 25 metres long and 4.5 metres wide, standing on a cut stone abutment, it was the first of its kind in the western hemipshere and now, because of its state of disrepair is on the UNESCO endangered monuments list.

Parade Square

Centrally located Parade Square holds possibly the finest collection of Georgian architecture in the Americas. A classical memorial to Admiral Rodney, who defeated the French in 1782 in the Battle of Les Saintes, dominates the northern side. An adjoining structure houses the National Archives (Mon–Thurs 9.30am–3.30pm, Fri 9am–3.30pm; free) containing a unique collection of records dating back to the seventeenth century.

Directly opposite the memorial on Parade Square is the Georgian-style parish **courthouse**, which replaced the original nineteenth-century structure destroyed by fire in 1986. On the west of the square is the porticoed, red-brick facade of the **King's House**, built in 1762, the residence of Jamaica's governors until the capital was moved to Kingston in 1872. A plaque can be seen commemorating a proclamation declaring full emancipation from slavery in 1838. A catastrophic fire destroyed all but the facade of the King's House over a century ago. Also on the west side of the square sits the former House of Assembly, once the house of the island's governing body and now the parish offices.

Cathedral of St Jago de la Vega

Barrett St • Daily 9am–5pm • Free • ☎ 984 2535, ⓦ facebook.com/CathedralChurchJamaica

The oldest cathedral in the English colonial empire, **St Jago de la Vega** stands on the foundations of the sixteenth-century Church of the Red Cross, and the black-and-white tiles in the aisle are thought to date from the Spanish building. Important monuments crowd the cathedral, many of them carved in England by leading sculptors of the time such as John Bacon and John Wilton, reflecting the status and wealth of the colony during the eighteenth century. Inside, two chapels, the Blessed Sacrament Chapel and the Lady Chapel, contain memorials to former governors. Outside, you can spend an hour exploring and deciphering the ancient gravestones under the mango trees.

Phillipo's Church

9 William St • Services Sun 6.45am, 9.45am & 6pm • ☎ 984 2551

Built in 1827 by Reverend James Phillipo, a Baptist minister who campaigned for the abolition of slavery, **Phillipo's Church** is another great example of Georgian architecture in the old town centre. Inside the church are two tablets dedicated to the minister, while outside in the yard you can find modest gravestones for him, his wife and child as well as a stone slab where it is thought shackles of slaves are buried. Phillipo is most famous for the establishment of "free villages" for emancipated slaves, one of which is nearby Sligoville.

ARRIVAL AND DEPARTURE	**SPANISH TOWN**
By bus Bus #21AX runs every 30min from New Kingston to the bus terminus at the main square on Burke Road; the journey takes approximately one hour.	**By taxi** A taxi from New Kingston costs about US$60 for two people, one way.

EATING

Charmz Restaurant and Lounge 36 Jobs Lane. The interior of this cookshop may be rustic, but the dishes bring locals daily for lunch on site or to take away. The plates of curry are a top choice (J$600) – the curry goat sells out quickly – as well as roti and baked chicken (J$400), served with sides of vegetables and rice. The wait can be long, arrive early or bring a good dose of patience. Mon–Sat 11am–3pm.

The Blue Mountains and the east

THE BLUE MOUNTAINS

The Blue Mountains and the east

Towering behind Kingston and enticingly visible from anywhere in the island's eastern third, the Blue Mountains conform with few people's mental image of Jamaica, land of sand, sea and reggae. Forming one of the longest continuous ranges in the Caribbean, their cool, fragrant woodlands are shrouded in mist and offer some of the best hiking on the island, including Blue Mountain Peak, the remarkable botanical gardens at Cinchona and estates producing some of the best and the most expensive coffee on earth.

South of the range, **St Thomas** is one of the country's poorest and least developed regions, despite a rich history. Tourist development remains negligible and there are only a handful of hotels, but these are good bases nonetheless to visit the delightful mineral springs at **Bath**, or the deserted beaches around **Morant Point Lighthouse**.

Contrasting in scenery and atmosphere, on the northern side of the mountains is the northeastern parish of **Portland**, justifiably touted as one of the most beautiful parts of Jamaica, with jungle-smothered hillsides cascading down to postcard-perfect Caribbean shoreline. Though increasing, particularly at the luxury end, tourism is less conspicuous here than in other resort areas, but that's all the more reason to come – the wetter climate supports some stupendous natural scenery, including beautiful waterfalls and the magical **Blue Lagoon**. The parish capital, **Port Antonio**, has plenty of historical charm, while inland you can hike in pristine **rainforest** or take a gentle rafting trip on the **Rio Grande**. Some of the island's best **beaches** are also found here, and they're far less crowded than those further west, with lovely places to stay to boot: from surf-pounded stretches at Long Bay and Boston Bay to calm and idyllic Frenchman's Cove and Winnifred Beach, visitors come to Portland to chill out and experience a lower-key Jamaica than found elsewhere.

GETTING AROUND | THE BLUE MOUNTAINS AND THE EAST

By public transport Most points along the coast are reachable by minibus and route taxi, though you'll need a car to explore much of the interior.

By car The main A4 highway runs all the way around the coastline of Portland and St Thomas, while the A3 connects Kingston with Annotto Bay on the north coast (known as "the Junction Road", this is an exquisitely beautiful stretch). The B1 from Kingston to Buff Bay via Irish Town provides a narrow and winding route through the mountains that is mostly well paved.

The Blue Mountains

The **Blue Mountains** begin where Kingston ends, and a starker contrast would be hard to imagine, with the chaotic concrete maelstrom fast replaced by lush tranquillity and staggering natural beauty. The mountains are named for the mists that colour them from a distance, and their craggy slopes form an unbroken, undulating spine across Jamaica's easternmost parishes, a fabulously fertile wilderness with a surprisingly cool,

BLUE LAGOON

Highlights

❶ **Hiking in the Blue Mountains** From the arduous ascent for sunrise at Blue Mountain Peak to the nearly-as-spectacular climb to Cinchona Botanical Gardens, hiking in the region is the perfect antidote to beach inertia. See page 92

❷ **Dine at EITS Café** Enjoy the freshest Caribbean ingredients in a spectacular mountain setting. See page 93

❸ **Port Antonio** Small, historic town with lots of character set around two pretty bays. See page 105

❹ **The Blue Lagoon** One of the most impressive natural sights in Jamaica, made famous in the film of the same name. The "bottomless" lagoon features a curious mix of warm sea and cool fresh water. See page 114

❺ **Winnifred Beach** The most atmospheric beach in Portland and one of the last with universal public access: ride a horse and eat in a basic yet superb restaurant. See page 114

❻ **Rafting on the Rio Grande** The best rafting trip in Jamaica, pioneered by Errol Flynn. The bamboo rafts glide serenely down the river, taking three hours to reach journey's end. See page 122

HIGHLIGHTS ARE MARKED ON THE MAP ON PAGE 88

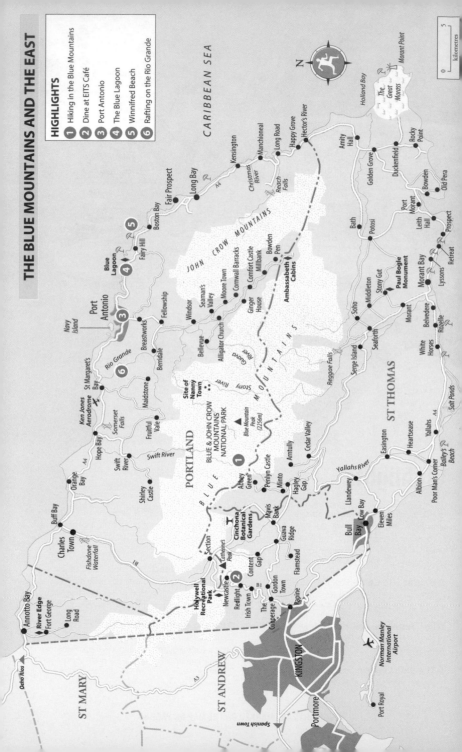

THE BLUE MOUNTAINS AND THE EAST

HIGHLIGHTS

1 Hiking in the Blue Mountains
2 Dine at EITS Café
3 Port Antonio
4 The Blue Lagoon
5 Winnifred Beach
6 Rafting on the Rio Grande

CARIBBEAN SEA

ST MARY

Ocho Rios

Annotto Bay
River Edge
Fort George
Long Road
Charles Town
Buff Bay
Fishdone Waterfall

PORTLAND

Orange Bay
Shirley Castle
Swift River
Hope Bay
Swift River
Fruitful Vale
Somerset Falls
Maidstone
Berridale
Breastworks
Fellowship

St Margaret's Bay
Ken Jones Aerodrome
Navy Island
Port Antonio

Rio Grande

Blue Lagoon
Fairy Hill
Boston Bay
Fair Prospect
Long Bay

A4

Kensington
Christmas River
Reach Falls
Happy Grove
Hector's River
Long Road
Manchioneal
Holland Bay

JOHN CROW MOUNTAINS

Windsor
Seaman's Valley
Moore Town
Cornwall Barracks
Comfort Castle
Millbank
Bowden Pen
Ambassabeth Cabins

Bellevue
Alligator Church

Quoha River

BLUE & JOHN CROW MOUNTAINS NATIONAL PARK

Site of Nanny Town
Stony River

Blue Mountain Peak (2256m)

MOUNTAINS

Ginger House

BLUE

Section
Catherine's Peak
Cinchona Botanical Gardens

Holywell Recreational Park

Newcastle
Redlight

Irish Town

Content Gap

Mavis Bank

Guava Ridge

Abbey Green
Penlyn Castle
Minto
Hagley Gap

Cedar Valley

Amtully

Reggae Falls

Serge Island

Bath
Potosi
Port Morant
Leith Hall
Retreat
Prospect

Amity Hall
Golden Grove
Duckenfield
Bowden
Old Pera
Rocky Point

Morant Point

The Great Morass

Morant Bay
Paul Bogle Monument

Stony Gut
Middleton
Soho
Seaforth
Morant
Belvedere
Rozelle
White Horses
Lyssons
Salt Ponds

ST THOMAS

Serge Island
Easington
Heartsease
Yallahs

Yallahs River

Llandewey
Low Bay
Bull Bay
Eleven Miles
Poor Man's Corner
Albion
Bailey's Beach

Flamstead
Gordon Town
Gordon Town
Guava Ridge
The Cooperage
Papine

B1

ST ANDREW

KINGSTON

Spanish Town

Portmore

Port Royal

Norman Manley International Airport

N

0   5
kilometres

wet climate. The dense forest provided perfect cover for the Windward Maroons (see page 120) during the seventeenth and eighteenth centuries, and today's sparse population is concentrated in settlements like **Gordon Town** and **Newcastle**.

The northern slopes of the mountains are covered by a huge quilt of dense, primary forest, but deforestation had, in the past, badly affected the southern side, where chunks were cleared by coffee planters and (catastrophically) hurricanes Gilbert and Ivan in 1988 and 2004. To try to protect the wilderness from further devastation, 200,000 acres were designated the **Blue and John Crow National Park** in 1993, to manage natural resources for long-term sustainable use and generate income opportunities through ecotourism (see ⓦblueandjohncrowmountains.org). To assist with the latter, **hiking trails** were created within the forest's interior, often following ancient mule trails over the mountains.

Tourism here, though on the rise, is small-scale, with just a few hotels and budget options – but most have spectacular locations. **Coffee** is the mainstay of the local economy, and excellent **tours** for those keen to see how the stuff is produced are to be found at the coffee factory at **Mavis Bank** and at plantations such as **Craighton Coffee Estate**. Dark and earthy, Blue Mountain coffee is considered one of the world's best by

THE MOUNTAIN ENVIRONMENT

The Blue Mountain range is Jamaica's oldest geographical feature, formed in the Cretaceous period (between 144 and 65 million years ago). Though the peaks are named for their cerulean tint when seen from afar, some of the rock is actually coloured blue by crossite minerals.

MOUNTAIN TREES AND PLANTS

Categorized as montane (high-altitude woodland), the **forests** are mostly native bilberry, soapwood, sweetwood and dogwood evergreens, with a few blue mahoe, bitter wood and teak trees, but the eucalyptus and Caribbean pines introduced in the 1950s are also having an impact. The primeval-looking cyathea (**tree fern**), with its diamond-patterned trunk and top-heavy fronds is particularly distinctive; the tallest are more than 150 years old. Below the dense canopy are **shrubs**, of which the red tubular flowers of the cigar bush are the most identifiable. Every tree trunk or exposed rock is festooned with brightly coloured epiphytes (plants that grow on other plants), including inexhaustible swathes of dirty lime-coloured old man's beard. Wild strawberries, raspberries, blackberries and rose apples provide a free feast, and you'll doubtless encounter prickly climbing bamboo, the only variety native to Jamaica; each one blossoms simultaneously with tiny white flowers once every 33 years – due next in 2050. Alongside are over five hundred species of **flowering plant**, including 65 varieties of orchid. Begonias, blue iris, agapanthus, lobelias, busy lizzies and fuchsias proliferate, while wild ginger lilies lend a delicate perfume.

ANIMALS AND BIRDS

Other than mongooses, coneys and the wild pigs that roam the northern slopes, there are few **mammals**. You may hear the scuffles of feral cats, mice and rats in the undergrowth, and a few Jamaican yellow boas (non-venomous) inhabit the lower slopes. The presence of bats is poorly documented; you're most likely to see them around the limestone slopes of the John Crow Mountains to the east. By contrast, **bird life** flourishes – incredibly, there are twenty-eight species here that can only be found in Jamaica. As a result, forests ring out with the evocative whistle of the rufous-throated solitaire, and buzzing hummingbirds (the national bird), white-eyed thrushes, mockingbirds, crested quail doves (known as mountain witches), blackbirds, and Jamaican todys add to the cacophony, backed by the squeaking mating call of tree frogs.

INSECTS

The mountains are the sole habitat of one of the rarest and largest **butterflies** in the world, the six-inch **giant swallowtail**, but its distinctively patterned dark brown and gold wings rarely flutter into view – again, the warmer John Crow range yields the most sightings. Insects, on the other hand, are multitudinous – in summer it's common to see thousands of **fireflies** (known as peenie-wallies) clustering on a single bush and lighting it up like a Christmas tree.

2

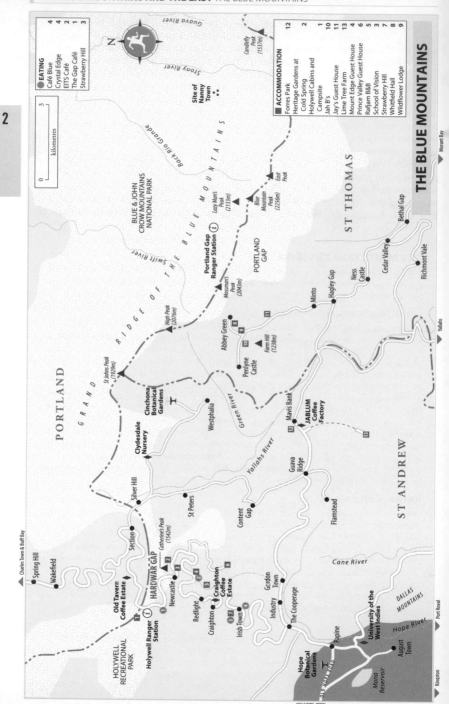

THE BLUE MOUNTAINS

● EATING

Café Blue	4
Crystal Edge	4
EITS Café	2
The Gap Café	1
Strawberry Hill	3

■ ACCOMMODATION

Forres Park	12
Heritage Gardens at Cold Spring	2
Holywell Cabins and Campsite	1
Jah B's	10
Jay's Guest House	11
Lime Tree Farm	13
Mount Edge Guest House	4
Prince Valley Guest House	6
Rafjam B&B	5
School of Vision	3
Strawberry Hill	7
Whitfield Hall	8
Wildflower Lodge	9

experts, and prices reflect that assessment, though you can usually find it cheaper here – at hotels, coffee factories or direct from the farmers – than anywhere else. Visitors also come here to hike up **Blue Mountain Peak** or to follow the well-maintained trails at **Holywell** or around Lime Tree Farm – superb trekking, for which you'll nonetheless need to be well prepared. Elsewhere, the botanical gardens at **Cinchona** are a delightful spot, a magical splash of colour 5000ft up.

GETTING AROUND
THE BLUE MOUNTAINS

BY PUBLIC TRANSPORT

Minibuses and route taxis The major routes from Papine to Redlight (via Irish Town), Gordon Town and Mavis Bank are served by minibuses and route taxis (J$150–J$250), though schedules are non-existent and frequency poor – it's always best to travel first thing in the morning or to arrange transport through your hotel. If you're travelling by route taxi, avoid starting out on a longer route on a Sunday (you should be able to get into Kingston, however).

BY CAR

Mountain roads You'll need a car to get the most out of the mountains. The principal access road, the B1 (Gordon Town Road), leads straight from Papine in northeast Kingston though the southern edge of the Mona Valley before winding upward into the riverine hills. Continuing straight ahead at tiny hamlet The Cooperage leads to Gordon Town and then

Mavis Bank, the main access point for Blue Mountain Peak. Turning left at The Cooperage, the road climbs precipitously up to Irish Town, the army barracks at Newcastle and onwards to Section before descending (equally precipitously) to Buff Bay on the north coast. At research time, this road was in good repair, but bear in mind that this latter section of the route is prone to landslides during hurricanes; confirm its condition before travelling.

Driving conditions Roads throughout the mountains come in for heavy assault during the wet season so expect significant bone-rattling, though you won't need a 4WD unless you plan to head off the main routes, such as to Cinchona or Abbey Green. Though roads appear wide enough only for a single vehicle, snorting delivery trucks still barrel up the slopes, sounding their presence with mighty blasts on the horn. It's wise to turn off the radio here and listen out, while also announcing your own presence with regular toots.

The Cooperage

The B1 from Papine follows the Hope River, which carries floodwater into the Mona Dam, its banks reinforced with high concrete walls. Wrapped around a road junction, the small village of **THE COOPERAGE** is named for the Irish coopers who worked here in the early nineteenth century, making the wooden barrels in which Blue Mountain coffee was shipped abroad. A left turn here leads up a precipitous winding road through the western section of the mountains and ultimately down to Buff Bay on the north coast – while continuing straight ahead takes you eastwards towards Mavis Bank and Blue Mountain Peak (see page 99).

Irish Town and Redlight

Settled by Irish coopers (hence the name) who worked in the valley below, **IRISH TOWN** is a small farming community located at just over 3000ft above sea level (around five twisting kilometres from The Cooperage), and now dominated by one magnificent **hotel**, *Strawberry Hill* (see page 93) – easily the best close to Kingston. The brainchild of Island Records magnate Chris Blackwell, this former coffee plantation opened as the first hotel under his Island Outpost brand in 1994, and offers a fabulous panorama from Kingston harbour to Spanish Town on one side, and of a lush Blue Mountain valley on the other. Bob Marley was brought here to convalesce after being shot in 1976, and many other artists have stayed here over the years – among them the Rolling Stones, U2, Stevie Wonder and Sting; the hotel's conference room contains numerous photos of the stars and Island's collection of gold and platinum discs from sales of Bob Marley's albums (open by appointment). Even if you can't afford to stay here, **eating** at *Strawberry Hill* is a must (see page 93).

This section of the mountains offers a greater choice of accommodation and eating than the Mavis Bank area to the east, and has a larger population, scattered between

2

HIKING AND BIKING IN THE BLUE MOUNTAINS

Most places to stay in the mountains are a good starting point for information and guided tours, with some offering ascents or ridge walks directly from their properties. Cycling is also an attractive option; several hotels offer day-long biking expeditions, calling in at small coffee farms and private homes, including *Mount Edge Guesthouse* (see page 93) and *Forres Park* (see page 97).

Shifting weather conditions and ecological protection projects mean that of thirty recognized hiking **trails** in the national park, only twenty or so are open at any given time; weather updates and trail accessibility information is available at the main **ranger station**, located at Holywell, and at smaller stations at Portland Gap and Millbank (not always manned). Ordnance survey maps are also on display. You can get information over the phone from the Jamaica Conservation and Development Trust in Kingston, which runs the park (see below). Bear in mind that adventures in the rainy season (May–June & Sept–Oct) pretty much guarantee getting drenched.

All the usual, common-sense guidelines apply to mountain hiking and biking. Bring decent boots or training shoes, plentiful **drinking water** (pine bromeliads hold much water between their leaves, but as they're home to insect nymphs and tree frogs, you'll only want to sup in an emergency), snacks, insect repellent and a torch.

It's almost always advisable to use a **guide** in the Blue Mountains; given changeable weather conditions and poor maps (alongside few obvious landmarks), it's very easy to get lost. Security can also be a problem for unaccompanied hikers, particularly on the Kingston side of the mountains. A guide will ensure your safety, clear overgrown paths and provide an informed commentary.

GUIDES AND TOUR COMPANIES

Blue Mountain Bicycle Tours Ocho Rios ☎ 974 7075, ⓦ bmtoursja.com. An excellent option for a day-long downhill bike tour. They'll drive you up to Section and let you freewheel 29km or so down towards the north coast, via the One Drop and Fishdone waterfalls and an attractive brunch spot and bar at Springhill. US$129 including transfer, brunch and refreshments.

Forres Park Mavis Bank ☎ 927 8275 or ☎ 977 8141, ⓦ forrespark.com. This hotel, spa and coffee farm organizes hiking and cycling tours, guided birding trips (US$150/1–3 people; includes transport) and peak hikes (US$190/2 people).

Jamaica Conservation and Development Trust 29 Dumbarton Ave, Kingston ☎ 960 2848/9, ⓦ blueand johncrowmountains.org. Conservation organization that manages trails at the Holywell park and organizes various day-hikes, including across the old Maroon Cunha Cunha Pass between the Blue and John Crow mountain ranges; US$20–50.

Mount Edge Between Redlight and Newcastle ☎ 944 8151 or ☎ 944 8973, ⓦ 17milepost.com. A very friendly guesthouse with a limitless range of customized tours, standard trips to Blue Mountain Peak (US$60/person) and guided cycling tours (US$80/ person, 4hr) and cycle rental (US$15/day).

RafJam Redlight ☎ 944 8094 or ☎ 426 3667, ⓦ rafjam.com. Set in a wonderfully atmospheric location with river hiking and swimming nearby, this guesthouse provides professional guides for treks to a Rastafarian camp settlement and to Blue Mountain Peak (among others) as well as horseriding (US$60/2 people).

Sun Venture 30 Balmoral Ave, Kingston ☎ 924 4515 or ☎ 408 6973, ⓦ sunventuretours.com. A very experienced option for Blue Mountain and island-wide hikes; includes various day-long mountain walks (US$120) as well as treks to the peak with a night in a mountain lodge (US$230). Prices are based on groups of four with transport included.

Irish Town and **REDLIGHT**, a couple of minutes' drive beyond along the B1. You'll pass a ridiculously high boundary wall between the two communities, known locally as the Great Wall of China, built by the owner to protect against landslides. Redlight itself is named for the former brothels that kept the Irish coopers entertained. It's a charming, laidback place with staggering views and a couple of basic rum/provision shops. Hiking from here, the **Gordon Town Trail** loops downhill, passing through small coffee plantations and precipitous fields of broccoli and scallion. The trail offers opportunities for swimming, with plenty of mini-waterfalls and deep pools; it's easy to follow once you get onto it – ask anyone in Redlight to direct you to the start, from where it takes about two and a half hours to get to Gordon Town.

Craighton Coffee Estate

Tours Mon–Sat 9am–5pm, 45min–1hr • US$25 • ☎ 944 8033, ⓦ ucc.co.jp/eng

Between Irish Town and Redlight, the road passes the near-vertical driveway for **Craighton Coffee Estate**, a private plantation owned by Japanese company UCC, who offer inviting tours of the 200-year-old plantation house (with its assortment of Japanese mementos and coffee oddments), a walk through the coffee farm and tastings; it offers a good insight into the process, from plant to production.

ARRIVAL AND DEPARTURE   IRISH TOWN AND REDLIGHT   2

By minibus and route taxi Redlight (via Irish Town) is served by minibuses and route taxis from Papine in Kingston (J$200). Schedules are non-existent, however –

it's best to travel first thing in the morning or to arrange transport through your accommodation. Sunday frequency is very poor.

ACCOMMODATION

★ **Mount Edge Guest House** 1.5km north of Redlight ☎ 944 8151 or ☎ 944 8973, ⓦ 17milepost. com; map p.90. Clinging to the side of a deep valley, this laidback and artistic guesthouse has phenomenal views and features simple, clean rooms inside the main house (shared bathroom) and separate en-suite rooms of a higher standard just outside. The home of wily local personality Michael Fox, it's gained a new lease on life via his daughter Robyn, with the addition of the excellent *FITS Café* restaurant (see below), plus a yoga deck and an organic farm. Breakfast US$5 extra. US$45

Prince Valley Guest House Newcastle Road ☎ 892 2365, ⓦ princevalleyguesthouse.com; map p.90. Tucked into a coffee- and fruit-filled corner of the mountains, the highlight here is the beautiful self-built Treehouse, wrapped around a mango tree. The four other rooms vary, but are spacious and comfortable with private bathroom. Rates include morning coffee, toast and seasonal fruit. Home-cooked meals (US$12) upon request. Rooms US$35 per person, treehouse US$40 per person

★ **Rafjam B&B** Just under 1km east of Redlight ☎ 944 8094 or ☎ 426 3667, ⓦ rafjam.net; map p.90. Ask for a room over the river at this supremely tranquil family-run guesthouse and coffee farm nestled in the valley below Redlight. Rooms are good value, the best one carved into the rock, while excellent Jamaican food with an international twist is served at the *Tiki Bar and Grill*. Camping available (negotiable). US$70

Strawberry Hill Irish Town ☎ 944 8400, ⓦ straw berryhillhotel.com; map p.90. Easily the classiest hotel in the wider Kingston area, maintaining an unpretentious Jamaican feel despite its often traditional colonial decor. Thirteen cottages are perched right on the hillside, made from local materials and boasting hand-carved fretwork and muslin-draped mahogany four-poster beds with heated mattresses (it gets cold at night). The beautifully landscaped gardens feature unusual Jade vines and a glorious infinity pool and deck affording breathtaking views. A state-of-the-art spa tops off this most luxurious retreat. Includes a continental breakfast. US$385

EATING

Café Blue Irish Town ☎ 944 8918, ⓦ jamaicacafeblue. com; map p.90. Italian-style coffee shop with a great range of Blue Mountain lattes and cappuccinos (J$350–550), inviting cheesecakes and an assortment of Blue Mountain-themed gifts. The coffee here is sourced from the Clifton Mount Estate, tours of which can be arranged from the shop. Mon–Thurs 8am–6pm, Fri–Sun 7am–8pm.

Crystal Edge Irish Town ☎ 944 8053; map p.90. A less formal meal is available at this very friendly and spacious diner with an outside terrace and great views over the valley. Serves up lovely soups like *janga* (crayfish) or red-peas, and delicious jerk chicken and pork (J$300–1000). Tues–Sun 8.30am–7pm.

★ **EITS Café** Mount Edge Guest House, 1.5km north of Redlight ☎ 944 8151 or ☎ 944 8973, ⓦ 17milepost. com/eits-cafe; map p.90. This new and exciting

restaurant offers stunning views and a scrumptious range of dishes using the freshest organic produce from the farm below. Try the innovative salads with nuts or anchovies, the outstanding lamb or the homemade pesto (mains US$12–30). Chicken smoked in a barrel offers a new take on an old Jamaican classic. Live jazz Sun. Book in advance. Daily noon–9pm.

★ **Strawberry Hill** Irish Town ☎ 944 8400, ⓦ island outpost.com; map p.90. Take in a panoramic view of the capital over a romantic dinner on the Great House terrace, or the unmissable Sunday brunch buffet (worth every cent of US$45). The sublime food is a combination of fresh ingredients and sophisticated international cooking, like baked crab backs with tropical remoulade and more conventional jerk chicken roti or plantain-crusted snapper. Mains US$25–45. Reservations required. Daily 8–10.30am & noon–10pm.

Newcastle

NEWCASTLE, an old British military base established by Major William Gomm in 1841 to escape the yellow fever raging on the hot, swampy plains below, sits 4000ft up from Redlight. The main road cuts across the **parade ground** of the Jamaica Defence Force, which still features old cannons and the insignia of the various regiments stationed here during the past century or so. The nearby military graveyard remembers the dead of that period with its neat, white crosses.

The views from the base across the mountains and down to Kingston are dazzling and almost vertiginous, while behind you, immediately above Newcastle, **Catherine's Peak** (5060ft) – named after Lady Catherine Long, the first woman to climb it (officially, at least) in 1760 – marks the highest point in the parish of St Andrew. You can make the steep, misty hike to the pylon-topped summit of Catherine's Peak via a concrete road that branches off the B1 just north of Newcastle and winds its way up, affording excellent views of Kingston when the mist clears.

The winding lane past Newcastle cuts through mist-covered **coffee plantations** and dense woodland for a couple of kilometres to the mountain pass at **Hardwar Gap**, named for a British army captain who supervised the construction of the road from here to Buff Bay. The atmospheric **Gap Café** (see below) was constructed in the 1930s and originally designed as a way station for those traversing the mountains by horse and carriage.

ARRIVAL
NEWCASTLE

By public transport There is no public transport to Newcastle; however, hitching a ride from infrequent passing vehicles at Redlight is possible.

ACCOMMODATION

Heritage Gardens at Cold Spring Newcastle ☎ 960 8627 or ☎ 978 4438, ⓦ heritagegardensjamaica.com; map p.90. A delightful two-bedroom cottage (rent whole or by the room) is attached to a larger house and set in landscaped gardens, part of the grounds of a former coffee plantation established by Irish naval officer Matthew Wallen while posted to Newcastle. Features a long, shady veranda and large bathroom with tub, and the hosts are friendly and welcoming. Includes breakfast. US$65

School of Vision Newcastle ☎ 482 0701, ⓦ him-school ofvision.blogspot.co.uk; map p.90. Immerse yourself in Rasta culture at this small community guesthouse with a dazzling location. The five guestrooms are basic but clean, the vibe is great, and there is superb ital food on offer. Guests can also take park in the Saturday Sabbath, as well as chanting and drumming. US$15 per person

EATING

The Gap Café Hardwar Gap ☎ 319 2406 or ☎ 361 4192; map p.90. A few twists in the road beyond the Newcastle barracks is this atmospheric restaurant serving sandwiches as well as Jamaican lunches like coconut fish, oxtail and curried goat (J$1700–2200). The charming garden terrace is a perfect place to sink a cocktail or a beer, with stunning views when not enshrouded in mist. Thurs–Sun 10am–5pm.

Holywell Recreational Park

100m beyond *The Gap Café* (see above) • US$10 • ☎ 960 2848, ⓦ blueandjohncrowmountains.org

At over 4000ft above sea level, the mountain air at **Holywell Recreational Park** is deliciously fresh, fragrant and cool – aided by a thick mist that, when it clears, provides a spectacular unbroken view over the shimmering streets of Kingston, Port Royal and Portmore. The three hundred acres of parkland are latticed with enjoyable, well-maintained hiking trails. Check in at the **ranger station** near the entrance before you set off on a walk, as rain can sometimes wreak havoc overnight and leave some trails impassable. You'll also need to be accompanied by a ranger for some of the more difficult routes (sturdy boots advised). Near the entrance you'll find a picnic spot with tables, covered gazebos, water taps and a toilet.

Holywell trails

The best of the walks is the gentle **Oatley Mountain Trail** (1.2km; 40min), an easy, varied circular hike through tunnel-like jungle. There are a couple of lookout towers and viewing platforms from which to enjoy the views, and several information boards explain the flora and fauna found in the area. You can continue on to the **Waterfall Trail** (1.3km; 1hr 30min), a mildly testing scramble along a river bed to the Cascade Waterfall; however, landslides have reduced the icy waters and swimming hole to a trickle. Oatley Mountain was extensively replanted with Caribbean pines after Hurricane Gilbert, and though it unfortunately suffered further damage during Ivan, it remains a sanctuary for a wide variety of birds. To the east lies Mount Horeb and the ecologically sensitive (and so off-limits) Fairy Glades Trail, where pines are outnumbered by the twisted trunks of soapwood and dogwood trees laden with clusters of orchids.

2

ACCOMMODATION	HOLYWELL RECREATIONAL PARK

Holywell Cabins and Campsite ☎ 960 2848, ⓦ blue andjohncrowmountains.org; map p.90. It's possible to rent one of the secluded on-site cabins in the park, ideal if you want to do some extended exploration. Each sleeps two to four people; they're no-frills but certainly attractive, with varnished wood floors plus a fireplace, kitchenette and marvellous views. Camping is also available. Camping per person US$5, cabins US$50

Old Tavern Coffee Estate

Green Hills, 1 km or so beyond Holywell • ☎ 865 2978 or ☎ 924 2785, ⓔ oldtaverncoffee@gmail.com

The 120-acre **Old Tavern Coffee Estate** is run by David Twyman from his family's unmarked cottage, which hangs vertiginously just below the mountain road. In 1997, after a drawn-out row with the government, David's parents, Dorothy and Alex Twyman, became the first growers in the country to process their crop from their own home-based facility. This advance signalled a greater openness in the industry: licensing processes were streamlined, and a plethora of producers were born. As coffee growers go, however, the Twymans arguably remain the most experienced, and their three roasts and subtler peaberry bean make for the best Blue Mountain coffee in Jamaica. Currently, the estate does not offer official tours, but there are hopes for them in the future; email for further information.

Section to Buff Bay

SECTION, three kilometres past Old Tavern, is a friendly if slightly dishevelled little settlement straggled around a fork in the road. Home to several small-scale coffee farmers, it is a good place to enquire about hiking guides or to buy some coffee (a pound of beans should cost about J$1300). Turning to the east here takes you around switchback turns towards **Silver Hill** and Clydesdale (see page 96), while turning northwards carries you briefly up and then steeply downwards for around seventy minutes to the Maroon settlement of Charles Town (see page 122) and then the coast at Buff Bay. The upper sections of this road are prone to collapse during hurricanes and heavy storms – ask around in Irish Town, Charles Town or Section if it's open before you travel.

The views along this entire route, through the mountain gaps, planted with neat rows of coffee, are fantastic. Fourteen kilometres before Buff Bay, a dip at **Fishdone Waterfall** offers a natural power shower and wide, clear pool of cool water; turn left just before the white Silver Hill bridge at a sign for the Avocat Primary School.

Gordon Town

GORDON TOWN is the only sizeable settlement in the Blue Mountains, reached from The Cooperage in the Blue Mountains foothills (see page 91). The route along the Gordon

Town River provides lots of swimming spots, and if you're heading to a remote area the town is worth stopping at to stock up on final supplies. It's built around a neat central square with a couple of snack bars and the usual giggling gaggles of smartly turned-out schoolchildren. Confusingly, the main road continues by taking an un-signposted turn eastwards across a narrow bridge; it deteriorates as it twists around hairpin bends all the way to Mavis Bank and beyond, but a little care and plenty of toots on the horn still make this a very enjoyable drive. Coffee aside, the main motivation for visiting the settlement is undoubtedly hiking; with the peak temptingly close and legions of fabulous walks nearby, you'd be crazy not to test out some of the trails.

Clydesdale

The northern fork from hilltop junction **Guava Ridge**, five kilometres east of Gordon Town, takes you eight kilometres up a steep and precarious slope into the heart of coffee country, through the tiny hamlet of **Content Gap**, and onward to **Clydesdale**, tucked into a remote pocket of the mountains and accessible only by foot or 4WD. An old coffee plantation, it was converted into a nursery in 1937 by the Forestry Department with row upon row of Caribbean pines, networked by several paths that make for a pleasantly shady walk. Sadly, the plantation is no longer functioning as a financial enterprise – its buildings have long been abandoned and are in a state of advanced disrepair – but it's still a lovely, tranquil spot, and usually completely deserted, so you'll need to bring a guide. Sun Venture Tours (see page 92) runs day-trips up to Clydesdale and on to Cinchona, including along a hiking trail to a small, icy-cold waterfall and river pool on the Clydesdale River, known locally as the **Fountain of Life** for its supposedly healing properties. This was once a picnic and swimming spot, popular among locals and Kingstonians, a fact attested to by the now-derelict changing rooms; some people still make the tough journey up from Kingston.

Cinchona Botanical Gardens

Daily dawn to dusk • Free • Contact Jamaica National Heritage Trust in Kingston ☎ 922 1287, ⊕ jnht.com • Camping permitted (negotiable)

Most people hike to **Cinchona Botanical Gardens** from Clydesdale, though it is possible to drive all the way from Westphalia or Mavis Bank in a 4WD (guide needed; see page 92) up the rough road that snakes through the precipitous coffee groves covering Top Mountain. The gardens are at the summit, and their semi-orderliness is a surprise after the rugged and wild hillsides below. Clinging to the ridge opposite Blue Mountain Peak and overlooking the Yallahs River valley, the ten-acre maintained gardens were initially a commercial venture, planted with Assam tea and cinchona trees – which produce quinine, used as an anti-malarial before the advent of modern drugs – in 1886. However, the inaccessibility of the site and competition from Indian plantations led to the project's decline, and it became a government-run public garden in 1968. Botanical research is still occasionally carried out here.

Despite obvious recent neglect, the gardens have a magical feel, with eucalyptus whistling in the breeze, and Norfolk Island pine, Japanese cedar, weeping cypress, rubber and camphor trees flourishing in the mist. The vivid flowerbeds are bursting with blooms, and wild coffee smothers the slopes. You can see the whole layout from above on the **Panorama Walk** (preferably accompanied by one of the gardeners – leave a tip), which takes you through a tunnel-like thicket of Holland bamboo and eventually back to the main house, an ancient oblong of stone that still contains most of its original fittings. Other guided (unsigned) trails are also available, among the most rewarding the sweaty ten-kilometre hike down to Mavis Bank, the six-kilometre hike to Catherine's Peak and the historic (and now somewhat impenetrable) sixteen-kilometre **Vinegar Hill Trail** to Buff Bay, an old Maroon trading route that the British used to transport supplies from Kingston to the north coast.

Flamstead

Flamstead, just under three kilometres southwest of Guava Ridge, is worth a visit for jaw-dropping vistas over Port Royal and the Caribbean. Once the site of a great house and plantation that was home to Governor Edward Eyre and British Admiral Horatio Nelson, the house was ruined by a series of hurricanes, though you can meander freely around the grounds (no set opening hours) and tip a gardener to let you into the tiny on-site **exhibition** on the property's history.

Mavis Bank

2

MAVIS BANK is picturesquely nestled in the Yallahs River valley, a more isolated part of the mountains. The neatly arranged settlement is the last full-scale village on the route to Blue Mountain Peak, but it is also ideally placed to explore the surrounding ridges and Cinchona Botanical Gardens (see page 96). There's little to Mavis Bank itself: the town's single street consists of a police station, several no-frills rum shops that also sell basic foods, a couple of churches and a smattering of homes. You can start the hike up to Blue Mountain Peak from Mavis Bank along the steep and strenuous Farm Hill Trail from the church, but given the distance it's much more sensible to begin from Abbey Green, just over eight kilometres northeast (see page 98). If you're driving and plan to go on to Abbey Green, unless you're in a sturdy 4WD you'll want to park in Mavis Bank in the lay-by opposite the police station and arrange return transport onwards. Although it's just about possible to drive on to Hagley Gap in a normal car, it's certainly not for the terrain beyond, and parking there can be a problem.

Mavis Bank Coffee Factory

West side of the village • Mon–Fri 10am–2pm • US$10 • Phone in advance ☎ 977 8015

The **Mavis Bank Coffee Factory** is Mavis Bank's main attraction, owned by the National Investment Bank of Jamaica and the Munn family. In business for around a hundred years and handling some seventy thousand bushels of coffee per year from six thousand farmers, the factory is Jamaica's main Blue Mountain coffee processing plant, and it is here that the precious beans are graded, roasted and packaged under the **JABLUM** consortium name. Beginning with an obligatory infusion of steaming caffeine at the on-site coffee bar, the tour takes you on an engaging journey "from the berry to the cup" through every part of the working factory, and at the end you can buy bags of beans far cheaper than in the shops.

ARRIVAL AND DEPARTURE   **MAVIS BANK**

By public transport Route taxis and minibuses leave when full from Papine to the Central Square in Mavis Bank. The journey takes 1hr 30min (about J$250).

ACCOMMODATION

Forres Park Mavis Bank ☎ 977 8141, ⓦ forrespark. com; map p.90. A charming, friendly hotel and coffee farm with luxurious (though not large) rooms with king-size beds and a shared veranda in the main house, and more economical timber cabins nearby. Good Jamaican food is available (daily by pre-order, non-guests welcome), as well as spa treatments. With 28 endemic bird species in the area, the property appeals to specialist birders, though hiking and mountain-biking tours are also available. Cabins US$90, rooms US$121

★ **Lime Tree Farm** Tower Hill District, Mavis Bank

☎ 446 0230, ⓦ limetreefarm.com; map p.90. The most impressive setting of any hotel in Jamaica, this coffee estate, co-owned by the grandson of former governor Hugh Foot, appeals as much to hikers as to lovers of seclusion; the views are outstanding and fruit trees of all varieties lie between the surrounding coffee terraces. The four spacious cottages are supremely comfortable, and delicious meals by Jamaican chef Keisha are served on your veranda or on a communal terrace. All-inclusive, with pick-up from Mavis Bank, and they offer reasonably priced tours and birding to all neighbouring peaks. US$285

Hagley Gap and around

HAGLEY GAP, reached via a rocky track across the Yallahs River ford from Mavis Bank, is a steeply inclining and untidy one-street village where you can buy basic last-ditch provisions and get a hot meal from one or two small-scale cookshops. You'll likely notice the village's poverty, at least partly the product of dependence on a volatile coffee market, alongside the associated risk of crop wipe-out during hurricanes (see page 99). A US-led development NGO, the Blue Mountain Project (ⓦbluemountainproject.org), has implemented programmes in basic health care, clean water and economic development, partly funded by a tourist homestay programme (see website for details).

The ascent north from Hagley Gap is along one of the least road-like roads in Jamaica, with huge gullies carved through the clay by coursing water; you'll need a powerful 4WD with a high clearance. Shortly after embarking on this tortuous route, you pass through (much prettier) **MINTO**, a drawn-out roadside community where proud locals have planted their gardens with brightly coloured flowers and shrubs.

Abbey Green

Starting point for treks to Blue Mountain Peak, the smattering of buildings that make up **ABBEY GREEN** lie at some 4500ft above sea level. It's a completely different world to the Jamaica below it, where wind shrieks through eucalyptus trees and seemingly impenetrable mists billow over the mountainside only to evaporate after a few rays of sun. It's an intensely beautiful place, and you're unlikely to meet anyone save the odd coffee grower or scallion farmer.

ARRIVAL AND DEPARTURE   ABBEY GREEN

Arrival here is only possible in a **4WD** – arrange transport through your tour guide or accommodation. Abbey Green hostels offer Land Rover pick-up from Mavis Bank for US$50 per vehicle (maximum six people).

ACCOMMODATION

Three rustic **hostels** act as bases for peak hikes (see page 99) and provide guides to the peak for around US$60. Whichever lodge you choose, it's a good idea to arrange to have a hot meal prepared ready for your return from hiking; you'll need it. Be aware that these places, located in exquisitely beautiful spots, also require the cost of 4WD transportation.

Jah B's Abbey Green ☎377 5206, ⓦjahbguesthouse. com; map p.90. A simple, friendly dormitory-cum-guesthouse run by a Bobo Rasta coffee and fruit farmer, with large portions of Ital food available (phone to order; US$12 for dinner). Rooms are divided between a wooden shack and a newer concrete house – view a couple before you decide. One of Jah B's sons, Razza, is often available to guide you to the peak (US$60). Dorms US$20, doubles US$50

Jay's Guest House Hagley Gap ☎321 8204, ⓦjays guesthouse.com; map p.90. Friendly, cheerful and brightly decorated spot high up in the mountains, with transportation available to and from the property. Helpful staff coordinate peak hikes, coffee farm tours and trips to swimming holes, and there are stellar home-cooked meals on offer. Dorms US$25, doubles US$60

Whitfield Hall Abbey Green ☎878 0514, ⓦwhitfield hall.com; map p.90. Rustic is the optimum word here at this atmospheric old coffee-planters' great house. Yellowing books line the walls of its huge communal sitting room and there's a large blackened fireplace, while low ceilings and an old-fashioned kitchen add to the archaic feel. Oil lamps cast shadows throughout the rooms of (fairly uncomfortable) bunks (plus two doubles), and you'll almost certainly meet other hikers preparing for the climb. Meals are available by advance order (US$9). Camping is available. Camping per person US$10, dorms US$20, doubles US$55

Wildflower Lodge Abbey Green ☎364 0722; map p.90. A recently upgraded, though no-frills, modern two-storey house that has double rooms and bunks, plus a kitchen and communal dining room, set in gorgeous flowered gardens. Meals are cooked to order (US$8). Dorms US$20, doubles US$50

Blue Mountain Peak

Undeniably the most rewarding hike in Jamaica, **Blue Mountain Peak** (7402ft), the highest point on the island, seems daunting but isn't the fearful climb you might imagine. It is magnificent by day, when you can marvel at the opulence of the canopy, the thousands of orchids, mosses, bromeliads and lichens, the mighty shadows cast by the peak and the coils of smoke from invisible dwellings below. It's also thrilling by night when, after a magical moon-lit ascent, Kingston's lights occasionally twinkling in the distance, you find yourself at Jamaica's zenith as a new day dawns.

From Abbey Green, the **climb to the peak** is around thirteen kilometres, and can take anything from three to six hours depending on your pace. If you're staying at one of the hostels, you can start at around 1am and catch sunrise at around 5.15 to 6.15am, depending on the time of year. A full moon also means you'll get natural floodlighting – otherwise, take a flashlight. Signposts make much of the route easy to follow without a guide, but in this remote area it's sensible to go with someone who knows the way. Don't stray onto tempting "short cuts" – it's illegal, you'll damage the sensitive environment and you'll almost certainly get hopelessly lost. Rescue patrols can take days to mobilize effectively, by which time you'll be in serious trouble.

Blue Mountain Peak is the furthest you can go into the Blue Mountains, as thick forest and treacherous terrain means that even the burly pig hunters seldom venture further east, preferring to enter the John Crow range from Millbank in Portland (see page 120).

The peak trail

The first stretch of the trail, a steep series of switchback turns through thick forest aptly named **Jacob's Ladder**, is said to be the most arduous, and you'll appreciate arriving at the halfway point at **Portland Gap Ranger Station** (7km), where you can rest at the gazebo, top up water and let the rangers know that you're walking the trail (leave a note if you arrive in the early hours).

Once past Portland Gap, it's another five and a half kilometres to the peak through twisted montane and then low-lying elfin forest, in which the gnarled soapwood and dogwood evergreens are so stunted by low temperatures, exposure and lack of nutrients that they grow no higher than 8ft. You're still only about 6000ft up, but you might already be a little dizzy from the rising altitude; if so, go slowly and eat a high-energy snack. At 7000ft, the plateau at **Lazy Man's Peak** is where some call it a day, but it's certainly worth struggling on for another twenty minutes.

BLUE MOUNTAIN COFFEE

Don't leave the island unless you've had some **Blue Mountain coffee** – one of the smoothest brews you'll ever find, and the low-caffeine content means you can enjoy copious amounts.

Coffee trees from Ethiopia were introduced to Jamaica in 1728 by Governor Sir Nicholas Lawes, and they flourished on the cool slopes of the Blue Mountains. Cultivation reached new heights of excellence during the first half of the nineteenth century, when expert coffee growers arrived from revolution-torn Haiti, soon meeting an increased demand from European coffeehouses. Jamaica became one of the world's main coffee exporters, producing up to fifteen thousand tons of beans per year.

In the nineteenth century, Britain abolished preferential trade terms on coffee, and direct competition with the coffees of South America crippled small Jamaican farmers. The decline continued into the twentieth century, and it was only after World War II that the Jamaican government took belated steps to save the Blue Mountain plantations. It established **quality guidelines** for both cultivation and processing, stipulating that only coffee grown at a certain altitude and on the regional soil type could claim the Blue Mountain name (you'll see coffee produced in Mandeville called High Mountain and elsewhere around the island Low Mountain). This exclusivity heightened the coffee's cachet and helped to underpin its reputation as one of the world's finest.

2

The peak

If you've arrived at the peak before dawn, you'll be completely bowled over. The inky black slowly melts into ever-intensifying pinks, oranges and purples until finally a hint of wispy blue heralds the sun and reveals the surrounding ranges. It's quite possible you'll be here alone, the highest person in Jamaica and feeling – literally – on top of the world. As the sun burns off the mist, the spectacular panorama becomes recognizable; you can make out Cinchona and, on a good day, Buff Bay and Port Antonio's Navy Island to the north and Kingston, Portmore and coastal St Thomas to the south.

St Thomas

St Thomas, nestling below the Blue Mountains, is the most neglected of Jamaica's parishes, and as a result, its villages are somewhat impoverished with meagre facilities for tourists. For some, however, the region offers a slice of the "real" Jamaica, untouched by the demands of tourism. The main attractions are the rambling old spa town of **Bath** in the foothills of the mountains, and also remote **Morant Point**, where a candy-striped lighthouse overlooks a stunning beach. A couple of waterfalls in other areas are interesting diversions, though there's little to do in the parish capital, **Morant Bay**, except to reflect on one of the bloodiest periods in Jamaica's volatile history. The parish's friendly people remain probably the biggest draw, and largely due to the presence of the descendants of free Africans, St Thomas is the cradle of Jamaica's African-based religions (see page 277), with roadside Kumina sessions found frequently.

ARRIVAL AND DEPARTURE   **ST THOMAS**

By public transport The main road to Morant Bay is served by regular minibuses, with route taxis continuing from there to Port Antonio, but it's difficult to reach more remote locations without a car.

Bull Bay

The A4 hugs the coastline east of Kingston, past the tiny settlements of **BULL BAY** and **COW BAY**, named for the manatees that were caught and slaughtered here in the seventeenth and eighteenth centuries. These days Bull Bay is more well-known as a **surfing** destination, with young groups of Kingstonians catching the decent waves that roll in off the Atlantic. The sport was pioneered here by Billy "Mystic" Wilmot, and together with his sons he now runs a surf school, *Jamnesia* (⚲jamnesiasurf.com), at the western end of town.

Yallahs

YALLAHS, sitting just east of the boulder-strewn mouth of the **Yallahs River** (which appears unfeasibly wide and bare in dry season), is best known for its **salt ponds**, said to have been created by the tears of an English estate owner distraught when his brother married the woman he loved. Bacteria occasionally go on the rampage here, turning the ponds a reddish colour, and scientists reckon that present archeo-bacteria are among the earliest of Earth life forms. University of West Indies research teams study the pond's ecosystem – particularly artemia, shrimp-like creatures that are one of the few animals able to survive. East of the salt ponds, **Rozelle Beach** offers swimming opportunities on its popular brown-sand strip.

Morant Bay

Three kilometres east of Rozelle, Bustamante Bridge takes you into dusty **MORANT BAY**, parish capital of St Thomas and best known for having witnessed some of the ugliest moments in Jamaica's post-emancipation history. Edna Manley's grim-faced statue of National Hero **Paul Bogle** stands in front of the courthouse here, where he was hanged after leading the 1865 **Morant Bay Rebellion** (see below); a plaque honours the protestors who died alongside him. The courthouse you see today replaced the original building razed in the rebellion. Bogle is buried behind it with those tipped into a mass grave here after the uprising, and only afforded a proper burial when they were dug up by chance in 1965. Today, a memorial erected "in gratitude from the generation who now realize that they did not die in vain" marks the spot, poignantly dedicated to those "who fell because they loved freedom", and National Heroes Day is celebrated annually in October (see page 58). Elsewhere, the attractive 1879 red-brick **Anglican church** is of passing interest, as is the bustling **market** (Mon–Sat daylight hours). A series of unassuming villages lie just east of town – the first, **LYSSONS**, notable chiefly for its palm-fringed **beach**.

2

THE MORANT BAY REBELLION

In August 1865, Baptist Deacon **Paul Bogle** – supported by **George William Gordon**, a wealthy Scottish-Jamaican member of the National Assembly – led an 87-kilometre march from St Thomas to Spanish Town to protest racial inequality in front of the island's governor, Edward Eyre. A generation after the abolishment of slavery, living conditions for Jamaica's black population remained abysmal, with food shortages, lack of access to property and high taxation. Once the marchers reached Eyre, they were turned away, and returned to St Thomas with plans to create a "state within a state" at **Stony Gut**, Bogle's home village. Unnerved by the force of the uprising, the police had two of Bogle's supporters arrested on trumped-up charges of assault and trespass. On October 7, Bogle and his men marched to Morant Bay, surrounding the courthouse and disrupting proceedings. Despite the protest's peaceful nature, the authorities issued a warrant for Bogle's arrest.

COLONIAL AUTHORITY RESPONSE

On October 11, Bogle and his men again marched into Morant Bay, raiding the police station for arms and attacking the courthouse where the council was meeting. Eighteen soldiers and council members were killed; the courthouse was burnt to the ground, and arms, gunpowder and foodstuffs were taken from the town's shops. Unrest quickly spread, and government troops arrived on October 12, too late to quell the disturbance. Fearing that the whole country would be engulfed, authorities gave free rein to the army, and the protesters were crushed with brutal ferocity. A staggering 437 people were **executed**, another six hundred men and women flogged, and over a thousand homes razed to the ground. Bogle evaded capture and fled to the hills, where he remained undetected for several days. In Kingston, Governor Eyre declared martial law in St Thomas and wrote a warrant for the arrest of George William Gordon, who was hanged outside the Morant Bay courthouse on October 20. There was nowhere for Bogle to hide; he was captured at Stony Gut on October 23 and went to the gallows two days later. His last words quoted slave leader Sam Sharpe from 1831: "I would rather die upon yonder gallows than live in slavery."

JAMAICA AFTER THE REBELLION

The rebellion marked a key political and social watershed for Jamaica. Governor Eyre was immediately recalled to England and stripped of his position, and the island came under **direct rule** from Britain until reforms in education and the legal system could be put into place – policies that, previously, never would have gotten past the local elite. Though progress for the poor was still painfully slow, Bogle's defiant legacy ensured that Jamaica remained relatively peaceful until well into the next century. The Jamaican government eventually recognized Paul Bogle (and George William Gordon) as National Heroes, and they are honoured on Heroes Day, held every year on the third Monday in October. In 2017, the Jamaican Parliament took Bogle and Gordon's exoneration one step further by revoking all criminal charges against them, an emotional stroke of litigation that was met with islandwide jubilation.

By public transport Minibuses and route taxis pull up next to the petrol station on the coast road.

Services The library, 31 Queen St (Mon–Fri 8am–

5.30pm, Sat 8.30am–5.30pm), holds interesting material on Paul Bogle.

ACCOMMODATION AND EATING

Brown's Guesthouse East of Morant Bay at Prospect ☎ 982 6205, ⓦ brownsguesthouseja.com. This supremely friendly guesthouse is run by the senior yet enigmatic Mr Brown. The immaculate, home-style rooms have TV and a/c, and there are meals on request. J$5500

Fish Cove Leith Hall Main Road, Port Morant ☎ 893 7103. At this restaurant just across the main road from the shoreline, a couple of kilometres east of town, you can choose your fish from a coolbox. Escovitched or steamed and served with bammy, the food here is supremely fresh (J$1000 upwards). Fish tea and conch soup are also on offer

(J$300). Daily 11am–11pm.

Golden Shore Beach Resort Winward Drive, Lyssons ☎ 982 9657, ⓦ goldenshorehotel.com. Right on the beach, this attractive and relaxing hotel has cool, airy, tiled rooms with a/c and TV, plus there's a restaurant and bar. US$65

Village Green Restaurant 14 Church St ☎ 734 5193. Right by the Shell petrol station as you head in from Kingston, this no-frills canteen has a large inexpensive lunch menu with fish stew (J$400), red-peas soup (J$200) and vegetable chop suey (J$300). Mon–Sat 8am–3pm.

Stony Gut

Paul Bogle's birthplace, the village of **Stony Gut** (see page 101) sits inland of Morant Bay. Central to Jamaica's history, it was from here that Deacon Bogle built the bedrock of support that enabled him to lead his rebellion. Opposite the Methodist church, a heavily hurricane-damaged lane leads down to Bogle's simple memorial, the **Stony Gut Monument**, atmospherically shaded by Otaheite apple trees and bearing a plaque that outlines his deeds. Bogle's great-grandson was caretaker of the site for many years and was interred behind the monument in 1995.

Reggae Falls at Hillside Dam

At **Reggae Falls**, a large man-made waterfall pouring over the Hillside Dam, shallow but fast-flowing waters meander along the improbably wide, boulder-strewn bed of the Johnson River. The road here is reached from Morant Bay by continuing straight ahead through residential Seaforth, and then taking a right turn (in effect going straight ahead) before the Morant River bridge. Walk along the riverbank and after a few minutes you'll reach the dam, once a hydroelectric plant; these days water cascades over to create a deep swimming pool. It's a fabulously secluded place and you're unlikely to meet another soul, though go in a pair or group to be sure of safety.

Bath

The little-visited village of **BATH** stands at the edge of the John Crow Mountains. Born when an escaped Spanish slave stumbled across hot mineral springs in the late 1690s, it was discovered that the waters could cure wounds. The same slave's owner sold the spring and some 1130 acres of land surrounding it to the British in 1699 for £400; they swiftly carved a road through the hills and erected a spa building here in 1747.

Bath Botanical Gardens

Bath, St Thomas • Daily dawn to dusk • Expect to give a local J$500 for entrance • Contact the Jamaica National Heritage Trust in Kingston ☎ 922 1287, ⓦ jnht.com

In the 1700s, Bath glittered in the colonial spotlight, but just a century later it fell from grace through a combination of political disputes and hurricane damage. A reminder of its heyday is to be found at the **Bath Botanical Gardens** established in 1779, adjacent to

THE BREADFRUIT AND THE BOUNTY

The starchy, nourishing **breadfruit** – about which eighteenth-century Captain Cook rhapsodized: "If a man plants ten of them… he will completely fulfil his duty to his own and future generations" – is a mainstay of Jamaican tables. While it's islandwide today, the breadfruit's journey from seed to plate was far from seamless, and over the centuries the story of its origin has grown to become a legend of the Caribbean seas.

Setting sail from England in 1787, the HMS *Bounty*, commanded by **Captain William Bligh**, was assigned the task of procuring breadfruit plants from their native Tahiti. After a dangerous journey around Cape Horn, captain and crew were garlanded with flowers before loading up the breadfruit plants and moving on. Three weeks later, on another arduous crossing with a captain who seemed to care more for his plants than for his men, the ship's crew mutinied. Bligh was cast adrift in the Pacific with a handful of loyal followers, while the rest made for Ascension Island and their place in history. Incredibly, Bligh survived. He found his way back to England, where he was cleared of any blame and entrusted with another ship, HMS *Providence*, to complete his mission. The Jamaican House of Assembly conferred him a substantial gift of 500 guineas to encourage his endeavours, and the *Providence* left England in 1791, finally delivering the breadfruit to the island in February 1793. The plants were propagated at Bath Botanical Gardens and eventually spread throughout the island.

the dilapidated Anglican church. This was where many plants – including cinnamon, jacaranda, bougainvillea and mango – were first introduced to the island. You'll still see descendants of the **breadfruit trees** brought from Tahiti by Captain Bligh of HMS *Bounty* fame (see above) in 1793, alongside guava trees, royal palms, bamboo and crotons. The annual **breadfruit** festival in September commemorates the seminal event in Jamaican history.

Bath Fountain Spa

Fountain Road, Bath • Daily 8am–9.30pm • From J$500, including towel and robe • ☏ 703 4154 • Reached by following signs up a twisting road for 1.5km from the town centre

Taking the waters at the rambling old **Bath Fountain Hotel and Spa** remains the main attraction for visitors to the village. The spa has ten small cubicles, each with a sunken tiled bath. The water is high in sulphur and lime, and has one of the highest mineral contents of any mineral water in the world.

Bear in mind that outside the hotel and spa you will most likely be accosted by a group of hustlers offering to take you to the open-air spring at the hotel's rear. This hot and cold "Sulphur River" is a pleasant spot (water from the two springs is diverted to the spa inside and mixed to provide a bath of a more even temperature). Here, massages are on offer, though the quality varies; use common sense precautions, and be upfront about pricing. If you prefer solitude, the best time to visit is between 6–7am.

Hiking trails lead from the spa for kilometres across the Blue Mountains; the best is the Cunha Cunha Maroon trading route through the John Crow range to Bowden Pen (see page 118) – for a guide contact the Jamaica Conservation and Development Trust (⊛jcdt.org.jm) or Sun Venture Tours (see page 92).

ARRIVAL   BATH

By public transport Route taxis run daily to Bath from Morant Bay (45min), Port Antonio (2hr) and Manchioneal (1hr); there is no fixed timetable.

ACCOMMODATION

★ **Bath Fountain Hotel** Bath ☏703 4154, ❸bath fountain@gmail.com. Crossing the threshold onto this delightful property, once a Swiss hospital, is like stepping back into the 1930s. Rates include free access to the baths, which on a one-night stay you'll probably want to enjoy two or three times, making it very good value. Rooms are comfortable, and tasty Jamaican meals and fruit juices are also available, for guests and non-guests alike (J$1200–3000; available daily but call in advance). **J$4800**

The southeast tip

The far southeastern corner of the island, beyond Bath and Port Morant, is a seamless feast of banana, sugar and coconut plantations, the least developed yet one of the most picturesque corners of Jamaica. The slightly dishevelled communities of **Golden Grove** and **Duckenfield** hold neat but dilapidated rows of homes on stilts, accommodating cane cutters working at the Duckenfield sugar plantation, while **Rocky Point Bay** has a delightfully secluded beach and a fleet of small fishing boats.

Morant Point

The cane fields and the mangroves of the Great Morass, a wide, forested wetland, lead to the serenely isolated hundred-foot **Morant Point lighthouse,** the highlight of St Thomas (ask locals for directions from the Duckenfield sugar factory; the route is sometimes impassable in the rainy season except by 4WD). The lighthouse itself, now solar- and wind-powered, was cast in London in 1841 and put up here by Kru men from Sierra Leone, among the first free Africans to be brought to the island after the abolition of slavery. Tip the lighthouse keeper to climb to the top; deserted and windswept, with Atlantic surf crashing onto the rocks, there's a magnificent panorama of the Blue Mountains, the vast mangrove swamp and gorgeous **Holland Bay**, a deserted swath of fine white sand and crystalline water overlooked by a few ragged palms – the perfect place to live out your Robinson Crusoe fantasies. If you can't face the drive, arrange a tour here by boat with *Zion Country Cottages* (see page 119).

Portland

Portland, north of the Blue Mountains, is generally considered one of the most beautiful of Jamaica's parishes – a rain-drenched land of luscious foliage, sparkling rivers and pounding waterfalls. Eastern Jamaica's largest town, **Port Antonio**, is an attractive destination in itself, but most visitors prefer to base themselves along the exquisite coastline heading east, containing fabulous beaches, the **Blue Lagoon** and a number of exquisite hotels. The surf-pounded stretches of sandy beach at **Long Bay** and **Boston Bay** are well-established destinations for budget travellers, who come for the waves and chilled-out atmosphere – while long-standing vendors at Boston Bay trade in authentic jerk pork and chicken. The gorgeous waterfalls at **Somerset Falls** and **Reach Falls** are within striking distance wherever you stay, while heading into the **John**

BANANAS

There are over fifty varieties of **banana** in Jamaica, and they have a glorious range of colour and texture: some are yellow when ripe, some green, some black; some are two inches in length, some are enormous. A few bananas are lemony in flavour, while others are sweet like sugar. There is one universal rule, however: no matter the colour or size, if your banana doesn't come away easily from the stem, the fruit is unripe, and you will be disappointed with the taste. For the best flavours, head to the market or (even better) a roadside stand. Anything handed to you from a box is agricultural, and won't taste as good as fruit from someone's garden.

In the nineteenth century, Portland had a booming banana business, with production output hitting thirty million stems a year. The arrival of **banana ships** at the wharves was signalled by blasts on a conch shell, followed by frenetic activity as labourers cut stems and carried the fresh fruit off the estates and onto waiting trucks. At the dock, the banana stems were taken to tallymen, who ensured that each had the nine hands required to count as a bunch – hence, in the banana boat song, *Day-O*, "six hands, seven hands, eight hands, bunch!".

Jamaica shifted its export trade over to pineapple and papaya in the twenty-first century, but in Port Antonio, on Boundbrook Wharf (see page 107), you can still see the loading docks and a number of working banana boats.

Crow Mountains in the interior you can be poled down the **Rio Grande** on a bamboo raft or hike through the rainforest along the centuries-old trails of the Windward Maroons (see page 120).

Brief history

Portland's **history** is distinctly one of boom and bust. The parish was officially formed in 1723, one of the last to be settled, despite Port Antonio being blessed with two natural harbours. Reports of the difficult terrain and the constant threat of Maroon warfare had deterred would-be settlers, though eventually the Crown was obliged to offer major incentives, including land grants, tax exemptions and free food supplies. The early economy was dependent on sugar until a surprise replacement crop – **bananas** – proved perfect for Portland's fertile soil towards the end of the nineteenth century (see page 104). Port Antonio boomed, ushering in a golden era of prosperity with businessmen pouring in, and in 1905 the town's first **hotel** was built on the Titchfield peninsula. Cabin space on banana boats was sold to curious tourists, who rubbed shoulders with the rich and famous – publishing magnate William Randolph Hearst, banker J.P. Morgan, actress Bette Davis – swanning in on their private yachts.

The boom proved to be short-lived, though the high-end tourism it had helped to engender remained. With the enthusiastic patronage of movie stars like Errol Flynn (see page 117), Port Antonio's place in the glitterati's global playground was assured, and Jamaica's first luxury hotel was built at Frenchman's Cove – to this day a testament to faded glamour. The movie business injected much-needed capital, too, in the 1980s and 1990s – films shot here include *Cocktail*, *The Mighty Quinn*, *Club Paradise* and *Lord of the Flies*. Its natural water features and beauty spots remain open to anyone who cares to find them – a lower-key Jamaica that's a welcome change for many visitors travelling the island.

2

Port Antonio

The days of movie stars coming to stay in **PORT ANTONIO** are long gone, and these days the town feels a little isolated. That said, sandwiched between the mountains and the sea, this somewhat sleepy place has a charm all its own – there are many remaining timber buildings and with a smart marina and plans to develop Navy Island and the Titchfield peninsula, things seem to be stirring once again. There's not a huge amount to see here and there's little in the way of watersports or shopping, but "Portie" is a friendly and beguiling place with a bustling central market and a couple of lively nightspots.

The town is easily navigable, with two main streets, and you can walk the handful of sights in a couple of hours. **West Palm Avenue** runs into **West Street** (from the western entrance of Port Antonio to the central clock tower), while **Harbour Street** cuts through the middle. To get your bearings, walk the steep climb up to the now defunct *Bonnie View Hotel* from the town centre; while the hotel itself is now closed you'll get a great view over the entire town.

Most people find Port Antonio something of a relief after the harassment of the north coast, and any hassle you do encounter tends to be fairly half-hearted. Even so, don't wander off the main streets after dark, and also be wary of police roadblocks east of town.

The town square

The obvious starting point for a stroll is Port Antonio's **central square**, with a landmark **clock tower** opposite the red-brick, two-storey Georgian **courthouse** (now housing the NCB bank), built in 1895 and fronted by an elegant fretworked veranda supported by cast-iron columns courtesy of William MacFarlane in Glasgow, Scotland. With the post office next door, the area is always busy with people on business. Looking

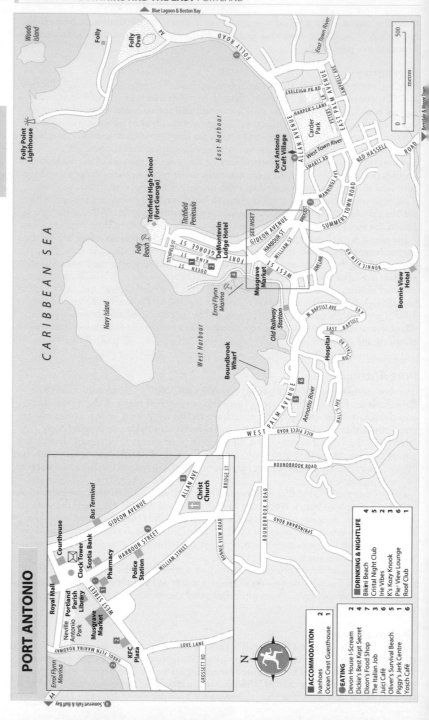

Blue Lagoon & Boston Bay

Woods
Island

Folly

Folly

Folly Oval

FOLLY ROAD

East Town River

Folly Point
Lighthouse

East Harbour

EVELEIGH PK. RD

HARPER'S LANE

ALLAN AVENUE

PETERS LANE

CAMPBELL AVE

EAST PALM AVENUE

Carder
Park

Port Antonio
Craft Village

West Town River

SMARTT RD

MANNING'S AVE

SUMMERS TOWN ROAD

RED HASSELL ROAD

Berridale & Moore Town

CARIBBEAN SEA

Titchfield High School
(Fort George)

Titchfield
Peninsula

Folly
Beach

Errol Flynn Marina

TITCHFIELD ST

KING ST

QUEEN ST

DeMontevin
Lodge Hotel

SEE INSET

GIDEON AVENUE

FORT GEORGE ST

WILLIAM ST

HARBOUR ST

WEST ST

BRIDGE ST

Musgrave
Market

LANE LANE

BONNIE VIEW RD

Bonnie View
Hotel

East Harbour

Navy Island

West Harbour

Boundbrook
Wharf

Old Railway
Station

W. BAPTIST AVE

EAST BAPTIST AVE

FALL RD

Hospital

HALL'S AVE

Arnotto River

WEST PALM AVENUE

RICE PIECE ROAD

BOUNDBROOK ROAD

SPRINGBANK ROAD

500

metres

0

N

PORT ANTONIO

Errol Flynn
Marina

Royal Mall

Neville
Antonio Park

Musgrave
Market

KFC
Plaza

ERROL FLYNN MARINA ROADWAY

Courthouse

Clock Tower

Scotia Bank

Pharmacy

Portland
Parish
Library

Police
Station

WEST STREET

Bus Terminal

GIDEON AVENUE

ALLAN AVE

Christ
Church

BRIDGE ST

HARBOUR STREET

WILLIAM STREET

BONNIE VIEW ROAD

LOVE LANE

GROSSETT RD

BOUNDBROOK ROAD

SPRINGBANK RD

Somerset Falls & Buff Bay

A4

ACCOMMODATION	
Ivanhoes	2
Ocean Crest Guesthouse	1

EATING	
Devon House I-Scream	2
Dickie's Best Kept Secret	4
Dixon's Food Shop	7
The Italian Job	3
Juici Café	6
Oliver's Survival Beach	5
Piggy's Jerk Centre	1
Yosch Café	6

DRINKING & NIGHTLIFE	
Bikini Beach	4
Cristal Night Club	5
Irie Vibes	2
K's Kozy Knook	3
Pie-View Lounge	6
Roof Club	1

northwards to the other side of the square, your eyes can't help but be drawn to the **Royal Mall** (formerly the **Village of St George**), a mishmash of architectural styles from medieval to Tudor and Renaissance built over the old Delmar Theatre. Somehow its striking, opulent exterior, richly embellished with murals and sculptures, manages to complement its surroundings.

Errol Flynn Marina

Daily 9am–11pm • ☎ 715 6044, ⓦ errolflynnmarina.com

Port Antonio has long been recognized as having one of the loveliest natural harbours in the world. It was the first place in Jamaica to receive tourists back in the nineteenth century, and now redeveloped, the small but sophisticated **Errol Flynn Marina** is designed to appeal to yachts of all sizes and small cruise ships. The elegant landscaped gardens come as something of a shock after negotiating the commotion of Port Antonio's streets, and though secured behind enormous gates, it's a down-to-earth spot, with locals enjoying ice cream on the waterfront and a bar and restaurant. The northern end of the development is where you'll also find the town's only sandy beach – a thin strip with palm trees and a bar behind.

If you're in town in late October, check out the prestigious **Port Antonio Blue Marlin Tournament** (☎ 927 0145, ⓦ jamaicasportsfishing.com) held here, attracting serious anglers from all over the world, and accompanied with numerous obligatory night-time goings-on.

Titchfield

The northern part of the town, the **Titchfield peninsula**, juts out into the sea and divides Port Antonio's **twin harbours**. The tip of the peninsula once held the British **Fort George**, whose ancient cannons and crumbling walls today form part of Titchfield High School, alive with noisy open-air lessons and frenetic games of football and netball. The short wander up from town takes you past the **DeMontevin Lodge** hotel – high-Victorian gingerbread architecture at its best – and the unexciting ruins of the **Titchfield Hotel**, Port Antonio's first, once owned by Errol Flynn. The peninsula is largely somnolent and peaceful, characterized by large and rather dilapidated wooden houses, while the town's only proper strip of sand, **Folly Beach**, has been tidied up, planted with palms and removed from the public domain.

Navy Island

The largest of the small islands that dot the Portland coast, **NAVY ISLAND** lies just off the mainland, and is closed to the public. The British Navy used it in the eighteenth century – hence the name – and Captain Bligh landed here in 1793, bringing yet more breadfruit from Tahiti (see page 103). A later adventurer, Errol Flynn, immediately bought it as a private retreat for entertaining Hollywood starlets – one of the myriad Flynn myths says that he lost it in a poker game less than a decade later. The 64-acre island, covered in lush vegetation, good beaches and trails, now belongs to the Port Authority; it's rumoured that an upmarket resort will be built on the site, but until then Dickie's son (see page 110) can take you on a cruise around it.

West Street

The compact **Musgrave Market** (Mon–Sat, daylight hours) is the liveliest spot in the centre of town; friendly, easy-going and crammed with stalls selling appetizing fruits and vegetables, it also has a busy trade in fish, meat and clothes, and a handful of jerk chicken barrels at the end of the day. Up West Street, past numerous shops, the battered old timber Railway Station built in 1896 and the grassy lawn where the **ferry** used to leave for Navy Island, **Boundbrook Wharf** is the loading point for the few bananas still shipped off the island (see page 104). This is the place that inspired the banana boat song *Day O* – "Work all night for a drink of rum, daylight come and me wanna go home". Today the backbreaking work is much simplified, with bananas packaged centrally and mechanically loaded.

Port Antonio Craft Village

Allan Ave (known locally as Folly Rd) • Daily 9am–8pm

A collection of raised wooden workshops and stalls housing the best of Portland's craftspeople, the new craft market was opened with fanfare in 2013 at a cost of some J$40 million (the original structure built in 1998 was never used). The market has an enviable location fronting the East Harbour, and it's also a perfect spot to see the sunset with refreshments provided by stalls serving coffees, drinks and meals. A few of the craftspeople here are really talented and you may well find souvenirs to bring home: look out for figures and furniture by master woodworker Rockbottom.

Folly Point and around

Folly Point, at the end of Allan Avenue (known locally as Folly Road), which runs east along the coast, is the second of the town's peninsulas. Covered with low-lying scrub, it's home to a cricket ground, and at its end, a **lighthouse**. You'll need to attract the attention of the keeper to let you into the pretty flowered garden that surrounds the lighthouse and they'll expect a donation; you can't climb the lighthouse but you're free to walk over the rocks in front of it, a favourite fishing spot.

Before you reach the lighthouse, a right fork brings you to the **Folly**, the sorry ruin of what was, briefly, one of the grandest houses in Jamaica. Built in 1902 for American banker Alfred Mitchell and widely applauded as a model of mock-Grecian architecture, the concrete house was a model of ostentation – until the roof collapsed in 1935, a victim of shoddy construction and the short-sighted use of salt water in the cement. Only the pillars and half a staircase remain standing, though restoration has made some improvements. Quirky and evocative, the shell's dramatic presence has not been lost on film-makers – it's been featured in movies and music videos by Shabba Ranks and Lauryn Hill. Just across the water, tiny **Woods Island** was once connected by a stone causeway, and Mitchell had a small zoo built on it for his pet monkeys. Swimmers can cover the short distance to create their own private retreat, though take care as undercurrents can be strong.

ARRIVAL AND INFORMATION   PORT ANTONIO

By bus There's a twice daily Knutsford Express (see page 22) service between Montego Bay and Port Antonio. It departs Montego Bay at 8.45am and 4.40pm.
Destinations Montego Bay (6am & 4pm; 3hr 45min); Ocho Rios (6am & 4pm; 2hr).
By route taxi and minibus Route taxis and minibuses from Kingston (2hr 30min) and Ocho Rios (2hr 30min) leave when full and pull in by the seafront on Gideon

Avenue, which is also the place to get public transport onwards to the beaches and other places of interest – route taxis run along the main road as far as Long Bay or Manchioneal; you'll pay around J$160 to Frenchman's Cove, J$200 to Boston Bay and J$250 to Long Bay.
Tourist information Information is available informally from tour operators at the Errol Flynn Marina (entrance opposite Royal Mall; Mon–Fri 8.30am–4pm).

GETTING AROUND

By route taxi Taxis congregate on Gideon Avenue (see above); or call the Port Antonio taxi cooperative/JUTA (☎ 993 2684).

By car Eastern Car Rentals, 16 West St (☎ 993 3624, ⓦ portantoniocarrentals.com); prices start at US$55/day.

TOURS AND ACTIVITIES

Boat tours and fishing Enquire at the Errol Flynn Marina (☎ 715 6044) for current operators for deep-sea fishing or a sunset cruise; the town is famed for its blue marlin fishing competition in late October each year.
Guides and tours Independent guide Joanna Hart

(☎ 859 3758) offers an exceptional highlights tour of Port Antonio with emphasis on the history and culture of the area (2hr 30min; US$50/person, minimum two people). You can also enjoy all of the main draws with tour company Attractions Link (☎ 993 7076, ⓦ attractionslink.com).

BEACH, ERROL FLYNN MARINA

2

Scuba diving Lady G'Diver, based at Errol Flynn Marina (☎ 995 0246, ⓦ ladydiver.com), offers dives (from US$90 for two dives), 3–5 day PADI certification courses (US$400) and equipment rental (snorkels and fins US$10).

Volunteering The Portland Rehabilitation Management shelter (☎ 993 9166, ⓦ prmhomeless.org) has an active volunteer programme in the local hospital and homeless refuge.

ACCOMMODATION

Though there are a few worthy places to stay in Port Antonio, there are much better options, for all accommodation budgets, in the communities just east of town (see page 111).

Ivanhoes 9 Queen St ☎ 993 3043, ⓦ go-jam.com; map p.106. Scrupulously clean and tidy no-frills guesthouse in a flower-filled garden opposite the ruins of the old *Titchfield Hotel*. Each of the appealing, reasonably priced rooms has a fan and a private hot-water bathroom. Breakfast available. **US$55**

Ocean Crest Guesthouse 7 Queen St ☎ 993 4024, ⓦ go-jam.com; map p.106. Small, simple yet smart guesthouse with six rooms with private hot-water bathrooms, some with a/c. Guests can use the large kitchen and dining area, though meals are available, and there's a sunny terrace with a view over the harbour. **US$50**

EATING

Port Antonio offers a number of inexpensive Jamaican eating choices, with two great vegetarian options. Look out for barrel barbecues around town at sunset; some do scrumptious foil parcels of spicy curried conch with okra.

Devon House I-Scream Errol Flynn Marina ☎ 715 4479; map p.106. All the creamy ice cream you could wish for on a hot evening is available here; flavours include pistachio, coffee and soursop (J$350). Daily noon–9pm.

Dickie's Best Kept Secret Main road just west of town ☎ 809 6276; map p.106. Easily missed as it's nestled on a knoll as you round the far bend of Port Antonio's West Harbour, this simple wooden shack is a surprising and fun choice. Served in owner Dickie's kooky lounge, the moderately priced (US$30) five-course dinners include dishes like ackee on toast, garlic lobster, steamed fish and veg options; order the morning before you want to eat. Breakfast also available. Daily 6–10pm.

Dixon's Food Shop 12 Bridge St; map p.106. Take-out joint with tables upstairs serving delicious home-made vegetarian food – tofu stew, stir-fried veg and salads – at rock-bottom prices. Wholemeal bread daily, plus garlic and raisin loaves each Friday; juices available. Mon–Fri 11am–3pm.

★ **The Italian Job** 29 Harbour St ☎ 573 8603; map p.106. Excellent restaurant with an Italian owner, serving pizza by the square slice (J$400), as well as carbonara pasta and homemade ravioli (J$1100), with a sideline in chicken or beef fajitas. You can't go wrong with the delicious

tenerina chocolate torta accompanied by a Blue Mountain espresso for dessert. Tues–Sat noon–10pm.

Juici Café Craft Village, Allan Ave ☎ 349 9167; map p.106. Inventive juices are the name of the game here at this little stall next to *Yosch Café*. Juices (seasonal) such as soursop, guava and mango are all made with care; plain chocolate and mixed fruit smoothies are also available. Mon–Fri 9am–10.30pm, Sat & Sun noon–10.30pm.

★ **Oliver's Survival Beach** Allan Ave ☎ 384 4730; map p.106. Really excellent and inexpensive Ital food and jerk fish (J$600) and soups (J$250) are served at this very basic and easy-going little shack with outdoor tables by the water. Daily 9am–11pm.

★ **Piggy's Jerk Centre** Intersection of Harbour and West sts; map p.106. The area's best jerk chicken (J$400), also great soup (J$200) and festival (J$50) can be found at this characterful waterfront stand. Take-away only. Daily noon–9pm.

★ **Yosch Cafe** Craft Village, Allan Ave ☎ 993 3053; map p.106. Surprisingly sophisticated café/bar serving club sandwiches, burgers, seafood and thin crust pizza (J$800), alongside espressos, and drinks in the evenings. Mon–Sat 9am–11pm, Sun 1–11pm.

DRINKING AND NIGHTLIFE

Port Antonio is a lively place in the evening – especially at weekends – and even in the daytime there are a few good bars (which also serve food). Bear in mind that the town's clubs get going late and continue to the wee hours. If you want to join the locals, the rum shacks along Allan Avenue (known locally as Folly Rd) are great spots for a drink on the water's edge.

BARS

★ **Bikini Beach Bar** Errol Flynn Marina ☎ 715 4288; map p.106. Current hot spot for an afternoon or evening drink, with a loud reggae soundtrack right on the beach. Cocktails

J$700, plus seafood and burgers available (J$900–2500). Mon–Thurs 11am–midnight, Fri–Sun 11am till late.

★ **Irie Vibes** KFC Plaza; map p.106. A great spot with a view over the harbour, hidden away down the lane behind

KFC. A pool table, sports screen and decent reggae-hip hop sound-track keep punters happy. Mon–Sat noon–2am, Sun 4pm till late.

K's Kozy Knook Allan Ave; map p.106. The archetypal Jamaican drinking hole. You may get a Red Stripe or a shot of Scotch or Appleton here, but you'll probably be the only one not fuelled by overproof: the circular bar draws a motley collection of white-rum drinkers, with chitchat and dominoes action. Daily noon–midnight.

Pier View Lounge 21 West Palm Ave; map p.106. Friendly upstairs bar known as *Beenie Bob's Place*, with a balcony and late hours, occasional live music and frequent oldies' hits nights. Daily 2pm–3am.

CLUBS

Cristal Night Club 19 West Palm Ave ☎ 288 7657; map p.106. Currently the most popular spot for young clubbers

trying out their moves to the latest dancehall, *Cristal* treads a fine line between normal and self-declared "exotic" (strip club) depending on the night (ask around or at the gate if you're not sure). Regular Thursday "Road Block" parties have become a permanent fixture on the Portland nightlife calendar, bringing something of the downtown Kingston street dance vibe into the countryside. Cover J$500. Daily 10pm–late.

★ **Roof Club** 11 West St ☎ 844 3298; map p.106. Long-standing fluorescent streamer-bedecked nightclub that retains something of the 1970s–'80s feel it had when it opened. With a country-wide reputation for a relaxed yet lively night out, it's busiest for Thursday's "Ladies' Night" and on Saturdays, when DJs pump out an eclectic mix of reggae/dancehall, soca, hip-hop and R&B. Cover J$400. Wed–Sun 10pm–late.

East of Port Antonio

Made all the more alluring for its delicious sense of faded glamour and relative lack of visitors, the rugged stretch of coast east of Port Antonio is one of the most attractive parts of Jamaica. It's a fairy-tale landscape of lush, jungle-smothered hills rolling down to a coastline studded with fantastic beaches, such as **Frenchman's Cove**, **San San** and **Winnifred**, and swimming inlets like the **Blue Lagoon**, a fabulous aquamarine pool of salt and fresh water made famous by the eponymous 1980 movie. A series of super-smart hotels vie for business with a handful of less expensive guesthouses (though none are as cheap as you'll find in town), while for **eating** you can plump for romantic international feasts accompanied by live jazz or mento at the salubrious restaurants of the region's best hotels – most of which are open to non-guests – or more authentic Jamaican cooking at **Winnifred Beach** and the **jerk stands** at **Boston Bay**.

GETTING AROUND
EAST OF PORT ANTONIO

By route taxi Route taxis ply the main road east of Port Antonio; however they're often already full and are infrequent after 7pm on weekdays; there is less frequency at weekends. Expect to spend time waiting on the road for transport, or else spending J$1000–1500 for a taxi charter to Port Antonio, depending on the distance.

Turtle Cove

Pretty **Turtle Cove**, the first cove east of Port Antonio, is preceded by the new luxury *Trident Hotel* (see page 112) and its sister property, the fantasy **Trident Castle** – a huge, white Disney-like edifice which looms up suddenly. It began life in the 1970s as an extravagant home (yet a relatively modest one compared to what would come) for the late European baroness and eccentric local celebrity Sigi Fahmi. She was forced to sell after financial troubles, and new owner Earl Levy got increasingly carried away with elaborate additions. Robust enough outside to have survived Hurricane Gilbert with barely a lost slate, inside it boasts classic antique decor and has been deemed opulent enough to be used in videos by the likes of 50 Cent and Snoop Dogg, not to mention hosting other stars such as Eddie Murphy and Canadian rockers Arcade Fire. The property, complete with its own woodland and separate chapel, is now operating as a luxury hotel owned by Jamaican-Canadian banking tycoon Michael Lee Chin.

Facing Trident Castle directly across the bay is the **Jamaica Palace** hotel and restaurant (see page 112), Sigi Fahmi's second European chateau fantasy once she had vacated the first. With interminable quirkiness from its 1980s heyday, the gigantic black-and-white tiled patio and swimming pool in the shape of Jamaica must be seen to be believed.

ACCOMMODATION

TURTLE COVE

Bayview Eco Resort and Spa Clear Spring District ☎ 993 3118, ⓦ bayviewecoresort.com; map p.112. This small, renovated hillside hotel is the best-value property close to Port Antonio, with two grades of room, one double the price of the other. All have attractive wood panelling, fans and a/c, while the more expensive ones are larger, have king-size beds and TVs. Also a pool, great views, spa and lovely flower garden. Breakfast included. <u>US$114</u>

Trident Hotel Anchovy ☎ 633 7100, ⓦ thetridenthotel.

com; map p.106. Spectacularly renovated, this historic hotel now boasts chic modern and contemporary design and one of Jamaica's most inviting infinity pools, alongside a superb restaurant and an exclusive yet down-to-earth atmosphere. Thirteen ultra-private villas lie along the top of low coral cliffs, each with its own infinity plunge pool above the sea, HD cinema screen, outdoor tubs and a host of other comforts. Spa and small private beach on site, plus guest access to Trident Castle (see page 111). <u>US$720</u>

EATING

Jamaica Palace Williamsfield ☎ 957 3838, ⓦ jamaica-palacehotel.com; map p.112. Elegant European restaurant with a menu that's big on steaks, plus some German dishes. Expensive in the evening (mains US$20–35), lunch here is much more reasonable with tasty burgers and grilled fish (US$10–15), plus Jamaican soups. While you're here, take a tour of the property, which includes obscure sculptures by the former owner. Daily 8am–11pm.

★ **The Veranda & Mike's Supper Club** Trident Hotel, Anchovy ☎ 633 7100; map p.112. Streets ahead of the

competition, *Trident's* restaurant serves easily Jamaica's best fillet steak (US$45), while the menu accompanying the live music at *Mike's Supper Club* offers exquisite and innovative fare like baby octopus served on crostini (US$13), and Jamaican Run Down with crayfish and conch (US$35). Entertainment, courtesy of the house jazz band (with top guest singers), has quickly made the *Supper Club* a high point of the Portland entertainment calendar. Veranda Daily 7am–9.30pm; Mike's Supper Club (reservations recommended) Sat 6pm–midnight.

Frenchman's Cove

Daily 9am–5pm • US$10 for non-residents • Guided horseriding US$70/hr (☎ 466 0563)

At **Frenchman's Cove**, the eponymous hotel – with lavish tropical gardens and stunning beach – was once one of the area's most sumptuous, frequented by royalty and A-list celebrities in the 1950s and 1960s. Though the hotel is not as it once was, the grounds are still beautifully maintained. The **beach**, though small, is one of the most splendid in Jamaica, with a curve of fine sand enclosed by verdant hills, and a freshwater river, its bottom alluringly lined by white beach-sand, running straight into the sea (arrive early in the morning for maximum quietude). Sun loungers and food and drink are available. The neighbouring property also offers **horseriding** trips, which take in the hills and the picturesque shoreline of San San Beach.

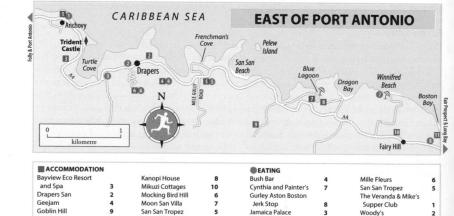

■ ACCOMMODATION					
Bayview Eco Resort and Spa	3	Kanopi House	8		
Drapers San	2	Mikuzi Cottages	10		
Geejam	4	Mocking Bird Hill	6		
Goblin Hill	9	Moon San Villa	7		
Great Huts	11	San San Tropez	5		
		Trident Hotel	1		

● EATING					
Bush Bar	4	Mille Fleurs	6		
Cynthia and Painter's	7	San San Tropez	5		
Gurley Aston Boston Jerk Stop	8	The Veranda & Mike's Supper Club	1		
Jamaica Palace	3	Woody's	2		

San San and around

Mon–Fri 10am–4pm, Sat & Sun 10am–5pm • ☎ 776 4402 • US$8 or J$800

San San Beach, three kilometres east of Frenchman's Cove, is a narrow but gorgeous strip of white sand beside a wide crescent bay, with rich reefs a few yards from the shore that provide excellent snorkelling. The beach is also well-equipped, with showers and a bar and restaurant. If you're bathing here, be careful of sea urchins which can be found both on the sand and in the water. Opposite the beach is the tiny but beautiful **Pelew Island**, also known as Monkey Island despite a lack of primates. It's great for snorkelling or lazing if you're up to the swim out there.

2

ARRIVAL AND DEPARTURE

SAN SAN AND AROUND

By route taxi Route taxis frequently ply the route to Port Antonio (J$250) and Long Bay (J$200); Mon–Sat (daylight hours), less often at night and on Sundays.

ACCOMMODATION

★ **Drapers San** Just over 1km west of San San Beach ☎ 993 7118 or ☎ 362 4771, ⓦ go-jam.com; map p.112. Funky, friendly, Italian-run guesthouse with an eclectic collection of rooms, some with shared bathroom; all have fan but no a/c or TV. Breakfast is included in the rates, and tasty Italian or Jamaican evening meals are also available. US$65

★ **Geejam** San San ☎ 993 7000, ⓦ geejamhotel.com; map p.112. Beyoncé, Amy Winehouse, Katy Perry and Alicia Keys have all stayed at this hip hotel in recent years (visit the recording studio and tinkle on the piano used in Keys' hit *This Girl Is On Fire*), and it's easy to see why: maximum seclusion is maintained, with forest walkways between seriously classy villas and eco-huts, while great inspiration is drawn from the astonishing view of the coastline. Each unit offers sleek linen and batik fabrics, digital accessories and sea-facing verandas; some have a steam room and outdoor jacuzzi. In addition, there's a bar/restaurant, gym, pool and access to a private beach. US$700

Goblin Hill San San ☎ 993 7443, ⓦ goblinhill.com; map p.112. A genteel complex of villas with a classy whiff of old Jamaica. With lovely contemporary decor, each villa is staffed with its own cook and housekeeper, and TVs have access to hundreds of films. There's a pool, bar and tennis courts on site, as well as extensive grounds that offer grand views of San San. US$205

Mocking Bird Hill Drapers ☎ 993 7267, ⓦ hotel mockingbirdhill.com; map p.112. Eco-friendly hotel set in a peaceful location in the hills above the coastline and filled with sculptures and paintings by artist and co-owner Barbara Walker. The airy rooms feature bamboo furniture and balconies, and there's a pool and a good restaurant. US$246

San San Tropez San San ☎ 993 7213, ⓦ sansantropez. com; map p.112. This genial Italian-run property, best known for its restaurant, also offers a family suite sleeping four (for the same price as for two). The rooms have a/c and cable TV, some have king-size beds and other queen, and there's a pool on site. US$120

EATING

Bush Bar Geejam, San San ☎ 993 7000; map p.112. The atmospheric terrace in the forest is the ideal setting for enjoying high-end delights like seafood in spicy coconut sauce (US$30), with great cocktails at the bar and lounge chairs to relax in. Listen to fantastic house mento band The Jolly Boys (sixty-plus years in the business and covering pop hits like Amy Winehouse's "Rehab") on Friday nights here – check the schedule and book in advance. Reservations essential. Daily 6pm–midnight.

Mille Fleurs Mocking Bird Hill Hotel, Drapers ☎ 993 7267; map p.112. A soothing terrace setting with wonderful views and some imaginative and delicious concoctions based on fresh ingredients and Jamaican staples. There's a daily vegetarian option, and the puddings are sublime. Daily 8–10.30am, noon–2.30pm & 7–9.30pm.

★ **San San Tropez** San San ☎ 993 7213; map p.112. Flavoursome and authentic dishes by the Italian owner: home-made spaghetti and *fettuccini* with tomato, seafood or pesto sauce (US$18–25); fantastic thin-crust pizzas (J$20); and Italian-style grilled fish with tomatoes. The crème caramel, made on site, is delightful. Daily 6–10pm.

★ **Woody's** Drapers ☎ 993 7888 or ☎ 886 2961; map p.112. The burgers here are homemade but this certainly isn't fast food: wait in the gazebo of this friendly café-cum-restaurant while they're cooked to order (J$500) and served with plantain, fries and delicious ginger beer. Veggie burgers and other sandwiches are also available, as are Jamaican staples like fish and curry goat (J$1800), if ordered in advance. Mon–Sat noon–9pm, Sun 1–7pm.

2

The Blue Lagoon

Swimming free • Rafting US$37/person (US$75/couple), rafts fit 3–4 people; tours are 45min–1hr • Snorkelling off Monkey Island an additional 45min and US$10/person • Trips easily organized on arrival, or call rafting legend Becky Hill (☏ 575 7381), who also runs tours by moonlight • Motorboat US$20/person; boats fit up to 12 people; tours are 30min

The **Blue Lagoon** is where 14-year-old nymphet Brooke Shields (and now-obscure cherub Christopher Atkins), playing child castaways on a deserted island, frolicked naked in the movie of the same name. Enclosed by high cliffs and forest, which give a deep green tint to the noticeably turquoise depths, the lagoon is a result of several underwater streams running down from the mountains. The whole effect is very picture-postcard, and swimming here is serene, with a layer of chilly fresh water covering warm waves of warm sea below. The lagoon drops to 198ft at its deepest spot – just enough for World Freediving Champion David Lee to set a one-time world record here: in 2002 he dived without assistance to 167ft in three minutes 45 seconds. Scuba/watersports operator Lady G'Diver (see page 110) offers dive packages and courses in specialist freediving at the lagoon.

One of the best ways to see the lagoon is by taking a velvety spin around the water on a **bamboo raft**. Knowledgeable guides slip you past almond trees, sea cotton, mangroves and exclusive villas, including the ones where Tom Cruise was filmed in *Cocktail* and *Knight and Day.* Throughout, the bright, translucent waters beckon, and you can opt to plunge in, snorkel, or simply peer off the sides for views of the sea grass and fish below. Fun (but noisy) motorboat rides are also on offer.

On the lagoon's western side, a slice of land has been acquired by Lee Chin of *Trident* fame (see page 112), and the seriously creative designers at *Geejam* (see page 113) are tasked with building a spectacular contemporary restaurant and villas in keeping with the serene surroundings, likely to open in 2019.

ARRIVAL AND DEPARTURE   **THE BLUE LAGOON**

By route taxi Taxis often ply the route to Port Antonio (J$200) and Long Bay (J$150); less frequency at night and on Sundays.

ACCOMMODATION

Kanopi House Dragon Bay Rd, Blue Lagoon ☏ 632 3213, ⓦ kanopihouse.com; map p.112. An eco-sensitive first for Jamaica, in that these secluded luxury cabins were built amidst towering banyans without felling a single tree. Paths snake down to the lagoon's mouth, where you can indulge your Blue Lagoon swimming fantasy direct from the property, while the friendly (if laidback) staff make you feel part of the family. Meals on request, or stock up beforehand and use your cabin's kitchenette. A backpacker rate is also

available for a small twin cabin which does not feature on the website. Cabin U̲S̲$̲8̲0̲, doubles U̲S̲$̲3̲0̲0̲
Moon San Villa Main Rd, Blue Lagoon ☏ 993 7777, ⓦ moonsanvilla.com; map p.112. Partially refurbished, this spacious and attractive villa lies 300ft from the lagoon and has five bedrooms that can be rented individually or together, with shared kitchen and living room. Includes breakfast, free use of a boat and passes to the Blue Mountain Bicycle Tour (see page 92). U̲S̲$̲1̲5̲5̲

Winnifred Beach

Horse rides J$500 • Monkey Island boat trips US$25/person (1hr)

Winnifred Beach (also known as Fairy Hill Beach) is one of the most appealing beaches in all Jamaica; to get there, turn left and then immediately right just east of the *Jamaica Crest Hotel* at the start of **Fairy Hill** village, following the road for a kilometre through a neat housing scheme before descending through the forest. You can drive right down onto the beach if it hasn't been raining; if it has, park where the tarmac ends and continue on foot.

Used as the setting for the Robin Williams movie *Club Paradise*, the wide, golden crescent of sand is supremely laidback and justly popular with Jamaicans. The small reef just offshore is perfect for snorkelling (you'll need to bring your own gear) and protects the bay from the waves, ensuring clear, calm, bright-blue water that shelves gently from the sand. At weekends, local operator Scotty offers children's horse rides along the sands, and fishermen will provide boat trips to nearby Monkey Island. At the western end, a small mineral spring offers a freshwater rinse.

Given Winnifred Beach's secluded beauty it's perhaps no surprise that the government attempted to authorize a private villa development here, threatening the beach's public access like so many others on the north coast. In 2015, after the entire community – from fruit sellers to luxury hotel owners – banded together to keep the beach in the public domain, the Urban District Council's ruling was overruled, and the threat of privatisation successfully quashed.

2

ARRIVAL AND DEPARTURE
WINNIFRED BEACH

By route taxi Taxis ply the route to Port Antonio (J$200) and Long Bay (J$130) from Fairy Hill on the main road. It's a 20–30min walk down to the beach.

ACCOMMODATION

Mikuzi Cottages Fairy Hill ✆ 978 4859 or ✆ 843 6859, ⓦ mikuzijamaica.com; map p.112. Rustic yet gorgeous three bedroom cottage with funky decor, shared bath, kitchen, and veranda, and a range of smaller, one-bed studios of varying quality, all at the top of the rutted track down (10min walk) to Winnifred Beach. Per room US$30

EATING

★ **Cynthia and Painter's** Western end of Winnifred Beach ✆ 562 4860 or ✆ 909 8453; map p.112. Some of the best food in Portland is available at this shack painted in Jamaican colours at the beach's western end. Delicious, delicately seasoned platefuls of ackee and saltfish, chicken and fish (US$6–7) and wonderful grilled lobster (US$15): food is cooked to order so you're best off phoning in advance or putting in a lunch request as soon as you arrive. Daily 9am–6pm.

Boston Bay
Surfboard and boogie-board hire US$15/day

The once-large public beach at **BOSTON BAY** is now largely eroded as a result of damage caused by hurricanes Gilbert and Ivan. Nonetheless, the little sand that's left is still pretty and is the base for taking in some of the best **surf** in Jamaica – you can hire boogie- and surfboards from local residents on the beach.

Regardless, Boston has long been better known for its collections of **jerk stands**. Jerking of meat originated in this part of the country – the Maroons hunted wild pigs and smoked the meat to preserve it – and the pork and chicken on sale here is some of the best in Jamaica. If possible, save your trip here for Thursday to Sunday, when there are more visitors and the meat is likely to be fresher. If you've room in your bags, buy a jar of the fiery homemade jerk sauce – you won't find better anywhere.

ARRIVAL AND DEPARTURE
BOSTON BAY

By route taxi Taxis often ply the route to Port Antonio (J$350) and Long Bay (J$150); less frequency at night and on Sundays.

ACCOMMODATION

Great Huts ✆ 353 3388, ⓦ greathuts.com; map p.112. Unusual option in a superb location atop low cliffs with a small private cove. Run by American doctor Paul Rhodes, the resort offers a slightly eccentric take on Jamaica's African origins, with a collection of tents and huts – from rustic dorm style to luxurious – connected by winding paths; all have fans and mosquito nets, some have a tub or jacuzzi. Breakfast included, and healthy Jamaican-international meals are available. Paul is an active supporter of local charities and long-stay volunteering is available (see page 110). Dorms US$40, doubles US$85

EATING

Six or seven almost identical **stalls** vie for your business on arrival at Jamaica's most famous **jerk** destination. You'll pay around J$1000 for half a chicken and J$700 for half a pound of pork; both are best eaten with roast yam or breadfruit (US$3–4), a festival dumpling (US$1) or even a hunk of hard-dough bread bought from the small shop across the road

(US$1). The stalls are all quite similar and the numerous on-commission **touts** can be aggressive, but if in doubt head to *Mickey's* or *Little David's*, the first and last stalls on the same side of the small lane at the village's western end (most are open daily 8am–9pm).

Gurley Aston Boston Jerk Stop 20m west of the jerk shacks, up the hill ☎ 849 7853; map p.112. Some might say this new smarter jerk restaurant goes against the traditional grain here – but if the Boston jerk touts are too much you'll no doubt appreciate the calm of its shaded bar and tables. Owned by a Boston family, its jerk is cooked the traditional way and at similar prices. Daily noon–10pm.

Long Bay

Unusually for Jamaica's sparsely developed eastern tip, a mini-tourist industry has existed in **LONG BAY** for close to thirty years; its wide crescent of surf-pounded honey sand and great surf attracts a constant trickle of visitors, and a few have chosen to settle and open guesthouses.

It's a far cry from north coast resorts – simple, friendly beach bars draw locals, visiting Jamaicans and tourists alike, and the whole place feels a bit like Negril might have in the 1960s: laidback and vaguely alternative, with a lot of ganja smoking and general hanging out. That said, the counter-culture atmosphere is not immune to the twinned ravages of poverty and crack cocaine; robbery at rented villas and assaults are not unheard of, and while this shouldn't put you off visiting (there's no reason to believe it's worse here than elsewhere) it's worth remembering that the beach idyll also has its limits – and that you should take precautions.

There isn't much to the village, which has grown up piecemeal either side of the main road. The north end of the beach is where you'll find a small **surf** scene (though the more enclosed swells at Boston Bay are rated better by professionals). The beach bars can help you find a board, and they'll also know of anyone who'll take you out **fishing**. **Swimming** is excellent here, too, particularly if you're feeling a little jaded about the usual placid Jamaican shores, but watch out for a dangerous undertow and riptides; it's best not to swim out further than you can stand. Try, also, to get up early for the staggering **sunrise** over the ocean. The almost separate, and quiet, community of Rose Garden lies up a steep rutted track at the south end of the bay – it has great views and a couple more guesthouses.

ARRIVAL AND DEPARTURE
LONG BAY

By public transport Route taxis run daily to Long Bay from Port Antonio (50min) and cost about J$350. These become very infrequent after 7pm and on Sundays.

By car Be aware that there's no petrol on sale between Port Antonio and Long Bay – the first station you'll reach is just as you enter the village.

ACCOMMODATION

Long Bay is not free from theft, so at night (and on the beach even in the daytime) be sure to lock the door to your room or villa.

The Glass House Northern end of Long Bay ☎ 891 0516, ⊛ themorgansglasshouse.wordpress.com. Smart and good-value five-bedroom house rented whole or by the room, with a large veranda, right on the beach. Boasts eclectic, homely decor and use of a kitchen. Services of a cook/cleaner are optional. US$80

Jamaican Colors Ross Craig, 5km south of Long Bay ☎ 893 5185 or ☎ 407 4412, ⊛ hoteljamaicancolors.com. Set in a beautiful spot on the cliffs with a walkway down to a private cove, the seven smart and colourful two- to four-person bungalows have hot-water bathrooms, a/c and TV/DVD. There's a swimming pool and jacuzzi, and the French owners serve great pizza and classic French dishes

at the on-site bar. Continental breakfast included. US$90

Likkle Paradise Just off main road, mid-way along the bay ☎ 913 7702. Two rooms in the home of knowledgeable Herlette Kennedy (guests share the kitchen). Attractive decor, a peaceful flowery garden and a good view of the centre of the beach from the small upstairs veranda make this an appealing option. US$50

Monica's Hide-Out Main road, mid-way along the bay ☎ 843 3328. Very basic, though reasonable, option with two bedrooms (one twin) in a small wooden house, each with tiled floor, fan and tiny private bathroom. Friendly atmosphere and central-beach location. US$30

Palm Yard Northern end of Long Bay village

ERROL FLYNN

For many, the bumpy six-kilometre route between Boston Bay and Long Bay, with its great views of pounding surf and rolling pastureland, will always be known as **Errol Flynn country**. The erstwhile screen idol bought a 2000-acre estate here in the 1950s, and his widow, Patrice Wymore, managed the groves of coconuts and guavas and its grazing beef cattle here until her death in 2014. The prime seafront property had already been on sale for some years, but her passing may well speed the pace of change.

By the time he arrived in Jamaica in 1947, Errol Flynn's movie career was already in decline. The era of the swashbuckler was drawing to a close, and the Australian actor – star of classic movies like *The Sea Hawk* and *Captain Blood* – had begun to fall from favour with the studios. Nonetheless, coming ashore in his famed yacht *Zaca* (now moored in Monaco and allegedly still haunted by Flynn's face and the sounds of a wild party), Flynn quickly worked his way into local legend. Well known for his powers of seduction, formidable drinking and addiction to gambling, the star reputedly lost Navy Island (see page 107) off Port Antonio in an unfortunate poker bet.

Flynn loved Jamaica, buying the *Titchfield Hotel* in Port Antonio, plus Navy Island, and later, with his third wife **Patrice Wymore**, setting up a ranch near Boston Bay. A string of celebrities attended the wild parties at his hotels – but unsuccessful efforts to resurrect his movie career and continuing bouts of heavy drinking and ill health were already taking their toll. During his final years, Flynn spent much of his time at Titchfield with the teenage actress Beverley Aadland. On his death in 1959, Aadland asked that Flynn be buried in Jamaica, but Wymore insisted that his body go to Hollywood. Today, despite the tarnishing of his reputation through tales of his exploitation of local girls, many people in the area remember the one-time heartthrob with affection.

2

399 8126 or 464 4988, lingunie@icloud.com. Just across from the beach in a palm and fruit-filled garden, this genial and tidy family home with a Rasta vibe offers two rustic yet comfortable rooms, sleeping up to three, with fans and tiled floors. The owner's sons are keen surfers and boards are available for hire. A good Jamaican breakfast is extra. Rates are per person. US$25

Pimento Lodge Rose Garden, southern end of Long Bay, up the steep hill 882 5068, pimentolodge. com. Attractive eight-room hotel with expansive sea views and large, colourful grounds, including an organic fruit and vegetable garden. The various standards of rooms are all bright and spotless (all have a/c), while there's a stunning pool and circular bar. US$155

Rose Garden Pool Villas Rose Garden, southern end of Long Bay, up the steep hill 445 7872, in US 1 707 323 2081. Gorgeous one-bed studio with its own pool as well as a no-frills three-bedroom house, located high above the bay. Good discount for renting whole property. US$70

Seadream Villa Northern end of Long Bay beach 890 7661. Right on the beach, with a wonderful veranda over the sea and large living/dining room, this three-bedroom villa is the best of the seafront options as its live-in caretaker, David, is on hand to cook, make drinks, drive (all additional, however, breakfast is included) and ensure a secure stay. US$100

EATING AND DRINKING

Ask around for the location of weekly dances (Fri–Sun); they tend to rotate around East Portland to draw the biggest crowd. Be aware that seasonal storms and hurricanes nearly always hit hard at Long Bay, often requiring beach bars to shut down and rebuild in a new location.

★**Chill Out** Towards the southern end of the beach 571 7005. The village's principal (and newly rebuilt) beach bar and restaurant serves great-value food and drink under a thatched roof right by the ocean (try the excellent steamfish). Plus it has a great sound system. Daily 10am–11pm.

Cliffhanger Restaurant and Lounge Ross Craig, 5km south of Long Bay 860 1395. This trendy place, perched right atop the cliffs close to *Jamaican Colors*, draws a young uptown crowd from Kingston and Port Antonio for higher-end dining and DJ parties. It serves a range of inviting seafood dishes (US$20–30) and is a great place to chill out with a drink. Tues–Sun 11am–10pm.

Jamaican Colors Ross Craig, 5km south of Long Bay 893 5185 or 407 4412. The classiest place to eat locally. French owner Bob cooks reasonably priced lobster, calamari and steaks (US$25), and serves great cocktails. Reserve in advance. Daily noon–10pm.

Y&V Restaurant Northern end of Long Bay, near the petrol station 432 2577. Yvette's basic little cookshop – painted in bright Rasta colours – serves some of the best (and cheapest) food in the village, including brown stew chicken, cowfoot and fish to order (J$250–500). A good breakfast option, too. Mon–Fri 7am–9pm.

DIRECTORY

Internet The library, behind the post office, has internet access (Mon–Fri 9am–5pm).

Post office Just off the main road (Mon–Fri 8am–1pm; ☎ 879 7254).

Supermarket A small supermarket at the southern end of the village sells basics (plus ice cream and alcohol).

Manchioneal and around

The road south of Long Bay passes by some marvellously rugged coastline and, before crossing the Christmas River, you'll pass **Kensington**, the birthplace of Father Hugh Sherlock who composed Jamaica's national anthem in 1962. Enclosed by a tunnel-like covering of trees and utterly pitch-black at night, the hairpin-bend stretch of road nearby is locally known as "see me no more". A couple of kilometres further, the road inches into the pretty fishing village of **MANCHIONEAL**. Here, brightly painted stalls selling roast fish and conch soup border the road, while there's also a petrol station and a couple of local cookshops. Canoes line up on the sand of the naturally enclosed harbour separating Manchioneal from Long Road just to the south. Ask around for sightings of **manatees** (locally known as sea cows) here; they can occasionally be seen gambolling in the water.

Reach Falls

Between Manchioneal and Long Road, 5km west from the main road • Wed–Sun 8.30am–4.30pm; ticket booth closes at 4pm • US$10 • ☎ 276 8663, ⓦ udcja.com/reach-falls • A round-trip, private taxi from Port Antonio to the falls costs around US$50

Dazzling countryside surrounds **Reach Falls**, one of the loveliest spots on the island, with the Drivers River running through sumptuous rainforest before cascading over the falls into a wide, green pool. The thirty-foot waterfall allows for an invigorating water massage, and (if you can muster the courage) there's an exhilarating jump from the top. You can also go on a thirty-minute (guided) climb upriver – picking your way across slippery rocks and swimming through deep pools. You can ask at the visitor centre to be taken to the base of **Mandingo Cave** beyond (guide US$20), though it's quite a tricky climb. Movie fans might recognize Reach Falls as the place where an amorous Tom Cruise cavorts with his lady love in the film *Cocktail*.

HIKING IN THE RIO GRANDE VALLEY

Hiking in the lower limestone valleys of the John Crow Mountains is entirely different from the Blue Mountains – hotter and wetter; you may want to use a waterproof jacket, though staying wet and cooling off at mineral springs could well be a wiser alternative. A guide is essential for most hikes: ask at *Ambassabeth Cabins* in Bowden Pen (see page 120) or *Sister Ivy's* in Cornwall Barracks (see page 119) for local help; otherwise book a **tour** in Port Antonio with **Valley Hikes** (Unit 41, Royal Mall; ☎ 993 3881), **Attractions Link** (☎ 993 7076, ⓦ attractionslink. com) or Kingston-based **Sun Venture Tours** (☎ 408 6973, ⓦ sunventuretours.com). Rates range from US$40 per person for a half-day to US$175 for a two-day trek to Moore Town – all operators can also arrange home-stays with local families.

RIO GRANDE TRAILS

A couple of trails (Road End or Scatter Water Falls, from Berridale) can be done without a guide, but most hikes follow old pig-hunters' routes or even former council "roads" – now heavily overgrown – and require the help of an expert. Among the best trails are: the **Cunha Cunha Pass** (10km; 4hr) following the old Maroon "**Freedom Trail**" finishing close to Bath in St Thomas; the **Guava River Trail** (11km; 7hr) from Bellevue, with plentiful waterfalls; from **Coopers Hill** through untouched forest to the site of eighteenth-century hideaway **Nanny Town** (16–24km; 2 days), a scattering of overgrown ruins that remains an important symbol of Maroon history, allegedly haunted by the ghosts of vanquished British soldiers; and **White River Falls** (6km; 7hr), starting from Millbank, a tough and slippery climb through virgin forest to a series of seven cascades.

Zion Country Cottages Long Road ☎871 3623 or ☎451 1737, ⊛zioncountry.com. Just across the bay from Manchioneal and offering gorgeous views of the harbour, this eco-friendly complex spreads down the cliffs to a small shingle beach with hammocks, while flowers and plants wreathe the pathways. Run by enthusiastic Dutchman Free-I, the four bright cabins share showers, and dinner is also available. Free-I offers excellent informal tours of the surrounding area, including hikes along the volcanic rocks of the local coastline to impressive blowholes and natural pools, as well as excursions into the mountains and to Morant Point. Includes breakfast. US$60

2

The Rio Grande valley

Portland's interior – the **Rio Grande valley** – is a fantastically lush and partially impenetrable hinterland of tropical rainforest and waterfalls. The **Rio Grande**, one of Jamaica's major rivers, pours down from the John Crow Mountains through a deep and unspoilt valley of virgin forest. Despite its beauty, the area is little explored; many people do **rafting trips** (see page 122), but there is also superb river and mountain **hiking**.

Many of the rivers and springs here are named after local Maroon (see page 120) leaders – Nanny, Quao, Quashie and Quako – and the major remaining Maroon settlement is **Moore Town**. If you're craving rustic isolation, some of the other **villages** beyond have lovely settings and fascinating names – Alligator Church, Comfort Castle – indeed, the only thing holding up booming ecotourism here is the abominable road, which in its higher reaches is barely navigable by car.

Moore Town

MOORE TOWN is one of Jamaica's principal Maroon settlements, founded, so the legend goes, by chieftain of the Windward Maroons, **Nanny** (see page 121), in the mid-eighteenth century. In 2003, this stalwart community at the end of a winding, rocky road was declared a **UNESCO** site, and designated one of the "Masterpieces of the Oral and Intangible Heritage of Humanity." Traditional Kromanti language can still be heard here, and Moore Town remains a real piece of tradition and African heritage. When visiting, you should, as a matter of protocol, check in with the Maroons' **colonel** – the present chief, Colonel Wallace Stirling, who assumed leadership in 1995, lives some way up the village. There's no charge for looking around, but donations are welcomed. **Bump Grave**, a monument to the "indomitable and skilled chieftain" Nanny – and said to be the place she's buried – is in the town's small central square.

Alternatively, you can find a local guide and hike the forty minutes up to the fabulous pools at **Nanny Falls**, or organize a longer trek through an **operator** (see page 118).

By route taxi Moore Town is served by daily yet infrequent route taxis from Port Antonio. Very few run on Sundays.

By car You can drive to Moore Town, though the road beyond the turn off for Berridale rafting trips at Fellowship is heavily pot-holed.

ACCOMMODATION AND EATING

There are few cookshops in this area, with limited tourism and residents always cooking at home. If you arrive early in the day however, and meet the colonel, you should be able to set up dinner in a local home. If you want to stay, you'll also be limited to lodging with a local family, or continuing to *Sister Ivy's*.

Sister Ivy's Cornwall Barracks, 2km from Moore Town ☎806 0161. Super-picturesque Cornwall Barracks is where the formidable Ivelyn Harris rents out a simple, mosquito screened, one-room cabin with double bed in her lushly planted garden. Sister Ivy is an expert herbalist and alternative-medicine practitioner. Meals can be arranged. US$60

2

THE WINDWARD MAROONS

When the Spanish left Jamaica in 1660, they armed their newly freed slaves and encouraged them to fight a guerrilla war against the British. Calling the guerrillas *cimarrones* (meaning wild or untamed), the word was corrupted by the British to **Maroons**. With their numbers boosted by escaped slaves from sugar plantations, the Maroons set up small communities in inaccessible locations, with the **Windward Maroons** establishing themselves in the Blue and John Crow mountains and the Trelawny Maroons making a base in Cockpit Country (see page 189). The groups raided British settlements for weapons and supplies, and by the 1720s they had become a serious threat to colonial order.

The Windward Maroons had their headquarters 2000ft up at **Nanny Town**, virtually inaccessible to British soldiers, who were unfamiliar with the terrain. They only discovered it after a slave led them there in 1728, and were periodically slaughtered on their forays into the rainforest to destroy it. Eventually, in 1734, army captain Stoddard dragged swivel guns up the south side of the John Crow Mountains and bombarded Nanny Town, destroying most of the 140 homes and forcing the Maroons to move south. Still, the British couldn't flush them out – five years later a peace treaty was signed, giving the undefeated Maroons an independent status that they retain today, as well as 500 acres of land in the Rio Grande valley.

Today, full-blood Maroons, or those who know they have Maroon blood, are fiercely proud of their heritage and their contribution to Jamaican freedom. Though there has been a peaceful assimilation into the wider Jamaican population, you'll still hear the traditional Kromanti language spoken in mountain villages such as Moore Town (see page 119).

Millbank

Little-visited **MILLBANK** – the last sizeable village in the Rio Grande valley – nestles deep in the John Crow Mountains, eight kilometres south of Moore Town (take the right fork at Seaman's Valley via **Alligator Church**, where a perilous bridge crosses the river), and contains one of the three national park **ranger stations** (see page 92). This is prime Maroon country, and many of the village's elders – a healthy diet and clean mountain air mean many are pushing 100 – will happily tell you historical tales, while younger locals can escort you to former Maroon settlements. The setting is spectacular: rainforest surrounds you and the perfume of wild ginger lilies hangs heavy; it's also the starting point for several **hikes** (see page 118), among them to the seven high cascades of **White River Falls**.

ACCOMMODATION AND EATING   MILLBANK

★**Ambassabeth Cabins and Campsite** Bowden Pen, 5km southeast of Millbank ☎395 5351 or call JCDT ☎960 2848. The only place to stay in the area is a 30min walk southeast of Millbank. Driving is possible in dry weather; otherwise you might be able to get a lift in a 4WD from the ranger station. Run by knowledgeable local Linnette Wilks, the basic wooden cabins have no electricity but fresh mineral-water-fed taps – and bags of atmosphere. Traditional Maroon meals are prepared on an open fire, and local guides are available. Arrange your stay in advance; the owners can organize transport from Kingston or Port Antonio. **US$30**

West of Port Antonio

The A4 winds west from Port Antonio, crisscrossing an old railway track and threading through tiny villages peppered with stalls selling fruit and vegetables. You can stop for a freshwater splash at **Somerset Falls**, head inland to the Maroon community of **Charles Town** and stay at the **River Edge** retreat near **Annotto Bay**.

St Margaret's Bay

Tiny **ST MARGARET'S BAY**, eight kilometres west of Port Antonio, is where the Rio Grande empties into the sea underneath an iron bridge dating from 1891. Just by the bridge, a side road leads towards **Rafters' Rest**, a pretty colonial building serving as journey's end for Rio Grande rafting trips (see page 122). You can also usually book a cheaper excursion here from a posse of touting operators – though it never beats experiencing the real thing. Past Rafters' Rest, St Margaret's Bay proper is an appealingly neat settlement spreading back from the roadside, and once served as the last-stop-but-one of the Jamaica Railway – the old railway station itself serves as a simple bar and cookshop.

ARRIVAL AND DEPARTURE   ST MARGARET'S BAY

By minibus Minibuses run along the main road between Kingston (2hr 15min) and Port Antonio (15min) hourly at peak times, and to/from Ocho Rios (four daily; 2hr 15min).

ACCOMMODATION

★ **Rio Vista** ☎ 993 5444, ⓦ riovistajamaica.com, A beautifully situated hotel on a bluff with stupendous views of the Rio Grande, and the Blue Mountains as a backdrop. Offering attractive rooms in the main house or a self-contained one-bed villa with kitchen, there's also a pool and the helpful staff serve delicious Jamaican meals on request. Doubles US$100, villa US$165

Somerset Falls

Between St Margaret's Bay and Hope Bay • Check ahead; closed at time of research

Lush landscaping marks the entrance to **Somerset Falls**, part of the cascading Daniels River. Guides lead you up a stairway to have dip in the "cool pool", and there is a boat ride through gorge-like rocks to the spectacular "hidden falls" beyond, cascading into a 20ft deep pool perfect for a natural power shower. At research time, Somerset Falls was closed, but as one of Jamaica's most beautiful swimming areas, locals were hopeful it would reopen soon.

Hope Bay

HOPE BAY is home to a string of shops and rum bars, with Linton's **Crafts Shop** selling woodcarvings, jewellery and drums at cheaper prices than in Port Antonio. Take a journey inland for marvellous **river swimming** in the upper reaches of the Swift River, a half-hour drive through cocoa groves and mountain valleys (turn left at the small suspension bridge).

Buff Bay and around

Farmers come to sell their wares in the covered market at easy-going **BUFF BAY**, a good starting point for trips into the Blue Mountains; you may also wish to poke around **St**

NANNY OF THE MAROONS

Though there is a scarcity of written documentation to tell the tale, verbal histories abound with figures and praise for the Maroon's most famous leader, **Nanny**.

An eighteenth-century chieftain of the Windward Maroons, Nanny's prowess in waging guerrilla warfare against the British was so extraordinary, it was widely believed she wielded supernatural powers (one oft-repeated legend is that bullets ricocheted off her rear end, reversing and killing her attackers). During her decades of leadership, Nanny's formidable skill enabled the Maroons to wreak terrific havoc on British troops and estates; meanwhile, invaders were easily thwarted from reaching the Maroons' home base of Nanny Town. It is also said Nanny would venture into plantations to liberate slaves and guide them back to Nanny Town, an enclave ingeniously situated in a steep, secluded corner of the mountains. In addition to her remarkable work on the battlefield, Nanny is credited with successfully preserving **West African traditions**, including a number of folk legends and songs.

A National Hero, Nanny is among those honoured on **Heroes Day**, held every year on the third Monday in October. At her gravesite in Moore Town (see page 119), a monument stands in her honour, but perhaps the most endearing and widespread tribute to her legacy is the $500 bill, which carries her image.

2

RAFTING THE RIO GRANDE

Once a means of transporting bananas, **rafting** down the majestic Rio Grande is now Portland's most popular attraction, ever since Errol Flynn raced with his friends in the 1950s. It's a delightfully lazy way to spend half a day, although the sun can get fierce.

From the put-in point at **Berridale**, ten kilometres southwest of Port Antonio, the thirty-foot bamboo rafts (each with a raised seat) meander down the river for two hours through outstanding scenery, poled downstream by a captain and stopping periodically for swimming, waterfall hunting or to buy snacks. Tickets are sold by TPD Co. (daily 9am–4pm; US$100/raft; ☎ 968 3441). The trip is one-way, terminating at Rafters' Rest in St Margaret's Bay (see page 120), so if you're **driving**, leave your car at Berridale and have an insured driver take it down for US$15, or else use a **taxi** – to Berridale and then back to Port Antonio from Rafters Rest costs around US$40. If you're desperate to save cash, the Berridale route taxi from Port Antonio (J$220) runs close by the put-in point, and route taxis to Port Antonio from Buff Bay pass the entrance to Rafters' Rest regularly.

A recent popular addition to the trip downriver is to arrange a lunch en route cooked by master chef Belinda, who descends on foot from the hills with the freshest ingredients and cooks delights like curried fish, jerk pork or crayfish right there on the river bank. Order through your hotel or call Belinda directly on ☎ 389 8826.

Local legend Becky Hill (☎ 575 7381), who also guides tours of the Blue Lagoon (see page 114), runs laudable trips of the river for US$90/raft, or you can find people touting **unofficial rafting trips** in Port Antonio and St Margaret's Bay. Don't hand over the cash until you've finished the journey at Rafters' Rest, and don't go with anyone who makes you feel uncomfortable.

George's Anglican church on the main road, dating from 1814 when it replaced the original structure built in 1681.

East of town, more awesome views of the Blue Mountains are accompanied by relentless fields of coconut palms and banana groves which line the road. At one time they formed part of the United Fruit Company's **Kildare Estate** until Panama Disease devastated the banana crop in the 1920s. The former great house is unfortunately now in a state of disrepair.

ARRIVAL AND DEPARTURE

BUFF BAY AND AROUND

By minibus Minibuses run along the main road between Kingston (1hr 45min) and Port Antonio (45min), and to/from Ocho Rios (1hr 45min).

EATING

★ **G&B Jerk Centre** Victoria St, just east of town ☎ 452 2172. Fans of jerk pork can indulge at *G&B*, which offers high-quality meat drawing on the owner's Maroon roots from the Buff Bay Valley. There's a small bar too. Half chicken J$800, pork J$1400/lb. Daily 10am–midnight.

Charles Town Asafu Yard

3km inland of Buff Bay • Donations welcome • Call in advance • ☎ 445 2861, ⊕ maroons-jamaica.com

CHARLES TOWN, a settlement of Maroon origin (see page 120), is home to an interesting museum, the **Asafu Yard**. Local Maroons are glad to guide people around the drums, crafts and displays on spiritual traditions and medicinal plants, while the area also provides good hiking to an old coffee plantation and reconstruction of a traditional Maroon village 3km upriver.

Section

Further inland from Charles Town, the road spirals dramatically up into the Blue Mountains past Fishdone (see page 95) and One Drop waterfalls before arriving at **SECTION**. The upper part of this route was closed for six years following collapses during Hurricane Ivan in 2004, and given on-going risk from storms it's sensible to ask around in Charles Town if the route is open. For now, with tourism between the mountains and the north coast at Buff Bay possible, efforts have been made to encourage visitors to take in this attractive river valley.

Annotto Bay and around

ANNOTTO BAY, sixteen kilometres west of Buff Bay, is a busy, tatty little market town (if you're there in May or June, be sure to pick up some of the extraordinary mangoes) named after the red annotto dye once produced here. The red and yellow **Baptist church**, right on the main road and built in 1892, has an entrance guarded by old cannons, the meagre remains of British Fort George.

The countryside **inland of Annotto Bay**, sheltering under the eaves of the Blue Mountains, makes a welcome change from coastal vistas; turn in at the Annotto Bay All Age School and follow signs to **River Edge** for wonderful river swimming, fifteen minutes' drive through banana groves and a flower farm.

2

ARRIVAL AND DEPARTURE   **ANNOTTO BAY AND AROUND**

By minibus Minibuses run along the main road between Kingston (1hr 30min) and Port Antonio (1hr), hourly at peak times, and to/from Ocho Rios (four daily; 1hr 30min).

ACCOMMODATION AND EATING

Human Service Station Main Rd. Just east of town and right by the sea, this longstanding diner is famed for its steamed fish (J$800–1500), and has been in business for over thirty years. Also serves fried chicken (J$400) and (if you're in luck) conch or fish soup (J$300); all washed down with a natural juice. Mon–Sat 9am–10pm, Sun 11am–6pm.

River Edge Fort George, 6km south of Annotto Bay ☏ 385 4943, ✉ riveredge99@hotmail.com. Built around the cool, clear waters of the Pencar River, this friendly, family-run combination of restaurant, swimming spot and retreat has relaxing pools and even offers massages. Stay in a choice of airy dorm beds or private studio apartments with cooking facilities. Camping also available with showers and bathrooms nearby. Camping US$10, dorms US$15, apartments US$25

Ocho Rios and the north coast

DUNN'S RIVER FALLS

Ocho Rios and the north coast

The north coast is the most developed area of Jamaica outside the capital, boasting numerous things to do and an energetic atmosphere. Highway upgrades between Montego Bay and Ocho Rios have effectively halved journey times between the two cities, opening up most of the coastline to new resort and villa developments. With many villages and towns running seamlessly into the next, it's sometimes hard to know where each urban area starts and ends. The attraction of the north coast is nonetheless clear as soon as you leave the main road: barrelling through the diverse parishes of St Mary, St Ann and Trelawny, there is stunning scenery – sweeping cane and coconut plantations, mangrove swamps, luscious farmland and kilometres of white-sand beaches with reefs less than a hundred feet out to sea. Though Ocho Rios enjoys a tempting set of all-inclusive hotels, be sure to spend time beyond the resort gates with the overlooked water holes, quiet gardens and densely rainforested hilltops that are the beating heart of this astoundingly lush region.

Much development is centred on the "garden parish" of **St Ann**, so called because of the area's immensely fertile soil. St Ann has also spawned luminaries such as **Marcus Garvey**, **Bob Marley** and **Winston "Burning Spear" Rodney**, and is considered by some to be the spiritual centre of the island. The nucleus of the parish and the home of the famous **Dunn's River Falls**, **Ocho Rios** offers solid dining options, excellent recreational activities and a decent nightlife scene. Just a few kilometres to the east, the quiet coastal communities of **Oracabessa** and **Port Maria** are disturbed by little other than birdsong, with deserted coastline ideal for hiking and waterfall hunting. West of Ocho Rios, down-to-earth **St Ann's Bay** has an intriguing memorial to its most famous native son, Marcus Garvey. Further west, sporadic tourism development is interspersed with peaceful villages like **Rio Bueno** and **Duncans** – and a few fantastic beaches. **Inland**, winding, leafy lanes pass through marvellous scenery; smack in the middle of St Ann is Bob Marley's birthplace and the site of his mausoleum, where a cache of Rasta guides welcomes hordes of reggae disciples.

Ocho Rios

Light years away from the sleepy fishing village of a few decades ago, **OCHO RIOS** (usually just called "Ochi") is a small but bustling city that's a hotspot for tourism. Each week thousands of cruise-ship passengers disembark here, and Ochi is fully geared up to meet them with numerous in-bond stores, appealing restaurants and several smartly packaged attractions. Beach lovers might prefer the lengthy strips of hotel-lined

FIREFLY

Highlights

❶ Shaw Park Botanical Gardens Ochi's stunning, little-visited garden boasts views down to the city and a magnificent array of tropical flowers, trees and palms. See page 133

❷ Spanish Bridge Forego the hullabaloo of popular Blue Hole in favour of this crystalline swim spot and its seventeenth-century bridge. See page 134

❸ Sugar Pot Beach After a dip in the azure waters of Rio Nuevo Bay, head to *Sugar Pot Ruins Restaurant* for rum punch and curried coconut fish. See page 141

❹ Firefly Noël Coward's hilltop home oozes history and has one of the best views on the island and his former beach house below is an intriguing and good-value accommodation option. See page 144

❺ Robins Bay A visit to this peaceful community feels like you've taken a step back in time, and you're ideally placed for exploring the north coast's unspoilt countryside. See page 147

❻ Stush in the Bush Excellent, independent-minded farm tour and a superb dining experience that's one hundred percent organic. See page 152

HIGHLIGHTS ARE MARKED ON THE MAP ON PAGE 128

OCHO RIOS AND THE NORTH COAST

HIGHLIGHTS

1. Shaw Park Botanical Gardens
2. Spanish Bridge
3. Sugar Pot Beach
4. Firefly
5. Robins Bay
6. Stush in the Bush

CARIBBEAN SEA

N

Port Antonio

Port Maria

Ocho Rios

St Ann's Bay

Runaway Bay

Discovery Bay

ST MARY

ST ANN

ST CATHERINE

TRELAWNY

CLARENDON

MANCHESTER

DRY HARBOUR MOUNTAINS

HIGHWAY 2000 NORTH-SOUTH LINK

0   3
kilometres

sand in Negril and Montego Bay, but for outdoor variety, Ochi outshines its siblings: waterfalls, river swims, lush fern foliage and serene botanical gardens are just a stone's throw away from city shores. Ochi's walkable downtown boasts a certain infectious energy, and the fact that its town and tourist area are one and the same means there's less of the "sitting duck" atmosphere of the Montego Bay strip. Harassment here, too, has become only a minor irritation.

Brief history

"Ocho Rios" is a corruption of the Spanish name *chorreros*, referring to the "gushing water" of the many local waterfalls – there are not "eight rivers" here. In contrast to its poetic name, the town has a somewhat violent history as the site of several bloody battles that took place when Spanish governor **Don Christobal Arnaldo de Yssasi** refused to give in to the British after their capture of the island in 1655. Major skirmishes took place at Dunn's River in 1657, Rio Nuevo in 1658 and Shaw Park in 1659, when Yssasi's men were attacked by a group led by his erstwhile ally, **Juan de Dolas**, a former slave who had defected to the British. In 1660, Yssasi fled the island, but local Spanish legacy remains in a smattering of place names such as the fragrant **pimento** tree, first discovered by the Spanish in St Ann and commercially planted here ever since.

The **British** left a more pervasive mark, with their huge sugar cane, system of slavery, lumber and cattle farms, though most planters were absentees. Ocho Rios remained little more than a fishing harbour until the twentieth century, when **tourism** and **bauxite** began to physically sculpt the land. In 1923, a great house at Shaw Park became Jamaica's first exclusive **hotel**, and by 1948 it had been joined by the *Sans Souci Lido*, *Silver Seas* and *Dunn's River* (now *Sandals*). Recurrent crop failures led local planter **Alfred DaCosta** to chemically analyse the St Ann earth in 1938, finding that the soil contained high levels of **bauxite**, the chief raw material used to produce aluminium. Foreign companies Reynolds and Kaiser bought up huge tracts of land, and in 1968 forty acres were reclaimed from behind what is now Ochi's Main Street. The harbour was dredged, and Reynolds built a deep-water pier, while Jamaica's Urban Development Corporation imported sand and built another jetty for cruise ships. More than three decades later, their efforts have brought about the established resort town of today.

Main Street

Compact enough to explore on foot, the busy streets of Ocho Rios boast two great markets (one for crafts, one for fruit and vegetables). If your schedule allows, visit the fruit market on a Saturday morning – you'll see it come alive with dressmakers, shoe sellers, even nail salons, in addition to the daily stalls that tout phenomenally fresh produce. Running parallel to the sea, **Main Street** is divided into two halves by the imposing seven hundred-room *Moon Palace* hotel, right in the middle of town. Main Street houses the majority of hotels, bars, shops and restaurants, as well as the post office. Opposite the clock tower and forking off towards the sea from Main Street, vibrant **James Avenue** has a number of colourful little restaurants and several no-frills nightclubs.

Mahogany Beach

The clamour of Ocho Rios's Main Street recedes as you head to the east of the centre, but one place you shouldn't pass by is **Mahogany Beach**, officially only open to those staying at *Carib Resort* or on Cool Runnings Cruises, but covertly also open to passersby. Set in landscaped gardens just past the *Hibiscus Lodge* hotel, it occupies a pretty strip of sand and is usually quiet. Good snorkelling and swimming is to be had,

3

plus it boasts a beach bar and grill, natural spring pool and massage hut. At weekends, jerk meat and fish is sometimes grilled outside and there's an uptown party atmosphere.

Ocho Rios Bay beach

Daily 8.30am–6pm; last entry 4.30pm • US$3

Most of the town's tourist activity centres on the main **beach** – variously known as Mallards, Turtle and Ocho Rios Bay. Tucked under the hotels and accessible from the western end of Main Street near the *Pier View* and *Sandcastles* hotels, the white-sand beach is wide and well maintained, with showers, changing rooms, bars and plenty of activity. Being a town beach, it's quite casual, with a nice mix of tourists and locals.

Island Village

Main St • Most shops daily 9am–6pm

At the far western end of both the beach and Main Street, the **Island Village** shopping complex is a popular place to spend an hour or two, designed to emulate Caribbean architecture, with wooden stalls in washed-out ice-cream colours selling classy holiday souvenirs, clothes and jewellery. The latest Hollywood releases can be seen at the Cove Cinema here (𝕆675 8804). The mall is centred around a large square that has a striking bronze statue of Bob Marley, guitar in hand.

● EATING		■ ACCOMMODATION	
The Almond Tree	3	The Blue House	2
Calabash Ital Restaurant	9	Carib Ocho Rios	
Devon House I-Scream	12	Condominium	6
Evita's	7	Chrisann's	3
The Healthy Way	13	Couples Tower Isle	1
The Lyming	8	Hermosa Cove	5
Island Coffees Café	14	Hibiscus Lodge	9
Miss Merle's Fish Joint	15	Jamaica Inn	4
Miss T's	2	Kaz Kreol	4
Mom's Homestyle	10	The Lion House	12
Restaurant	6	Little Shaw Park	
Passage to India	11	Guest House	11
Reflections	5	Pineapple Court	10
Reggae Pot	4	Reggae Hostel	13
Toscanini	1	Silver Seas	8

■ DRINKING & NIGHTLIFE		● SHOPPING	
Amnesia	2	Craft Market	2
Glenn's Restaurant and		Harmony Hall	1
Cocktail Lounge	1		
John Crow	5		
Margaritaville	4		
Oceans 11	3		
Ocho Rios Village Jerk Centre	6		

WATERSPORTS, BOAT CRUISES AND RIVER ADVENTURES

Although there isn't that much underwater at Ocho Rios's main beach – you'll find richer pickings east of the harbour or at the reef at the bottom of Dunn's River – the sand is lined with watersports concessions. Prices are set and displayed at boards by the entrances, and offerings range from jet packs and banana boats to water-skiing (see page 135). Kayaks and windsurfers are also on hand. Half- or full-day deep-sea **fishing** for blue marlin or sailfish is available, as are glass-bottom boat rides along the coast to Dunn's River Falls. For divers, the best spots are Devil's Reef at the eastern end of town and a couple of shipwrecks further out to sea.

On most days, the coast reverberates to sound systems aboard **pleasure cruises**. Day-trips go to Dunn's River for climbing the falls (try to go on one that leaves early in the morning, before the crowds, or late in the afternoon), while romantic or soca sunset cruises enjoy the afternoon or early evening, usually with unlimited alcoholic drinks and snacks.

Some of the most fun activities are swimming, tubing, kayaking and rafting on the White River just to the east of Ochi (see page 134). Bear in mind that the rapids are only mildly challenging even after heavy rain. Nonetheless, fear of accidents has led to a degree of over-cautiousness by commercial operators; this notably doesn't include the lower key attraction Blue Hole.

3

Ocho Rios Fort

If you head west of town beyond Main Street, past the food outlets and bauxite factory gates, you'll reach longstanding **Ocho Rios Fort**, now in the shadow of giant docked cruise ships. The fort was built by the British in the seventeenth century and restored in 1780 to defend against a feared French attack, but there's little to see other than two cannons, taken from the now derelict Mammee Bay Fort west of town and placed here in the 1960s. The fort is also the starting point of the rather grandly named "**One Love Trail**" – a pretty three-kilometre footpath between the sea and the main road, giving easy access to Ochi's busiest tourist attractions: Mystic Mountain, Dolphin Cove and Dunn's River Falls.

Rainforest Adventures Mystic Mountain

2.8km west of Ochi · Daily 8am–5pm · ☎ 974 3990, ⓦ rainforestadventure.com · Bobsled (includes chairlift) US$69, canopy zipline (includes chairlift) US$113, chairlift only US$47, Tranopy (all three attractions) US$139

Serene **Mystic Mountain** boasts a kilometre-long chairlift over forest canopy all the way up to the hilltop, where you'll find a visitor centre with restaurant, pool with waterslide and a small yet absorbing exhibition on Jamaica's myriad sporting achievements. From here the attraction draws on Jamaica's *Cool Runnings* fame with a fun and fast two-person "bobsled" roller-coasting through the trees, while nearby a series of canopy ziplines is one of the island's best. Constructed with the environment in mind – equipment was brought in via helicopter in order to avoid damaging any trees – the site works harmoniously with the landscape, and as an attraction, it feels tranquil instead of touristy.

Dolphin Cove

3.5km west of Ocho Rios, close to Dunn's River Falls · Daily 8.30am–5.30pm · ☎ 974 5335, ⓦ dolphincoveja.com · US$69, includes snorkelling and water park access · Dolphin encounters daily, times vary; check website · US$99–398, book in advance online for discounts

The main draw of the **Dolphin Cove** theme park is the chance to swim with bottlenose dolphins and (docile) bottlenose sharks, kept in a fenced-off section of the bay (changing facilities and lockers on-site) – the normal entrance fee will enable you to see the dolphins swimming. There are a variety of programmes allowing anything from a "handshake" and a "kiss" to a swim with dorsal pull and photos included; book a few days ahead. While swimming with dolphins is undeniably a great experience, there remain doubts about the capture and trade of wild dolphins for use in theme parks. The owners inevitably maintain that dolphin welfare is their primary concern; for

CRUISE SHIP SCHEDULES

Because Ochi is a popular **cruise ship** port of call, some of its sights – particularly between December and March – occasionally swarm with visitors. If you're seeking solitude, schedule your sightseeing for the afternoon: cruise ships dock early in the morning, and are usually filled up with their guests and back out to sea by 2pm. Avoiding tour groups in general is a good idea and you can call attractions before heading out, just to check if they are expecting any large groups.

further information visit the Jamaica Environment Trust website at Ⓦjamentrust.org. Elsewhere in the complex, there's a pool containing sharks and rays, a "Jungle Trail" with stops for petting macaws and touching starfish and snakes, a small beach where you can rent snorkel equipment and canoes, and a restaurant and gift shop.

Dunn's River Falls

4km west of Ocho Rios • Daily 8.30am–4pm, beach closes 6pm • US$20, plus a tip for the guide; water shoes for rent (US$7) or purchase (US$17) • Free lockers • ☎ 974 2857, Ⓦ dunnsriverja.com

Jamaica's best-loved waterfall and a staple of tour brochures, **Dunn's River Falls** are overdeveloped but still breathtaking, and remain the island's major tourist honeypot. Masked from the road by restaurants, craft shops and car parks, the wide and magnificent 600ft waterfall cascades over rocks down to a pretty tree-fringed white-sand beach. There's a lively reef within swimming distance, and snorkel gear is available to rent from several touts.

Impressively proportioned, with water running so fast you can hear it from the road below, the falls are surrounded by dripping foliage and more than live up to their reputation, despite the concrete and commerciality. The main activity is climbing up the cascade, a wet but easily navigable hour-long clamber. The step-like rocks are regularly scraped to remove slippery algae, and the thing to prevent a stumble is to form a hand-holding chain led by one of the very experienced guides. It's thoroughly exhilarating, as you're showered with cool, clear water all the way up – wear a bathing suit. There's a restaurant and bar, and full changing facilities at the beach and at the top of the falls. Hundred-strong queues frequently form along the beach; to avoid the crowds arrive at opening time or late in the afternoon (last climb at 4pm), when cruise passengers are already aboard their ships.

Little Dunn's River

2.7km west of Ocho Rios (1.3km east of Dunn's River Falls) • Daily dawn to dusk • Free

An alternative to the crowds and admission price of Dunn's River Falls are the **unmaintained waterfalls** at Little Dunn's River, a kilometre down the road (opposite Mystic Mountain). Free, and more of a local scene, Little Dunn's harbours a small collection of streams that flow gently down sloped boulders into a tranquil, shallow bay. The rocks are fun for clambering about, or, if you're feeling particularly brave, you can start the day here with a polar bear-style shower under one of the waterfalls.

Turtle River Falls and Gardens

Eden Bower Rd, Ocho Rios • Mon–Sat 9am–4pm • ☎ 974 5114, Ⓦ turtleriverfallsandgardens.com • US$20 • To reach the gardens, go 500m up steep Eden Bower Rd from Dacosta Drive, more or less opposite Island Village; the entrance is just past *Evita's* restaurant

Turtle River Falls and Gardens, one of Ochi's attractive botanical gardens, features fourteen separate wide and climb-able waterfalls cascading through fifteen acres of tropical forest and flowered clearings. The one-hour tour (included in the fee) shows you the best of the falls and provides a guide to the park's plants and the brightly plumed birds, which feed from your hands in the walk-in aviary. The pool and swim-up bar is left over from the property's former life as the *Enchanted Gardens Hotel* – and now back in use they particularly appeal to the cruise passengers who come up here en masse when a ship is docked.

Shaw Park Botanical Gardens

Shaw Park Rd, 2.5km southwest of Ochi's centre · Daily 8am–5pm · US$10, plus a tip for your guide · ☎ 974 2723

Shaw Park Botanical Gardens sits a mere 550ft above sea level but boasts stunning aerial views nonetheless. The former grounds of a long-gone hotel, nowadays Shaw Park is a little-visited attraction, which only adds to its appeal. Its 25-acre garden was creatively planted by the aptly named Flora Stewart, and is resplendent with unusual flowers, plants and trees – including hibiscus, bougainvillea and a huge banyan with swingable vines. Set amid lush, unending shades of green, there's also a near-perpendicular waterfall (but there's no swimming).

Konoko Falls and Botanical Garden

Shaw Park Estate, 2.5km southwest of Ochi's centre · Daily 8am–4.30pm · US$20 · ☏ 622 1712, ⓦ konokofalls.com

Well worth your time, the intimate **Konoko Falls and Botanical Garden** is a much more packaged attraction than nearby Shaw Park Botanical Gardens, with a café and gift shop. Wooden walkways allow easy viewing of the heliconias, anthuriums, hot pink ginger lilies and rampant vines, and flowerbeds are bisected by streams teeming with mullet, koi, crayfish and turtles, with occasional glass panels providing a view of the underwater goings-on. Housed in an elegant cut-stone building, the **museum** has a limited but thoughtful collection of exhibits, from Taíno *zemis* (talismans used to ward off evil spirits) to a nineteenth-century man trap, photographs depicting post-abolition life and displays on St Ann parish's own revolutionaries Marcus Garvey and Bob Marley. The (Dunn's River-esque) falls are in a beautiful spot overhung by mahoe trees.

Fern Gully

Heading out of Ocho Rios on Milford Road (shortly after the Shaw Park turn-off) brings you into **Fern Gully**, a densely vegetated and steeply inclining five-kilometre stretch of the A3/A1 road (which eventually leads to Kingston), made famous by the arboreal splendour of the four hundred or so varieties of fern that smother the roadside banks. First planted in the 1880s, the ferns are overhung by tall trumpet and mahoe trees, which filter the sunlight to create a cool, green-tinged tunnel. Moist and sheltered, the gully environment is ideal for plant life.

FAITH'S PEN

Once a Jamaican street-food institution, **Faith's Pen** has been hit hard by the opening of Highway 2000, which redirected countless patrons. Still, the aroma-intensive stalls (some 26km south of Ocho Rios), blackened by years of barbecue cooking, do a worthy trade among drivers looking to avoid the toll road to Kingston. Vendors serve variations on a theme (go for the cook with the longest queue to find the tastiest food): roast yam and saltfish, jerk chicken or pork, ackee and saltfish, roast corn, curry goat, mannish water or fish/conch soup, alongside beers and natural juices. Food sells for between J$500 and J$1200, and you eat at benches, with whizzing cars and the strains of Irie FM serving as background music.

You can reach Faith's Pen in twenty to thirty minutes' drive from Ocho Rios: take the A3 through Fern Gully, continuing through emerald-coloured fields to the quiet village of **Moneague**. Stay on the A3 (avoiding the Highway 2000 to Kingston); five minutes after passing Moneague, you'll see Faith's Pen on the right-hand side of the road.

MI DIAL STUCK PON IRIE FM

In amongst the glamorous frontages of all-inclusive hotels, the studios of **Irie FM** are marked by a colourful billboard opposite the Coconut Grove shopping centre. Irie was Jamaica's first reggae-only station and remains the island's most popular – airwaves were previously dominated by American soul, gospel and country. Since its first transmission in 1990, Irie has championed the cultural legitimacy of a musical genre branded subversive until the early 1970s. Today, the station provides the soundtrack for the nation. Wherever you go, you'll hear the music, the popular talk shows and the patois jingles: "Irie FM – a fi wi station" or "My radio dial stuck pon Irie FM, and guess what – me nah bother fix it". Steel Pulse, Burning Spear, Aswad and Third World, among many others, have recorded at Irie's Grove Studios, and the station has brought a bit of Kingston-style culture to Ochi.

White River

Ocho Rios's urban sprawl has in effect annexed the villages surrounding it: to the east, past the Irie FM studios, Main Street merges into the A3 coast road and crosses the bridge over the sluggish **White River**, which marks the parish boundary of St Ann and St Mary. Several tour operators offer tubing and rafting here (see page 136), accessed from various points on Bonham Spring Road (turn inland just west of the bridge), while there are many spots for river swimming and the sumptuous Sandals Golf and Country Club.

Irie Blue Hole

Thatch Hill Rd, 10km from Ocho Rios • Daily 8am–6pm • 1–2hr guided tour obligatory • US$10 plus tip, US$5 to rent water shoes • To get here, turn left (east) at Lodge Square, follow the road down for 1km, then turn right onto the unsignposted track at the JPS electric substation

A collection of marvellous river pools, one of them the deep eponymous **Irie Blue Hole**, offers excellent swimming below waterfalls on the White River. The attraction is a classic case of Jamaican DIY-tourism, though how long authorities permit guides to work here without board approval remains to be seen. On arrival you're approached by a group of blue-shirted, enthusiastic locals who run the tours (many of them make their living entirely from it), and decide among themselves who will act as your guide through the river pools. If you haven't brought water shoes or flip-flops you'll need to rent them from a makeshift stall. You're then taken some fifteen minutes up-river, with a number of beautiful diving spots, a rope swing and a couple of deep blue pools along the way, including the blue hole itself, and – if you're brave – into a large cave hidden behind the largest waterfall. Aim to make your visit around 3pm; earlier, Irie is often swamped with tour buses and cruise ship passengers.

Spanish Bridge

Thatch Hill Rd, 20min drive from Blue Hole • Free

If you'd like to get out on the river, but are interested in something a little less commercial than busy Blue Hole, continue driving along Thatch Hill road for another twenty minutes beyond the electric substation. The route becomes terribly rough (though you're rewarded with visions of virgin rainforest), until terminating at a spectacular natural pool called **Spanish Bridge,** named for the beautiful seventeenth-century bridge that spans the river here – a vestige of Spanish colonization. Beneath the bridge, the water is cool and clear, there are a few chickens and dogs about, and a happy mix of locals and tourists entertain themselves with a rope swing and drinks from two small bars.

Bamboo Beach Club

6km east of Ocho Rios • Daily 9am–10pm • ☎ 975 5122, ⓦ bamboobeachclub.com • US$11 entrance; US$59 all-inclusive including entertainment

Known to locals by its former name, Reggae Beach, **Bamboo Beach Club** is one of Jamaica's most picturesque curves of yellow sand, with shady palm groves and old almond trees, and cliffs protecting it at either end. Unfortunately, the site has acquired a bit of a fenced-in tone, with cruise ship parties coming in for an all-inclusive eating option, and entertainment from drummers and costumed dancing girls. If you want to enjoy the beach and are prepared to pay the entrance price you might want to go on a quieter day; phone to check when would suit you.

ARRIVAL AND DEPARTURE OCHO RIOS

By bus The Knutsford Express intercity service (ⓦ knutsford express.com) to/from Falmouth and Montego Bay (7–9 daily; 2hr) and Kingston (7–9 daily; 1hr 45min) operates from the Island Village parking lot at the west end of Main St.

By minibus Minibuses work similarly to route taxis (see below) but run longer distances, including to Port Maria (about J$250), Runaway Bay (about J$250), Kingston

(J$500) and Montego Bay (J$800).

By plane Charter companies AirLink Express (ⓣ 940 4870, ⓦ intlairlink.net) and Tim Air (ⓣ 952 2516, ⓦ timair.net) fly to Ian Fleming International Airport from Montego Bay (30min), Negril (1hr) and Kingston (30min). The airport is 16km east of Ocho Rios; a cab to town should cost about US$25.

GETTING AROUND

By route taxi For shorter or in-town distances, the best way to get around is by route taxi, which ply set paths and are shared by an ever-revolving group of passengers (see page 24). Identified by their black and white checkers and a destination on the side, during daylight hours, Mon–Sat, route taxis originate at the bus terminus, behind the fruit and vegetable market. In the evening and on Sundays, route taxis leave from various points around the clock tower in the heart of town (ask at the clock – drivers call out their destinations). For most drives around town, you'll pay about J$150; trips to Boscobel or Oracabessa will cost about J$250.

By private taxi Expect to pay about US$12–14 to charter a taxi from downtown to the Tower Isle area east of town or to Dunn's River Falls; plentiful tourists can also mean inflated fares – if in doubt, haggle. JUTA (ⓣ 974 2292) and Maxi Taxi (ⓣ 974 2971) are both reliable taxi firms.

By car Many international rental firms have branches in Ochi. Otherwise the following local companies may give you a better deal: Caribbean Cars, 99A Main St (ⓣ 974 2123, ⓦ caribbeancarrentals.net); Sunshine, 154 Main St (ⓣ 974 2980); and Villa, Shop 7, Coconut Grove (ⓣ 974 2474).

INFORMATION AND TOURS

Tourist information Information desks are located at the Cruise Ship Pier and at TPDCO, upstairs in Ocean Village Plaza on Main Street (Tourist Product Development Company; Mon–Thurs 8.30am–5pm, Fri 8.30am–4pm; ⓣ 974 7705) – both have details of activities and useful local maps, while the latter can advise on hotels. Weekly print newspaper The North Coast Times (ⓦ northcoasttimesja.com) is a decent entertainment resource.

Independent drivers Reliable drivers for local sightseeing are Mahlon Bentley (at The Lion House; see page 136; ⓣ 917 0039), Dawn Clarke (ⓣ 774 1202), Dalton Fletcher (ⓣ 859 4522 or ⓣ 995 3800) and Clifton Riley (ⓣ 375 8174). Drivers charge depending on distance (expect US$100–200/day), but make sure you negotiate in advance which stops will be made.

ACTIVITIES

BIKING

Blue Mountain Bicycle Tours ⓣ 974 7075, ⓦ bmtours ja.com. Reliable local operator offering excellent downhill mountain cycling in the Blue Mountains, including transport (US$129; see page 92).

BOAT TRIPS

Cool Runnings Catamarans ⓣ 974 2446, ⓦ cool runningscatamarans.com. Day-trips to Dunn's River for snorkelling and climbing the falls (4hr; US$126) and romantic or soca sunset cruises (3hr; US$75).

DIVING AND SNORKELLING

Garfield ⓣ 544 4354, ⓦ garfielddiving.com. Long-established Ochi scuba operator, also offering snorkelling

at the reef and Dunn's River aboard a glass-bottom boat (US$30) plus fishing charters (from US$645).

Resort Divers ⓣ 881 5760 or ⓣ 863 1472, ⓦ resort divers.com. Five-star PADI operator offering a full range of half- to seven-day courses (US$100–695), plus snorkelling and boat trips (US$30–60), and deep-sea fishing for blue marlin or sailfish (from US$650).

LAND TOURS

Chukka Cove Adventure Tours ⓣ 656 8026, ⓦ chukka. com. International mass-market operator offering a variety of tours: tubing (US$65), including a combination with a canopy zipline tour (US$89), takes place at their landscaped "village" high up the White River valley; there's also an ATV/quad-bike tour beyond St Ann's Bay (US$115) and the

3

OCHO RIOS VILLA RENTALS

There are hordes of **villas** around Ocho Rios, renting for anything between US$1000 and US$20,000 per week (and sometimes beyond) – some represent excellent value, especially those that have room for larger groups. Many can be booked through JAVA (Jamaica Association of Villas and Apartments ☎974 2508, ⊛javavillas.org), whose website also has special offers for immediate rental. A particular highlight is *Te Moana* (☎974 2870, ⊛harmonyhall.com; US$200), offering two funkily designed spacious cottages, each with one bedroom, large living area, kitchen, bathroom and French windows opening onto the veranda. Perched atop low cliffs 1.5km from town, the property has steps down to its own beach and reef, and use of kayaks and paddleboards is included.

Zion Bus Line to the Marley Mausoleum (US$115; see page 155). Prices include hotel pick-up.

Yaaman Prospect, St Mary ☎974 5335, ⊛yaaman adventure.com. Focused on Prospect Plantation, a kilometre east of town, and managed by Dolphin Cove (see page 131), the former haunt of planter Harold Mitchell offers jitney rides through fields of sugar, coconut, pimento, lime, ackee, breadfruit and soursop, stopping to spot butterflies and sample fruits. Also has a camel safari, buggy rides, culinary tour, Segway scooters, and horse rides down to Jamaica's first hydroelectric plant at White River gorge (tours 2–5hr; US$40–199).

PAINTBALL

H'Evans Scent Freehill, St Ann ☎427 4866, ⊛hevans scent.com. Property in the hills above St Ann's Bay, offering paintballing (J$3950) and the island's most economical (non-canopy) zipline (J$4250), in the hills above St Ann's Bay.

RAFTING

Calypso Rafting ☎817 8433, ⊛calypsorafting.com. Long-established operator offering calm rafting (US$55 for two) and tubing (US$25/person) on the White River, alongside fishing and boat charters (from US$600).

ACCOMMODATION

In addition to the numerous all-inclusives, condo resorts – blocks of family-friendly, self-catering apartments grouped around a pool – are popular in Ochi. Budget travellers are less well catered for, though there are still a few rooms around for less than US$50 (if you're stuck, remember to scout ⊛airbnb.com).

GUESTHOUSES AND HOSTEL

★ **The Blue House** White River, 4km east of town ☎994 1367, ⊛thebluehousejamaica.com; map p.130. Superb B&B with tasteful rooms and large luxurious bathrooms. The highlight is undoubtedly the best Jamaican-fusion cooking on the island, courtesy of "The Barefoot Chef", with Chinese, Indian and international influences. Dinner is served family-style with a range of dishes (US$30), while the genial hosts are a mine of information. There's a pool, sundeck and lounge, plus river bathing nearby, all great for relaxation. Outstanding, imaginative breakfast (such as cassava pancakes with banana and walnuts) included. US$218

★ **Hermosa Cove** Hermosa St, 1.5km east of town ☎974 3699, ⊛hermosacove.com; map p.130. A dreamy collection of bright, handcrafted villas (one is even in a treehouse) that look as though they could have been lifted from the pages of *Peter Pan* and *Robinson Crusoe*. There's a triplet of swimming pools that tier down to the sea, plus nature trails, a yoga studio, two restaurants and spa services. US$400

★ **The Lion House** Breadnut Hill Rd, 5km south of Ocho Rios ☎917 0039, ⊛thelionhousejamaica.com; map p.130. Perched in the hills, in a stunning location 1500ft above the sea, this cosy and colourful guesthouse is run by former restaurant owners and current operators of an organic farm. It will come as no surprise, then, that meals (available on request) are sublime, served high in the sky on the spacious veranda, with views of soursop, moringa, pimento, coconut trees and the inn's own trail leading down to the gully. There's an *irie* breeze, solar hot water and ceiling fans (no a/c). Route taxis stop directly in front of the house. US$40

Little Shaw Park Guest House 21 Shaw Park Rd ☎974 2177, ⊛littleshawparkguesthouse.com; map p.130. Easy-going, family-owned place set in gardens above town. The homely rooms have cable TV, fan and private bathrooms; the studios have kitchen facilities and all have a/c. Doubles US$55, with kitchen US$65

Reggae Hostel 19 Main St ☎974 2607, ⊛reggae hostel.com; map p.130. The party vibe at the roof bar/grill is the major bonus of this hostel right in the middle of town, close to the beach. The six and eight-bed dorms are simple but clean with lockers and a/c; the doubles offer no frills but are comfortable enough, with their own bathrooms; and there's a kitchen area with microwave, fridge and tea and coffee. Dorms US$25, doubles US$60

APARTMENTS

Carib Ocho Rios Condominium Main St ☎ 974 0305; map p.130. Quiet and quaintly furnished apartments in a number of two-storey buildings overlooking attractive Mahogany Beach, with manicured gardens and access to the sea. All units have small balconies and ocean views; some have a/c and TV. US$110

Chrisann's Tower Isle ☎ 975 4467, ⓦ chrisannsbeach resort.com; map p.130. Good-value, attractive condo resort east of town. Clean, well-maintained studios and one- to three-bedroom apartments with a/c, cable TV, fully equipped kitchen and access to the pool and mini private beach. US$108

HOTELS

Couples Tower Isle St Mary ☎ 975 4271, ⓦ couples. com/resorts; map p.130. Opened as the world's first all-inclusive concept hotel in the 1950s, *Couples Tower Isle* retains a chic exclusivity from those days. Jamaican-owned, it boasts the best beach of Couples' Ocho Rios properties as well as an "au-naturel" (nudist) island just offshore, accessed by private boat. While rooms are not large they're certainly comfortable, the best with grand sea views, but you may want to spend more time in the relaxing communal areas, which include a swim-up bar, award winning spa, five restaurants and consummate fitness and watersports facilities. All-inclusive US$299

Hibiscus Lodge 83–87 Main St ☎ 974 2676, ⓦ hibiscus jamaica.com; map p.130. This very attractive hotel is set back from the road in beautiful gardens, but has sea access and a sun deck to the rear. The clean and pleasant cliffside rooms all have balconies, while the good restaurant (the attached bar has swinging seats) also boasts a fine sea view. Guest use of pool, jacuzzi, and tennis court. Rates include breakfast. US$150

★**Jamaica Inn** Main St ☎ 974 2514, ⓦ jamaicainn. com; map p.130. The most elegant and traditional hotel in Ochi has a gorgeous private beach, pool, helpful staff and one of the island's best spas, right over the ocean. Wonderfully spacious and private villas occupy half the property, all with modern fabrics and ocean view – and represent excellent value for groups of four or six. Traditional rooms have large ocean-facing verandas. No children under 10, long trousers and a collared shirt required for dinner. US$569

Kaz Kreol White River Bay ☎ 631 4548; map p.130. Straddling the boundary between St Ann and St Mary, this laudable spot is smack on the beach with rooms at the right price. Accommodations are standard motel fare, and the property could benefit from an update, but the staff is caring, continental breakfast is included and you are steps from the turquoise sea. US$65

Pineapple Court Pineapple Place ☎ 974 2727, ⓦ pineapplecourthoteljamaica.com; map p.130. Just off Main St and a short walk from the beach, rates at this budget-friendly hotel include a full breakfast, and the immaculate guestrooms are stocked with a kettle, fridge and microwave. There's a lovely swimming pool. US$75

Silver Seas 66 James Ave ☎ 974 2755, ⓦ silverseashotel. com; map p.130. Faded yet wonderfully atmospheric hotel with a peaceful ambience, despite its downtown location. Rooms are simple with colourful fabrics; all have sea views and private verandas. Large garden, pool and bar on site. US$90

EATING

There's a high standard of eating choices in Ochi, with Italian, Indian and American options vying for custom alongside Jamaican staples. Downtown places are often open from breakfast through dinner, while more established restaurants stay open until late. Jerk chicken vendors wheel out their oil-drum barbecues near the clock tower once the sun sets, the air filling with the heady smell of charcoal smoke and spicy grilled meat.

CAFÉS AND SNACKS

Devon House I-Scream Island Village; map p.130. On the beach side of the plaza, this tiny take-away shop consistently has a great range of flavours – try the Devon stout, grape nut or (surprisingly good) Red Stripe beer. Mon–Wed 10am–7pm, Thurs–Sun 10am–9pm.

Island Coffees Café Island Village ☎ 384 9578, ⓦ island coffeesltd.com; map p.130. Sip a Blue Mountain espresso (US$2) or cappuccino at one of the tables overlooking the plaza (free wi-fi), or enjoy an iced or hot coffee with rum cream, whisky or Tia Maria. Decent sandwiches and wraps (US$5) can be bought here to take to the beach. Daily 6am–9pm.

RESTAURANTS

The Almond Tree Hibiscus Lodge, 83–87 Main St ☎ 974 2813, ⓦ hibiscusjamaica.com; map p.130. A romantic and smart clifftop setting with friendly service and a great Jamaican and international gourmet menu. Superb seafood (US$20–30) is the highlight, though burgers and a couple of Jamaican favourites and pasta dishes are available (US$10–15). Daily 7.30am–10.30pm.

Calabash Ital Restaurant Boswell Plaza, 9 DaCosta Drive ☎ 570 5565; map p.130. Surprisingly sophisticated vegan restaurant, serving Ital stews, nutmeggy porridge, veggie burgers, tasty beans and lentils (US$5–8), and a good range of natural juices and soy ice cream. Mon–Sat 8.30am–10pm, Sun 10.30am–8pm.

★**Evita's** Eden Bower Rd ☎ 974 2333, ⓦ evitas jamaica.com; map p.130. For thirty years, *Evita's* has served up great pasta on a gingerbread veranda overlooking the bay. There's a large choice of starters, salads and soups; for mains, try the wonderful seafood linguine, or "Lasagne Rastafari" with ackee, callaloo and tomatoes (US$20–40). Tiramisu á la Eva is ingeniously made with rum and Tia Maria – and named after the inimitable and welcoming owner who keeps the atmosphere fun. Photos of her with numerous visiting celebrities (LL Cool J, Kofi Annan, Uma Thurman, for example) adorn one wall. Daily 11am–11pm.

The Healthy Way 54 Ocean Village Plaza ☎ 974 9229; map p.130. Smart and efficient vegetarian restaurant and take-away, offering veggie/tofu burgers and patties, porridges, soups, fresh juices, cakes and a different main dish (J$800–1200) each day. The friendly owner is a mine of information on healing juices and tonics. Mon–Sat 9am–5pm.

★ **The Lyming** A3 Rd, at Walkerswood (opposite the post office), 12km south of Ocho Rios ☎ 917 2812; map p.130. Overlooking a lush rolling valley, this in-the-country gem serves traditional, well-cooked Jamaican fare like jerk pork and chicken (J$1100), a soup of the day and bread pudding (J$350). Sunday brunch (J$2000) is a must. Mon–Thurs 11am–9pm, Fri & Sat 8am–10pm, Sun 8am–9pm.

★ **Miss Merle's Fish Joint** White River, under the Road Bridge ☎ 595 2250; map p.130. A great cool spot on a hot day, this teensy stand serves up sublime fried fish (two daily varieties, such as snapper and barracuda; J$1200). Order your meal with festival (fried dumplings) or bammy, and enjoy on rustic seats by the river. Also makes a great way to cap off a rafting trip, easily organized here. Daily 9am–6pm.

★ **Miss T's** 65 Main St ☎ 795 0099, ⓦ misstskitchen. com; map p.130. This colourful restaurant and tidy garden is an oasis of calm in the middle of Ochi (a block east of the clock tower; parking is available northwards down a tiny lane from Main St). The helpful staff serve up great oxtail (US$20) while the ackee and bammy starter is delicious, as is the curried goat. The well-stocked bar also has a good range of natural juices. Mon–Thurs noon–9pm, Fri & Sat noon–10pm.

★ **Mom's Homestyle Restaurant** 7 Evelyn St ☎ 974 2811; map p.130. With a reputation since the 1980s for serving the best food in town, it offers a pick of ackee, salt-mackerel or callaloo for breakfast (US$6), and lunch and dinner highlights such as curry goat, brown-stew pork and shrimp rundown (US$9–13). Mon–Sat 8am–10pm.

Passage to India 2 Turtle Beach Rd, Cruise Ship Pier ☎ 795 3182, ⓦ passagetoindiaja.com; map p.130. Attractively decorated restaurant right by the water that cooks up excellent Indian cuisine. The menu is comprehensive: tandoori meats, chicken jalfrezi, rogan josh and lots of seafood and vegetarian options (try the Goanese Shrimp or Lamb Madras). Lassi yoghurt drinks and desserts are also available. Mon–Fri J$800 lunch special. Daily 11am–10pm.

Reflections 2 Market Square, 2nd floor (no sign) ☎ 398 3810; map p.130. Interesting and well-spiced vegetarian food (think jerk tofu wrap with mango or a grilled veggie sandwich) served up by a Bobo Rasta who has cooked in the kitchens of some of the island's best hotels. Excellent juices (guava-pineapple, mango-carrot, June plum), too. Eat in the cheerfully painted dining room (around J$250 for juices or J$600 for lunch). It's located in a nondescript building adjacent to the fruit and veg market, and a little tricky to find – ask a local if you're stuck. Daily 10am–10pm.

Reggae Pot 86 Main St, opposite Hibiscus Lodge ☎ 890 3748; map p.130. Right on Main St, just beyond the central hustle bustle, this bright little spot serves classic Ital fare (around J$500–600 for lunch) and natural juices, eaten outdoors under the big umbrella. Daily 9am–9pm.

★ **Toscanini** Tower Isle ☎ 975 4785; map p.130. Under the eaves of pretty Harmony Hall, a ten-minute drive east of the centre, this is Ochi's best restaurant. The menu features all the Italian classics, from carpaccio to home-made pasta and meat dishes such as veal escalope with prosciutto and parmesan (US$25–45), and there are also daily specials and vegetarian options. Service is great, and the puddings are sublime. Tues–Sun noon–10pm.

DRINKING AND NIGHTLIFE

In addition to the places listed below, another possibility is an evening pass to one of the all-inclusive hotels (from US$85) such as *Couples* or *Sandals*, which includes food, drinks and entertainment. A number of restaurants (see page 137) also function as bars: *Evita's* holds occasional theme nights with dancing and regular local musicians while *Toscanini* offers a sophisticated bar ambience. Finally, James Avenue hosts several bars, usually pretty harmless and good fun, though it can be seedy and you might not want to walk it late at night.

BARS

Glenn's Restaurant and Cocktail Lounge Tower Isle ☎ 975 4360; map p.130. Friendly out-of-town restaurant serving Jamaican food plus steaks (decent but a bit overpriced), though it's the bar ambience that makes it worth the trip – great inexpensive drinks, 1970s decor, tinkly jazz as background music and occasional live performances.

Daily 8.30am–11pm.

John Crow 10 Main St ☎ 974 5895; map p.130. Decent bar with sports screens, reasonably priced cocktails, a friendly vibe and live music on cruise ship days. Also has fast food and nibbles (good jerk sausage) with tables out in the open air to watch the world go by. Daily 9am–1am.

Oceans 11 Turtle Beach Rd, Cruise Ship Pier ☎974 6896; map p.130. Right where the ships dock, this slick spot with loud dancehall attracts the cruise hordes at daytimes, and at night gets lively – karaoke on Tues and oldies on Sun, with occasional live music. Serves as a great club warm-up spot for nearby *Margaritaville* or at other times for an inexpensive beer or cocktail, with a seafood restaurant too. Daily 11am–1am.

Ocho Rios Village Jerk Centre 14 DaCosta Drive ☎974 2549; map p.130. The jerk here is reasonable (you'll get more authentic fare at *Scotchies Too* out of town; see page 149), but this place is also a popular spot for an inexpensive drink and dance, especially on weekend evenings, when it's open late into the night. It also has monthly soca/reggae parties – check hoardings for details. Daily 11am–2am (or later).

CLUBS

Amnesia 70 Main St ☎571 3572; map p.130. Located above the Mutual Security building, this is a proper nightclub with two indoor a/c dancefloors and outdoor bar area. Schedule frequently changes but presently Thursday is the busy Ladies' Night when women get in free, Saturday is party night and "Sipping Sundays" are a good time to relax. Cover J$500–1000. Daily 8pm till late.

Margaritaville Island Village ☎675 8800, ⓦmargarita villecaribbean.com; map p.130. Part daytime family-fun venue with pool and water slide, part all-hours bar, this Jamaican institution is best known for its wet 'n' wild club nights, attracting hordes of locals and tourists. Specializing in potent cocktails and other drinks promotions, there are plenty of theme nights; check flyers for a full programme. Daily 10am–10pm.

SHOPPING

Ochi's Main Street houses numerous open-air **shopping plazas** filled with duty-free shops. It's best to look for souvenirs in the craft markets themselves; start from the back, where stalls see less visitors and often have better deals. Bartering is expected – it's considered an enjoyable part of Jamaican culture. A good rule of thumb is to halve the seller's initial asking price and negotiate from there.

Craft Market Main St; map p.130. Ochi's main market has over the years enticed many a soul to leave Jamaica laden with "Yeh mon it irie" T-shirts. Yet among the dross you'll find really nice T-shirts, paintings and sculptures, and vendors have a wicked line in sales banter. This is also the best place to get the latest dancehall mix CDs alongside old favourites (around J$200 each). Daily 8am–7pm.

Harmony Hall Tower Isle ☎975 4222, ⓦharmonyhall. com; map p.130. This wonderful art gallery and shop set in a beautifully restored Great House exhibits a variety of local and national artists' work; you can buy prints by renowned contemporary Jamaican artists as well as Caribbean books. Tues–Sun 10am–5.30pm.

DIRECTORY

Doctors Dr Osmond Tomlinson 65 Main St (☎974 2610) is very reputable. Also try the Medical Care and Surgical Center at 110 Main St (☎974 9987, ⓦmedicalcareja.com).

Hospitals The nearest is at St Ann's Bay (☎972 2272), a fifteen-minute drive from Ocho Rios. In an emergency call ☎119; for a private ambulance, call AmbuCare at ☎978 2327.

Money and exchange Most of the banks are located on Main St near the craft market, with several ATMs. The best rates for exchanging money are at the cambios; there's one

near the clock tower and a number in the shopping centres.

Police The police station (☎974 2533) is on Evelyn St behind the Texaco garage that faces the clock tower; in emergencies call ☎119.

Post office Main St, opposite the main craft market (Mon–Fri 8am–5pm).

Telephones Phonecards are available all over: at the post office, gas stations, supermarkets and pharmacies. Digicel, 70 Main St, sells local network SIM cards for as little as $5.

East of Ocho Rios

East of Ocho Rios, tourism recedes and the road glides through some of the most beautiful scenery on the north coast. Following **Boscobel**, location of the region's small airport (see page 135), the main settlements are **Oracabessa** and **Port Maria** – slow, close-knit communities where tourism has taken hold in a sensitive manner, with small guesthouses and restaurants peppering the roadside. Low-key glamour has a lengthy history here, however, having long been a haunt of the rich and famous. Noël Coward and James Bond creator Ian Fleming both lived here and their old homes, **Firefly** and **Goldeneye**, have been preserved. Firefly is a modest museum with a stunning setting,

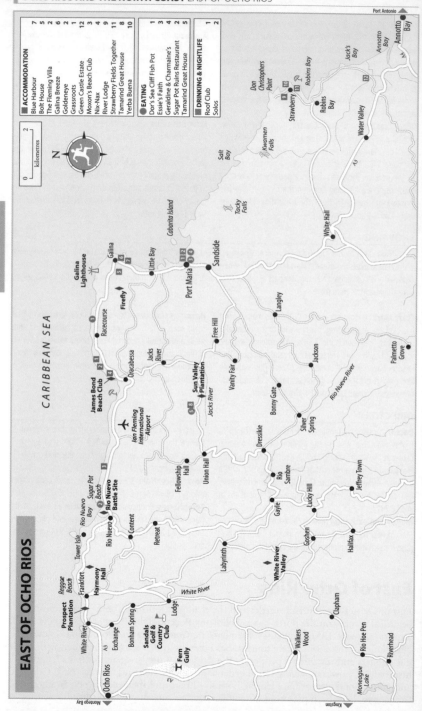

EAST OF OCHO RIOS

ACCOMMODATION

Blue Harbour	7
Bolt House	5
The Fleming Villa	2
Galina Breeze	6
Goldeneye	2
Grassroots	1
Green Castle Estate	12
Moxon's Beach Club	3
Nix-Nax	4
River Lodge	9
Strawberry Fields Together	11
Tamarind Great House	8
Yerba Buena	10

EATING

Dor's Sea Cliff Fish Pot	1
Essie's Faith	3
Geraldine & Charmaine's	4
Sugar Pot Ruins Restaurant	2
Tamarind Great House	5

DRINKING & NIGHTLIFE

Roof Club	1
Solos	2

while *Goldeneye* is the centrepiece of the most exclusive villa complex in Jamaica. Beyond Port Maria, the road swings inland and the coastline extends in an unbroken series of forested outcrops interspersed by deserted, volcanic-sand beaches and beautiful waterfalls reachable only on foot or by boat. Hiking uncovers breathtaking vistas – best undertaken from **Robins Bay**, where eco-minded accommodations offer reasonably priced guides and tours. Push further inland and you are firmly off the tourist trail, smack in the gorgeous scenery of the **St Mary interior**. Market communities like **Dressikie** and **Gayle** have numerous local swimming spots; ask around for directions if you're feeling adventurous.

Rio Nuevo Battle Site

10km east of Ocho Rios, signposted just north off the A3 Hwy • Mon, Wed & Thurs 9am–3pm • US$5 • ☎ 922 1287, ⓦ jnht.com

A new housing development has almost obscured the **Rio Nuevo Battle Site** (pronounced "No-vo"), centred around a rather nondescript (though signed) monument 150 yards from the road on the ocean side. Commemorating the final skirmish in 1658 that made Jamaica a British rather than a Spanish territory, the area was donated to the Jamaica National Heritage Trust who have created a small yet mildly interesting exhibition on the area's Taíno, Spanish, Maroon and British heritage. Despite this, few tourists visit and you're more likely to find courting couples enjoying the sea breeze under the shade of bamboo.

Follow the road down beyond the battle site (turning down opposite the police station) to find **Rio Nuevo Bay**, with shady trees and a gorgeous swath of public yellow sand that's undiscovered by developers.

Sugar Pot Beach

Rio Nuevo Bay, 12km southeast of Ocho Rios • Daylight hours • J$400 • ☎ 852 7135, ⓦ sugarpotruins.com • Take the A3, pass *Couples Resort*, follow the descending hill into Tower Isle; at the bottom, go through the Cool Oasis petrol station and bear right to the beach

Around the bend from where the Spanish lost a decisive battle to the British (see above), this enchanting beach has a stellar restaurant and bar, velvety soft sand, jewel-toned waters and only a few blissed-out souls taking advantage of it all. There's a small fee to swim, or you can skip the water in favour of rum punch with a view of the lapping waves.

EATING   SUGAR POT BEACH

★ **Sugar Pot Ruins Restaurant** Rio Nuevo Bay, through the Cool Oasis service station ☎ 852 7135; map p.140. Dreamily located on an under-the-radar beach, this relaxed bar-restaurant serves classic Jamaican fare like oxtail with mash and curried coconut fish (mains start at J$800; seafood J$1500 and up). The food is served in a breezy, tin-roofed hut, and you can jump in the water while your meal is cooking (beach access J$400). The bar has fresh piña coladas, punches and daiquiris (around J$500). Daily 9am to around 6pm(weather dependent)..

Oracabessa

Lit in the afternoons by an apricot light that must have prompted its Spanish name, *Orocabeza* ("Golden Head"), **ORACABESSA** is a delightfully sleepy little town, with friendly citizens and a mere handful of tourists visiting at any one time. Some 20 kilometres east of Ocho Rios, it is centred on a covered fruit and vegetable market (main day Friday), a police station and a few shops and bars. A hub for the export of **bananas** until the early 1900s, the wharves around the small natural harbour closed in 1969, taking with them the rum bars, gambling houses and most of the workers. It took until the mid-1990s for Oracabessa to begin to develop as a low-key resort, when the **Island Outpost** corporation (whose owner, Chris Blackwell, famously produced Bob Marley and has family connections with the area) bought up seventy acres of prime land – from Jack's River to the *Goldeneye* estate at the town's eastern outskirts. British reggae group UB40 also set up Oracabessa Records here, and artists frequently record in their studios above the town (not open to the public).

East of the petrol station, Oracabessa merges into the residential community of **Racecourse** (named after a long-gone donkey-racing track), and where gates, walls and trees mask **Goldeneye** (see page 143), the resort surrounding the unassuming white-walled bungalow designed and purpose-built by Ian Fleming, sometime military man and creator of James Bond.

James Bond Beach Club

Off Main St at the end of the Old Wharf Rd (signposted just west of Oracabessa) • Daily 9am–8pm • US$5 • ☎ 975 3665

The **James Bond Beach Club** comprises a stylish strip of sand with a collection of brightly painted changing rooms, a bar and a restaurant, yet it receives a mere handful

007'S JAMAICA

From Errol Flynn to Beyoncé, Jamaica has always attracted the rich and famous, but the island also served as inspiration for the ultimate (albeit fictional) symbol of glamour – **James Bond**. As a commander in the Naval Intelligence Division (NID) of the British army, Bond's creator, Ian Fleming, first visited Jamaica in 1943. Staying in the Blue Mountains, he was immediately taken with the island's sensual pleasures and declared that he'd be back to put down permanent roots after the war. By 1947, he'd paid £2000 for a plot of land on Jamaica's north coast that had once served as Oracabessa's racecourse, and engaged local workers to build the elegant beach house that he'd designed himself. Naming it after a bungled NID anti-German operation he'd been involved in, **Goldeneye** became his winter retreat and a source of competition with neighbour **Noël Coward**, who insisted that his Blue Harbour (see page 144) was far superior to Fleming's spartan bachelor pad.

IAN FLEMING AT GOLDENEYE

A series of magazine articles penned by Fleming on the joys of his island paradise soon lured a fashionable set to Jamaica, and Goldeneye played host to luminaries such as Sir Anthony and Lady Eden, Truman Capote, Lucian Freud, Graham Greene, Evelyn Waugh and Cecil Beaton. Cocktails by the pool and snorkelling with his "Jamaican wife" Blanche Blackwell (mother of Island Records' Chris Blackwell) soon began to take up most of Fleming's time. It wasn't until his other lover and soon-to-be wife, Lady Anne Rothermere (ex-wife of the British newspaper baron), became pregnant in 1952 that he got down to any serious writing. He cranked out **Casino Royale** on a rickety old Remington typewriter with the jalousies shut to block out the distracting sea view.

Clearly besotted with the island, Fleming exploited the Jamaica connection by taking his hero's name from the author of the classic book *Birds of the West Indies* – and many of his characters were inspired by Jamaican friends. Pussy Galore, in the *Goldfinger* novel, was said to be a tongue-in-cheek representation of Blanche Blackwell. Two novels, *Doctor No* and *The Man with the Golden Gun*, were set here (scenes for the movie versions were filmed in Kingston and Westmoreland respectively), and the island served as the fictional San Monique in *Live and Let Die*. And of course 007 wouldn't have dreamed of drinking any other coffee than his favourite Blue Mountain brew. Fleming later wrote "Would these books have been born if I had not been living in the gorgeous vacuum of a Jamaican holiday? I doubt it."

BOND ON FILM

Fleming returned to Goldeneye each January to spend two months writing, but the years of hard drinking and partying began to take their toll and by the late 1950s his health had seriously deteriorated. Fleming survived long enough to supervise Cubby Broccoli's movie version of *Dr No*, filmed in Jamaica with Chris Blackwell as location manager. In the first few months of 1964, Fleming returned to Goldeneye and wrote his last 007 novel, *The Man with the Golden Gun*, infusing the pages with a strong sense of nostalgia for Jamaica. Though his Bond novels had by then sold some forty million copies, Ian Fleming died (on August 12, 1964) without ever really knowing what a sensation he had created. Four months after his death, the release of the movie version of *Goldfinger* signified the beginning of worldwide Bond mania.

of visitors during the week. Locals do venture down at weekends, however, and the expansive oceanfront lawns, often used to stage large-scale concerts such as Boxing Day's **Teen-Splash**, make a wonderfully breezy outdoor venue. For most people though, snorkelling to see the stingrays that live in the waters surrounding the beach, or a glass-bottom-boat tour around the reef (revitalized as a result of the Oracabessa Foundation's fish sanctuary, see ⓦoracabessafoundation.org) are the order of the day. The small adjacent **Fisherman's Beach** is an equally appealing place to swim, and there are shacks on the sand selling seafood meals and drinks.

Sun Valley Plantation

3km from Jacks River • Daily except Sat 9.30am–2pm; best to call ahead for scheduling • US$15 • ☏ 995 3075, ✉ sunvalleyjamaica@ gmail.com • To get here, turn onto the inland road at the far western end of Oracabessa, through the village of Jacks River, from where signposts lead you another 3km to the gate

One of the north coast's most attractive plantations, **Sun Valley** offers one of the best tours of its kind in Jamaica, with plenty of insight into the development of crops on the island, linking ecology to plantation politics and agricultural exports and providing lots of room for questions and personal attention. The fascinating growth processes of bananas, coconuts, and sugar are explained, and the tour, which takes in trees and flowers, as well as the crops themselves, finishes with drinks, a light meal and fruit tasting.

ARRIVAL AND DEPARTURE | ORACABESSA

By minibus and route taxi During daylight hours, minibuses and route taxis frequently ply the route between Oracabessa and Ocho Rios (J$200); less frequency at night and on Sundays.

ACCOMMODATION

The Fleming Villa Main Rd, Racecourse ☏ 622 9007, ⓦ theflemingvilla.com; map p.140. Ian Fleming's beautifully restored Jamaican home and two satellite cottages are available as a villa rental sleeping up to twelve with full staff on hand, and offering maximum seclusion with access to the private beach where Fleming cooled his toes. Fleming wrote almost all the 007 novels within these walls, and for inspiration designed the windows to frame the sea view like large pictures. His desk still sits in the corner – and the chic decor combines tradition and modern touches. Use of all *Goldeneye*'s facilities included. **US$10,000**

★ **Goldeneye** Main Rd, Racecourse ☏ 622 9007, ⓦ goldeneye.com; map p.140. Centred around Ian Fleming's villa retreat (see page 142), this is Jamaica's most exclusive hotel and a regular haunt of the rich and famous. The one- and two-bedroom villas are indescribably inviting, with peerless attention to detail, outdoor bathrooms and every amenity. Disconnect by swimming or kayaking across the serene lagoon to the simple but sophisticated spa, or enjoy a matchless breakfast at the open-air counter-culture *Bizot Bar* while gazing at the white powder beach and infinity pool. Staff exude laidback Jamaica while understanding all the little details, imitating the rhythms that parent Island Records (see page 285) propelled with immense success worldwide. **US$1100**

★ **Grassroots** Main Rd, Racecourse ☏ 566 8997; map p.140. Two bright studios next to Goldeneye, each with kitchen and bathroom; one situated in a charming little cottage that's blessed with both an indoor and outdoor shower, the other a second-floor property with skylight, high ceilings and a veranda fringed in foliage. Owned by artist Rani Carson, a Rasta from New York, meals are available upon request and the home is a ten-minute stroll to the local beach. **US$40**

Moxon's Beach Club Main Rd, Boscobel, 7km west of Oracabessa ☏ 975 7023, ⓦ jfactoratmoxons.com; map p.140. Situated between Oracabessa and Ochi, this hip hotel offers good-value luxury and has a reef offshore. The original owner was Timothy Moxon who played Strangeways in *Dr No*, and the hotel had a long list of celebrity patrons in the 1960s. Today, the gorgeous restaurant/bar is right over the ocean and the rooms are painted in deep yet tasteful colours; some have attractive verandas. **US$185**

Nix-Nax Off Main St ☏ 975 3364; map p.140. A friendly, if very basic, guesthouse run by long-time resident Domenica. *Nix-Nax* is a local institution with clean dorms and rooms above a school, attracting backpackers and volunteer parties. There's a communal kitchen, the walls are adorned with consciousness-raising adages, and alternative therapies are available. Per person **J$2000**

★ **Tamarind Great House** Crescent Estate (near Jacks River), 8km south of Oracabessa ☏ 995 3252, ⓦ tamarindgreathouse.com; map p.140. The sumptuous but unpretentious home of this welcoming English family boasts ten spacious and good-value guest rooms, all with

3

four-poster beds. There's a pool, as well as beautiful views of the surrounding orchards and valley below. Sailing and snorkelling trips are available, as are gourmet meals, including a full English breakfast. U$$105

EATING

Dor's Sea Cliff Fish Pot Main Rd, Racecourse ☎ 508 9670; map p.140. Stop at this jovial, circular bar perched atop a cliff at the eastern end of Racecourse, which serves superlative fresh fish, lobster, shrimp (J$1000–2000) and conch soup (J$250), plus fried chicken with wedges (J$500). Daily 8am–10pm.

★ **Tamarind Great House** Crescent Estate (near Jacks River), 6km south of Oracabessa ☎ 995 3252; map p.140. Host Gillian Chambers cooks up delicious three-course meals (around US$30), served on the *Great House*'s elegant veranda. You'll need to book in advance and take a charter taxi from Oracabessa if you don't have your own transport. Open daily by reservation only.

Firefly

20km east of Ocho Rios on the Main Road (A3), Port Maria • Mon–Thurs & Sat 9am–5pm • Guided tour US$10 • ☎ 725 0920, ⓦ firefly-jamaica.com

Jamaica's most northerly tip, five kilometres east of Oracabessa at the Galina Lighthouse, marks your arrival in playwright Noël Coward's country. It was while at his former beach house, **Blue Harbour** (now a superb if quirky guesthouse; see page 146) that Coward stumbled upon the historical site that was to become **Firefly**, perched on the hilltop high above. He bought the land from the brother of Blanche Blackwell (see page 142) for £150, and from its construction in 1956 until the playwright's death in 1973, Firefly was the Jamaican home of both Coward and his partner, actor Graham Payn. Now it remains the area's only organized attraction.

The house was built on the site of a former **Taíno settlement** – with artefacts found both here and across the hillside – before later becoming the stamping ground of pirate extraordinaire Sir Henry Morgan (see page 80), who used it as a vantage point during his reign as governor; slits in the wall of the bar, carved to hold guns, recall buccaneer days. Acquired by Island Outpost in 1992 (this arrangement is under review at the time of writing, with the museum's future uncertain), the house remains much as Coward left it: his studio with a painting on the easel; the drawing room – where illustrious guests from Sophia Loren to Audrey Hepburn and Joan Sutherland were entertained – complete with polished piano; kitchen cupboards full of yellowing bottles; and the table freshly laid as it was on the day the Queen Mother came to lunch in 1965. Coward died here and is buried on the property. A statue of him by UK-based artist Angela Conner overlooks his favourite view. Even if you're not a Coward fan, it's worth coming up to Firefly for the panorama alone; possibly the best on the island, taking in Port Maria bay and Cabarita Island, with the peaks of the Blue Mountains poking through the clouds.

Port Maria

A series of twisting outcrops protecting a natural harbour mark your arrival in the diminutive capital of St Mary, **PORT MARIA**. As you round the last bend, a stunning view of tiny and forested **Cabarita Island** is revealed, right in the middle of the bay and well known for its variety of bird species. Once one of Jamaica's most picturesque towns – nestled around a crescent bay with lots of cut-stone and faded gingerbread fretwork alluding to more auspicious times – it's now rather a scruffy place with little to keep you. West of the centre and marked by two sizeable royal palms at its gates is the quaint cut-stone **St Mary Parish Church**, dating back to 1861, with the weathered gravestones of its cemetery extending down to the sea. Nearby, in the middle of the playing field, is a monument to freedom fighter **Tacky** (see page 146), while the covered "ben-dung" fruit **market** (main day Friday) – so called as you must literally

3

> ## THE TACKY REBELLION
>
> In the late eighteenth century, Port Maria saw one of Jamaica's bloodiest rebellions against slavery, an uprising that sowed the seeds for emancipation eighty years later. Led by an escaped slave known as **Tacky** (a European spelling of the Ghanaian name Tekyi, meaning "the great"), who was said to have been a chief of Akan descent, the rebellion sparked violent protests throughout the island, and sought the creation of an all-black colony. The revolt began on Easter Sunday 1760, when Tacky and a small group of slaves from local estates murdered their overseers and marched to Port Maria, killing the storekeeper at Fort Haldane and seizing arms and ammunition. Five months of fighting ensued, with £100,000 worth of damage to nearby plantations. However, the thousand-strong slave army could not compete with British military force, which utilized the **Maroons** (duty-bound by the parties' 1739 treaty) in guerrilla warfare. The rebellion was savagely quashed and severe punishments meted out: Tacky was captured by Maroon marksmen and killed, his head cut off and displayed on a pole in Spanish Town; others were chained to stakes and burned alive, gibbeted or hung by irons, as an example to others contemplating sedition. It's said, however, that in one last defiant gesture, Tacky's sympathizers removed his body under cover of night and gave him a proper burial. After Tacky's death, many of his followers committed suicide rather than live enslaved. Three hundred Africans died fighting, with fifty more captured and executed. Only sixty whites lost their lives.

"bend down" to get items spread out over the ground – is a maze of dingy paths winding through piles of yams, bananas and assorted local produce.

A bridge crossing the murky Ochom River brings you into the centre of Port Maria, where the streets of yellow stone and timber are laid out in a rough grid. At the eastern end of town is Pagee Beach, where you can arrange a combined fishing trip and visit to Cabarita Island (approx US$25/person). Boats are moored at one end of the greyish sand, which, although strewn with sea grass, extends in a long picturesque sweep backed by palms. If you're here in early August come along to the annual **Fisherman's Regatta**, held on the first Wednesday after Independence Day, which showcases a fishing competition as well as lining up all the local sound systems along the town's streets.

ARRIVAL AND DEPARTURE   PORT MARIA

By minibus and route taxi During daylight hours, minibuses and route taxis frequently ply the route from Port Maria to Oracabessa (J$120), Ocho Rios and Annotto Bay; less frequency at night and on Sundays.

ACCOMMODATION

A number of hotels and guesthouses lie just north of Port Maria, and there's a nice variety among them – everything from small hotels to guesthouses with history.

Blue Harbour Castle Garden, 3km north of Port Maria ☎ 725 0289 or ☎ 575 586 1244 in the US, ⓦ blueharb.com; map p.140. Built in the 1950s by playwright Noël Coward to house his guests (including Marlene Dietrich and Katharine Hepburn), the main house – with a veranda on two sides – as well as the three villas (4–12 beds) In a vertiginous flowery garden, all have astonishing sea views and may be rented as a whole or room-by-room. The owner has done an excellent job of preserving the original colonial property, and yet the atmosphere is whole-heartedly Jamaican, with friendly, laidback and helpful staff. There's a saltwater pool, a tiny beach and plenty of seclusion. The full-board option is a good deal at US$120 per person (two-night minimum); without meals, it's US$50 per person. **US$120**

Bolt House Galina, 5km north of Port Maria ☎ 486 8092, ⓦ bolthousejamaica.com; map p.140. Gorgeous villa built by Blanche Blackwell (mother of Island Records impresario Chris) on a bluff below Firefly, which affords similarly stunning views of Port Maria bay. Beautifully furnished and boasting walls hung with contemporary art, the villa epitomizes classy, secluded luxury, with two bedrooms, dining and living rooms and a lovely pool, all set in landscaped gardens. Rates are for up to four people, including day passes to *Goldeneye*. **US$2400**

Galina Breeze 5km north of Port Maria ☎ 994 0537, ⓦ galinabreeze.com; map p.140. Tempting little hotel with a stunning perch right over the sea. Rooms are decked out in cheerful tropical shades, and there's a salt-water swimming pool, restaurant, jerk centre and a staff that goes above and beyond. **US$100**

EATING

Port Maria has plenty of small, salt-of-the-earth restaurants serving tasty Jamaican food. There are some great eats; just don't expect anything fancy, however: it's mainly food stands and shops.

Essie's Faith 10 Main St ☎ 994 2352; map p.140. Tasty Jamaican food (J$400–900) is served at this joint in the town square next to Courts department store. For decades, the restaurant was run by Miss Essie herself, who held the reins here until well into her eighties. Essie passed in 2016, but her restaurant continues as a landmark of the area. Daily 7am–midnight.

Geraldine's & Charmaine's 48 Warner St ☎ 507 1222; map p.140. A brightly striped exterior welcomes you into this family-run restaurant with natural juices and sublime Jamaican cooking. Breakfast sees the likes of callaloo and saltfish, while lunch and dinner have fried chicken, oxtail and curry goat (J$300–900). Very local spot. Daily 7am–10.30pm.

DRINKING AND NIGHTLIFE

Roof Club 10 Main St; map p.140. Above *Essie's* is the open-air *Roof Club*, the only late-opening bar in town, which has dancing and a local scene and gets going late at weekends. Wed–Sun 8pm–2am.

Solos Pagee Beach; map p.140. A long-standing no-frills bar situated at the east end of town, with the freshest cooked-to-order fish around (J$600–1200). It also hosts dancehall nights most weekends. Daily noon–11pm (or later).

3

Robins Bay

A series of small villages and estates around 23km from Port Maria, **ROBINS BAY** is the ideal place to explore the stunning section of coastline between Port Maria and Annotto Bay, the last part of the north coast without development. Tourism here is based largely around the tranquil Rasta-oriented community of **Strawberry**, named after the *Strawberry Fields* campsite popular with American hippies in the 1970s, whose free-love shenanigans drew sighs of consternation from local people. An earlier claim to fame is that the campsite's pretty white-sand cove was where Spanish governor, Don Christobal Arnaldo de Yssasi, fled the island in 1657 as the British closed in.

Signposts for *Robins Bay* and *Strawberry Fields Together* indicate the turning from the main road, and the road meanders along a craggy section of coastline past the hotel, working plantation and orchid houses of Green Castle Estate (a left turn after a kilometre). A right turn at the signed crossroads in the village beyond leads you past the incongruous concrete of *Robins Bay Village Resort* and down into Strawberry. The community itself, perennially laidback, just has a couple of basic, quiet, friendly bars that offer Jamaican food, and you can look out for local fine artist/sculptor Busha, who has some of the most detailed wood carvings to be found anywhere in Jamaica (ask for directions).

OUTDOOR ACTIVITIES AT ROBINS BAY

East of Port Maria the road swings inland, allowing the coastline to remain undeveloped, with disused plantations, long-gone villages and a plethora of fruit trees growing wild. A hiker's paradise, there are scores of attractive black-sand beaches and deserted **waterfalls** to explore – notably **Kwamen Falls**, a twenty-foot drop into a deep blue lagoon, and **Tacky Falls**, better accessed by boat but equally impressive. The staff at the listed accommodation (see page 148) can set up guides and tours along the coastline from Robins Bay, whether on foot or by boat (US$25–100). More leisurely pursuits include fishing trips, with river gorge hiking, natural whirlpool massage and rock climbing. Day passes to *Strawberry Fields Together*, including the cove, cost J$800, which covers access to showers as well as volleyball, table tennis and the use of a barbecue and wood-burning pizza oven. A short hike upstream directly from the River Lodge property passes a series of impressive rock pools and cliffs, eventually opening out into a clearing with bamboo towering overhead.

By chartered taxi There's no public transport to Robins Bay, so you'll need to charter a taxi. From Port Maria, it will cost around US$50.

ACCOMMODATION

Green Castle Estate Robins Bay ☎ 881 6279, ⓦ gc jamaica.com; map p.140. Supremely relaxed and secluded, the rooms in the main house here are smart and comfortable, with use of a pool, but the highlight are the views of the 1650-acre plantation all the way down to the sea. A cook prepares satisfying meals following a day's hiking or birdwatching – ideal here given the estate's wide variety of fruits and flowers – or touring the 300-year old plantation to see the orchid houses or coconut oil factory. US$180

River Lodge Robins Bay ☎ 995 3003, ⓦ river-lodge. com; map p.140. A restful, alluring complex built around the restored ruins of a Spanish fort. Rooms make full use of the remaining stone walls, and offer attractively minimal decor with shared or private bathrooms. In rainy season, you can swim in the river running through the property; the beach is a short walk away. A thatched restaurant/bar serves plentiful fresh fish, and the yoga deck is surrounded by lush forest. Breakfast included. US$60

Strawberry Fields Together Robins Bay ☎ 337 6127, ⓦ strawberryfieldstogether.com; map p.140. This breezy complex has its own stunning cove and a collection of cottages and villas offering varying levels of luxury. Some offer a kitchenette, and one comes with a raised jacuzzi, a breakfast bar over the sea and a natural wood interior. Volunteer groups are particularly welcome, and good food (including vegetarian) is served – try the sweet plantain porridge. All-inclusive eco-adventure packages available. Breakfast included. Cottages US$90, villas US$260

Yerba Buena Robins Bay ☎ 318 7855, ⓦ yerbabuena farmjamaica.com; map p.140. Run by an international Rasta family, this beautiful property has three rustic, comfortable cabins, which dot the shoreline beside a magnificent beach. The owners double as beekeepers and farmers, and the grounds are a veritable Garden of Eden – avocado, cashew, ackee, mango and guava are among some of the many plants. You can sign up to learn about beekeeping and essential oils. US$60

West of Ocho Rios

West of Ochi, the coast road sees plenty of tourist traffic, though the invasiveness of large-scale development is generally restricted on the beachside – such as at the established resort neighbours of **Runaway Bay** and **Discovery Bay**. Elsewhere, low-key guesthouses and boutique hotels can be sought out. With its thriving market and Georgian architecture interspersed with weather-beaten clapboard houses, **St Ann's Bay** is the small, unpretentious capital of St Ann, while the ruined Spanish capital of **Seville** is just a few minutes away. Further west, the boundary of St Ann and Trelawny parishes marks a distinct change in the landscape, from languid hills to rugged hillocks. Undeveloped yet energetic interior communities like **Brown's Town** and **Alexandria** perch on the fringes of Cockpit Country (see page 189), close to the stunning cross-country B3 route to Mandeville (see page 250). Inland, **Bob Marley's Mausoleum** remains the major attraction.

Mammee Bay

If you're a James Bond fan, you'll be interested to know that six kilometres west of Ochi, behind the Roaring River generating station (also known as Laughing Waters), is the private beach where Ursula Andress emerged from the sea as Honey Ryder in *Dr No*. Otherwise, the area is urbanizing fast and is now dominated by the 846-room *ClubHotel Riu Ocho Rios* at **MAMMEE BAY**, a kilometre beyond. On an attractive spit of white sand named after the Mammee apple trees that grew here, the Benidorm-style all-inclusive has broken the peace somewhat. Nonetheless the beach is still gorgeous, especially further down from the resort. If you want to visit, either walk from Roaring River or enter via the Mammee Bay Estate, a villa development whose gates are right next to the Hotel Riu entrance. Tell gate security that you'd like to visit the restaurant and they'll let you drive down and park right by the sand (and use the toilet and shower facilities).

St Ann's Bay

Attractive **ST ANN'S BAY** stretches up the hillside entirely inland from the coast road. Characterized by its porticoed shop-fronts, sloping streets and old-fashioned atmosphere, it's small enough to cover on foot in an hour, with two central thoroughfares, Bravo and Main streets, meeting in a crossroads. The Main Street shops and **market** hog the action, and dominating from the top of the street is the town's distinctive 1860 **courthouse** (observation gallery open to the public). In the middle of a nearby roundabout, Christopher Columbus strikes a noble pose above sunken ships, and just before the road forks, the pretty Catholic church of **Our Lady of Perpetual Help** is constructed of stone reclaimed from an earlier structure – Peter the Martyr Church, the first stone church in Jamaica, built in 1524 by the Spanish in nearby Sevilla la Nueva (see page 151). The quieter left fork of Main Street holds the **library** (Mon–Fri 9.30am–5.30pm, Sat 9.30am–3pm; ☎972 2660), with its **Marcus Garvey memorial statue** out front proclaiming the words "We Declare to the World – Africa Must Be Free". The house where he was born is a private residence, but a parade in his honour takes place every August 17, and the library itself is a good source of information on Garvey's life (see page 150).

Windsor Mineral Spring

At the far eastern end of town, by a rough track beyond the Windsor Girls' Home • Donation of J$1000 expected

The small yet remarkable **Windsor mineral spring** (known as "Fire Hole") is strangely understated. Looked after by a couple of local guys, the muddy hole bubbles with sulphur gas and can be lit to impressive effect, with flames dancing across the water. Reggae artists have used the site in music videos, but visitors are few and far between save from an occasional tour group.

ARRIVAL AND DEPARTURE

ST ANN'S BAY

By minibus and route taxi Minibuses and route taxis run frequently to St Ann's Bay from Ocho Rios (J$150). Intercity services between Montego Bay and Ocho Rios will stop on request on the main A1 road, a kilometre from St Ann's Bay's centre.

ACTIVITIES

Roxborough Beach Spa Off the A1, near the Cool Oasis service station ☎334 7469. Heavenly beachside massage parlour where you can get your nails painted listening to the Caribbean Sea. Manicure JMD$700, pedicure JMD$1500, full-body massages JMD$4000 and up. Appointments recommended. Mon–Sat 10am–6pm.

ACCOMMODATION AND EATING

Staying in St Ann's Bay has its advantages, especially if you have your own vehicle; you escape the bustle of Ochi while being close enough to enjoy its good points, as well as take in the inland sights and scenery. For eating (beyond what's below), the usual selection of patty- and cookshops lines Main St.

★ **Anglers** Windsor Rd ☎794 8449. Signed from the main highway, this smart, breezy and enduringly popular restaurant serves excellent seafood – try the escovitched fish (J$900–2700), fish tea or "crack conch" (J$1000) – marinated, deep-fried pieces of tender meat so-named because, like the drug, they keep you going back. Friday evenings are busy around the bar with a DJ and sound-system. Free wi-fi. Daily noon–2am.

★ **Scotchies Too** Drax Hall, 1km east of St Ann's Bay ☎953 8041. Extending its winning Montego Bay formula (see page 176), this order-at-the-counter restaurant serves traditional and good-quality jerk chicken, pork and sausage (J$500–1100) in attractive gardens. The well-stocked bar here is also a good place to stop and banter with the locals. Mon–Sat 11am–11pm.

TeresinaJamaica Top Rd, Sussex Estate ☎594 7020, ⊕teresinajamaica.com. This well-presented three-bedroom chalet has views over the hills. The rooms boast wooden floors, private bathrooms, ceiling fans and small verandas, and great Jamaican food is served by housekeeper Miss Ruth. Includes breakfast. **US$89**

3

3

MARCUS GARVEY

Born at 32 Market St in St Ann's Bay in August 1887, the **Right Excellent Marcus Mosiah Garvey** was one of the most powerful black rights activists of the twentieth century. His outspoken denunciations of colonialism and racism and his concrete efforts to unite and empower the African diaspora influenced politicians, musicians and academics alike. Rastafarians call him a **prophet**, and his philosophies form the basis of their faith (see page 279).

EARLY YEARS

Reputedly of Maroon descent, Garvey was the son of a master stonemason with an uncompromising attitude, who pursued multiple lawsuits against those who had slighted him on racial grounds. Though lack of funds ended the young Garvey's formal schooling at fourteen, he continued to study privately and spent long hours in his father's library. Prodigious from an early age, Garvey was made foreman of his uncle's printery at eighteen. But small-town living offered scant opportunities, and in 1906 he moved to Kingston and found work as a printery foreman – a significant coup when supervisors were usually white. As an activist in the fledgling trade union movement, Garvey was disturbed at the injustice meted out to black workers, and he left in search of better prospects in Costa Rica. There, he worked on a banana plantation and set up workers' newspapers to publicize the deplorable conditions for West Indian migrants. During a stint in England in 1912, he read up on black nationalists at Birkbeck College, and Booker T. Washington's seminal text *Up From Slavery* informed Garvey's increasing militancy.

THE UNIVERSAL NEGRO IMPROVEMENT ASSOCIATION

In 1914, Garvey returned to Jamaica and formed the **Universal Negro Improvement Association** (UNIA) "to champion Negro nationhood by redemption of Africa; to make the Negro race conscious, to advocate self-determination, to inspire and instil racial love and self-respect". But Jamaica's middle classes weren't ready for such radicalism, and Garvey immigrated to the US in 1916 to seek a more sympathetic audience. Black Americans identified so strongly with him that by 1920 the UNIA had become the largest black pressure group ever to exist in the US, with a membership of millions. Though outlawed in most of the colonies, Garvey's self-published *Negro World* achieved the largest circulation of any black newspaper in the world. With the financial backing of thousands who bought shares, Garvey formed the **Black Star Line** Shipping Company to foster trade links between black nations and enable repatriation to the African homeland.

ACTIVISM AND THE BLACK STAR LINE

Though known principally as a "Back-To-Africa" advocate, Garvey was equally concerned with improving the situation of blacks wherever they found themselves. He assaulted post-colonial nihilism, countered feelings of inferiority and powerlessness fostered during enslavement, and advocated black pride by emphasizing the historical achievements of Africans: "Up you mighty race, you can accomplish what you will". Garvey was seen as subversive by white America, and his supporters saw his 1922 two-year imprisonment on a trumped-up mail-fraud charge as an attempt to muzzle the message. Pressure from UNIA members secured his release, but in 1927 he was deported back to Jamaica on a wave of publicity. A loss of momentum ensured that the Black Star Line foundered, and Garvey never recaptured his early success. Tiring of constant battles with authority, he moved the struggle to the UK, where he died in obscurity in 1940. His importance was only recognized posthumously – in 1964 his remains were returned to Jamaica and interred in Kingston's National Heroes Park. In the 1970s, reggae music inspired a resurgence of Garveyism in Jamaica, with Rastafarian musicians like Burning Spear immortalizing his life and work. Today, Marcus Garvey's ideas remain central to the Jamaican national consciousness.

Priory

The village of **PRIORY**, just under two kilometres west of St Ann's Bay, is a favoured selling spot of jerk vendors (also keep an eye out for insanely good sweet potato pudding) and home to an appealingly deserted, clear water public beach. Though unremarkable today, it's built close to a former Taíno settlement and a sixteenth-century Spanish village at Sevilla la Nueva (just to the east) – while the **Seville Great**

House and Heritage Park is one of the island's true heritage sites. Priory offers a couple of accommodations, ideally located to attend the three annual festivals that take place west of town at Grizzly's Plantation Cove: the stellar Rebel Salute reggae festival in January; **Jamaica Epicurean Escape**, a culinary festival held in May; and the **St Ann Carnival**, in April.

Seville Great House and Heritage Park

Turn inland from main A3 Road, 2km southeast of Priory and 4km west of St Ann's Bay • Daily 9am–4pm • Free • ☎ 972 2191, ⓦ jnht.com

Occupying a former sugar plantation, Taíno village and Spanish settlement, the **Seville Great House and Heritage Park** is an interesting diversion. Refurbished with the help of the Spanish-Jamaican Foundation (ⓦ spanishjamaicanfoundation.org) – which channels funding from Spanish-owned hotels – the museum that takes up the larger part of the Great House celebrates the birth of the nation from its three separate origins; Taínos, Africans and Europeans. The displays include numerous artefacts such as Taíno *zemis* (talismans to ward off evil spirits), as well as describing the customs and cultures of each group. Outside, replica Taíno and African huts provide an idea of what the early settlements looked like. The wide lawns at the front of the property also serve as the venue for the Easter Monday **kite festival**, attracting flyers from all over the world and thousands of spectators, a lively **Emancipation Jubilee** festival (31 July & 1 Aug), as well as a mid-October **Heritage Expo**, with cultural performances from groups nationwide.

Sevilla la Nueva

Main A3 Road, 1.5km east of Priory and 3km west of St Ann's Bay • Visits via Hooves horse rides (2hr; US$70) • ☎ 972 0905, ⓦ hooves-jamaica.com

Hidden in cattle pastures and woods on the beach side of the highway (marked by a commemoration plaque), the ruins of the old village of **Sevilla la Nueva** – Jamaica's first Spanish settlement – are now dotted with crumbling remains: a waterwheel, parts of Peter the Martyr Church, a sugar mill, the 1509 castle-home of the first Spanish governor, a Taíno village and slave settlement. The only way to see Sevilla la Nueva is on an excellent **horse ride**, courtesy of Hooves, which meanders from the great house to the ruins, finishing up at the sea, where you can ride your mount into the water.

CHRISTOPHER COLUMBUS AND THE TAÍNOS AT SEVILLE

The north coast, specifically St Ann's Bay, was where **Christopher Columbus** first sighted Jamaica. Sailing in during his second voyage in 1494 to claim new territories for King Ferdinand and Queen Isabella of Spain, the conquistador was so impressed that he named the bay area **Santa Gloria**. He was rather less enamoured during his fourth and final voyage in 1503, when his unseaworthy caravels forced his crew to spend an unhappy year marooned here, awaiting rescue from compatriots in Hispaniola. Plagued by illness and worried by a partial mutiny, Columbus used bribery and superstition to coerce indigenous Taínos into providing his sailors with food.

Columbus died in Spain in 1506, but his son **Diego** was appointed Governor of the Indies. He directed **Juan de Esquivel** to establish the first Spanish colony on the island, **Sevilla la Nueva**, in 1510. Situated on the site of the Taíno village of **Maima**, during the course of just fifty years, Sevilla la Nueva all but eradicated Jamaica's Amerindian population. The *encomienda* system of serf labour – the antithesis of the unfettered Taíno lifestyle – was brutally enforced, and *caciques* (Taíno chiefs) selectively murdered. With their society in tatters and forms of authority destroyed, the Taínos were enslaved. Alongside Africans, transported to the island by the Spanish for the purpose, Taínos were conscripted to build the new city. The Amerindians were unable to bear a life of slavery; ill treatment and, particularly, European diseases, eradicated those who didn't commit suicide. But while the Taínos expired, New Seville rapidly developed into a sizeable town, with churches, irrigation and a wharf. Its occupation lasted only until 1534, however, when the marshy, disease-inducing environment was abandoned in favour of Villa de la Vega, or Spanish Town.

STUSH IN THE BUSH

Brainchild of Lisa and Chris Binns, **Stush in the Bush** (Zionites Farm, Freehill, St Ann; ☎ 562 9760, ⓦ stushinthebush.com; US$70 with a fresh pizza dinner or US$95 with full vegetarian spread; reservations necessary) is an innovative **organic farm-to-table tour** with as much focus on fine ingredients and flavoursome food as on ecological sustainability. Rustic bush and high-end stush (poshness) collide here, with their gorgeous self-built and off-grid cabin also the focus for a product line in tasty chutneys, herb marinades and deluxe cooking sauces made from home-grown ingredients. The tour takes in education on farming methods and food quality alongside tasting a variety of unusual fruits and vegetables. You can pick your own micro-greens to cover delicious thin-crust pizza made outdoors in front of you (think plantains, peppers and fresh pesto), or opt for a fuller vegetarian spread, eaten for lunch or by evening torchlight, all washed down with stushy sorrel squash or lemongrass iced tea.

ARRIVAL AND DEPARTURE   PRIORY

By minibus and route taxi All intercity services between Montego Bay and Ocho Rios will stop on request on the main A1 road at Priory. Local route taxi services from St Ann's Bay and Runaway Bay also serve Priory.

ACTIVITIES

Horseriding Chukka Cove Adventure Tours (☎ 972 2506, ⓦ chukka.com) offer a number of excursions from their prestigious equestrian facility and polo ground 1.5km west of Priory. Trips include a fabulous 2hr beach horse ride, swimming your snorting mount below barren volcanic cliffs, used as a backdrop for scenes from the cinematic epic *Papillon* (US$79), and an ATV/quad-bike tour through forest and along a river bed (US$115); hotel transport and drinks are included.

ACCOMMODATION

Circle B Farm Signed 2.5km inland from Priory ☎ 913 4511. Turn inland at the western end of the village to find this budget dormitory/guesthouse, a friendly option on a working farm with communal kitchen. Camping is also available. Pitches U̲S̲$̲1̲5̲, dorms U̲S̲$̲2̲5̲, doubles U̲S̲$̲5̲0̲

Cranbrook Flower Forest

3km west of Priory • Daily 9am–5pm • US$10 • ☎ 891 1101

Cranbrook Flower Forest is an exquisitely landscaped, 130-acre nature park with grassy lawns, tilapia fishing pond, resident peacocks and a swift-running river with marvellous swimming pools for adults and splashing children alike. No boomboxes or vendors are allowed, and it's the perfect place for a picnic or barbecue in the purpose-built gazebos. Beyond the pond and lawns, pathways overhung with tropical flowers, tree ferns, orchids, philodendrons and sheaves of giant bamboo run parallel to the riverbank. Strategically placed steps lead down to the deeper pools, but for the best swimming you'll need to walk a kilometre to the **riverhead**, a gorgeous 20ft-wide pool where the river gushes up from the rocks. Surrounded by lush greenery, the turquoise water is cool and refreshing.

Runaway Bay

The mini-resort of **RUNAWAY BAY** basks in isolated indolence halfway along the north coast, with little in the way of either natural beauty or manufactured attractions. Theories abound as to the **naming** of the bay; while it's assumed that "runaways" were Spanish troops fleeing the British in the seventeenth century, it more likely refers to Africans who made the risky 145-kilometre canoe trip to Cuba and freedom.

Runaway Bay is a lackadaisical melee of no-frills rum joints and commercial centres running along a five-kilometre strip from the satellite community of **SALEM** to the east, where you'll find the majority of shops and restaurants, to the main "square", marked by a post office and the road to Brown's Town inland. **All-inclusive hotels**, which have fenced in the best stretches of beach, are spread throughout, but as all holiday business takes place inside them the town itself is pretty somnolent. For swimming, sugary-sanded if narrow **Flavours beach**, opposite the Rubis petrol station, is popular with locals (and has occasional sound systems on Sundays), and the **fisherman's beach** at Salem is less pristine but full of atmosphere. Even better is to jump in a route taxi to lovely Puerto Seco beach in Discovery Bay.

ARRIVAL AND DEPARTURE
RUNAWAY BAY

Minibuses and route taxis Minibuses and route taxis from Montego Bay and Ocho Rios arrive and depart from points all along the main road through Runaway Bay. Route taxis to Brown's Town depart from the junction of the main road with the B3.

By car Car rental is available from Salem Car Rental (Main St, Salem; ☎ 973 4167, ⊛ salemcarrentals.com.jm).

ACTIVITIES

Diving and snorkelling Runaway Bay is well-blessed with good snorkelling and dive sites, including sunken ganja planes. Local operator Resort Divers (Sharkies Beach, Salem; ☎ 881 5760, ⊛ resortdivers.com) offers trips to all local reefs and sites, as do operators based further afield like Jamaica Scuba Divers (☎ 381 1113, ⊛ scuba-jamaica.com).

ACCOMMODATION

There are many luxury villas, which can be cost-effective for large groups – contact JAVA (☎ 974 2508, ⊛ javavillas.org).

The Cardiff Hotel & Spa Rickets Drive, Cardiff Hall ☎ 973 6671, ⊛ thecardiffhotel.com. Outstanding (if sometimes a little confused) service due to its designation as a HEART hotel training school, set amid immaculate gardens overlooking Runaway Bay's golf course, with a pool and beach shuttle. The comfortable double or twin rooms are business-like with TV, a/c and private bathrooms. US$130

House Erabo Salem ☎ 973 4813, ⊛ house-erabo.com. An attractive and spotless three-bedroom (all with en-suite bathrooms) guesthouse on the western edge of town, with steps leading down to a small private beach. US$45
Piper's Cove Salem ☎ 973 7156, ⊛ piperscoveresort jamaica.com. A smart complex of modern one-bedroom holiday apartments in a pretty landscaped garden with pool and private beach. Studio US$95, apartment US$116

EATING AND DRINKING

Runaway Bay's fancy restaurants are all within hotels, and as most people head into Ocho Rios for their **nightlife**, the bay is not exactly jumping – though occasional sound systems are advertised. Non-guests can buy an evening pass to most of the all-inclusives (US$60–90) covering dinner, drinks, a floorshow and disco. A number of bars line the main road, some of which serve as go-go clubs with plenty of semi-naked gyrating late into the night.

Devon House I-Scream Main St, Salem ☎ 973 7292. Twelve flavours of Jamaica's famous creamy ice cream are available at this basic-looking shop, including wonderful fruity delights like soursop and cherry. Daily 10am–6pm.
Isabella's Cardiff Hotel & Spa, Rickets Drive, Cardiff Hall ☎ 973 6671, ⊛ thecardiffhotel.com. For semi-fine-dining, come to this hotel training school, which offers imaginative Jamaican and international cuisines (US$10–20), including a popular Sunday Brunch – served with a lovely seafront view. Daily 8am–10pm.

Luvinya Café and Juice Bar 10 Main St ☎ 505 0117. Lovely little vegetarian and vegan spot with great smoothies and a variety of local and international dishes such as curried plantain, ackee rundown, and salads with hummus and veggie "steak". Save room for the ganja cookies. Mon–Sat 7.30am–8.30pm, Sun 8am–6pm.
★ **Sharkies Seafood Restaurant** Salem Beach ☎ 973 5472. Succulent lobster, conch, shrimp and roast fish dinners (US$10–20) are served up alfresco at this beachside diner with occasional live bands. Daily 10am–10pm.

Discovery Bay

Calmer than Runaway Bay, the crescent harbour of **DISCOVERY BAY** is dominated by the red-stained sphere of the Kaiser **bauxite** plant, from where much of Jamaica's two million tons of "red gold" is exported annually to US refineries. The plant also acted as

"Crab Cay", the fictional base of Dr Julius No in the first of the James Bond movies. Contrary to popular belief, Discovery Bay does not hold the dubious honour of being the place where Columbus first stepped onto Jamaican shores; that accolade goes to Rio Bueno, a few kilometres down the road.

The eastern curve of Discovery Bay's horseshoe is dominated by luxurious villas, and on the opposite outcrop, the University of the West Indies Marine Lab (T 973 2241) houses the island's only **decompression chamber**.

Green Grotto Caves

Between Discovery Bay and Runaway Bay • Daily 9am–4pm • 45min guided tour, US$20 • T 973 2841, W greengrottocavesja.com

Green Grotto Caves is the area's sole managed attraction. The site has a nature park with fishing (you catch, they cook for an additional fee), while the limestone caves themselves are expansive and well lit, with an underwater lake 120 feet below sea level. The grotto may have been used as a hideout by fleeing Spanish troops and as a Taíno place of worship, but in more recent times it gained notoriety as a nightclub – a surfeit of gyrating dancers badly damaged the delicate formations, which have fortunately now mostly grown back. Guides are properly trained and informative, and they work hard at injecting humour into their tours.

3

Puerto Seco Beach

In the centre of Discovery Bay

Puerto Seco beach offers gleaming sand, crystal-clear water and a gently shelving shoreline that's good for children. The name means "dry harbour", in reference to Columbus's reluctance to land in a bay with no source of fresh water. At research time, the beach was on the cusp of reopening after a two-year renovation; if you're in the area, don't miss an opportunity to pop over and see if you can dive in.

ARRIVAL AND DEPARTURE — DISCOVERY BAY

By minibus and route taxi Buses and route taxis from Montego Bay and Ocho Rios arrive and depart from the A1/B3 intersection in Discovery Bay. Route taxis to Brown's Town depart from the junction of the main road with the Brown's Town road at the eastern end of the bay.

EATING

Ultimate Jerk Centre Opposite Green Grotto Caves T 973 2054, W ultimatejerkcentre.com. A large and lively place serving up delicious helpings of authentic Boston-style pork and chicken, and plenty of white rum. Daily 10am–11pm.

Brown's Town

Both the B3 from Runaway Bay and the inland road from Discovery Bay lead high in the hills to bustling **BROWN'S TOWN**, a sizeable inland community with fantastic views and a booming central **market**. Pillars of sugar cane, yams and dasheens caked in red alluvial earth are ferried in by farmers and sold by formidable female higglers, while bootleg name-brand clothing and knick-knacks sell by the bucketload. Even the shops are worthy of a look – Direct Books on Main St (T 975 2247) is a treasure-trove of ancient books with yellowing covers, postcards and intriguing miscellanea, while nearby **restaurants** are good for Jamaican food. If you're on the island during the holidays, do your best to get here for the **Christmas Eve street party**, featuring numerous sound systems, the entire town out on the road and the market open late.

ARRIVAL AND DEPARTURE — BROWN'S TOWN

By minibus and route taxi Minibuses and route taxis run along the main A3 route to Brown's Town, and stop in its Central Market Square.

ACCOMMODATION

New Meditation Heights Hotel 10 Huntley Ave ☎ 975 9180. Clean, cheerful guesthouse with soft double beds and fans; rooms have TVs, a/c and small private bathroom. Located at the top edge of town; take a left fork beside the Cool Oasis petrol station. US$45

Bob Marley Centre and Mausoleum

Nine Mile · Daily 9am–5pm · US$25 · ☎ 843 0498

A throng of would-be "community guides" greet you outside the **Bob Marley Centre and Mausoleum** and former home of the king of reggae. The location is beautiful: red-earthed pastures, distant Cockpits and the sweeping hills and gullies of the Dry Harbour Mountains are a photographer's dream, and suitable for the home of the original "Natural Mystic". That said, in many ways the centre is a disappointment, with the abundance of concrete and high prices giving the impression of a theme park cut off from the community, and guides inside the complex not entirely convincing in their roles. There is inevitably also large amounts of hustle to contend with outside the complex when you bring thousands of high-earning tourists into a poor community and region each week – you'll doubtless be offered overpriced ganja and much more, with some hustlers finding it difficult to take no for an answer. There's also a sizeable gift shop and unremarkable vegetarian restaurant inside the complex.

The tour

Once you've paid the entrance fee, a Rasta guide takes you into the centre proper. There's a prayer space at the first plateau, sometimes occupied by orthodox Rastafarians, and to the right is the wooden shack where Marley lived from age six to thirteen, still furnished with his original bed and decorated with tapestries, paintings and photographs. Opposite is a barbecue where he cooked up Ital feasts during rural retreats, and the "meditation stone" where he rested his head for contemplation, immortalized in the song *Talkin' Blues*. You leave cameras and shoes outside before entering the **mausoleum**, the marble slab holding Marley's remains encased by walls painted with angels and Rasta colours. A stained-glass window filters red, gold and green sunlight over the stone, while candles, incense, fresh flowers and handwritten tributes make the mausoleum an affecting and contemplative place.

ARRIVAL AND INFORMATION · BOB MARLEY CENTRE AND MAUSOLEUM

By charter taxi You can make your own way here in a taxi charter: a round-trip from Ochi or Runaway or Discovery bays should cost US$80–100.

By organized tour Chukka's Zion Bus Line (☎ 972 2506, ⓦ chukka.com; US$115 from Ocho Rios; 5hr) operates a vehicle designed to look like a 1970s Jamaican country bus, with a pumping Bob Marley soundtrack, though cynics may find the ambience too "gift-wrapped Jamaica". A straightforward bus tour is operated by Tourwise (☎ 974 2323, ⓦ tourwiseltd.com; US$80 from Ocho Rios; 5hr).

By car Take a left turn from the B3 at Alexandria onto a (signposted) narrow road, through the communities of Alva and Ballintoy; you'll know you're in Nine Mile when you see the red-gold-and-green flags of the Cedella Marley Primary School flying high. Continue another few minutes and turn directly into the compound car park on the left, rather than risk the "parking assistants" on the road.

Festivals The centre comes alive each February 6 on Marley's birthday, sometimes featuring one of the Marley children (contact the Rita Marley Foundation ☎ 928 2929, and check Jamaica entertainment websites).

Rio Bueno

RIO BUENO is a quiet harbour town of crumbling eighteenth-century buildings, used as backdrop in the 1965 film *A High Wind in Jamaica*. Now cut off from the main highway, which bypasses the town, you'll need to look for the two turnings east and west of the village carefully; they're easily missed. It's popularly agreed that the "crescent harbour" in Rio Bueno was where **Christopher Columbus** – having spent a night

BOB MARLEY – KING OF REGGAE

The legacy of the ambassador of reggae is impossible to over-emphasize, with his lyrics today continuing to strike a chord across every social stratum. Born February 6, 1945, **Robert Nesta Marley** was the progeny of an affair between 17-year-old Cedella Malcolm and 51-year-old Anglo-Jamaican soldier Captain Norval Marley, stationed in the Dry Harbour mountains as overseer of crown lands. Marley's early years, surrounded by a doting family and the rituals of rural life, had a profound effect on his development. His African heritage was of utmost importance to him, and he revelled in the cultural life of Kingston, where he spent most of his later life. Marley was known as a spiritual individual, emanating energy and charisma, but he was also a lover, fathering twelve children by eight women including those by his wife, **Rita Anderson**, his 1966 marriage which lasted until he died. Appropriately enough, his 1970s membership of the Rastafarian sect the Twelve Tribes of Israel gained him the name Joseph, "a fruitful bough" according to the Bible.

THE WAILERS

Fusing African drumming traditions with Jamaican rhythms and American rock guitar, Marley's music became a symbol of unity and social change worldwide. Between 1961 and 1981, his output was prolific. Following their first recording, *Judge Not*, on Leslie Kong's label, Beverley's, his band, the Wailers (Marley, Bunny Livingstone and Peter Tosh), went on to record for some of the best producers in the business; most agree that their finest material was recorded in collaboration with volatile genius Lee "Scratch" Perry. In 1963, the huge hit *Simmer Down* meshed perfectly with the post-independence frustration felt by young Jamaicans, and the group's momentum of success began in earnest. International recognition came when the Wailers signed to the Island label – owned by Anglo-Jamaican entrepreneur Chris Blackwell, whom Marley saw as his "interpreter" rather than producer. The first Island release was *Catch a Fire* in early 1973, and the eleven albums that followed all became instant classics. With the help of Blackwell's marketing skills, reggae became an international genre. Differences with Blackwell led to the departure of Livingstone and Tosh in 1974, but Marley continued to tour the world with a new band called *Bob Marley and the Wailers*.

POLITICS AND PEACE CONCERTS

In the run-up to a performance at the 1976 Smile Jamaica concert – staged by the government to quell rising tensions in a factionalized election campaign – gunmen burst into Marley's home and tried to **assassinate** him. The attempt was bungled, and most of the shots hit manager Don Taylor (who made a full recovery), though Bob and Rita took bullets as well. Undeterred, a bandaged Marley went on stage, choosing to leave after the concert to recover and record in Britain and the US, a period which produced the album *Exodus*. Two years later, he returned to perform at the historic **One Love Peace Concert**, the result of a short-lived truce between the political garrisons of the PNP and JLP. He was the headline act of a line-up that also included Peter Tosh spitting vitriol at the politicians, and Marley ended his performance by enticing arch-enemies Michael Manley and Edward Seaga on stage to join hands in a show of unity. But Marley's call for unity and freedom was not restricted to Jamaica; one of his greatest triumphs was performing the protest anthem *Zimbabwe* at the independence celebrations of the former Rhodesia.

MARLEY'S LEGACY

In the midst of a rigorous 1980 tour, Marley was diagnosed as suffering from cancer; he died a year later in Miami, honoured by his country with the Order of Merit. Marley died without making a will, and years of legal wrangles resulted in his widow being granted the lion's share. The Rita Marley Foundation (ritamarleyfoundation.org) continues to sponsor the development of new artists and to manage Bob's legacy, and many of the Marley children have also forged their own musical careers. Ziggy, Cedella and Sharon found success as the Melody Makers, while Damian "**Junior Gong**", his son by 1976 Miss World Cindy Breakespeare, is an established star with four albums and three Grammys to his name. **Stephen Marley** has found success as both producer and recording artist, US-based Ky-Mani has had a number of reggae-hip-hop hits, and grandson Skip Marley is an up-and-coming songwriter recently featured in Katy Perry's "Chained to the Rhythm".

anchored off St Ann's Bay during his "discovery" of the island in 1494 – decided to land, recording the bay's rapidly running river and horseshoe dimensions in his diary. Columbus made a lucky choice as Rio Bueno also boasts one of Jamaica's deepest harbours. History is also present in the form of a ruined British **fort**, named after secretary of war Henry Dundas, and dating back to 1778, and in the blue- and white-painted **St Mark's Anglican church**, built at the sea's edge in 1833. The original **Baptist church** was burnt to the ground by hostile Anglicans – the present incarnation above town was erected in 1901.

Dornoch Riverhead

Take the road to Woods Town (south from the main road just east of Rio Bueno) and continue towards Jackson Town; it's hidden from the leafy lane and you may need local help · a rough track crosses the road where you can park up and walk the final 270 metres westwards

If you're after more pastoral delights, head for a swim inland at the (hard to find) source of the River Bueno, **Dornoch Riverhead**, a deep, cliff-edged swimming hole surrounded by silk cotton trees and throngs of mosquitoes. Baptist missionary and anti-slavery activist William Knibb (see page 183) baptized converts here, and a spiritual, slightly spooky ambience lingers. On the way, you'll enter a landscape strewn with the crumbling chimneys of unidentifiable sugar factories and stone churches built by Baptist missionaries.

Duncans

Silver Sands beach entry US$25 · Daily 9am–6pm

With the highway speeding off towards Montego Bay, it's easy to miss the turning for **DUNCANS**, a peaceful village huddled under the hills of Cockpit Country, with a clock-tower timepiece that hasn't worked for almost thirty years. Most visitors passing through come to stay at the restful and secluded **villas** of *Silver Sands* (see below), a wide and windswept beach with powdery white sand and superlative swimming – accessed from just west of town. The **coastline** here is sublime, though the *Silver Sands* beach has a hefty day fee for non-guests and is totally out of the reach of locals. A neighbouring public beach, just west of the Silver Sands entrance, is unfortunately rocky, though swimming is possible.

ACCOMMODATION

DUNCANS

Silver Sands Just north of the village ☎ 954 7606, ⓦ my silversands.com. There are around a hundred privately owned holiday villas here, decorated in varying styles and degrees of luxury. Many of these holiday homes are rented out for a minimum of three nights: villa sizes vary from studios- to eight-bedrooms but all are very comfortable. A twelve-person villa rents for around US$7000/week, but there's plenty available at the less expensive end. **US$150**

3

Montego Bay and Cockpit Country

RAFTING ON THE MARTHA BRAE

Montego Bay and Cockpit Country

Jamaica's second-largest city, the seaside settlement of Montego Bay is one of Jamaica's premier tourist honeypots. Framed by a cradle of hills and sitting pretty in a sweeping natural harbour, with fabulous beaches hemmed in by a labyrinth of offshore reefs, it's furnished with enough natural attributes to fill any brochure, and its slick tourism suits the commercial, easy-access tastes of cruise shippers. Long accustomed to visitors, Montego Bay remains the reigning old madam of Jamaican resorts: absorbing, spirited and lively, particularly during its world-renowned summer reggae festival, Sumfest.

The coastline to the east of town has been snapped up by upmarket all-inclusives, pieced out alongside souvenir malls and golf courses; the most famous of these is at **Rose Hall,** taking full advantage of its massively embellished legend of Voodoo, romance and betrayal. The sun-bleached Georgian-era town of **Falmouth,** aside from the recent arrival of twice-weekly cruise ships, remains marooned from the action of the North Coast Highway and offers a welcome respite from the resort ethic – as well as providing the unusual prospect of a night-time swim in its nearby phosphorescent lagoon. Inland, the landscape rises sharply as you enter rural St James, where districts such as **Montpelier** and **Kensington** were once absorbed by huge **sugar estates,** worth the trip alone for their magnificent settings covered with acres of citrus. The verdant **Great River valley** here offers good freshwater **swimming** as well as **tubing** or **rafting** in the silky green waters, or hand-feeding a hummingbird at the beautiful **Rocklands Bird Sanctuary** high above the bay.

Less than two hours' drive from the centre of Montego Bay lies an area so untouched by any kind of holiday development that it's something of a parallel universe to the coastal resorts. The mainly uninhabited limestone hillocks of **Cockpit Country** are the antithesis of palm trees and concrete, and the few settlements that cling to the edges of this almost lunar landscape are some of the most beguiling on the island. Some are still home to descendants of the mighty **Maroons,** enslaved Africans who escaped and waged war against the British. Though **Accompong,** on the southern side of the Cockpits, is still a semi-autonomous state governed by a Maroon council, the Trelawny Maroons of western Jamaica welcome visitors, and as a result, the west is one of the better places to learn a little Maroon history firsthand.

Montego Bay and around

MONTEGO BAY, or MoBay, as it's locally known, nestles between the gently sloping Bogue, Kempshot and Salem hills, and extends some eight kilometres west to the haunts of the suburban rich at Reading and to the plush villas and resorts of Ironshore and Rose Hall sixteen kilometres to the east. Planeloads of foreigners flood in every day, seduced

DOCTOR'S CAVE BEACH

Highlights

❶ Doctor's Cave Beach Powdery white sand and gin-clear waters make this the ultimate place to take a dip in the warm Caribbean. See page 165

❷ Horseriding Swim your mount through the sea from the sumptuous *Half Moon* hotel stables. See page 173

❸ Meal at the Houseboat Bar and Grill Gourmet Jamaican food in a lovely setting on the waters of Bogue Lagoon. See page 176

❹ Greenwood Great House More atmospheric and of greater historical interest than nearby Rose Hall, the museum at

Greenwood provides a glimpse into the lives of nineteenth-century plantation owners. See page 182

❺ Falmouth Boasting some of the most impressive Georgian architecture in Jamaica, this small market town has a lively but unhurried atmosphere, and a compelling monument to the abolishment of slavery. See page 182

❻ Cockpit Country adventures Descend into deep caves, visit an eighteenth-century Maroon settlement and hike in the unique egg-box hillocks of Cockpit Country. See page 190

HIGHLIGHTS ARE MARKED ON THE MAP ON PAGE 162

by a heavily marketed Caribbean dream of swaying palm trees, lilting reggae and cocktails at sunset, and the city in many ways still delivers, building on its success with a new influx of hip resorts such as Zoëtry and Breathless. It has also achieved fame as the base for Jamaica's summer reggae festival, **Sumfest** (see page 177) and the college antics of Spring Break inject shots of adrenalin at other times of the year.

Montego Bay itself is made up of two distinct parts: touristy **Gloucester Avenue**, vigorously marketed as the "Hip Strip", and the city proper, universally referred to as

"**downtown**". The split between the two is so sharp that the majority of tourists never venture further than the Strip on foot, dividing their time between the unbroken string of beaches, shops and restaurants, though the air of enforced tourist-friendliness can be a bit disquieting. Downtown offers a more accurate and vibrant picture of Montegonian life, and, though it's short on specific sights, the markets here provide MoBay's best shopping possibilities. Nearby, past the **Freeport cruise ship pier,** are a handful of marina-facing restaurants and resorts, including a Yacht Club popular with residents.

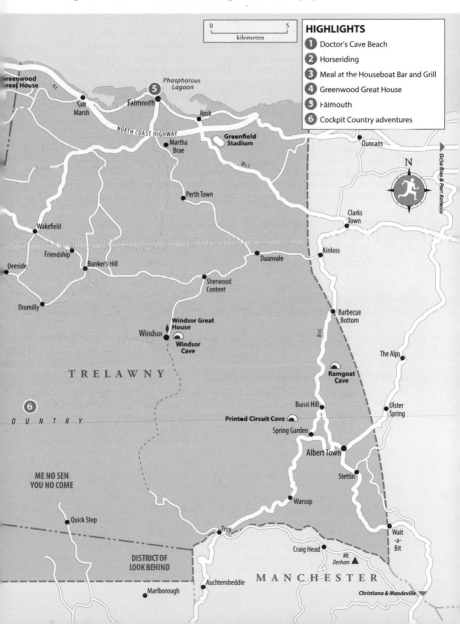

HIGHLIGHTS

1. Doctor's Cave Beach
2. Horseriding
3. Meal at the Houseboat Bar and Grill
4. Greenwood Great House
5. Falmouth
6. Cockpit Country adventures

Brief history

When Columbus anchored briefly in Montego Bay in 1494, he was charmed enough to name it *El Golfo de Buen Tempo* (The Bay of Good Weather). The Spanish were less romantic, dubbing it *Manterias*, a derivation of *manteca* (pig fat), after the lard they produced and shipped from here in large quantities. Eventually, the English corruption, "Montego", stuck. By the time the Spaniards hastily fled the island (see page 256), the city was little more than a village. Its subsequent development was heavily influenced by two factors. First was the presence of the **Maroons** in neighbouring Cockpit Country (see page 189), an African-Jamaican band of militarily skilled former slaves whose frequent attacks on British settlements kept the town from prospering until the peace treaty of 1739. By this time, plantation **sugar production** was booming, the harbour was thronged with ships, and lavish cut-stone town houses and inns were spreading back from the waterfront. The 1831 **Christmas Rebellion** (see page 170) nonetheless nearly destroyed it. The most important of the violent slave revolts that prefaced emancipation began in the foothills behind the town, and saw almost every estate in the area burnt to the ground.

After the collapse of the sugar trade, Montego Bay spent a hundred-odd years in limbo, and it was not until the early twentieth century that it entered another period of growth, beginning when Sir Herbert Baker advocated the redemptive powers of the Doctor's Cave waters, north of the city's centre. MoBay metamorphosed into the ultimate **tourist town**; rich North Americans and Europeans built holiday homes around Doctor's Cave, or arrived on banana boats to stay in the town's first hotel, the *Casa Blanca*. The town's population increased fourfold between 1940 and 1970, with Jamaicans from all over the island moving in to work at the hotels. In the 1960s, the Freeport peninsula in the south was constructed on reclaimed land, assuring its position as a premier port of call for Caribbean cruises. The beaches were attractively overhauled in the 1990s and in 2017 the "Hip Strip" was undergoing a facelift; determinedly tourist-friendly, MoBay feels on the upswing.

The Hip Strip: Gloucester Avenue and the beaches

Though it stretches for less than three kilometres, Montego Bay's glittering **Hip Strip** is the focal point of many a Jamaican vacation. Dazzling **beaches** with protected offshore coral reef are located here, leading to development of the whole of **Gloucester Avenue**

MONTEGO BAY MARINE PARK TRUST

Until 1991, MoBay's offshore reefs remained open to attack from plunderers, spear fishers, divers, boat anchors and industrial pollution. To stem the destruction, **Montego Bay Marine Park Trust** (☎ 952 5619, 🌐 mbmpt.org) was created, Jamaica's first national park with environmental regulations enforced by rangers. Running west from Sangster International Airport to Great River, just past Reading, the park comprises sixteen square kilometres of coral reef, sea-grass and mangrove, divided into conservation, recreation and port zones. Within the park, it's illegal to mine sand, damage or move coral, shells and seaweed, fish without a permit, spear-fish – and drop litter, too. Other initiatives have included the introduction of buoys along the major reefs, so that pleasure-cruise snorkelling stops don't result in damaged coral, the replacement of small mesh used for fish and lobster traps with larger mesh to allow young specimens a chance to reach maturity, and annual reef fish counts, to assess conservation success. Though funding and lack of policing resources make it difficult to run the permit system, patrols and education projects aimed at educating fishermen (and their children) on alternative means of income do take place, alongside numerous restriction signs. Tours with park rangers are available (phone the number above), and donations in cash or kind (particularly depth gauges) are gratefully accepted. If you'd like to learn more, visit the Resource Centre on the top floor of the row of shops and offices adjacent to the *Pier One* restaurant and night club (see page 176).

and stretching north into **Kent Avenue**. The Strip goes all out to cater to tourists' every need, but its shiny commercialism does make it feel a bit unreal, as though visitors and Jamaican workers here are all playing out designated roles in a sort of open-air tropical theme park.

Though Gloucester Avenue runs parallel to the sea, the water is mainly obscured by buildings. The only place to fully appreciate the seep of the bay is from the Strip's only **green space**, around Walter Fletcher Beach; it's a favourite spot for football, and there are a few benches to take in the view.

Fort Montego
Fort St

The southern end of the Strip – across from Aqua Sol theme park – has a truncated, easily missed upper section (Fort Street), running parallel. Here you'll find an uninspiring hulk of stone next to a small craft market (see page 179); built by the British to guard against foreign attack, **Fort Montego** dates back to the eighteenth century but its cannons were fired only twice, both times with disastrous results. In a salute to celebrate the capture of Havana in 1760, one cannon misfired and killed a gunner, while in 1795 the fort mistakenly opened fire on one of its own vessels, the *Mercury*, carrying a cargo of dogs to hunt down Maroons; inevitably, the shots missed.

Walter Fletcher Beach
Gloucester Avenue

Opposite the fort, **Walter Fletcher Beach** is a wide expanse of curving yellow sand that is popular with locals. Closed in 2017 for renovations, it formerly sported watersport facilities like jet skiing and glass-bottom boat rides, plus tennis and basketball courts and a go-kart track. Though it was unclear what the beach's update would bring, the plan at the time of this update was to expand on the facilities here.

Margaritaville
Midway along Gloucester Ave • Daily 10am–4am • Daytime entry free; special events US$30 all-inclusive; nightclub covers vary (see page 178) • ☎ 952 4777, ⓦ margaritavillecaribbean.com

A mini-watersports park-cum-restaurant-cum-bar, the neon facade of **Margaritaville** rudely shatters the bucolic illusion of a tranquil Caribbean shoreline created by the Walter Fletcher Beach park. Part of musician and businessman Jimmy Buffett's concept-empire of nightclubs and restaurants, this is a temple to crazy tropical fun featuring a 110ft water slide, water trampolines and floating sun decks, while a smoking volcano belches vomit-like lava down the walls. The complex is at its peak during February's Spring Break, when wet T-shirts and beer-drinking competitions combine with fun in the jacuzzi; nonetheless, off-season it's a fairly decent place to hang out, with a reggae and pop soundtrack and a bar and outdoor eating deck jutting out over the sea.

Doctor's Cave Beach
Northern end of Gloucester Ave • Daily 8.30am–sunset • US$6 • ☎ 952 2566, ⓦ doctorscavebathingclub.com

The magnificent **Doctor's Cave Beach** is Montego Bay's premium portion of gleaming white sand, located amid the parade of bars, cafés and tax-free in-bond shops at the northern end of Gloucester Avenue. The beach was put on the map in the late nineteenth century when Doctor Alexander McCatty founded the Sanatorium Caribbee, a private bathing club that's still in existence. In the 1920s, English chiropractor Sir Herbert Baker was so impressed by the curative potential of the waters that he published an article extolling their efficacy. The beau monde flocked and MoBay's tourist industry was born. The city's very first resort hotel, the *Casa Blanca* (now closed) backs onto the western end of the beach. The rapidly deepening, crystal-clear waters really are the best in town and facilities are excellent, though it does get

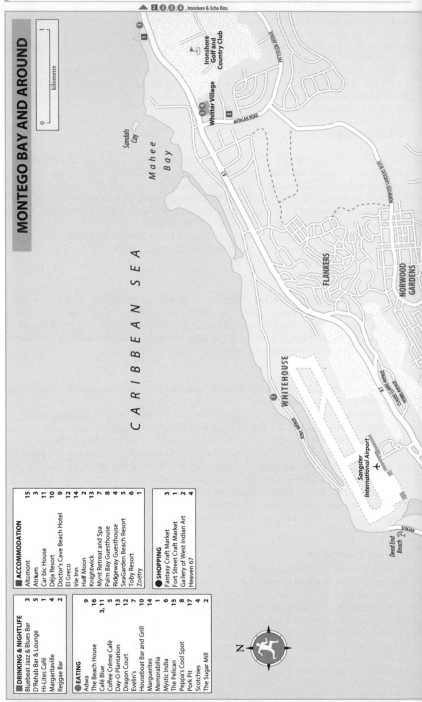

MONTEGO BAY AND AROUND

Ironshore & Ocho Rios

Ironshore Golf and Country Club

Whitter Village

MORGAN ROAD

Sandals Cay

Mahee Bay

CARIBBEAN SEA

FLANKERS

NORWOOD GARDENS

WHITEHOUSE

Sangster International Airport

Dead End Beach

N

0 kilometre 1

■ DRINKING & NIGHTLIFE	
Bluebeat Jazz & Blues Bar	3
D'Rehab Bar & Lounge	5
Hi-Lites Café	4
Margaritaville	2

● EATING	
Adwa	9
The Beach House	16
Café Blue	3, 11
Coffee Crème Café	5
Day-O Plantation	13
Dragon Court	12
Evelin's	7
Houseboat Bar and Grill	10
Marguerites	14
Memorabilia	1
Mystic India	6
The Pelican	15
Peppa's Cool Spot	8
Pork Pit	17
Scotchies	4
The Sugar Mill	2

■ ACCOMMODATION	
Altamont	15
Atrium	3
Car bic House	11
Déja Resort	10
Doctor's Cave Beach Hotel	9
El Greco	12
Irie Inn	14
Half Moon	2
Knightwick	13
Mynt Retreat and Spa	7
Palm Bay Guesthouse	8
Ridgeway Guesthouse	4
SeaGarden Beach Resort	5
Toby Resort	6
Zoëtry	1

● SHOPPING	
Fantasy Craft Market	3
Fort Street Craft Market	1
Gallery of West Indian Art	2
Heaven 67	4

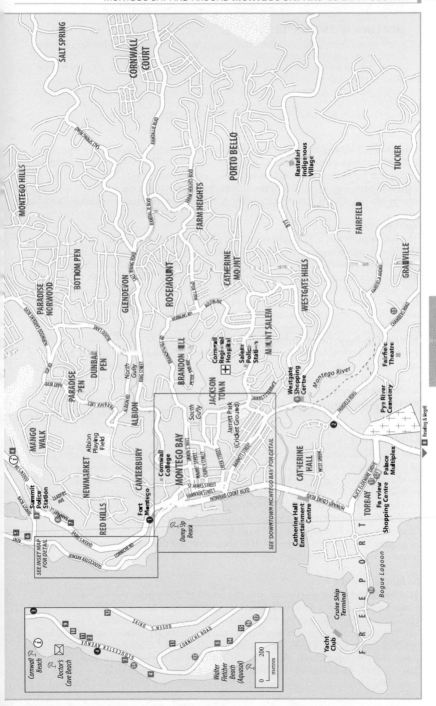

very crowded at weekends. Beach umbrellas, sun loungers or snorkelling equipment are available (at high cost), and there are beautiful corals offshore. The membership-only **clubhouse** (of interest to repeat visitors at an annual cost of US$250 per family) offers a games room, a gym and steam room, but the regular changing rooms are also well equipped. There are several snack counters, as well as a reasonable restaurant and bar.

Kent Avenue

The hotels peter out as Gloucester becomes **Kent Avenue** at the junction with Sunset Boulevard, which continues to hug the coast before ending abruptly at the Sangster airport runway wall. The thin but attractive parallel strip of public sand, **Dead End Beach** (also known as Buccaneer or Sunset Beach) is shallow, with good snorkelling, and is popular with Jamaicans. Viewing the sunset from here is fabulous, accompanied by street drinks vendors and car stereos (pick your location by music style), though the atmosphere is plagued by occasionally startling landings and takeoffs.

Sunset Boulevard and Queen's Drive

Away from the sea, **Sunset Boulevard** is home to a few forlorn shops and bars, countless car-rental outlets and the rather grand **Summit Police Station**, which boasts its own pool. At the airport roundabout, the boulevard meets **Queen's Drive**, a fast traffic route looping across the hill above (locally known as "top road"). The views over the bay are fantastic.

Downtown

After the flamboyance of the Strip, **downtown** MoBay announces itself with a curve of grass-fringed white sand at the southern end of Gloucester Avenue. Though you might not want to go there alone, **Dump-Up Beach** is a decent place to swim or chill out; soccer matches take place here, alongside occasional markets and packed gospel meetings with dressed up locals overflowing the marquees erected for such occasions. At the wide crossroads with Queen's Drive at the end of the Strip, Howard Cooke Boulevard shoots off to the south, passing the turn-off to *Pier One* nightclub, a couple of playing fields and the **Catherine Hall Entertainment Complex**, stage show venue and home of Reggae Sumfest (see page 177).

St James Street

St James Street is the main route into the centre of town from the Strip and a clamorous affair, with dancehall flooding out from store-fronts and all manner of pushcarts and vehicles jostling for space with the thick human traffic. A short way along, a small sunken garden area houses the **parish library** (Mon–Fri 9.30am–5.30pm, Sat 9am–4pm; ☏952 4186), which carries a fair stock of Caribbean books (reference possible for non-members). Adjoining St James Street through to adjacent Orange Street is lively **Gully Market** (the correct name, William Street Market, is seldom used); hard-dough bread and callaloo are sold from supermarket trolleys, and fruit and veg spill over.

Orange Street

To the east, running parallel to St James Street, **Orange Street** is another busy downtown thoroughfare; on its north side, it forks with sweetly monikered "Love Lane", and passes the red-earthed playing fields of MoBay's main high school, Cornwall College.

Sam Sharpe Square

Sam Sharpe Square, at the intersection of St James and Market streets, is the heart of downtown, characterized by its central fountain, permanent stream of honking traffic, and jumble of old and new architecture. **The Cage**, now a craft shop, was originally built in 1806 as a lock-up for disorderly seamen and escaped slaves; inmates damaged the original wooden walls to such an extent that in 1823 they were replaced by the red-brick and stone structure that stands today. In 1811, the belfry was installed, used to ring out a 2pm curfew; after a second ring at 3pm any slaves still on the streets were locked up. Just outside, freedom fighter and National Hero Sam Sharpe (see page 170) is commemorated in a rough **bronze statue** by Jamaican sculptor Kay Sullivan; Sharpe was executed by the British (along with hundreds of other enslaved Africans) here in 1832; the square was renamed to honour him in 1976. To the east, the corner of Market and King street holds the hulking **Burchell Memorial Baptist Church,** where Sam Sharpe lies buried, while the western section of Market Street, towards the main craft market (see page 179) and the sea, has been pedestrianized.

Montego Bay Cultural Centre

Sam Sharpe Square • Tues–Sun 9am–5pm • US$8 • ☎ 876 971 3920, ⓦ montegobayculturalcentre.org

The dynamic **Montego Bay Cultural Centre**, the city's beating historical and artistic heart, blocks out the downtown din with air-conditioning and a calm, smart ambience. Housed inside a handsome Georgian-style structure, the centre was thoroughly refurbished in 2014, and, under the aegis of Kingston's **National Museum** (see page 55), hosts exhibits on Jamaican history such as post-emancipation life, the exportation of bananas (with an interesting boat model), the Taínos, and local handiworks; there is also a theatre and

4

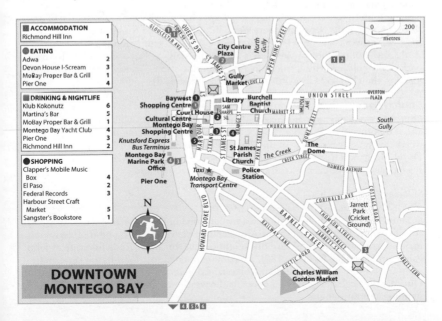

SAM SHARPE AND THE CHRISTMAS REBELLION

During the course of just over a week, slavery in Jamaica received the blow that would kill it forever. The **Christmas Rebellion, or Baptist War,** began on December 27, 1831; by its end on January 5, 1832, sixty thousand slaves had razed nearly 160 sugar estates, causing damage to the value of £1 million – then a massive drain on the British exchequer. It was the largest slave uprising in Jamaican history, and set the stage for the system's abolishment in 1834.

The rebellion was led by **Sam Sharpe**, slave of a MoBay solicitor and a brilliant deacon of the town's Burchell Memorial Baptist Church. By reading international newspapers, Sharpe learned about English anti-slavery sentiments, and became convinced that emancipation in Jamaica was imminent – a reality that planters were trying to suppress. A powerful orator, Sharpe formed a **secret society** that sought wages for employment, and with this basic human right as foundation, plans took shape for the non-violent withdrawal of enslaved labour over the Christmas period. Talk of the insurrection spread fast through St James estates, and planters became uneasy as December 1831 drew to a close. By the night of the 27th, passions were running high. Peaceful protest soon degenerated into anarchy; tipped off by estate owners, the militia were out in force, and some resisters responded by lighting bonfires at the highest point of the Kensington estate, starting a full-scale **rebellion**. Other fires followed suit and within days western Jamaica was burning as the cane fields and great houses were destroyed one by one. The response of the British militia was brutal. Though damage was predominantly restricted to property and only fourteen whites died, soldiers gunned down one thousand slaves, and magistrates handed down a further three hundred execution orders during the emotional six-week trial that ensued. Sharpe – who took full blame for the events in an attempt to exonerate other resisters – was hanged in the MoBay square that today bears his name. His last words, later echoed by fighter Paul Bogle (see page 101), were "I would rather die upon yonder gallows than live in slavery." He was buried in the harbour sand, though his remains were later exhumed and interred in the vault of Burchell Memorial Baptist Church (see page 169), where there is an affecting memorial to him.

events space. Though petite, the centre packs an educational punch: it's one of the few exhibitions in western Jamaica to address the realities of slavery, the plantation economy and resistance fighters like Paul Bogle and Sam Sharpe.

In addition to its historical displays, the centre has rotating art shows (updated every three months) in its **National Gallery West**. Brainchild of the Kingston museum (see page 54), artworks here run the gamut from Caribbean animation to avant-garde works and modern canvases by Marcia Biggs and Mallica "Kapo" Reynolds. To the back of the cultural centre, fenced in away from the street, is a monument to fighters killed in the 1831–32 Christmas Rebellion (see page 170).

Church Street

Church Street is the most architecturally interesting of downtown's busy thoroughfares, and is dominated by St James Parish Church (see below). Facing the church is the weathered yet elegant facade of the **Town House**, constructed in 1765 by merchant David Morgan; it has served as a private home, church manse, Masonic lodge, synagogue, hotel (Queen Victoria stayed here) and restaurant.

St James Parish Church

Church St • If locked, ask at the rector's office opposite or call ☎ 952 2775

St James Parish Church, built from creamy cut stone in the shape of a Greek cross, was considered the showpiece of the parish when completed in 1782, and it underwent major repairs after the 1957 earthquake. Inside, the virtues of Rosa, first wife of John Palmer of Rose Hall (see page 180), are commemorated in a John Bacon verse and sculpture set to the left of the altar, while stained-glass windows depict the Crucifixion. Outside, the neglected graveyard contains the weathered graves of planters, many standing at erratic angles.

Barnett Street

The roads surrounding **Barnett Street** are a raucous belt of lively shops, mini-malls and traffic, with hole-in-the-wall emporia vying for space with neon signs and sidewalk vendors, fighting to be noticed against a background symphony of reggae and shouts of "sky juice" and "peanuts and melons". Shopping here is certainly not of the duty-free and T-shirt variety. Barnett Street holds a notorious **police station** and lock-up, a run-down colonial structure where inmates sleep ten to a cell on concrete floors and officers make appeals for donations. On the northern side, you'll find the **Montego Bay Transport Centre**, terminus and starting point for most of the city's route taxis (see page 172).

At the southern end of Barnett Street (close to the turn upwards for Jarrett Park; see page 173), the road passes over the Montego River and the scenery either side opens up and takes on an incongruously lush aspect. Giant bulrushes and emerald reeds flourish in the greyish water and egrets roost in poinciana and palm.

Charles William Gordon Market

Fustic Rd

Straddling the disused railway tracks, **Charles William Gordon Market** (also known as Fustic Market; main days Fri and Sat) is a visceral whirl of tarpaulin-covered mounds of earthy yams alongside deep-orange pumpkins, spring onions and thyme, and a kaleidoscope of fruits, while numerous higglers (pedlars) make up temporary beds beside their pitches in the pungent indoor meat section. Though the market received a limited refurbishment and reorganization in 2013, pedlars and hustlers spill out onto the surrounding streets and it's not the safest of areas. Come here if you're already well accustomed to the island, or with a Jamaican to guide you.

Rastafari Indigenous Village

3km east of downtown • US$35 2hr tour, US$45 with lunch, all visits must be booked in advance • ☎ 285 4750, ✉ rastafariindigenousvillage@gmail.com

The **Rastafari Indigenous Village** is a working community that shatters myths about the world's most stereotyped religious movement. Developed by members of the IION Station Rastafari in Montego Bay, its two-hour tours are quite good – you're led through medicinal gardens, a drumming circle and the housing collective, all the while listening to an enlightening talk on the movement's history and conception of nature, and its place in today's world. If you're enthusiastic for all things Rasta, call ahead about having an Ital lunch, learning artisan crafts or studying bush-healing methodologies. Also, keep an eye out for special events here; well-known musicians are known to perform.

Freeport Peninsula

The **Freeport Peninsula**, backed to the south by the mangroves of the Bogue Lagoon and to the north by commercial wharves and the **cruise ship pier**, is a collection of upscale shops and restaurants. Past here are a series of smart apartment complexes and the yellow high-rise *Sunscape Splash* resort. It's worth coming over for a sundowner on the roof of the *Houseboat Bar and Grill* (see page 176), or a game of pool and a tasty lunch at the posh **Yacht Club** (ⓦmobayyachtclub.com), ostensibly for members only but the bar is accessible to all; it's easily reached by route taxi.

Ironshore

With endless reefs and postcard-perfect beaches, the coast east from central Montego Bay has long been the preserve of expensive hotels, and a number of brand-new mammoth all-inclusives and condos together with glitzy shopping malls ensure the upmarket feel lingers. The plush residential belt of **IRONSHORE** is home to palatial private residences and three of the island's best **golf courses** (see page 173). Among the large developments you can still find the occasional appealing bar or **restaurant**, however, such as *Scotchies* jerk centre, living-museum-cum-bar *Memorabilia* and MoBay's only South Asian restaurants.

ARRIVAL AND DEPARTURE

MONTEGO BAY AND AROUND

BY PLANE

Sangster International Airport (ⓦmbjairport.com; ticket, flight and baggage information line ☎ 952 3124) is right by the sea, 1.5km from Gloucester Ave; there's a 24-hour cambio and ATM machines. Luggage trolleys aren't permitted past immigration, but red-capped porters will carry your bags for a small charge (US$5).

Getting into town Larger hotels provide free airport transfers; the JUTA and hotel booths in the arrivals area run bus transfers for the few guests heading to large Negril and Ocho Rios hotels that have not booked their accommodation and transfer in advance; space allowing, independent travellers may be able to jump in one for US$25–35/person. Alternatively you can charter a taxi from the omnipresent JUTA drivers outside. A ride to Gloucester Ave, Queen's Drive or downtown should cost no more than US$10; if you're on a very tight budget and travelling light, you could consider flagging down one of the local route taxis (see below) that circle the Arrivals gate, and run down the Strip into downtown MoBay.

Car rental Numerous car rental booths can be found in arrivals, including: Island (☎ 929 5875, ⓦ islandcarrentals.

com), Budget (☎ 953 0534) and Hertz (☎ 952 4250). Rates are decent (US$50/day) and there are reductions for weekly rentals.

Airlines The following are all based at the airport: Air Canada ☎ 952 5160; Airlink ☎ 1 888 247 5465 or ☎ 940 6660; American Airlines ☎ 971 7379; Caribbean Airlines ☎ 1 800 523 5585; Delta ☎ 971 1284; JetBlue ☎ 1 800 538 2583; Spirit ☎ 1 877 211 1546; United ☎ 1 800 864 8331; Virgin Atlantic ☎ 876 974 2323.

BY BUS

The best option for inter-city travel is on Knutsford Express coach services (ⓦknutsfordexpress.com), which depart from their own terminus at 10 Harbour Circle, close to Pier One and the main craft market. Cheaper minibuses also run to all island destinations from the busy downtown transport centre, where Barnett St meets Howard Cooke Blvd; note that they leave when full, and it can be a cramped ride (see page 24). From either terminus, chartering a taxi to Gloucester Ave or Queen's Drive will cost around US$10. Cheaper shared taxis are also available to points all over the city; ask somebody to show you the relevant departure point.

GETTING AROUND

On foot If you're staying on the Strip, walking is the best option with all attractions reachable on foot – and you shouldn't experience any problems even at night, but downtown it's better to walk in company until you get your bearings.

By route taxi Public transport around town is provided by route taxis (see page 24) that ply set paths, convenient for short hops along the Strip or to get to the beaches if you're not staying right on Gloucester Ave. They charge around J$200 per person, and J$300–500 for trips out of town (bear in mind that rates change constantly with inflation and fluctuating petrol prices). Most start at the Montego Bay Transport Centre on Barnett St (see page 171), but you can flag them down anywhere en route.

By private taxi If you want to charter a private taxi there are legions of drivers along Gloucester Ave – be prepared to haggle and always settle the price before you get in; most rides from Gloucester Ave around town cost US$10. Route taxis congregate at the Transport Centre, where Barnett St meets Howard Cooke Blvd (prices are always less downtown than on the Strip). You'll often get a better (and cheaper) sense of Jamaica by hiring a local driver and doing

some independent sightseeing. Freeman Peddie (☎859 1340) and Chester of Chester Tours Experience (☎587 3584) is recommended; fees vary according to distance and petrol prices, but it's a good idea to budget around US$160 per day for two people, or US$45 per person per day for groups of four or more.

By car Tailbacks at rush hour (7.30–10am & 4.30–6.30pm) and a very flexible interpretation of rules make driving a frustrating experience; nonetheless it is a good option for independent sightseeing. Between 7am and 2am there are parking charges between *Margaritaville* and the plaza in front of Fantasy Craft Market; pay at the shops east of Doctor's Cave Beach. Outlets selling permits close at 8 or 10pm – though restrictions are rarely enforced after 5pm. Avoid the whole scenario by parking in the lots up the hill opposite Margaritaville or close to Cornwall Beach.

Car rental Reliable local companies tend to be based along Sunset Boulevard/Queen's Drive, close to the airport: Alex's, 1 Claude Clarke Ave (☎940 6260); Prospective, 2 Federal Ave (off Queen's Drive; ☎ 952 3524, ⓦ prospectiverentacar. net), Danjor, 34 Queen's Drive (☎940 2679, ⓦ danjorcars. com); Horizon, 2 Sunset Blvd (☎952 0185).

INFORMATION AND TOURS

TOURIST INFORMATION

The Jamaica Tourist Board office (Mon–Fri 8.30am–4pm, Sat 9am–1pm; ☎ 952 4425) is at 18 Queen's Drive, opposite the airport, offering maps, flyers and limited advice on hotels, restaurants and attractions. Musical concerts, festivals and special club nights are usually announced by banners and on the radio.

TOUR OPERATORS

Hundreds of tour companies operate out of Montego Bay; most have booths at the airport and offices along Gloucester Ave and offer similarly priced trips to plantations such as Croydon (see page 188) and great houses like Rose Hall (see page 180) or Greenwood (see page 182). Standard tours usually mean sitting with twenty others on an a/c bus and paying for the privilege, though you may be able to set up a more personalized trip, for example with the drivers mentioned above.

Barrett Adventures ☎ 382 6384, ⊚ barrettadventures.com. Interesting options, from customized packages to waterfalls and plantations as well as activities like hiking in Cockpit Country, horseriding and snorkelling. US$60–160.

Caribic Vacations 69 Gloucester Ave ☎ 979 3421, ⊚ caribicvacations.com. Longstanding operator that organizes standard trips to major sights all over the island, including Dunn's River Falls, the Appleton Estate and cycling in the Blue Mountains. From US$75.

Chukka Caribbean St Ann ☎ 979 8500, ⊚ chukka. com. The biggest operator on the island offers river-tubing along the Great River (5hr), jeep "safaris" into the St James interior (4hr), with swimming and a waterfall climb; and plenty of ziplining options in which you buckle on a harness and swing through the treetops. US$89–185.

Yardie Tours Offices in Montego Bay and Falmouth ☎ 567 5619, ⊚ yardietours.com. Stellar local tours ranging from horseriding, to tubing and kayaking, paintball and a visit to Green Grotto Caves close to Runaway Bay (see page 152). US$65–199.

ACTIVITIES

CRICKET

Jarrett Park Creek St (uphill, well past the Dome) ☎ 952 0045. MoBay's cricket ground and the original site of Reggae Sunsplash (Bob Marley performed here in 1979). Even if you're not a cricket fan, attending a match (tickets US$7–10) is highly entertaining, as much for the dancehall that booms out during breaks in play as for aficionados' impassioned commentaries. Tickets sold at the gate, but arrive early for high-profile matches.

GOLF

Half Moon Golf Club Half Moon Resort, Rose Hall ☎ 953 2560, ⊚ halfmoon.com. Sumptuous eighteen-hole course with professional academy, clubhouse, putting green and restaurant.

Ironshore Golf and Country Club Ironshore ☎ 953 3107. Challenging eighteen-hole course with a mini amphitheatre at the final hole.

White Witch Course Hyatt Ziva Rose Hall ☎ 632 7444, ⊚ whitewitchgolf.com. An exclusive eighteen-hole course aimed at resort residents but open to non-guests (from US$159).

HORSERIDING

Half Moon Equestrian Centre Half Moon Resort, Rose Hall ☎ 953 2286, ⊚ horsebackridingjamaica. com. Some of the island's best horseriding is found here, an immaculate facility that's home to many ex-racehorses. The best option is the 1hr 45min Beach Ride (US$140), a stroll through gardens and onto the beach, where you ride into the waves, swimming your horse back to shore.

Dressage, horse-jumping and polo lessons are also on offer (US$100), as are pony rides for kids (US$30). Mon–Sat 9am–5pm.

RAFTING

Bamboo rafting is available at Lethe Estate (see page 187) or Martha Brae (see page 185).

WATERSPORTS

Montego Bay is justifiably famed for its turquoise waters and reefs, some swimmable from the beach. Deeper reefs are alive with fish, rays, urchins and occasional turtles and nurse shark. Pamphlets and information are available from the Montego Bay Marine Park Trust office (see page 164). Jet ski hire (30min; US$90) and glass-bottom boat trips (30min; US$25) are on offer at the main beaches.

SPORT-FISHING BOAT RENTAL

Available from Marlin Madness (☎ 574 8662) and Reel Magic (☎ 771 4367).

DIVING AND SNORKELLING

Guided dives (around US$75), certification courses (from US$400) and diving and snorkelling equipment rental (from US$25), as well as snorkelling tours, are offered by: Captain's Watersports and Dive Centre, located at the *Hilton*, *Holiday Inn*, *Secrets*, *Round Hill*, and *Half Moon* resorts (☎ 953 3048); Jamaica Scuba Divers, based at *Duncans* (☎ 381 1113, ⊚ scuba-jamaica.com); and Seaworld Jamaica at *Cariblue Hotel and Scuba Resort* at Rose Hall (☎ 953 2180, ⊚ diveseaworld.com).

4

BOAT TRIPS AND CRUISES

Boat trips, with an open bar and lunch, depart from Pier One downtown and sail around the bay, with a stop for reef snorkelling.

Dreamer Catamaran Cruises Gloucester Ave ☎979 0102, ⓦdreamercatamarans.com. Tours aboard one of two beautifully maintained catamarans sail along the coast, stopping for snorkelling and at *Margaritaville*'s water slides – and ladies get a foot massage (3hr cruise US$88 including transfer). Family cruises in the morning, while afternoons are a racier, adults-only affair.

ACCOMMODATION

Most people stay adjacent to the beaches along buzzing **Gloucester Ave** – aka the **Hip Strip** – but quieter options are available on **Queen's Drive**, above and to the east of the Strip, which has fabulous sea views and is connected to Gloucester Ave by route taxi. There are a few worthy **budget** places near the beaches, and places **downtown** are all considerably cheaper. Many hotels include free airport transfers and beach shuttle. It's rarely difficult to find a vacancy, unless you hit town during Sumfest (August) or the Jazz Festival (January). Montego Bay's swankiest resorts (as well as most of the all-inclusives) are out east at suburban Ironshore and Rose Hall, in addition to *Round Hill,* 17km west (see page 187).

THE HIP STRIP: GLOUCESTER AVENUE AND AROUND

Altamont West 33 Gloucester Ave ☎620 4540, ⓦaltamontwesthotel.com; map p.166. An excellent option, close to the action and Walter Fletcher Beach. The modern, business-like rooms have useful amenities like hairdryers and CD players, while there's a pool, sun deck and great restaurant/wine bar. Breakfast included. US$125

Caribic House 69 Gloucester Ave ☎979 6073, ⓦcaribic vacations.com; map p.166. Small hotel by Doctor's Cave Beach, run by an excellent tour outfit (see page 173) and popular with budget travellers. All of the three room categories are well organized, with a/c and fridge; some share a communal balcony over the street. US$80

Déja Resort 92 Gloucester Ave ☎940 4173, ⓦdeja resort.com; map p.166. Centrally located, close to Doctor's Cave Beach, this small, friendly hotel has guest-rooms decorated in ocean hues, a kid's play area, a restaurant and an outdoor pool and jacuzzi. There is an all-inclusive option if required. US$185

★**Doctor's Cave Beach Hotel** Gloucester Ave ☎952 4355, ⓦdoctorscave.com; map p.166. One of the better Strip hotels, opposite Doctor's Cave Beach. Communal areas have funky decor and tropical landscaping, plus there's a pool, jacuzzi, restaurant, bar and gym. The bright rooms are pretty uniform, but the real draw is the very friendly atmosphere. Includes continental breakfast. US$99

El Greco Queen's Drive ☎940 6116, ⓦelgrecojamaica. com; map p.166. Complex of slightly faded, self-contained apartments/suites perched high above the Strip (access via a lift from opposite Doctor's Cave Beach); an excellent choice if you want some independence. Modern, with balconies and kitchens; there's a pool and tennis courts; rates include breakfast and beach pass. US$115

Irie Inn 39 Gloucester Ave ☎526 5867, ⓦtheirieinn. com; map p.166. Appealing and inexpensive self-contained apartments in a wonderful location. All have tiled floors, big bathrooms and a living area with kitchenette. US$65

★**Knightwick** Corniche Rd ☎952 2988; map p.166. Several large, comfortable rooms in an elegant hacienda-style family guesthouse, conveniently situated up the hill opposite *Margaritaville*. A good breakfast (included) is served on the veranda. One of the best options in town, with bargain triple rooms (US$90). US$70

Mynt Retreat and Spa 9 Ramparts Close ☎622 5530, ⓦmyntretreat.com; map p.166. Tucked away on a quiet cul-de-sac and yet right in the heart of the action, this bed and breakfast-meets-hotel has seven cosy guestrooms, charming Moroccan design details, and a spa. Plus it's just steps away from wonderful *Peppa's* restaurant (see page 176). US$160

Ridgeway Guesthouse 34 Queen's Drive ☎952 2709, ⓦridgewayguesthouse.com; map p.166. Conveniently located behind tourist information and near the airport, this homely and friendly guesthouse has eight lovely rooms with tiled floors (fan or a/c), wooden furniture and marble bathrooms; some have fridges, kettles and sea views. Free beach shuttle. US$80

SeaGarden Beach Resort 8 Kent Ave ☎1 844 742 7778, ⓦseagardenjamaica.com; map p.166. This elegant and traditional 140-room resort has its own private beach club across the road, two fine, intimate restaurants plus piano and wine bars (one with a dancefloor), a large pool, and facilities for children. The decor is bright, contemporary and tasteful. Choose a poolside room away from street noise. All-inclusive. US$400

Toby Resort Cnr Gloucester Ave & Sunset Blvd ☎952 4370, ⓦtobyresorts.com; map p.166. Long-established place with an appealing location in pretty gardens, within easy walking distance of the beaches. The comfortable, refurbished rooms have rattan furnishings, and there are two pools, a restaurant and two bars. US$155

DOWNTOWN

★ **Richmond Hill Inn** Richmond Hill, off Union St ☎ 952 3859, ⓦ richmondhillinnja.com; map p.169. Former planters' house and one of MoBay's best hotels in the 1970s: delightful touches from that period remain. The lofty setting offers easily the best views in town, while a great breakfast is served and communal areas include a pool and lots of greenery. Bright rooms have tiled floors, a/c, TV, microwave, fridge and patio (some have a view). Excellent value. US$155

SOUTH OF DOWNTOWN

Palm Bay Guesthouse 14 Bogue Crossing ☎ 952 1795, ⓦ palmbayguesthouse.com; map p.166. A busy budget guesthouse just off the shared-taxi route into town. Neat, tiled floor rooms have fan or a/c, phone and cable TV. Jamaican restaurant plus shaded bar/jerk centre. US$65

IRONSHORE

Atrium 1084 Morgan Rd ☎ 953 2605, ⓦ atriumironshorehotel.com; map p.166. Just off the main road, by the Blue Diamond Shopping Centre, these spotless, tiled, modern apartments have full kitchens and living areas, and there's a pool on site. Good online discounts available. US$125

★ **Half Moon** ☎ 953 2211, ⓦ halfmoon.com; map p.166. Paradise on earth: established in 1954, this genteel hotel (which has played host to Jackie O and Queen Elizabeth, among many elegant others) has 197 rooms dotting a postcard-perfect, two-mile beach. Harmoniously landscaped amid centuries-old trees, there's legions of swimming pools (54 at last count), an equestrian centre (see page 173), spa, golf course (see page 173), tennis courts and the splendid *Sugar Mill* restaurant (see page 176). Its open lobby has old-world features like chess sets and art books. US$420

Zoetry Mahoe Bay ☎ 1 888 496 3879, ⓦ zoetryresorts.com; map p.166. Stylish all-suite resort that caters to your every need: thrice-daily maid service, personal butler, organic meals, top-shelf alcohol and unlimited international calls. Some rooms have private pools. All-inclusive. US$223

EATING

Montego Bay's resort status ensures a fair share of swanky international **restaurants** alongside the usual Jamaican places. Some restaurants offer free pick-ups for dinner guests, especially those furthest from the centre. If you're in the mood for a serious splurge, head west of town to *Round Hill* in Hopewell (reservation required), a supremely romantic candlelit affair (see page 187), at the other end of the scale, there are a string of stalls to the west of Hopewell churning out seafood for an enthusiastic local crowd.

CAFÉS AND SNACKS

Café Blue Shoppes at Rose Hall (on main road) ☎ 953 4646, ⓦ jamaicacafeblue.com; map p.166. Gourmet coffees made with beans from their own estate and Blue Mountain spring water, panini and good selection of cakes (J$800–1300), served in a cool a/c lounge. A second branch can be found inside the Fontana pharmacy at Fairview Shopping Centre (Alice Eldemire Drive; daily 8am–8.30pm). Mon–Fri 8.30am–5.30pm, Sat 10am–5.30pm.

Coffee Crème Café Whitter Village (upper level), main road, Ironshore ☎ 953 4588, ⓦ thecoffeencremecafe.com; map p.166. Serves a range of coffees, panini and cakes, plus ice cream, smoothies, salads and burgers, at reasonable prices (J$400–1000). Free wi-fi. Mon–Thurs & Sun 8am–8pm, Fri & Sat 8am–10pm.

Devon House I-Scream Baywest Centre, Strand St ☎ 940 4060; map p.169. Creamy ice cream galore as well as french fries at this small branch of the best islandwide brand. Unusual flavours are accompanied by old classics like coconut, rum 'n' raisin, and pineapple (J$350–800). Mon–Sat 10am–7pm.

RESTAURANTS

Adwa City Centre Mall, Harbour St; Westgate Shopping Centre, Barnett St ☎ 952 6554; map p.169. Two branches of this fabulous vegetarian/vegan takeaway – a good place to pick up lunch before heading on excursions. Serves breakfast (porridge, wholewheat ackee, veg or tofu patties; J$300–600), and lunch (salads, veg stew, curried tofu or meals of pulse/vegetable combinations; J$500–1300), plus smoothies, juices and power drinks. Daily 8am–9pm.

The Beach House 29 Gloucester Ave ☎ 622 7494; map p.166. A busy bar at night but also the best place on the Strip for a sit-down Jamaican breakfast, taken on the trendy plant-filled veranda – take advantage of reduced rate buffets (Sunday brunch is a highlight at US$16) and lunch specials. Mon–Thurs & Sun 9am–1am, Fri & Sat 9am–3am.

★ **Day-O Plantation** Lot 1, Fairfield Ave, 5km east of downtown ☎ 952 1825, ⓦ dayorestaurant.com; map p.166. This elegant and romantic hillside restaurant in a plant-wreathed colonial building feels a world away from flimsy tourist spots. The Jamaican and international food is wonderful; smoked marlin, jerk snapper and conch Creole, plus grilled fillet steak with Béarnaise sauce, oxtail and curried goat, and a spicy fruit and veg "Curry Caribe" (US$20–40). Great service. By reservation only. Daily 6–11pm.

Dragon Court Fairview Shopping Centre, Alice Eldermire Drive ☎ 979 8822; map p.166. Best Chinese in town, with a plush a/c dining room, and a huge menu,

4

including veggie choices, dim sum and sushi (J$700–1400). Takeaway/delivery available. Mon–Sat 11am–10pm, Sun 10.30am–10pm.

★ **Evelin's** 2 Kent Ave, Whitehouse ☎952 3280; map p.166. Basic Indian-Jamaican seafood joint by the water (turn right after *Sandals*), serving all things piscatorial with rice, bammy or, unusually, roti, the last a great accompaniment to the curried conch or Indian dhal (from US$5). Great cooking and inexpensive. Daily 8am–9pm.

★ **Houseboat Bar and Grill** Freeport Rd ☎979 8845, ⓦthehouseboatgrill.com; map p.166. Fantastic, unique setting in a converted houseboat moored on Bogue Lagoon. You board by way of a rope-pulled launch, and a window in the floor allows perusal of the marine life gliding underneath. The sophisticated menu offers imaginative takes on local seafood (choose-your-own lobster) and meat and vegetarian choices (US$25–40). You might find the signature black bean soup, spicy shrimp or surf 'n' turf. Desserts are satisfyingly indulgent, and service is great. Daily 6–11pm.

Marguerites Gloucester Ave ☎952 4777; map p.166. Right on the seafront next to *Margaritaville*, and with tables under the stars or in the open-sided dining room, this is perfect for a romantic dinner, with faultless formal service, upscale atmosphere and a delicious continental menu specializing in seafood (US$30–50); the crème brûlée is excellent. Daily 6–10.30pm.

★ **Memorabilia** 27 Mahoe Bay, Rose Hall (on main road, near the fishing village) ☎377 0224; map p.166. An unexpected, Cuban-owned beach bar and restaurant worth the drive east of town (just after *Coyaba* resort). Decked out with all manner of oddments and photos, the friendly bar is well stocked and the menu covers Jamaican and international foods (J$700–1500)– you'll get some of the best steam fish in MoBay here (J$1200–2000) – while the music mix is as eclectic as the furniture. Daily noon–2am.

★ **MoBay Proper Bar & Grill** Fort St ☎940 1233; map p.169. Brilliant, inexpensive little place on the approach to the Strip, offering a welcome alternative to the all-encompassing Americana hereabouts. Jamaican lunches and dinners (red-pea soup, stewed chicken, steamed or brown-stewed fish, curried conch; J$500–1500), all served up on the veranda or indoors. Popular Friday night fish fry. Daily 11.30am–1am.

Mystic India Whitter Village, Ironshore ☎953 9460, ⓦmysticindiajamaica.com; map p.166. This friendly and authentic tandoori house boasts a large menu that includes numerous vegetarian options. Unusual offerings include a shrimp pakora or Afghan kebab starter (US$10), Goanese shrimp curry (US$17) or lamb rogan josh (US$16). Free hotel pick-up. Daily noon–10pm.

The Pelican Gloucester Ave ☎952 3171, ⓦpelican grillja.com; map p.166. This long-established, mid-priced restaurant is a MoBay institution, and its leatherette booths are the perfect spot for a reliable Jamaican meal. Highlights include cornmeal porridge or Ameri-Jamaican breakfasts (US$8–12), lunch specials (from jerk chicken to cowfoot; US$12–20) and desserts (rum pudding and coconut- or banana-cream pie). Free hotel pick-up after 6pm. Daily 7am–10.30pm.

★ **Peppa's Cool Spot** Ramparts Close, behind the Grandiosa Hotel ☎433 9617, ⓦpeppascoolspot. com; map p.166. Beloved by locals and tourists alike, this hidden gem has a lovely alfresco setting and organic international dishes like home-smoked chorizo sausage with potatoes (US$10), haddock and prawns topped with a cheese crumb (US$13) and miso chicken with sticky rice (US$13). Mon–Fri 2–11pm, Sat 1pm–12.30am, Sun 2–10pm.

Pier One Howard Cooke Blvd ☎952 2452, ⓦpierone jamaica.com; map p.169. With tables laid out along a breezy pier and great views down the coastline, this is a pleasant spot for lunch or dinner, with burgers, salads and fish or steak sandwiches alongside Jamaican dishes as well as scallops in Red Stripe or seafood pasta (US$12–30). Free hotel pick-up. Becomes a major Montego Bay club some nights of the week. Mon 11am–midnight; Tues, Thurs & Sat 11am–11pm; Wed 11am–1am; Fri 11am–4am; Sun noon–midnight.

Pork Pit Gloucester Ave ☎940 3008; map p.166. The Strip's obligatory jerk spot, and very good it is too, with a shaded dining area and well-seasoned, inexpensive, chicken, pork, shrimp, ribs and fish grilled over a proper pimento-wood fire (J$500–1200). There's yam, festival or hard-dough to help soak up the pepper, and a tasty, hearty pumpkin or chicken soup, too. Mon–Thurs & Sun 11am–11pm, Fri & Sat 11am–midnight.

★ **Scotchies** Ironshore (on main road, opposite the Holiday Inn) ☎953 8041; map p.166. A bit out of the way, but worth the effort if you're after some excellent jerk cooking; pork, chicken, fish and seafood (J$500–1100) are served with festival, breadfruit, yam or sweet potato at palm-thatch-shaded tables set back from the road. Daily 11am–11pm.

★ **The Sugar Mill** Spring Farm Drive, Rose Hall ☎953 2211, ⓦhalfmoon.com; map p.166. Located on the grounds of a former sugar plantation, this atmospheric restaurant is the *Half Moon* hotel's signature dining spot (see page 175) and one of Jamaica's best restaurants. The menu is Caribbean-American fusion; expect dishes along the lines of callaloo and kale salad, crayfish bisque, and sea bass with coconut milk and plantains, served under dangling lamps and swaying palm fronds. Including drinks (there's a renowned rum collection), you'll spend around US$100 per person. Reservations recommended. Daily 6–10pm.

SUMFEST: JAMAICA'S PREMIER REGGAE FESTIVAL

Every year, Jamaica's best-loved art form overwhelms Montego Bay as **Reggae Sumfest** takes to the stage. The build-up is frenetic: flights are overbooked, beaches throng with fans and the line-up – which reads like a reggae hall of fame – is worried over on radio talk shows. By the time sound and light equipment arrives, the city's hotel rooms are booked out and every scrap of cardboard is appropriated by entrepreneurs to be sold as "reggae beds" – an essential piece of equipment for tired legs.

Sumfest's origins date back to 1978 when revellers enjoyed five nights of roots reggae at Jarrett Park. This "**Reggae Sunsplash**" captured international attention and a year later organizers announced a killer line-up with Bob Marley at the helm. The quintessential 1980s shows drew huge crowds in a heady combination of rum and ganja, and "good musical vibes" were the order of the days. By the mid-1990s, legal wrangles left Sunsplash outshone by its new Montego Bay competitor **Reggae Sumfest**, which today remains Jamaica's most popular festival. The party was marred slightly in 2005 when obscenities and homophobic lyrics led to a (temporary) ban on Beenie Man and other locally popular artists – in the eyes of some this was evidence of sanitization in the quest to appeal to foreigners – but its draw for tourism dollars, especially from Jamaicans overseas, is simply immense. It continues to attract some brilliant line-ups, with sets in recent years from Bounty Killer, Beenie Man, Sean Paul, Aidonia, Stephen Marley, Masicka and the late John Holt, plus huge international stars like Ne-Yo, Alicia Keys and Nas. And with 60,000 tickets sold, it remains unmissable.

THE LINE-UP

Sumfest usually takes place between mid-July and early August, kicking off with a beach party on the Sunday featuring top sound systems, fashion shows and food stalls. A Monday music cruise often follows, with Tuesday's **All White Party,** staged at *Pier One*, a slightly smarter affair.

Sumfest proper takes place just along the road from *Pier One* at the Catherine Hall Entertainment Complex. Thursday's show is a showcase for raw dancehall – the mostly local crowd is packed to the rafters to see the current biggest names in the industry. Jamaican audiences know their music and are notoriously hard to please; people waste no time demonstrating their appreciation with firecrackers or setting a lighter to a stream of hairspray – or not, with some blistering heckling and, occasionally, bottle-throwing. By the time Alkaline or Mavado take to the stage in the early hours, the atmosphere is truly electric. Shows usually good-natured despite on-stage rivalries, and aside from lyrics and posturing you'll be treated to some truly rude dancing courtesy of Dancehall Queens. Friday and Saturday nights have a more international feel. The new generation of roots artists add a cultural flavour, and grizzled old dreads wave enormous sticks of ganja in the air. A fabulous PA bounces all your favourite tunes around the hills surrounding the town.

TICKETS AND INFORMATION

Entry (tickets are much cheaper when purchased online in advance) to the Sumfest beach party costs around US$25, the White Party US$29, while the Monday street party is free. Dancehall night is US$50 and Reggae Night is US$54. An all-events pass (around US$167) covers entry to all the main nights, and a VIP version (around US$300), gives access to the backstage and front of stage areas. For more **information**, check out ⊚ reggaesumfest.com.

DRINKING AND NIGHTLIFE

Montego Bay has many lively **nightspots**, but aside from the buzz around *Margaritaville*, you have to search them out. Doctor's Cave Beach is great for a drink at sunset, and some of the restaurants listed above double up as bars: *Houseboat Bar and Grill* is superb for cocktails and bar snacks (happy hour 5.30–7pm), with Friday night attracting the expat crowd; *Memorabilia* has a wonderful bar with a private section of beach; while the *Beach House* is a lively spot at weekends. At the other end of the scale, the "Dead End" beach, at the end of Kent Ave (beyond the Strip), is often busy with Jamaicans taking a drink and listening to music at sunset. **Live music** is surprisingly thin on the ground, with all-inclusive resorts snapping up local performers. If you're lucky you'll catch a full-moon party at Doctor's Cave or Cornwall Beach, a sound-system jam at by the beach or other one-off events advertised on Irie FM or on posters. The large music events of the year are Jamaica Jazz and Blues in January (see page 32) and Reggae Sumfest in July/August (see above).

BARS

Bluebeat Jazz & Blues Bar Gloucester Ave ☎ 952 4777; map p.166. Upmarket, icily a/c (and non-smoking) little bar with dark decor, jazz-themed pictures on the walls and an outside deck. Offers fancy cocktails, cheap beer (US$5) and great live jazz or blues daily. Daily 9pm–1am.

D'Rehab Bar & Lounge 33 Gloucester Ave ☎ 620 9826, ⊕ drehabsportsbar.com; map p.166. A "no drop pants, ganja smoking, expletive language and loitering" sign greets your arrival at this late bar just above the Strip, with pool tables, a fine veranda and super-loud reggae and hip-hop. Daily noon–2am.

Hi-Lites Café 19 Queen's Drive; map p.166. Very sleepy bar with Red Stripe, Appleton and a few other Jamaican drinks staples available (J$300–600). Sporadic opening hours but a great escape from the Strip and worth visiting for the wonderful view across the bay. Daily 11am–10pm.

Martina's Bar 1 Howard Cooke Blvd ☎ 953 6557; map p.169. Next to Freeport Police Station, this is an attractive circular outdoor bar with a large lawn and own car park – a laidback spot drawing a mature crowd, with frequent DJs spinning older reggae music. Food and fresh juices available. Daily 11am–midnight.

★ **MoBay Proper Bar & Grill** Fort St ☎ 940 1233; map p.169. The best place on the Strip to get a flavour of downtime Jamaican-style, drawing a loyal crowd for veranda drinks or a round of pool; board games are kept behind the bar. Pool and skittles tournament Tues, DJ jam on Wed, karaoke Thurs, old hits Fri and jazz on Sun. Daily 10am–2am.

Montego Bay Yacht Club Freeport ☎ 979 8262, ⊕ mobayyachtclub.com; map p.169. The great and the good of MoBay society, as well as visiting yachties, come here to hang out and sink martinis (US$10) in plush surroundings. The club is members only, but the bar is open to all. Daily 10am–11pm.

Reggae Bar 47 Gloucester Ave; map p.166. Tiny rooftop bar with a pool table and well-stocked bar, serving rum, *mojitos,* and more rum (US$8–12), with a reggae soundtrack. Right on the Strip amid the action. Daily 11am–midnight.

Richmond Hill Inn Richmond Hill, off Union St ☎ 952 3859, ⊕ richmond-hill-inn.com; map p.169. A lovely spot for a sunset drink by the pool. The setting – on its very own hill at the top of Union St – is spectacular and intensely romantic; the view covers the whole bay. Daily 7am–7pm.

CLUBS

MoBay's club scene gets going late, from 11pm or midnight. Don't be surprised if you find that there's rather a lot of go-go (strip) clubs around – they draw a mixed crowd of men and women, but with regular "freaky" shows they're not for the faint-hearted. If you're well up on dancehall culture ask around for street dances downtown, in the flavour of those in downtown Kingston; they sometimes happen around the malls on Barnett St.

Klub Kokonutz Main Rd, Reading (3km southwest of MoBay) ☎ 620 8498, ⊕ klubkokonutz.com; map p.169. A traditional indoor a/c nightclub, drawing big crowds for its sporadic parties featuring big-name DJs and singers. Otherwise you're not likely to find it packed, though it can be good fun and has karaoke on Mondays and occasional retro parties. "Dress to impress" – though in reality tourists will be let in as long as men are not in shorts. Mon–Sat noon–2am.

Margaritaville Gloucester Ave ☎ 979 8041, ⊕ margaritavillecaribbean.com; map p.166. Hugely popular bar-cum-restaurant-cum-club – if you're looking for guaranteed action, this is it, and if you don't mind sunburnt tourists, it's great fun. Big sports screen TVs, 52 different flavours of margarita and 32-ounce "bongs of beer" keep the atmosphere buzzing, and nights run to various themes, always with a packed dancefloor. Theme nights include "Ladies Night" and "Bare-as-you-dare"; Sat is busiest with big-name DJs. Cover Mon, Tues & Sun US$6, Wed–Sat US$15. Daily 8pm till late.

★ **Pier One** Howard Cooke Blvd ☎ 952 2452, ⊕ pieronejamaica.com; map p.169. Popular MoBay old-timer, with a roster of club nights and sports events shown on big-screen TVs. The waterside setting is great for a drink anytime, but best is the packed Friday night Pier Pressure, with dancehall, hip-hop, R&B and soca on the decks and a mostly local crowd demonstrating all the latest dances. Mon 11am–midnight, Tues, Thurs & Sat 11am–11pm, Wed 11am–1am, Fri 11am–4am, Sun noon–midnight.

ENTERTAINMENT

Fairfield Theatre Fairfield Rd, 3km east of downtown ☎ 781 8792. Catch one of the excellent Montego Bay Little Theatre Movement productions at this atmospheric venue which promotes Jamaican playwrights. Check their Facebook page for details.

Montego Bay Cultural Centre Sam Sharpe Square ⊕ montegobayculturalcentre.org. A theatre and events space hosting occasional Jamaican roots plays.

Palace Multiplex Fairview Shopping Centre, Alice Eldemire Drive ☎ 1 888 429 5722, ⊕ palaceamusement.com. Shows all mainstream Hollywood releases. Tickets J$1050.

SHOPPING

Countless malls are given over to tax-free **in-bond shopping** for the cruise ship crowd, with jewellery, perfume and leather goods; City Centre Plaza on Fort St is the least ostentatious, and The Shopping Village in Ironshore, easily the most upscale, with numerous attractive Caribbean designer boutiques. The Montego Bay Shopping Centre – usually referred to as the LOJ (Life of Jamaica) Mall – on Howard Cooke Boulevard is better for general purchases, with clothes shops and a branch of Fontana Pharmacy, great for gimmicky souvenirs, while the nearby Baywest Shopping Centre on Harbour and Union streets is similar. Browse the untouristy stores downtown on St James and Barnett streets for miscellaneous odds and ends like red, gold and green necklaces and car-mirror tassels.

CRAFT MARKETS

Fantasy Craft Market Gloucester Ave, opposite Cornwall Beach; map p.166. This diminutive market is tucked behind a row of duty-free stores and take-outs and is oversold by its vendors, but you may pick up a bargain. Daily 8am–7pm.

Fort Street Craft Market Fort St; map p.166. Tucked away around steep steps up to Queen's Drive, this market is worth a look, though it tends to be a little more expensive than the main craft market downtown. Daily 8am–7pm.

Harbour Street Craft Market Between Harbour St and Howard Cooke Blvd; map p.169. MoBay's main craft market is a surprisingly hassle-free place to shop if you don't treat the inventive sales pitches as bamboozling (vendors expect a bit of bartering). Packed with straw and wicker-work, belts, clothes, jewellery, T-shirts and woodcarvings, the two-hundred-odd stalls sell every type of Jamaican craft, and there are a couple of decent, cheap, local places to eat. Daily 7am–7pm.

GALLERIES

★ **Gallery of West Indian Art** 11 Fairfield Rd, Catherine Hall ☎ 952 4547, ⊛ galleryofwestindianart. com; map p.166. Just past the left-hand turn-off for Fairfield, a side road to the west leads to this higher-end gallery with a marvellous repository of artworks from Jamaica and the wider Caribbean. It's renowned for hand-carved and painted wooden animals, and is a great place to pick up prints and original works, and to learn about the local arts scene. Mon–Fri 10am–5pm.

RECORD STORES

Downtown record stores and street boom boxes offer the Jamaican speciality of custom-made reggae CDs (around US$5) as well as albums on CD.

Clapper's Mobile Music Box Church Lane Car Park; map p.169. Quality sound-system session CDs and bootleg recordings of stageshows on sale (US$5); ask for a test play before you buy. Mon–Sat.

El Paso 3 South Lane ☎ 952 9133; map p.169. Right by Sam Sharpe Square, this upstairs shop has a counter all the way around with vinyl plastered to the walls. Good back catalogue and CDs too. Second branch at the Baywest Centre (same opening hours). Mon–Sat 9am–6pm.

Federal Records 14 Strand St ☎ 952 7541; map p.169. Worth a visit for the enthusiasm of owner Ainsworth Palmer, coupled with his large collection on CD and vinyl. Mon–Fri 9am–5pm, Sat 9am–2pm.

BOOKS, SOUVENIRS AND CAKES

Heaven 67 Gloucester Ave ☎ 412 0191 or ☎ 940 1505; map p.166. A souvenir shop right by Doctor's Cave, offering a superior selection of jewellery, books, artworks and clothing. Mon–Sat 9am–7pm, Sun 11am–4pm.

Sangster's Bookstore Baywest Shopping Centre ☎ 952 1122, ⊛ sangstersbooks.com; map p.169. MoBay's principal bookshop, selling fiction, reference and children's titles, plus stationery. There's a second outlet at 9 Upper King St. Mon–Sat 8.30am–6pm.

DIRECTORY

Consulates Only the Canadian Consulate (☎ 538 3025) and US Consulate (☎ 953 0620) have offices in Montego Bay; the former on Gloucester Ave, the latter in Whitter Village. UK citizens should call the British Honorary Consul (☎ 936 0700). Embassies and other consulates are all based in Kingston (see page 75).

Doctors Most hotels have a doctor or nurse on duty or on call. A recommended practitioner is the holistically minded Dr Anthony Vendryes (☎ 971 9459).

Hospitals Cornwall Regional Hospital, Mount Salem (☎ 952 5100), is the best public hospital outside Kingston. The best private institutions are Doctor's Hospital in Fairfield (☎ 952 1616). In an emergency dial ☎ 119 for an ambulance.

Immigration Immigration Office, Floor 3, Overton Plaza, 49 Union St (☎ 952 5381; Mon–Thurs 8.30am–4pm, Fri 8.30am–4pm); for visa extensions, go early to avoid the queues.

Laundry Most hotels have a laundry service, but there are some fairly good coin-operated laundries. Try Fabricare at 4 Corner Lane (☎ 952 6987) and Westgate Plaza (☎ 940 0492).

Money and exchange FX Trader, above the *Pelican* restaurant on the Strip (Mon–Sat 9am–5pm), is best for exchange. Cambio King, at the Casa Montego mini-mall opposite Doctor's Cave, is also good. Banks with ATMs congregate at Sam Sharpe Square; there are also ATMs on Gloucester Ave near Cornwall and Doctor's Cave beaches and at the airport.

Pharmacies There are plenty of pharmacies downtown. Try Best Care, 10 St James St (Mon–Sat 9am–10pm, Sun 9am–9pm); Fontana, Fairfield Shopping Centre (Mon–Sat 8am–9pm, Sun 10am-4pm) and Montego Bay (LOJ) Shopping Centre (Mon–Sat 8am–7pm).

Police Montego Bay has four police stations. Visitors are usually told to take crime reports directly to the Tourism

Liaison Unit at Summit station on Sunset Boulevard (☎ 952 1540). Other stations are located in Catherine Hall (☎ 952 4997) and downtown at 14 Barnett St (☎ 952 1557). In an emergency, dial ☎ 119.

Post offices The two main post offices are on the corner of Fort St opposite the library, and at 120 Barnett St.

East of Montego Bay

Away from the shops and the beaches, there's plenty to see around Montego Bay. East of town, the **Greenwood Great House** has a quiet charm and seductive natural beauty, and the wealth of Georgian architecture at sleepy **Falmouth** is certainly worth a few hours of your time. Falmouth is the parish capital of **Trelawny**; the region is best known for both its magnificent yams (sixty percent of Jamaica's yam crop is grown here) and as the home of world record sprinter Usain Bolt (see page 266). Trelawny's history is dominated by the plantation era; at the height of the plantocracy there were 88 **sugar estates** here worked by tens of thousands of slaves.

Rose Hall

9.5km east of MoBay • Daily 9.15am–9.15pm • US$20 (US$18 online) • ☎ 953 2323, �🌐 rosehall.com

Romanticized plantation history comes into its own at **ROSE HALL**, site of the infamous **Rose Hall Great House**, the inspiration for Jamaica's best-loved piece of folklore. Built between 1770 and 1780 by planter and parish custos (mayor) John Palmer, the dazzling white stone structure, surrounded by gardens and a bird-filled pond, is difficult to miss. The 45-minute tours (by flashlight after 6pm) make much of the embellished legend of Annie Palmer, the "White Witch of Rose Hall" (see below); starting in the gift shop, you gasp at blurred photos sent in by previous visitors

---

THE WHITE WITCH OF ROSE HALL

Jamaica's most famous horror story centres on **Annie Palmer**, the "White Witch of Rose Hall". A beautiful young woman, Annie Mary Patterson's early years are cloaked in mystery. Born in either England or Ireland, she was the only child of small-time property owners John and Juliana Patterson, who brought her to live in Haiti, where she learned the Voodoo art. The date of her arrival in Jamaica is unknown, but it's said that she came to Kingston as a fresh-faced seventeen-year-old in search of a husband. She was granted access to high society and her brooding good looks soon captured the attention of John Palmer, incumbent of Rose Hall and grand-nephew of its architect, also John Palmer. They married in March 1820, but the union was not a happy one; seven years on and bored with her insipid husband, Annie took a young slave lover. Palmer found out and whipped her severely; Annie took her revenge by poisoning his wine and smothering the dying man with a pillow. She went on to murder two more husbands and seduce and murder a succession of white book-keepers and black slaves. She was a cruel and sadistic mistress even to those slaves she wasn't sleeping with, meting out excessive punishments for misdemeanours.

However, Annie's cruelty proved to be her undoing, and she was **murdered** in her bed in 1831. No one knows for sure whose hands encircled her neck, but some accounts point to an old and powerful balmist whose pretty granddaughter had been in competition with Annie for the attentions of a young English book-keeper until the older woman set an "ol' hige" vampire upon her rival, killing her within a week.

Gripping as it is, there's barely a shred of truth in the story (though it's retold in bodice-ripping style in Herbert de Lisser's novel; see page 294). Annie Palmer did exist (she's buried in a concrete grave, where the tour of the property concludes; see above), but by all accounts she had no discernible tendencies to sadism or lechery. She may have become confused over the years with Rosa Palmer, the original mistress of Rose Hall, who did have four husbands, but she was said to be unwaveringly virtuous. Nonetheless, most Jamaicans believe in something more sinister, and visiting mediums swear to strange visions and buried effigies in the grounds, while the house retains a vestige of creepiness.

THE CORAL GARDENS MASSACRE

The grounds of Rose Hall Great House are lovely, though these too have a violent (and authentic) past. On Good Friday in 1963 the district was the site of the "**Coral Gardens Massacre**", a bloody altercation between police and Rastafarians – then commonly viewed as vicious, anti-white, drug-crazed maniacs – whose right of way through the Rose Hall grounds to their vegetable plots was being threatened by property speculators developing the house into the tourist attraction it is today. After months of contention, a petrol station was set on fire, and a policeman sent to investigate was attacked by machete-wielding Rastas. During the ensuing bloodbath eight people were killed (Rastas, policemen and civilians), and an unofficial "war on Rastas" was declared islandwide, with hundreds thrown into jail and their locks forcibly sheared off.

Each Easter, the killings are commemorated by Rastafarians at Sam Sharpe Square (see page 169) in MoBay. Reconciliation with this difficult piece of history took a strong step forward in 2017, when the Jamaican government issued an official apology denouncing the "brutality, injustice and repression" that characterized the incident. In addition, a trust was set up for survivors and the groundwork laid for a heritage site in St Catherine.

that supposedly show the face of an unknown woman in the mirror or a bat in a chandelier, and gawp at Annie's bedroom, symbolically redecorated in shades of red, and the terrace from which she allegedly pushed a maid to her death. As the house was unoccupied and widely looted during the nineteenth century, almost all of its current contents have been transported from other great houses or from overseas. The silk wallpaper and magnificent mahogany staircase are attractive (if not from the right period), and the fake food laid out on the dining table adds a touch of kitsch.

ARRIVAL AND DEPARTURE | ROSE HALL

By car Coming from MoBay, turn inland just east of the Montego Bay Convention Centre, 1.5km before *Hilton Rose Hall*.

By minibus or route taxi Route taxis and minibuses ply this route to the east of MoBay (Mon–Sat daylight hours, quite frequent; less on Sun and in evenings).

ACTIVITIES

Sugar Mill Falls Water Park Hilton Rose Hall Resort, 1.5km west of the Great House ☎ 953 2650, ⓦ rosehall resort.com. Jamaica's largest water park, Sugar Mill Falls offers cascading waterfalls, a thrill slide, a "lazy river" for tubing and swimming, and several pools. It's great fun for kids and adults alike, and non-guests can buy a day pass that includes all food and drink (US$85 adults, US$65 children) – good value if you spend the whole day here. Daily 11am–5pm.

ACCOMMODATION

Hyatt Rose Hall Main Rd, Rose Hall ☎ 953 2800, ⓦ hyatt.com. This huge, super-luxurious property feels like a country unto itself, combining the *Hyatt Zilara* (adults only) and *Ziva*. The 427 classically decorated rooms come with every imaginable amenity; facilities include a large beach, the White Witch golf course, a spa, pools and legions of restaurants and bars. Sun loungers are equipped with flags to raise to order a drink without moving more than your hand. Both beach and atmosphere are all manufactured impeccably. **US$460**

Greenwood

Coastal development becomes more sporadic between Rose Hall and the diminutive village of **GREENWOOD**. Bar an enormous *Iberostar* complex and the odd villa development, the coast road passes scrubby mangrove swamps and opens up to a magnificent sea view. At Greenwood's eastern edge, some enterprising locals have landscaped a pretty little slip of white sand and clear water known as **Citizens Beach**. It's a lovely, breezy spot for a drink or a snack, particularly on Sundays when local families come down, and it occasionally serves as a venue for sound-system jams, too.

Greenwood Great House

435 Belgrade Ave (walking distance inland from the main road) • Daily 9am–6pm, via 45min tours (last tour at 5pm) • US$20 • ☎ 631 4701, ⓦ greenwoodgreathouse.com

Perched on a hill overlooking the sea, the classy stonework of **Greenwood Great House** is deservedly declared a National Heritage site and remains one of the best historical sights on the island. Surrounded by lush gardens, it has none of the flashy allure of Rose Hall (see page 180), but is of far more interest, retaining most of its original contents as well as a wonderfully listless, frozen-in-time eighteenth-century ambience. Built in 1790 by relatives of the Barrett family of Wimpole Street fame, the house contains the owners' original library and an eclectic collection of ancient musical instruments, a court jester's chair and custom-made Wedgwood china. The Barretts' seventy-foot veranda commands a panorama of the sea unbroken by land, and you really can see the curvature of the earth. The tour, which ends at a bar in the original kitchen, is more enjoyable than the breakneck run around Rose Hall. Though the Barretts owned 84,000 acres hereabouts, worked by some 2000 Africans, there's little information on the realities of the plantation era, other than a cursory reference to a man-trap used to catch escaped slaves and a leg-iron displayed like an ornament.

ARRIVAL AND DEPARTURE   GREENWOOD

By minibus or route taxi Route taxis and minibuses frequently ply the route between MoBay and Falmouth (less often on evenings and on Sun).

EATING

Chill Out Hut On main road ☎ 620 8720. Out on the main road, just west of Greenwood Great House, this justly popular beachfront hangout offers super-fresh seafood dishes, classic Jamaican fare like oxtail and curry goat and pasta dishes, too. Fun drinks, and a relaxed ambience. Daily 10am–11pm.

Far Out Fish Hut On main road ☎ 954 7155. Head for the main road at the eastern edge of Greenwood for this excellent locals' fish spot with a laidback seaside setting and a thatch-roof bar (prepare for slow service). Pick your fish from the catch of the day and have it roasted in foil or escovitched, and eat it with bammy and a cold beer (J$1300–1600). Daily 11am–11pm.

Falmouth

Trelawny's parish capital, **FALMOUTH** – 34 kilometres east of MoBay and named for the English birthplace of Parish Governor Sir William Trelawny – became the main port of call for sugar ships in the late eighteenth century. Slaves were traded and goods unloaded, while planters built elegant Georgian town houses.

Falmouth fell into a state of disrepair in the nineteenth century, which continued for well over a hundred years, but its long-held sleepy quality shifted in 2011 with the opening of a new deep-water **cruise ship dock** on the town's eastern seaboard. Divers were contracted to individually move over 150,000 valuable corals from a section of reef, thus making space to service the happy hordes disembarking from the largest cruise ships in the world. The development was nonetheless supported by most of the town, appreciative of the financial influx and the increase in the job market. Some residents were happy, too, to see the renovation of much of its best **Georgian architecture**. This includes some of Falmouth's most impressive constructions: **Tharpe House**, a block west of the port, the porticoed **post office** in the middle of Market Street, and the old **courthouse**, built overlooking the sea in 1815, are still in commercial or municipal use.

Outside cruise ship days and the immediate vicinity of the port, Falmouth remains an easy-going place, with a high concentration of two-hundred-year-old timbers leaning onto the tarmac, and once majestic properties now well-aged shelters for chickens and stray dogs. A wander through the streets provides an unadorned – and due to its slavery connection, sometimes chilling – glimpse into Jamaica's past. The best **beach** in the area is Burwood Public Beach, 6km east of town (just east of the *Royalton Sands* resort), off the main highway.

Brief history

In the late eighteenth century, Falmouth boasted 150 houses and a cage where the market now stands (similar to the one still on view in Montego Bay's Sam Sharpe Square – see page 169), used for locking up drunken sailors found on the streets later than the 6pm curfew. Slavery ended within fifty years of the town being declared parish capital in 1790, but Falmouth's natural harbour ensured prosperity, and the town thrived where others declined. The advent of the steamship – the first docked at Jamaican shores in 1837 – spelt the first step in Falmouth's decline. The harbour wasn't deep enough for larger vessels, and by 1890 the place had become something of a ghost town – traders left for Montego Bay or Kingston, and their houses began slowly to rot. In 1896, however, the Albert George Market was built, and Falmouth's status as **market town** still ensures a bustling centre, with fruit and veg, bootleg clothing and brightly coloured fripperies set out along the pavements, in traditional "bend down" style.

Water Square and around

Falmouth's centre retains its original grid formation, with main streets fanning out from **Water Square**, named in allusion to the town's status as the first in Jamaica to have piped water. The non-functioning central fountain marks the spot of a stone reservoir that once held fresh water pumped by waterwheel from the Martha Brae River. The square has numerous remaining renovated wooden shop-fronts, combined with cane and coconut vendors and crowds of shoppers. At the side of the square, the **Albert George Market building** (Mon–Sat 9am–5pm; free) holds a collection of bits and bobs from Falmouth's past alongside sandals, jewellery and t-shirts.

A block west of Water Square, on Market Street, the stately and carefully restored **Baptist Manse** is said to have been inhabited by Baptist preacher and white anti-slavery campaigner **William Knibb** (see below). Knibb called slavery "one of the most odious monsters that ever disgraced the earth", and his fiery campaigning across the United Kingdom went a long way towards its abolishment in 1834. A grassroots pioneer, Knibb used stirring theatrics to punctuate his powerful words; once, in front of a crowd of three thousand Londoners, he raised up, then tossed, human shackles to the ground in front of them, imploring his audience to treat Africans from the "same family of man".

Phoenix Foundry

Immediately striking as you enter or leave town to the east is the conical roof of the 1810 **Phoenix Foundry** behind the locked gates of **Central Wharf** (close to the new cruise ship terminal) – where sugar, rum and slaves were traded during the port's heyday – along with several dilapidated warehouses and disintegrating plasterboard set dressings from the filming of *Wide Sargasso Sea* in 2004.

William Knibb Memorial Baptist Church

Cnr King and George streets

The chunky **William Knibb Memorial Baptist Church** is where, on the momentous date of August 1, 1838 when Jamaican slaves were given full freedom, William Knibb declared "The Monster is Dead" to the crowd gathered to celebrate and thank the man who had been instrumental in the process. Slave irons, collars and whips were ceremonially buried under an affecting memorial that still stands in the grassy churchyard; Knibb is also buried here, at the back of the church. Inside the church, a marble plaque erected by "sons of Africa" depicts the interment of the implements, alongside the biblical quote "Ethiopia shall soon stretch out her hands unto God." Another plaque marks the demise of Knibb's twelve-year-old son, whose death was "occasioned by fever from excess of joy" when congregation members granted freedom to their slaves a year before formal emancipation, after concluding "slavery is incompatible with Christianity".

The Barrett House

1 Market St

Falmouth was built on land originally owned by plantation magnate Edward Barrett, and it was even once known as Barrett Town. The Regency-style **Barrett House** was built in 1799, with a brick base and weatherboard upper storey supported by wooden columns; the upper half has now completely disintegrated and there are sadly no immediate plans to restore it. The house also has a tenuous literary connection. Having survived his three sons, Barrett left his estate to his daughter on the condition that the man she married took the Barrett name – the house was built by her husband, Charles Moulton Barrett. The couple moved to England and had two sons, one of whom fathered the poet **Elizabeth Barrett Browning**.

Jamaica Swamp Safari Village

Foreshore Rd, 2km west of the town centre • Daily 9am–4pm • US$25 • ☎ 617 2798, ⓦ jamaicaswampsafari.com

The somewhat haphazard menagerie at the **Jamaica Swamp Safari Village** is the only place on the north coast where you can see Jamaican crocodiles (see them in the wild on a safari at Black River; see page 235). Ranging from tiny babies to an alarming fourteen-footer, the crocodiles lie in rather depressing small-zoo conditions – and with various other caged indigenous animals (endangered Jamaican yellow snake and coney, plus monkeys and raccoons) – you may decide you'll give the place a miss. Incidentally, it was here that Ross Kananga, the zoo's American founder, performed the stunt in *Live and Let Die* where James Bond used crocodile heads as stepping stones. Later the same year the safari village was also a location in the film *Papillon*, starring Steve McQueen.

Glistening Waters Luminous Lagoon

Rock, 4km east of Falmouth • Boat trips US$25 (35min) • ☎ 954 3229, ⓦ glisteningwaters.com

The community of **ROCK**, just east of Falmouth, is home to **Glistening Waters Luminous Lagoon**. Enclosed by a casuarina-covered promontory, the lagoon owes its name to the very impressive incandescent illuminations of microorganisms (one of only four similar locations worldwide), which can be viewed on small tours. After dark, the water shines bright turquoise when agitated, and you can see trails of fish. Tours (see below) include a boat trip in the early evening and the opportunity to plunge into the eerie depths surrounded by what appears to be glowing water (wear your swimsuit).

ARRIVAL AND DEPARTURE
FALMOUTH

By bus Knutsford Express (ⓦ knutsfordexpress.com) buses to Montego Bay and Ocho Rios arrive and depart from Glistening Waters, east of town (7–9 daily; 35min to Montego Bay, 1hr 45min to Ocho Rios); to get here, take a route taxi from Water Square.

By minibus and route taxi Minibuses and route taxis to Montego Bay, Discovery Bay and routes inland to Wakefield and Albert Town depart from outside Courts department store, close to Water Square.

INFORMATION AND TOURS

Tourist information A JTB information desk operates at the cruise port on ship days only; a more reliable information source is at Falmouth Heritage Renewal (see below). The Georgian Society of Jamaica has produced an informative booklet, *Falmouth 1791–1970*, about the town's history; it's available from the society's headquarters with sections online (☎ 479 9519, ⓦ georgianjamaica.org).

Boat tours Local man Michael Currie (☎ 466 2194, ⓦ faithfulwatersjm.com), operates a trip to the Glistening Water Luminous Lagoon (US$15) in his glass-bottom boat, with a relaxed attitude and reggae soundtrack.

Walking tours To learn more about Georgian Falmouth, contact staff at Falmouth Heritage Renewal Inc, 9 King St (☎ 617 3163, ⓦ falmouthjamaica.org), who organize walking tours. The organization led the restoration of large parts of the centre and runs an NGO focusing on youth training in carpentry and restoration.

Festivals Turn inland to Florence Hall from the highway at Rock for the under-used 25,000-seat Trelawny Stadium, constructed for the opening of the Cricket World Cup in 2007 and given a new lease of life as occasional venue for the high-profile Jamaica Jazz and Blues Festival (see page 32).

ACCOMMODATION AND EATING

There are loads of local cookshops around town, and two bar/restaurants at the cruise ship pier that are open on ship days.

Aunt Gloria's Bar & Grill Main Rd, Rock, 1.5km east of Falmouth ☎ 353 1301. The best home cooking locally is found east of town, serving typical Jamaican stewed or escovitched fish (by weight, from J$800), curry goat or fried chicken (J$400–800), accompanied by jerk chicken and pork (Fri–Sat only). Mon–Sat 7am–9pm.

Fisherman's Inn Main Rd, Rock, 2km east of Falmouth ☎ 954 3427. A small hotel with sweet, clementine-coloured guestrooms, a/c, a restaurant and a pool, backing onto the luminous lagoon next to Glistening Waters, with its own small marina. US$70

Glistening Waters Rock, 2km east of Falmouth ☎ 954 3229, ⓦ glisteningwaters.com. This slightly overpriced Jamaican seafood restaurant and bar by the marina of the phosphorescent lagoon serves decent lobster tails (US$35). Mon–Sat 10am–9pm, Sun noon–9pm.

Martha Brae Rafter's Village

Martha Brae Rd • Daily 9am–4.30pm (last raft puts in at 3.30pm) • Rafting trips US$65 per two-person raft, 1hr 20min • ☎ 952 0889, ⓦ jamaicarafting.com • Heading inland from Falmouth, a lone road threads from Water Square, under the highway and onward for about 4km to the village

The **Martha Brae River**, Trelawny's longest waterway, is notable chiefly for relaxing **rafting** trips. If you want to have a go, follow the signs from Falmouth to the put-in point at Rafter's Village, which has a small (underused) swimming pool, bar, and gift shop. The leisurely trip begins with a complimentary fruit drink and takes you past banks overhung with silk cotton, mango and towering banyan trees festooned with vines. There are a few craft stalls, floating bars and, after rain, a constant mosquito offensive – bring repellent. The Brae periodically hosts streams of cruise ship passengers; call ahead to confirm space and scheduling for the day.

4

Good Hope Great House

Good Hope, Bunker's Hill • Estate Pass US$49 • Daily 10am–5pm • ☎ 656 8026, ⓦ chukka.com • Accessed along a well-signposted but muddy and rutted road 10km or so along the Martha Brae road from Falmouth; transportation available through Chukka

Built in creamy English stone by John Tharp, the largest land- and slave- owner in Jamaica in the late eighteenth century, **Good Hope Great House** is now a stunning Georgian property overlooking a 2000-acre working plantation, ringed by the conical hillocks of Cockpit Country which are best seen when the mists roll away at dawn across the surrounding valleys. Now managed by Chukka Caribbean and a destination for mass adventure/historical tourism, an estate pass lets you tour the property, which includes an aviary, gardens, waterfall, swimming pool and challenge course.

David Pinto Ceramic Art

By appointment • ☎ 886 2866, ⓦ jamaicapottery.com

The workshop of master potter David Pinto, a famed craftsman whose art you can find both overseas and at galleries and elegant dinner tables across Jamaica, is also within the estate's boundaries. His beautifully crafted plates and sculptures are reasonably priced, while classes and workshops on clay pottery are held by arrangement.

ACTIVITIES   GOOD HOPE GREAT HOUSE

Zipline An all-day "thrill-seekers pass" (7hr; US$170) takes in a zipline through the trees, close to the Martha Brae River, from where you don your tube and navigate low rapids for 30min; the tour ends with a water slide.

ACCOMMODATION AND EATING

Good Hope Coach House ☎ 881 6869, ⓦ goodhope jamaica.com. The house is rented out as an exclusive villa with seven bedrooms and space to sleep fourteen. There are antique furnishings, a large lap pool and magnificent views of Cockpit Country, plus the property is surrounded by gardens full of flowers and hummingbirds. Villa weekly US$6200

South and west of Montego Bay

The smooth coastal highway towards Negril hugs the shoreline and offers beautiful views of the turquoise, reef-studded water. By contrast, the roads heading inland are overhung with the dripping foliage of the jungle-smothered interior, and pass over swift streams towards the Cockpit foothills. If you have your own transport, you'll be able to appreciate how spectacular the scenery is in this region.

The principal road south from Montego Bay veers away from the coastal highway by the traffic lights at **Reading**, a couple of kilometres east of Hopewell. The well-signposted B8 road heads straight up the tortuous ascent of **Long Hill** into the verdant **St James interior**, parallel to the Great River valley with occasional glimpses of lush palms and ferns in the chasm below. Most visitors venture here to tube the Great River or sail through the treetops at Lethe, though the area also offers more easygoing sights such as the gardens at **Ras Natango**, hummingbird visitation at the **Rocklands Bird Sanctuary** and the eco-oriented **Animal Farm**. The B8 rises to 2000ft before Anchovy and passes through the citrus groves of **MONTPELIER** (look out for rows of seasonal ugli fruit, a cross between a grapefruit and an orange), before the road forks; a right turn takes you over the interior mountains on an incredibly pretty route to Shettlewood and Sav-la-Mar (via the excellent Border Jerk stop), while a left fork passes through marvellous countryside to the unique German settlement of **Seaford Town**.

The rolling hinterland pastures of the **St James interior** was prime plantation territory for British colonists, and a few of the old estates (such as **Bellefield Great House**) have kept their land and opened it up to the public. Polished boiling pots and repointed stone mills illustrate the mechanics of the sugar industry, and lavishly restored great house interiors gloss over the planters' lifestyles. Annually in the tiny hamlet of **Kensington**, the key flashpoint of the 1831 Christmas Rebellion (see page 170), a "Flames of Freedom" torch run commemorates one of the most significant phases in Jamaican history. The insurgency that began here in St James – when a fire was started on the Tulloch Castle Estate – set the wheels in motion for the abolition of slavery in Jamaica.

4

GETTING AROUND   SOUTH AND WEST OF MONTEGO BAY

By car, taxi or tour The B8 is the route from MoBay to Savannah-la-Mar and the south coast, so traffic is pretty heavy. Public transport can be a problem in the rural areas beyond, so your best bet is to join an organized tour or hire a private driver (see page 172).

By public transport If you don't have a car, and would prefer to spare yourself the expense of chartering a driver, go to the Transport Centre in MoBay (see page 171), and tell a minibus driver, or a conductor, where you are headed outside the city. They can advise you as to which route taxi or minibus will get you closest to your destination.

Bellefield Great House and Gardens

6km southeast of Montego Bay • Tours by appointment only, Mon–Thurs; 2–3hr • US$56, includes Jamaican lunch • ☎ 952 2382, Ⓦ bellefieldgreathouse.com

Just outside the city, the pristine grounds of the ten-acre **Bellefield Great House** are viewable on a quieter, less harried tour than those of the area's more well-known plantation homes. Dating to the 1600s, Bellefield was a major sugar mill and production centre in the eighteenth-century, and visits here include a tour of the mill, where you sample sugarcane and learn about the cane-to-sugar process. After a visit to the antique-filled great house, lunch (there's a great jerk pit onsite) is served in the shade of a centuries-old guango tree.

Ras Natango Gallery and Garden

1 Ras Natango Way, Camrose District, 6.5km southeast of Montego Bay • Mon–Fri 10am–6pm, Sat & Sun by appointment • US$35, includes free shuttle from Montego Bay • ☎ 578 2582, Ⓦ rasnatango.com

Set high in the hills, the **Ras Natango Gallery & Garden** is a dazzling chromatic display of tropical flowers (including orchids, hot-pink ginger lilies and huge begonias), lush ferns and Natango's own artwork, displayed around the grounds as well as in the gallery. After the 45-minute guided tour, you are welcome to stroll the gardens, which are home to hummingbirds galore, and boast views of the mountains and the city down to the ocean.

Hopewell

The first sizeable town west of Montego Bay, the straggling residential community of **HOPEWELL** is famous mainly for its one **hotel**, *Round Hill*, draped across an entire hillside just east of town and one of the classiest in Jamaica. Designed in part by Ralph Lauren, with an elegant 36-room hotel building and 29 eclectically furnished villas, the 98-acre property exudes taste and opulence. JFK and Jackie, Audrey Hepburn, Clark Gable and Queen Elizabeth II gave the hotel a reputation for glamour that even today attracts an autograph book of famous names.

Aside from *Round Hill*, the **coastline** here is not ideal for swimming, but there are occasional sandy spots such as **Old Steamer Beach**, past the murky fishermen's beach, marked by the rusting iron shell of a wrecked boat, which gets packed in the early evening and on weekends when kids descend, dominoes slap down on veranda tables, and sound systems string up. Before moving on, visit the small **gallery** of local potter Sylvester Stephens, past the Shell petrol station on your left as you drive west. His garden has an interesting collection of giant pots and clay figures nailed to wooden posts.

4

ARRIVAL AND DEPARTURE — HOPEWELL

By minibus and route taxi Frequent route taxis and minibuses between Montego Bay and Lucea or Negril stop at Hopewell (less often in evenings and on Sun).

ACCOMMODATION AND EATING

A good stop for a seafood meal is directly in front of the fishing beach west of town, where a couple of simple places offer conch soup and steamed or fried fish.

Round Hill Hopewell ⓣ956 7050, ⓦroundhill.com. One of Jamaica's top resorts, with exquisite, spacious and elegant villas featuring natural woods and large French windows opening onto the Caribbean. On Mondays, the hotel hosts a wonderful candlelit beach party open to non-residents, with tables and chairs shifted onto the sand, barbecued food and live music (US$60/head). **US$600**

SHOPPING

Round Hill Resort Boutique Hopewell ⓣ940 2237, ⓦroundhill.com. Stocks excellent clothing, essential oils and scents, including Starfish candles and bathing products, as well as Blue Mountain coffee. Daily 8am–6pm.

Lethe

Lethe, Hanover • From Montego Bay head west and turn inland at Reading; after 8km turn westwards at Wiltshire village and continue a further 5km to Lethe • book in advance

Towards the top of Long Hill, the inland road from Reading, there's a well-signposted left-hand turn towards **LETHE**, a pretty village set amid cool and vividly green hills with a graceful stone bridge straddling the Great River, built by slaves in 1820. Aside from the scenery, the main reason to come to **Lethe** is for **rafting** and **ziplining** (see page 188); the one-hour rafting trip takes you past banks dripping with vines. Due to heavy rainfall, the water often takes on a muddy aspect, but it's still safe for swimming. There are a few turbulent shallow spots where the bamboo rafts scrape the bottom, but the raftmen are highly experienced. The five ziplines are proudly proclaimed as the longest in the Caribbean, and offer an enjoyable tour through the treetops.

ACTIVITIES	LETHE

Rafting Chukka (☎ 656 8026 or ⓦ chukka.com) offer one-hour guided trips at Lethe Estate (US$65 per two-person raft).

Ziplining Zipline Adventure Tours (ⓦ ziplinejamaica.com) have one-hour tours at Lethe Estate along five lines (US$90 including transfer).

Animal Farm and Nature Reserve

Copse, 3km south of Lethe • Daily 10am–5pm • US$10 • ☎ 899 0040 • Coming from Lethe: when the road curves, look out for a signposted dirt track to the left, which leads down to the farm

A delightful, environmentally conscious smallholding run on solar energy and biogas from pig dung, **Animal Farm** makes a worthwhile stop, especially if you're travelling with children. There's an array of exotic birds, cages containing mongooses and snakes, plus a petting zoo and herb garden, all of which are explained by knowledgeable guides. Children's donkey rides are available, and a path leads down for swimming in the Great River.

Rocklands Bird Sanctuary and Feeding Station

Wiltshire, St James • Daily 10am–sunset • US$20; morning guided walks US$20 • ☎ 952 2009 • Indicated by a battered sign along a potholed turn-off just before residential Anchovy, south of the Lethe turn-off from the B8

The fabulous **Rockland's Bird Sanctuary and Feeding Station** was the home of the late Lisa Salmon, a celebrated ornithologist. More than a hundred varieties of bird have been sighted here, including orange quits, vervain and the streamer-tailed doctor – Jamaica's national bird – the iridescent colouring and thrumming wings of this and the other hummingbirds make the prettiest visitors, however. Hummingbirds here are confident enough to drink sugar water while perched on your outstretched finger; feeding peaks at around 4pm. A nature walk is included in the entry fee, but serious ornithologists should call ahead for specific hikes with knowledgeable Fritz, who can take you on trails beyond the property.

The Catadupa Hills

The area between Montpelier and Seaford Town, at the fringes of Cockpit Country, is known as the Catadupa Hills – an immeasurably picturesque district of citrus and pineapple plantations, which occupy the last stretches of accessible land before the Cockpit hillocks make large-scale farming impossible. Accompanying the citrus are pretty villages like **ST LEONARDS** and the tiny hamlet of **MARCHMONT**. **CATADUPA** was once the main tourist stop on the train line from Montego Bay to Kingston; today, goats pick at the sleepers near the peeling paint of the gingerbread station house.

Croydon Plantation

Croydon, St James • Tues & Fri 9am–6pm • US$70 including transfer (6hr trip); negotiate price in advance if you have your own transport • ☎ 979 8267, ⓦ croydonplantation.com

Set amid the beautiful wooded Catadupa Hills, this working pineapple, citrus and coffee plantation was originally the birthplace of National Hero Sam Sharpe, the slave and Baptist preacher who led the 1831 Christmas Rebellion (see page 170). The somewhat overpriced tours of the plantation – especially popular with groups from cruise ships and north coast resorts – whisks you around the carefully constructed terraces where the fruits are grown, with a stop for a barbecue lunch with fresh juice and a Blue Mountain coffee.

Seaford Town

At first glance, **SEAFORD TOWN** is just another rural community, but you'll soon notice that a lot of the older residents are white. In 1834, after slavery had been abolished, the British administration sought cheap labour to work Jamaican fields. The result was the drafting of more than a thousand Germans, promised prosperity after a set period of indentured toil. Between 1834 and 1836, 251 Germans settled in Seaford Town, a 500-acre plot of land donated by Lord Seaford of Montpelier. Other immigrants scattered throughout the interior and blended in; Seaford Town remains the only Jamaican community to be deliberately established.

The new arrivals, many unused to farm labour, found life in rural Jamaica difficult, and when first-year rations ran out, became as impoverished as their neighbours. Hardship and tropical diseases depleted their numbers, and many survivors emigrated to the US. Enough remained, however, for their legacy to be obvious. Despite intermixing, a tradition of intermarriage within the community has ensured that quite a few of the town's residents still have blonde hair, blue eyes and (almost) white skin. Little German culture has been retained, however; traces are seen in older houses' pointy roofs and gingerbread fretwork – fast being eclipsed by new-builds – but very few people speak any German, and residents eat rice and peas rather than sauerkraut. The story of the town is the subject of an interesting documentary film; for more information see ⓦgermantownjamaica.com.

Seaford Town Historical Museum

Main St • Open upon request • US$2

The diminutive **Seaford Town Historical Museum**, on a grassy knoll below the Catholic church, tells the story of Seaford's German heritage, with photographs of the original settlers and a list of their names and occupations (one man was a comedian). It's usually locked; to gain access, ask around town for Roy Chambers, who will be happy to let you in.

ARRIVAL AND DEPARTURE   **SEAFORD TOWN**

By route taxi Route taxis leave from Montego Bay and Black River in St Elizabeth.

Cockpit Country

Pristine surroundings combined with a delightfully immersive experience (tour operators will likely find a place for you inside a local home) make **COCKPIT COUNTRY** unforgettable. A slice of raw wilderness, the area boasts Jamaica's most unusual landscape: an uncanny series of improbable lumps and bumps covering roughly nine-hundred square kilometres of Trelawny, St James and St Ann parishes, south of Montego Bay. Thousands of years of rainwater flowing over porous limestone created this rugged **karst topography** of impenetrable conical hillocks, dissolved on each side by a drainage system of sinkholes and caves. At its heart, Cockpit Country is a sanctuary of untouched beauty, particularly in the early mornings when low-lying mists and a silence broken only by bird calls give it an almost primeval feel.

The region is worthwhile not only for its fantastic scenery but also its incredible history. For Jamaicans, this is an area of significant struggle and pride, the place where the **Maroons** – enslaved Africans who escaped and fought guerrilla wars against the British – won their freedom. To learn more about Maroon history, head to **Accompong**, home to an important annual heritage festival (see page 194) and the site where, following the defeat of British forces in 1738, the parties signed a 1739 peace treaty. **Maroon Town** and **Flagstaff** are other places of historic interest, as it was in this area that the original Trelawny Town Maroons lived, before they were forcibly deported (see page 192).

Cockpit Country is largely uninhabited. Locals mainly congregate in the buffer communities like **Albert Town,** or the tiny ecological community of **Windsor** and its

HIKING AND CAVING IN THE COCKPITS

Well-organized **guided tours** are on offer to point out the rare plants and beautiful birdlife of Cockpit Country. Albert Town, Flagstaff and Windsor are the most accessible starting points, where you should hire a local guide – essential not only to stop you from getting lost but also in case of accident. The sixteen-kilometre **Barbecue Bottom** trail, a mix of under-canopy and open vistas, traces hillocks and limestone forests from Kinloss to Spring Garden, and offers stunning 360 degree views of Cockpit Country's flipped egg-carton landscape. Guides from the South Trelawny Environmental Agency (see page below) lead **hikes** here, highlighting significant aspects of the ecology, endemic bird species and medicinal plants as you go. Aim your visit for the early morning: by the time you've reached Barbecue Bottom, the mists in the valley will be coming up, creating a breathtaking fog in and around the hillocks.

Another great option is a trip to the gorgeous village of **Bunkers Hill**, where Cultural Xperience (see below) guides tours of Dromilly Cave, thought to be a former Maroon hideout, and then to a swimming spot in the Tangle River, where you can commune in the river near a waterfall. Superb Jamaican meals – anything from rice and peas with coconut milk, to rundown, roast yam, sweet potato and cornmeal pudding – are also on offer.

Cavers find Cockpit Country irresistible. Around 300 caves network the area; though the Printed Circuit Cave (see page 195) in Rock Spring is the most accessible. If you're interested in taking a tour around Printed's stalactites and mesmerizing dark corners, prepare for mud, snug spaces, shallow swimming holes and an unforgettable experience.

TOUR OPERATORS

Bunkers Hill Cultural Xperience Albert Town ☎ 370 2864, ⊛ bunkershilltourja.com. Wonderful, home-grown organization offering hikes and cave visits (one a former Maroon hideout, another inscribed with Taíno writing and carvings) in and around Bunkers Hill. River, hike and cave tour US$30.

Cockpit Country Adventure Tours Albert Town ☎ 393 6584, ✉ info@stea.net, ⊛ stea.net. Community-based trips are offered by this brilliant part of the South Trelawny Environmental Agency (STEA). Local guides are fully committed to sustainable community tourism and offer nature walks, birding, trips to wet caves like the Printed Circuit (see page 195), and hikes on a medicinal plant trail along Barbecue Bottom Rd. Caving US$60, birdwatching US$60, hikes from US$30.

Flagstaff Heritage Tours Flagstaff ☎ 421 3473, ⊛ flagstaffheritagetours.com. Run by charismatic

Maroon chief Michael Grizzle, this outfit offers two-hour walking and trekking tours around "Trelawny Town-Flagstaff", which boasts a rich Maroon history.

Jamaican Caves Organisation ⊛ jamaicancaves. org. National caving organization that leads cave explorations; if you're a serious caver you may be able to join one.

Sun Venture Kingston ☎ 924 4515, ⊛ sunventure tours.com. An excellent islandwide operator (see page 25); hikes from US$60.

Windsor Research Centre (WRC) Windsor Great House (see page 194) ☎ 997 3832, ✉ windsor@ cwjamaica.com, ⊛ cockpitcountry.com. Resident wildlife ecologist Susan Koenig leads informative walks for US$30 an hour, per person – for the best experience, go at night. Franklyn Taylor, aka Dango, warden of Windsor Cave, runs tours and hiking trips; if you're in the area, seek out his red, yellow and green shop, just before the turn up to the Great House.

neighbour **Sherwood Content,** birthplace of Usain Bolt. The region's economy is based on small-scale farming, and yam and coffee are important crops.

GETTING AROUND   COCKPIT COUNTRY

By car If you're coming from Montego Bay or Ocho Rios on the A1, the turn-off for Cockpit Country is in Duncans, with good signage at the junction.

By minibus and route taxi From Falmouth, Albert Town is well served by route taxis, with less frequent services to Sherwood Content. For the more remote community of

Windsor (see page 193), it's best to charter a taxi.

By organized tour An organized tour from MoBay (see page 173) is a good option if independent travel feels like too much hassle; most tour companies offer trips to Windsor or Flagstaff (see above).

Maroon Town

Easily accessed from Montego Bay via **Kensington** – which boasts huge historical significance as the place where the first fires of the Christmas Rebellion were lit (see page 170) – **MAROON TOWN** offers marvellous views over gaping valleys and a living connection with Maroon heritage (see page 192); John Crow vultures whirl high on the thermals and though you're only 24-odd kilometres from Montego Bay, the contrast couldn't be more striking.

Flagstaff Heritage Tours

Flagstaff, 4km southeast of Maroon Town • US$35 • ☎ 421 3473, ⓦ flagstaffheritagetours.com

Flagstaff Heritage Tours draws on the incredible history of the Trelawny Maroons. Local culture is exhibited at a small visitor centre with traditional foods, crafts and dramatic sketches, and there's a choice of three guided trails (2hr) through Cockpit Country's fascinating flora and fauna to the historical remnants of the British occupation of Trelawny Town, with explanation of Maroon traditions. A bed-and-breakfast programme also operates within host homes in the community (US$60), offering an excellent insight into life in the Jamaican interior; contact chief Michael Grizzle for more details (see page 190).

ARRIVAL AND DEPARTURE MAROON TOWN

By route taxi Route taxis leave frequently from the Montego Bay Transport Centre for Maroon Town, Mon–Sat during daylight hours; less often in the evening and on Sun.

By chartered taxi A chartered taxi will cost around US$40 from Montego Bay.

Accompong

Sitting on one of the steep hillocks that make up outer Cockpit Country, **ACCOMPONG** is one of the best places to learn about Maroon culture and heritage. Boasting breathtaking views, the town is ruled by a Maroon **colonel**, elected every five years – the current incumbent is police inspector Ferron Williams (if he's there, it's considered proper protocol to call on him when you arrive). Accompong colonels hold real power; they ensure citizens abide by the town's constitution, and mete out justice for petty crimes.

While Accompong retains its own unique identity, over the centuries, there has been somewhat of a natural assimilation into the greater fabric of Jamaican culture. That said, the Maroons, and subsequently, Cockpit Country and Accompong, holds an incredible pride of place for Jamaicans – this is where enslaved Africans found their freedom (see page 192). Though you might hear dancehall and hip-hop in Accompong more often now than traditional goombay drums and Akan chanting, locals place enormous value on their history and heritage – and some residents can claim direct descent to Maroon leaders Nanny (see page 121) and Cudjoe. For the best window into traditional Accompong, visit the annual **Accompong Maroon Festival**, held on January 6, with day-and-night celebrations (see page 194).

Brief history

Named after the brother of Maroon hero Cudjoe, Accompong came into being in 1739, when, as part of the peace treaty that ended the first **Maroon War**, the British granted the Maroon people 15,000 acres of land to create a semi-sovereign community; a missing zero in fact meant that only 1500 acres were made available, a matter of continuing contention. Several such communities, including Trelawny Town in St James, were also given land, and the Maroons set about a peaceful farming life. In 1795, however, a Trelawny Town Maroon caught stealing a pig in downtown Montego Bay was publicly flogged by one of the escaped slaves the Maroons had captured and returned to the plantations in accordance with the peace treaty. His

THE MAROONS

Comprised of enslaved Africans armed by retreating Spanish troops in 1660 (the Spanish thought the slaves would aid in fighting the British, but during battle, many left and fled to find freedom), alongside escaped slaves from British plantations, the **Maroons** (a corruption of the Spanish *cimarrones*, meaning "wild" or "untamed") lived in remote parts of the Blue and John Crow mountains in the east and Cockpit Country in the west of the island. Initially, most Maroons were of Kromanti descent, from the region of modern-day Ghana, and despite the upheaval of slavery, their shared language and traditions helped them to organize powerful communities in their new environment. As numbers grew, they periodically plundered British settlements for arms, animals and supplies, and they proved an effective deterrent to colonists who were considering settling in areas like Portland.

THE BRITISH RESPONSE

Although British soldiers made regular forays against them, the Maroons had become such a serious threat by the 1720s that forts and barracks were built at the edges of their territories, and British military might was turned towards wiping out this troublesome fifth column. Special troops were brought in, including a large party of Mosquito Indian trackers from Nicaragua but, in extremely difficult and confusing terrain, they were often outmanoeuvred by the skilled **guerrilla tactics** of the Maroons. In places that now carry evocative names like "The District of Look Behind", whole parties of British soldiers were slaughtered, though one was normally left alive to carry the message of comprehensive defeat back to the authorities.

By 1739, it was apparent that winning a war against this "invisible enemy" would be drawn-out and difficult. British commanding officer Colonel Guthrie and **Cudjoe**, the Maroon chief, agreed to terms where the Trelawny Maroons would stop attacking British settlements, return all future escaped slaves and provide assistance in the event of internal rebellion or foreign invasion. In return, the British acknowledged the Maroons' autonomy, permitting them fifteen hundred acres of land in Cockpit Country (around present-day Accompong), as well as the administration of justice in all cases except for those involving the death penalty. One year later, the Windward Maroons – those encamped in the Blue Mountains – signed a similar deal.

THE SECOND MAROON WAR

For two generations the peace held, and the Maroons lived as a sovereign state within Jamaica. Both sides kept to the agreement, most notably in 1760, when Maroons helped to suppress the **Tacky Rebellion**. However, in 1795, the public flogging of two Maroons in Montego Bay outraged the Trelawny Town Maroon community, and hostilities quickly flared again. Plantations were burnt and planters killed, and the British army rushed to quell this internal conflict. For a while, the **Second Maroon War** followed the path of the First, with soldiers ambushed as they ventured into unfamiliar territory, and the Maroons inflicting heavy losses. However, the British were better organized this time and had at their disposal both enormous hunting dogs imported from Cuba, and warriors and trackers from Jamaica's other Maroon settlements, including the Accompong Maroons. A peace offer was made by British General Walpole and the Maroons surrendered, although not until several days after the terms of the peace offer had lapsed. Using this pretext, the British revoked the promise that Maroons should be allowed to stay on their land, and five hundred of the Trelawny Town Maroons were **deported** to the freezing climate of Nova Scotia (although not before General Walpole had resigned in disgust at the authorities' duplicity). The deported Maroons stayed in Nova Scotia for just a year before setting sail for Sierra Leone – from where, generations earlier, many of their ancestors had been brought to Jamaica as slaves. Things came full circle in 1841, when a number of these same Maroons returned home to Jamaica.

Most of the Maroon communities in Portland (see page 104) and at Accompong (see page 191) remained relatively undisturbed by the ructions of the Second Maroon War and, protected by the 1739 peace treaty, continued to maintain a semi-independent status within the island that persists to this day.

kinsmen rebelled once again and the second Maroon War flared up. Though the Trelawny Town Maroons could muster only three hundred fighters, the British took no risks and sent in 1500 soldiers and hunting dogs to track them down and wreck their villages. Accompong, the only Maroon village that chose to remain neutral, was allowed to stand.

Main Street

Accompong is ranged along a precipitous main street; as you drive in you'll most likely be met by one of many locals acting as informal **tour guides** (JMD$2500/person for a tour of the village; JMD$6000 to the Peace Cave; this is a bit negotiable, however), who relate the town's history and introduce you to local characters. The **community centre** on Main Street contains a small museum (included in the price) with exhibits on Maroons as well as the wider history of Jamaica, with items such as calabash gourds, an Ashanti stool and goat-skin goombay drums. Next door is a skills training centre with computers and small library (book donations appreciated).

The village church sits atop a hillock overlooking the town and Main Street; on the lower half of Main Street there's a **memorial to Cudjoe**, co-signatory of the 1739 treaty.

Up to the Peace Cave

From the museum, you'll be led up the hill to the **Parade Ground**, once a lookout point, training ground and the site of Maroon court, and onwards to the sacred **Kindah Tree** (a 15min walk), a beautiful giant mango, adjacent to which there's a battered sculpture of a hand-less Maroon – a traitor to Cudjoe (it's said they would have cut his head off, but it would grow back). From here, you're led through undulating hinterland to the **Peace Cave**, a seventeenth- and eighteenth-century hideout used for stationing Maroons, who would warn their brethren of approaching British soldiers (signalled by an abeng horn), and also said to be where the 1739 treaty with the British was signed (the site of the accord is currently in dispute: new artefacts suggest it may have taken place near Flagstaff; see page 191). Note that it's a solid heart-pumping hour out to the cave, through tall grasses and (occasionally) buggy terrain – if there's been recent rain, the muck may make it practically impassable. That said, you're well rewarded with the views, with stellar vistas and hills cascading all the way down to the Appleton Estate (see page 247), and the cave itself, such an incredible piece of Jamaican history, it has to be one of the island's greatest highpoints.

4

ARRIVAL AND DEPARTURE | **ACCOMPONG**

By car There are several ways to get to Accompong, the easiest by driving north from Maggoty in St Elizabeth (see page 247) to Vauxhall, and following the signs. You can also drive up from Albert Town, skirting the southern edge of Cockpit Country along the B10/B6, through Troy, Auchtembeddie (notable for having the highest number of recorded land snail species in the world) then Oxford. Turn right into Balaclava, then on to Maggotty. If you're coming from Montego Bay, travel via Elderslie and Jointwood from the west. It's a fabulous drive with spectacular vistas. There is no public transport.

Windsor

Smack in the middle of Cockpit Country's accessible northern edge, **WINDSOR** is a gorgeous spot, cradled by high cockpits and with impossibly lush foliage permanently threatening to overtake the dirt tracks that serve as roads. Its largest property, Windsor Great House, dates from the early eighteenth century and was the cattle overseer's house for John Tharp (of nearby Good Hope fame; see page 185). The house (see page 190) is now a research station and base for exploring the cockpits; there's not much else to the tiny community (last count was fewer than ten residents) save for a few fields of coffee, swimming spots along the Martha Brae River (which rises by Windsor Cave) and unpaved tracks for nature lovers.

Windsor is reached via the tiny village of **Sherwood Content** (itself a 25min drive beyond the Martha Brae rafting station; see page 185), remarkable for the unlikely fame granted it by its most celebrated son, Usain Bolt, the 100m and 200m world record holder and Olympic sprint champion. A couple of signs decorate the village in the name of the "Lightning Bolt", and en route to Windsor at Coxheath you'll see his aunt's gift shop, *Miss Lilly's* and his parents' house, both painted in proud, bright green and yellow. Bolt himself ascribed his success to the strength of the Trelawny yams he grew up eating; there could be something in it given a host of other top sprinters (among them Ben Johnson and Veronica Campbell-Brown) were also born nearby.

ARRIVAL AND DEPARTURE   WINDSOR

By chartered taxi You'll need to charter a taxi to get to Windsor, around US$40 from Falmouth.

ACCOMMODATION

★ **Windsor Great House** Windsor ✆ windsor@cw jamaica.com, ⓦ cockpitcountry.com. The Great House's annexe is the best-equipped option in the community, with simple rooms and hot-water showers en suite; also, there are communal facilities in the main house, with cold-water showers (or you can bathe in the cool Martha Brae). Meals are taken on the huge veranda. Bear in mind that Windsor is primarily a research station: rooms are often booked up by visiting biologists and aren't really geared towards tourists. Though the mosquitoes are hellish, if you've even a passing interest in Cockpit Country or fancy a little solitude, this is a magical place for a night or two. At visitor's request and with a minimum of a group of four, the owners host a "Meet the Biologist" dinner (four courses, US$40 per head, plus alcohol, preceded by a field trip to the top of Windsor Cave), an ongoing activity to develop and fund research. Experience the allure of the Cockpits at night, with bats leaving their roosts and mosquitoes ceasing their attentions as the glowing fireflies and whistling frogs of the forest take over. US$55

Albert Town and around

If you fancy a more lively base for exploring the Cockpits than Windsor, head to **ALBERT TOWN**, a friendly hillside community and home of the excellent **South Trelawny Environmental Agency** (STEA) and its tour company, Cockpit Country Adventure Tours (see page 190).

ACCOMPONG MAROON FESTIVAL

Every January 6, Maroons from all over the island celebrate Cudjoe's birthday and the victory of Maroons over the British forces. Early in the morning, under a towering mango tree (known as the **Kindah Tree**), a black male pig (according to Maroon tradition) is roasted or boiled and eaten communally – bringing luck to all that partake. The highlight of the day (at around 10am) is when Maroon leaders, adorned by the carcoon leaves used as camouflage by their ancestors, return to the Kindah tree from **Old Town**, where they have eaten pork, performed rituals, and paid respect to their elders. Goombay drumming begins in complicated rhythms, and a hornblower sends the haunting tones of an **abeng** horn (a cow horn once used as a means of communication; still employed to call meetings, or if someone passes away) echoing across the hills. Drumming reaches a climax and the assembled mass joins in with call-and-response Akan war songs. The procession then moves through the village, heading to the monument for Cudjoe and finishing at the **Parade Ground** for speeches and whirling dancing, sprinkled with a traditional dash of white rum. Eventually, drums make way for towers of speakers, and the party continues all night, sometimes with live reggae. Note that there's an entry fee (usually around US$10 for foreign visitors) to the village festival, and that timings vary – get there in the morning, and go with the flow.

FLORA AND FAUNA OF THE COCKPIT COUNTRY

Soil forms only a thin cover over the Cockpit limestone, and as the rock soaks away most of the rainfall, the area's **plant life** has had to adapt in order to survive. As a result, visitors see a proliferation of species that make the most of their rather limited means. Bromeliads collect dew and rainwater in the tanks between their leaves, while the thick, waxy leaves of other plants, such as the tiny orchids that colonize dead wood, take advantage of high humidity. There's a huge range of **bird life**, including twenty-eight of Jamaica's 29 endemic species; this is one of the few places you'll see – and hear – profusions of boisterous Amazon parrots. With hundreds of caves, **bats** are common – 21 varieties are found on the island. The limestone also provides a perfect cover for the (non-venomous) **Jamaican boa**, or **yellow snake**. Prepare yourself for mosquitoes, which, unfortunately, are the most abundant wildlife. For more on the area's unusual environment, visit ⓦ cockpitcountry.com.

Some 65,000 farmers produce yams in Trelawny, a fact celebrated in Albert Town's annual **Trelawny Yam Festival**, a hugely popular celebration of the enormous tubers that are the backbone of the parish's economy, held on and around Easter Monday. Thousands of people, locals and tourists, fill the streets to witness culinary displays, best-dressed goat and donkey competitions, yam head-balancing races and ultimately the crowning of the Festival King and Queen. Associated events include a 10km road race, DJ and singing competitions and gospel concerts.

Printed Circuit Cave

Rock Spring, 5km outside of Albert Town • 2hr tour, US$60 • ⓣ 393 6584, ⓦ stea.net

4

A tour through **Printed Circuit Cave** is one of the highlights of Cockpit Country. Affable, environmentally-conscious guides strap you into a headlamp-topped helmet, and you're off on a dark scramble past stalactites and stalagmites, occasionally on your hands and knees through snug, mini-tunnels, and even into a cool pool with (harmless) crawfish that appear to glow pale blue (wear clothes and shoes you don't mind getting wet and muddy). It's incredibly quiet and as you traverse along, the dank, eerie chambers take on an almost hallowed quality. Note that, if you're nervous, bats are few and far between, and will most likely remain discreetly in their roosts (also, though it probably goes without saying, they bite fruit, not people).

The cave has a fascinating history. Used as a Maroon hideout in the eighteenth-century, local legend states it was also the stomping grounds of an Obeah man with an enchanted crocodile.

ARRIVAL AND DEPARTURE   ALBERT TOWN

By car The best route into Albert Town is via the B11 from the north coast through Duncans. At the junctions, keep an eye out for signs arrowing you toward Cockpit Country.
Transfers STEA (ⓣ 393 6584, ⓔ info@stea.net, ⓦ stea.

net). Email ahead to arrange for pick-ups (priced upon request) from Falmouth, Ocho Rios or Montego Bay.
Route taxi Route taxis run up frequently from Falmouth for around J$400.

ACCOMMODATION AND EATING

There's no formal accommodation in Albert Town, but STEA (contact for reservations; US$40) organizes lovely **bed and breakfasts** at the homes of local families, with meals at extra cost. Basic **cookshops and rum bars** surround the square.

Negril and the west

NEGRIL BEACH

5 Negril and the west

Split in two by the parishes of Hanover and Westmoreland, sybaritic Negril has a front-row sunset seat, the longest continuous stretch of white sand in Jamaica and a geographical remoteness that provides this ultimate chill-out town with a uniquely insouciant ambience. "Discovered" by wealthy hippies in the 1970s, Negril is immensely popular with those who favour fast living and corporeal indulgence – but even though the main menu items are still sun, sea, smoke and sex, there are plenty of natural attractions too, including the Great Morass, the Royal Palm Reserve and some marvellous reefs.

Away from this tourism magnet, **Hanover** is the island's smallest parish and, despite the deceptively steep-looking rise to the **Dolphin Head Mountains**, it's also the flattest, ensuring the island's lowest rainfall and invariably sultry weather. The decaying grandeur of sleepy **Lucea** has been slated for heritage development for years, but though there's now a large all-inclusive nearby there's little other development along its coastline, and deserted coves beg for exploration. To the south, the flat coastal plains of **Westmoreland** were once Jamaica's foremost **sugar-growing** area, and cane plantations still surround the main commercial town, **Savanna-la-Mar**. Inland, the watery attraction of **Mayfield Falls** offers a picturesque diversion, while eastwards quiet coastal villages backed by rugged hills project an air of pastoral neglect, with undeveloped beaches dedicated to fishing rather than aloe massages and sun loungers. Villages like **Bluefields**, its neighbour **Belmont** – birthplace of reggae revolutionary **Peter Tosh** – and **Whitehouse**, have real understated Jamaican charm and a good variety of boutique and villa accommodation, ideal if you want peace, quiet and few other foreigners.

Negril

Jamaica's shrine to permissive indulgence, **NEGRIL** metamorphosed from deserted fishing beach to full-blown resort town in three decades. By the 1970s, this virgin paradise with eleven kilometres of palms and pristine sand, offering beach camping, ganja smoking and chemically enhanced sunsets, had set the tone for today's free-spirited attitude. Thanks to deliberately risqué resorts like **Hedonism II**, Negril is widely perceived as a place where inhibitions are lost and pleasures of the flesh rule. The traditional menu of ganja and reggae (Negril has a deserved reputation for **nightlife** and **live music**) draws a young crowd, but the north coast resort ethic has muscled in, too. All-inclusives now pepper the coast and undeveloped beachfront land is sparse.

Negril's dramatic expansion and reputation as "sin city" certainly does draw an over-quota of **hustlers** – though an active year-round tourist police force prevents occasional

CORAL REEF, NEGRIL

Highlights

❶ Negril Beach Seven uninterrupted miles of brilliant white sand facing turquoise waters, and buzzing with entertainment. See page 201

❷ Sunset-watching An institution in Negril, where everyone heads to the cliffs of the West End for cocktails and the most spectacular sunsets in Jamaica. See page 205

❸ Snorkelling and scuba diving Negril's coral reefs are the finest in Jamaica, with a wealth of marine life, year-round warm water and excellent visibility. See page 208

❹ Abingdon Great House Step back in time at a newly restored seventeenth-century sugar estate tucked away in thick forest in Hanover. See page 218

❺ Mayfield Falls A series of waterfalls and river pools in the hills of Westmoreland whose natural beauty remains, for the present, unspoilt. See page 226

❻ Bluefields Bay Take in the lively coastal village feel here, with charming guesthouses, bars, hillside tours and engaging residents. See page 226

HIGHLIGHTS ARE MARKED ON THE MAP ON PAGE 200

5

edginess from becoming anything more than a minor irritation. The resort shrugs off minor annoyances and remains supremely chilled-out – conversations start and end with "Irie" or "no problem" – and addicts come back year after year for the best sunsets in Jamaica. Pristine kilometres of sand with comprehensive watersports, open-air dancing to rated Jamaican musicians, a wide range of eating and drinking joints and gregarious company are all on offer. For all its tourism-heavy scenery, laidback Negril preserves pieces of its Jamaican roots and opens its arms to all who venture here. As a result, many visitors have stayed on permanently, and the consequent blurring of the distinction between tourists and locals makes for a relaxed, natural interaction that's a refreshing change from other resort areas. For an entertaining introduction, read Mark Conklin's novel, *Banana Shout* (see page 293), based on the outlandish real-life events that shaped the beginnings of Negril as a tourist resort.

The "town centre" in Negril consists of a roundabout that feeds its three roads: beach-ward Norman Manley Boulevard, which runs parallel to Long Bay, Bloody Bay and the Great Morass wetlands; quieter West End/Lighthouse Road (renamed One Love Drive to the confusion of just about everyone) winding along the cliffs; and **Sheffield Road**, the less touristic route inland toward Savanna-la-Mar.

HIGHLIGHTS

1. Negril Beach
2. Sunset-watching
3. Snorkelling and scuba diving
4. Abingdon Great House
5. Mayfield Falls
6. Bluefields Bay

NEGRIL AND THE WEST

5

"RENT-A-DREAD"

Jamaica is a carnal kind of country, and monetary-based holiday liaisons are a well-established convention. Fuelled by tropical abandon and the island's pervasive sexuality, the lure of the "big bamboo" prompts some unusual partnerships. Middle-aged women strolling hand in hand with handsome young studs have become such a frequent sight that pejorative epithets – **"Rent-a-dread"** or **"Rastitute"** – for the young men who make a career out of these cynical liaisons have entered the lexicon.

The butt of many jokes, the stereotypical Rastitute is a muscle-bound model of the latest mini-trunks and sneakers, with a head topped off with dreadlocks – or extensions if he can't manage the real thing. However, not all gigolos come in the same package; a Rastitute can also appear as an Ital-style Rasta, wooing with talk of natural living and preaching sex with white tourists in the name of racial unity.

In a country of scant possibilities, becoming a gigolo is a very practical career move. Negril is a centre for this kind of trade-off, and many women regularly return for an injection of "Jamaican steel", some forming relationships that span several years' holiday time. As a result, single women are universally assumed to be out for one thing only – prepare yourself for a barrage of propositions.

Male tourists are less involved in the holiday romance scenario, but **female prostitutes** are common and men should expect to be frequently propositioned.

If you do choose to indulge in any kind of holiday liaison, practice safe sex; syphilis and HIV rates are high.

Brief history

Negril's isolation – before the coast road was laid in 1959, it was completely cut off from the rest of the island by the Great Morass – is central to its history. Even its Spanish name, *Punto de Negrilla* or "dark point", referred to its remoteness as much as to the black eels that once thrived in its rivers. During British rule, Negril's seclusion was used both to protect British ships and to attack Spanish vessels en route to and from Cuba. It also provided an ideal hideout for **pirates** in the eighteenth century (see page 202), and for the export of **ganja** in more recent years. In 1996, overzealous coast guards opened fire on a plane owned by Island Outpost boss Chris Blackwell, assuming that the cargo was drugs rather than, as was the case, members of the band U2 and country singer Jimmy Buffett; fortunately the volleys missed and a tragedy was averted. The town has also played a part in war: in 1814, fifty English warships and six thousand men, including one thousand Jamaicans from the West Indian Regiment, sailed from Negril to Louisiana to fight the Battle of New Orleans.

Though it's hard to imagine once you've seen today's overdeveloped strip, in the late 1960s Negril's population was under a hundred; it was only in the 1970s that the town's charms were brought to wider attention by hippies from overseas. Developers were quick to step in, and by the early 1980s the once-empty curve of beach was smothered with all the trappings of a full-blown resort. International attention was captured by tales of debauchery at the notorious *Hedonism II* resort, and Negril's reputation as Jamaica's devil-may-care hot spot was assured. Though summer hurricanes slow the pace of development by altering the shape of the beach, 1990s infrastructural projects and a new highway to Montego Bay in the 2000s ensured continued growth, often at the expense of local ecologies. Even Bloody Bay, until 2000 untouched by development, now has five all-inclusives on its sands. This said, particularly at the "cliffs" end of town, it is still more than possible to find the laidback charm and gorgeous scenery that first brought tourists here.

Negril Beach

Negril Beach (also known as **Seven Mile Beach**) is a near-perfect Caribbean seashore with inviting whiter-than-white sand and swaying palms and sea grapes. Bathing here is Negril's trademark feature; the water is translucent and still, and the busy reefs

NEGRIL'S WOMEN PIRATES

One of Negril's proudest moments came when the reign of **Calico Jack Rackham**, the most notorious buccaneer to terrorize Jamaican waters, was brought to an end here in November 1720. Rackham – called "Calico" in reference to his preferred underwear – and his crew had moored their captured sloop in Bloody Bay to celebrate recent plunders, unaware that their every move was being shadowed by one Captain Barnet of the British Navy. Made inattentive by rum punch, the pirates were quickly overwhelmed. Some surrendered instantly, but two, in particular, put up a mighty struggle – even turning their weapons on their more malleable crew members. Eventually, they were subdued – at which point naval officers were astonished to find that they were **women** in disguise. Famously bloodthirsty in battle, **Anne Bonney**, Rackham's former mistress, and **Mary Read** formed a ruthless double act and were instrumental in earning Rackham his infamy as a freebooter. At their trial, victim Dorothy Thomas noted that "they wore men's jackets and long trousers… each of them had a machete and a pistol in their hands, and cursed and swore."

Rackham was executed, his body displayed in an iron frame at the Kingston cay that now bears his name. Bonney and Read were also sentenced to death, but were spared when they declared themselves pregnant and were eventually reprieved. Anne Bonney disappeared from recorded history, while Mary Read died of yellow fever and is buried in St Catherine.

ornately encrusted. It's also packed with tourists, locals and holidaying Kingstonians, and while it's great for lively socializing – the banter runs as freely as the rum cocktails – the high concentration of human traffic inevitably draws vendors and high-octane hustlers. As well as the usual crafts, hair braiding and aloe massage (the last must have been invented in Negril), you'll be offered sex and drugs with alarming frequency.

Though many hotels guard "their" portion of beach with security and floating buoys, the law keeps beaches public up to the shoreline and you can walk the first couple of kilometres in an hour or so, though it's a hot and thirsty business in the sun. The beach is roughly divided by the bank of all-inclusives at the outcrop splitting Long Bay and Bloody Bay.

Long Bay

Stretching north from the roundabout, **Long Bay** by day is a rash of bronzing bodies and flashing jet skis, and by night a chain of bars dedicated to reggae, rum punch and skinny dipping. At the northern end, hotels give way to the grassy stretch of **Long Bay Beach Park**, with picnic tables, changing rooms and considerably fewer people; it's also the venue for the hilarious annual **Donkey Derby**, usually held early in February.

Kool Runnings Adventure Park

Norman Manley Blvd • Tues–Sun 11am–6pm • Waterpark only US$33; waterpark & adventure zone US$75; after 4pm US$19 • ☎ 957 5400, ⓦ koolrunnings.com

Ever a popular day out for adrenalin-fuelled kids and their families, **Kool Runnings Adventure Park** is a large complex across the road from the beach, which offers ten water slides (some forty feet high), tubing on a "lazy" river, as well as water cannons and giant tipping coconuts. Adding to the fun, a separate adventure zone offers various other activities such as paintballing, lazer combat and karting, plus kayaking, inflatable or (more traditional) bamboo rafting on the Great Morass, which the property borders (see page 204).

Bloody Bay

The final stretch of Negril's eleven kilometres of sand is crescent-shaped **Bloody Bay**. Named for the crimson innards of whales once butchered here, it's now home to two luridly coloured *Riu* hotels and a range of other all-inclusives – among them *Hedonism II* with its nude beach and swingers' month (much to the consternation of local Evangelicals), and the newer Royalton Resorts, occupying what was left of public white sands on this end. Northwards from here the coast is fringed by mangroves until it reaches the major horseriding centre **Rhodes Hall Plantation**, and a few kilometres further, beautiful **Half Moon Bay** (see page 218).

Booby Cay

Boats to the cay US$25

The small forested islet in the centre of Bloody Bay, **Booby Cay**, appeared in the epic 1954 movie *20,000 Leagues Under the Sea*, based on the Jules Verne novel. It's named after the **booby bird**, or sooty tern, an ocean dweller that takes a brief respite to lay eggs, though centuries of egg collection and hunting mean you're unlikely to spot one. Hotels hold barbecues on the narrow but attractive sands here, and you can

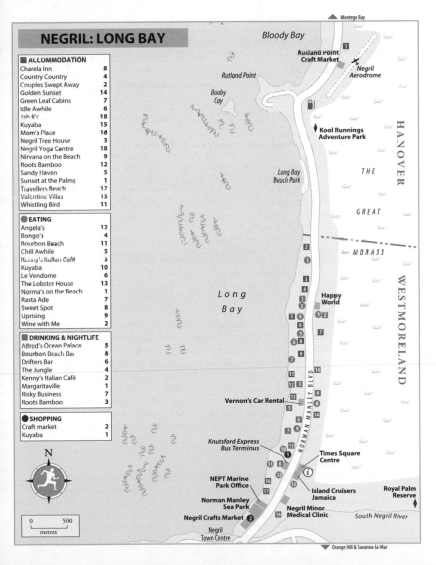

NEGRIL: LONG BAY

■ ACCOMMODATION
Charela Inn	8
Country Country	4
Couples Swept Away	2
Golden Sunset	14
Green Leaf Cabins	7
Idle Awhile	6
Jah B'r	10
Kuyaba	15
Mom's Place	16
Negril Tree House	3
Negril Yoga Centre	18
Nirvana on the Beach	9
Roots Bamboo	12
Sandy Haven	5
Sunset at the Palms	1
Travellers Beach	17
Valentine Villas	13
Whistling Bird	11

● EATING
Angela's	12
Bongo's	4
Bourbon Beach	11
Chill Awhile	5
Kenny's Italian Café	3
Kuyaba	10
Le Vendome	6
The Lobster House	13
Norma's on the Beach	1
Rasta Ade	7
Sweet Spot	8
Uprising	9
Wine with Me	2

■ DRINKING & NIGHTLIFE
Alfred's Ocean Palace	5
Bourbon Beach Bar	8
Drifters Bar	6
The Jungle	4
Kenny's Italian Café	2
Margaritaville	1
Risky Business	7
Roots Bamboo	3

● SHOPPING
Craft market	2
Kuyaba	1

Montego Bay

Bloody Bay

Rutland Point Craft Market

Negril Aerodrome

Rutland Point

Booby Cay

Kool Runnings Adventure Park

HANOVER

THE

Long Bay Beach Park

GREAT

MORASS

WESTMORELAND

Long Bay

Happy World

Vernon's Car Rental

NORMAN MANLEY BLVD

Knutsford Express Bus Terminus

Times Square Centre

NEPT Marine Park Office

Island Cruisers Jamaica

Royal Palm Reserve

Norman Manley Sea Park

Negril Minor Medical Clinic

South Negril River

Negril Crafts Market

Negril Town Centre

N

0 500 metres

Orange Hill & Savanna-la-Mar

5

ENVIRONMENT MATTERS

Rapid growth and unplanned development have had a devastating effect upon Negril's ecosystems. Norman Manley Blvd cuts straight through what was originally swampland, jet skis – now banned – and anchors have played havoc with the reefs and mangrove-felling has allowed the sea and hurricanes to slim down the precious beach and smother portions of reef with earth and sand that the trees once filtered. Homes built on captured land to deal with Jamaica's population explosion lacked water supplies, garbage removal and sanitation facilities until relatively recently. Now, thankfully, Negril has a US$15-million water treatment plant and reservoir, which has minimized the amount of untreated sewage flowing into the sea, although link-up is still proving beyond some people's means.

A 2012 study demonstrated that the shoreline at Long Bay has retreated on average 23cm every year since 1971 – a trend expected to accelerate with sea-level rise – and in 2016, the government scrapped a US$1 billion controversial project proposing to build two submerged breakwater structures to combat Negril's beach erosion issue, particularly in the Long Bay area. Stakeholders and NGOs pushed back, citing the potential damage this method would cause to the environment and businesses. The erosion issue is still being studied for other solutions.

ENVIRONMENTAL NGOS

With healthy support from Negril citizens, the **Negril Coral Reef Preservation Society** (NCRPS) has placed 45 mooring buoys at key points on the reefs and successfully lobbied for marine park status like that afforded the Montego Bay waters (see page 164 and ⦿ jpat-jm.net); it was granted in March 1998. The **Negril Environmental Protection Trust** (NEPT; ⦿ nept. wordpress.com) has a wider brief, declaring 128 square kilometres from Green Island to Salmon Point as the **Negril Watershed Environmental Protection Area**, with action required on all fronts: from reforestation projects to combating the burning of hardwoods for saleable charcoal, and to rescuing sea turtles deprived of their beach nesting grounds. An environmental education programme in local schools is also under way in collaboration with the Negril Education Environment Trust (⦿ neetja.com). Among other successes, NEPT also engaged larger hotels in the **Blue Flag Campaign**, which provides beach marine certification to those active on beach erosion and effective coastal management – not an easy task. To find out more about these groups, visit their Marine Park office next to the main craft market (☎ 957 3736).

usually get a fisherman to take you across – ask near the main craft market. Aside from sunbathing, there's decent snorkelling to be had at patches of reef just offshore.

Sheffield Road

Negril's centre is focused on the roundabout feeding the three main roads, with most visitors leaving the beach or cliffs only to change money, buy petrol or find a ride out of the area. **Sheffield Road** is nonetheless the least tourist-oriented part of town and the closest approximation of a real heart to the town, with the police station, market stalls, petrol station, restaurants and constant crowds dodging beeping mopeds. To the right of the roundabout are two rather tatty **shopping plazas** – Coral Seas Plaza and Plaza de Negril, the latter used by locals more than tourists; the car park in front is known as **Negril Square**, a base for taxi drivers, low-key hustlers and would-be guides. Nestled behind is **Red Ground**, a residential area that visitors seldom see but which houses most of Negril's permanent population.

Royal Palm Reserve

Sheffield, Negril • Daily 9am–6pm • Free (US$10 tip for informal guide expected) • Fishing or birdwatching tours US$10 • ☎ 364 7407, ⦿ jpat-jm.net • Take the signed left turn (northwards) from Sheffield Rd east of the Negril Hills golf course and continue for 2km

The 289-acre **Royal Palm Reserve** was created in the 1980s at the southern side of the **Great Morass** as a means of protecting this crucial wetland. While very sadly officially closed due to a lack of funding and visitor interest, it is still very much worth a visit and there's always someone on hand to show you around for a small tip. The royal palm cluster here is one of the largest single collections of the tree in the world; tall and magnificent but devoid of coconuts, the palms have a stately presence that lends the reserve a patently tropical air. Wreathed in creepers and vines springing up from the nutrient-rich bog below, the trees are thick enough in places to block out views of the hills behind. Fishing is possible in the peat channels, and there's a rickety birdwatching tower.

A tour of the reserve makes use of a system of boardwalks, which is the best place to view this rare habitat without getting wet (though boat trips are also available from the Kool Runnings Adventure Park; see page 202). Jamaica's second-largest **wetland** comprises six thousand acres of rivers, peat bogs and grasses that back right onto Negril's beach; fed by rivers from the Orange and Fish River hills, the area is crucial to freshwater supply, acting as a giant natural filter, protecting reefs from being smothered by silt and providing a sanctuary for insects, shrimps, rare plants and birds – commonly seen are Jamaican euphonias, parakeets and woodpeckers. Land crabs enjoy one of the few remaining perfect habitats in Jamaica and are a common sight during the summer breeding months. The morass has long been threatened by pesticide and sewage pollution and proposals to remove peat fuel, but so far the cut-and-drain activities of the government-owned Petroleum Company of Jamaica (PCJ) have been contained.

The onsite small **museum** is predictably desultory and poorly kept since NEPT withdrew its permanent staff, but there are still explanations of wetland ecosystems and bird varieties on the walls. The informal **guides** that are still to be found on site are unpaid and expect to accompany visitors on a 45-minute tour; most are informative and enthusiastic, however, and justify their tip. Dawn or dusk birdwatching as well as fishing for tarpon and tilapia are especially worthwhile activities here (also guided should someone be on hand).

The West End

Beyond the overpriced cocktails and hallucinogenic sunset-watching at the infamous *Rick's Café*, the **West End** cliffs are the last vestige of truly laidback Negril. The ostensible serenity, however, follows an extended period of economic decline in the late 1990s, when the more obvious appeal of the beach eclipsed its popularity. Nevertheless, decent reefs and the thrill of diving from a cliff straight into fifteen feet of the crystal-clear Caribbean remain unbeatable, and with some top accommodation options and several popular evening joints, life has been brought back to the area.

West End Road, re-branded as **One Love Drive**, begins at the roundabout in the centre of town and twists and turns along the cliffs for some five kilometres to Negril Lighthouse, whereupon it becomes Lighthouse Road and meanders onwards along the coast to Orange Hill (see page 222). The first stretch, up to the A FiWi (or Vendor's) Plaza, is the liveliest, with jerk shacks, bars, juice stalls and the odd craft stall on either side of the road, as well as one tiny **beach** where fishermen moor their canoes – check the cleanliness of the water if

---

NEGRIL SUNSETS

The **sunset view** from the West End, Jamaica's extreme westerly point, is the best you'll see. Most evenings the sky blazes with absurdly rich oranges, pinks and blues that intensify as the sun dips behind the horizon, eventually merging into the deepest of blues, with the moon reflected way out to sea. Sunset-watching is an institution; most bars and restaurants offer sunset happy hours and the half-hour or so before dusk is the closest the West End gets to hectic. Coach parties descend in droves upon Negril's biggest cliché, **Rick's Café**, the venue of sunset cliff-diving demonstrations (local boys dive and pose for tips); while the drinks flow at the bar and (very average) bands churn out Marley classics. Though the cliffs are at their highest around *Rick's*, many other hotels and **restaurants** are superb for a sunset drink and swim; best is probably the *LTU Pub* (next to *Rick's*), though the *Sands* bar at the *Caves* hotel has an exclusive air, and the *Rockhouse* boasts sea access from a stylish bar and restaurant, and complete seclusion. *Xtabi* also has a friendly attitude towards non-guests and a spectacular portion of cliff, with a network of underground caves.

5

you're thinking of swimming. The fancy King's Plaza and Sunshine Village shopping malls are just beyond, but the true West End begins over the next blind bend; the road narrows and the hotels that carve up the rest of the cliffs begin in earnest. Nonetheless, each resort is small-scale and by-and-large single storey – the relative quietude here can mean that you've got some of the best places entirely to yourself, especially off-season. After *Rick's*, development is thinner, with hotels interspersed with near-wild coastline.

Being limestone, the cliffs are also riddled with caverns. A popular network lies below the *Xtabi* restaurant, while the wonderful Jamaican *Pushcart* restaurant is located above spacious Joseph's Cave, made famous in movies *Dr No*, *Papillon* and *20,000 Leagues Under the Sea*, though sadly there is also no longer access from above (you can view it by boat, however).

Negril Point Lighthouse

The **Negril Point Lighthouse** stands a proud hundred feet above sea level at Jamaica's westernmost tip. Built in 1894, the 66-foot tower flashes a solar-powered beam sixteen kilometres out to sea, though it still contains the acetylene gas canisters that originally provided the power, the hand-wound pendulum that once regulated the beam and plenty of brass fittings. Port authority workers are usually willing to take you up all 103 leg-quivering steps (tip at your discretion). Look out for the quaint (listed) crumbling outhouses and the far-reaching roots of a huge silk cotton tree. Below the lighthouse

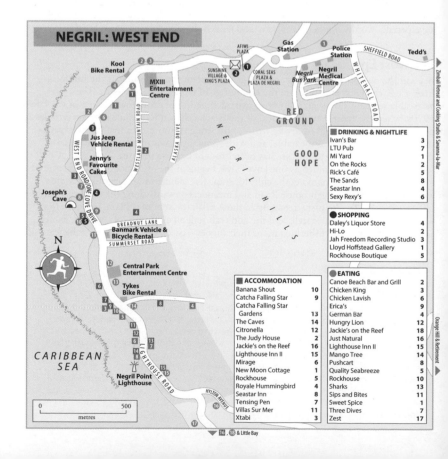

NEGRIL: WEST END

DRINKING & NIGHTLIFE

Ivan's Bar	3
LTU Pub	7
Mi Yard	1
On the Rocks	2
Rick's Café	5
The Sands	8
Seastar Inn	4
Sexy Rexy's	6

SHOPPING

Daley's Liquor Store	4
Hi-Lo	2
Jah Freedom Recording Studio	3
Lloyd Hoffstead Gallery	1
Rockhouse Boutique	5

ACCOMMODATION

Banana Shout	10
Catcha Falling Star	9
Catcha Falling Star Gardens	13
The Caves	14
Citronella	12
The Judy House	2
Jackie's on the Reef	16
Lighthouse Inn II	15
Mirage	6
New Moon Cottage	1
Rockhouse	5
Royale Hummingbird	4
Seastar Inn	8
Tensing Pen	7
Villas Sur Mer	11
Xtabi	3

EATING

Canoe Beach Bar and Grill	2
Chicken King	3
Chicken Lavish	6
Erica's	9
German Bar	4
Hungry Lion	12
Jackie's on the Reef	18
Just Natural	15
Lighthouse Inn II	15
Mango Tree	14
Pushcart	8
Quality Seabreeze	5
Rockhouse	10
Sharks	13
Sips and Bites	11
Sweet Spice	1
Three Dives	7
Zest	17

is a beautiful cove, now connected to the chic *Caves* hotel and reached via a precarious wooden ladder, with rocks smooth enough to lie on and an accessible small cave. Swimming can be risky here, with coastal winds whipping the sea into a frenzy.

ARRIVAL AND DEPARTURE   NEGRIL

By bus and minibus Daily Knutsford Express services (see page 22) to/from Kingston, Montego Bay, Ocho Rios, Sav-la-Mar and elsewhere arrive/depart from their office opposite Time Square plaza on Norman Manley Blvd, close to the beach. Minibuses to all destinations run to and from the bus park on Sheffield Rd. From either location, you can charter a taxi to the West End or beach for US$10, or take a route taxi passing along the road for J$250–350.
Destinations Kingston (8–12 daily; 4hr); Mandeville (2 daily; 3hr 10min); Montego Bay (every 30min; 1hr 30min); Ocho Rios (3 daily; 3hr); Savanna-la-Mar (every 15min, 45min).

By private taxi Private taxis charge anything from US$50 to US$80 for the MoBay to Negril ride.
By plane International Air Link (☎975 3773, ⊛intlairlink. net) offers a daily scheduled service (12min; US$140) from Montego Bay to Negril Aerodrome at Bloody Bay (☎940 6660); TimAir (☎952 2516, ⊛timair.net) also offers plane charters. Taxi fares to hotels are around US$10–15, though most hotels offer their own airport transfer service.
Airlines International Air Link (☎957 5924) and TimAir have offices at Negril aerodrome.

INFORMATION AND GETTING AROUND

Tourist information The helpful Tourist Product Development Company (TPDCO) is on hand for information, located at Times Square plaza on Norman Manley Blvd (Mon–Fri 9am–5pm, ☎957 9314, ⊛tpdco.org); it stocks freesheets with local maps, listings and news. Also worth checking out is ⊛negril.com for informa-tion on the latest goings-on.
By taxi Taxi companies include Rocky's (☎370 7915) and Kenny's (☎995 9410).
By shared taxi Shared route taxis run the length of the beach and West End Rd all day every day, charging around J$250–300 from the roundabout to the lighthouse or Bloody Bay – flag them down anywhere.
By boat If you're staying on the cliffs, you can flag down a glass-bottom boat on its way to the beach in the morning – *Famous Vincent Elvira* is a good choice, though at US$15 one way, it's not the cheapest way to travel.

Bike rental Bicycle hire costs around US$15–20 per day and is an excellent way to explore; rental is available from Jah B's on Norman Manley Blvd (☎957 4235, ⊛negril.com/jahbs) and Banmark (☎957 0196, ⊛banmarkjamaica.wix.com/banmark), Kool Bike Rental (☎957 9224, ⊛koolbikerental. tripod.com) and Tykes Bikes (☎957 0388, ⊖tonyvassell@yahoo.com), all on West End Rd. There's plenty of undeveloped land perfect for mountain biking beyond the West End; rental companies can suggest routes and guides.
Moped and dirt bike rental Mopeds and dirt bikes rent for US$25–50 per day from Happy World (☎957 4004, ⊛carrentalnegril.com) and Jah B's on Norman Manley Blvd (☎957 4235, ⊛negril.com/jahbs), and Banmark (☎957 0196, ⊛banmarkjamaica.wix.com/banmark) and Tykes Bikes (☎957 0388, ⊖tonyvassell@yahoo.com) on West End Rd.

TOURS FROM NEGRIL

As Negril tends to attract those who want to stay put and relax, **tours** are not such a big business. Most operators offer the same trips as from Montego Bay (see page 173), along with a few south coast tours; the best **standard trip** includes a crocodile search along the Black River (around US$85/person), together with a visit to the YS Falls and perhaps the Appleton Rum Estate; the nature tour to Mayfield Falls (US$75/person) is also a good bet. Aside from the destinations listed above, great day-trips (with similar prices) organized independently or through one of the recommended drivers include the **Blue Hole Garden** at Roaring River; the mountain cooking and farm tour at **Zimbali Retreats** (see page 224); or the **Bluefields Organic Fruit Farm** in Bluefields, easily combined with the Peter Tosh Mausoleum in Belmont. Reliable drivers for independent tours and airport pick-ups are listed below and The Negril branch of JUTA (☎957 9197 or ☎957 4620, ⊛jutatoursnegrilltd.com) also offers all the conventional tours. There are, of course, islandwide tour operators as well (see page 25).

OPERATORS
Joe Cool Taxi and Tours ☎390 1614.
Kenny Tours ☎995 9410 or ☎361 2534, ⊛kenny tours.com.

Orlando's Taxi and Tours ☎417 7002.
Paradise Travels ☎912 1432.
Rocky's Taxi and Tours ☎370 7915.

5

Car rental On Norman Manley Blvd: Dollar at Negril Aerodrome (☎ 957 4110), Happy World (☎ 957 4004, ⓦ carrentalnegril.com), and Vernon's at *Fun Holiday Beach Resort* (☎ 371 3078, ⓦ vernonscarrental.com); and on West End Road Jus Jeep (☎ 957 0094/5). Manufactured in Jamaica, Island Cruisers can be rented from their office on Norman Manley Blvd (☎ 422 2831, ⓦ islandcruiserjamaica.com).

ACTIVITIES

Cruises An excellent way to see the local coastline, daytime or sunset cruises by catamaran are usually made to Rhodes Hall Plantation or Half Moon beach (US$50–70/person); most include snorkelling and snacks or dinner and have an open bar. Try Cool Runnings (☎ 974 2446), Red Stripe (☎ 433 0178) or Wild Thing (☎ 957 9930).

Fishing Most glass-bottom boat operators (see below) also offer fishing. Rates vary (about US$50/person per half-day); you can also ask at the fishermen's beach behind the craft market. If you're really serious you can hire a sport fishing boat from Stanley's Deep Sea Fishing (☎ 957 6341 or ☎ 818 6363, ⓦ stanleysdeepseafishing.com), Sea Shell Charters (☎ 875 4167, ⓦ seashellnegril.com) and Winter Fresh (☎ 440 1119, ⓦ winterfresh.ca); bait, tackle and beverages are usually included (price from around US$400/half-day for up to four people).

Glass-bottom boats Operators for the classic Negril boat trip are well represented (US$25 for a 1hr 30min trip; min two people); they ply both beach and cliff coastlines touting for business for impromptu pleasure. Amongst the best-known operators are Famous Vincent Elvira (☎ 473 6910) and Mike's (☎ 847 7699).

Golf East out of town on Sheffield Rd, the Negril Hills Golf Club (☎ 957 4638, ⓦ negrilhillsgolfclub.com) is an extremely hilly and attractive eighteen-hole, 6600-yard, par-72 course. The topography makes for a challenging game, and there's a clubhouse and restaurant on site.

Scuba diving and snorkelling Two large reefs parallel to the West End and four along the beach make snorkelling and diving major Negril highlights. Despite environmental damage, parts of the reefs remain sumptuous, crowded with soft and hard coral, brilliantly coloured sponges and fish, octopuses, sea stars and even the odd turtle or nurse shark. There are several sunken wrecks that have become artificial reefs, including a ganja-smuggling plane that misjudged its landing at a Negril airstrip. Snorkelling equipment (US$20/day) is available at most hotels and all dive operators, which are based between the West End and along the first kilometre or so of beach: Dream Team Divers (☎ 957 0054, ⓦ dreamteamdiversjamaica.com); Marine Life Divers (☎ 957 3245, ⓦ mldiversnegril.com); and Sun Divers (☎ 957 4503, ⓦ sundiversnegril.com) are all reputable.

Watersports Water-skiing, parasailing, jet-skiing and canoeing are available from numerous operators along the first kilometre or so of beach. Go with a formal operator (such as *Ray's*; ☎ 957 5349) and sign papers in their office – accidents have been known to happen when renting informally, with no operator insurance.

Whitewater rafting Grade two whitewater rafting is available inland on the Cabarita River through Cabarita Expeditions (☎ 847 287 9900 or ☎ 298 6113, ⓦ cabaritaexpeditions.com; 3hr 30min; US$140/person including pick-up, instruction and lunch).

ACCOMMODATION

Negril Beach (Norman Manley Blvd) is the place to stay if you want to be right at the centre of the town's party culture. Many hotels have commandeered areas of beach with sun loungers and security, while smaller hotels and those on the inland side of the road (including a couple of backpacker hangouts as well as undistinguished apartment blocks) use whatever piece of sand is closest. Those inland back straight onto the Great Morass, so bugs can be a problem in rainy season. The **West End** is quieter with a degree of privacy, and boasts several of the loveliest hotels in Jamaica as well as some attractive budget options; bear in mind that those right over the (steep and open-access) cliffs are a bad choice if travelling with children. Much accommodation in Negril is in traditional palm-thatched or tile-roofed **cottages**; though cooler than concrete, many are ludicrously easy to break into. Wherever you stay, check doors and windows are secure and ID anyone before you let them in.

THE BEACH

GUESTHOUSES AND B&BS

Green Leaf Cabins Norman Manley Blvd ☎ 429 6438, ⓦ greenleafcabins.com; map p.203. Friendly, family-run cottages across the road from a popular stretch of Negril Beach, offering the best beach budget deal. Each cabin is basic but comfortable with private porch and bath, optional a/c or fan only, and fridge. On-site shop with patties and drinks. US$35

Jah B's Norman Manley Blvd ☎ 957 4235, ⓦ negril.com/jahbs; map p.203. Very appealing budget option in a family yard full of shrubs and flowers on the Morass side of the road. Wooden cabins are clean and comfortable, if basic, each with a bathroom, while decent Jamaican food and drink is served in the attached restaurant/bar. US$35

Mom's Place Norman Manley Blvd ☎ 957 3349; map p.203. Run by a friendly Jamaican couple, this is a simple and homely set of rooms by the beach. All have bright

5

decor, fans and private bathrooms; some have a/c. Café/bar on the premises. US$90

Negril Yoga Centre Norman Manley Blvd ☎957 4397, ⓦnegrilyoga.com; map p.203. Yoga centre and guesthouse overlooking the Great Morass offering cottages of varying degrees of comfort, surrounded by heaps of greenery. Wholefood cooking, a guest kitchen, and yoga and pilates classes available. US$45

Roots Bamboo Norman Manley Blvd ☎957 4479, ⓦroots bamboobeach.com; map p.203. Friendly, efficient and one of the most popular budget options, with numerous small cabins in a large flowering garden by the beach. Each cabin is cosy but slightly faded; some have private showers. Newer rooms offer private bath, mini fridge, large balcony, cable TV and spacious balcony with partial sea views. Camping is available with 24hr security, and there's a Jamaican restaurant on site. Right amid the beach action with regular reggae gigs on site. Camping US$20, cabins US$65

Valentine Villas Trombone's Place, Norman Manley Blvd ☎562 8435, ⓦvalentinevillas.com; map p.203. A small, family-owned property under shady trees: a wooden house offers four clean yet basic rooms (those upstairs are slightly smarter and have a larger veranda), while modern concrete garden rooms have soft colours and floor tiles and are slightly pricey. A bright and luxurious (US$240) "ocean suite" is right over the water – one of the nicest rooms in Negril. US$70

HOTELS

Charela Inn Norman Manley Blvd ☎957 4277, ⓦcharela. com; map p.203. Smart French-Jamaican-owned place with gardens, pool, four-poster beds and an air of cultured elegance. It's home to one of Negril's most popular fine-dining options, *Le Vendome* (see page 213), and folklore and jazz/reggae shows are held twice weekly. Five-night minimum stay. US$216

Country Country Norman Manley Blvd ☎957 4273, ⓦcountrynegril.com; map p.203. Brightly painted cottages set in a pretty garden with a small strip of beach. Rooms are spacious (each sleeps three) with fridge, cable TV and mosquito nets. Rates include breakfast, served at the attractive beachside bar/restaurant. US$205

Couples Swept Away Norman Manley Blvd ☎957 4061, ⓦcouples.com; map p.203. Extensive landscaped gardens, great facilities and an environmental-impact policy make this Jamaica's best large all-inclusive, aimed at couples seeking romance, relaxation or fitness-oriented breaks. Vast sports facilities include an Olympic-sized pool, tennis courts, yoga and watersports. The elegant, well-appointed rooms are accompanied by a beautiful spa and a variety of eating options; the highly rated nouvelle Caribbean and Thai restaurants may well be Negril's best dining options. All inclusive. US$385

Golden Sunset Norman Manley Blvd ☎957 4241, ⓦthegoldensunset.com; map p.203. Long-established

and reliable budget hotel, across the road from the beach, with a range of clean, plain, good-value rooms and cabins, private bath and private or shared kitchenette. US$50

★ **Idle Awhile** Norman Manley Blvd ☎957 3302, ⓦidle awhile.com; map p.203. Sophisticated small boutique hotel with beautifully designed rooms, all with TV, and a veranda with hammock and loungers. Includes free pass to *Swept Away*'s vast sports facilities and free shuttle to/use of sister property *Hide Awhile* over the cliffs. The beachside *Chill Awhile* restaurant (see page 212) is a lovely spot to relax. US$285

Kuyaba Norman Manley Blvd ☎957 4318, ⓦkuyaba. com; map p.203. A classy hotel: the king and honeymoon suites have stylish Mexican tiling, calico fabrics and large bathrooms with jacuzzi. More basic wooden cottages are also available. Good restaurant on site. Three-night minimum stay. US$197

Negril Tree House Norman Manley Blvd ☎957 4287, ⓦfacebook.com/negriltreehouse; map p.203. A clean, comfort-able and appealing complex of rooms and villas. The bar is built around a tree, and there's a restaurant, pool and jacuzzi, plus watersports and a massage room. Excellent buffet breakfast included. US$206

★ **Nirvana on the Beach** Norman Manley Blvd ☎957 4314, ⓦnirvananegril.com; map p.203. Attractive suites and three-bed wooden cottages with kitchens in a spacious, sandy beach garden (take a massage under the trees), dotted with sculptures and hammocks. Friendly atmos-phere and kooky decorative touches. Very reasonable for groups of four or more. US$240

★ **Sandy Haven** Norman Manley Blvd ☎957 3200, ⓦsandyhavenresort.com; map p.203. A chic aqua-marine lobby punctuated with ceramic sculptures sets the tone at this luxury boutique resort. Spacious beachfront and garden suites, ideally located right on the Negril Beach strip, with private balcony, soaking tub and shower, cable TV, mini-fridge and coffee maker. Swimming pool, jacuzzi, gym, friendly beachfront bar staff serving wonderful cocktails and food, and a gourmet Caribbean restaurant. Breakfasts are additional but the extensive menu is well worth it. US$433

Sunset at the Palms Norman Manley Blvd ☎957 5350, ⓦsunsetatthepalms.com; map p.203. On the morass side, elegant wooden cabins in lush tropical gardens at this private all-inclusive in Negril. The resort has access to a section of Bloody Bay beach across the road. All-inclusive price includes all food, sports and morning yoga. Non all-inclusive option available by arrangement. US$538

Travellers Beach Resort Norman Manley Blvd ☎957 4314, ⓦtbr.travel; map p.203. Family-operated, attractive blue and cream coloured bungalows and suites with private verandas flank a flowery garden, along a pathway leading to Negril Beach. Value-packed rooms include mini-fridge, cable TV, private verandas and glass showers. Swimming pool, gym, and beachfront restaurant deck boasting perfect sunset views, weekly Jamaican buffets and weekly live music. Look for frequent online deals; meal plans optional. Negril's long-established educational non-profit NEET has offices on site. US$109

★ **Whistling Bird** Norman Manley Blvd ☎ 957 4403, ⓦ whistlingbird.info; map p.203. Beach cottages (most with a/c, some have TV) set in a lovely overgrown garden with a cook-to-order restaurant offering decently priced meal plans. Private but also family-friendly. Good online specials available. Wheelchair access. US$209

WEST END

HOSTELS, GUESTHOUSES AND B&BS

★ **Catcha Falling Star Gardens** West End Rd ☎ 957 0279, ⓦ catchafallingstargardens.com; map p.206. Located right across the street from one of Negril's best bars, the *LTU Pub* (the property was formerly *LTU Villas*), these are spacious, great-value apartments in quiet gardens with an attractive pool. Each room has two double beds, a lounge and a fridge, some have balcony and a/c. US$76

The Judy House Westland Mountain Rd ☎ 424 5481, ⓦ judyhousenegril.com; map p.206. Homely, great-value cabins with bathroom, well-equipped kitchenette and deck (two have a/c), plus two small dorms with kitchenette. Set amid secluded flower gardens a short walk from the sea (turn in at the *Canoe Bar*). Dorms US$25, cabins US$60

Lighthouse Inn II Lighthouse Rd ☎ 957 4052, ⓦ lighthouseinn2.com; map p.206. Really attractive and good-value simple cabins are scattered throughout a beautiful garden – though it's a distance from the action. All have veranda and small kitchenette, and a breakfast and dinner package is available at the good on-site restaurant. Wheelchair-friendly. US$70

Mirage West End Rd ☎ 957 0390, ⓦ catchajamaica. com; map p.206. Quiet, small property perched on the cliffs with 12 spacious rooms with panoramic sea views. Take shade under the almond tree by the swimming pool or take the steps down the cliffs to swim and snorkel in the sea. Rooms feature mini-fridge, cable TV, coffee maker. Continental breakfast included, and use of beach facility at sister property *Charela Inn*. US$181

★ **New Moon Cottage** West End Rd ☎ 957 4305 or ☎ 417 6848, ⓦ newmooncottagenegril.com; map p.206. Clean, quiet, and bargain rooms with private bath in two cottages at a Jamaican family home, with communal kitchen. Camping available (US$25), and home-cooked meals to order. US$60

HOTELS

Banana Shout West End Rd ☎ 957 0384, ⓦ banana shoutresort.com; map p.206. Originally owned by Mark Conklin (whose Negril-based novel is reviewed on page 293), these clean and attractive cottages lie in gardens right atop the cliffs. Each unit has kitchenette, fan, hammocks on the veranda and Haitian artwork. There's a diving platform, sun deck, private cave and exceptional sunset views. Includes continental breakfast; bar and jerk grill on site. US$180

Catcha Falling Star West End Rd ☎ 957 0390, ⓦ catcha jamaica.com; map p.206. With an ideal clifftop location, featuring a range of private and attractive rooms, from wood-panelled cottages to apartments within a main villa; each has veranda and full amenities. Relax in the exquisite pool or enjoy superb food and cocktails at the popular *Ivan's Bar & Restaurant*. US$180

The Caves Lighthouse Rd ☎ 957 0270, ⓦ islandoutpost. com; map p.206. Gorgeous, romantic boutique hotel set behind Fort Knox-inspired gates. The eleven cottage-style rooms are funkily designed and equipped with batik bathrobes and every amenity, while the Aveda spa, sauna and Jacuzzi with sunset view are faultless; guests can have a massage in one of the caves below, with the sea lapping nearby. Three-night minimum stay; rates are all inclusive. US$722

★ **Citronella** West End Rd ☎ 460 8369, ⓦ citronella jamaica.com; map p.206. This private, tranquil property next to the *LTU Pub* offers luxury away from the oft-irritating resort schmaltz of today's Negril. Five luxuriously furnished self-catering cottages are set in sprawling cliffside gardens with sea access, and are especially good value for groups of four to seven. US$198

SPRING BREAK

Every year, between the end of February and Easter, ten thousand American college students arrive in Jamaica for **Spring Break** – and most head straight for Negril. Though not reaching the levels of debauched hype that Cancun has become famous for, it's a non-stop carnival of fun if you're 19, and a rude shattering of the (relative) peace if you're not. If wet T-shirt competitions, drinking challenges and dancing in piña colada-flavoured foam are your thing, then this is the time to head for Negril – otherwise be warned. *Margaritaville*, *Risky Business* and *Rick's Café* are the self-appointed headquarters for Spring Break; most other beach bars put on **special events**, and the season is sponsored by Red Stripe and Appleton. This is also a good time to hear **live music**, with some of Jamaica's best DJs and bands making the most of a large, enthusiastic audience.

Travel agents specializing in Spring Break packages include *Student Travel Services* (☎ 1 800 648 4849 in US, ⓦ ststravel.com) and *Sunsplash Tours* (☎ 1 800 426 7710 in US, ⓦ sunsplashtours.com). For further information check ⓦ negrilspringbreak.com.

5

★ **Jackie's on the Reef** Coast Rd, 5km east of the lighthouse ☎ 957 4997, ⓦ jackiesonthereef.com; map p.206. Wonderful holistic wellness retreat for body, mind and spirit; vibrant owner Jackie is the perfect advertisement for her treatments. Remarkably designed for those recovering from urban stress, the expansive airy rooms lie under a geodesic dome, with a large communal veranda and saltwater pool and massage hut on the shore. Other therapies include heated bamboo, reiki and past-life regression. Four-night minimum; rates include a tasty and wholesome breakfast and dinner plus daily yoga or meditation. Non-guests welcome, but must arrange a treatment/lunch in advance. US$175

★ **Rockhouse** West End Rd ☎ 957 4373, ⓦ rockhouse hotel.com; map p.206. Enviable location on a rock peninsula with ladders down into an azure cove; this is a unique, stylish and comfortable hotel. Thatched studios or villas, each with glass-door patio overlooking the ocean, outdoor shower, fan and bamboo four-poster bed. Excellent thatched restaurant (best breakfasts in town), while the innovative, super-relaxing spa and infinity pool take their place amongst Jamaica's very best. The hotel is Negril's leader in social responsibility, with its Rockhouse Foundation involved in a range of programmes. US$217

Royale Hummingbird Resort West End Rd ☎ 332 7211, ⓦ royalehummingbird.com; map p.206. Set on a lane back from the main road, this family-run resort offers 16 spacious and renovated rooms (with mini-fridge, terrace and cable TV) partly centred on a swimming pool and restaurant. Friendly staff and optional on-site restaurant meals. US$70

★ **Seastar Inn** Off West End Rd (turn inland just before Rick's Café) ☎ 957 0553, ⓦ seastarinn.com; map p.206. One of Negril's best bargains, *Seastar* somehow combines a friendly family feel with being a hot spot for live music two nights per week. Amid well-kept gardens, the rooms are quiet and spotless with private bath, a/c, fridge and TV, a pool and international menu available at the restaurant or brought to your room. Rates include a substantial breakfast and free daily beach shuttle. US$79

Tensing Pen West End Rd ☎ 957 0387, ⓦ tensingpen. com; map p.206. Stylish and exclusive retreat in pretty clifftop gardens. The imaginatively decorated wood and stone cottages of varying levels are graced with bamboo furniture and have an individual touch. There's a restaurant (breakfast included) and yoga room. The property's two cliffs are linked by a tiny suspension bridge. US$195

Villas Sur Mer West End Rd ☎ 957 0342, ⓦ villassurmer. com; map p.206. Unfailingly stylish throughout, this renovated property features sumptuous thatched wooden cottages with sea access via a cave under the road. A separate six-bed luxury villa is located on the clifftop, with marble bathrooms and breezy living room. Pool and jacuzzi on site. Three-night minimum stay. US$288

Xtabi West End Rd ☎ 957 0121, ⓦ xtabinegril.com; map p.206. Lovely West End veteran with flowering gardens and network of caves. The oceanside rooms are in wooden cabins with private sun deck and swimming platforms, or there are garden-side apartments with kitchen. Pool plus open-air restaurant/bar. US$100

EATING

Negril's cosmopolitan dining scene offers some of the finest cuisine in Jamaica. There are good **vegetarian** options alongside chicken and fish, and you'll also find a lot of **pasta** and **pizza**, with some restaurants run by Italian expats – popular with the large number of Italians who visit in the early summer. Jamaican food tends to be lower-priced, with numerous vendors in shacks along the first stretch of West End Rd selling roast or fried fish and soups, and **jerk vendors** wheeling out their oil-drum barbecues as dusk falls. Many of the smarter restaurants offer free pick-up; call in advance.

THE BEACH

Angela's Bar-B-Barn Hotel, Norman Manley Blvd ☎ 957 9793; map p.203. Decent, mid-priced Italian restaurant on a breezy and attractive upstairs terrace. Coffee, delicious thin-crust pizza, pasta dishes, and other Italian specialities (US$15–30). Daily 8.45am–11.45pm.

★ **Bongo's** Norman Manley Blvd ☎ 957 4330; map p.203. Set inside *Sandy Haven Resort*, Jamaican Chef Tyrone Guthrie heads this romantic indoor and courtyard restaurant that's open to non-guests. The Caribbean fusion menu has the likes of crab and corn chowder (J$385) and jerk chicken pasta (J$800) and plenty of beef and fish dishes, vegan and vegetarian options, local desserts and a mini wine cellar. Daily 6pm–10pm.

Bourbon Beach Normal Manley Blvd ☎ 957 4432; map p.203. Consistently tasty, fiery jerk chicken (J$550 for quarter) served on the go – with the best jerk sauce in Negril, and optional sides ranging from rice and peas to fries or festival – enjoyed on-site to the sounds of reggae. Daily 24hr.

Chill Awhile Idle Awhile, Norman Manley Blvd ☎ 957 9566; map p.203. Prices are a little high but the food is certainly tasty, with Jamaican breakfasts (US$8–15) and lots of seafood plus fresh juices, quesadillas, vegetarian pastas, salads and burgers (US$15–40) – all served up in attractive gardens on the beach. Daily 8am–11pm.

Kenny's Italian Café Norman Manley Blvd ☎ 957 4032; map p.203. A stylish spot on the Morass side, serving a full list of Italian thin-crust pizzas (US$12–18), plus pasta, salads, meat and cheese sandwiches (US$8–15), and Blue Mountain espresso. Free hotel pick-up. Daily noon–midnight or later.

★ **Kuyaba** Kuyaba Hotel, Norman Manley Blvd ☎ 957 4318; map p.203. Thatch-roofed, open-sided and upmarket restaurant with innovative decor and consistently good food. The frequently changing menu might include lobster in white wine and garlic, steak, snapper with coconut callaloo and vegetarian dishes (US$25–40). Great burgers and pepper shrimp at lunchtimes (US$16–28). Daily 7am–11pm.

Le Vendome Charela Inn, Norman Manley Blvd ☎957 4648; map p.203. Celebrated, sophisticated, expensive French/Jamaican cuisine – menu items include duck à l'orange, veal with velouté sauce, snapper in coconut, mussels au gratin (US$35). A five-course set menu, with vegetarian options, is available for US$75, plus home-made ice cream, bread and a decent wine list. Live jazz/cabaret twice weekly. Daily 11.30am–11pm.

The Lobster House Sunrise Club Hotel, Norman Manley Blvd ☎957 4293, ⊛sunriseclub.com; map p.203. Smart, friendly, Italian-run restaurant-cum-bar on the morass side. The wood-fired brick oven turns out probably the best pizza in all Jamaica (US$12–20), while honours are also due for the coffee – Blue Mountain, Italian style, unbeatable. The fine yet mid-priced Italian lobster (US$22–40) comes in ragu, cannelloni, crepes and more – and the pink gnocchi's tasty, too. Daily 8am–midnight.

Norma's on the Beach Sea Splash Hotel, Norman Manley Blvd ☎957 4041; map p.203. Formerly affiliated to late Jamaican master chef Norma Shirley, this moderately priced (US$16–40) Negril stalwart features nouvelle Jamaican cuisine, with creative salads, pastas, soups like pumpkin bisque with sherry, and fantastic seafood – try the marlin sushi. The breakfast and lunch menus are especially good value. Daily 8am–11pm.

★ **Rasta Ade** Norman Manley Blvd ☎529 0171; map p.203. A colourful beachfront bamboo shack serving excellent vegetarian and vegan fare by the sea. Veggie Platter (J$1000–1500), sandwiches (J$1200) and soups (J$700), enjoyed on shaded red-gold-green tables. The juice bar is equally popular for a tropical fruit heat break – a favourite is the Rasta Lemonade (J$400) with a fresh ginger mix. Daily 8am–8pm.

Sweet Spot Norman Manley Blvd ☎334 8292, ⊛sunrise club.com; map p.203. Bright yellow painted local restaurant serving up typical Jamaican breakfast, soups, rice n' beans dishes and specialties from curries (J$400) to oxtail (J$600). Fresh squeezed juices and other drinks available. Lunch or dinner get busy with locals picking up orders, though there's plenty of seating. Daily 8am–11pm.

Uprising Norman Manley Blvd (opposite Drifters Bar); map p.203. Tucked back a few steps from the main beach foot traffic, and popular with busy taxi drivers, a screened wooden shack turned central kitchen serves heaping plates of stews with rice and beans (J$400), fish (J$600), and other specialties. Limited seating, and best taken away to enjoy beachfront. Daily 11.30am–8pm.

★ **Wine with Me** Norman Manley Blvd ☎340 2108, ⊛facebook.com/winewithme2; map p.203.
An exciting addition to Negril, offering a chilled out, sophisticated wine bar setting. The coral red cosy interior booths and armchairs ooze romance, as does the dim-lit veranda and lawn side tables for al fresco dining. Delicious gourmet dishes and weekly Sunday brunch, ranging from pastas to whole fish served Jamaican-style (J$2000–2500). Ask for the scotch bonnet honey sauce, or the daily "wine down" two-glass special from 4pm–8pm from an extensive wine list and imported cheese selection; charcuterie options also available. Tues–Sun 10am–11pm.

SHEFFIELD ROAD

★ **Sweet Spice** Opposite the Texaco station ☎957 4621; map p.206. Known among locals as the best affordable Jamaican restaurant in Negril, *Sweet Spice* serves all the island's specials for breakfast, lunch and dinner at a high standard, plus a few unusual options, to take away or eat in (J$1000–1800). Daily 8.30am–10.30pm.

WEST END

★ **Canoe Beach Bar and Grill** West End Rd ☎878 5893; map p.206. A Jamaican-Canadian owned restaurant on the West End serving good-value international food – seafood pasta, potato wedges, burgers, sandwiches and cakes (all US$9–20). Great chilled vibe, occasional steel bands and singers, and set on its own tiny beach. Daily 10am–10pm.

Chicken King West End Rd (opposite MXIII) ☎459 1866; map p.206. Long-timer roadside restaurant with an extensive menu of jerk chicken, lobster, pork, fried fish, curries, roasted breadfruit and callaloo, all prepared on grills (expect to pay J$2500 for lobster, much less for everything else). Sit on wooden benches and tables facing the beach and a solid sea breeze. Daily 9.30am–11pm.

Chicken Lavish West End Rd ☎957 4410; map p.206. A choice spot for domino players, serving up breakfast, chicken and fish Jamaican- and Chinese-style, steaks and pork chops, plus lobster on occasion, all inexpensive (J$600–2000). Daily 9.30am–11pm.

Erica's West End Rd ☎889 3109; map p.206. Small shack featuring home cooking by Erica herself. Seafood is a speciality, with good low-priced, lobster (J$2000) and conch stew (J$800). Daily 8am–11pm.

German Bar West End Rd ☎471 6493 ⊛german-bar.com; map p.206. An expat haunt perched on the seafront, serving a variety of Schnitzel and Bratwurst, but equally popular for its extensive, delicious pizza menu (J$550). Tues–Sun 1–9.30pm.

Hungry Lion West End Rd ☎957 4486; map p.206. A walled courtyard affords privacy to eat some good vegetarian food, and seafood too: try the green lentil shepherd's pie, lobster in lemon butter and black bean chilli (US$10–20). Highlights are the coconut cream pie for dessert, and the colourful cocktails. Hotel pick-up available. Daily 6–10pm.

5

★ **Jackie's on the Reef** Coast Rd, a couple of kilometres from town ☎ 957 4997; map p.206. An innovative and health-food-oriented menu, served in a romantic and unusual setting. Moderately priced dishes (US$12–20) include grilled tuna with sesame noodles, sundried tomato pasta and marvellous chicken or black bean tacos, plus health-giving smoothies and juices. Lunch daily by advance order only.

★ **Just Natural** Hylton Rd ☎ 957 0235; map p.206. Relocated to just beyond the lighthouse, this inexpensive, sibling-run vegetarian, Ital and seafood spot serves great fresh Jamaican breakfast like callaloo omelettes and ackee (J$800–1200). For lunch, there's pasta or lobster burritos and at dinner Ital stews or grilled lobster (J$1000–2500), in a romantic garden with fairy lights. Daily 8am–9pm.

Lighthouse Inn II West End Rd ☎ 957 4052; map p.206. Imaginative, intimate restaurant set in an overgrown garden just before the lighthouse. An original mix of Caribbean and German/European cuisines and a homely feel make this one of the best mid-priced options (J$1200–2500). Complimentary pick-up. Daily 8am–9pm.

Mango Tree West End Rd ☎ 957 0185; map p.206. Small bar conveniently located opposite *Rick's*, serving small (J$350) or large-sized (J$450) portions of Jamaican dishes, from curries to stews and vegetables. There's a bar on-site with an old television blasting movies or sports if you choose to linger, and a couple of ramshackle wooden tables. Daily noon–9pm.

Pushcart West End Rd ☎ 957 4373; map p.206. A smart Jamaican restaurant and bar in a prime spot over Joseph's Cave, serving straightforward but high-quality food (the jerk pork and oxtail are highlights) at moderate prices (US$18–30). Service is friendly and professional, and it's also a great spot for an evening drink. Daily 11am–midnight.

Quality Seabreeze West End Rd ☎ 584 9030; map p.206. This funky, colourful wooden house veranda-turned-restaurant sits across from the sea and serves excellent seafood including lionfish (J$400–1500), octopus and conch. Beef and chicken options also available. Free pick ups offered with a dinner reservation. Daily 6pm–11pm.

★ **Rockhouse** West End Rd ☎ 957 4373; map p.206. One of Negril's finest restaurants, romantically set on a boardwalk right over the sea. Good value for money (mains US$23–45) and an imaginative menu including numerous crustaceans and Asian touches: try seafood bouillon in a coconut shell, or conch fritters. Steaks and burgers also available. Daily 8am–11pm.

Sharks West End Rd ☎ 428 8411; map p.206. Popular with locals and tourists alike for the big portions of good-quality Jamaican food and the very friendly service from Shark and family. Inexpensive (J$700–1600). Daily 8am–midnight.

Sips and Bites West End Rd ☎ 957 0188; map p.206. A large and very friendly open yard with eating at long tables, some undercover. Serves unadulterated Jamaican cuisine and fresh juices at very reasonable prices (J$500–1500); is very popular with taxi drivers for breakfast. Daily except Sat 8am–10pm.

★ **Three Dives** West End Rd ☎ 344 6850; map p.206. Popular and inexpensive (J$400–1500), this jerk centre is a Negril favourite, set in a cliffside garden, with particularly good lobster, a nightly bonfire and often a lively crowd. Mon–Sat 9am–11pm.

Zest West End Rd ☎ 632 0919; map p.206. Imaginative, secluded clifftop restaurant offering "cuisine of the sun" linked to famed Jamaican Chef Norma Shirley's son, Delius Shirley. Meals blend international and Jamaican influences, such as the jerked chicken penne pasta (J$2,575) and spicy curried crab cake (J$2300); callaloo and other vegetables sourced from the on-site organic plot. Daily 8am–9pm.

DRINKING AND NIGHTLIFE

Most **bars** want you to spend the sunset with them and offer happy hours as an incentive. As the cliffs give the best view, bars along the West End tend to be livelier at dusk, with the action most nights moving to the beach later on. If you want some local flavour, try the darkened interiors of the **rum bars** and **beer shacks** along Sheffield Road or West End Road near the roundabout. There is only one proper **club** in town, *The Jungle*, so most of the weeknight dancing is offered by **beach bars** using sand as a dancefloor – though there are a couple of West End options, too. A nightly rotation system shares business around. DJs play reggae, dancehall and dance music, and there is plenty of live music, from Marley covers to soul and jazz. Ask around to see what's happening – you can usually walk from one beach venue to another. Negril's risqué reputation means it has a number of go-go clubs: scantily-clad women gyrate for drinkers and post *Jungle* clubbers; these clubs draw a mainly local clientele of both sexes.

THE BEACH
Alfred's Ocean Palace Norman Manley Blvd ☎ 957 4669, ⓦ alfreds.com; map p.203. Busiest bar on the sand, with thrice-weekly live reggae (currently Sun, Tues and Fri) and crowds of vacationers dancing within their fenced-off section. Can be great fun but watch out for the hustlers on gig nights. Bob Marley covers earlier in the night, with raw dancehall later. Daily 11am till very late; shows 10pm–2am.

Bourbon Beach Bar Norman Manley Blvd ☎ 957 4434, ⓦ bourbonbeachjamaica.com; map p.203. Still known by many as *De Bus* (the trademark London bus used in 007 movie *Live and Let Die* has mysteriously disappeared from its entrance gate, however), there's DJs or live music every night here, while the jerk chicken is famously good. Upstairs offers shisha/hookah smoking in an Arabian lounge. Daily 6pm–2am or later.

★ **Drifters Bar** Norman Manley Blvd, 1.5km from the Negril roundabout ☎826 2116, ⓦfacebook.com/driftersbarnegril; map p.203. Run by ever-friendly former Drifters singer Luddy Samms, this is one of the top spots for music on the beach. Fri afternoons (2–7pm) feature the region's best singers at an R&B, soul and reggae jam, while there's also live music on Sun and karaoke on Wed. A three-night Blues on the Beach festival takes place each Jan. Traditional jerk to order. Daily noon–10pm.

★ **The Jungle** Norman Manley Blvd; map p.203. Negril's only purpose-built nightclub, across from the beach, with a gaming lounge, sports bar and jerk food. Thursday's "Ladies' Night" is one of the best and most popular club nights in the country, with seemingly half of western Jamaica's youth sweating and gyrating to a surprisingly original music selection (ladies free until midnight). Cover usually J$1000, but varies. Wed–Sun 9pm–5am.

Kenny's Italian Café Norman Manley Blvd ☎957 4032, ⓦfacebook.com/italiancafejamaica; map p.203. On the Morass side, this was the latest hotspot at the time of writing, especially busy as a *Jungle* warm-up Thurs–Sat. It draws a stylish 20s–30s crowd, enjoying the soft lighting, outdoor tables and house music DJs. Great bar (drinks US$5–12) and pizzas. Daily noon–midnight or later.

Margaritaville Norman Manley Blvd ☎957 4467, ⓦmargaritavillecaribbean.com; map p.203. Large and hugely popular American beach bar/restaurant with water trampolines, beach volleyball, two-for-one drink offers (US$6-15) and sports screens. Themed nights include karaoke or a bonfire beach party, and live acts, too – check schedule for details. Free hotel shuttle. Daily 11am–2am or later.

Risky Business Norman Manley Blvd ☎957 3008; map p.203. Beach venue for the wild, young and reckless, with live music and sound systems nightly – and inevitably drawing a varied crowd of tourists and hustlers. Inexpensive up- and downstairs bars and good jerk for snacking on later. Daily 6pm–2am or later.

Roots Bamboo Norman Manley Blvd ☎957 4479, ⓦrootsbamboobeach.com; map p.203. Still one of the best and liveliest places to have an inexpensive drink on the beach. The music's usually good-quality reggae and dancehall, with guest sound systems and live acts on Wed. Daily 6pm–2am or later.

WEST END

★ **Ivan's Bar** Catcha Falling Star, West End Rd ☎957 0390, ⓦcatchajamaica.com; map p.206. One of the best hotel bar-restaurants (open to non-guests after 5pm), rebuilt with driftwood oddities after damage from Hurricane Ivan. Excellent cocktails (US$10–20) and finger foods like crab cakes, jerk shrimp and strips of tenderloin, as well as a full dinner menu, all enjoyed in a supremely romantic terrace setting on the clifftop. Daily 5–11pm.

LTU Pub West End Rd ☎957 0382; map p.206. Laidback Negril stalwart offering cliffside drinking, diving, snorkelling and a moderately priced, mixed menu: seafood, stuffed jalapeno chillis and jerk favourites. Ask the barman to make you a Bob Marley – the five-shot red, gold and green special can take a while to get down (J$1000). Daily 9am–midnight.

Mi Yard West End Rd ☎957 4442, ⓦmiyard.com; map p.206. Two-floor inexpensive bar that's tourist-friendly but positively Rasta. Open for music, dominoes, drinking and jerk; live music on occasional Tues or Sat. Always busy once the beach bars start to slow down after 2am. Daily 24hr.

On the Rocks West End Rd ☎544 0295, ⓦontherocks negril.com; map p.206. Attractive cliffside circular bar

---

NEGRIL'S DRUG CULTURE

As any aficionado can tell you, Jamaica's best **ganja** (marijuana) – well-flavoured and incredibly potent – grows in the fertile local Westmoreland earth. The trade to eager tourists has always played a significant part in the local economy and many devotees make annual pilgrimages to find a place to chill out and partake of the local weed. Hearing hissing offers of "sensi" as you stroll the beach or walk the streets was no surprise even when the drug was illicit, but since the Government of Jamaica decriminalized the possession and consumption of up to two ounces (56 grams) of marijuana (see page 67), large chalkboard café signs openly invite you to come and "bake". However, don't feel that you can light up wherever you choose – marijuana smoking is generally prohibited in public spaces, so check with the establishment first. Time your trip for mid-December and you can experience Jamaica's first legalized marijuana event: the annual Rastafari Rootz Fest, with a Ganja Cup contest and live reggae performances.

Note that there's also a great deal of **cocaine** and **crack** use around town. It's not especially noticeable, but you might pick up on a certain furtiveness around the late-night beach bars. Negril is also one of the few places on the island where you're likely to be offered locally abundant (and legal) **magic mushrooms**, considerably larger and stronger than those in cooler countries. Some restaurants include them in cakes or omelettes and serve foul-tasting mushroom tea, for instance *Jenny's Favorite Cakes* (also serving up potent ganja cake) on the West End Road, while *Tedd's* on Sheffield Rd (ask a taxi driver for Tedd Brown's) mixes up mushroom-flavoured daiquiris and more.

5

in vogue for its loud Wed dancehall sessions on the large lawn, with an up-for-it crowd of locals and tourists arriving not before 11pm. Daily 6pm–2am or later.

Rick's Café West End Rd ☎957 0380, ⓦrickscafe jamaica.com; map p.206. The classic West End bar, fully rebuilt, overpriced and touristy, with a distinctly average Marley covers band – yet it still manages to win "best bar in the world" competitions. The high point is the traditional and impressive spectacle of local boys diving from the high cliffs at sunset. Daily noon–9pm.

The Sands The Caves, Lighthouse Rd ☎957 0270; map p.206. Negril's most exclusive hotel has an attractive public bar (US$8–20) to match – and it's markedly atmospheric, relaxed and unpretentious. Strictly for sunset only. Daily 4–8pm.

★ Seastar Inn Off West End Rd (turn inland just before Rick's); map p.206. This hotel's "Saturday One Love Reggae Show" has become a high point of Negril's entertainment scene, with live drumming, a house band and sometimes big name reggae acts. Also promotes a great karaoke night on Mondays, with high standards. Great burgers and other food, plus cocktails (US$7–12) available. Daily 11am–midnight or later.

Sexy Rexy's West End Rd ☎445 3740, ⓦsexyrexy negril.com; map p.206. Just beyond *LTU*, this infamous and inexpensive small shack has as good a clifftop view as anywhere in the West End. Rexy is an entertaining local character and tour guide and will cook up tasty fried fish if you're hungry. Daily, no set hours.

SHOPPING

CRAFTS AND SOUVENIRS

Dedicated craft shops pepper West End Rd; especially good are A FiWi Plaza (otherwise known as Vendors' Plaza or Hi-Lo Plaza), Sunshine Plaza and the ramshackle collection of huts opposite the *Rockhouse Hotel*. Times Square Plaza on Normal Manley Blvd and the new Boardwalk Plaza on Bloody Bay have numerous in-bond stores with souvenirs, jewellery, cigars, clothing and the like.

Craft market Norman Manley Blvd (at the round-about end); map p.203. The best place to buy crafts, with a hundred stalls and a full spread of merchandise. Be prepared for sales banter and a good haggle. Mon–Sat 9am–5pm.

Kuyaba The Beach ☎957 4318; map p.203. For high-quality carvings and unusual craft items, try this excellent hotel shop, which prides itself on stock that you can't find elsewhere in town, like painted tin "country buses" and brightly enamelled tropical fish. Daily 10am–5pm.

Lloyd Hoffstead Gallery Shop 34, A FiWi Plaza ☎957 3903; map p.206. Original sculpture and wonderful music-themed prints from this Hanover artist. Mon–Sat 9am–5pm.

Rockhouse Boutique Rockhouse, West End Rd ☎957 4373, ⓦrockhousehotel.com; map p.206. Best of the hotel shops, offering a pretty array of beach wraps and other

clothing, embroidered designer bags by Negril-based French designer Sophie Eyssautier, Starfish bathing products, CDs, books, pepper sauces and more. Daily 10am–6pm.

MUSIC

Try the group of small shops at Sunshine Village Plaza on the West End, which stock a good variety of Jamaican CDs.

Jah Freedom Recording Studio West End ☎957 0037, ⓦjahfreedom.com; map p.206. Recording facilities for local and international musicians; can arrange dub plates with top Jamaican artists. By arrangement.

FOOD AND DRINK

Try the stalls along Sheffield Rd for cheap fresh fruit and vegetables.

Daley's Liquor Store West End Rd ☎957 4434; map p.206. 1.5km from the roundabout, Daley's has a large selection, offers discounts on bulk buys of beer or spirits, and can deliver to your hotel. Mon–Fri 9am–5pm, Sat 9am–1pm.

Hi-Lo Sunshine Village Plaza, West End ☎957 4546; map p.206. Negril's best supermarket, walkable from the roundabout. Best for rum and Blue Mountain coffee. Mon–Fri 9am–6pm.

DIRECTORY

Internet Best service is from Surf n Talk, between Merrils 1&2 on Norman Manley Blvd (☎957 4795). Mi Yard on West End Rd (☎957 4442) is open 24hr (slow service).

Laundry West End Cleaners, off Hylton Ave at the top of Lighthouse Rd (☎957 0160); washing costs J$100 per pound, including soap.

Massage Massage is a Negril institution. Try *Jackie's on the Reef* (☎957 4997; see page 212), *Tanya's Secret Escape* (☎887 4918), or *Rockhouse* (☎957 4373; see page 212) (US$60–120) for a delightful massage right atop cliffs; numerous beach masseuses set up daily along Negril Beach, though quality varies.

Medical services Negril Minor Emergency Clinic, Norman Manley Blvd (☎957 4888; daily 9am–5pm with 24hr doctor on call); Omega Medical Centre, 2a Plaza de Negril (☎957 9223, ⓦomegamedicalservicesltd.com). Nearest hospitals are at Savanna-la-Mar (☎955 2533) and the Noel Holmes Hospital in Lucea (☎956 2733), though anything serious is dealt with at Cornwall Regional Hospital, Montego Bay (☎952 5100). In an emergency, dial ☎110 for an ambulance.

Money and exchange 24hr ATMs can be found at Scotiabank by the roundabout – although it is a less secure location roadside – and at the Bloody Bay gas station by the Negril Aerodrome; NCB in Sunshine Village has an

5

STAGE SHOWS AND SOUND-SYSTEM JAMS

Large **stage shows** featuring well-known reggae artists are advertised on roadside billboards and through a car-with-megaphone system, rarely starting before 11pm and going on until 2–5am. Main venues for large shows are *MXIII* and *Negril Escape* on the West End, and *Roots Bamboo*, *Bourbon Beach*, *Alfred's* or *Risky Business* on the beach; cover charges start at US$10. There are usually reggae extravaganzas around **Negril Carnival** – held in late April, with costume parades and all-night dancing – and at the **Bob Marley Birthday Bash** on February 6. The birthday of Westmoreland's own Peter Tosh, in October, sometimes also draws big-name acts. Aside from reggae, look out for Negril's **Blues on the Beach** festival, promoted by the team at *Drifters Bar* (see page 215) and planned to take place each January. At New Year, Easter and Independence Day in August it's always worth the forty-minute drive to Savanna-la-Mar for big-name, all-night dancehall shows. Sound-system jams also take place each weekend: Red Ground, Orange Hill and West End Road are the usual locations; ask around for what's happening. Jazz fans will find weekly gigs at *Roots Bamboo*, *Charela Inn* and *Drifters Bar*.

ATM, counters and wire-transfer facilities (Mon–Thurs 9am–2pm, Fri 9am–4pm); both banks offer exchange and credit cash advances – as do cambios FX Trader, by HiLo Supermarket, Sunshine Village (Mon–Thurs 9am–5pm, Fri & Sat 9am–5.30pm), and Banmark, Cnr of West End Rd and Summerset Lane (Mon–Sat 9am–6pm).

Petrol Negril has two petrol stations: on Sheffield Rd at the junction with Whitehall (daily 24hr), and Petcom by

Negril Aerodrome (daily 6.30am–11pm).

Pharmacies Baywatch Pharmacy, 11 Sunshine Village (Mon–Sat 9am–8pm, Sun 10am–6pm); Negril Pharmacy, 27 Plaza de Negril (Mon–Sat 9am–7pm, Sun 10am–2pm); Riverside Pharmacy, 1 Negril Shopping Centre, West End Rd (Mon–Sat 8am–7pm).

Post office West End Rd next to A FiWi Plaza (Mon–Fri 9am–5pm).

The northwest coast

Visitors destined for Negril tend to bomb along the highway to and from Montego Bay airport as quickly as possible, and consequently largely overlook the coastline of the parish of Hanover. Stopping at fishing villages cut off from the super-fast highway yields insouciant stares from locals, incredulous that you've torn yourself away from a resort. But the Hanover coastline has its more established attractions, too. The beautifully situated **Rhodes Hall Plantation** is an ideal spot for riding and diving, while there's swimming at the marvellously secluded **Half Moon beach**, a far cry from the resort onslaught. The bustling market town of **Lucea** breathes life into the area as you head northeast from Negril, with its fair share of architectural gems, now complemented by its own large all-inclusive and a second branch of the popular north coast attraction Dolphin Cove. The mini-museum at Alexander Bustamante's **Blenheim** birthplace is the only "official" historical site hereabouts, and as most people choose to remain within sight of the Caribbean Sea much of the inland **Dolphin Head** range of hills remains uncompromisingly indifferent to tourism.

Rhodes Hall Plantation

Hanover, 3km north of the resorts at Negril's Bloody Bay; 16km from Negril's centre • Daily 9am–6pm • Day pass US$15; horseriding US$60–70; lunch US$15 • ☎ 957 6422, ⓦ rhodesresort.com

North of Negril, long tracts of mangrove break occasionally for a villa or sea view, with the first point of real interest being **Rhodes Hall Plantation**. A historic sugar plantation now condensed into a 550-acre coconut, banana, plantain and pear farm, it has two private **beaches**, an offshore reef and a freshwater mineral spring bubbling under the brine. While the on site small-scale resort has fallen into neglect, **horseriding** remains the most popular activity undertaken here, with visitors arriving from Negril. Well-kept mounts trot into the hills, along the beach and past a pristine **mangrove swamp**, home

5

to a handful of Jamaican **crocodiles** – if you can't see any in the open section you'll usually find some sunning themselves in a fenced-off enclosure.

Half Moon beach and around

8km north of the resorts at Negril's Bloody Bay; 20km from Negril's centre • Daily 8am till late • US$5 (if not eating at the restaurant) • ☎ 531 4508, ⓦ halfmoonbeachjamaica.com • Minibuses and route taxis ply the route from Negril to Green Island and Lucea every 10min (Sun less frequently); ask the driver to stop at Half Moon beach

Full of the paradisiacal charm that originally brought tourists to Negril, the wide curve of white sand at unspoilt **Half Moon beach** offers no braiding booths or jet skis, just a little sea grass and some small islets (boat trips available). Nude bathing is acceptable and snorkelling equipment is cheap, while you can also arrange bamboo rafting, kayaking and horseriding in advance. The overgrown flat track behind the restaurant was once an illegal airstrip used for ganja smuggling. Bear in mind that all-inclusive groups do visit on Sundays so it can get crowded and rowdy at these times.

Abingdon Great House

8km north of the resorts at Negril's Bloody Bay; 20km from Negril's centre • Daily 11am–4pm • US$5 • ☎ 531 4508, ⓦ halfmoonbeachjamaica.com • Entrance path opposite Half Moon beach

North of Negril, tucked off the main highway across from the Half Moon beach entrance, a dirt road crossing through a wild forest and scrubland, filled with giant trees bearing fruits, leads to **Abingdon Great House**. Standing on a hilltop, this magnificent seventeenth-century all stone cream-colored colonial house is on land originally gifted in 1674 to Captain Roger James, a British royal navy officer from Abingdon, as a reward from the King of England. Finding Jamaica too hot to call home, his grandson inherited the land, completing the home in 1776 with a sugar plantation. Recently renovated, along with the main house, the adjacent sugar mill reveals a stunning piece of hand-quarried architecture that processed sugar cane, brought from the fields directly below and later turned into sugar and rum in the boiling houses. The site is operated by the owners of Half Moon beach – whose family inherited the land. Indian caves have been located on the vast property, with pottery chards and bones, as well as the original path that led to Negril before 1965, when there was no highway. The three rooms in the Great House basement were being renovated into a guesthouse as the time of this update.

ACCOMMODATION

HALF MOON BEACH

Half Moon Beach ☎ 531 4508, ⓦ halfmoonbeach jamaica.com. Set back within the trees behind the beach are seven wooden cabins ranging from very simple to semi-luxurious but all comfortable with veranda and either fan or a/c; perfect for a paradisiacal escape. The restaurant/bar offers excellent sandwiches, chicken and fish, as well as freshly caught lobster at US$20/lb. By arrangement you can have a private romantic dinner on the beach with your own musician – and weddings are also a speciality. <u>US$75</u>

Cousins Cove

Ten kilometres north of Negril's Bloody Bay, **Cousins Cove** offers lots of rootsy appeal, vividly portrayed in Guy Kennaway's hilarious novel about Jamaican village life, *One People* (see page 294). Visitors could be forgiven for thinking this is just another sleepy community, but a read of the book, with its insight into local politics, illicit shenanigans and life in the slow lane – yet yards from resort debauchery – quickly dispels the sentiment. Accessed by means of two turns off the main highway, the first (more scenic) turn-off is somewhat hard to find, and the second to the north of the village is confusingly marked "Davis Cove"; readers of the novel may understand the sign mix-up. Cousins Cove has a lovely enclosed bay and a couple of local bars to while away the evenings with dominoes, white rum and reggae, and from where you can arrange boat trips along the coast and to patches of reef.

ARRIVAL AND DEPARTURE

By minibus and route taxi Minibuses and route taxis ply the route from Negril to Lucea every 20min (Sun less frequently); stop on the main road at the northeastern-most exit to Cousins Cove, from where the village is a kilometre walk away.

ACCOMMODATION

Cliffhouse Cousins Cove, at the northern end of the village ⓦcliffhousejamaica.com. An attractive five-bedroom villa right over the water, with large, sumptuous rooms and numerous facilities such as a pool, tennis court and private woodland and reef. Sleeps ten; weekly rentals only. <u>US$5000</u>

Sweet Breeze Main Rd, Cousins Cove, just north of the village ⓦbit.ly/facebook_seabreeze. An attractive collection of simple rooms set in a grassy clearing with fruit trees, not far from Ron's Arawak Cave (see below). Also has space for camping. Room rates include a good breakfast. Camping <u>US$15</u>, cottages <u>US$50</u>

Ron's Arawak Cave

Lance's Day • Open sporadically 9am–5pm • US$10 • ☏ 426 63 15 • Signposted east from the main road, inland from Lance's Bay, 1.5km northeast of Cousins Cove

An impressive kilometre-and-a-half-long chamber, **Ron's Arawak Cave** has a number of intricate stalactite formations as well as faint markings on the wall made by bat guano miners – presumed to be Taino Amerindians – and is worth a visit if you're spending some time in the area and fancy a mildly eccentric trip with the eponymous Ron. His fun tours involve wandering deep into the cave while he recounts a raft of local tales, with flaming torches casting eerie shadows. Ideally you'll exit the cave at sunset, when the bats emerge en masse.

Lucea

LUCEA (pronounced Lucy) was a flourishing port town during the plantation era, its wharves thronged with ships exporting locally produced sugar. Even Henry Morgan (see page 80), during his respectable period as governor of Jamaica, moored ships here at **Bull Bay Beach**, a stunning cove just west of town. In slightly more recent times, **Lucea yams**, a tasty tuber with excellent storing properties, were exported in vast quantities to the Jamaicans who migrated in the nineteenth century to work on sugar plantations and the Panama Canal in Central America, and yams are still the mainstay of local agriculture – though these days, only the occasional shipment of molasses leaves the docks.

Despite being the capital of Hanover, Lucea is no showpiece; peeling paint pervades and even the best buildings display broken windows or sagging walls – a sharp contrast to the whitewashed faux-palace exterior of the sprawling *Grand Palladium Lady Hamilton Resort* just east of town. Nonetheless, it's a beguiling jumble of austere stone architecture and salt-and-sun-bleached clapboard houses, gaudy store-fronts and snack and rum bars, all clustered around a seething central bus park. Nearby, the **Cleveland Stanhope Market** spills out onto the streets on Saturdays (8am–2pm), selling local produce and household goods. Lucea's western portion contains many older buildings; noticeable is the cut-stone steeple of **Hanover Parish Church**, dating back to 1725 with some fine monuments, while the cemetery's walled area is a **Jewish burial ground**, presented in 1833 to the Jewish community who settled here during Lucea's commercial heyday.

Alexander Bustamante Square

The imposing exterior of the once-majestic Georgian **town hall** and old **courthouse** has been restored after decades of neglect, and overlooks the official (traffic-clogged) town square, formally dedicated as **Alexander Bustamante Square** by Britain's Queen Elizabeth in 1966, and used as a period set for parts of the movie *Cool Runnings*. The roof of the

5

courthouse is topped by an incongruously large **clock tower**. Still keeping perfect time after more than 170 years, the size of the clock betrays its misplacement – it was originally destined for St Lucia (Lucea's Spanish name was Santa Lucea) but arriving here by mistake, locals became so attached to it that they refused to exchange it for the modest timepiece originally ordered, raising the difference through public collections. The tower was built with funds from a local German planter, hence the distinctive nippled rooftop dome of a German army helmet.

Rusea's School
Watson Taylor Drive (main A1 road) • Mon–Sat 8am–4pm • Free

Close to the sea (and behind the parish church), **Rusea's School** was established in 1777 by a benefaction from French religious refugee Martin Rusea, so grateful for the help he received when washed ashore at Lucea that he bequeathed his estate to the parish; disgruntled relatives contested the will for ten years after his death in 1764, without success. The school moved to the present site, an old army barracks, in 1900.

Just past the school, through a small truck-repair yard, near-derelict **Fort Charlotte** was restored in 1761, though no one is sure when the foundations were first laid. Three original cannons remain, and it has a sweeping view across the harbour.

CHIEF BUSTA

Wild-haired and brutishly handsome, **Sir William Alexander Bustamante**'s physical stature, charismatic appeal and legendary appetite for women earned him a fond notoriety in the ribald world of Jamaican politics. Born Alexander Clarke on February 24, 1884, into an impoverished family working on the Blenheim estate, Bustamante rose to political prominence through a mixture of insight, cunning and cynical manipulation of the illiterate populace who worshiped him as "**Busta**" or simply "Chief".

THE UNION YEARS

Bustamante left Jamaica at 19 in search of better prospects, and his years away are veiled in mystery, though he's said to have laboured and cut cane alongside other migrants. He returned nearly thirty years later with an assumed surname and enough wealth to become a small-time moneylender, a shrewd move that gave him clandestine influence before he entered the political arena. The Jamaica that Bustamante returned to was still languishing under Britain's firm imperial grip. Working conditions for those lucky enough to have a job were abysmal, and the polarities between the ruling class of whites and mixed race "browns" and the black majority were as sharp as ever. Settling in Kingston, Bustamante began to win workers' support through outspoken condemnation of inequality. By 1938 his "fire and brimstone" warnings of racial violence and black revolution (designed to scare the colonial authorities into action) were almost realized; fanned by Bustamante's inflammatory rhetoric, a violent confrontation between police and workers broke out at the West Indies Sugar Company in Frome, Westmoreland, sparking a wave of strikes that brought the island to a near standstill. Eclipsing the tentative support for black nationalist labour leader St William Grant, Bustamante formed the **Bustamante Industrial Trade Union** – still the main union today – and became the leader of the labour movement among the rank and file.

THE JAMAICA LABOUR PARTY

In 1940, distressed at the volatility of his speeches, the government seized on Bustamante's union involvement and imprisoned him as the ringleader of the 1938 unrest. On his release in 1942, he formed the **Jamaica Labour Party** and swept to victory in the island's first election in 1944, trouncing his first cousin Norman Manley's People's National Party so decisively that Manley lost even in his own constituency. Though the PNP enjoyed a few years of power between 1955 and 1961, it was the JLP that ruled through independence in 1962, and Sir Bustamante (he was knighted by Queen Elizabeth II in 1954) who danced with Princess Margaret during the ensuing celebrations. He remained active in politics until 1967 and died a National Hero on August 6, 1977, at the age of 93.

The Lucea Infirmary

Next to the Hanover Museum • ☎ 956 2947 • If you wish to donate or volunteer, contact ☎ 350 0077 or ✉ DrPaulShalom@yahoo.com

A residential home for the elderly, the newly rebuilt **Lucea Infirmary** is a modern, functional building, but like many social institutions in Jamaica in dire need of funding and equipment. A visit here in 1995 inspired American gerontologist Paul Scott Rhodes (of *Great Huts* fame; see page 115) to set up JAFIS, a charity that brings financial and practical aid, such as wheelchairs and sheets, to a number of hospitals and homeless shelters around Jamaica, and also encourages visits to residents.

ARRIVAL AND DEPARTURE   LUCEA

By bus All minibuses connecting MoBay and Negril stop at Lucea's central bus park (every 45min; 50min to both destinations).

By taxi Reliable local firm Kenny Tours (☎ 995 9410 or ☎ 361 2534, ⊛ kennytours.com) have cars and minibuses for all taxi services as well as tailor-made tours.

ACCOMMODATION

Global Villa Esher, 1.5km west of Lucea ☎ 956 2916, ⊛ globalvillahotel.com. This business-like but friendly guesthouse offers clean, a/c rooms with tiled floors, cable TV and a decent sea view – a good choice if you're looking to stay in a more rural area. The on-site restaurant/bar serves good Jamaican food to advance order, including a range of vegetarian choices. US$50

Dolphin Head Mountains

Dividing Lucea and the north coast from the flat sugar plains of Westmoreland to the south, the **Dolphin Head Mountains** are a languid series of low-lying hills said to resemble a dolphin – though no one seems to know *where* you get this perspective. The range rises to 1789ft and is known for its abundant bird life, plus 23 endemic plants including species of orchid and bromeliad. Most of the hillocks are partially cultivated by small-scale farmers, and there's none of the cool air or remoteness of full-scale ranges like the Blue Mountains. There are no **organized tours** in the area, though you may be able to arrange an ad hoc guide at the tiny village of **Askenish** on the Lucea East River, the nearest settlement to the highest peak, or at Mayfield Falls in Westmoreland (see page 226).

Blenheim

BLENHEIM, a twenty-minute drive from Dyas, up the hills from central Lucea, was the birthplace of National Hero Alexander Bustamante (see page 220). The shack in which Jamaica's first prime minister grew up has been converted into a small but interesting **museum** (daily 9am–5pm; J$600; contact the Jamaica National Heritage Trust/JNHT to gain access in case it is closed when you visit; ☎ 922 1287, ⊛ jnht.com) celebrating Bustamante's life and achievements. Though the building was gutted by fire late in 2005, refurbishments have largely been completed and the beautiful grounds make a great picnic spot with plenty of shade and staggering views of lush hillsides covered in vegetation.

Kenilworth Great House

Signposted just south (inland) from Eddie's Highway Pub, close to Mosquito Cove, 8km east of Lucea • Daily 9am–5pm • Free • ☎ 953 5315

Inland of Mosquito Cove, horses graze in clipped pastures dotted with the odd run-down windmill, relics of the plantation days when the land was part of the Kenilworth estate. A superb example of old industrial architecture, Kenilworth's **great house** now serves as the HEART (Human Employment and Resource Training) Academy, a further education college. There are no guided tours, but you can go in and have a look around the surrounding mills, boiling houses and distillery, all now under the protection of the Jamaica National Heritage Trust.

Sandy Bay

The settlement of Sandy Bay is strung out along a lengthy swath of beach some sixteen kilometres west of Montego Bay. At its eastern end, a towering **waterwheel** at the roadside marks its most famous location, old **Tryall Estate**, a once huge sugar plantation destroyed in the Christmas Rebellion (see page 170), and which is now Jamaica's most prestigious **golfing retreat**, with the hotel based around the plantation's refurbished great house and boasting its own large section of off-limits beach.

ARRIVAL AND ACTIVITIES
SANDY BAY

By minibus and route taxi All minibuses and route taxis connecting MoBay with Negril and Lucea pass Sandy Bay and the Tryall Estate (every 30min; 40min from MoBay).

Chukka Caribbean Adventure Tours Blue Hole Bay Estate ☎ 656 8026, ⓦ chukka.com. This well-organized company offers two trips from its Sandy Bay base, which draw large parties from Montego Bay cruise ships and all-inclusives there and in Negril. The classic "Horseback Ride 'n' Swim" tour (2hr 30min; US$79) takes riders through lush mountain scenery and the shallow waters of the Blue Hole

Bay Estate, while an ATV quad-bike "safari" (2hr; US$115) makes use of the inland dirt trails.

Tryall Club Tryall Estate ☎ 956 5660, ⓦ tryallclub.com. Until 1996, Tryall hosted the annual Johnnie Walker golf tournament, due to its well-kept, smoothly undulating eighteen-hole course. Reputedly it's the most challenging on the island, though you'll need deep pockets to examine it; non-*Tryall Club* guests pay US$95 for nine holes or US$150 for eighteen holes per round plus mandatory caddie service. The club also offers tennis coaching at all levels, from US$60.

EATING

Pachie's Main A1 road, just past Tryall Estate ☎ 425 7150. Directly on the highway yet facing the seaside, this popular seafood haunt lets you pick your fresh catch – lobster in season, lionfish and conch (from J$1300) –

before cooking it on the outdoor grills while you watch. Plates come served with all the local favourites, including traditional, crispy Hanover breadfruit soaked in salt water and fried. Daily 11am–11pm.

Southwest Jamaica

After Negril's glittering hedonism, southwest Jamaica, with its slow fishing villages, fewer organized attractions and less serviceable roads, can come as quite a surprise. Restaurants remain wholeheartedly traditional, with mannish water and eye-rollingly insouciant service. Locals tend to be more genuinely friendly and, unfettered by high-rises, the countryside is magnificent.

Alluvial plains occupy the western half of Westmoreland parish, with the multi-tributaried **Cabarita River** meandering down from the Dolphin Head Mountains through vast cane fields, to arrive at the parish's concrete capital, **Savanna-la-Mar**, where brisk trade and honking horns fight against the soupy humidity. A few kilometres inland from Sav-la-Mar, **Roaring River** marks its entrance above ground with a spectacular blue swimming hole, having carved out an inky cave on its way, and more fabulous swimming is available at **Mayfield Falls**.

Hills rise up once more to the east of the parish beyond Savanna-la-Mar, hiding lush stretches of coastline and beach with reef-fringed shallows below at the contiguous fishing communities of **Bluefields**, Belmont and Whitehouse; a series of **low-key hotels** and guesthouses are perfect to appreciate the area's unhurried charm.

The Negril Hills

East from the cliffs at Negril's West End, the terrain alternates between the dry limestone peaks of the **Negril Hills**, habitat of non-venomous **yellow boa snakes** occasionally seen slithering across the road, and the basins below with their lush fields of sugar cane. The first community of any size is **ORANGE HILL**, some six kilometres from Negril, with flower-surrounded duck ponds and a host of quietly convivial **bars** – though the village's greater islandwide fame is undoubtedly for the strength of its ganja, grown in the surrounding fertile hills. Orange Hill merges into residential **RETIREMENT**, home to the distinctive **Jurassic Park Art Garden** (no set price or opening hours; tips appreciated), marked by a giant cast-iron pterodactyl on its gate. This is the creative outlet of local ironworker Daniel Woolcock, whose enormous sculptures of flamingos, hibiscus flowers and a five-foot-long centipede overlook a basketball court, a sporadically open bar and a shady gazebo.

Little Bay

An extremely attractive, tranquil piece of coastline with a couple of low-key eateries and a range of budget to guesthouse accommodation options, **LITTLE BAY** is only thirteen kilometres from Negril yet feels light years away. The only formal attraction hereabouts, signed from the road, is the Blue Hole Mineral Spring (see below), which has breathed new life into the district, slowly but steadily reviving. At the western end of the community is the pleasant inlet of **Homer's Cove** (also known as **Brighton Beach**). The once pristine beach here was mostly eroded for sand mining, but it's still a nice place for a swim and there are a few vendors selling drinks and snacks. Round the bend eastwards and you arrive in Little Bay proper, with its curve of yellow sand a better bet for swimming. Patches of reef are great for unhurried snorkelling, while the sheltered bay is a good location for sea kayaking.

Although it is locked up behind high gates due to protracted ownership disputes, you may still be able to find someone to take you into the garden of **Bob Marley's Place**, an attractive wooden seafront house built by Marley in 1972 for himself and girlfriend Esther Anderson, which became the setting for *Talking Blues*. There's a small mineral spring pool next to the house, large enough to swim a couple of strokes.

ARRIVAL AND ACTIVITIES LITTLE BAY

By route taxi Infrequent route taxis go from the bus park in Negril to the main crossroads in Little Bay via Little London (Mon–Sat hourly or less; 40min).

By car From Negril, head to Orange Hill and its neighbouring village Retirement, just east. Take a right turn at the fork here, where the road then weaves its way back down to the coast.

On foot and by bike You can also arrive in Little Bay along the beautiful, rugged coastline directly from Negril, on a dirt track. The trail in fact continues 6km eastwards

from here, too, to Broughton, location of a beautiful long fisherman's beach.

Blue Hole Mineral Spring Brighton, Little Bay ☎ 860 8805, ⍟ blueholejamaica.com. Here you can take a gorgeous plunge into a clear blue hole in the limestone cliffs; deep, invigorating and refreshing. Part of the joy is watching local guys diving and flipping their way into the pool — but there are also drinks, food and reggae on hand. US$10. Daily 8am–6pm.

ACCOMMODATION

Judy House Backpacker Hostel Little Bay ☎ 957 0671, ⍟ judyhousenegril.com. Tucked at the back of a sprawling garden entrance, an octagon shaped cottage fits six individual beds, and there are separate private rooms with or without kitchen in a separate building. Located steps from the sea and surrounding beaches, *Judy House* is run by the friendly Brit owner of sister-hostel in

Negril. There's a cook shop across the road. Dorms U̲S̲$̲1̲5̲, camping U̲S̲$̲2̲0̲

Richies on the Beach Little Bay ☎ 368 0376, ⍟ richies onthebeach.com. Small and friendly hotel set in a garden right by the beach. The four simple a/c rooms have a large shared veranda, and great, reasonably priced Jamaican food is served on a terrace overlooking the sea. U̲S̲$̲9̲0̲

Little London

A massively expanded settlement at the heart of Westmoreland's sugar-cane fields, **LITTLE LONDON** lies sixteen kilometres from Negril, and now spans some six kilometres of roadside en route to Savanna-la-Mar. The town's population was once dominated by Indians who came to work as indentured labourers in the cane fields, though inter-mixing has long since blurred ethnic origins. Since the Indians arrived in the

5

mid-nineteenth century, the wetlands between here and the coast have been employed for the cultivation of **rice**, but though it remains a crop for local consumption, sugar still reigns supreme as local employer. There's little of interest in the town itself, though routes inland offer a couple of diversions.

Frome Sugar Factory

Frome, 8km north of Little London • ☎ 955 6080 • Tours by arrangement; US$15 expected

The flat savannah lands north of Little London and Savanna-la-Mar have proved ideal for the cultivation of cane, long meaning strong ties to the **sugar industry**. Jamaica's biggest cane-processing factory lies at **FROME** and handles most of the cane from neighbouring plantations (see below). Though the **sugar factory** is not officially open to the public, you can arrange a tour by calling ahead.

ARRIVAL AND DEPARTURE	**LITTLE LONDON**
By minibus and route taxi All minibuses and route taxis connecting Negril with Sav-la-Mar stop in Little	London (every 10min in either direction; 15min to Sav-la-Mar, 30min to Negril).

ACCOMMODATION AND EATING

Zimbali Retreat and Cooking Studio Canaan Mountain, in the southern fringes of the Dolphin Head Mountains, 20min north of Little London ☎ 252 3232, ⊛ zimbali-retreats.com. Resolutely roots, *Zimbali* offers the chance to chill out among beautiful hillside scenery, follow organic food from farm to table and learn something of rural Rastafarian life – though it comes at a price. You can stay as a guest in simple but comfortable cabins (meals and tours included), or visit for the day to enjoy a farm and river tour or a cookery lesson and dinner. The latter (US$75) offers you a choice of meat or vegetarian foods cooked before your eyes by an entertaining professional chef – while live drummers provide the beats. <u>US$360</u>

BITTERSWEET STRUGGLES

The centre of some of Jamaica's most violent labour disputes, **Frome sugar factory** (see above) was built in 1938 by British company Tate and Lyle's subsidiary West Indies Sugar Company, and was at the time the most modern facility in the West Indies. Constructed during a period of high unemployment, it drew job-seekers from across the island in their thousands. Most were unlucky, and even those who were given jobs received a pittance far lower than the salary they'd been promised. Under the fiery leadership of **Alexander Bustamante** (see page 220), the workers banded together in protest. The dispute swiftly turned ugly; cane fields were set on fire and a full-scale riot broke out on May 3, 1938. The unrest left four dead from police bullets and one hundred demonstrators, including Bustamante, in jail. Further industrial disputes through the twentieth century ensured that Frome's volatile reputation for collective bargaining endures.

For years Jamaican sugar was a loss-making enterprise run by the government-owned Sugar Company of Jamaica. The industry's decline since its 1960s heyday came to the fore with the removal of preferential tariffs to the EU for former colonies in the 2000s – a crippling effect, but deemed to be in the interest of fair and free trade by the World Trade Organization. In reality, Jamaica's problems were exacerbated by cheaper (and increased) global production, and the country's inability to invest in technology through three decades of poverty had made its plants obsolete. After a brief, failed flirtation with a Brazilian bio-energy giant, three plants including Frome were finally sold to Chinese firm COMPLANT in 2011, which released much-needed investment for the beleaguered industry. Plans to diversify into other products like ethanol and molasses now generate excitement, but this is offset by fears of re-mechanization with the inevitable loss of hundreds of manual jobs. With food production largely undercut by cheap imports, diversification is limited, and Frome today remains the largest single employer in western Jamaica. Two hundred years after sugar gave the British Empire unprecedented wealth, the bargaining power of organized labour seems to be replaced by Jamaica's ability to bargain in a world of Chinese expansion and global competition.

Savanna-la-Mar

5

Capital of Westmoreland it may be, but there's little to keep you in commercial **SAVANNA-LA-MAR** (known to most people simply as **Sav**). It's the area's main shopping centre, but as the profusion of low-lying concrete keeps the air still, it's a hot and uncomfortable place and most people depart as quickly as possible. As it lies almost at sea level, successive hurricanes have flattened Sav through the centuries; in 1748 the wind drove the sea far enough up needle-straight thoroughfare **Great George Street** that boats were left dry-docked in the middle of the road. Today, most of the main street is taken up with pharmacies and general stores selling an assortment of imported designer bootlegs, though this is also the place to go if you want true yardstyle string vests, bandannas, barely-there dancehall attire or **reggae music** from street vendors, all at half the price of those at Negril. Great George Street ends abruptly at the seashore, where you'll find a rough-around-the-edges fruit and vegetable **market** (Mon–Sat 7am–1pm), and two remaining high walls of an eighteenth-century fort that the British never completed.

ARRIVAL AND DEPARTURE
SAVANNA-LA-MAR

By bus and minibus Knutsford Express services to/from Negril (2 daily; 45min), Montego Bay (2 daily; 45min) and Kingston (3 daily; 4hr) stop at the Dunbar Mall, off Barracks Road at the eastern end of town. Minibuses connecting these and other south coast and inland destinations stop at the bus park 600m west, close to Beckford St (if you're heading east you may be able to get transport at Dunbar).

ACCOMMODATION

Hotel Commingle 7 Hudson St ☎918 1011. Smart, clean, a/c and business-like, the *Commingle* comes as quite a shock when compared to the rest of Sav outside. Rooms are comfortable, breakfast (included) is served in the dining room or on the tiled patio outside and there's also a pool. <u>US$70</u>

Roaring River Park

10km northeast of Savanna-la-Mar • Mon–Fri 9am–5pm • US$15 • By car, drive 4km north from Petersfield, turning left at the sign through the cane fields — you may need directions to find it

Formerly one of Westmoreland's most visited sights, at the time of writing the lack of management at **Roaring River Park**, located at the community of Roaring River, has ensured its descent into a nightmare of hustling and overcharging by unofficial "tour guides", and until this is resolved visits are not recommended.

If the situation appears to be better by the time you're in the area (ask at your accommodation or with tour companies or drivers if that's the case), the location is nonetheless really pretty and worth visiting. An extensive cave network is surrounded by river gardens with watercress growing wild along banks planted with palms and crotons, and the forested hillside rising up unbroken beyond. Concrete walkways and lighting let you appreciate the full magnitude of the caverns, which range from broom cupboard to auditorium in size. Bats flit about, and there are two mineral pools for a disquieting swim in pitch-blackness – the water is said to rejuvenate. The caves are marred only by graffiti carved into the rock and jagged edges where the quartz has been levered off and sold. Official park guides should be available via the ticket office.

Blue Hole Garden

10km northeast of Savanna-la-Mar • Daily 8am–6pm • US$15 • ☎370 8033 • By car, drive 4km north from Petersfield, turning left at the sign through the cane fields – you may need directions to find it; continue beyond Roaring River Park (where hustlers may well attempt to draw you in), turn left and continue through the village – the garden is 1km further on the right

The gorgeous **Blue Hole Garden** is a great antidote to the hustle of nearby Roaring River Park; no guide is necessary, helpful staff answer any questions you might have and the whole place offers an enticingly serene ambience. Located within a relaxed Rasta-oriented community, the blue hole itself is overhung with trees and flowers, a thirty-foot-wide natural spring of refreshing chilly azure water which is said to be bottomless – the true depth has never been charted. The surrounding gardens are well kept and packed with unusual trees, anthuriums, narcotic white trumpet flowers and every variety of heliconia. There is also a sculptured pool in which to immerse yourself amid gushing mini-waterfalls.

ACCOMMODATION AND EATING
BLUE HOLE GARDEN

Blue Hole Garden Roaring River ☎ 955 8823. Offering a wonderfully tranquil atmosphere, it's well worth experiencing the *Blue Hole Garden*. A smart three-bedroom wooden cottage is located on the hillside directly above the garden, and has a kitchen, living room and large veranda with a marvellous view, and is rented with staff included. while two simple thatched cabins sit right inside the garden (with mosquito screen and outdoor shower and

toilet). Camping is also allowed. Camping US$20, cabins US$40, cottage US$450

Lover's Café Blue Hole Garden, Roaring River ☎ 955 8823. The Jamaican menu here is excellent, considering that it's a relatively remote spot, and includes vegetable patties (US$5), garlic bread, spicy dumplings and fish and Ital options (US$12–20), washed down with fresh juice. Order by phone in advance. Daily noon–7pm.

Mayfield Falls
26km from Sav-la-Mar • Daily 9am–dusk • River walks US$20 plus tip; hiking guide from US$25 • Original Mayfield Falls ☎ 610 8612 or ☎ 792 2074

On the southern slopes of the Dolphin Head Mountains (see page 221), 22 mini-cascades and numerous swimming spots on the Cabarita River make up **Mayfield Falls**. The Original Mayfield Falls tour operator based at the side of the river offers the experience of a tranquil guided walk through bamboo-shaded cool water with swimming holes every twenty yards – a fabulous, sensuous treat compared to the contrivances of the more famous Dunn's River Falls further east (see page 132). Wear a swimming costume and bring water shoes (also rented on site) as the stones are tough on bare, wet feet – while mosquitoes can also be a problem. You'll at time be wading in chest-high water, so though you can ask the guide to keep cameras and other personal effects in a waterproof bag, avoid bringing a host of valuables with you. Hiking guides are also available for walks in the surrounding hills.

ARRIVAL AND DEPARTURE
MAYFIELD FALLS

By car Mayfield Falls is not the easiest of places to find: signs dot the route from Frome and Roaring River (and from Tryall via Pondside in Hanover), but you may have to ask for directions multiple times.

By organized tour To avoid getting lost, go with a local or join the Original Mayfield Falls' round-trip tour from Negril or MoBay (US$85 including lunch).

Bluefields
BLUEFIELDS is where pirate Henry Morgan sailed from to attack Panama in 1670, and the calm seas and sheltered bay have attracted every generation of Jamaican settler. The most interesting building is the privately owned but now virtually derelict **Bluefields House**, uphill from the police station. It was once a temporary home to Philip Gosse, "father of Jamaican ornithology" and inventor of the modern aquarium, who researched *Illustrations of the Birds of Jamaica* and *A Naturalist's Sojourn in Jamaica* during an eighteen-month residence in 1844–45. In the gardens stands a **breadfruit tree** said to be one of the first in Jamaica, planted by Captain Bligh when he brought seedlings from Tahiti (see page 103). These days, the most famous (occasional) resident is Usain Bolt, who's said to favour the region's calm (and its real estate opportunities) when he's not enjoying city life in Kingston.

Low-key **Bluefields Beach**, the narrow, white-sand public beach here, gets very busy with Jamaicans at weekends – though weekdays you'll have it largely to yourself. To find it follow signs to Bluefields Beach Park, once an active space of food and drinks, now in a lull.

Bluefields Organic Fruit Farm
Located just off the main road after Bluefields Beach in the Blue Hole community • Daily 9am–5pm • US$15 • ☎ 373 6435, ✉ keithr44@yahoo.com

A ten-minute drive uphill from the coastline, **Bluefields Organic Fruit Farm**'s near 22 verdant acres of meticulously landscaped fields brim with Jamaica's most colourful home-grown fruit trees, fenced and guarded by goats. Bluefields native and owner Keith Wedderburn takes you on a hike of this family-operated organic farm – entirely free of pesticides – and while identifying over 40 species of trees and tasting ripe fruits like June plum, sweetsop, mango, star fruit, pears and honey bananas, he'll also explain their medicinal properties. Vegetables grow here as well, including large pumpkins, breadfruit, allspice pimento, and scotch bonnet. Birds flock to this lush landscape daily, like the Jamaican Crow, adding to the all around country yard vibe. A surprise awaits those who brave the last, steep hike to the top of the farm – where a near-completed guesthouse will soon offer a farm stay for a full Bluefields experience.

ARRIVAL AND DEPARTURE   BLUEFIELDS

By minibus or route taxi Minibuses and route taxis ply the route between Whitehouse and Sav-la-Mar, stopping at Bluefields on request (every 20min).

By car Bluefields lies some 18km southwest along the A2 from Sav-la-Mar.

ACCOMMODATION AND EATING

Bluefields Bay Resort ☎ 383 7449. No frills, peach-coloured resort with lovely seafront views. Spacious, basic rooms with wooden furniture include cable TV, kitchenette and a private terrace. Continental breakfast included, served at the resort's bar-restaurant. U$$70

★ **Dor's** Crab Shack ☎ 471 4984. Directly along the main road, in a sprawling, seafront wooden dining room or a breezy over-the-water *palapa*, Miss Dor serves the best crab back (from J$400) and seafood specialties – brown stew fish and steam fish – this side of Bluefields and Belmont. Frequent tour stop, and local road trip favourite. Fried chicken and pork also served. Daily 9am–6pm.

Belmont

Birthplace and later home of reggae-revolutionary **Peter Tosh** (see page 228), **BELMONT** is a slow coastal village with a lot of life going on beneath the surface, stretching back from the main road into the hills above. Just three kilometres from the public beach at Bluefields (and 19km from Sav-la-Mar), Belmont has its own deserted fishing beach at the village's southeastern end which in some ways is even more attractive – and you'll always meet some interesting locals while you're there. Offering a range of **accommodation** from basic to exclusive, the village is certainly a great place to relax, swim, take a boat trip, and discover rural south coast Jamaican life.

The region southeast of town as you continue along the A2 (though long forgotten by all but the most learned and aged locals) is known as **Surinam Quarters** in honour of the English who resettled here when the former British colony was captured by the Dutch in 1667. The scenery becomes drier, with swaths of pasture and plenty of cattle.

Peter Tosh Mausoleum
Located at a signed entrance toward the eastern end of Belmont, just off the main road • Daily 9am–5pm • US$12

Thankfully the burial place of the late reggae icon (see page 228) is much less of an affair than the Marley mausoleum in St Ann (see page 155) and is often deserted. The small red-gold-and-green **mausoleum** is decorated with stained glass, photos and press cuttings. Upgrades by Tosh's family – his mother lives in a modest house at the back of the property – means there's now a small car park, along with CDs and T-shirts on sale and hand-painted signs that exhort you to light up a spliff on your way in.

5

PETER TOSH

Consciously controversial, **Peter Tosh** (born McIntosh) was Jamaica's best-known lyrical agitator. Born an only child in Belmont on October 19, 1944, he was raised by an aunt in the west Kingston tenement yards dominated, at the time, by the explosion of harmony groups that transformed post-independence Kingston into a hotbed of aspirations. Every newly arrived country "bhuttu" (or bumpkin) wanted to be a singer and Tosh followed suit, embarking on a mission to reveal home truths from a ghetto perspective. He saved to buy his first guitar and in 1964 formed vocal trio the Wailers with teenage allies Bunny Livingstone and Bob Marley. In 1972 they signed to Chris Blackwell's Island label, and recorded *Catch a Fire* and *Burnin'* together while Tosh put out tracks on his own Intel Diplo HIM label (Intelligent Diplomat for His Imperial Majesty), all the time becoming increasingly bitter over pay and personal disputes with the man he referred to as "Whiteworst". By 1974, he and Bunny Livingstone had gone their separate ways.

ROOTS REGGAE REVOLUTIONARY

Having already earned a reputation as the Wailers' social conscience and an uncompromising egotist, Tosh took on the mantle of chief critic of what he called Jamaica's **"Babylon shitstem"** (system), publicly berating politicians for double standards and hypocrisy, and lighting spliffs on stage with a cool disregard for the law. His bellicose militancy did him no favours with the island's police; in 1975 he was busted on a trumped-up ganja charge and beaten to within an inch of his life. As soon as his wounds had healed, he answered back with *Whatcha Gonna Do*, a cocky release chiding the futility of police brutality, smokers' anthem *Legalize It* and the defensive *Can't Blame the Youth* – inevitable airplay bans ensured record sales and Tosh cemented his position as the roots reggae revolutionary.

Tosh stayed in Jamaica, but his status and fortune – collaboration with the Rolling Stones in 1978 and a deal with EMI attracted global recognition – drew awkward parallels with the sufferers' lot he espoused. In a country where money and fame draw a barrage of demands from old friends, causes and shady characters, the intensely spiritual and suspicious Tosh began to display signs of paranoia, believing himself both a victim of an establishment assassination conspiracy and haunted by duppies. His prophecies of destruction were fulfilled on September 11, 1987, when **gunmen** opened fire in his living room, killing him and two friends, and wounding five others. Rumours concerning the motive spread, some arguing that renowned "bad man" assassin Dennis "Leppo" Lubban was exacting financial retribution for a prison stint he saw as Tosh's rap, others muttering of a government-backed gagging.

Remembered by Jamaicans as a formidable ladies' man with a razor-sharp wit, Tosh himself provided his best biography: the "Red X" tapes, shot on scratchy film in a darkened room, show him philosophizing on his mantra, reggae and Rastafari and form part of the essential Tosh documentary *Stepping Razor Red X*.

ARRIVAL AND INFORMATION

By minibus or route taxi Minibuses and route taxis ply the route between Whitehouse and Sav-la-Mar and stop in Belmont on request (every 20min). Although running frequently on weekdays, transport is very infrequent evenings and Sundays.

BELMONT

Tourist information and services For local information, as well as internet access, visit the Bluefields People's Community Association (☎ 373 6435) at Belmont "Square" – the main crossroads at the village's northwestern end.

ACCOMMODATION

Horizon Main Rd, at the southeastern end of Belmont ☎ 955 8823 or ☎ 602 942 7633 in US. Delightful guesthouse with two smart cabins, each with kitchenette (though a cook is available) and a wonderful outdoor shower. Small private beach and jetty with sea kayaks on hand, plus tours available. US$130

★ **Luna Sea Inn** Main Rd, in the middle of Belmont ☎ 383 6982, ⓦ lunaseainn.com. Right on the rocky

shoreline in the centre of Belmont, the renovated *Luna Sea* has the perfect location and promises the friendliest staff, ecofriendly energy and comfortable a/c rooms. There's a gazebo over the water for chilling out, boat trips are available and good Jamaican and international food is served at the *Cracked Conch Café* (see page 229), where the included breakfast is also served. US$130

★ **Nature Roots (aka Brian's place)** "Cotch-a-tree"

area, Belmont ☎384 6610, ⓦnatureroots.de. A bare-bones, budget option a short walk from the sea and tucked within the village. Two simple cabins are rented whole or by the room, each with kitchenette and basic bathroom. Rasta owner "Doc" Brian is a fountain of knowledge on the area and does excellent nature tours to track down birds

and butterflies; meals available. US$30

Shades Cottage "Cotch-a-tree" area, Belmont ☎441 1830, ⓦshadescottage.com. Next to *Nature Roots*, Bigga and family rent out seven rooms, each with a double, twin or three beds. There's a bar squeezed in between the cabins; meals are provided on request. Negotiable for longer stays. US$35

EATING

Cracked Conch Café Luna Sea Inn, Main Rd ☎383 6982. Opened in 2015, this seafront café-restaurant offers delectable conch fritters and soup to accompany a drink at the water's edge, as well as fish, burgers and international dishes (US$10–20). Daily 11am–9pm.

★ **Prince's Bar and Restaurant** Main Rd ☎503 9501.

Right next to the Peter Tosh mausoleum in a shack in Rasta colours, join top local cook Cutta and Tosh's young nephew Kenial for Red Stripe, rum and delicious fried chicken or curried conch or goat (J$500–1300). Mon–Sat 8am–midnight, Sun 2pm–midnight.

SHOPPING

Studio Black Main Rd ☎459 9918. Pick up one of Belmont artist Jah Calo's vibrant pieces of Rastafarian-inspired art, from paintings to sculptures. The colourful art shack is hard to

miss on the main highway between Bluefields and entering Belmont, before reaching the Peter Tosh Memorial, for which he has also painted murals. Daily 9am–5pm.

Culloden and Whitehouse

At one time these two villages in the southeastern corner of Westmoreland parish were easily distinguishable separate entities, but, as with much development in Jamaica these days, there's now just one extended urban area. A prominent south coast fishing port, **WHITEHOUSE** offers little beach life but plenty of commercial bustle with a fruit and vegetable **market** (Wed & Sat) and **fishing beach**, where on afternoons you can see huge hessian bags of flapping specimens weighed and bartered over, while women scale furiously. Boats return here from trips that can last as long as a week, with the fish transported islandwide. A variety of basic stalls at the market cook up a taste of the fresh catch at lunchtime – washed down with white rum, and a reggae beat to aid digestion.

Whitehouse's satellite **Culloden** boasts greater sleepiness and all the decent accommodation hereabouts; the *Sandals South Coast* (formerly *Sandals Whitehouse*) lies just to the north, the first full-scale resort on Jamaica's south coast on a formerly beautiful beach-fringed isthmus and crocodile swamp, with a large reef just offshore.

ARRIVAL AND DEPARTURE   CULLODEN AND WHITEHOUSE

By minibus or route taxi Minibuses and route taxis ply the route between Whitehouse and Sav-la-Mar (every 20min; 45min to Sav), Whitehouse and Black River (every 45min; 35min), and minibuses from Sav to Kingston also

pick up at Whitehouse Square heading east (hourly; 3hr). Although running frequently on weekdays, transport is very infrequent evenings and Sundays.

ACCOMMODATION

ARC-Jamaica (aka Jim's Place) Culloden by the Sea ☎963 5503, ✉jmplax@rogers.com. Purpose-built by a Canadian architect, playwright and set designer, this octagonal retreat offers artists and holidaymakers an inspirational sea view plus child-friendly pool and solar hot water. The three comfortable self-catering apartments have mosquito nets, verandas and a large bathroom, but no a/c, and sleep up to six; a housekeeper/cook can be arranged. US$75

★ **Elaine's Chateau** Culloden by the Sea, Culloden

☎963 5004, ⓦelaineschateau.com. Panoramic Caribbean sea views, an infinity pool, a veranda restaurant and three intimately-sized, well appointed rooms make Elaine's a delightful find on the quiet south coast. Spacious rooms feature electronically coded doors, king size bed, cable TV, mini-fridge, and en-suite bathroom. Tasty Jamaican and international meals and drinks are available and the sunsets from the terrace are spectacular. For the active crowd, owner Elaine can take you on a two-hour challenging hike through Whitehouse's hilly communities and forest. US$130

The south

ALLIGATOR HOLE

The south

Mass tourism has yet to reach Jamaica's southern parishes – the beaches aren't packed with sun-ripened bodies and there still remain some great off-the-beaten-track places to visit – so if you want to catch a glimpse of Jamaica as it was before the tourist boom, head south. Though without the turquoise seas and white-sand beaches of the north, Jamaica's southern coastline is among the most spectacular on the island. The scenery is wild and unspoilt, with fishing boats, giant cacti and goats standing sentry at the roadside and thickets of makka thorn bushes, wetland morass and twisted mangroves giving way to glimpses of undeveloped coves, the volcanic sand twinkling in the sunlight. It takes a bit of extra effort to get here, and you'll need a car or a tour to see some of the more remote highlights, but it's definitely worth it.

The parishes that make up south-central Jamaica are immensely varied, with the landscape ranging from mountain to scrubby cactus-strewn desert, and from typically lush vegetation to rolling fields more redolent of the English countryside. To the west, in the beautiful parish of St Elizabeth, **Black River** is the main town, an important nineteenth-century port that today offers popular **river safaris** and a handful of attractive colonial-era buildings. If you're after somewhere to stay and swim, **Treasure Beach** is a better target; it's an extremely laidback place with lovely yellow-sand beaches and some unique accommodation options that are fast making it a major destination in the south. As for touring around, you can make for the **Appleton Estate rum distillery** on the Cockpit fringes, the fabulous **YS waterfalls** or drive around the tiny villages of the attractive and untouristed **Santa Cruz Mountains**.

Further east, the parishes of Manchester and Clarendon are less diverse but scenic areas. Manchester, with its cool evenings and misty mornings, has the major town of **Mandeville**, a very English inland touring base that makes a pleasant, if unspectacular, change from the coast, and the much smaller market town of **Christiana**, an unspoilt retreat with a single, delightful old hotel. Along the coast, there's marvellous river and sea swimming, and some great fish restaurants at **Alligator Pond**, while the combination of mineral spring and black-sand beach at **Gut River** provides one of the most picturesque spots on the entire island. The parish of Clarendon is total farming country, with large citrus groves in the north and sugar-cane fields everywhere else, but it offers a handful of unusual places to visit including the mineral spa at **Milk River**.

Although remnants of the once lucrative **bauxite** industry are still around (in the form of massive empty factories and dried-up red mud lakes), it is **agriculture** that has been and continues to be, despite St Elizabeth's dry climate, the main stay of the local economy, producing most of the country's agricultural surplus – which is why the area is known as Jamaica's "breadbasket". Recently, **tourism** has begun to make an impact, though it is unlikely ever to approach north-coast levels. The emphasis is on small-

APPLETON ESTATE RUM DISTILLERY

Highlights

❶ Black River safari Jamaica's longest river, complete with water hyacinths, mangroves full of roosting egrets and surprisingly tame crocodiles. See page 235

❷ Turtle-watching tours Join a sunrise hike from May to November and witness hawksbill turtles nesting and hatching on the black sand beaches of Treasure Beach. See page 240

❸ Jack Sprat, Treasure Beach Funky and laidback, this is the quintessential south-coast beach bar. See page 242

❹ Milk River Spa This wonderfully ramshackle colonial-era spa hotel offers the chance to soak away aches and pains in the second-most radioactive water in the world. See page 246

❺ Pepper shrimp, Middle Quarters Spicy and delicious, the peppered river shrimp sold at the roadside here are legendary. See page 247

❻ YS Falls Surrounded by spectacular rainforest-edged farmland, the falls here come equipped with a Tarzan-style rope swing over the water. See page 247

❼ Appleton Estate rum distillery tour Hemmed in by the egg-box Cockpits in the gorgeous Nassau Valley, the scenery here is as spectacular as the effect of tasting seventeen luscious varieties of rum and liqueurs. See page 247

HIGHLIGHTS ARE MARKED ON THE MAP ON PAGE 234

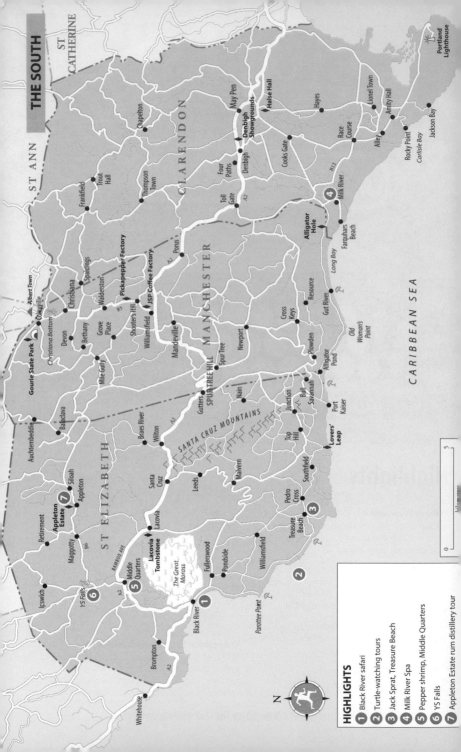

PEDRO CAYS

If you spend any time in this part of Jamaica, you'll appreciate the importance of the local **fishing industry**. Tiny fishing villages are scattered along the coast, with boats pulled up on stretches of the beach; even in tourist areas like Treasure Beach, fishing remains vital to the local economy. Many of the fishermen make month-long trips to the **Pedro Banks**, a series of sandy cays in rich, but treacherous, fishing waters some 129km south. Over the years, full-scale communities have become established on these tiny blips in the ocean, and the abandoned behaviour of the fishermen and the few women who live on them semi-permanently are the stuff of local legend. However, things on the cays are more organized these days, with a police post ensuring some semblance of order, and two-way radio transmitters. The cays are the preserve of Jamaica's hardiest fishermen, so not a destination for a day-trip, but if you want to try your hand at fishing JA-style, ask around at any of the fishing villages.

6

scale, community-based, environmentally friendly tourism, avoiding the disruption to traditional lifestyles that the industry has caused elsewhere on the island.

GETTING AROUND   **THE SOUTH**

By bus and minibus Regular buses and minibuses ply the main routes between Kingston and Negril, giving easy access to the main towns of May Pen, Mandeville, Santa Cruz and Black River. From these centres, a network of buses and route (shared) taxis fan out to smaller towns like Christiana, Treasure Beach and Malvern. Car-less travellers can also opt for taking a relay of route taxis that link with each other to trek to smaller towns where most public transport doesn't go.
By car Driving is the best way to see the hidden parts of the south. Many of the main attractions in the interior, like YS Falls and Appleton, are somewhat off the beaten track and can be hard to reach without your own set of wheels. That said, Jamaican roads are not for the faint-hearted and in the south they are notoriously bad. Potholes packed with marl or gullies on the smaller, coastal roads (a result of poor drainage and a series of bad hurricanes in the last few years), will, if you approach them aggressively, take the bottom out of your car or at least damage your tyres.

Black River

Although it's St Elizabeth's largest town, **BLACK RIVER** is a quiet spot, and most travellers only nip in briefly to take a boat trip on the river in search of crocodiles, or stay a couple of nights whilst exploring the delights of western St Elizabeth. It wasn't always this way, though: in the mid-nineteenth century the town derived substantial wealth from the trade in logwood, used to produce black and dark-blue dyes for the textiles industry and exported in great quantities from Black River's port. For a brief period the trade helped to make the town one of the most influential in Jamaica, with electricity, the telephone and the car all first introduced to the island here, and a big racecourse built to the west of town. However, with the introduction of synthetic dyes, the trade in logwood began to dry up, and today, the only signs of those illustrious days are some wonderful but decrepit old gingerbread houses.

The waterfront

The nicest thing to do in Black River itself is to take a stroll along the **waterfront**, particularly attractive around sunset, and check out the old wooden buildings, many with gorgeous colonnaded verandas and gingerbread trim and most in a perilous state of near-collapse. The **Waterloo Guesthouse**, built in 1819, is reputed to have been the first place in Jamaica to get electricity – installed to provide air conditioning for racehorses kept in the old stables – and to have boasted the island's first telephone. Nearby, the **Invercauld Hotel** (no longer a hotel and now home to a medical school) was built in 1889. With its lavish fretwork and spacious floor plans, it reflects the confidence of the town during its heyday. As you head back towards the town centre,

6

EXPLORING THE GREAT MORASS

There is no better way to explore the Great Morass than with **safari boat tour** – even if the word "safari" promises rather more excitement than it delivers. You do have a virtually guaranteed sighting of **crocodiles** (albeit fairly tame ones, most of which answer to their names), and there are some marvellous **mangrove swamps** where you can normally spot flocks of roosting egrets as well as whistling ducks, herons and jacanas, and you may come across the occasional shrimp- or crab-fisherman in his dugout canoe. To go on the one-hour tour, head to Black River's dock where, with luck, you won't have to wait long to board; call ahead for definite departure times however, and there is a minimum passenger load of three unless you are willing to pay an additional charge. Ask your tour operator about stopping at *Miss Lou's*, for some scrumptious crabs and a cold beer.

TOUR OPERATORS

Two recommended operators (both based in Black River) are:

J. Charles Swaby's Black River Safari Boat Tours 1 Crane Rd ☎ 965 2513. US$20. Daily 9am–3.30pm.

St Elizabeth River Safari Riverside Dock ☎ 965 2374. US$20. Daily 9.30am–3pm.

---

you'll see goats roaming the grounds of **St John's**, the tidy parish church; it dates from 1837 and has marble monuments to Robert Munro and Caleb Dickenson, benefactors of two of the schools at nearby Malvern.

Black River and the Great Morass

The main reason most people come to the town is for a **boat safari** on the **Black River** itself, which, at 71km, is Jamaica's longest. The river – so named because the peat moss lining the river bottom makes the crystal-clear water appear an inky black – is fed by various tributaries as it makes its way down from Balaclava, on the Manchester/St Elizabeth border. It's the main source for the **Great Morass** – a 201-square-kilometre area of wetland that spreads north and west of Black River and provides a swampy home for most of Jamaica's surviving crocodiles as well as some diverse and spectacular bird life. It's the best place to spot the crocodiles, a rapidly dwindling bunch now protected by law, who once lived in great numbers around the coast of Jamaica until hunting and the deterioration of the swamplands began to take their toll.

Parottee

Just beyond Black River, going east is secluded **Parottee**, which has also begun to promote tourism. Visitors are slowly coming to this quiet fishing village to explore nearby swamplands and go birdwatching, take boat tours to **Pelican Bar** (see below), or simply enjoy the kilometres of pristine, all-to-yourself, golden-sand beaches just beyond the main road.

Pelican Bar

1km off Parottee Point (11km west of Treasure Beach) • Daily 11am–6pm • Boats to *Pelican Bar* depart from *Basil's Bar* at the end of the Parottee main road (US$15/person; ☎ 369 2565)

A main Treasure Beach activity, **Pelican Bar** provides a thrill to the first-timer who heads off this fishing village coastline to the ramshackle, wooden bar on stilts in the middle of the sea. Order snapper with rice and beans, then take a swim until food and sunset arrive. There's a new souvenir shack attached to the main bar, but there's no obligation to shop. For the 45min boat journey from Treasure Beach, seek out a boat captain at Frenchman's Bay; they can pick you up anywhere along the coastline, up to Great Bay (see page 239).

ARRIVAL AND TOURS   BLACK RIVER

By bus and minibus Buses and minibuses stop in the typically chaotic bus park behind the market, just off the High St. Buses are operated by independent drivers and don't typically work to schedule but are fairly regular (every 15–20min) especially Monday to Saturday and during daylight hours; fares start at about J$150 and run up to J$300.

Destinations Bluefields (45min); Luana (for connections to Negril and Kingston; 30min); Middle Quarters (30min); Savanna-La-Mar (1hr 30min); Treasure Beach (40min);

Whitehouse (1hr).

River tours See page 236.

Way Back When Black River Heritage Tour St John's Parish Church, Black River ☎ 530 6902, ⓦ real-jamaica-vacations.com. Black River native and local historian-tour guide Allison Morris conducts a walking tour of the parish's historic capital providing guests with an entertaining insight into the colourful past of this small town. Thurs–Sun; advance booking required; US$25.

ACCOMMODATION AND EATING

Given that few tourists stop over in Black River, much less Parottee, there aren't really many places around town worth staying at.

Cloggy's on the Beach Crane Rd ☎ 570 2647. Fresh seafood is the order of the day in this seaside town and *Cloggy's* has a lovely setting by the sea, with tables under thatched gazebos, on the sand or inside by the bar. This is the best place in town for curry shrimp (J$1500) or lobster (J$1400), or a plate of fish (J$1200), served with rice, bammy and festival. Daily 10am till late.

Waterloo Guesthouse 44 High St, Black River ☎ 965

2278, ⓦ waterlooguesthouse.com. Unfortunately, guests rarely stay in the original hotel building – a tattered version of its former lovely self built in the nineteenth century to commemorate the Battle of Waterloo. There are sixteen basic but well appointed rooms to choose from at the back of the property, all with mini fridge and TV, facing a swimming pool – sufficient for an overnight stay or two. **US$77**

Treasure Beach

South of the main A2 road between Black River and Mandeville, snoozy **TREASURE BEACH** is the bright spark of south-coast tourism. A string of laidback fishing villages tucked under the Santa Cruz Mountains amid some of Jamaica's most beautiful countryside, the area is the ultimate antidote to the island's more commercialized resorts. Tourism is very much a community concern here: many of the accommodation and eating places are owned by local families, and as there are no fenced-off all-inclusives to create a barrier between the locals and the visitors, everyone mixes easily together. One of the safest areas in Jamaica, this tight-knit, proud community has both a solid tourist infrastructure and a strong sense of its own

---

BOAT TRIPS FROM TREASURE BEACH

Frenchman's Bay is the departure point for **boat trips** along the coast, a brilliant way to see the area. You'll probably be approached by various operators on the beach (some of whom have questionable safety standards); best plan is to ask at your hotel who they recommend someone to you, or get in touch with Captain Dennis Abrahams (☎435 3779, ⓔdennisabrahams@yahoo.com), an excellent and experienced boatman whose fishing pirogue is the fastest (and one of the most comfortable) in Treasure Beach.

A popular excursion is to **Pelican Bar** on a sandspit offshore from Parottee Point (see page 236). Ask to combine it with a ride along Pedro's Bluff. Other boating excursions offered by Dennis include a trip to Landacre beach for sunbathing and snorkelling (1–4 hr; US$250). He'll also take you to *Little Ochi* (see page 245; 3hr 30min; US$130); a ride up the coast and along Black River to see the crocodiles (4hr; US$130); and line fishing (US$70/hr). All prices are for two people, and there are good reductions for larger groups.

Joseph "Blacka" Brown (☎376 9944) is another reliable tour operator who offers a popular Kingfish Cook-Out tour – a day-long trip (weather permitting) that takes you to a private beach where he will cook up kingfish or lobster and serve drinks (US$300/2 people).

Fort Charles & Black River

N

Billy's
Bay

ACCOMMODATION

77 West	1
BeBe's Place	8
Calabash House	11
Golden Sands	7
Irie Rest	2
Ital Rest	15
Jakes	9
Katamah	6
Mar Blue Villa Suites	13
Ocean View Guest House	12
Shakespeare Cottage	5
Sunset Resort Hotel	10
Taino Cove	14
Treasure Beach Hotel	4
Two Seasons Guest House	3

EATING

Frenchman's Reef	4
Gee Whiz	10
Gold Coast	9
Jack Sprat	6
Jakes	7
Lobster Pot	12
M&D Bar	8
Mellow Yellow	5
Mother Earth Ital Cafe	11
Smurf's Café	3
Strikie T's	1
The Singing Chef	2

Frenchman's
Bay

Swaby's
Plaza

Breds Treasure
Beach Sports Park

Calabash
Bay

Kingfisher
Plaza

Old
Wharf

Great Pedro
Pond

Police Station, Pedro Cross, Lovers' Leap, Junction & A2

Police Station

PEDRO PLAINS

DRINKING & NIGHTLIFE

Dougie's Bar	5
Eggy's Bar	2
Fishermen's Bar	3
Jack Sprat	4
Pelican Bar	1

SHOPPING

Callaloo	1
Treasure Hunt Craft Shop	2

Great
Bay

Great
Bay

Back Seaside

GREAT PEDRO
BLUFF

0 ——— 500
metres

TREASURE BEACH

traditional values. It's a tiny spot, with no neon beach-bars or jet skis or sun loungers on the beaches, and attracts a mix of hip, bohemian jet-setters and young backpackers who simply want to unwind and absorb Jamaica's gentler, more pastoral side.

The **Santa Cruz Mountains** rise up from the sea just east of Treasure Beach and run northwest, providing a scenic backdrop for the village and protecting the area from rain clouds coming from the north. As a result, Treasure Beach has one of the driest climates in the country, and the scrubby, desert-like landscape – red-earth savannahs strewn with cactuses and acacia trees – is often reminiscent of the African plains. Despite the dry weather, though, this is very much farming country, and you'll see rolling plantations of carrots, scallions, thyme, onions and watermelons scattered around the area. You may also notice that many of the residents have a very distinctive appearance – red or blonde hair; blue, green or yellow eyes; light skin and freckles – that is said to be the result of intermarriage between locals and a crew of Scottish sailors who were shipwrecked here in the nineteenth century. Whatever the reason, Treasure Beach's "red" men and women, as they're known, are famed islandwide for their unusual beauty.

There's a good and ever-expanding range of **accommodation** options here, including a delightfully eclectic collection of villas and beach cottages to rent, some great places to **eat** and a couple of diverting attractions, while the bays that make up the area feature some spectacular undeveloped golden-sand **beaches**. You'll probably stay on the long sandy sweep of **Frenchman's Bay**, where tourism has largely displaced fishing as the main industry, or smaller **Calabash Bay**, where you can still see brightly coloured fishing boats pulled up on the beach below the newly constructed villas and guesthouses. To the east, **Great Bay** remains a basic fishing village with a sprinkling of guesthouses and villas and some spectacular scenery – the beach here is the safest to swim in Treasure Beach – while west of Frenchman's Bay the road runs out of town past **Billy's Bay**, home to some of the more upmarket villas in Treasure Beach, some pretty, deserted beaches and a lot of goats.

Frenchman's Bay, Calabash Bay and Billy's Bay

Spread on either side of the main coast road, Treasure Beach has no town centre as such, though things are busiest between *Jakes* in **Calabash Bay** and the *Treasure Beach Hotel* at the western corner of Frenchman's Bay, where restaurants and hotels line the road. Billy's Bay is also now up and coming, with a host of new villas and local restaurants. Most people divide their time between their hotel and the beautiful undeveloped **beaches**, most of which have fine black sand, body-surfable waves and crystal-clear water once you get out past the breakers; however, you'll need to watch the **undertow**, which can get strong at times; ask locally about present conditions. The best swimming is along the wide sweep of **Frenchman's Bay**, where there are few underwater rocks and several beach bars for snacks and drinks. The sweep of sand here is wide enough for late-afternoon football games amongst local lads, and it's a great spot to watch the sun go down.

Great Bay

On the outskirts of Treasure Beach, a turn-off from Pedro Cross police station leads to **Great Bay**, least geared for tourism of Treasure Beach's mini-communities, but perhaps the most physically beautiful, with a fabulous beach that is safe to swim and a sprinkling of low-key guesthouses. This is primarily a fishing community, as demonstrated by the large Fishermen's Co-op building on the beach where the paved road ends, and many of the locals are regulars at the Pedro Banks (see page 235). Aside from exploring the beach (there are several paths over rocky outcrops that lead to secluded coves) and eating fresh lobster, the only other thing to do in Great Bay is to head for **Back Seaside**. Back Seaside is a magnificent portion of undeveloped coastline in the shadow of Lovers' Leap that's home to numerous types of cacti, tall golden grass and age-old thatch palms, all of which support several species of sea birds. On the other side of the Great Pedro Bluff, and reachable via a fifteen-minute walk through strangely English-looking pastureland (only the palm trees give the game away), it's a great spot for a coastal walk or a spot of shell collecting.

Lovers' Leap

11km east of Treasure Beach • Daily 9am–7pm • J$300 • ☎ 965 6887 • Signposted off the main road at Southfield

At some point, most Treasure Beach visitors take a trip out of town up to the sheer cliffs of **Lovers' Leap**, where the Santa Cruz Mountains drop nearly two thousand feet to the sea. According to legend, two young lovers – slaves at a nearby plantation – came here while running away from their owners. They were followed to the edge of the cliffs and, preferring to die rather than be separated again, threw themselves into the sea. It's hardly gripping stuff, but there's a bar on site – recently renovated and run by *Jakes* – with a balcony that takes in the breathtaking sea-to-sky view, making it a good spot for an evening drink with live jazz while watching the sun go down.

ARRIVAL AND DEPARTURE	TREASURE BEACH

By car If you're driving, there are several approaches to Treasure Beach. From the main A2 road between Santa Cruz and Mandeville, turn right at Gutters (opposite a large petrol station) and follow the road south towards

Nain and then Junction, where you veer right and head through Southfield and roughly 25 minutes later Pedro Cross, just north of the coastline. A turn-off to the left at Pedro Cross leads towards the coast – continue straight,

6

TURTLE-WATCHING TOURS

It is still a little known fact that Treasure Beach is Jamaica's second most important **turtle-nesting site** after Ocho Rios. Last year, 20,000 hawksbill turtles hatched on these shores, along the secluded beaches of Billy's Bay and Fort Charles. A new **Natural History Museum** in Fort Charles (Tues–Sat 9am–noon; ☎ 562 3855) aims to shed light on these creatures and the importance of conservation, and offers visitors turtle tours in season. From May to November, you are likely to see turtles nesting or hatching as the little ones make their way to the sea. Get in touch with the museum or with Carvel Ebanks (☎ 304 7778), the town's "turtle whisperer."

past the police station and down a narrow winding road and you'll see a sign to the left for Great Bay or straight to Treasure Beach. You can also get to Pedro Cross from Santa Cruz via Malvern, a spectacular but bumpy drive on a badly pot-holed road. From Black River, you can either take the A2 to Santa Cruz and turn south there, or take the small signposted right turn from the A2 just past Parottee at Fullerswood, from where a tiny, winding road runs though a series of quiet hamlets and then descends towards the coastline into Treasure Beach.

By private transfer Without your own transport, the easiest way to get here is to organize a private transfer:

Treasure Tours (☎ 965 0126, ⦿ treasuretoursjamaica.com; US$210 from Kingston for up to three people, US$140 from MoBay for up to three people) and most local hotels can organize pick-ups from Kingston or MoBay airports as well as transport for excursions.

By public transport Public transport links with Treasure Beach are not great, although several minibuses and route taxis run daily from Black River (40min) and from Mandeville via Junction or Santa Cruz (you'll have to change bus/route taxi; 1hr 30min). A regular taxi to Treasure Beach costs around US$55 round-trip from Black River, more from Mandeville.

GETTING AROUND AND TOURS

By bike As signs dotted along the roadsides announce, Treasure Beach is "bike country", and given the inconsistent state of the roads, periodically reduced to gullies following the severe flooding that has hit the area in recent years, a bicycle is an excellent way to get around. Damian "Reds" Parchment (☎ 586 2837) rents his mountain bikes for individual use (US$25/day) and for guided tours of the area, and he also operates hiking trips. Tours include two- to three-hour bike rides (US$60/person) and a hike in the Santa Cruz Mountains towards Malvern (US$75/person).

By scooter Scooters are another great option (☎ 543 1457 ⦿ treasuretoursjamaica@gmail.com). Pick up is in front of

Smurf's Café, and you go on a practice run before heading out. US$40/day, or US$35/day for 4 days or longer.

Treasure Tours ☎ 965 0126, ⦿ treasuretoursjamaica. com. If you're interested in seeing the YS Falls, Gut River, Alligator Pond or other parts of the island from a base here, try this locally operated tour company that offers a more personal experience. Run by the friendly, efficient and knowledgeable American émigré Rebecca Wiersma, Treasure Tours also offers transfers from MoBay and Kingston airports (as well as other resorts), hotel, villa and guesthouse booking and a taxi service for Treasure Tours guests staying in the area.

INFORMATION

Tourist information There is a new tourist office in Kingfisher Plaza (Mon–Sat 9am–5.30pm; ☎ 965 0126), run by a Destination Management Organization made up of long-running hotels and tour operators. The town also has an old but useful website for background information, ⦿ treasurebeach.net. Otherwise, most hotel and guesthouse operators are happy to share their local knowledge and arrange excursions.

Banks The first-ever ATM – from Scotiabank – in Treasure Beach was installed in 2017 at *Jack Sprat*. There are no cambios or full service banks in town; the nearest are in

Southfield, Santa Cruz, Black River or Junction, a bustling town at the crossroads of Alligator Pond and the coastal communities (including Treasure Beach).

Internet Most hotels including *Jakes* and *Sunset Resort* provide wi-fi to guests and non-guests hanging out at their restaurants; otherwise bring your own laptop and surf with a sea view and a cold beer at *Jack Sprat* (see page 242), the first public "hotspot" in the area. BREDS Source in Kingfisher Plaza (Mon–Sat 9am–5.30pm; ☎ 965 0748) has a small internet café and provides basic business services including scanning and printing.

ACTIVITIES AND SPAS

The Breds Treasure Beach Sports Park and Academy Treasure Beach Main Rd ☎ 965 0748. Located down a dusty lane just off the main Treasure Beach Road, the park

is as great a place to catch a local cricket or football match as it is to have a run round the pond and pitches, play (for the kids) in the nautical-themed playground, work out at the open gym or enjoy a game of tennis. A swimming pool was being built at the time of this update. Entrance is free except on some game days. Call ahead to book the tennis courts.

Driftwood Spa Jakes Hotel, Calabash Bay ☎ 965 3000, ⓦjakeshotel.com. Treasure Beach's only full-service spa, offering an array of treatments including traditional massages, facials, mani-pedis, scrubs and wraps. Yoga is also available most weeks in season and based on teacher availability out of season. Driftwood Facial (75min) US$115, Sea and Sand Sensation Scrub (45min) US$95. Daily 9am–5pm.

Joshua Lee Stein ☎ 389 3698, ⓦjoshualeestein. com. A freelance therapist and long-time Treasure Beach

"character", Joshua will visit you at your villa or can meet you at the Driftwood Spa (see above) to offer his unique Intuitive Bodywork Massage that blends various traditional techniques with movement and healing energy. 1hr US$80.

Shirley Genus ☎ 827 2447. Based in a small enclave beside her home at the entrance to Treasure Beach, Shirley is a herbalist and self-professed healer offering a great herbal steam bath prepared with organic herbs – a fantastically soothing experience. Rates include round-trip transport from local hotels; a 15min steam with a 1hr massage is US$90.

ACCOMMODATION

There is a wide variety of **accommodation** in Treasure Beach, from full-blown resorts and chic boutique hotels to numerous guesthouses and villas, the latter charging lower rates (US$50 per double is average) than in more developed parts of the island. More places are springing up all the time and, in addition, seemingly every other house is a rentable **villa**; these vary from simple beach cottages to luxurious and elegant homes with all mod cons. Expect to pay upwards of US$175 a night, with most villas – especially between November and April – requiring bookings to be a minimum of three nights. Websites worth checking for villa rentals include ⓦtreasurebeach.net and ⓦvrbo.com.

OLD WHARF

★ **Mar Blue Villa Suites** ☎ 965 3408; map p.238. A stylish boutique hotel on a secluded stretch of beach, run by a friendly couple, with fabulous attention to detail. Spotless and fresh, and a stone's throw from Calabash Bay beach, the rooms have balconies overlooking the sea and the veranda villa suites have king-sized beds, and living areas. There is a two-bedroom suite with wheelchair access, and a small pool on the property. US$111

Taino Cove ☎ 845 6103, ⓦtainocove.com; map p.238. Quiet and secluded, this two-storey tastefully decorated boutique hotel features striking African-inspired art throughout, with twelve en-suite rooms with high, artisan-designed wooden ceilings. There's also a pool, a vegan restaurant, and small private beach cove. Breakfast is included US$165

CALABASH BAY

Calabash House ☎ 818 9830, ⓦcalabashhouse. com; map p.238. Right on the sea, this colourful, artsy guesthouse offers four simply decorated rooms in the main house with private bathrooms as well as two cottages (US$10/day a/c surcharge) for rent. There is also a communal kitchen and large dining and living room in the main house, where meals are provided on request. US$95

★ **Jakes** ☎ 965 3000, ⓦjakeshotel.com; map p.238. *Jakes* is a unique and imaginative spot. The quirky rooms have all been decorated in earthy colours, with attention to detail particularly evident in the shell and coloured-glass mosaics in the outdoor showers. There's a fabulous saltwater pool, a TV/library/games room, a good restaurant and a bar that draws a genial local crowd. *Jakes* also manages several nearby villas – rates start at US$700 a night. US$115

Ocean View Guest House ☎ 965 0126 or ☎ 369 1859, ⓦtreasuretours.com; map p.238. Homely beachfront house with traditional Jamaican furnishings, including four-poster beds in each of the fan-only bedrooms. There is a communal kitchen and living area and a large shared veranda facing the sea. Nearest swimming hole is a five-minute walk. Ask for room 1 if travelling in a large group or with kids. US$50

Sunset Resort Hotel ☎ 965 0143, ⓦsunsetresort. com; map p.238. An incongruous and delightfully kitsch resort in a lovely seaside setting, *Sunset's* rooms are spacious, with satellite TV; self-catering cottages are also available. There's a good restaurant on site. US$137

FRENCHMAN'S BAY

BeBe's Place ☎ 433 0252, ⓦbebesplace.com; map p.238. Three cottages – two trimmed in fretwork and one in a Moorish design – offer a total of five rooms at this simple but neat property. Three rooms have queen-size beds, two have two twin beds each, and one cottage has a kitchen and rooftop deck. Great location, just across from the beach. US$55

Golden Sands ☎ 965 0167, ⓦgoldensandstreasure beach.com; map p.238. A long-standing budget option in a prime position right on Frenchman's Beach. The basic, tiled-floor rooms are either on the beach or a stone's throw from the beach, with fan or a/c, screened windows and en-suite bathrooms. All share a communal kitchen. There are also three-bedroom apartment options with kitchen and dining room but no a/c. US$55

★ **Katamah** ☎ 567 9562 ⓦkatamah.com; map p.238. Facing a lovely stretch of Frenchman's Bay, the laidback, bohemian-chic *Katamah* is run by a Jamaican husband-wife team, and offers eco-designed cottages and rooms decked in Morocco-meets-Bali flare, with private or shared bathrooms. Choose the new "Berry Suite" with kitchenette and private balcony for its oasis-like feel – other cabins have Asian-style outdoor shower and ocean-facing patios for a cool sea breeze (one unit has a/c). There's also a lively, communal beachside kitchen stocked with drinks and barbecue grill, and ample seafront spaces for lounging in hammocks. Furnished tents are available in high season. Doubles US$130, glamping US$60

Shakespeare Cottage ☎ 965 0120, ⌨ marycroteau.com/sc; map p.238. Excellent budget option, with four basic but clean rooms in the original building, all with fans and shared bathrooms, and a kitchen for guests to use. In addition, there are three simply decorated, fan-only en-suite rooms in a newer building; rooms on the top floor have small balconies with sea views – there's also a one-bedroom cottage for rent. Doubles US$26, cottage US$60

Treasure Beach Hotel ☎ 965 0110, ⌨ jamaicatreasurebeachhotel.com; map p.238. In the middle of Treasure Beach, this hotel remains the largest resort in the area with two pools, extensive gardens and a restaurant and bar. The oceanfront suites are newer and all have a/c and satellite TV. US$140

BILLY'S BAY

Irie Rest ☎ 965 0034, ⌨ irierestguesthouse.com; map p.238. Extremely friendly place set back from, but within walking distance of, the beach. Rooms are simple and inviting, with en-suite bathrooms; some have huge screened verandas. There's a cool communal area with a stereo and satellite TV. Two of the apartments have kitchens. Great value. US$40

Two Seasons Guest House ☎ 571 0818, ⌨ 2seasonsguesthouse.com; map p.238. Three-storey guesthouse tucked down a lane towards the scrubby mountainside of Treasure Beach, offering ten spacious rooms, ideal for groups. Some have a/c and kitchenettes, and all have cable TV. There is a pool, and breakfast is optional and at added cost but worth it, served by friendly staff. Best used as a base if you have a car, due to its distance from the main road. US$80

77 West ☎ 965 0034, ⌨ 77west.net; map p.238. A series of steps lead down to the ultra-sleek, all-white property with sweeping views over the sea and rocky shores, with an infinity swimming pool as its centrepiece, plus the secluded beach beyond. Five minimalist white and blue rooms complete the picture, with stone floors, shutters and small verandas. The seaview restaurant terrace is open to the public. US$115

GREAT BAY

Ital Rest ☎ 421 8909 or ☎ 473 6145, ⌨ italrest.com; map p.238. There are only four rooms (in two cottages) for rent at this gentle, friendly and beautifully landscaped place, which is within walking distance of a lovely swimming cove. The two bedrooms – one upstairs and one downstairs – in each cottage can each sleep up to three people. Ask to rent an upstairs bedroom for the views and the breeze – there is no electricity. There's a small bar with a ping-pong table, meals (vegetarian and vegan possible) are available on request, and bike rental is also offered. US$50

EATING

Evenings are pretty low key in Treasure Beach, but there are an increasing number of excellent food options, most offering, unsurprisingly, locally caught seafood. Most of the places are small-scale affairs, but a few – *Jakes, Sunset Resort, 77 West* – accept credit cards. If you're cooking for yourself, you'll find several small **grocery stores** in Treasure Beach with a limited selection of goods – but for a big shop, you'll need to go to Black River, Southfield or Junction. Vans selling fruit and vegetables pass through Treasure Beach a couple of times a week; ask locally.

Frenchman's Reef Treasure Beach Main Rd, Frenchman's Bay ☎ 965 3049; map p.238. Relaxed, family-run restaurant and bar serving reasonably priced drinks and tasty local dishes and international favourites such as burgers and pizza in a great location right on the beach. Occasional live entertainment in the evenings. Daily 8am till late.

Gee Wiz Maylen Plaza, Main Rd, Treasure Beach ☎ 573 5988; map p.238. Vegan and vegetarian meals for lunch and dinner such as curried pumpkin and stewed veggie chunks (J$500), as well as freshly pressed juices and shakes. What the roadside location lacks in ambience the conversation with genial owner/chef Delroy Brown and freshness of the food make up for. Meals cost about J$600 and prepared to order – call in advance. Daily 11.30am–7.30pm.

Gold Coast Kingfisher Plaza, Calabash Bay ☎ 391 2458; map p.238. Husband- and wife-run cookshop that's best for takeaway as it lacks atmosphere. Delicious Jamaican food, including curry goat (J$500), stew chicken (J$450) and rice and peas. Lunch only. Mon–Sat 9am–6pm.

★ **Jack Sprat** Calabash Bay, just past Jakes ☎ 965 3583; map p.238. With tables under sea-grape trees and a sandy path down to the beach, this is the perfect place for a relaxed meal. Shellfish (conch, shrimp and lobster in season) as well as fish cooked any style are served with bammy, rice and peas, and salad (J$1576). There is also a hearty conch soup available alongside tasty pizzas (bases are handmade on the spot, and toppings include fresh pineapple and proper pepperoni; from J$1200). Pastries, cakes and Devon House ice cream satisfy the sweet tooth, and prices are reasonable. Daily 10am–11pm.

Jakes Calabash Bay ☎965 3000; map p.238. Open-air restaurant within *Jakes* hotel (see page 241), this is usually one of the busiest places in town, serving moderately priced Jamaican dishes with a sophisticated twist. The blackboard menus change daily; highlights include Jakes' jerk burger (J$1087), pumpkin soup (J$604) and home-made coconut ice cream (J$420). Tables are under shady trees, and there's a good, if small, wine list. Daily 7.30am–10.30pm.

Lobster Pot Great Bay ☎456 871; map p.238. Barefoot and buttoned-down beach shack that serves great local fish and lobster cooked to order. There's also a bar inside making it a great place to eat, swim and watch the sunset. Try the curry lobster (J$1000). Meals are made to order, so call in advance. Daily 9am till late.

★ **M&D Bar** Calabash Bay ☎438 5005; map p.238. Run by the formidable Maureen Powell and her partner Delvin, *M&D*'s is a bar and well-stocked grocery, also known for its weekend jerk conch, chicken and pork and a massive pot of deliciously spicy conch soup (J$300). A quarter of chicken costs J$350. Mon–Fri 7.30am–8pm, Sat 9am–10pm.

Mellow Yellow Frenchman's Bay ☎365 1097; map p.238. The freshest Italian-Jamaican fare in town. Sample the jerk chicken pasta (J$1500), callaloo lasagne or pizza in an authentic Treasure Beach roadside veranda setting. Tues–Sun noon–10pm.

★ **Mother Earth Ital Cafe** Old Wharf ☎275 8499; map p.238. Located at Taino Cove, Empress Thandi Wise serves only the freshest Jamaican health food – from land to pot – at this poolside, beachfront bistro. Breakfasts include porridge with coconut, or callaloo power smoothies (J$1200); Sunday brunch features roti wraps (J$1500) and kale salads (J$1100), among other picks, with live jazz. Ask to sample housemade ganja wine or banana wine; pair it with dessert. Tues–Sun 8am–5pm.

Smurf's Cafe Frenchman's Bay ☎504 7814; map p.238. Serving up some of the most delicious and well-priced breakfasts in the area (all mains, including ackee and saltfish, and omelettes and pancakes cost J$550). Tasty breads and pastries are available to order, as well as freshly ground coffee beans. Mon–Sat 6.30am–2pm; dinner on request.

Strikie T's Billy's Bay ☎899 6436; map p.238. Community hotspot in Billy's Bay that serves up delicious Jerk (J$700 for chicken) in a thatched roadside hut. Cosy up with the locals at communal tables, grab a drink from the bar and enjoy the sights and sounds while your meal is cooked to order. Nov–April Mon–Sat 2pm till late.

The Singing Chef Billy's Bay ☎422 5211, ⓦfacebook. com/thesingingchefjamaica; map p.238. Cosy, thatch hut dining terrace run by a local family, serving fresh lobster (J$1800) and seafood specialities. Stay on past dinner to see Chef Elliot Kerron come out and sing with his guitar. Daily 11.30am–11pm.

DRINKING AND NIGHTLIFE

Treasure Beach isn't a nightlife hot spot and, during the week, evenings out will generally consist of after-dinner **drinks** at any of the restaurants listed above or at the area's few bars, which often keep quite late hours if the punters are drinking. In addition to the places listed below, there are numerous rum shops in and around town for a spot of white-rum drinking and ol' talk. Things get busier on the weekends, with the occasional special event happening at local bars or in the hotels; for a dancehall fix ask locals about street dances in the area (a party that usually spreads from a local rum bar to the middle of a road) or listen out for "town-criers" (cars that drive around with loudspeakers strapped to their roofs) who announce everything from plays to parties.

Dougie's Bar Jakes Hotel, Calabash Bay ☎965 3000; map p.238. Relaxed hotel bar that's usually filled with a friendly crowd of sophisticates and locals. A great spot for a sunset cocktail or a glass of wine. Daily 10am until late.

Eggy's Bar Frenchman's Bay ☎420 3274; map p.238. The first beach bar shack you'll see as you turn right out of *Waikiki*, *Eggy's* is a Treasure Beach institution – no-frills, simple drinking; occasional grilling of fresh catch; and always lots of locals (particularly fishermen) catching up on gossip. Great at sunset. Daily 9am till late.

Fishermen's Bar First lane on the right after Jakes and before South Jammin', Frenchman's Bay ☎379 9780; map p.238. *Fishermen's* has a small indoor disco, occasional live music and a pool table out back, plus a thatched bar and restaurant fronting the lane. This easy-going local hangout is a reliable if slightly shady spot –

attracting local guys who might throw out a pick-up line or two or offer to sell you drugs – but is open long after everywhere else has closed. Very popular at the weekends with both locals and tourists. Daily 7am–2am.

Jack Sprat Calabash Bay ☎965 3583; map p.238. A good place for a drink or to catch local/international games on the massive screen, *Jack Sprat* also hosts the best New Year's celebration in town and a Thursday movie night under the stars; it is the most likely venue to have live music during the season. Daily 10am–11pm.

Pelican Bar 45min by boat to Parottee Point; map p.238. This ramshackle wooden bar attracts crowds from as far as Negril for its setting in the middle of the Caribbean Sea (see page 236). Sunsets here are perfect, with a swim, even if the rum punches (J$800) and beers (J$500) are priced for tourists. Daily 11am–6pm.

6

6

SHOPPING

Callaloo Frenchman's Bay ☎390 3949; map p.238. A delightful boutique selling locally made beach chic sundresses, T-shirts, jewellery, kids' clothing and homewares, designed and hand-crafted by French former fashion designer Sophie Eyssautier who now lives in the community. Worth a visit even if only browsing. Daily 9am–6pm.

Treasure Hunt Craft Shop Old Wharf ☎965 3878, ⓦ tbwgjamaica.com; map p.238. The Treasure Beach Women's Group stock this gift shop with unique items handmade by the area's local artists – including woven bags, lignum vitae earrings, or signature hand painted starlights. Craft workshops are occasionally held here. Mon–Fri 9am–3pm, Sat 9am–1pm.

East of Treasure Beach

The road leading east out of Treasure Beach rises and dips through the hilly farming communities of **Pedro Cross**, **Flagaman**, **Southfield** and **Top Hill**, winding its way along with dramatic views of the sea until reaching the bustling town of **Junction** – where all the roads from the coast rise to meet in one chaotic main square. The drive itself is incredibly picturesque, taking in the quilt-like farming landscape, colourful street bars, watermelon vendors and the incongruous, massive homes of returned residents who have opted for the cooler climate of the hills. Once off the main road that leads to Junction, and moving towards the southeast coast, the terrain around every hairpin corner begins to change again, going from urban to rural to completely wild and arid, ending in the dusty but scenic fishing town of **Alligator Pond**. Here you'll find little more than a couple of tasty seafood spots – worth the trip – and a quiet black-sand beach that you can usually claim all for yourself. On the way back out of town, just right of the main road (there is no signpost so ask if uncertain), is the south coast road, built with a vision of local tourism development now long forgotten. Although completely undeveloped and a little desolate in places (you wouldn't want to break down here as it could take a while before anyone passes by), the road itself is in good shape and makes an interesting way to go off the beaten track towards May Pen. For kilometres, there's not much to see except rugged, sparse cacti and thatch-strewn coastline and then thick overgrown reeds edging the road as you approach the morass – but if you persevere the drive will eventually take you past cooling Gut River and alongside the Canoe Valley observation area for a chance to see one of Jamaica's remaining manatees. Most travellers who take this route do so to get to the world famous – albeit in desperate need of funding – **Milk River Spa** in the quiet, dusty town of Milk River, where you can take a soothing dip in the mineral waters before reconnecting with the A2 towards May Pen.

Alligator Pond

At first glance, the ramshackle fishing village of **ALLIGATOR POND** is not one of the most attractive spots on the south coast. But if you're passing, it's worth stopping to get the feel of a part of Jamaica pretty much unsullied by tourism, and to eat some superb **seafood**. Where the main road into Alligator Pond opens up into an unofficial town square, a dirt road to the right leads to several small shacks selling lobster and fish fresh from the boats.

There's no tourism scene here as such, but there's a bar at the water's edge, and local families arrive at the weekends for a day on the beach. It's also a great spot for watching the sunset – or the moonrise over the hills, which slip down to the sea in the unmistakeable shape of an alligator's head.

ARRIVAL AND DEPARTURE	ALLIGATOR POND

By car Alligator Pond is 16km east of Treasure Beach, and reachable from the A2 via a direct road from Gutters.
By bus You can catch a route minibus from Mandeville (J$250) and Junction (J$150).
By route taxi Route taxis run roughly three to five times daily (Mon–Sat) from Mandeville (1hr 30min) and Junction (40min).

EATING

Little Ochi Alligator Pond ☎ 852 6430 or ☎ 878 6090, ⓦ littleochie.com. Once the most popular of the seafood shacks in town is *Little Ochi* with its unique collection of tables housed in brightly painted fishing boats on stilts overlooking the beach. There's always a steady trade here, but it's particularly busy on weekends, with hungry folk pouring in from Mandeville and even as far as Kingston, and reggae blaring from columns of speaker boxes. The fish, shrimp, lobster and conch – hand-selected by you and cooked in every way possible alongside bammy and festival – certainly taste good eaten in the sea air though not as fresh as in the past, and the wait can be considerable: an hour or more at busy times. Try the jerk crab for J$1500 or garlic shrimp for J$1900. Daily 9am till late.

★ **Oswalds** Alligator Pond ☎ 381 3535. Giving *Little Ochi* a run for its money, nearby *Oswalds* up the beach is the best current choice especially on days when the area gets packed (public holidays and most Sundays). With a bird's-eye view of the fishermen bringing in their nets, *Oswalds* offers a great low-key, personal feel on a small dining deck by the sea. Try the finger-licking jerked snapper or lobster (J$1100) – taste-wise it's hard to beat. Daily 10am till late.

Canoe Valley

The drive from Alligator Pond to Alligator Hole and Milk River is what Jamaicans call a "lonely road" (with a shiver of misgiving), but it's a lovely drive through an isolated area known as **Canoe Valley**, or the Long Bay Morass, much of it along the coast, with goats and sea birds usually your only company. The area is barely touched by development and remains a naturalist's paradise, with the dry, cactus-strewn slopes in the west giving way to mangrove swamps as you head further east – brilliant for birdwatching. In several places, you can access the beautiful, completely deserted stretch of brown-sand **beach** along Long Bay. It's not really a place to swim – the water is usually rough and currents strong – but it's a marvellous spot for a walk, with plenty of driftwood and shells to collect.

Gut River

One of the most picturesque places on the south coast, **Gut River** runs under the road towards the sea, emerging in a clear blue stream edged by coconut palms and huge aloe plants, where you can swim and watch frigate birds and egrets flap lazily around. Unfortunately, developers have recently taken over the land adjoining and although no current plans are in place to build anything specific yet, they have put up a massive wall making the river difficult (but not impossible) to access. These semi-built structures and the interest of the new owners means that on weekends, especially Sundays, the spot draws a crowd and often a sound system too; best to visit early in the morning on a weekday.

Alligator Hole

South Coast Rd, Canoe Valley • Daily 9am–4pm • Free

A tiny nature park that gives a peek into the surrounding morass, **Alligator Hole** is most famously the part-time home of a small number of **manatees** (see page 246). It's a peaceful place to stop, with a small visitor centre housing displays on the mammals and Caribbean ecosystems. If you're lucky, you'll see the manatees come in for their daily feed, usually in the late afternoon, supplied by the caretaker-managers who hang out by the park, drinking, playing dominoes and selling cold beer and soft drinks. It's a truly paradisiacal spot in all its stillness and natural glory, allowing visitors an otherwise unattainable glimpse into the healthy and active morass, and its wildlife, flora and fauna. **Crocodiles** (known locally as alligators) also inhabit the area, although they are seen less often, and lots of people swim in the cool, clear waters here (which is safe, despite the presence of crocodiles).

Milk River

There's little to the village of **MILK RIVER**, a couple of kilometres inland from Alligator Hole, other than the spa (see page 246), the usual crowd of schoolchildren and a smattering of churches, although there are rumoured plans to build a large all-inclusive

6

MANATEES

The **manatee** – an aquatic mammal that looks rather like a large, fat seal with a bigger snout and a smile – is found in the warm waters of the Atlantic Ocean and in the Caribbean Sea. Known locally as the sea cow, it's a very secretive creature; little is known about its reproductive habits, for example, and scientists have found it tricky to monitor its numbers. The nature park at Alligator Hole is the only place in Jamaica where you've an excellent chance of seeing them in the wild.

Fully grown, manatees can reach up to fourteen feet in length, although the great size is no cause for concern as they are strictly vegetarian – eating as much as four hundred kilos of sea grass per day – and known for doting on each other and their young. Columbus probably spotted them when he first came to Jamaica in 1494 (although he claimed that he had seen mermaids), and there were certainly plenty around back then.

Sadly, their slow and gentle lifestyle meant that they were (and are) easy prey for fishermen; accordingly, even though they are now protected, fewer than three thousand are believed to survive in the Caribbean and only a hundred in Jamaica.

hotel close to the spa. The river itself is named for its colour in the early morning, when it is shrouded in mist; swimming is not a great idea, given that the river is home to a number of crocodiles. Three kilometres beyond the spa, past rows of giant cacti, is the tiny fishing village of **Farquhars** which has, at its western end, a passable black-sand beach where you can swim in the ocean. Expect lots of good-natured attention from the locals, as tourists very rarely venture this far.

Milk River Spa

At the *Milk River Hotel*, Main Rd ☏ 610 7745 or ☏ 618 0268 · J$600/15min

The **hot mineral springs** at Milk River were first discovered in the early eighteenth century. Mineral spas were subsequently built in the area – first opened to the public in 1794 – and are today housed in the basement of the *Milk River Hotel*. Renovations on the main **baths**, including new tiles and mosaic designs, have added to its appeal, as well as the opening of three additional, larger baths at the far end of the hotel – only open on special occasions. Many of the guests at the hotel and spa are return visitors who swear by the curative powers of the water for a range of ailments from rheumatism to gout, nerve diseases and sciatica. Other visitors find their curiosity tinged with concern about the high radioactivity levels of the baths – more than fifty times that of the waters at Vichy in France – although the staff will assure you that this is quite harmless so long as you don't stay in for more than fifteen minutes at a time.

ARRIVAL AND ACCOMMODATION   MILK RIVER

By bus or route taxi There is no bus or taxi service that runs from Alligator Pond to Milk River although a private taxi can be arranged in town for about US$40 each way. Buses and taxis run daily about every two to three hours from May Pen to Milk River.
Milk River Hotel Main Rd ☏ 610 7745 or ☏ 618 0268, ✉ hotelmilkriver@yahoo.com. A lovely old wooden building with comfortable, if rather sparse, mostly en-suite rooms and inexpensive meals on offer. Though there's nothing spectacular about the area, the dry climate and the laidback atmosphere make it a decent place to spend a night. You get free use of the spa if you're staying here. Rates include breakfast and dinner. <u>US$137</u>

Central St Elizabeth

The A2 highway speeds inland from Black River, passing through some attractive countryside before making the long climb up Spur Tree Hill to **Mandeville**. The main road passes through **Bamboo Avenue**, with its walls of tall bamboo, and there are several interesting detours worth taking, particularly in the interior of St Elizabeth. There are gorgeous **waterfalls** at YS, **hiking** possibilities in the **Black River Gorge** and the quiet and completely untouristed villages of the **Santa Cruz Mountains**. You can also visit a **rum factory**, beautifully placed among fields of sugar cane at Appleton, on the southern edge of Cockpit Country.

Accommodation options in the area are limited and you may want to consider visiting on day-trips from a base on the south coast or in Mandeville.

YS Falls

4km north of Middle Quarters • Tues–Sun 9.30am–3.30pm • US$17; canopy zipline US$42 • ☎ 997 6360, ⓦ ysfalls.com

YS (pronounced "why-ess"), an area dominated by the **YS farm**, is the home of the magnificent **YS Falls**. The name is thought to derive from the farm's original owners in 1684, John Yates and Richard Scott, whose initials were stamped on their cattle and the hogsheads of sugar that they exported. Today the farm covers around 2300 acres and raises pedigree Red Poll cattle – a breed that you'll see all over the country. The YS Falls, a series of ten greater and lesser waterfalls, are great fun. A jitney pulls you through the estate and along the banks of the YS River to a grassy area at the base of the falls, where there are changing rooms and toilets. You can climb up the lower falls or take the wooden stairway, which leads to a platform beside the uppermost and most spectacular waterfall. There are lianas and ropes for aspiring Tarzans, and pools for gentle bathing at the foot of each fall as well as two spring-water swimming pools on the flat, one with private cabanas, perfect for lounging. For the more adventurous, there's a **canopy tour**: once strapped to a harness you can zip through the treetops starting at the top of the waterfall and finishing just before the spring-water swimming pool. Early morning is a good time to go, before the afternoon clouds (and the bus tours) draw in; take a picnic and a book and you can comfortably spend a few hours loafing around the gardens. Cold beers, soft drinks, coffee and simple snacks are offered in the well-stocked gift shop.

ARRIVAL AND DEPARTURE

YS FALLS

By public transport Buses run along the main A2 highway south of YS between Black River and Santa Cruz. Ask the driver to drop you at the junction, and you can usually find taxis waiting to run passengers up to the YS farm (around J$200).

Maggotty

MAGGOTTY, east of YS and eleven kilometres from the main A2 highway, resembles a small Wild West frontier town. It's a dry, dusty place, most of whose inhabitants work at the **Appleton Estate** rum distillery nearby (see below).

The Appleton Estate Rum Tour

Appleton, 5km east of Maggotty • Mon–Sat 9am 3.30pm • US$25 • ☎ 963 9216, ⓦ appletonrumtour.com • Lunch can be arranged with 24 hours' notice and at an additional cost of US$15 per person • You'll need a car to get here, or you can take a route taxi or bus from Maggotty for about J$150

The **Wray and Nephew rum distillery** at **APPLETON** – under heavy expansion and renovation at the time of writing – has a great setting in the Nassau Valley among

---

PEPPA SWIMPS

Undeniably a highlight of driving along the south coast is the opportunity to indulge in a bag of salty, Scotch-bonnet-spiced boiled **pepper shrimp** – otherwise known as **peppa swimps** – fished from the Black River and sold at **Middle Quarters**. Feel free to sample from the proffered bags before you buy; reckon on around J$500 for a small bag. Buy some to add to your picnic if you're heading to the YS Falls or take a few minutes out to crunch them on the roadside and have a chat with the women. Incidentally, don't be intimidated by the fiercely competitive approach of the sellers – they are often all members of the same family and if one is lagging in sales for the day, she will usually be thrust forward to clinch the deal. If available, try the equally delicious *janga* (shrimp) soup (J$300).

6

RUM AND RAISON D'ÉTRE

Rum – once known as rumbullion or kill-devil – is Jamaica's national drink, and you couldn't choose a better place to acquire a taste for the stuff. Jamaica was one of the first countries to make rum commercially and it still produces some of the world's finest. Overproof is the drink of choice for the less well-off – it's cheap, lethally strong (64 percent alcohol) and, supposedly, cures all ills. If you can't handle the overproof, the standard **white rums** are the basis for most cocktails, while more refined palates go for the **darker rums**. During the ageing process these rums acquire colour from the oak barrels in which they are stored and, as they get older, they slip down increasingly smoothly with no need for a mixer.

Distilling of sugar-cane juice started in Jamaica during the years of Spanish occupation, stepping up a few gears when the British took over in 1655 and rum became famous as the drink of the island's semi-legitimate **pirates** and **buccaneers**. The production process hasn't changed much over the centuries, although it has become fully mechanized, putting a number of donkeys out of work in the process. The sugar cane is squeezed to extract every drop of its juice, which is then boiled and put through a centrifuge, producing molasses. In turn, the molasses is diluted with water, and yeast is added to get the stuff fermenting away. After fermentation, the liquid "dead wash" is sent to the distillery, where it's heated, and the evaporating alcohol caught in tanks. It sounds simple enough – and it is. But when you discover that it takes ten to twelve tonnes of sugar cane to produce half a bottle of alcohol, which is then blended with water and a mixture of secret ingredients (molasses is almost certainly among them) to make the finished product, you begin to appreciate all those fields of swaying cane a little more.

thousands of acres of sugar-cane fields. At 250 years old, this is one of the oldest rum producers in the English-speaking Caribbean and the best known of Jamaica's several brands. All of the rum produced here is sent for blending, barrelling and bottling in Kingston – though some barrels are sent back here to age in a warehouse viewed during the tour.

The hour-long **Appleton Estate Rum Tour** starts with a complimentary drink and video session, followed by a visit to the factory (heavy with the sweet scent of molasses) and the cobwebby, ageing house, and then outside to an old sugar press, where donkeys used to walk in circles to turn a grinder that crushed juice out of the sugar cane. Today it's all mechanized, though a donkey has been put back into service to demonstrate old techniques. The tour concludes in a "tavern", where you get to sample all seventeen kinds of rum and various rum-based liquors. Though you're free to drop in, it's a good idea to call ahead to arrange a guided visit, if only to avoid your visit coinciding with a big tour party.

Apple Valley Park

5km east of Maggotty · Daily 10am–5pm, by reservation only · US$13, includes lunch · ☎ 487 4521

Located on a 169-acre family farm, **Apple Valley Park** opens for the few who venture here and reserve ahead for a day surrounded in beautiful green landscape, including a lake, a forest reserve and pools. Fun outdoor activities include paddling, kayaking, swimming and hiking excursions to hidden falls on the property.

ARRIVAL AND DEPARTURE   MAGGOTTY

By car The road north from the A2 highway is in far better condition than the road running east–west between Maggotty and YS.

By minibus Infrequent minibuses run to Maggotty from Black River and Santa Cruz a handful of times a day (predominantly during school hours – 7am–3pm) and take about 45min. Route taxis run from the Texaco at Tombstone (in Lacovia) to Maggotty.

Bamboo Avenue

For several kilometres on either side of the main A2 highway, halfway between Middle Quarters and Lacovia, *Bambusa vulgaris*, Jamaica's largest species of bamboo, has grown up to create a pretty arch over the road. **Bamboo Avenue**, as it is fondly known, was once almost completely shaded by the bamboo, but the sun now streams in through gaps created by Hurricane Gilbert and, some say, by official neglect. There are several rest stops along the road where you can get a jelly coconut or a cold beer.

Lacovia

The village of **LACOVIA**, one-time capital of St Elizabeth, was once an important inland port for shipping sugar and logwood down to Black River for export. Today it is most notable for its **twin tombs**, just outside the Texaco petrol station, believed to contain the bodies of two young men killed in a local duel in 1723. One of the deceased is identified as Thomas Jordan Spencer and the coat of arms on his tombstone suggests a connection with the family of Britain's Winston Churchill and Lady Diana Spencer.

Santa Cruz

If you're in this part of the country, sooner or later you're likely to pass through **SANTA CRUZ**, the main settlement along the A2 and reckoned to be the hottest place in Jamaica. This rapidly expanding market town, once famous as a livestock trading centre, is noisy and frenetic at the best of times, and there's no particular reason to stop off here, although you can fill up on fresh patties and delicious juices on the Main Street.

Malvern

The road south from Santa Cruz to Treasure Beach and the coast is a beautiful (if slow) drive over the Santa Cruz Mountains. The drive takes you through a series of tiny villages and the quiet town of **MALVERN**. Like Christiana further north (see page 252), this is one of Jamaica's coolest towns, at around 2500ft above sea level. In the early twentieth century, it was an important summer retreat for foreigners and wealthy Jamaicans, though it's now almost bereft of tourists. Apart from a handful of top-notch schools and colleges established here in the 1850s, there's not much to the town, although the presence of returning residents who've made their money abroad is injecting an air of affluence – with grand houses springing up on the hilltops – and it's a pretty place to explore for a little while.

Spur Tree Hill

At **Gutters**, on the Manchester/St Elizabeth border and a turn-off for Treasure Beach, the A2 begins the long and rather tortuous climb up **Spur Tree Hill** to Mandeville. Once known as "man bump", the switchbacking hill provides dramatic views over the southern plains, the Santa Cruz Mountains, and down to the sea, and there are a couple of good **bars** and **restaurants** where you can stop off and enjoy the view.

EATING   SPUR TREE HILL

All Seasons Spur Tree Hill Rd ☎ 583 8483. *All Seasons* serves a great jerk pork and chicken and an excellent jerk pork sausage at weekends. A quarter of jerk chicken is J$380, and quarter-pound of pork J$350. Guests can opt to eat in the mini restaurant/bar area (itself not very decorative) but with an amazing view of the valley below or you can sit in the more atmospheric smokehouse on bar stools. Daily 10am–11pm.

Neville's Curry Goat Spur Tree Hill ☎ 507 8308. A sweet and friendly, one-table "one-stop" cookshop and bar, frequented by truckers and locals alike – a curry goat meal costs about J$500. Daily 10.30am–8.30pm.

6

Claudette's Top Class Restaurant Spur Tree District, across from Hood Daniel Depot ☎ 964 6452. Run by Miss Claudette and her hard-working team of ladies serve Jamaican cookshop staples (fried chicken and curried goat J$500, breakfast of ackee and saltfish J$350) in a simple but decent setting along the main road. Daily 8.30am–6pm.

Mandeville

You can almost feel the wealth in **MANDEVILLE**, Jamaica's fifth-largest town. Founded in 1814, the big money started to arrive here in the 1950s as a result of a now-defunct but once highly profitable **bauxite industry** that grew up around the town. More recently, returning expatriate Jamaicans, attracted by the cooler climate (you'll need a sweater in winter) and the relatively low crime rate, have begun to invest their accumulated savings in large homes and small businesses around town, and Mandeville has grown at an unprecedented rate. Tourism has dipped in the last few years, although from the early days of the *Mandeville Hotel* in the 1890s, the town was popular with British soldiers who came to escape the heat of the coastal areas and to recuperate from their fevers and diseases. To this day the town still retains something of its early colonial air – most noticeably at the very English **Manchester Golf Club**, just west of the town centre. For sightseeing, a car is definitely a major asset; although you can see everything in the town centre on foot, getting out to the local coffee **factory** (see page 251) will require your own wheels.

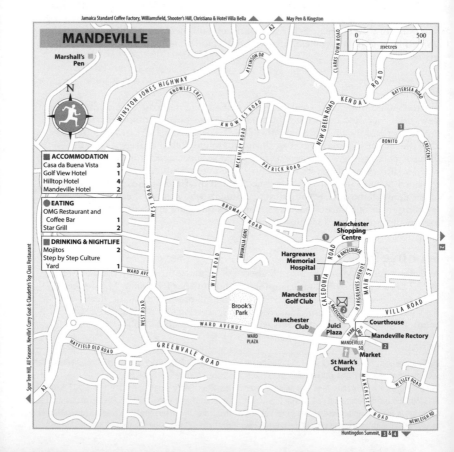

COMMUNITY TOURISM

The creation of big tourist "ghettos" on Jamaica's north coast has completely disrupted traditional lifestyles there and means that, often, the only contact overseas visitors have with Jamaicans is when they're serving drinks or driving tour buses. In the face of its own gradually developing tourist scene, Jamaica's south coast, where the absence of large-scale beach resorts offers visitors more of a feel of the "real" Jamaica, is keen to escape such insensitive development. Planners and hoteliers continue to show increasing interest in the concept of "**community tourism**", which aims to contain and control tourism by fostering closer connections between the tourists and the community. In Mandeville, Diana McIntyre-Pike of **Countrystyle Community Tourism Network** (☏ 507 6326, ⓦ accesscommunitytourism. com) can put together tailor-made tours of the island with themes including "Marvellous Mandeville", for instance, and a trip to Resource Village in Manchester, where you can learn how to make traditional bammy bread. The cost is US$60 per person including lunch and a community/host guide but not transport. She can also arrange homestays (US$40–60).

Mandeville Square

The town's first buildings were set out around **Mandeville Square**, a rather unkempt grassy space now also known as Cecil Charlton Park after a former mayor, and this is the best starting point for a brief walking tour of the centre. Built in 1819, **St Mark's Church** is on the south side of the park, behind the massed ranks of taxis, buses and vendors. The interior is pretty ordinary, but, as usual, there are plenty of goats nosing around in the churchyard, and you could happily spend a few minutes wandering among them and checking out the nineteenth-century tombstones. On the other side of the park, the limestone **courthouse** is one of Mandeville's original buildings, completed in 1820 and still normally crowded, while the **rectory** (now a private home) alongside the courthouse dates from the same year. The nearby **police station** – once the town jail and workhouse – is the last of Mandeville's original structures.

Jamaica Standard Coffee Factory

Main Rd, Williamsfield • Mon–Thurs 9.30am–11.30am or 1.30pm–3.30pm • J$1250 • ☏ 963 4211

The **coffee factory** of Jamaica Standard Products is a couple of kilometres north of the town centre in Williamsfield. The factory roasts, grinds and packages beans for the superior Blue Mountain coffee as well as JSP's own – High Mountain – and Baronhall brands, grown at lower elevations. Since seventy percent of coffee drunk in Jamaica is instant, most of the coffee packaged here is exported – largely to Japan. The hour-long tour of the coffee plant, conducted by staff members and with an entirely uncommercial air, is informative, taking you through all stages of processing from grading the beans to roasting – and the entire place smells wonderful. Tours are by reservation only, and a dress code is enforced – no sleeveless tops, shorts or skirts, no see through clothing or flip-flops. Afterwards you have a chance to buy the products at excellent prices.

ARRIVAL AND DEPARTURE
MANDEVILLE

By bus and minibus Buses arrive and depart from the south end of Mandeville Square. The town's main taxi rank is alongside.

Destinations Alligator Pond (45min); Christiana (40min); Junction (45min); Kingston (1hr 30min); Montego Bay (2hr 30min); Santa Cruz (45min).

By car There are three separate entrances to town signposted from the highway – it's simplest to take the middle one, at the major roundabout, and follow New Green Rd all the way into town.

ACCOMMODATION

Most accommodation in Mandeville is aimed at business travellers, but there are also guesthouses and Airbnb options perfect for anyone just passing through.

6

Casa da Buena Vista 29 Chellaston Drive ☎ 431 7163 ✉ lisa.lueyen@gmail.com; map p.250. Lovely guest-house set on a quiet residential street. Two well-appointed apartments (US$30/day a/c surcharge) with kitchenette, bathroom and living area, sit beside a beautifully landscaped and shaded fruit garden. The included breakfast is delightful, served in the communal outdoor dining room where a constant breeze flows. Hostess Lisa is full of excellent recommendations, and offers car-hire services. US$75

Golf View Hotel 51/2 Caledonia Rd ☎ 962 4477, ⓦ thegolfviewhotel.com; map p.250. Modern, well-equipped hotel designed around a central courtyard with a pool. The en-suite rooms, either a/c or fan, have attractive wood furnishings, cable TV and a balcony, and there's a restaurant and bar on site. US$134

Hilltop Hotel Northern Caribbean University, Manchester Rd ☎ 963 7013, ✉ hilltophotel@ncu.edu.jm; map p.250. Clean, spacious and comfortable en-suite rooms, and a communal kitchen for preparing snacks and hot drinks. Most guests are visitors to the university; staff are friendly and helpful, and panoramic views over Mandeville are incredible. Rates include breakfast. US$75

Mandeville Hotel 4 Hotel St ☎ 962 2460, ⓦ mandevillehoteljamaica.com; map p.250. One of the oldest hotels in Jamaica, this is a pleasant and easy-going place to stay right in the heart of town. The rooms and studios are a bit on the plain side but have amenities such as cable TV. Facilities include a nice restaurant, bar and large pool. US$44

EATING

Mandeville has a couple of good **restaurants** but more fast-food options at the ubiquitous malls (particularly at the Manchester Shopping Centre). The central bus park at twilight is your best bet for jerk chicken and delicious roast yam.

OMG Restaurant and Coffee Bar Cobblestone Plaza, 1 Brumalia Rd ☎ 962 7251; map p.250. This brightly painted, modern restaurant-café serves tasty local and international food at a moderate price – lasagne is J$880, ackee and saltfish is J$560. There is a bar upstairs that serves frozen drinks and wine, and they also serve brunch on Sundays. Mon–Fri 7am–11pm, Sat 8am–2am, Sun 12.30–8pm

Star Grill 20 South Racecourse Rd ☎ 527 5053, ⓦ stargrilljm.com; map p.250. Predominantly a takeaway restaurant that serves traditional Jamaican and international dishes in a lively setting (stewed chicken is J$450, shrimp pasta J$1390). The small dining area on the second floor is outfitted with oversized lanterns and rain curtains. Mon–Thurs 10am–10pm, Fri & Sat 10am–11pm, Sun noon–8pm.

DRINKING AND NIGHTLIFE

As you'd expect from such a peaceful town, Mandeville's **nightlife is** generally tame, but there are couple of spots to look out for, including a Thursday night live reggae band performance at *Step by Step Culture Yard*.

Mojitos Elethe Mall, 25 Caledonia Rd ☎ 622 2352; map p.250. Small bar with a modern feel, about 15min out of town, serving up cocktails (from J$650) and light meals to a dolled-up clientele. Mon–Sat 3pm–midnight, Sun 5.30pm–midnight.

Step by Step Culture Yard Bonito Crescent ☎ 435 1711; map p.250. Enjoy live roots reggae from artist Coco Tea's official recording band, hailing from Mandeville, and performing in their spacious house yard turned bar and concert space every Thursday night.

Christiana

CHRISTIANA is a small market town for the surrounding agricultural community, where potatoes, yams, ginger, coffee and cocoa are grown. Lofty and cool, three thousand feet up in the hills, the town was a popular resort for "old-style" tourism in the 1940s and 1950s, when beaches and tanning were less fashionable than they are today. If you have a car, Christiana also makes a decent base for visiting Appleton and Maggotty to the west (see page 247) or Bob Marley's mausoleum to the northeast in Alexandria (see page 155).

Christiana Bottom

A hike to the lush gorge at **Christiana Bottom** is the big thing to do here. Take a right turn by the post office in town and then follow the left fork at the crossroads to a

> ## DENBIGH AGRICULTURAL SHOW
>
> A three-day fair in the Denbigh showgrounds just west of the town of May Pen, the **Denbigh Agricultural Show** (ⓦ jas.gov.jm/denbigh.html) features displays of agricultural produce from each of the country's fourteen parishes, exhibits of prize livestock and a coronation event for the Miss Jamaica Farm Queen. There's also plenty of live entertainment, including singers, dancers and reggae bands, and the usual array of food vendors and craft stalls. Now in its seventh decade, the show makes for a great family day out; it's normally held over the last weekend in July or the first weekend in August.

6

standpipe where you can park if you're driving (though it's perfectly walkable from the centre of Christiana). Continue down an often muddy track through prolific ferns and bamboo to a **waterfall** and a cold but refreshing pool. (It's not easy to find the way, so if you get lost ask for the "blue hole".)

Gourie State Park

North of town, beyond the village of Coleyville • Daily during daylight hours • Approx. US$30 for two people • Call ⓣ 870 5052 or ⓤ 8/2 8045 in advance and Forestry Department officer Otway Elliott will organize a guide • To get to the park from Christiana, turn left off the main road towards Albert Town at the signposted potato-processing factory; follow the road, bearing left, and keep going until you reach a gate saying Forestry Department

The **Gourie State Park** has a number of lovely hiking trails through its pine woods; the cool air up here makes for especially pleasant hiking. Trails lead into the forest from the gazebo in the clearing at the end of the rough (but driveable) pine-lined road that leads from the entrance gate. To the left of the gazebo are the **Gourie Caves** and **Oxford Caves**, which offer challenging caving, some through underground river pools. The routes are tricky and a guide is strongly recommended.

ARRIVAL
By minibus or route taxi Regular minibuses and taxis run up Shooter's Hill (on the Winston Jones Highway) from Mandeville and head straight into town; expect to pay J$150–300 one way.
By car Turn left off Winston Jones Highway onto the B6.

CHRISTIANA
Turn right at T-junction passing the Pickapepper Factory on your left (staying on the B6). At next T-junction turn left on B5 and head up the hill past Walderston Post Office. Continue onto B10 until reaching the centre of town.

ACCOMMODATION
★ **Hotel Villa Bella** ⓣ 964 2243, ⓦ hotelvillabella. com. The lone hotel in Christiana, *Hotel Villa Bella* is one of the most delightful small hotels in Jamaica. There is no pool or unnecessary trippery, but the place retains a colonial-era feel and is dotted with interesting curiosities – plenty of Art Deco furniture, nineteenth-century china, old prints and the hotel's original guest book from 1941.

Villa Bella is also the best place to organize a guide to take you to Christiana Bottom and Gourie State Park (see above). The *Hummingbird Restaurant* (open for guests only) serves standard international and Jamaican fare at moderate to expensive prices and has a nice indoor dining area (you'll find it's too cold to eat outside in the winter). US$60

CANE-CUTTERS

Contexts

History

The first inhabitants of Jamaica were the Taínos, indigenous Americans who spoke an Arawak language and are thought to have arrived in Jamaica around 900 AD, making their way from present-day Venezuela and Guyana aboard dugout canoes. A peaceful people whose subsistence depended on farming and fishing, they lived in scattered settlements all over the island. Estimates of Taínos numbers at the time of Columbus's arrival in Jamaica are hugely varied, but it's possible that there were as many as a million. Although Taínos living in the small islands of the eastern Caribbean were raided by the reputedly more warlike Caribs, there's no evidence of Carib attacks on Jamaica.

The arrival of the Spanish

Christopher Columbus first set foot on Jamaica on May 6, 1494, when he landed at Rio Bueno on the north coast during his second "voyage of discovery" in search of a western sea route to Asia. He had little interest in Jamaica (which he named Santiago), but claimed it for Spain nonetheless. During his fourth and final voyage in 1503, he made an unfortunate return, his ships running aground on the coral reefs at St Ann's Bay (see page 149), but Spanish settlement of Jamaica didn't begin in earnest until 1510, when a group of settlers from Hispaniola headed by Governor Juan de Esquivel set up a base at Sevilla Nueva, near modern-day Ocho Rios on the north coast, and set about searching for gold. They didn't find any, and nor was Sevilla a good site; surrounded by swampy land, the tiny Spanish population soon found its numbers threatened by fever. In 1534, King Charles I permitted a transfer of the capital, and the Spanish decamped south to Villa de la Vega, known today as **Spanish Town**, which remained Jamaica's capital until 1874.

Though farms were established throughout the island, Spanish Jamaica remained largely undeveloped, serving mostly as a stopping-off point between the mother country and the richer colonies of the Spanish Main. Nonetheless, the Spanish still managed to obliterate almost every trace of the native population, who fell victim to European diseases in their thousands and suffered severely from the legendary cruelty of the Spanish; by the time of the British conquest in 1655, the entire Taínos population had been all but wiped out.

Because the Taínos didn't provide the labour force that the Spanish required, they began importing **slaves** from Africa within a decade of arriving in Jamaica, and there is evidence from this period of the first escaped slaves, the *cimarrones* or **Maroons** (see page 192), who gradually developed settlements of their own and who were to prove a constant thorn in the side of the British after 1655.

900 AD	**1492**	**1510**
Taínos arrive in Jamaica from the South American mainland, naming the island Xaymaca.	Columbus lands on the north coast. A few Spanish remain, and are present 11 years later when he returns and is shipwrecked off St Ann's Bay.	Sevilla la Nueva settlement is established and gold prospecting begins across the island. The first Africans are brought over as slaves.

The British conquest

Spanish Jamaica was not a well-protected colony; in 1596, for example, English adventurer Sir Anthony Shirley landed with five hundred men at Passage Fort near present-day Kingston and completely **sacked** Spanish Town. Spain provided little or no assistance in defending the place, and gave scant impression of caring for its colonists.

In 1654, Britain's "Lord Protector" Oliver Cromwell, distrustful of sections of his armed forces whom he suspected of plotting the restoration of the monarchy, decided to send them against Spain's American possessions, far away from home. The British were well aware of the immense Spanish wealth in the area; for over a century, British pirates and buccaneers like Sir Francis Drake had been making a good living from looting Spanish ships and cities. Cromwell sent fifteen vessels under the command of General Robert **Venables** and Admiral William **Penn**.

After a disastrous first assault on Hispaniola, they set sail for neighbouring Jamaica, which they knew to be a modestly prosperous and poorly defended place, and landed at **Passage Fort** in May 1655. After the previous sackings, there were few Spanish left to fight for Jamaica; the capital was quickly overrun. The Spanish did hold off the British on the north coast, however, and in 1657, forces sent over from Cuba engaged the British at Los Chorreros, present-day Ocho Rios. In 1660, troops led by British governor Edward D'Oyley finally defeated the Spanish at the battle of **Rio Nuevo**, near Ocho Rios. As they fled for Cuba, the Spaniards freed and armed their slaves to continue the fight; these freed slaves proved an important boost for the growing band of **Maroons**. Penn and Venables, meanwhile, returned to Britain with little booty to show for their efforts and, despite the ejection of the Spanish, were promptly imprisoned in the Tower of London.

Port Royal and the buccaneers

Immediately after the British conquest of Jamaica, defence of this newly won prize became the first priority. **Fortifications** were built on either side of Kingston harbour, with five separate forts created on the uninhabited island of **Port Royal**. In 1661, Edward D'Oyley became Jamaica's first non-military governor and, in 1664, the first **local assembly** was summoned. Sir Thomas Modyford became governor and encouraged local **buccaneers** to make Port Royal their base for attacks on Spanish dominions. These buccaneers had started out as a ragged collection of outlaws living on the island of Tortuga; by the mid-seventeenth century, they had evolved into a disparate but skilled collection of pirates, attacking ships around the region. The British saw a way of using buccaneers to their advantage. By giving them official sanction as **privateers** and letting them use Port Royal as a base, they would provide some defence for the young colony; equally important, they would harass the Spanish enemy, attacking their cargo ships, and would be obliged to deliver ten percent of their haul to the British authorities in Jamaica.

Port Royal became a boom town. The security provided by the forts and the wealth of the privateers encouraged traders to set up, exporting sugar and spices and importing slaves and supplies for the growing population. Although Spanish Town remained the capital city, government figures set up home on the island alongside the merchants, and Port Royal became one of the wealthiest places in the world. However, its ascendancy was

1534	1660	1665	1670
Spanish settlement moves south to the location of today's Spanish Town.	A large force sent from England by Oliver Cromwell finally defeats the Spanish at Rio Nuevo.	Port Royal becomes one of the world's wealthiest cities, based on piracy of gold from Spanish ships.	Buccaneer Henry Morgan is rewarded with the Jamaica governorship by the British.

short-lived; a devastating **earthquake** in 1692 plunged most of Port Royal into the sea, and sent its residents fleeing for a new home across the harbour in modern-day Kingston.

Pirate Henry Morgan becomes governor

By the 1670 **Treaty of Madrid**, the Spanish recognized British rule in Jamaica, and the brief era of the privateers was over, though there was to be one last fling the following year. Henry Morgan, most famous of the privateers, launched an attack on the Spanish colony of Panama, sailing from Bluefields Bay on Jamaica's southwest coast. Though he claimed that he was unaware of the peace treaty, Morgan and Governor Modyford were recalled to Britain. Modyford was sacked to appease the Spanish, while Morgan, having insinuated his way into royal favour, was made lieutenant-governor in Modyford's stead, returning to Jamaica with a new brief – to stamp out piracy by persuading his former colleagues to turn to a life of peace.

Naturally enough, many of the privateers, now officially termed "**pirates**" to mark their loss of favour, refused to give up their thrilling and financially rewarding lifestyles and continued to torment shipping in the Caribbean throughout the eighteenth century. But their heyday was past, and a succession of high-profile successes by the authorities – particularly the capture in 1720 of Calico Jack Rackham (see page 202) – inexorably turned the screw on the remaining bandits.

Sugar and development of the Jamaican economy

Though initially unimpressed with his new possession, Oliver Cromwell soon came to appreciate Jamaica's strategic importance, and issued a proclamation encouraging emigrants from Britain and other parts of the Empire with offers of land grants and other financial incentives. Jamaica began to mutate from an insignificant colony into a much-prized possession, and the key factor in this change was **sugar**. Though first planted in Jamaica by the Spanish, cultivation of sugar cane became a major phenomenon only under British rule, and as Europe developed an ever sweeter tooth, the number of sugar estates here grew by leaps and bounds, expanding eightfold between 1673 and 1740. During the eighteenth century, the island became the biggest producer of sugar in the world.

Many of the **planters** were absentee landowners who spent most of their time in Britain and delegated control of their estates to overseers. These planters amassed extraordinary fortunes from their Jamaican estates, and this wealth brought with it significant political power and influence in London. This, in turn, was used to nourish and protect the sugar trade, with huge duties levied on sugar imported from elsewhere and the price of Jamaican sugar kept artificially high. Given the lavish lifestyle led by the planters in Britain, practically none of the profits of sugar were ploughed back into developing Jamaica, although every plantation had its **great house**, the elegant hilltop mansions that still survive to this day.

Slavery

The success of the sugar industry and the wealth of the planters was, of course, predicated upon the appalling inhumanity of **slavery**. The development of the sugar

1692	1729	1739
Port Royal is destroyed by a massive earthquake; its remaining residents relocate to Kingston.	The emerging planter class gains devolved power to form a new Jamaican assembly.	A peace treaty is signed between the British and the Maroons, thus ending the First Maroon War, originally begun in the 1660s.

estates called for a mammoth workforce and, with no indigenous labour available, the planters embarked in earnest upon the importation of slaves from Africa.

The slave journey

The **slave trade** in the Caribbean was dominated by British merchants, whose ships sailed first to the west coast of Africa carrying trinkets and other goods to barter for the human cargo. From Africa, ships loaded with slaves sailed direct to Kingston, the region's key transshipment point, where those strong enough to have survived the **Middle Passage** leg of this transatlantic trade triangle were unloaded into warehouses and sold at auction. From there, the ships would return to Britain, now laden with Jamaican sugar, rum and spices. It's estimated that in total between **twelve and fifteen million** people were transported from Africa as slaves, the majority to the Caribbean and Brazil, and they brought great wealth to the traders, reflected – among other things – in the development of the major port cities of London, Bristol and Liverpool.

Little attention, meanwhile, was paid to the plight of the West Africans, drawn principally from the tribes of the Coromantee, the Fula, the Ashante, the Ibo and the Mandé. As the needs of the colonies expanded, **raiding parties** were sent into the African interior to hunt for more victims, who were marched across the continent to stockades on the coast. From there, the journey to the Americas took between six and twelve weeks with Africans enduring the most deplorable conditions imaginable – kept in chains in the hold of the ship, packed into galleries one above the other and jammed into spaces so small that they couldn't stand or lie at full length. With no sanitation facilities and barely any food, up to two million died of disease or malnutrition; many committed suicide if the chance arose, leaping from the ship rather than continue in captivity.

Plantation reality

Despite the high rate of loss, it continued to be profitable for the slavers to ply their trade, and every year, several thousand Africans survived the Middle Passage to become labourers on the estates or, on a smaller scale, domestic workers in the homes of white settlers. Unsurprisingly, many of those transported – uprooted from home and family and prohibited from using their own language – found the prospect of life on the plantations impossible, and there was continual **conflict** between slaves and slave owners. **Living conditions** for the slaves were invariably squalid, and discipline was brutal, with severe punishments meted out to any wrongdoer – in his 1740 treatise *A New and Exact Account of Jamaica*, Charles Leslie noted of Jamaica's planters that "no Country exceeds them in a barbarous treatment of slaves, or in the cruel Methods that they put them to death". Torture, designed as much to humiliate as to punish, was commonly inflicted, and followed by a slow, painful death.

Slaves were at the whim of cruel overseers, few of whom would ever be called to account, however badly they treated those in their charge. **Religion** went some way to improve living conditions – converted slaves were usually given Sundays off to attend church, while church leaders encouraged planters to treat slaves as human beings rather than "chattels" – and when food supplies to the island were disrupted in the 1770s during the American War of Independence, slaves were often allowed to cultivate and market their own foodstuffs. Yet this was hardly an altruistic gesture – malnourished

1740	1760	1770
Jamaica becomes the biggest sugar producer in the world. The resulting capital underwrites Britain's rise as a world power.	The Tacky Rebellion lasts for five months until a brutal end in Port Maria.	The eight-month-long Second Maroon War takes place in Trelawny.

slaves did less work, so it was in every planter's interest to keep his "chattels" alive at the least possible cost to himself. For every slave owner who made some small effort to ensure the physical well-being of his slaves, there were ten more who cared little or nothing for their condition – it was easier and cheaper simply to buy some more should any slaves die or be put to death. Life on the plantations remained unimaginably horrible for all but the slave owner and his family.

Rebellion

Given the conditions on the estates, it's hardly surprising that **slave revolts** were a feature of Jamaican life from the time of the British conquest right up until emancipation in 1838, always dreaded by the authorities and invariably crushed with appalling brutality. Dissenters were severely flogged and their wounds rubbed with salt, lime and pepper before being slung up from the waist in the sun for several days; they were then taken down to have the soles of the feet and the armpits seared, the heart and entrails removed and burned in front of the alleged "victims" of their crime (if still alive); the heads of hanged or burned slaves were routinely cut off and displayed on poles as a warning to others considering revolt. Despite such grisly punishments, slave rebellions in Jamaica – occurring, on average, every five years during the eighteenth century – were both more numerous and on a larger scale than in the United States or elsewhere in the British West Indies.

There were a number of reasons for this. The island's mountainous **geography** encouraged rebels by providing places to escape and hide, while the high level of absentee slave owners also encouraged revolts either through the cruelty of the overseers or, conversely, because of a lack of attention to the risks of rebellion. In addition, **social and religious ideas** fermented disorder, with abolitionists arguing the case against slavery at the turn of the nineteenth century. Meanwhile, the creation of the first independent black-led republic in the world following Toussaint L'Ouverture's 1799 revolution in **Haiti** provided slaves with a concrete example of a successful revolt.

Though brutally crushed, Tacky's rebellion in 1760 (see page 146) was the major slave revolt of the eighteenth century, while the 1831 **Christmas Rebellion**, led by Sam Sharpe (see page 170), was the most serious slave uprising in the island's history. The scale of the rebellion and the brutality with which it was crushed intensified the abolition debate, both in Jamaica and in Britain, and accelerated the emancipation that Sharpe had been seeking.

Foreign skirmishes and domestic insurrection

The eighteenth century saw the Jamaican authorities plagued as much by the threat of **foreign invasion** as they were by domestic insurrection. Skirmishes with French troops from nearby San Domingo led to a frenzy of **fort building** around the coast (and in parts of the interior, to contain the threat of the Maroons), and all of Britain's great naval commanders served time here, many of them based at Port Royal. The presence of such force undoubtedly contributed to the fact that there was not to be another foreign invasion. Though the French took advantage of Britain's preoccupation

1831	**1832**	**1834**
The Christmas Rebellion unites 20,000 Jamaicans in a revolt against the British; the riots lead to the abolishment of slavery.	Mixed-race "mulattos" are awarded equal legal status to whites.	The Emancipation Act is passed in Britain, officially ending slavery. Forced "apprenticeships" continue until 1838, however.

with the 1775 **American War of Independence** and launched a series of invasions that left Britain's West Indian possessions limited to just Jamaica, Barbados and Antigua, Jamaica itself was saved from invasion by Britain's conclusive victory at the Battle of **Les Saintes** off the Windward Islands in 1782, which saw the destruction of the French Navy by British forces under Admiral Rodney, and removed the threat of attack from the island for several generations.

Planters and "mulattos"

Without the threat of invasion to contend with, the early eighteenth century saw Jamaica consumed with problems more close to home, as conflicts arose between the interests of the early settlers and those of the mother country. As **Creole** society developed, and a new generation of whites who had actually been born in Jamaica grew up, there were increasing demands for political power to be kept entirely on the island. Accordingly, in 1729 the British Crown recognized the **local assembly** as the source of all legislation on Jamaican matters, replacing the Crown's governor as the chief authority on the island.

Throughout the eighteenth century, power remained in the hands of the white planter class, with the right to vote given only to property owners. Gradually, given the sexual proclivities of the planters, who routinely enforced sex on their female slaves (planter diarist Thomas Thistlewood chronicled some 4000 sex acts with 138 women during his time in Jamaica), a "mulatto" or **mixed-race class** emerged who looked to their white fathers for an education and opportunities that were denied to people of pure African origin. Although this mulatto class was not officially granted equal rights until 1832, many of its members exercised considerable political influence and were to prove far more sympathetic to the black cause than white planters had been.

Emancipation

In the early nineteenth century, forces inside and outside Jamaica brought about a sea change in the fortunes of the different racial groups. In 1807 the British parliament prohibited its colonies from trading in slaves, but the **abolition of slavery** itself – heavily opposed by the West Indian lobby, who feared the collapse of the local economy – was not finally passed until 1834. Despite the islandwide jubilation, the slaves were not yet given unconditional freedom; they were expected to continue working for their former masters, unpaid, for a six-year "apprenticeship". In 1838 the apprenticeship system was abandoned and the former slaves were, at last, free to demand wages or work elsewhere. Many left the hated estates at the first opportunity, establishing small farms on squatted or rented land, or settling in the "**free villages**" set up by missionaries throughout the island. Plots of land were either sold or donated to former slaves, who in turn helped to build the church and school that the villages were based around.

Alternative labour

The drain of workers from the estates, and the reluctance of many estate owners to pay proper wages, forced them to turn to alternative sources of cheap labour. Already, during the 1830s, when the white ruling class was keen to avoid seeing Jamaica's fertile interior settled by black ex-slaves, 1200 Germans had been brought to the island and

1845	1860	1865
The migration of 35,000 Indians begins, brought to Jamaica as indentured labourers to sustain sugar production.	Paul Bogle leads a non-violent protest of racial inequality to the governor's office; it is brutally repressed by the British, but leads to civil rights reform.	Cultivation of bananas begins as a new export crop, encouraged by American businessman Lorenzo Dow Baker.

granted land at present-day Seaford Town (see page 188) once they had worked on the estates for five years. Other workers were brought from China, the Middle East and other parts of Europe, but India was to provide the great majority of the new **indentured labour**. Under a scheme approved by the Jamaican assembly in 1845, 35,000 **Indians** were brought to the island before the Indian government banned further traffic in 1917. The estate owners promised that, once the workers had paid off the cost of their passage from India, they would be able to earn decent money to send home, before returning themselves at the end of their contracts. In practice, the Indians became the new slaves – working for scant pay under terrible conditions – and the majority never had the chance to return home.

Sugar starts its decline

The sugar industry took another major blow in 1846, when the Sugar Duties Act forced Jamaica's sugar producers to compete on equal terms with others worldwide; simultaneously, the development of **beet sugar** contributed to a drop in price and reduced demand for cane sugar. Although the industry was far from dead, this series of setbacks forced the island to end its reliance on a single crop. **Banana** cultivation was introduced in the 1860s and, for a while, became the boom crop as demand for the new fruit soared in Europe and America. By the end of the nineteenth century, the older economic pattern of the Jamaican community had faded completely and a new organization was emerging.

Post-emancipation problems

Jamaica's estate owners were given a total of £20 million compensation for the loss of their slaves (most of which went to repay debts owed to merchants in Britain). There was no such compensation for the former slaves, for whom life remained incredibly difficult. Their first problem was **land**. Without somewhere to grow crops, black Jamaicans had little choice but to return to the plantations as poorly paid wage-labourers; getting their own land guaranteed a degree of independence and provided a bargaining tool for higher wages. The planters were equally aware of this issue, however, and made it as hard as possible for the ex-slaves to get land, imposing high rents and taking action against squatters who tried to occupy unused land. The second issue was the one-sided **administration of justice**; the planter class dominated the magistrates' courts and imposed heavy-handed penalties for squatting and other minor wrongs.

Rebels and politics

The downturn in the country's economy that followed the abolition of slavery and the introduction of free trade in sugar also took its toll on the former slaves. Wages were kept pitifully low, taxes were imposed and unemployment rose as plantations were downsized or abandoned altogether. As food shortages intensified, unrest among Jamaica's black population grew, eventually coming to a head in 1865 when the **Morant Bay Rebellion** (see page 101) broke out in St Thomas. Fearing that the uprising would spread throughout the island, Governor Eyre ordered a tough response from the armed forces. Little mercy was shown, as 437 people (including the rebellion's leader, **Paul Bogle**) were killed or executed, and thousands more beaten and terrorized.

1866	1872	1907
Following the Morant Bay Rebellion, Jamaica's legislative assembly is disbanded and direct British rule resumes, with new reforms.	The capital is transferred from Spanish Town to Kingston.	Kingston suffers a devastating earthquake, and two hurricanes follow in the ensuing decade, all increasing poverty.

This brutal suppression caused horror throughout Jamaica and Britain, and provoked change in the colony. Governor Eyre was ordered back to Britain and dismissed for his part in the atrocities, while his assembly abolished itself and, in 1866, Jamaica became a **Crown Colony**, with direct rule from Britain via a legislative council. Although this set back the cause of responsible government on the island for almost a century, it enabled certain reforms to be passed that would never have got past the planters and their representatives in the assembly. New courts were established, a police force created and the Church of England was disestablished on the island. Roads and irrigation systems were improved, more money was spent on education, and in 1872 the capital city was transferred from Spanish Town to **Kingston**. This move was long overdue; most of Jamaica's trade – from slaves to rum – had been processed through Kingston's harbour for two centuries, bringing colossal wealth in its wake, and by any criteria the city was the right place for the seat of government.

There were downsides to the changes, of course. Taxes were raised to finance the reforms, and the unrepresentative political system frustrated the island's fledgling democratic movement for nearly eighty years. On the whole, the new system kept the peace while preserving the status quo; the whites retained all political and social authority, while the blacks were mollified to the point that there was little threat of upheaval for the rest of the century. Nonetheless, landowners bemoaned the government's financial extravagance and inefficiency, while black leaders pointed to the lack of any radical change.

Away from politics, meanwhile, the 1890s saw the arrival of the island's first **tourists**, many sailing from North America on the banana boats that plied between the east coast and Port Antonio in Portland.

Jamaica in the twentieth century

The early twentieth century saw considerable **economic prosperity**, with particular booms in the banana and tourism industries. And the new wealth was no longer confined to the whites – **George Stiebel**, Jamaica's first black millionaire, used his fortune to design some fine buildings, particularly Devon House in Kingston, and his example proved an inspiration to others. Inevitably, though, most of the new wealth bypassed the black masses, and serious **poverty** remained throughout the island. People were increasingly drawn to the new capital city to look for work, but many were left stranded in Kingston slums with little prospect of income or employment. **Natural disasters** also took their toll. In 1907, the capital was partially flattened by a devastating earthquake, and there were major hurricanes throughout the 1910s.

By the 1930s, as the **Great Depression** took hold worldwide, the positive effects of the economic boom had pretty much evaporated. The banana crop had been decimated by disease, and never regained its former export heights, while sugar revenues fell precipitately as demand dried up. Unemployment spiralled, and riots in Kingston and around the island became commonplace, as did **strikes**; in 1938, a major clash between police and workers of the West Indies Sugar Company factory at Frome left several dead. Protests and looting followed islandwide, and in the wake of the dispute, strike leader **Alexander Bustamante** founded the Caribbean's first **trade union** – the Bustamante Industrial Trade Union (BITU). An associated political party was born,

1920	1938	1943
Marcus Garvey begins to preach black consciousness and social upliftment, increasing pressure for political reform.	The Bustamante Industrial Trade Union and Norman Manley's People's National Party (PNP) are founded.	Alexander Bustamante forms the Jamaican Labour Party (JLP) to rival Manley's PNP.

too, with the foundation of the **People's National Party (PNP)** by the lawyer **Norman Manley**. Both events gave a boost to Jamaican nationalism, already stirred by the campaigning of black-consciousness leader **Marcus Garvey** during the 1920s and early 1930s, and increased the pressure for political reform and improvement in the condition of the workers.

World War II and the road to independence

Jamaica served as an important Allied base during **World War II** (and thousands of islanders contributed to the war effort more directly by volunteering to fight for Britain), while the need to provide increased supplies of food to the mother country led to the expansion of sugar and other food industries. Economic development continued by way of both increased tourist arrivals and the emerging bauxite industry, which began commercial export in 1952.

On the political front, a **new constitution** in 1944 introduced universal adult suffrage, and the same year saw the first elections for a locally based government to work in conjunction with the British-appointed governor. The vote was taken by the **Jamaica Labour Party (JLP)**, formed by Bustamante in 1943 after he split from Manley's PNP. The two parties gradually drifted in different ideological directions, with the JLP adopting a liberal capitalist philosophy and Manley's PNP leaning more towards democratic socialism.

When the PNP finally took over the reins at the 1955 election, one of Norman Manley's first priorities was the issue of independence. As it was impractical for Caribbean colonies to "go it alone", the idea of a West Indian confederacy was floated; by 1958, the ill-fated **West Indies Federation** was launched, with its capital in Port of Spain, Trinidad. However, it never really stood a chance. Jamaica refused to accept the principle of federalism, arguing that it must be allowed to protect its own economic interests, even where these clashed with the other islands, while traditional inter-island rivalries left many Jamaicans suspicious that they would have to subsidize their smaller, less successful neighbours. In a **referendum** called by Manley in September 1961, Jamaica voted categorically to leave, prompting the Federation's rapid disintegration. Disheartened though they were, the British had little choice but to accept the decision of the electorate. Within a year they had granted Jamaica its **independence**.

Independence and the Manley era

On August 6, 1962, Jamaica became an independent state within the British Commonwealth, with Bustamante as its first prime minister. The early years of independence were marked by rising prosperity, as foreign investment increased, particularly in the bauxite industry. The JLP continued in power until the key **elections of 1972**, when Jamaicans rejected the JLP's US friendly liberal economic programme and voted in droves for the PNP, now led by Norman Manley's charismatic son Michael. The next eight years of PNP rule represented a crucial period for Jamaica. Until 1972, economic and political power had rested predominantly with white and mixed-race Jamaicans. **Michael Manley**'s rousing slogans, such as "Power for the people" and "Better must come", the latter borrowed from Delroy Wilson's hit reggae tune, exemplified his desire to improve the conditions of the black majority and to challenge the status quo.

1944	1952	1962
Jamaica's first constitution allows for universal adult suffrage. A Jamaican parliamentary election is won by Bustamante's JLP.	Commercial export of bauxite begins for aluminium smelting in the US.	Jamaica achieves independence within the British Commonwealth on August 6, with Bustamante as its first prime minister.

His **major reforms** included a minimum wage, a literacy campaign, the distribution of land to small farmers, more public housing and an improvement in funding for the island's education and healthcare sectors – all of which were financed by businesses that had been largely protected from taxation, in particular the internationally owned bauxite industry. The strategy backfired, however, when the bauxite companies promptly scaled down their Jamaican operations, reducing the country's foreign-exchange earnings, and this blow was compounded when the 1973–74 oil crisis further increased pressure on government spending. In the light of this, Manley sought to promote a greater degree of **self-sufficiency**, encouraging the use of Jamaican, rather than imported, products. In **foreign affairs**, meanwhile, Manley rejected close ties with the US in favour of friendship with Fidel Castro's Cuba. Needless to say, the American reaction was furious; economic sanctions were applied and foreign investment nosedived. Fearing higher taxation and even the introduction of communism, wealthy white Jamaicans left in large numbers, withdrawing their capital and skills at the time they were most needed.

Jamaican politics became increasingly polarized and antagonistic, with the JLP (by now led by **Edward Seaga**) launching blistering attacks on the "communist" administration. The 1976 election – won by the PNP again – saw a disturbing increase in **political violence**, particularly in the ghetto constituencies of Kingston, which the political parties had turned into "**garrisons**" by distributing guns to their supporters and encouraging them to drive away opponents through intimidation. Manley's response to the violence was to impose a **state of emergency**, establishing a non-jury "Gun Court" and passing severe anti-crime legislation that allowed it to impose life sentences for anyone convicted of unlawful possession of a firearm.

The PNP's **second term** sounded the death knell for Manley's brand of democratic socialism. Foreign investment had fallen precipitately, local capital had been withdrawn from the island and, despite the empty shelves in the supermarkets, the cost of imports continued to outstrip exports. The government turned to the International Monetary Fund for assistance, and the resulting curtailment of public spending and the drastic cuts in social programmes alienated many erstwhile supporters. Violence flared again during the 1980 election campaign, with hundreds of people killed in shoot-outs and open gang warfare. Amid the carnage, the Jamaican people turned to the JLP for a new vision for their country.

The JLP in power

The first foreign leader to visit the newly elected President Ronald Reagan in Washington, Edward Seaga's **realignment** of the two neighbouring countries was perhaps his most important change in policy. The US took steps to open its markets to foreign imports and to encourage outward investment, most notably with the enactment of the Caribbean Basin Initiative (economic aid in return for free elections and cooperative governments), and foreign capital began to find its way back to Jamaica. However, Seaga was obliged to continue the cutback of government services, and his honeymoon with the Jamaican people proved short-lived. A snap election in 1983 was boycotted by the PNP, but, as re-elected prime minister, Seaga was unable to give the island's economy the boost it required, and rising poverty and unemployment combined with his lack of charisma led to a fall in support. In 1989,

1972	1973	1974
At the election, Jamaicans reject the JLP's US-friendly economic policy and vote in Manley's son on a socialist PNP ticket.	Withdrawal of the bauxite companies combined with the international oil crisis creates serious recession in Jamaica.	Support for Castro and Cuba leaves Manley and Jamaica under US sanctions. Wealthy Jamaicans begin leaving en masse.

Michael Manley was returned to office, and the PNP were to remain in government for the next eighteen years.

The PNP years

Despite widespread fears of a return to the politics of the 1970s, the new-look Manley administration proved very different. The emphasis now was on continuity of policy, and although foreign relations with Cuba were restored, there was no more anti-American rhetoric. The demands of the World Bank and the IMF continued to be met and a generally liberal economic policy followed. In 1992 Manley resigned the premiership on the grounds of ill health, leaving his successor, **P.J. Patterson**, to continue the policy of continuity. The first black man to become Jamaica's prime minister, Patterson went on to defeat Seaga and the JLP in the 1993 general election, a loss from which Seaga never fully recovered; having lost successive elections in 1997 and 2002, Seaga resigned from politics in 2004.

Despite having limped to victory for a further two terms, the PNP received a much-needed shot of adrenalin in 2006, when Patterson resigned as the PNP's leader and **Portia Simpson Miller** became Jamaica's first female prime minister. Far removed from the white (or nearly white), male, upper-class hegemony that has dominated Jamaican politics since independence, and employing plenty of Christian rhetoric along with the spin, "Mama P" initially proved hugely popular. A tightly contested election in 2007 brought the JLP into power for a term, but Simpson Miller was returned to office at the beginning of 2012. Perhaps due to Jamaicans realizing that the parties no longer offer any discernible ideological difference – or that a history of election violence had brought little in terms of pay-off – the late 2011 poll was the least violent in the country since 1972.

Jamaica today

Twenty-first-century Jamaica is an intriguing mix of extreme juxtapositions. This tiny developing country with its brutal history of slavery and social injustice has nonetheless managed to produce a succession of truly remarkable writers, musicians and athletes, not to mention dictating many of the defining features of youth culture the world over, from dreadlocks to pseudo-patois and musical inspirations. But for all its successes and its sense of inherent hipness, contemporary Jamaica presents serious challenges.

The Jamaican economy

The backbone of the island's economy now rests on bauxite, tourism and the **remittances** that overseas Jamaicans send to family back home, the latter two each accounting for a colossal thirty percent of GDP. A huge amount of money is spent on promoting Jamaica as a **tourist** destination, and a steady increase in visitor arrivals (over two million overnight visitors in 2016, plus over a million more cruise ship passengers) is no doubt affirmation of the immense appeal of Jamaica's cultural and physical attributes. **Bauxite** production has long recovered from the blow the industry took in the 1970s, although sharp falls in prices worldwide following the recession have meant lower earnings overall – and as the island's processing plants are foreign-owned, aside from wage labour relatively little of the industry's profits remain in Jamaica.

1976	1980	1988
With Manley's PNP winning the election against Edward Seaga's JLP, Kingston communities become political "garrisons", with violence between the two parties.	Seaga's JLP comes to power amid a bloodbath on the streets. Realignment with the US brings foreign capital but continued spending cuts.	Hurricane Gilbert strikes Jamaica head-on, the worst storm in decades, with 200 deaths and 400,000 left homeless.

USAIN "LIGHTNING" BOLT

Born in 1986 in Sherwood Content, a quiet, rural community in Cockpit Country, sprinter **Usain Bolt** grew from humble beginnings into one of the world's most successful and best-known athletes. After running track at William Knibb Memorial High School in Falmouth, Bolt moved to Kingston to train with the prestigious Jamaica Amateur Athletic Association (JAAA). From then onwards, beginning with the 2002 World Junior Championships, Bolt's skill on the track was practically superhuman. In 2008, he competed in his first Olympic Games, setting three world records and garnering three gold medals – in the 100m, 200m and 4x100m race. He found similar success at the 2012 and 2016 Olympics, resulting in a "triple-double," so called because he won the gold medal at all three competitions for both the 100m and 200m. By 2016, Bolt had snagged a staggering **eleven world titles**, the most ever achieved. Announcing his retirement from the international games in 2017, Bolt set his sights on playing **professional football**: he has reportedly been in talks with Sir Alex Ferguson about signing for Manchester United.

The potential of **agriculture** remains vast, with great products and superb farming conditions. Non-traditional exports such as ackee and seafood have made significant increases in recent years, while premium Blue Mountain coffee continues to fetch high global prices. However, the gradual phasing out of preferential tariffs to European markets for Caribbean producers following a WTO ruling – in effect ending four hundred years of colonial trade – has left much of the Caribbean reeling. In Jamaica, banana exports all but collapsed, unable to compete with huge operations in Latin America by three US giants. Nonetheless, since 2012 bananas have made a limited comeback, exporting to non-producing Caribbean islands and also value-added juice extract to international markets. The impact on the **sugar** industry was more far-reaching, with overseas aid and loan-based bailouts preventing the industry from total disintegration. In 2011 the JLP sold the (formerly public) Sugar Company of Jamaica to a Chinese firm, which so far seems to have released much-needed investment (see page 224), and ethanol production (as a gasoline additive and as a cleaner-burning fuel) is now tipped as sugar's saviour in the future. Ultimately, small-scale farming remains as it does for much of the world – a difficult way of life that's subject to the volatility of climate change and international trade markets. That said, Jamaica is an incredible fertile island, and the majority of backcountry residents earn at least a bit of their income from farming, plus practically everyone has a fruit tree or two in the backyard to help put dinner on the table.

Jamaica's foreign **debt burden** is unfortunately now US$9.4 billion and unemployment stands at around twelve percent; the glamour of the tourist resorts belies a lot of poverty both in Kingston and rural areas. Government debt repayment and spending has been justified by significant expansion of mass tourism, with concessions to unscrupulous developers at the expense of environmental quality and small-scale fishing. New Chinese involvement in infrastructural, heavy industrial and agricultural projects is seen as either saviour or peril depending on which side of the political fence you stand.

1989	1992	2006
After a decade of deep austerity and social tension, Manley is returned to power in a more centrist administration.	P.J. Paterson becomes Jamaica's first black leader, taking over the PNP from Manley. He remains prime minister for fourteen years.	Portia Simpson-Miller, Jamaica's first female prime minister, takes over the PNP leadership, but loses the 2007 election to the JLP's Bruce Golding.

Crime, violence, and drugs

A major issue for most Jamaicans – and the one that makes the most headlines overseas – is **crime**: despite recent improvements the island still has the sixth-highest per capita murder rates in the world – around 1200 per year, or three per day, and a terrible reputation for violent crime in its inner cities. The "garrison communities" established during the 1970s are run by gangsters known as "area leaders" or dons, and they – with the help of their contacts in every walk of Jamaican life, from the police to the government to the army and coastguard – have turned the island into a key trans-shipment point for cocaine being smuggled from South America to the US, with criminality brought to sophisticated and brutal levels. In 2011, images of street battles between the Jamaican armed forces and the biggest don's ghetto army were beamed around the world; his eventual arrest led to his extradition to the US.

This appears to have tempered the scale of downtown Kingston's organized crime – at least far more than previous initiatives such as **Operation Kingfish** were able to (where British police officers were installed within the Jamaica Constabulary). Cynics, however, point to the fact that the police fatally shoot at least two hundred Jamaicans each year as evidence that so-called **vigilante justice** has been unofficially adopted as the principal way for the police to deal with violent crime. The 2014 case of Mario Deane may have brought things to a head on this matter: the 31-year-old, arrested for a cannabis joint in Montego Bay was found dead in his cell, with police first alleging he had fallen from his bunk and then asserting he had been beaten by cell mates. In 2015, the Jamaican government moved towards decriminalizing marijuana; possession of two or less ounces is now treated as a petty offense (a ticket instead of jail time), and residents are permitted to grow up to five ganja plants at their property. The move, met with jubilation and relief among Jamaicans, aims to pave the way for the on-island development of medical marijuana facilities, as well as, more importantly, give a bit more breathing room to the countless Jamaicans who value this part of their culture.

Sport and culture

In the sports arena, Jamaica has plenty to celebrate. The island's **athletes** provoked ecstatic national celebration at the 2012 Olympics in London, notching up four each of gold, silver and bronze medals, with unrivalled sprinter Usain Bolt (see page 266) accounting for three of the golds and successfully defending his world records achieved at Beijing in 2008. Bolt solidified his place in the history books at the 2016 Olympics, when he completed a "triple-double", snagging gold medals for the third time in both the 100m and 200m race. Team Jamaica also consistently wows at the World Championships, with numerous medals. Sporting success is a truly awesome feat for such a tiny nation, especially one that doesn't have the resources of economic strongholds such as the US and the UK. Culturally, too, Jamaica remains a world leader, with the country's musicians – from the pre-eminent Bob Marley and his son Damian "Junior Gong" to countless dancehall DJs and roots artists – topping the charts in every corner of the globe.

2011	2012	2015
Chinese company COMPLANT buys the Sugar Company of Jamaica, in effect ending five hundred years of state involvement in the sugar industry.	The PNP and Portia (as she's known across Jamaica) return to government on a ticket of lower crime and Chinese cooperation.	Marijuana is decriminalized: carrying two ounces of ganja for personal use is legalized, and residents are permitted to grow five plants per household.

The environment

From parched savannah plains and dry limestone forest to low-lying rainforest and wetland swamps, with richly vegetated, undulating hills and lush pastures in between, Jamaica's landscape and topography vary immensely, and harbour a rich array of plant, bird and animal life.

With a total area of more than sixteen hundred square kilometres, Jamaica is the third-largest island in the Caribbean archipelago, after Cuba and Hispaniola. Unlike many of its neighbours, however, more than half of it stands over 1500ft above sea level, providing mist-shrouded peaks as well as brilliant white-sand beaches. Other than the metamorphic, sedimentary and igneous volcanic rocks of the Blue Mountains – Jamaica's oldest geological feature – most of the island's surface area is covered with soft, sedimentary **limestone**, at its thickest in central and western areas such as Cockpit Country, where rivers have carved out a labyrinthine network of conical hillocks surrounded by deep sinkholes and caves.

Trees and shrubs

Though Jamaica's deforestation rate is high, some thirty percent of the island is still shrouded in a thick cloak of trees, and even in urban areas, there's plenty of green to be seen. Trees are often planted for their shade-giving properties; the **guango**, with its bromeliad-smothered spreading branches, is common, but the most arresting and majestic is the towering **silk cotton**, which often reaches more than 130ft in height, its huge buttressed roots spreading elegantly to meet the ground. Naturally buoyant and easily carved, silk cottons were hollowed out into dugout canoes by Taínos, and their fruits contain the cotton-like kapok. **Logwood** is extremely common and was once grown commercially for the dark-blue dye extracted from the trunk and roots. In 1893 it surpassed cane and coffee as the island's main export, but synthetic alternatives subsequently ended the trade. Bees flock to the perfumed yellow blossoms, and logwood honey is said to be the best available. The **annotto** was also exploited for the intense orange-red dye extracted from seed pods growing in clusters around its attractive pink flowers. Taínos used it as their principal body paint and it was a prime commodity during Spanish occupation, though it's extremely rare today.

You'll encounter the marbled, blue-tinted wood of the **mahoe**, the national tree, in countless craft items. Fast-growing and indigenous, the mahoe has a short straight

---

THE HURRICANE EFFECT

Jamaica's geographical location and geological origins make the island highly susceptible to the elements, particularly during the rainy seasons (roughly May–June and Sept to mid-Oct), when tropical waves, as storms are called, cause islandwide flooding, landslides and road closures. These are mere trifles, though, in comparison to the devastation wrought by the **hurricanes** that blow through the region between June and November each year. Though many bypass the island entirely, Jamaica has suffered extensive hurricane damage over the years, most notably from **Allen** in 1980, **Gilbert** in 1988, **Ivan** in 2004 and **Dean** in 2007, the latter sweeping through the south and east coats and causing such devastation that Prime Minister Portia Simpson-Miller postponed the general election and declared a month-long state of emergency while the island licked its wounds and repaired the worst of the damage. Ivan, meanwhile, was even more devastating, resulting in seventeen deaths, thousands of destroyed homes, power lost for days and severe damage to banana, coffee and sugar production, fisheries and roads.

> ## ALOE VERA
>
> Jamaicans are so convinced of the curative power of fast-growing **aloe vera** or "sinkle bible" (a corruption of the botanical name *sempervivum*) that many dispense with titles altogether and simply call it the "healing plant". Noticeable for its thick, spiny-edged clusters of leaves growing close to the ground, aloe is the workhorse of Jamaican healing. It's used to treat sunburn (for which it's particularly effective), heat rashes, cuts, bruises, burns and all insect bites; mixed with water to make an eye wash that soothes conjunctivitis; used to condition sun-damaged hair; prepared as a treatment for skin conditions like eczema and psoriasis; and drunk with garlic to cleanse the blood – a daring feat, as it's very bitter.
>
> Rastafarians use aloe in place of the biblical hyssop for purging or purification. Aloe plants flourish throughout the island and in rural areas you can usually get a stem for free; it's much more effective (and hygienic) to use aloe straight from the plant than in a preparation. To extract the gel, slice the stem in two, cut off the serrated edges, lightly scrape the mauve jelly and wipe it on. Be careful not to get it on clothing – it can leave a stubborn stain.

trunk that grows up to 65ft, broad leaves and distinctive hibiscus-like flowers that change from yellow to orange and deep crimson as they mature. The rich red wood of Jamaican **mahogany** is regarded as some of the best in the world, but has been so heavily exported that few trees are left – the custom of stripping the bark from young trees to extract a dye also helped to decimate populations. Those remaining grow in remote areas such as Cockpit Country and the Blue and John Crow mountains, and can attain a height of 130ft.

The archetypal Caribbean tree, the **palm** comes in numerous shapes and sizes. Ornamental varieties include the **royal palm**, a 100-foot-high specimen that's often planted along driveways to impressive effect; close relative the **cabbage palm** manages a whopping 130ft and has thicker, messier-looking fronds. There are several pseudo-palms in Jamaica, of which the most attractive pretender is the magnificent **travellers' palm**, a member of the banana family – the name refers to mini-ponds at the base of the leaves that provide a convenient water source. Fronds fan out from the base in an enormous peacock's-tail shape that can measure 30ft.

Flowering trees and shrubs

If you fly over Jamaica's interior or look closely at any rural panorama, you'll notice occasional patches of deep red, courtesy of the **African tulip** or "flame of the forest"; flowering sporadically throughout the year, its clusters of blooms often cover entire outer branches. Known for the gorgeous crown of deep-scarlet blossoms that adorn many a hotel garden, the **poinciana** or "flamboyant tree" also produces long brown seed pods, often polished and used as shaker instruments. More familiar as a Christmas pot plant in temperate climes, the **poinsettia** grows into a lovely tree here, with a huge spread of bright green leaves that turn deep red in the cooler winter months. Twenty-nine varieties of **cassia**, meanwhile, provide showy cascades of blossoms, most commonly in pink or yellow; equally common is the **bauhinia** or "poor man's orchid", a prolific purple-flowered shrub with cloven-hoof-shaped leaves. The blossom of the tree of life, **Lignum vitae** – so called because of its many medicinal uses – is Jamaica's **national flower**, a subtle, light-blue shower. Highly resinous, its wood is heavy enough to sink in water and was extensively used in shipbuilding and as a suitably painful material for truncheons.

Fruit trees

Bearing Jamaica's national fruit, the ubiquitous **ackee** is identifiable by its crimson seed pods, which burst open when ripe to reveal the edible yellow arils. Almost as prevalent are the spreading branches of the **breadfruit**, decorated by serrated, hand-like leaves and pockmarked, matte-green fruits. **Cashew** trees are common and produce both fruits and nuts. Similar in appearance to red ackee pods, cashew "apples" produce the nut but can also be cooked and eaten. The oily liquid in the shell is poisonous, while the sap produces an indelible ink. The source of many a souvenir, the large globular fruits of the **calabash** are hollowed and dried for use as dishes and containers, or filled with pebbles to make maracas. **Cocoa** trees are easily identifiable, with shiny dark-green or red leaves and ten-inch oval pods that grow in clusters from branches or sometimes the trunk, turning from light green to brown when ripe; the sweet pulp around the beans inside can be eaten when raw.

Versatile **coconut palms** are everywhere, with every part of their fruit used – be it for food or floor mats. The Jamaica Tall coconut palm has been largely eradicated by lethal yellowing disease (you'll see the frond-less trunks dotted around) and has been widely replaced by the hardier hybrid **mayapan**, a squat ten-footer with straggly yellowed leaves and orange-tinted nuts. Diminutive **guava** trees grow wild throughout the island and are also cultivated commercially for their green-skinned, pink-fleshed fruits, but the king of the fruit trees is the **mango**, in many varieties, with their dense covering of finger-like leaves and branches heavy with fruit during the summer season.

Coastal trees

Jamaica's surviving **mangrove swamps** are central to the health of coastal ecosystems, affording protection from hurricane surges, filtering earth sediments and nutrients and providing a protected nursery for fish and crustaceans. Nonetheless, those on the north coast continue to be under an unprecedented and short-sighted assault for hotel resort development, which began in the mid 1990s and which has seen fish stocks plummet, with small-scale fishing livelihoods taking a hit. Elsewhere, mangrove has also been cleared for sand mining, or removed for use in charcoal kilns. Though not naturally a coast-dweller, the **Indian almond** flourishes along the length of Jamaica's shores. Branches grow symmetrically, and the nuts can be eaten once the outer pods turn brown. A staple of all Jamaican beaches, the **sea grape** varies considerably in shape according to its environment; on exposed shores it lies low and twisted, but with less buffeting it can attain a height of 50ft. The flat, round leaves are distinctively veined and turn a deep red as they mature. Once they've turned purple, the grapes are edible, if a little sour. Fortunately very rare and definitely one to avoid is the **manchineel**,

---

GANJA CULTIVATION

Jamaica's most infamous crop, **ganja** (marijuana) is not particularly easy to raise; many cultivators liken the task to bringing up a sickly child. Seeds must first be carefully germinated, then planted in open ground and stringently guarded against pests and birds. As buds attain maturity, farmers spend increasing amounts of time at the plot, feeding, watering and tending the crop as well as defending the valuable stems against thieves. Some farmers use pesticides and expensive conventional fertilizers, though this is frowned upon and seen to taint the real thing; organic fertilizers like bat guano are preferred to ensure top potency. Though there are two annual growing seasons, ganja is mainly reaped between August and October, when the buds have received the full benefit of the long summer sun. Plants can reach a height of 7ft, and are usually grown among other tall crops in remote and usually small plantations. After harvesting, the outer leaves are discarded and the potent buds hung up and cured.

Growers can face losing all in **eradication programmes** conducted by the Jamaica Defence Force as the fields reach maturity. Helicopters scour the hills for plantations, while ground crews sweep the countryside burning or spraying the plants with herbicide. Unscrupulous soldiers are known to accept a bribe in return for burning only a portion of the fields or not arresting the farmer, though as many policemen sell or smoke cannabis themselves, undocumented and profitable confiscations are reputedly common. That said, since decriminalization in 2015, you can no longer be locked up for growing for personal use – all residents are legally allowed to raise five plants. You now see marijuana growing where you never did before, and it feels like every household has a plant or two.

which grows to about 40ft, with a wide-spreading canopy dotted with indistinct green fruits and flowers, all of which are extremely poisonous – even standing below a manchineel during rain incurs blistering. Luckily, you're only likely to chance upon a manchineel in the most remote areas, and even there, run-ins are extremely unlikely.

Plants

Of Jamaica's abundance of plants, some of the most striking are the **cacti** that flourish in the dry scrub of the Hellshire hills and south coast plains. Some, such as the two **dildo** varieties, grow as tall as 20ft, stretching skywards between clumps of viciously thorned **makko** bushes. The inner stems of **torchwood** cacti are dried and lit as home-made torches in rural areas and bear a yellow fruit, while the **dildo pear** has a red fruit; both are edible. **Prickly pear** and the "smooth pear" or **cochineal cactus** are also common, the latter known as "roast pork" for its taste when cooked. Of climbing varieties, most spectacular is the **queen of the night**, which boasts a huge and powerfully scented flower that only blooms after dark. The endemic **god okra**, with its edible stems and crimson fruits, is often vested with supernatural powers as its aerial roots spread so far over rocks and trees from their triangular main stem that they appear to have no earth to support them. The epiphytic **spaghetti cactus**, meanwhile, has 6ft skinny green stems that hang down from dead or living trees, and bears miniature white flowers and berries. The flat-lobed prickly **tuna** cactus is widely used in bush medicine, said to cure dandruff, reduce swelling and relieve chronic pain.

Jamaica's **vines** are equally unusual. The rampant forest **cacoon** has a huge circular bean pod the colour of a burnished conker, while strings of shiny red and black seeds from the **John Crow bead vine** turn up on craft stalls islandwide. The rare, triffid-type **duppy fly trap** bears the largest flower in Jamaica – an eight-inch, purple heart-shaped centre from which 23-inch fly-catching spurs extend. A rotting-meat odour attracts flies to the inside of the flowers, where they are covered in pollen and released to pollinate other plants. Growing prolifically throughout the island, the mimosa family's fascinating **shame'o'lady**, resembling a miniature bracken, closes its leaves to expose thorns on its stem at the slightest touch as protection against foraging animals. Equally intriguing is the epiphytic **wild pine bromeliad**, its 3ft pineapple-like leaves flourishing wherever there's a tree to host it. The rainwater collected between the leaves supports a variety of insects and even frogs, and the most protected specimens boast a pale crimson flower.

Flowers

Jamaica's rich soil supports 3003 varieties of flowering plant (twenty-eight percent of which are "endemic", or only found in Jamaica), from the lavish exotics of the lowlands, exported worldwide, to the delicate irises, begonias and azaleas of cool mountain climates and the hibiscuses, ixoras and bougainvilleas that feature in almost every garden. A favourite of hotel landscapers, the brush-like deep-pink bracts of the **red ginger** hide the small, white true flower that grows from each tip once fully open. A close relative is the **torch ginger**, which boasts one of the showiest heads in the world, a deep-crimson cluster of thick waxy petals nestled among leaf blades that grow to 15ft. Also ubiquitous are the forty vividly coloured varieties of **heliconia**. Most popular are the various red shades of aptly named **lobster claw** and the red, gold and green cascade of the **hanging** heliconia, which looks like a series of fish hanging from a rod. Equally prevalent is the **anthurium**, a heart-shaped and shiny red, pink or white bract with a long stem protruding from the centre, and the spectacular **bird of paradise**, a mauve, bent stem which resembles a bird's head graced by a deep-orange crest.

Jamaica boasts 237 species of **orchid**, approximately 25 percent of which are endemic; many are so small that you'll need a magnifying glass to appreciate them, such as the pea-sized **Lady Nugent's purse**, commonly seen in the Blue Mountains and Cockpit Country.

BUSH MEDICINE

Many Jamaicans, particularly in rural areas, still make frequent use of "**bush medicine**" or "**balm**". A system of African herbal medicine introduced to Jamaica by slaves, it was fundamental to Maroon civilization for three hundred-odd years and is used to treat anything from the common cold to impotence. Herbs are taken as an infusion or decoction (usually as a tea), as a poultice, or in a hot "bush bath". Many households have a pot of cure-all **bush tea** permanently on the hob, made up of diverse ingredients like lemon, fevergrass, soursop, breadfruit leaves and pepper elder. Perhaps the most widely used single herb is **cerassee**, a climbing vine made into a very bitter tea – you can buy ready-made teabags if you develop a taste. It's said to cure practically everything, but is particularly good as a blood purifier and allegedly discourages mosquitoes.

Inevitably, there are loads of plants geared around **male virility** – chainy root, jack-in-the-bush, medina, janta (or cow-hoof leaf), quassia – the list of "front-end lifters" goes on and on, and many concoctions are now commercially bottled (see page 29). Ganja is boiled into a tea for asthma and eye problems; **leaf of life** is said to conquer colds, hypertension and bronchial problems; **tuna cactus** is used to treat dandruff, nerves and chronic pain such as arthritis. Many of the medicinal herbs have wonderfully fanciful names; among the best are **search mi heart** and **shame'o'lady**, both used for colds and stomach problems, but the prize goes to **ram goat dash along**, good for arthritis and debility.

Healing properties are also attributed to simple **fruits and vegetables**. Soursop is said to calm the nerves, and its leaves are used to help testy babies go off to sleep. Papaya (paw-paw) is reputed to relieve indigestion; guava leaves are good for diarrhoea; tamarind soothes itchy skin and chicken pox; and coconut water cleanses the bladder.

Hedges and fences are beautified by several varieties of flowering shrub; the ubiquitous bougainvillea ranges from red to deep magenta, white, orange and pink. **Hibiscus** take on an abundance of hues and shapes but are distinguishable through the generic pollen-tipped stamen that grows from the centre. The lacy coral hibiscus has a cluster of tiny curling red petals and an unusually long stamen topped by another red frill, and there are hundreds of hybrid varieties.

Fauna

Aside from its creepy crawlies and bats, Jamaica's animal life isn't as noteworthy as its flora, and there are few large mammals. **Camels** made a brief and inopportune appearance in the eighteenth century, transported by planters to carry sugar and rum on the estates, but their preference for smooth ground and sand dunes made them unsuited to Jamaica's uneven and precipitous terrain. They spooked other livestock and had more or less died out by the late nineteenth century, when historian Edward Long described them as "the most useless animals on the island". Planters also introduced the **mongoose** in 1872, which quickly wiped out the Jamaican cane and rice rat population, as well as decimating the island's snakes. Together with rats and mice first introduced via the galleys of Spanish ships, burgeoning populations of mongoose pose a significant threat to other Jamaican creatures, including the hutia or **coney**, a nocturnal rabbit-sized rodent that lives in hollowed trees or rock crevices. The only other indigenous mammal is the **bat**, of which there are 21 varieties; Jamaicans call them all "rat-bats" (the country's huge moths are called rat-bats, too). Some bats are solitary tree-dwellers, but huge colonies inhabit Jamaica's caves, from which their droppings, or guano, have been harvested as a fertilizer, particularly prized for its effect on ganja plants.

Birds

Approximately 250 species of bird frequent Jamaica's skies, though many are migratory or come to the island only to breed. There are 25 indigenous species and 21 varieties found nowhere else in the world, which represents a greater level of endemism than in any other Caribbean island. Quick-moving, brightly coloured **hummingbirds** epitomize Jamaican bird life at its most spectacular; the red- or black-billed streamertail, or **doctor bird**, is the national bird, though only males have the characteristic trailing double tail-feathers (reminiscent of an old-fashioned doctor's coat) and iridescent green breast. At under two inches, the **vervain** or bee hummingbird is the second-smallest bird in the world. Its darting aerial techniques, surprisingly loud squeaky call and insect-like buzzing are far more notable than its grey-brown plumage. Another common nectar addict (and a frequent visitor to hotel breakfast terraces), the black-and-yellow **banana quit** punctures flowers with its curved bill and often hangs upside down from a twig to ensure a favourable feeding position, while glossy black, sharp-beaked **greater Antillean grackles** are to Jamaica what pigeons are to England. Noisy and social, they live in groups and their harsh clacking call, broken by a gentler whistle, forms a constant background music. Commonly seen around cattle, the **white egret** often roosts on a ruminating rump in a mutually rewarding relationship that provides the egret with a constant supply of insects and the cow some relief from bloodsuckers.

Few sights are more evocatively Jamaican than the sight of a distant **John Crow vulture** swooping high over the hills. Though ugly and awkward on the ground, this scavenging carrion bird comes into its own in the air as it scans the land for the scent or sight of dead meat. Typically scrawny, its messy black plumage and bald red neck and head make it a convenient euphemism for people considered dirty, lazy or ugly. Easily recognizable by its harsh rasping cry is the 2ft **red-tailed chicken hawk**, dark brown and black with a white breast and russet tail feathers, which feeds on rats, mice and occasionally chickens. Jamaica has two types of night-hunting **owl**, both surrounded by superstition. The eerie cry of the **"screech owl"**, or white owl, is said to bring bad luck, despite its useful function as a vermin exterminator, while the **Jamaican brown owl** or "patoo" feeds on moths and lizards, and has a deep, hoarse cry that's said to be a harbinger of death and destruction – it's certainly disquieting on a dark night.

Reptiles and amphibians

There are 24 species of **lizard** in Jamaica including the **iguana**; the rare endemic Jamaican version, *Cyclura collei*, grows up to 5ft in length. However, most of the lizards you'll see are one of the seven varieties of *Anolis*: *lineatopus* has a mixed pattern of brown markings, while *Anolis grahami* and *garmani* are bright green and can darken their skin if threatened. A variety of gecko, **croaking lizards** provide a throaty night-time call and are extremely common. There are six species of **snake** in Jamaica, none of which are poisonous. The largest is the Jamaican **yellow boa**, which grows to around 7ft and is bright yellow/orange when young, maturing into a beautiful yellow and black; during the day it rests in trees and sinkholes and is rarely seen. Popularly called the trophy dophy, the **thundersnake**, cream-coloured with rows of brown squares along a russet stripe, is said to be able to soothe sprains; chunks of its body are marinated in white rum, which is rubbed into the skin – its willingness to be handled makes it easy to catch. Jamaica's two species of **grass snake** (*Arrhyton funereum* and *dromicus*), also known as black snakes, both attain a size of about a foot and are uniformly brown with a white underside; they're found under logs or leaf litter.

A south coast swamp inhabitant, the American **crocodile** was so extensively hunted that it's been classed as endangered and protected by law since 1971. The Black River Morass is one of the last places it lives wild, growing up to 12ft. Generally nonaggressive unless threatened, Jamaican crocodiles live mostly on small fish. There are 22 varieties of **frog** in Jamaica. Since their introduction in 1890 by the then-governor's wife Lady Blake, who apparently found their sound soothing, whistling frogs provide a regular night-time chorus throughout the island. There is one variety of **toad**, commonly called "bull frog", introduced from Barbados in 1844 as an insect killer, but most often seen squashed flat on country roads.

Insects

By far the most noticeable Jamaican insects are the 120 varieties of **butterfly** and **moth** ("rat bats" to Jamaicans), which appear in all shapes, sizes and colours. Most striking but extremely rare is the 6in **giant swallowtail** butterfly, seen only in the lower slopes of the eastern John Crow Mountains, matched in size by the multiple species of giant moth. **Spider** species are comparatively few, and though there are none of the huge and hairy tarantula types, there are some pretty big ones; the orange, red and black **silk spider** measures around 6in. Its many-layered webs are an arachnaphobe's nightmare; at 3ft wide with attachment lines extending as far as 6ft, they have been known to trap small birds. Encountered only by the foolishly inquisitive, **brown** and **black widows** live under rocks and leaves and, though dangerous, do not carry a fatal bite. Often referred to as "white ants", Jamaica's seventeen species of **termite** construct the lumpen nests you'll see on tree trunks.

Marine life

Much diverse marine life is found around Jamaica's reefs. The sixty or so coral varieties include rotund **brain** coral, patterned with furrowed trenches; branching umber **elkhorn** and **staghorn**; stalagmite-like **pillar** coral; and cool-green **star** coral. Extremely striking are the **gorgonian** group of intricate soft coral **sea plumes**, **sea whips** and purple **sea fans**. Around the reefs, brilliant yellow **anemones** and red, brown, purple and green **sponges** provide a splash of colour, some growing up to three feet in diameter. **Crabs**, **Caribbean spiny lobsters** and spotted **moray eels** inhabit the crevices between corals. Harmless unless provoked, when they can inflict serious bites, morays open and close their mouths in a constant snarl as they draw oxygenated water over the gills. The patches of sandy seabed and sea-grass fields between harbour spiny black **sea urchins**, and the less spiky round white urchins. **Sea cucumbers** are long, thin and off-white, sifting through the sea floor to feed on deposited nutrients, while five-armed orange and green **starfish** and queen **conch snails** move slowly along, encircling grass blades with their stomachs to ingest encrusted organisms. One of the most stunning inhabitants of the sea floor is the flat manta or **stingray**, often partially buried in sand. Though nonaggressive, it has a serrated tail-spine that is venomous but can only be used if the ray is partially immobilized by a bite or a badly placed foot.

Despite the effects of overfishing, there are still over seven hundred varieties of fish in Jamaican waters. The commonest include multicoloured **parrot** fish, electric-blue creole **wrass**, red and yellow **snappers**, ornate **damselfish**, striped **grunts**, glassy **sweepers**, spiny **puffers**, and rarer **tarpon** and **trigger fish**. The slender yellow and blue **trumpetfish** suspends itself vertically in the water awaiting smaller victims to drift by and into its mouth. Larger specimens include **grouper**, **jackfish**, **kingfish**, **tuna**, **marlin**, **bonita** and **wahoo**. The scourge of spear fishermen, silvery-sleek predatory **barracudas** impart a nasty bite if provoked, though the common **nurse shark** is benign unless attacked or cornered. In deeper water, **dolphins** are a common companion to boats.

Though increasingly rare, hawksbill and loggerhead **turtles** still lay their eggs on Jamaican shores, despite the continuing threat of capture. The Caribbean **monk seals** that once inhabited offshore cays are now believed to be extinct, and Jamaica's cutest sea mammal, the **manatee**, or sea cow, is extremely endangered; there are only about a hundred left in Jamaican waters, mostly along the less-developed inlets of the south coast.

Threats to the environment

The Jamaican environment has long suffered the effects of unplanned development and a lack of environmental awareness. Few of its **reefs** are now the beautiful underwater gardens presented on hotel brochures, and what is left is under serious threat. Studies report that 95 percent of the island's reefs have been damaged over the last twenty years as a result of overfishing (and destructive practice), as well as sand mining, coral collection, industrial pollution and mass tourism. Dynamiting and chemical bleaching – stunning fish up to the surface for an easy catch – are thankfully now rare, but had a disastrous effect on reefs, which depend upon clean, clear water for their survival. A symptom of high sea temperatures worldwide, coral bleaching is reported on ninety percent of reefs around Jamaica's shores – killing the algae within the polyps and starving the still-living coral.

On land, **deforestation** and its associated problems are a major concern. Slopes stripped both by human hand and as a result of hurricane damage are overly susceptible to soil erosion and landslides, threatening hundreds of already rare animal and insect species and wreaking havoc with the island's ecosystems. Deforestation has been particularly severe in the Blue Mountains, which represent the watershed for the entirety of eastern Jamaica, causing annual droughts and floods. For an island with such a high rainfall, Jamaica is in the perverse situation of facing a permanent drought entirely of human making. In the Yallahs Valley, a century of misuse – slopes cleared for coffee cultivation or slash-and-burn farming techniques – has left the area vulnerable to the torrential rainy season deluges, which have flooded the valley and dumped huge amounts of earth onto former farmlands, leaving the slopes above bald and impossible to cultivate. The situation became so desperate that the government intervened as early as 1961, creating the Yallahs Valley Land Authority to rehabilitate the area through planting Caribbean pine, mahoe and eucalyptus to restabilize the slopes, although a lack of funding has resulted in poor maintenance and the flooding is ongoing.

Bauxite mining, meanwhile, has come at a heavy price: caustic red mud deposits are often inadequately disposed of and seep into the watersheds to poison rivers and lakes. Elsewhere, though eighty percent of household waste is collected by the government, the remaining twenty percent is simply dumped in open areas and gullies, resulting in poor hygiene, increasing levels of vermin and polluted water.

Non-governmental organizations

Thanks to the efforts of **nongovernmental conservation organizations**, there has been a marked increase in public awareness of environmental issues over the last decade. Jamaica has established three **national parks** (Montego Bay Marine Park, Negril Marine Park and the Blue and John Crow Mountains National Park), while areas offshore of Oracabessa, Portland Bight and Bluefields – in St Mary, St Catherine and Westmorland parishes respectively – have also been designated protected areas for fish and reef conservation. A number of further sites are proposed for protected status, including Black River and the coastline around Port Antonio. In 2017, after years of debate, Cockpit Country won itself a protective boundary, eliminating the threat of bauxite and limestone mining in the region – a huge coup for this slice of Jamaican wilderness, which boasts hundreds of endemic species and a number of sacred Maroon heritage sites. The Goat Islands recently received similarly good news: in 2016, the government ditched plans to build a huge transshipment port here with the Chinese government, and in 2017, word was received that the islands would officially be declared a wildlife sanctuary.

ENVIRONMENTAL AND CONSERVATION ASSOCIATIONS

Environmental matters in Jamaica are the responsibility of the **National Environmental Planning Agency** (Ⓦ nepa.gov.jm), which ensures (with sometimes negligible success) sustainable development and devises and enforces environmental legislation. The **Jamaica Conservation and Development Trust** (Ⓦ jcdt.org.jm), has responsibility for Jamaica's national parks, among other things, while the website of the **Environmental Foundation of Jamaica** (Ⓦ efj.org.jm) has links to some of Jamaica's many environmental NGOs, which are useful for obtaining information on specific environmental concerns throughout the island; the **Jamaica Environment Trust** (Ⓦ jamentrust.org) is another source of up-to-date information on environmental issues.

Religion

With over 250 denominations and the world's highest number of churches per capita, religion is a Jamaican vocation, and in this fundamentally non-secular society, faith features in every aspect of daily life. Popular ideology is governed by biblical dogma, and most Jamaicans are devoutly religious and have an astonishing ability (and propensity) for quoting lengthy passages of scripture. Sunday piousness is fervently observed, reggae stars devote entire performances to unadorned preaching and the most popular newspaper agony columnist is addressed "Dear Pastor". Churches are at the heart of all Jamaican communities, providing subsidized housing, education, healthcare and a strong social focus – and this centrality is fundamental to Jamaican religion, in all its myriad forms.

Religious development

The antecedent of most contemporary Jamaican religious groups and Christian sects is a wider **African religious tradition** that arrived with the first wave of slaves. As the white ruling class didn't deign to give their "chattels" Christian religious instruction until the late eighteenth century, African religions flourished under the British plantocracy, with the constant influx of new slaves keeping belief systems and practice alive – something the planters attempted to quash by banning drumming and persistently breaking up ceremonies.

Moravian, Baptist and Methodist **missionaries** began arriving in the late eighteenth century, however, and slowly set about proselytizing increasing numbers of slaves, while also attempting to convince the planters that slavery in itself was inherently unchristian. A mass church culture was born, and as Sunday mass became the only sanctioned gathering for slaves, it planted the seed for the abolishment of slavery, as firebrand preachers used their sermons to whip congregations into political action.

After slavery was abolished, the British took a belated interest in the spiritual lives of black Jamaicans and tried to "civilize" them into orthodox Christianity, but the majority of former slaves preferred to practise aspects of their folk culture or combine their traditions with western Christianity. The time was ripe for a uniquely African–Jamaican phenomenon. Some twenty years after the abolition of slavery, a new **religious fervour** swept Jamaica, initially carried along by the momentum of the newly popular Native Baptists and other Christian denominations but essentially resting upon the Revival, Pukkumina, Zion and Myal Afro-Jamaican religious groups that have remained active in Jamaica ever since. The **Great Revival** of 1860–61 was one of several religious revivals (others took place in 1831, 1840, 1865 and 1883) that signified a resurgence both of religious practices banned under slavery and of a desire among blacks to rediscover and celebrate their African origins. It marked the beginning of a Jamaican religious tradition that threatened carefully constructed colonial hierarchies, and white Jamaicans were horrified at this "grossly perverted religious fervour" and "scenes of debauchery and hideous caterwauling".

The Native Baptist Church

By the end of the nineteenth century, the white Jamaican elite was panic-stricken by the phenomenal popularity of the church led by self-declared messiah **Alexander Bedward**. His August Town branch of the Native Baptist Church adapted conventional theology, proffering a combination of black power and faith healing – Bedward blessed the waters of Hope River and thousands flocked to Kingston for baptism or a miracle cure. He also prophesied that he would sprout wings and fly to Zion on December 31, 1921, and Bedwardites from all over Jamaica and the Caribbean descended upon Kingston to witness his departure; Bedward stayed put, but used the mass gathering as an opportunity to spread the message. Inevitably, Bedward's black-nationalist tendencies led to several clashes with the state; in 1895 he was tried for sedition but acquitted on the grounds of insanity, and eventually he was arrested as a vagrant and committed to Kingston's Bellevue asylum, where he died in 1930.

Christianity

Christianity arrived in Jamaica with the Spanish, who built the island's first **Roman Catholic** church at Sevilla la Nueva in St Ann (see page 151) in 1524. The British promptly outlawed Catholicism in 1655, and it was not freely practised again until 1792; of the eighty percent of Jamaicans who describe themselves as Christian today, only around six percent are Catholic.

The British divided the island into the ecclesiastical **parishes** that remain today and established what later became known as the **Anglican Church of Jamaica**. Other groups include the Baptist Church, first brought to Jamaica by African-American ex-slaves George Lysle and Moses Baker in 1783. The **Native Baptist movement**, as it was then known, incorporated numerous African rituals into more orthodox forms of worship and was widely supported at its peak, with impressively large and still-functioning churches springing up all over the Jamaican interior throughout the nineteenth century. Baptist preachers, such as Sam Sharpe and Paul Bogle (see pages 170 and 101), were instrumental in the revolts that led to the abolishment of slavery and post-abolition rights in Jamaica; the Baptists were also the first to set up **free villages** for former slaves, and became a main instigator and provider of free education for black Jamaicans.

Approximately ten percent of Jamaicans are **Methodists**, which in Jamaica is a faith strongly influenced by the African religious tradition and often connected to Revivalism (see below). Methodism arrived on the island in 1789, when missionaries from the Wesleyan Missionary Society set up the Coke church in Kingston, and assured potential converts that their own religious traditions would survive within the ambience of the Methodist Church.

In more recent years, the fundamentalist tenets of US Bible-Belt churches have also proven immensely popular, with many Jamaicans becoming **Seventh-Day Adventists** and **Jehovah's Witnesses**, while the Pentecostal Church and the Church of God also have significant followings.

Revivalism and Kumina

Essentially spiritualistic, the **Revival** movement combines African and European religious traditions into a uniquely Jamaican form. It centres on the African acceptance of a synthesis between the spiritual and temporal worlds, an animist philosophy of a supernatural power that organizes and animates the material universe. Spirits are seen to have a distinct influence upon the living and, accordingly, must be respected, pacified, praised and worshipped through ritual dances, offerings and prayer. There are two branches within Revivalism: **Zionism** and **Pukkumina**. More overtly Christian, Zionism deals only with the heavenly spirits and angels of the Bible, while the more African Pukkumina worships earthbound "ground spirits" such as deceased ancestors. Known as bands (the collective plural is always used), Revivalist congregations have a female (**mother**) or male (**shepherd** or **captain**) leader who acts as general adviser and governs meetings. Ceremonies are held in consecrated **mission/seal grounds** or

poco yards, which are specifically designated by spirits and marked by a tall central pole flying coloured flags to attract passing spirits and identify the site. The **tabernacle** – decorated with symbolic candles, fruits, herbs, flowers and holy pictures, and containing an earthenware jug of water used in the rituals – is either in the open air, a temporary bamboo structure or, increasingly, a concrete building. Liturgies include the singing of "**Sankeys**" (hymns penned by the American evangelist Ira David Sankey), dancing, drumming, clapping, and multiple-spirit possession (sometimes called **trumping**). Once inside a physical host, the spirit becomes an adviser to the whole flock and is controlled by the shepherd, who interprets messages received in tongues or through the movements of the possessed. The drumming, chanting and dances are all of African origin, as are the traditional goatskin burru or kette drums (see page 284). Today, Revivalism is concentrated in the eastern end of the island, and its followers wear flowing white or coloured robes and cover their heads in a turban-style wrap.

Usually described as the most African of Jamaican religious groups, **Kumina** (also concentrated in the east) is less formally organized than Revival. Though still centred on connections between spiritual and temporal worlds and the evocation and worship of ancestors, it focuses on music to a far greater extent – call-and-response chants backed by complicated, hypnotic drumming rhythms provide the music for the worshippers, who dance around the drummers in a ring and often "catch the spirit", as possessions are called. Though a relatively obscure practice today, Kumina has made an indelible mark on Jamaican culture; the intricate and precise patterns of its **drumming** have had far-reaching influence upon latter-day forms such as reggae, and Jamaica's national dance company, the NDTC, incorporates numerous Kumina movements into performances.

Obeah

Obeah or "science" (from the Ashante term *obayi*, meaning a malicious spirit) is the belief in a form of spiritual power that can influence events – from curing disease to providing good fortune or wreaking revenge. Though dismissed by many as nonsense – and theoretically outlawed, though prosecutions are rare – obeah, or "duppy business", is taken seriously, and it's not uncommon for Jamaicans, particularly in rural areas, to call upon the services of an obeah practitioner, who (for a fee, of course) will invoke or dispel a curse. They often give their supplicants bags of special powders – comprised of roots, herbs, ashes, earth (perhaps grave dirt), blood, feathers – to sprinkle on the subject and bring on the desired effect, which is reversible only by a more powerful obeah-man.

The jiggery-pokery of obeah also manifests itself in ghosts or **duppies**, as they're called in Jamaica. The idea of the duppy originates from the African belief that each person has two souls; after death, one goes up to heaven while the other may linger in the temporal world and can be easily persuaded by an obeah-man to do good or evil to the living. Believers consult obeah-men if they feel they've been "fixed" or cursed, and there are countless rituals, charms and substances used to ward off or invoke the spirits. A traditional superstition warns that when walking on lonely roads at night, you should carry handfuls of stones or matches and drop them as you go to ensnare any inquisitive ghoul – unable to count beyond three, the duppy is forced to remain on the spot in a perpetual inventory.

Alongside the ghosts of regular people, there are also specific fiends that haunt children's bedtime stories and have become intermeshed with Jamaica's folklore and culture. The **Ol' Hige** is a bloodsucking hag who leaves her skin at night to seek out succulent babies and feast on their blood. A crossed knife and fork and Bible kept near a child's crib are said to ward off her attentions, but she can only be stopped by finding her skin and dousing it with salt and pepper. The **Rolling Calf** is a night phantom that appears as an enormous red-eyed bull draped with clanking chains and walking with

AFRICAN DEATH RITUALS

Believed to be a prime time for the release of wicked duppies (evil spirits; see page 278), **death** in Jamaica is traditionally surrounded by rituals designed to smooth the passage from one world to another. If a death occurred at home, mirrors were turned against walls to prevent reflections that could portend further deaths, and the house was ritually swept out with new palm brooms. The deceased would be washed by two family members who began at the head and feet and met in the middle, and the body was then placed with their head at the foot of the bed to confuse any lurking duppies. These practices are fast dying out, however, but one tradition that's still often observed is the **Nine Night**, originally staged over the nine days and nights following a death. During this time, friends and relatives meet to remember and celebrate the deceased and ensure that their duppy doesn't return to haunt the living; food is cooked and consumed, stories told, sound systems are played and rum is imbibed. One of these nights is starkly differentiated from the rest, however: on the evening known as the "dead yard", candles are lit, there is no music, drinks or food, and the tone is quiet and meditative.

a sickly rolling gait; to see it is dangerous and to be attacked means certain death. The only duppy to appear during the day, the **River Mumma** combines the African belief in a river spirit with the Western mermaid legend. Appearing as a ravishing young woman, she sits near deep pools on river banks and exposed rocks, bewitching passing males with her beauty; once beguiled, the love-struck victims are pulled down to the river bed and drowned.

Rastafari

From the reds, golds and greens that colour everything from dresses and jewellery to shop hoardings, the outer trappings of Jamaica's most visible religious movement are on proud display across the island. **Rastafari** has influenced all aspects of society, from art to politics, academia, language and particularly music, but the movement was not always looked upon favourably. The last sixty years have seen a complete societal volte-face from widespread revulsion and persecution (a favourite police pastime in the 1960s was to arrest Rastas on ganja charges and shear off their locks – as sacrilegious as the cutting of hair is to Sikhs) to the warmly embraced acceptance and respect for Rastas that you'll find in Jamaica today.

The expression of Rastafarianism is both varied and diverse. Visitors to the island may see dreadlocks and assume the wearer is Rastafarian. But there are actually as many Rastafarians without dreadlocks as there are Jamaicans with dreadlocks who are not Rastafarian. Rastafarianism is as much a way of life as it is a religion or a belief structure. It is up to each Rasta to create his or her own way, embracing the tenets that she or he has aligned with – it is an individualistic religion. Some Rastas will be vegan; some only consume raw foods; some will eat meat or fish. But all Rastas have a consciousness around a natural (or "Ital") way of eating and being. Rastas are mindful of what they put into their bodies as well as the environment around them. They work to "live clean", both in home and body. Another important principle of Rastafarianism is the belief that there is no afterlife. To Rastas, heaven isn't a concept of "where you go when you die" – heaven is here and now.

Garvey's prophecy and Haile Selassie

The Rastafari faith has its roots in the teachings of black activist and National Hero **Marcus Garvey** (see page 150). He advocated an anti-imperialistic, pro-black philosophy and prophetically urged Jamaican followers to "Look to Africa, where a Black King shall be crowned." When **Ras Tafari Makonnen** was crowned Negus of Ethiopia in 1930, taking the title **Emperor Haile Selassie**, King of Kings, Lord of Lords, Conquering Lion of the

Tribe of Judah, many Jamaicans looked to their Bibles and interpreted his title as proof of divinity. Garvey was christened the Black Moses and Selassie became a messiah sent to redeem black people from their suffering at the hands of white oppressors.

Rastafari places Africans as the direct descendants of the original Hebrew Israelites, and Africa as the promised land, offering a restructuring of black identity and an emphasis on black culture lost and maligned by centuries of "slave mentality". As a colonized country, Jamaica is part of the white, Western system of corruption and "downpression" – **Babylon** – which will ultimately destroy itself through its own innate wickedness in an appropriately apocalyptic manner.

Except for Bobo Ashantis (who look to Prince Emmanuel; see page 282), the first tenet of Rastafari is the acceptance of Haile Selassie as the second coming of God, or **Jah**. The **Kebre Negast**, the Ethiopian version of the Christian Bible, places him in a legendary line of Ethiopian kings stretching directly back to King Solomon and the Queen of Sheba; it states that the Ark of the Covenant (and therefore the God of Israel) rests in Ethiopia rather than Jerusalem, and that Selassie was the 225th incarnation of the divinity – a latter-day Christ. Selassie never acknowledged himself as a god and was said to be frightened rather than gratified by the adulation he received.

Repatriation and the Babylon shitstem

A second central doctrine of Rastafari is African **repatriation**. This became a real possibility through Haile Selassie's gift of land at Shashamene in Ethiopia for black people to return home to. Though the few who made the journey found life in Shashamene considerably harsher than it was in Jamaica, the belief in Africa – particularly Ethiopia or **Zion** – as a spiritual home persists amongst all Rastas. More recently other groups of Jamaicans have settled quite successfully in Ghana. Younger followers, though, largely point to Selassie's 1966 public comments, in which he advised Rastafarians to "liberate themselves in Jamaica": the new cry of "liberation before repatriation" emerged in the 1970s. Traditionally, Rastas do not vote and refuse to enter the corrupt world of "politricks", but following Selassie's words, the movement became intensely political, with popular adherents such as Peter Tosh publicly decrying the manifestations of the bloodsucking Babylon "shitstem" (system). This politicization was taken further early in the new millennium, with several Rastas standing for office in local and national elections. Meanwhile, Rasta groups appealed to their head of state, Queen Elizabeth, for reparations to compensate for slavery; the request was denied on the grounds that the UK "can't be held responsible for something that happened 150 years ago". Reparations talks remain on the table, however, and the Jamaican government was actively pursuing them in 2017.

Early advocates

One of the most provocative early sympathizers with the **Rastafarian** movement was **Claudius Henry**, head of the self-made Kingston-based African Reform Church and something of a charlatan. Aligning himself with Rastas through public speeches on white corruption and the necessity of repatriation, in 1959 he enraged the poorest sections of Jamaican society through the sale of thousands of cards purporting to be tickets back to Africa. Hundreds of eager exiles sold up and descended upon Kingston on October 5, only to be disappointed as Henry reneged on his promises. The movement was further discredited when Henry's church was raided and a quantity of detonators, guns, swords and conch shells packed with ganja were seized. Henry was imprisoned, but reports that his son was training a crack team of armed Rastas in preparation for an overthrow of the government led to a national manhunt and an islandwide state of emergency – a public-relations disaster for a movement that prides itself on pacifism and tolerance.

Among early Rasta elders of a more sincere nature, **Leonard Howell** stands out as one of the most influential father figures. He established a Rasta commune at **Pinnacle**, an abandoned great house near Sligoville in St Catherine, where converts lived a self-sufficient lifestyle praising Jah, growing food crops and cultivating ganja. Despite countless police raids, the community flourished for more than thirteen years until Howell's 1953 arrest and permanent committal to the Bellevue asylum. Those Pinnacle members who were not incarcerated drifted back to the slums of west Kingston, establishing the Back'o'Wall and the Dungle strongholds described in Orlando Patterson's seminal novel *The Children of Sisyphus* (see page 294) and setting up Jamaica's oldest Rastafarian camp at Bull Bay, east of Kingston. (Howell's descendents still occupy the land to this day, however, and the Jamaica National Heritage Trust declared the site a national monument in 2009.)

Politricks, reggae and resistance

By the late 1950s, Rastafari was a serious faction in the volatile sphere of Jamaican religion, with at least fifteen different sects practising in Kingston alone. Yet the wider view, fuelled by hysterical press reports, was of a drug-crazed, violent underclass plotting the mass murder of white Jamaicans. Police harassment ensued throughout the 1960s, with Rastafarian communities bulldozed without notice and countless followers beaten, thrown into jail and relieved of their locks. However, come the 1970s, things began to look more favourable for Rastafarians. Poor Jamaicans in their thousands began to identify with the movement's militant analysis of a wicked state and its apparent disdain for the lot of the black sufferer. Michael Manley was the first politician to use the Rasta faith to his advantage. During a visit to Ethiopia in 1970, Manley was presented with an ornamental staff by Haile Selassic, a sacred relic that

---

RASTA RITUALS

Most Rastafarians abide by **basic principles** based on interpretations of the Bible. Proverbs 15:17 – "Better is a dinner of herbs where love is, than a stalled ox and hatred therewith" – is the source of the strict **Ital** (natural and unprocessed) **diet**: no salt in cooking, no meat (pork, lobster and shellfish are particularly avoided, though many Rastas eat small fish – anything larger than twelve inches is probably predatory and representative of cannibalistic Babylon), and few dairy products. Animal by-products such as lard are also prohibited, as are alcohol, cigarettes and chemical stimulants. However, **ganja** – or "herb", as Rastas prefer to call it – is seen as a religious sacrament, as referred to in Psalms 104.14 "He causeth the grass to grow for the cattle, and the herb for the service of man." Though many followers smoke pretty much continually to aid their meditations, or "reasonings", ganja is primarily used at prayer meetings, when the communal pipe (chalice, cutchie or chillum) is stoked with the finest herb available, blessed with a prayer and passed round the group. Alleged to have first grown around King Solomon's grave, the "holy herb" is said to enable deep penetration of thought as well as permitting a higher level of spirituality that transcends the petty distractions of the Babylonian world. **Reasoning** is central to the Rastafari faith, designed to reveal truth and elucidate the wickedness of the world and the Rasta position within it. Alongside these ad hoc sessions, Rastafarians hold more organized gatherings, centred on drumming and reasoning and known as **grounations** or **nyabinghis**.

Dreadlocks are also believed to be a biblical directive; Leviticus 21:5 commands that "They shall not make baldness upon their head, neither shall they shave off the corner of their beard, nor make cuttings in the flesh." Orthodox Rastafarians cover their hair in a wrap or a knitted hat called a **tam**, believing it indiscreet and immodest to show it off. The reference to cutting the flesh informs Rasta opposition to surgery; most prefer to trust in herbal **bush medicine** and supplement their diet with a variety of stamina-building fruit drinks and herbal tonics such as the "roots wine" concoction consumed by Rastas and nonbelievers islandwide.

Finally, the Rastafarian **colours** of red, black, gold and green have a deep significance. Red symbolizes the blood spilled in Jamaican history, black is the African skin of 97 percent of the population, gold is the hope for the victory over oppression and green represents the fertile land of Jamaica – and Ethiopia.

he dubbed the "**Rod of Correction**" and transported to every election meeting in every small village during the 1972 election campaign. Always up for a little showmanship, Jamaicans greeted the appearance of the sacred rod with evangelical fervour, and Manley reinvented himself as the Rastas' ally, employing their lexicon in speeches and calling himself the "people's Joshua", able to lead Jamaicans into deliverance. He swept to victory on election day with the tacit support of the Rastafarian community and its many sympathizers.

Governmental recognition of Rastafari was lent untold weight by the worldwide influence of **Bob Marley and the Wailers**, who brought international attention to Jamaica and forced an acknowledgement of the movement's legitimacy at home, and suddenly – almost overnight – the tide of public antipathy turned. Dreadlocks became chic, and reggae Jamaica's number-one export, but these halcyon days were short-lived. Conspiracy theories about infiltration by the CIA were supported to a degree even by Manley, who believed that his programme of "economic socialism" was deliberately destabilized by the US government. Twinned with the death of chief ambassador Marley in 1981, this general degeneration meant a loss of international prominence and local momentum, but Rastafari continues to develop its political and ideological strategies on home ground, remaining one of the most unique and fascinating of contemporary religions.

Though true figures are probably far greater, it's estimated that there are around 100,000 Rastafarians in Jamaica today.

Sects

Though there have been many attempts to coordinate the Rastafarian movement, there are hundreds of divergent belief strands, sects and methods of worship. Some prominent Rastas (including several of the Marley family) have moved towards the more Christian-oriented **Ethiopian Orthodox Church**, while others have joined the **Twelve Tribes of Israel** sect (as Marley himself did for awhile). Well-organized and well-connected, Twelve Tribes is now one of the more prosperous branches of Rastafari, with chapters in the UK and America. Members are encouraged to read a chapter of the Bible every day and are assigned a name and a colour based on twelve "houses" related to birth months and corresponding to the twelve tribes.

Another important sect, the **Nyahbinghi** look to Haile Selassie as an embodiment of the almighty, and cover their dreadlocks with tams. Generally self-employed and individualistic, the group comes together for events such as the Ethiopian New Year or Selassie's coronation, holding five- to seven-day long ceremonies where the drumming is continuous and the fire is not allowed to die. These celebrations, also called Nyahbinghi, are set in large, round buildings called "tabernacles".

At the other end of the spectrum, members of the reclusive and strictly orthodox **Bobo** sect are the high priests of Rasta, following the teaching of the late Prince Emmanuel Charles Edwards in choosing to reject wider society and live self-sufficiently in semi-rural communes called **camps** (the largest being at Bull Bay, just east of Kingston), wearing their locks wrapped tightly in a cloth turban rather than the conventional knitted tam, and sometimes dressing in long, flowing robes. Members sell palm brooms and leather sandals made on site, which can be used to purchase foodstuffs that the commune is unable to produce.

Music

Close your eyes practically anywhere in Jamaica and you'll hear music. Radios blare on the street, minibuses pump out nonstop dancehall and, come Friday or Saturday night, the vibrations of a thousand sound systems waft through the evening air. Music is a serious business here, generating an average of a hundred record releases per week (the highest anywhere in the world) and influencing every aspect of Jamaican culture from dress to speech to attitude. Reggae, and specifically DJ-based dancehall, dominates, but Jamaicans are catholic in their musical tastes: soul, hip-hop, jazz, rock'n'roll, gospel and the ubiquitous country and western are all popular.

The evolution of Jamaican music

Jamaica has long been a musical island. The simple rhythms of the Amerindian Taínos were adopted by the Maroons; and the drumming, Coromantee chants and songs of their Myalist religious ceremonies and related **Kumina** dance movement became the island's first established musical form. Principal instruments included the bamboo and Coromantee nose flutes, abengs (cow horns), conch shells and strum-strums – home-made banjos fashioned from a hollowed calabash strung with horsehair. These provided the melody, but by far the most important instruments were the gumbe and ebo **drums**, supplemented by **percussion** from shakers, scrapers and graters. But while the Maroons were sounding their drums and abeng horns through the hills, plantation slaves were expressing themselves in a considerably more restricted environment. Recognizing the drum as a principal instrument of African warfare, the British tried to smother the provocative music of their minions, going so far as to prohibit "the beating of drums, barrels, gourds, boards or other such-like instruments of noise".

Yet African musical traditions survived, most notably in the annual **Jonkonnu** masquerade parade, contemptuously dubbed "Pickaninny Christmas" by the whites. Jonkonnu was originally a religious ceremony using music and dance to evoke spirits

---

TRADITIONAL JAMAICAN DANCE

The syncretism of African and European culture in the plantations and beyond is particularly visible in Jamaican traditional **dance**. Much of it emanates from the moves performed at Myal or Revival religious ceremonies, and most dances are purely African, often revolving around "dip and kotch", up-and-down movements or shuffling, hip-swinging styles that parallel the counter-clockwise movements of ritual dance. One of the most interesting dances is **etu**, traditionally danced at Nine Night ceremonies (see page 279). It revolves around a process called "shawling", where the Revival Queen throws a scarf around the neck of a fellow dancer who is ceremoniously dipped back, giving each individual a chance to demonstrate some solo footwork from the standard pose of a slight but flat-footed bent-kneed crouch. Still actively practised in Portland, **brukins** is danced to celebrate the emancipation of Africans from slavery; groups of red and blue sets perform in a mock contest before the king and queen of each colour.

Many of Jamaica's most well-known dance forms are incorporated into performances by the island's professional dance companies, and you can see practically every style ever danced at the annual Heritage Festival held each summer in Kingston.

– and named for its principal rhythmic component, the jawbone of a cow or horse played by scraping a stick across the teeth – and appropriated on the plantations to become a secular travelling pantomime. It incorporated British fife and drum marching rhythms and featured the fixed characters of a cow- or horse-headed leader followed by a king, queen and policeman, with companies of **Set Girls**, grouped by coloured sashes and skin tone. Jonkonnu has pretty much died out today, although it is resurrected as a tourist attraction around Christmas time. Other celebrations, such as those marking the end of the plantation year, were more European in flavour, with English maypole and morris dancing, and French quadrilles.

Folk songs

Another significant development was the rise of the **folk song**, created by workers in the cane and banana fields as a way to alleviate the arduous hard labour – an oral tradition that survives today. In the enormous canon of Jamaican folk music, there are traces of African, British, Irish and Spanish musical and vocal traditions, and heavy doses of Nonconformist hymns, arrangements and singing styles. Each of these influences is blended with characteristic Jamaican wit, irreverence and creativity. There are songs for courting, marrying, digging, drinking, playing ring games, burying – and just for singing, too. One of the all-time classics is "Hill and Gully Rider", a timeless ode to transport on an island strong on hills and weak on roads.

Reggae roots: burru to mento

After emancipation, the arrival of free African workers rekindled support for the less European aspects of Jamaican music and society. The Great Revival of 1860–61 (see page 276) saw a massive resurrection of support for Myal, Kumina and Afro-Pentecostal religious forms, all of which used drumming, chanting and singing as an integral part of worship. The new prominence of the master **burru** drummer and his topical, wickedly humorous social commentary signified the return of the **drum** to the heart of Jamaican music. A version of the West African griot (a travelling one-man information agency who brought gossip and news to rural communities), the burru man originally accompanied fertility rites and played in plantation cane fields to keep machetes swinging to a steady pace, but later became a sort of smutty strolling minstrel. Characterized by their innuendo and wicked wordplay, burru songs dealt with situations seen as taboo in everyday speech. Musically influenced by Pukkumina and Revivalist drumming, the burru man would accompany himself on a three-part set of drums known today as **akete**, beating out complicated rhythms that would eventually work their way into Rastafarian music and develop into ska, rocksteady and finally reggae.

Over time, burru men added a booming rhumba box (a wooden box with a hole on one side covered by metal strips that are plucked for an elementary bass sound) and home-made bamboo fifes, piccolos and fiddles to their repertoire. By the turn of the twentieth century, groups of burru men were banding together to perform at jump-ups and parties, singing souped-up and sophisticated versions of traditional folk songs – burru had become **mento** and Jamaican popular music was born. With a syncopated rhythm that got hips gyrating and bodies dipping forward or back in Kumina-esque abandon (a style of movement revived in the "bogle" dance of the early 1990s), pelvis-centred mento was closely related to calypso – the music of Trinidad and Tobago – through both a predilection for rhythmic and lyrical bawdiness and its humorous social commentary. Mento dominated the Jamaican music scene for the first decades of the last century. You'll still see mento trios – often referred to as calypso bands – performing welcome songs or forming the "authentic culture" portion of shows at hotels, while Portland parish has seen a resurgence of the genre with regular performances by classic mento band the Jolly Boys (see page 113).

Big bands to ballads

By the early 1940s, mento was waning in popularity as thousands of young Jamaicans left the island to fight for Britain in World War II or find work in Cuba, Latin America and the US. They returned with a taste for new rhythms and musical styles – rumba, salsa and merengue – as well as new musical technology – phonograph records and cheap radio sets, widely available and affordable for the first time. Taking their influence from black Americans Count Basie and Duke Ellington, meanwhile, **big bands** such as the Eric Deans Orchestra found moderate success playing international standards and cleaned-up versions of mento hits at hotel floor shows. The best of these were put on vinyl by West Indies Recording Limited (WIRL), a record label owned by then-entrepreneur and later prime minister Edward Seaga. However, despite the quality of these tightly orchestrated performances, the big bands were bypassed by the majority of Jamaicans in favour of the radio stations beaming black-American R&B from transmitters in Florida.

Jams in the tenement yards

By the early 1950s, Jamaica's music scene was concentrated in a few pockets of southwest Kingston that were later to spawn the island's best-known musical luminaries. The desperately poor communities of Trench Town, Jones Town, Denham Town and Greenwich Farm offered plenty of dancehalls and street corners where quick-thinking impresarios like **Duke Reid**, **Prince Buster** and **Clement "Coxsone" Dodd** played for the people on huge mobile disco sets, taking the latest R&B or blues to areas where few could afford to see a big band play live. Reid and Dodd were the first to exploit the full commercial potential of the **sound system** (see page 289), vying with each other to see who could spin the best selections (often acquired on record-buying sorties to the US), and employing the braggadocio that characterizes today's dancehall posturing. An ex-policeman who always carried a firearm, Reid was prone to arrive at a dance dressed to the nines in sequins and leather, his guns cocked and ready to discipline any contenders to his throne.

Building the studios

By the mid-1950s, R&B's star had faded and the fickle Jamaican consumer was tiring of American imports. Quick to catch on to a new opportunity, men like Reid, Dodd and Leslie Kong began recording music themselves – primarily soft and soulful ballads – using established vocalists and players who had cut their teeth on the big-band circuit. The Gaylads, Jackie Edwards, Owen Grey, Jackie Opal, Laurel Aitken and Bunny and Skully were backed by some of the best musicians Jamaica has ever produced – Roland Alphonso, Tommy McCook and "Deadly" Headley Bennett on saxophone, Don Drummond and Rico Rodriguez on trombone, Jerome "Jah Jerry" Haines and Ernest Ranglin on guitar, Lester Sterling on trumpet and keyboard virtuoso Jackie Mittoo. Initially, the producers used the WIRL and Federal studios to record, but as soon as finances allowed, Reid and Dodd (among others) built their own rudimentary studios, naming them after their most popular labels, **Treasure Isle** and **Studio One** respectively. Around this time, too, Chris Blackwell founded **Island Records**, which would go on to become arguably the most famous label in Jamaican music. It was a halcyon age for Jamaican music, a time of cooperation and innovation.

Ska licks

Musicians and singers began flirting with the philosophies of **Rastafari** by the late 1950s. Some went down to the Dungle district of Kingston or Adastra Road in the Rasta-dominated Wareika foothills and jammed with master drummers like **Count Ossie** and his **Mystic Revelation of Rastafari** band. Reworked in 1993 to massive commercial success by Jamaican DJ Shaggy, the band's track "Oh Carolina" was one of their most influential recordings, a perfect example of the fusion of Kumina drumming, harmonic singing and unique rhythm that was later to develop into ska, rocksteady and finally reggae. The Rasta drummers became well known on the Kingston entertainment scene via their regular performances at the popular *Vere Johns Opportunity Knocks* variety show (held every week at the Ambassador Theatre in Jones Town), and went on to perform regularly at other Kingston venues.

For Jamaican musicians, the late 1950s and early 1960s were a time of intense creativity, a period of exploring new rhythms and pushing the boundaries of jazz, R&B and Rasta drumming – an explosive combination that sometimes saw drummers and instrumenta-lists pitched against sound-system wattage. Meanwhile, session musicians were conducting their own experiments, using the exaggerated shuffle rhythm of R&B and syncopated mento sounds. Somewhere along the way, the staccato, guitar-and-trumpet-led sound of **ska** emerged and captured the Jamaican musical imagination with effortless ease.

Following independence from British colonial rule in 1962, the future seemed full of possibilities. You can hear the euphoria in the music of the time – joyous, up-tempo ska tunes that seem now not to express a care in the world – and the small independent record labels in west Kingston were at the cutting edge. Ska lyrics provide a window into the evolution of Jamaica and its music. With its home-grown roots and dance-floor beat, ska expressed the mood of the ghetto dweller. Tommy McCook grouped together the cream of the session musicians to form the now-legendary **Skatalites**, who released a host of massively popular instrumental tracks, like "Guns of Navarone", and backed most of the era's popular singers – including Millie Small, who shot to international fame with "My Boy Lollipop" and gave Chris Blackwell's Island label its first smash hit. Other prominent ska tracks included Justin Hinds and the Dominoes' "Carry Go Bring Come", the Ethiopians' "Train to Skaville" and a host of others on Beverley's, Federal, Treasure Isle and Coxsone Dodd's Studio One and Coxsone labels.

Rude boys to rocksteady

As the post-independence glow began to fade, Jamaica's ghetto youth became increasingly dissatisfied with their meagre slice of the pie, and the **rude boy** era of police brutality and ghetto dissent began. Rude boys were cinematically celebrated by Jimmy Cliff's portrayal of urban rebel Ivan in *The Harder They Come*, and musically documented in early Wailers cuts like "Rule Them Rudie" and "Let Him Go (Rudie Get Bail)". Their fractious stance also generated the Wailers' 1964 "Simmer Down", an appeal for calm among the youth.

While the musical critique of free Jamaica continued in releases like the Skatalites' 1966 "Independent Anniversary Ska", subtle changes occurred in the music itself as Jamaicans began to demand something more leisurely. Producers acquiesced and began to slow down the tempo, guiding their artists toward a more benign lyrical output. The rude-boy lament continued in cuts like "007 (Shanty Town)" from Desmond Dekker and the Aces, but by 1966 Hopeton Lewis had produced "Take It Easy", and Stranger and Patsy were singing emollient **rocksteady** tracks about love and relationships in "When I Call Your Name". "Happy Go Lucky Girl" and "Only A Smile" by John Holt and the Paragons, "Queen Majesty" by the Techniques and "I Caught You" by Brent Dowe's Melodians also did something to temper the pressure in west Kingston. Characterized by the addition of the "one drop" drumming style and a more melodic tone, rocksteady carried the swing and swiftly eclipsed the ska sound. The king of the era was **Alton Ellis**, who put a name to the movement with his "Get Ready Rock Steady" track. It was a prolific time for Jamaican music, with labels like Studio One and, primarily, Treasure Isle pumping out the tunes, many set to rhythm tracks that still continue to be heard to this day (see page 287). However, rocksteady was a short-lived movement, and by 1968 it had been superseded by the tighter guitars, heavier bass and sinuous rhythm of reggae.

Reggae to roots rock

So many artists contributed to the development of **reggae** that it's impossible to say who originated the genre – it's most likely that this ubiquitous Jamaican sound developed organically as a natural progression from rocksteady, but Toots and the Maytals' 1968 single "Do The Reggay" (sic) certainly cemented a name that Rastafarians may tell you derives from *rex*, meaning king. Hence reggae is the "king's music" – an apt allegory, as the appearance of reggae coincided with an explosion in the popularity of the Rastafarian movement.

From 1970 onwards, Jamaican music took an increasingly religious stance, with its main lyrical themes drawing reference from the tenets of Rastafari: repatriation, black history, black pride and self-determination. "**Roots and culture**" were the lick, and reggae became fully-fledged protest music. It was anathema to the establishment, who saw a menacing, subversive message from a dirty and violent source and banned it wherever possible – though the rum-bar jukeboxes played whatever the radio stations wouldn't. It wasn't until after Bob Marley and the Wailers signed with Island Records in 1972, to international acclaim (see page 156), that reggae was given islandwide approval for the first time.

A time of intense musical productivity, the 1970s stand out as the classic period of Jamaica's best roots reggae. But while **Burning Spear** was singing "Marcus Garvey" and "Slavery Days" and Joseph Hill's **Culture** provided apocalyptic warnings in the song "Two Sevens Clash", the era also offered a sweeter side; the angelic crooning of more mainstream artists like **Dennis Brown** and **Gregory Isaacs** found an eager audience, their style becoming known as **lovers' rock**. Though their lyrics rested mostly on love and affection, lovers' artists also had some bite; tracks like Junior Byles' "Curly Locks" (a song about the controversial move of falling in

THE ART OF THE RHYTHM TRACK

Through what's known in Jamaica as the **rhythm track**, the bass lines and chord sequences laid down during the rocksteady and reggae eras have become the foundation for practically all Jamaican music recorded thereafter. Realizing that there are only so many chords to play, or pressed for time when studios charge by the hour, the island's musicians and producers have capitalized on the best chord and bass-line combinations, manipulating and reinterpreting them so often that most of the classic rhythm tracks have established names, usually gleaned from the song title with which they first appeared. Working as full-time studio session musicians throughout the rocksteady and early reggae eras, the likes of singer, bassist and arranger Leroy Sibbles and the "rhythm twins", **Sly Dunbar** and **Robbie Shakespeare**, created many of the rhythms that backed hundreds of 1970s' reggae cuts and are still reworked into today's dancehall. Producer Bunny Lee, meanwhile, was one of the first to release multiple versions of a song backed by the same rhythm track; today, this has become normal practice, with all the prominent Jamaican artists recording a vocal version over whatever rhythm track is currently in vogue. Within contemporary dancehall, certain rhythms – from "punany" and "pepper-seed" in the 1980s and 1990s to "dutty wine" and "willy bounce" in the new millennium – become hugely popular, with specialized dances to go with them (as Usain Bolt demonstrated to the world at the 2008 Beijing Olympics with his performance of the "nuh linga" dance).

The upshot is that listening to Jamaican music can feel like an exercise in déjà vu; you may or may not have heard a particular song before, but once you've listened to a fair portion of rocksteady and early reggae, you'll certainly be familiar with most of the classic rhythm tracks. And once you've listened to the radio for a couple of hours, you'll get to know the currently popular dancehall rhythms.

love with a Rastaman) highlight the uneasy relationship that Rasta and reggae still had with wider Jamaican society.

Dub to DJ business

As the 1970s wore on, studio technology became increasingly sophisticated. Producers began manipulating their equipment, using reverb or echo machines, overdubbing techniques and snatches of dog barks or gunshots to produce some of the most arresting and penetrating music ever to emerge from Jamaica – **dub**. Employing a remarkable level of inventiveness with often limited means, Jamaican engineers such as dub pioneers **King Tubby**, **Prince Jammy** and **Scientist** predated the advent of the digital sampler by ten years and brought reggae back to basics, stripping down songs so that only bass, drums and inflections of tone remained. Snippets of the original vocals were then mixed in alongside sound effects and two-line DJ sound bites. Like ska, dub remained a primarily instrumental music for a short time. Before long, scores of DJs clamoured to produce a dub voice-over, and producers plundered their archives and released dub versions of old cuts, while DJs provided the voice-over and even vocal tracks had a dub flip-side.

The cult of the **DJ** had begun in the sound systems, with resident DJs improvising a couple of lines of introductory patter at the beginning of a record. The ecstatic crowd responses encouraged them to spin it out, and soon they were delivering full-length monologues over the music, discussing topical events as well as the state of play on the dancefloor. The craft was mastered by **U-Roy** – inspired by the earlier efforts of Count Machouki and Sir Lord Comic – who released talk-based singles to great success throughout the 1970s with roots sound systems like the venerable King Tubby's Hi-Fi, Stur-Gav, Tippertone, Sir George and Killamanjaro providing the backing for their live appearances. Meanwhile, the DJs' trade was expanded when Big Youth started talking over ("toasting") records in his cultural style, followed by the likes of King Stitt, Dennis Alcapone, I-Roy, Jah Stitch, Tappa Zukie, Prince Jazzbo and Dillinger, whose "Cocaine Running Around My Brain" scored a hit in the UK. As the violent elections of 1976 and 1980 saw the pressure in Kingston building up, the sound systems multiplied and the DJs "chatted" on the mike about the times, analysing the position of the ghetto youth in Jamaica from a dread perspective and offering cultural distractions by setting the Psalms to song. Newcomers U-Brown, Ranking Joe, Josey Wales, Charlie Chaplin and Trinity continued in the same vein, touring Jamaica and the Caribbean with sound systems, and paving the way for the dancehall explosion of the 1980s.

Marley's legacy

In 1981, the Jamaican reggae industry was left in shock as Bob Marley succumbed to cancer and the music fraternity realized the enormity of their loss. Jamaica came to a standstill for two days as mourners viewed his coffin and lined the roads to watch the entourage on the final procession to Nine Mile. Though not the greatest singer to emerge from Jamaica, Marley's influence and songwriting talent were immeasurable, and following his demise, reggae struggled to regain its direction and purpose. Groups like **Black Uhuru** recorded a succession of roots albums for Island, but the musical tide had already turned towards the DJ, and Marley's legacy of cultural consciousness began to seem less appropriate to the world of cocaine-running and political warfare in the ghettos.

Successive further blows were also taken by the roots reggae legacy. Marley's fellow Wailer, the uncompromising genius Peter Tosh (see page 228) was killed in 1987, followed by the tragic death in an explosion in 1994 of staunch Rastafarian singer **Garnet Silk**. In 1993, when "gun and gyal" lyrics had become the sole signifiers, this young man had managed to conquer the dancehalls, his immense popularity starting

THE CULT OF THE SOUND SYSTEM

Since the mid-1950s, when Duke Reid and Coxsone Dodd discharged the first shots in a battle of heavy wattage, mobile discos known as **sound systems** have been intrinsic to the Jamaican music scene. Laying the foundations of each stage in reggae's development, sound systems provide an opportunity to test crowd response to new lyrics or rhythms and inspire Jamaicans to follow their sound of choice with vehement loyalty. A simple arrangement of high-powered amplifiers and huge columns of speakers customized to give a heavy, belly-rolling bass, the sound system began as a way of bringing the music to those who couldn't afford nightclub or stageshow cover charges. And so it remains; the sound system jam is now the major form of entertainment for young Jamaicans, with outdoor events such as the legendary Passa Passa and the many subsequent street dances breaking new artists and tunes and — of course — allowing the opportunity to display prowess at the dances that go with each new rhythm. Some sound system devotees go to hear their favourite **selector**, the man who employs an almost clairvoyant intuition to play just what the crowd wants, while others come for the prospect of hearing DJs chatting live lyrics. Overall, though, it's the unique "dancehall vibe" that most people come to savour, with patrons dressed to the nines in the very latest fashions, dancing in the light of the inevitable video camera or posing for the photographers from local dancehall websites.

Since the early days when Dodd would set up on an opposite Kingston corner to Reid and try to poach his crowd with a mightier bass and a craftier playlist, **rivalry** has been central to sound-system culture. The battle to be known as the best is fought out at "**clashes**", where two sounds play on one night, and crowd appreciation is the mark of the winner. Buying a larger amp or a new set of speakers is one way of achieving dominance, but the most popular method is still to spin an exclusive track voiced over by the latest DJ or singer (though CDs have replaced the "dub-plate" acetates of the vinyl era).

Today, the main players in the Jamaican sound-system scene are the inimitable **Stone Love**, whose raw reputation and killer selectors still prompt followers to travel for miles to hear them play; Killamanjaro and Bass Odyssey offer elite competition. And the sound system phenomenon isn't restricted to Jamaica, either, with Mighty Crown from Japan, King Addies from New York and "Ramjam" Rodigan from the UK being three of the more popular sets from overseas, all of which play regularly in Jamaica.

a resurgence of cultural reggae. Later in 2009, one of Jamaica's very sweetest voices went silent with the death of the "Crown Prince of Reggae", Rastafarian **Dennis Brown**. Nonetheless, hope for sustaining "conscious" music in the 1990s and beyond continued with the likes of the very popular Rasta artists and groups like Morgan Heritage, Luciano and Richie Spice, using musicians rather than keyboards and writing their own material.

Slackness in the dancehall

These days, you're more likely to be assailed by a clamorous barrage of raw drum and bass and shouty patois lyrics than hear Bob Marley or Burning Spear booming out from Jamaican speaker-boxes. Known as **dancehall** (because that's where it originated and where it is best enjoyed) or bashment, this is the most popular musical form in contemporary Jamaica. The genre first surfaced around 1979 and was fully established in 1981 when flamboyant albino DJ **Yellowman** exploded onto the scene with his massive hits "Married in the Morning", "Mr Chin" and "Nobody Move". Yellowman's lyrical bawdiness and huge popularity signified the departure from roots reggae and cultural toasting (the original term used to describe the Jamaican talking-over-music that inspired US rappers) to the sexually explicit and often violent DJ-ism that took hold in the 1980s. Though none were rawer than Yellowman, who added energetic stage performances and self-deprecating humour to the expletives, other DJs – fuelled by a positive response from their Jamaican

DANCEHALL QUEENS

Weekends in Jamaica mean sound-system dances islandwide, and here, **fashion** goes hand-in-hand with the music. Parties are a time to let loose and forget the domestic drudgery in favour of some of the rudest dancing and most glittery glamour on the planet – as demonstrated in the Jamaican movie *Dancehall Queen*, named for the women who rule Jamaican sound-system parties.

Whether it's a latticework leatherette G-string and bra ensemble or a concoction of carefully arranged silver plastic straps, topped off with a neon wig, thigh-high boots or killer heels, dancehall wear is loud, proud and deliberately ostentatious. The outfits are for one purpose: the sheer hype and self-promotion of making an impression at a party and performing the suggestive gymnastics of the latest dances to mesmerizing effect. **Dancehall Queens** are the icons of sound-system culture, a league ruled for years by an uptown Kingstonian named Carlene, whose killer dress-sense, athletic dancing style and charismatic personality earned her the local status of a Hollywood film star. Carlene's hold on Jamaica remains strong: her day-to-day life still makes the news, and in 2016 she was awarded a Queens of Reggae Island award for her contribution to the music industry. The queens are a fascinating slice of Jamaican nightlife; you can experience their artistic phenomena firsthand at Montego Bay's annual Dancehall Queen competition (see page 33).

audience – emulated his lewd approach, and sexually explicit lyrics – or "**slackness**" – began to proliferate.

In 1985, Wayne Smith's hit "Under Me Sleng Teng" – voiced for a King Jammy's rhythm of the same name – heralded the start of the computer age in the dancehall. Studios switched from analogue to digital recording formats, and producers seized upon computerized rhythms as a quicker and cheaper way of putting out a record. The mixing board became an instrument unto itself, with a new breed of producers like Bobby Digital, Donovan Germaine, Mikey Bennett, Dave Kelly, Jeremy Harding and Patrick Roberts becoming the Reids and Dodds of the 1990s, and DJs becoming the island's biggest stars. Vocalists also clamoured to ride the digital rhythms – singers like Frankie Paul, Michael Palmer, Little John, Barrington Levy and Pinchers all got the sweetness out of the rhythms – while after years in the business Sanchez, Beres Hammond and Wayne Wonder still provide love songs for the romantically inclined today.

Dancehall is massive in contemporary Jamaica, though it's not to everyone's liking. Many charge the genre with wider moral decline as the DJs become the gangsta rappers of reggae, with flash cars, designer clothes and, in some cases, a seemingly limitless enthusiasm for automatic firearms and sex. Homophobia, too, is a regular theme; although high-profile DJs such as **Buju Banton** (whose 1988 song "Boom Bye Bye", written when he was 15, has become synonymous with Jamaican anti-gay sentiments) have bowed to pressure from campaigners and no longer perform their more inflammatory hits overseas (Banton himself is jailed in the US until late 2018 on a complicated cocaine charge), many still publicize their views while back in Jamaica. However, though some dancehall does seem intent on a glorification of violence and bigotry, much of it simply reflects the lives of hundreds of thousands of ghetto dwellers for whom brutality and prejudice are a daily reality. Essentially, dancehall is a raw, rude, hard-core music designed to titillate and tease its Jamaican audience on home ground and beyond. Whether you like the lyrics or hate them, it's unlikely you'll be able to resist dancehall's compelling rhythm and infectious hype, and while you're in Jamaica, it's futile to try.

Reggae in the twenty-first century

Undoubtedly, dancehall has dominated Jamaican music through the 1990s and into the new millennium. Masses of artists have come and gone. Shabba Ranks, Buju

Banton, Super Cat and Chaka Demus and Pliers represent some of the biggest names of "old", while the long-drawn-out feud between stalwart DJs **Beenie Man** and **Bounty Killer** rumbled on – seemingly partly for effect – for a decade until at least 2007. Big-name Rasta artists like Capleton and Sizzla played a significant part in the scene, while dancehall favourites Lady Saw, Mr Vegas and Elephant Man have already become the rearguard in this fast moving scene.

Dancehall also made moves into the pop arena: Grammy Award-winner Shaggy scored worldwide hits with "Boombastic" and "It Wasn't Me" in 1995 and 2000; platinum-selling uptown boy **Sean Paul** scored several No.1s on the US Billboard chart in the 2000s, and Grammy-winner **Damian "Junior Gong" Marley** shot to global fame on the back of his brilliant 2005 second album, *Welcome to Jamrock*, a sizzling record with guest performances from his Marley brothers Stephen and Ziggy as well as a slew of international names.

THE PRODUCERS

From the late 1950s to the late 1960s, **Duke Reid** and **Coxsone Dodd** dominated Jamaica's music scene, commanding heavyweight respect among the music fraternity and churning out the majority of the island's hits. This pair of musical titans are widely credited with controlling Jamaican recording as the industry shifted focus from ska to rocksteady. Their "big fish in a small pond" reputation has shaped the way that the industry works at a basic level: a producer raises enough funds to buy a studio, he then hires a team of musicians or a master keyboard programmer to lay down the rhythm tracks, and scouts for a talented arranger to look after the daily running of recording sessions and audition hopeful vocalists. The producer then selects the right combination from his pool of vocalists, songs and rhythm tracks, puts it all together, presses vinyl copies and releases the record, inevitably taking no chances on its success by handing out favours – payola – to ensure the tunes are played on the radio and at dances.

INDEPENDENTS AND UPSETTERS

Though the reign of Dodd and Reid remained unchallenged until the late 1960s, the prevailing mood had changed by the early 1970s. Artists got sick of being paid a single fee while the producers reaped the royalties, and in house arrangers baulked at doing all the work while the producers sat back and enjoyed the rewards. As starting a label was merely a matter of raising the funds for studio time and record pressing, a new breed of **independent producer** emerged. Many lasted no longer than a couple of releases, but the likes of Jack Ruby, Harry "J" Johnson, Bunny "Striker" Lee, Henry "Junjo" Lawes, Sonia Pottinger and Clancy Eccles had more staying-power, and produced some of the finest reggae of the era. The most instrumental independent producer, though, was the eminent "Upsetter", **Lee "Scratch" Perry**, who started out as a bouncer for Prince Buster and graduated to running Coxsone's Studio One, where he worked with Marley and the Wailers on the definitive singles ("Small Axe", "Sun Is Shining", "Duppy Conqueror", "Satisfy My Soul") that were later reworked on albums for Island Records. In the late 1960s, Perry built his **Black Ark** studio and established the famous Upsetter label, releasing classic tracks such as Junior Murvin's "Police and Thieves", Max Romeo's "Sipple Out Deh (War Inna Babylon)" and the Congos' definitive roots reggae LP *Heart of the Congos*. Perry remained at reggae's cutting edge until the late 1970s, becoming one of the chief innovators of dub as a patron of the late King Tubby. But his legendary – and often consciously cultivated – mental instability (planting records in his garden, burning down his studio in a fit of pique) and refusal to compromise his increasingly eccentric musical vision led to a decline in sales.

The digital age of the 1980s heralded a new era for reggae, as producers were able to release material with even fewer resources behind them. Big names such as Prince Jammy churned out electronic dancehall rhythms alongside fellow luminaries Bobby Digital, Gussie Clarke, Mikey Bennett and Donovan Germain, Philip "Fatis" Burell and Steely and Cleevie, while Dave Kelly and Jeremy Harding carried the swing throughout the 1990s and are still producing today.

Dancehall nonetheless continued in its classic abrasive form into the late 2000s and early 2010s, with numerous releases by the likes of Busy Signal, Konshens and female star Spice, while old rivalries were eclipsed by the new dancehall kingpins **Vybz Kartel** (**"Gaza"**) and **Mavado** (**"Gully"**); most young Jamaicans chose their side. The feud came to an abrupt halt in April 2014 with Kartel's life imprisonment for murder (he has continued to release tracks during his incarceration, however; fans speculate his new music is produced by smartphone wizardry, while Kartel's lawyers maintain the hits come from a treasure trove of material that was unreleased at the time of his arrest). His prison sentence has done nothing to halt the appeal of dancehall in Jamaica and Kartel's influence – he's also released a clothing line and an autobiography – seems only to have grown from behind bars.

Conscious revival

Yet throughout dancehall's "slackest" periods, more "conscious" artists, many of them Rasta and preaching peace and respect, have been present in the background – very often overlapping older and newer rhythms. Top performers like Tarrus Riley, Jah Cure, Queen Ifrica, Tanya Stephens, Etana and Tessanne Chin have all established themselves in the scene since the turn of the millennium, while old masters like Beres Hammond continue to write occasional hits.

In an exciting evolution, the emergence of an advanced guard of new artists appears to be shifting cultural consciousness and Rastafari from the background of the dancehall scene to the forefront of mainstream culture. Eminently talented Rasta performers like Chronixx, Jah9, Proteje, Sevana, Dre Island, and Kabaka Pyramid combine old and new styles of reggae and ride dancehall rhythms as well as or better than the rest. These new, young role models, offering conscious lyrical content, encapsulate a new musical era.

Books

The selection below represents the best available books written about Jamaica, alongside some of the authors' personal favourites. All are available from general websites or from specialist Caribbean publishers such as Sangsters (ⓦsangstersbooks.com), UWI Press (ⓦuwipress.com), Peepal Tree (ⓦpeepaltreepress.com) and LMH (ⓦlmhpublishing.com). Titles marked with ★ are particularly recommended.

TRAVEL AND DIARIES

Patrick Leigh Fermor *The Traveller's Tree*. The classic Caribbean travelogue describing Leigh Fermor's visit in the late 1940s before tourism had really started, though only the last chapter covers Jamaica, with specific reference to the developing Rastafari movement in west Kingston.

★ **Linda Gambrill** (ed) *A Tapestry of Jamaica*. A collection of the best articles from thirty years of Air Jamaica's brilliant in-flight magazine. Covering sport, music, travel, fashion, people, art, history and folk tales, as well as a whole section on the inimitable Miss Lou, this is an essential collection, made all the more poignant by the sheer love of the island that comes through in the final "memories" section.

★ **David Howard** *Kingston*. Comprehensive treatment of Jamaica's irrepressible capital, with a solid historical perspective alongside plenty of informed social commentary and a trot around all the sights and sounds of Kingston.

Brian J. Hudson *The Waterfalls of Jamaica*. A wide-ranging ode to Jamaica's gorgeous cascades (though not a guidebook in the practical sense), it looks at the main waterfalls and their exploitation as tourist attractions, with illustrations ranging from eighteenth-century prints to contemporary photographs. Food for thought as you idle away an afternoon at YS or Reach.

Matthew Lewis *Journal of a West Indian Proprietor*. Fascinating diaries of Lewis, an early nineteenth-century English novelist, describing his brief visits to his Jamaican estates and cataloguing the lifestyle and living conditions of the island's slaves.

Lady Maria Nugent *Journal of Residence in Jamaica 1801–5*. Lady Nugent was the wife of one of Jamaica's governors, and her diary, though often naive and patronizing, paints an interesting picture of how the "ruling class" lived.

★ **Chris Salewicz** *Rude Boy – Once Upon a Time in Jamaica*. Part history of Jamaica, part travelogue written by a true Jamaica-phile, it evokes some of the innate paradoxes of Jamaica with humour and delicacy.

★ **Frank Fonda Taylor** *To Hell with Paradise*. Exhaustive history of the beginnings of the Jamaican tourist industry, with great black-and-white photos and early adverts. Offers some marvellous insight into the prejudices and condescension of the first visitors.

Anthony Winkler *Going Home to Teach*. Engaging story of novelist Winkler's own experiences as a white Jamaican returning to live on his native island during the "anti-white" climate of the late 1970s. Very good on the politics of the period.

FICTION

Russell Banks *The Book of Jamaica*. Narrated by an academic who bases himself in Jamaica while writing a novel about the Maroons, this is a slow starter that eventually manages some compelling commentary on island society in the 1970s, from the prejudices of his landlords and the magic worked by a Maroon colonel to the lifestyles and attitudes of the Jamaicans that live around him.

★ **Louise Bennett** *Anancy and Miss Lou*. Jamaica's oral tradition of storytelling may be fading, but these are the classic folk tales told in patois by the late Louise Bennett, the greatest of modern Jamaican storytellers.

★ **Margaret Cezair-Thomson** *The True History of Paradise* and *Pirate's Daughter*. Poignant and beautifully written, the former is a history of Jamaica as told by various generations of a Jamaican family, from the Scottish wife of a planter to an African ex-slave to a modern-day uptown girl in Kingston.

The latter is a brilliantly imaginative tale of a Portland family whose lives become intertwined with Errol Flynn, with evocative descriptions of their life with him on Navy Island.

Colin Channer (ed) *Iron Balloons*. Written by participants in the Calabash Writers Workshop, an offshoot of Jamaica's marvellous literary festival (see page 32), this pacey collection of short stories, set in Jamaica and the US, gives voice to some wonderful new writers alongside more established names such as Kwame Dawes and Channer himself.

Colin Channer *Waiting In Vain*. This tale of a modern-day romance between a Jamaican man and an American woman perfectly evokes the Jamaican communities of England, New York and Jamaica itself. Great holiday reading.

Mark Conklin *Banana Shout*. Engaging and occasionally hilarious account of an American draft dodger's adventures as he sets up home in Negril during the 1970s.

Herbert de Lisser *The White Witch of Rose Hall*. A blend of Gothic horror and purple prose, this richly embellished account of the island's best-known ghost story tells the tale of Annie Palmer, mistress of Rose Hall Great House, whose three husbands all died in suspicious circumstances (see page 180).

Perry Henzell *Power Game*. Long, entertaining story of power-seekers at different levels in Jamaican society – politics, the army, the banks, the drug trade. Henzell catches local language and atmosphere with the same skill he used in his movie *The Harder They Come*.

★ **Marlon James** *John Crow's Devil, The Book of Night Women* and *A Brief History of Seven Killings*. Probably Jamaica's most exciting new writer, James centres the first on the battle for the soul of the village of Gibbeah; a powerful, perfectly paced novel with crackling dialogue and a riveting plot. The latter two are equally brilliant, respectively taking on slavery and urban violence (*Killings* starts with attempted 1976 assassination of Bob Marley) in all their dark complexity.

Evan Jones *Stone Haven*. Long-winded but readable historical novel that picks its way through modern issues, from 1920s attitudes to colour to the problems of post-independence.

★ **Guy Kennaway** *One People*. Entertaining and brilliantly funny take on life in a tiny coastal town in Hanover parish. It perfectly evokes rural Jamaican life, from the patois chat to the clandestine shenanigans of the locals. Essential.

★ **Roger Mais** *The Hills Were Joyful Together, Brother Man* and *Black Lightning*. *Hills* is a bleak, compelling picture of life in a Kingston ghetto in the 1950s, with a harsh look at law and order Jamaica-style, by one of the country's earliest novelists. *Brother Man* details the emergence of Rastafari in Kingston via the gentle "Brother Man" himself, while *Black Lightning* is an intense and atmospheric account of the life of a brooding sculptor living in the Jamaican bush.

Alicia McKenzie *Stories from Yard*. With settings ranging from a Brazilian beach to the streets of Kingston, this wide-ranging collection of short stories is sweet, funny and sometimes very sad.

Terry McMillan *How Stella Got Her Groove Back*. In McMillan's lightweight but enjoyable tome, this semi-autobiographical tale tells the story of a holiday romance that turns serious, written as a result of the author's experiences during holidays in Negril.

Brian Meeks *Paint the Town Red*. Moving portrayal of an uptown Kingstonian's first day of freedom after serving a prison term for his involvement in a politically motivated shooting in the run-up to the 1980 election. The descriptions of life in the ghetto are particularly gripping – and brutal.

★ **Orlando Patterson** *The Children of Sisyphus*. Famous, uncompromising picture of the poorest of Kingston's poor,

fighting for survival on the margins of society, and of Dinah, a prostitute who tries to leave them behind and move up in the world. One of the first novels to try to present a fair picture of the Rasta community.

★ **Geoffrey Philp** *Benjamin, My Son*. A Jamaican living in Miami returns to the island for the funeral of his father, a politician loosely modelled on several recognizable Jamaican leaders, and becomes embroiled in the shady world of Jamaica's political scene: gunmen, obeah-men and all.

V.S. Reid *The Jamaicans*. Juan de Bolas was a slave liberated by the Spanish when the English captured the island in 1655. Reid's fictionalized account tells of his life in hiding and struggle against the English.

Jean Rhys *Wide Sargasso Sea*. Poignant, beautifully written view of post-emancipation Jamaica, with Antoinette, a young Creole girl, and Rochester, her English boyfriend, trapped by declining financial circumstances and his inability to understand the realities of local life. Written as a prequel to Charlotte Brontë's *Jane Eyre*.

Kim Robinson & Leeta Hearn (eds) *Twenty-two Jamaican Short Stories*. Excellent short-story collection that covers some of the more chilling psychological aspects of Jamaican life. Venerable authors include Olive Senior, Dennis Scott, Hazel Campbell and Trevor Fearon.

Tony Sewell *Jamaica Inc*. Gripping and intelligent fictional history of a strangely familiar political family dynasty.

Sistren Collective *Lionheart Gal*. Recently reissued, this brilliant collection penned by members of the Sistren Theatre Collective sheds light onto the hopes, dreams and realities of women's lives in Jamaica, and though the island has gone through many changes since the initial publication, all the voices strike a contemporary chord and, as most are written in patois, provide a lovely window into the local lingo.

Vanessa Spence *The Roads Are Down*. Excellent and amusing first novel of a cross-cultural love affair, set in modern-day Kingston and the Blue Mountains.

Michael Thewell *The Harder They Come*. Novel inspired by Perry Henzell's brilliant movie, telling the story of Rhygin – country boy turned rude boy – who comes to Kingston and gets caught up in gangs and ganja.

★ **Anthony Winkler** *The Great Yacht Race, The Painted Canoe* and *The Lunatic*. Set just before independence, *The Great Yacht Race* is a hilarious look at the lifestyle of Montego Bay's erstwhile "ruling class" as the lawyers, journalists and hotel owners go through scandal after scandal in preparation for their annual boat race. *The Painted Canoe* is a powerful, evocative tale of a Jamaican fisherman and his relationship with the sea, while *The Lunatic* is a poignant but amusing tale of a Jamaican madman, who wanders the island talking with the trees and bushes, and his encounter with Inge, a sexually voracious German tourist (see page 78).

HISTORY AND POLITICS

Warren Alleyne *Caribbean Pirates*. Alleyne debunks the myths about the region's leading pirates – from Blackbeard to Henry Morgan – in a series of brief portraits.

Clinton Black *Port Royal* and *Tales of Old Jamaica*. *Port Royal* is a solid history of the city once known as the "wickedest place on earth"; *Tales* has brief accounts of some of the key events in the island's past, recalling the capture of Jamaica by the British, the story of Three-Fingered Jack Mansong, and the female pirates Anne Bonney and Mary Read (see page 202).

★ **Trevor Burnard** *Mastery, Tyranny and Desire*. Based around the diaries of Thomas Thistlewood, who kept a regular journal during his forty years as a plantation owner in Jamaica, this compelling and accessible book provides a chilling insight into life in the colonial era, from Thistlewood's obsessive detailing of his sexual exploits to the routine punishment and humiliation he meted out to his slaves.

★ **James Ferguson** *A Traveller's History of the Caribbean*. Concise and well-written overview that provides a good introduction to the region's history.

John Gilmore *Faces of the Caribbean*. Excellent and essential sociohistory of the Caribbean, covering everything from slavery to reggae, cricket and the environment.

Michelle Harrison *King Sugar – Jamaica, the Caribbean and the World Sugar Economy*. Solid history of the Jamaican sugar industry – and the fortunes it made for British planters.

Rupert Lewis & Patrick Bryan (eds) *Garvey: His Work and Impact*. Twenty-one articles on the historical background to Garveyism, his influence on Jamaica and his worldwide legacy.

Michael Manley *The Politics of Change – A Jamaican Testament*. Interesting overview of the proposed transformation of the island under Manley's PNP government, written as it got underway in the early 1970s.

★ **Carey Robinson** *The Iron Thorn: The Defeat of the British by the Jamaican Maroons*. Written by a journalist, historian and former head of the Jamaica National Trust, this historic account offers a balanced and informed perspective on the Maroon Wars, from both sides of the battlefield.

★ **Tony Sewell** *Garvey's Children: The Legacy of Marcus Garvey*. Readable account of Garvey's black-power movement and the inspiration it has provided for black nationalists in Jamaica and abroad.

Philip Sherlock & Hazel Bennett *The Story of the Jamaican People*. A chunky yet readable tome that provided a revisionist history of the island when it was published in 1998. It focuses on the Afro-Jamaican experience of slavery and resistance, culture and religion, rather than colonizers' or politicians' perspectives.

RELIGION, CULTURE AND SOCIETY

Leonard Barrett *The Rastafarians* and *The Sun and the Drum*. The former is one of the most comprehensive accounts of the eponymous movement, explaining its origins and politics and looking at related religious movements like the Twelve Tribes of Israel sect. The latter is an in-depth look at the influence of African traditions in Jamaican culture, including language, witchcraft and folk medicine.

★ **Derek Bishton** *Black Heart Man – A Journey into Rasta*. Succinct, well-researched foray into the origins and development of the Rastafarian movement in Jamaica, with discussion of Garvey and a host of lesser-known black theorists.

Adrian Boot & Michael Thomas *Babylon on a Thin Wire*. Evocative photographic portraits of 1970s Kingston from one of the most renowned photographers of Jamaican culture, backed up by cynical and informed text.

Lloyd Bradley *Bass Culture – When Reggae Was King*. Very readable history of reggae written, for once, by a man of Jamaican origin rather than a US academic. Entertaining and pretty comprehensive, though a bit short on contemporary detail.

★ **Barry Chevannes** *Rastafari Roots and Ideology*. Comprehensive, accessible study of Rastafari, tracing the history of the movement and detailing religious practice, and with a chapter dedicated to orthodox Bobo dreads to boot. Essential reading.

★ **Laurie Gunst** *Born Fi' Dead*. Gripping account of the dark side of political and drug-related violence in Jamaica, reissued with a new postscript. Ably researched with the help of Jamaicans in Kingston and New York, this traces the development of Jamaican posses from political lackeys to drug-trafficking gangsters.

★ **Polly Pattullo** *Last Resorts – The Cost of Tourism in the Caribbean*. Important, well-researched critique of the tourist industry and its impact on the Caribbean islands.

M.G. Smith, Roy Augier & Rex Nettleford *Report on the Rastafari Movement*. Published in 1960, this was the first academic study of Jamaica's home-grown religion. A dated but accurate description of the contemporary make-up, history, beliefs and rituals of Rastafari.

★ **Ian Thompson** *The Dead Yard*. An absorbing exploration of contemporary Jamaica that paints a depressingly accurate portrait of the realities of Jamaican life at home and in the diaspora. Though the headline-friendly title is an indication of authorial melodrama, this is nonetheless an exemplary commentary on Jamaica's history and current affairs, and makes essential reading.

MUSIC AND ART

★ **Steve Barrow & Peter Dalton** *The Rough Guide to Reggae*. Out of print but still available, this is the definitive handbook on reggae music, with sections on the UK, US and African scenes as well as a comprehensive rundown on things in Jamaica.

Cedella Booker *Bob Marley*. Very personal account of Marley's life and death written by his mother, light on the music but heavy on family anecdotes, plus the occasional (and most entertaining) catty swipe.

★ **Adrian Boot & Chris Salewicz** *Bob Marley – Songs of Freedom*. Boot's fabulous photos and Salewicz's spot-on text make this one of the better Marley bios, with lots of input from the family and first-hand interviews.

★ **David Boxer & Veerle Poupeye** *Modern Jamaican Art*. Lavish tome with text from Jamaica's premier art historians, and high-quality plates of the best and most familiar works.

★ **Jeremy Collingwood** *Bob Marley – His Musical Legacy*. Coffee-table heavyweight, lavishly illustrated with little-seen photographs as well as shots of contemporary magazine covers, record labels, concert flyers and newspaper clippings, all of which set the tone for the informed and sensitive text on Marley's career from downtown Kingston to inter-national stardom. Detailed discography, too.

Lee Jaffe *One Love – Life with Bob Marley and the Wailers*. An American photographer who hung out with Bob et al. in the 1970s, Jaffe tells his story via interviews with Roger Steffens. The text is interspersed with Jaffe's wonderful photographs (some previously unpublished), which perfectly document the era.

David Katz *Solid Foundation* and *People Funny Boy. Solid Foundation* is a history of Jamaican music from mento to the dawn of dancehall, as told by the musicians themselves. The two hundred-plus interviews include producers (Coxsone Dodd, Prince Buster, Junjo Lawes), musicians (Sly and Robbie) and essential artists, from the Skatalites and Toots and the Maytals to Burning Spear, U-Roy and Frankie Paul. Katz's *People Funny Boy* is the definitive biography of the eccentric genius Lee "Scratch" Perry.

★ **Beth Lesser** *King Jammy's* and *Dancehall*. The former is a brilliant bio of the Waterhouse dancehall maestro, which provides the definitive lowdown on the man himself as well as a host of artists from Wayne Smith to Bounty Killer. *Dancehall* gives a wider overview of the scene in Jamaica from the 1980s onwards.

★ **Chris Morrow** *Stir It Up*. LP-sized tribute to Jamaican record-cover artwork, with all the best efforts in full colour.

Norman C. Stolzoff *Wake The Town and Tell The People*. Though written from the somewhat academic and anthropological perspective of a non-Jamaican, this provides some solid background to the sound-system scene, from the genre's early days to a blow-by-blow account of a Killamanjaro dance.

Petrine Archer Straw & Kim Robinson *Jamaican Art*. Comprehensive account of the development of modern Jamaican art, well illustrated with the work of all of the major painters and sculptors, from Edna Marley to Kapo.

Don Taylor *Marley and Me*. Taylor was Bob Marley's one-time manager, and his chatty if rather badly written account – focusing on girlfriends, politics and controversy – is more sensationalist than White's (see below).

Timothy White *Catch a Fire*. Exhaustive and loving biography of Bob Marley (including a detailed discography), with an in-depth look at the early Jamaican music scene; plenty of obeah, superstition and supposition on the thoughts and feelings of the great man and those who surrounded him.

FLORA AND FAUNA

C. Dennis Adams *Flowering Plants of Jamaica*. Useful introductory guide to Jamaican flora.

James Bond *Field Guide to Birds of the West Indies*. The classic bird book, from which Ian Fleming took the name of his fictional hero, though generally considered to have been supplanted by the Downer/Sutton book.

Audrey Downer & Robert Sutton *Birds of Jamaica: A Photographic Field Guide*. The definitive field guide on the island's birds, with handy sections on the island's principal habitats and birding "hot spots".

★ **Alan Fincham** *Jamaica Underground*. The ultimate guide to caving in Jamaica, with reams of background info and some three hundred plans of the island's caverns, sinkholes and underground rivers.

Eugene Kaplan *A Field Guide to the Coral Reefs of the Caribbean and Florida*. Attractive guide to the region's reefs.

G.W. Lennox & S.A. Seddon *Flowers of the Caribbean; Trees of the Caribbean; Fruits and Vegetables of the Caribbean*. Handy pocketsize books, with glossy, sharp, colour pictures, and a good general introduction to the region's flora.

FOOD AND DRINK

Norma Benghiat *Traditional Jamaican Cooking*. Handy and engagingly written guide to the island's traditional dishes, from ackee and saltfish to curry goat and rice and peas, with all of the classic recipes and a lot more. *The Food of Jamaica*, by Benghiat and John Demers, is another reliable option.

Mike Henry *Caribbean Cocktails and Mixed Drinks*. All of the classic recipes, based mostly on rums and fresh juices.

★ **Caroline Sullivan** *Classic Jamaican Cooking*. The Jamaican version of Mrs Beeton, little changed since its first publication in 1896. Excellent recipes, anecdotes and the essential "Herbal Remedies and Household Hints".

Helen Willinsky *Jerk – Barbecue from Jamaica*. Do-it-yourself jerk manual.

Language

Tune into the talk-show-dominated radio and you'll soon see that Jamaicans enjoy nothing better than a good debate, taking great delight in outwitting each other in verbal battles. Although the official language is English, patois is the working mode of expression.

An incredibly creative and constantly evolving idiom, patois develops with new words regularly coined to suit every development; many fall into common use with astonishing speed.

- There is no gender distinction between "he" and "she", with women commonly referred to as "him": "Wha! Shelley pregnant! Him never tell me!"
- "H" is often not voiced, but makes up for the discrepancy by adding itself to plenty of other words. Hence "So yu is 'Enry from Hin-glan, don't?" ("don't" is used to mean "aren't you", or "isn't it?").
- There are plenty more random additions and absences: "shrimp" is often "swimp", "spliff" is "scliff", "vex" is "bex", "little" is "likkle", "ask" is "aks".
- Plurals are either ignored or conveyed by adding "dem"; hence "two feet" becomes "two foot", and "the girls are cooking for me" is "de gyal dem a cook fi mi". In contrast, "you" is divided into singular and plural forms: "yu" and "unu" (sometimes "oonoo") respectively.
- Possession, such as "my car" or "their house" becomes "a fi mi car" and "a fi dem house".
- If somebody calls you "fatty", "whitey" or "big batty gyal", they are (usually) simply being direct rather than attempting to insult. Follow Jamaicans in their directness and convey your meaning as simply as possible. Don't waste time with unnecessary pleasantries – "please" and "thank you" will suffice (though don't pass someone on a country road without wishing them good morning/afternoon/evening).

Rasta linguistics

The Rasta challenge to all things Babylonian includes an assault upon all that "downpresses" the black man via language. As a means of resistance, Rastas have reclassified words as a way of correcting perceived racial bias and turning negatives to positives; hence greeting someone with "hello" might illicit the cool response "We're not in hell and I'm not low". Rasta linguistics is one of the most creative elements of Jamaican patois, breaking down words, analysing syllabic connotations and reading significance into every nuance; hence understand becomes **overstand** (because if you comprehend something, you're above it rather than beneath it), oppress (up-press) becomes **downpress**. The most recognizable aspect of Rasta linguistics is the use of "I" to emphasize unity (Inity) and positivity as well as to protest against the coercive control of language. Hence all right becomes **I-rie**, create becomes **I-rate**, continually becomes **I-tinually**, creation is **I-ration**. Selassie I is interpreted as proof of Haile Selassie's omnipresence: **Selasee eye**. It isn't difficult to see why there are so many cryptic messages embedded in 1970s roots-reggae lyrics.

PATOIS GLOSSARY

The common words and phrases below have been written semi-phonetically, a sometimes clumsy medium but the only way in which to convey their sound in the available space.

Ago Verb meaning will or going to do something: "Me ago check yuh tomorrow".

Almshouse Militant or negative behaviour, a favourite attitude during sound-system clashes.

Babylon Government or the established and oppressive social system; also an insulting title for police.

Baby mother/father A person with children.

Badmind Jealous, covetous, bad intentions.

Bakra White man, traditionally a slave owner, probably derived from the Ibo "mbaraka".

Bandulu Trickery or a swindle.

Bashment A big party or dance.

Batty Backside/bottom.

Batty riders Lycra shorts or hot-pants, as modelled by Dancehall Queens.

Bhuttu Unsophisticated, simple country bumpkin; used as an insult. Also used these days for any uncouth, rude person.

Big up Boost yourself up (verb), a compliment. "Big up yourself on your shoes".

Blood Principally a swear word used with claat and hole. Can also be used as a respectful greeting signifying unity, as in "Wh'appen, blood?"

Blouse and skirt An exclamation of surprise.

Bly An opportunity, or second chance: "De rain gimme a bly – me nah haffe go a wuk".

Boderation Annoyance, irritation.

Bombo Offensive expletive meaning backside, usually used in conjunction with claat or hole: "Move yu bombo-claat face from me".

Bow Verb meaning to indulge in oral sex; "**bow cat**" is a participant.

Brawta A little extra to make a better bargain, usually employed when bartering in a market: "Gimme me brawta, nuh?"

Breed To get pregnant, or be pregnant: "Mi wan' breed dat gal before year-end".

Broughtupsy Good manners as a result of a careful upbringing; often used to reprimand someone: "Dat child have good broughtupsy!"

Bruddah Friend, Brother usually male: "Yes mi bruddah!" **Bredren** is the plural form, used both as a noun and as an adjective; **breds** is the shortened version.

Bruk Broken or out of money.

Brukout To let loose, usually at a party. Can also be more of a negative, such as to go wild or get in a fight.

Buck To meet somebody: "Me will buck up wid yu later".

Bumper Large backside/bottom.

Bun or **burn** Literally, burn. Used in terms of smoking: "Me bun de ganja long time"; as a condemnation: "Bun out de politician dem"; and to connote infidelity: "She give him bun with a nex man".

Cha Exclamation, usually of surprise or distaste: "Cha! Me nah wan no man inna me life".

Chalice Pipe for smoking ganja, usually communally.

Charged Intoxicated, stoned: "Me get charged las' night".

Check Pay a visit: "Me ago check yu tomorrow". Also a term of platonic or sexual appreciation, as in "Me check fe di man's argument", and as a term for sexual advances: "De young bway try check big woman".

Claat/clot Literally, cloth, used with Raas and bumba as an expletive: "Tek yuh blood-claat hands off me!"

Cook an' curry Everything's been taken care of, as in "Me clean de whole house; everyting cook an' curry now".

Copasetic Cool, good: "Everyting copasetic".

Cork Full, as in "the dance cork tonight".

Cotch Rest up, chill out: "Sit dung and cotch with me". Also a verb to mean where a person sleeps: "Me a cotch by Evelyn's". Also used to denote bracing something: "Cotch de wheel wid' a rock".

Craven Greedy, desperate.

Criss Attractive, beautiful: "Maxine a criss, criss gyal", or "Your clothes is criss."

Criss-biscuit Anything of excellence.

Cuss-cuss Argument.

Cut-eye A malevolent look: "Pure cut-eye me get from him".

Daggering Aggressive, athletic dancing, usually of a sexual nature.

Dally To go: "Me mus dally now".

Dawta Young woman, interchangeable with **sistah**.

Dead-stock Quiet, a non-event: "Dem promote pure dead-stock dance".

Dealing Dating, being in a relationship.

Dege-dege Small, measly: "She gimme one dege-dege piece of yam".

Deh-pan Doing it, in control of matters: "Me deh-pan the repairs, man". **Deh-bout** is to be somewhere: "Him deh-bout somewhere inside".

Diss Disrespect: "Him a diss de programme" ("He's rudely disrupting our plans").

Don Literally a ghetto "area leader", but also used to describe any respected male: "Him a de don".

Draw card To trick or deceive; pull something sneaky.

Dread A person with locks (not necessarily of Rastafarian faith), or an adjective used to describe a bad situation: "De times dread".

Duh-duh Be somewhere: "Me duh-duh" ("I am here").

Dun know Used to express total agreement (as in "I/ you/we already knew it").

Duns/Dunsa Money.

Dutch pot Heavy cooking pot.

Dutty Dirty, nasty or sleazy.

Dweet Do it: "Me dweet sweet, sis".

Ends A place, usually somewhere to chill out: "Mi deh pon a ends, still" ("I'm here relaxing").

Facety Impertinent, rude: "De touris' facety to rass".

Favour Resemble.

Feel no way Don't worry about it.

Flex A person's way of behaving: "Ah so me flex, my yout" ("That's how I operate, young man").

Flop Losing face, usually in public and often associated with the performance of an artist or sound system.

Fren/Friend Apart from the usual meaning, can be used (rather confusingly) to refer to one's sexual partner.

Frenemy False friend.

Fuckery Irritating, bothersome, out of order: "Dis man is pure fuckery" ("This man is badly behaved").

Galang Expression meaning "Go away".

Gallis Man who has a way with the ladies.

Ganja Marijuana.

Gate Home: "Check me at me gates".

Gravalicious Greedy or avaricious.

Grind To have sex. A **grindsman** is a man particularly skilled between the sheets.

Guidance An inspirational goodbye meaning "Let God be with you".

Gwan Go on or carry on (verb). Also used to mean "go away" or "going to".

Gweh Go away.

Gyal Girl or woman.

Heartical Conscious, esteemed person: "He's my heartical bredren" (pronounced "artical").

Herb Ganja, herbal marijuana.

Higgler Female market-trader, or a woman who brings goods to Jamaica from abroad to sell.

High grade Premium-quality ganja.

Hol' it down Be cool and restrained, to be on a low profile or stay quiet.

Hottie-hottie An attractive female.

I an' I Rasta-speak meaning me, I, we, mine, myself. **I-man** equally applies.

Idren Friends or **bredren**.

Irie Adjective meaning fine or good: "You lookin' Irie tonight". Also used as a greeting.

Ital Anything natural (an Ital car wash is a river) or pure (a spliff without tobacco). Also describes Rastafarian meatless food cooked without salt.

Iyah Greeting to a friend: "What a gwan Iyah".

Jacket Child raised by a man who isn't his father (the father usually doesn't know).

Jamdung/Jamdown Jamaica. **JA** and **Jamrock** are also frequently used.

Jinnal Con man/woman or trickster.

Joe Grind Term for a man sleeping with someone else's partner.

Jook Stab or pierce: "De rass fish hook jook me".

Juggling Sound-system tactic of playing several tracks on the same rhythm, mixing them smoothly via two decks. Also just playing records in a dance.

Kiss me neck! An expression of surprise: "Kiss me neck! Price of rice gone down!"

Labrish Gossip, small talk. **Labba-labba** is to talk too much.

Let off Give something: "She nah let off she tings".

Lick To strike a blow: "(H)im a lick down the pear tree". Also to smoke: "Me a lick de chalice Iyah". Also an adjective meaning hot: "Beenie Man a de lick!" ("Beenie Man is the best").

Lick shot Literally or figuratively firing a gun to demonstrate appreciation in the dancehall.

Licky-licky Taking more than you have the capacity to take.

Likkle more See you later.

Live blanket Human body: "Darlin', you need a live blanket?" ("Would you like to have sex with me?")

Lock off Cease, desist; also keep a low profile.

Maaga Thin, skinny.

Mampy Big-boned woman, not necessarily derogatory.

More time Another way of saying "See you soon".

Mule A person that smuggles drugs internally.

Murderation Violence: "De fight was pure murderation!"

Natty Used as an adjective or adverb to describe dread-locks, also a greeting to a Rasta. "Wh'appen, Natty?"

Navel string Umbilical chord/placenta; it's traditional for a new baby's navel string to be planted under a sapling.

Nuff A person who likes to be "seen plenty".

Nyam To eat, from the Hausa word "nyamnyam".

Obeah Jamaican witchcraft.

One love Greeting or farewell salutation. "**Love**" is used in the same way: "Love Iyah".

Ongle Only.

Pappy show Something utterly ridiculous and foolish.

Passa passa A disturbance, hullaballoo or scene, often caused by gossip. Adopted as the name of Jamaica's most popular street-jam.

Par Hang out with.

Pardner Savings club, where each member makes a weekly contribution, and in turn gets a whole week's collection.

Pikney Child.

Pirogue Fishing canoe.

Pon On or upon.

Prentice Apprentice or protégé, usually young man; also shortened to prenta.

Quail-up Fade, shrink, cower.

Queen Respectful title for a woman, usually a Rastaman's partner.

Raas Loosely translated as backside ("Mi fall dung pon me raas"), and an expletive when used with claat or hole: "That man is one nasty raashole". Can also express surprise or emphasize a point: "Wha de raas claat man a deal wid?"

Raggamuffin Respected and wily ghetto sufferah, often used in a musical context. Also used to refer to "street" style.

Rahtid Mild expletive or an expression of surprise.

Ramp Usually used in the phrase "ramp wid", meaning to interfere with or irritate.

Ras Rasta (abbreviation), often a respectful greeting: "Wha'ppen, Ras?"

Rastitute See **Rent-a-Dread**, below, and box, p.199.

Reason Discuss and debate a subject.

Red Used to refer to a lighter-skinned person: "See de red man deh". Red also describes someone who has been smoking ganja.

Red-eye Greedy, envious.

Rent-a-Dread A man with locks making a living out of sexual relationships with tourists.

Respect Perhaps the most commonly used greeting or farewell in Jamaica.

Roughneck Ragamuffin rascal.

Rucktion Commotion, dispute.

Rude bway Bad boy.

Runnings Happenings, things that are going on: "Bway, runnings hard dis year" ("Things are tough this year").

Rush Assail: "Watch dem rush de gates" ("Look at them forcing their way in").

Salt Used as a verb to describe something unlucky or gone wrong; as in "Windies gwine lose the series – we salt fe true".

Science Obeah.

Screw Be annoyed, and look like you are. A **screw face** is a miserable character.

Seen Understand or comprehend what someone is saying. Usually used as a reply to a statement, as in "Uh-huh".

Sensimillia High-grade ganja; also shortened to **sensi**.

Session Sound-system jam: "Stone Love session gwine be wicked!"

Shock-out Looking good: "Me ago shock-out tonight ina mi criss new suit".

Shotta Rude boy, with all the appropriate notoriety that such status demands.

Sick Slang term meaning good: "Mavado new tune is sick!"

Siddung Sit down, often used by DJs to describe their lyrical flow: "Me siddung pon de riddim".

Sinting Something.

Sistren Woman/women generally, or close female friend.

Skank Rip off, con: "Me get skank at the mechanic today". Also an old-time dance.

Sketel Promiscuous, provocatively dressed woman.

Skin-teet Smile.

Skull Play truant from class or take a sickie from work.

Slackness Improper, lowdown, dirty, base behaviour; also used to describe rude dancehall lyrics.

Slam The sexual act.

Smalls Small change: "Beg you a smalls, boss?"

Spar Friend.

Spliff Marijuana joint.

Star Used as a salutation or qualifier in greetings: "Wh'appen, star".

Stoosh Snooty, condescending from a position of assumed superiority. Also means something of quality.

Sufferah Poor but righteous ghetto-dweller.

Sweetboy Attractive, well-dressed young man, perhaps financially supported by his lover.

Talawah Small but strong, applied to Jamaica itself in the motto: "She little but she talawah".

Tan Stay or stand: "Tan so back" ("Hold back").

Tek set To follow someone around or annoy them: "De youts tek set pon me all day, me never get no break".

Ting Object or partner: "A my ting dat" ("That's my girlfriend"). Also the Jamaican pronunciation of "things": "Tings a gwan rough sah".

Trace To curse somebody or quarrel.

Version A cut of a popular rhythm-track.

Vex(t) Irritated or annoyed.

What a gwan "What's going on?"

Wine/Wind Dance closely and suggestively, as per Tony Matterhorn's hit *Dutty Wine*.

Windies West Indies cricket team

Wuk Regular work, or sex.

Wutless Combination of worthless and witless: "Pure wutless bway me meet at the show" ("I met some awful men at the show").

X-amount Huge, incalculable amount: "Me have x-amount of loving".

Yahso Here: "Park yuh car yahso".

Yard Home; also used as an alternative name for Jamaica: "No where no better dan Yard".

Yush An alternative for "hello".

Small print and index

A ROUGH GUIDE TO ROUGH GUIDES

Published in 1982, the first Rough Guide – to Greece – was a student scheme that became a publishing phenomenon. Mark Ellingham, a recent graduate in English from Bristol University, had been travelling in Greece the previous summer and couldn't find the right guidebook. With a small group of friends he wrote his own guide, combining a contemporary, journalistic style with a thoroughly practical approach to travellers' needs.

The immediate success of the book spawned a series that rapidly covered dozens of destinations. And, in addition to impecunious backpackers, Rough Guides soon acquired a much broader readership that relished the guides' wit and inquisitiveness as much as their enthusiastic, critical approach and value-for-money ethos. These days, Rough Guides include recommendations from budget to luxury and cover more than 120 destinations around the globe, from Amsterdam to Zanzibar, all regularly updated by our team of roaming writers.

Browse all our latest guides, read inspirational features and book your trip at **roughguides.com**.

Rough Guide credits

Editor: Rachel Mills
Commissioning Editor: Edward Aves
Cartography: Carte, Katie Bennett
Managing editor: Rachel Lawrence

Picture editor: Aude Vauconsant
Cover photo research: Roger Mapp
Senior DTP coordinator: Dan May
Head of DTP and Pre-Press: Rebeka Davies

Publishing information

This seventh edition published in 2018 by
Rough Guides Ltd

Distribution
UK, Ireland and Europe
Apa Publications (UK) Ltd; sales@roughguides.com
United States and Canada
Ingram Publisher Services; ips@ingramcontent.com
Australia and New Zealand
Woodslane; info@woodslane.com.au
Southeast Asia
Apa Publications (SN) Pte; sales@roughguides.com
Worldwide
Apa Publications (UK) Ltd; sales@roughguides.com
Special Sales, Content Licensing and CoPublishing
Rough Guides can be purchased in bulk quantities
at discounted prices. We can create special editions,
personalised jackets and corporate imprints tailored to
your needs. sales@roughguides.com.

roughguides.com
Printed in China by CTPS
All rights reserved
© Rough Guides, 2018
Maps © Apa Digital AG and Rough Guides Ltd
All rights reserved. No part of this publication may be
reproduced, stored in or introduced into a retrieval system,
or transmitted in any form, or by any means (electronic,
mechanical, photocopying, recording or otherwise) without
the prior written permission of the copyright owner.
A catalogue record for this book is available from the
British Library
The publishers and authors have done their best to
ensure the accuracy and currency of all the information in
The Rough Guide to Jamaica; however, they can accept
no responsibility for any loss, injury, or inconvenience
sustained by any traveller as a result of information or
advice contained in the guide.

Help us update

We've gone to a lot of effort to ensure that the seventh
edition of **The Rough Guide to Jamaica** is accurate
and up-to-date. However, things change – places get
"discovered", opening hours are notoriously fickle,
restaurants and rooms raise prices or lower standards. If
you feel we've got it wrong or left something out, we'd like
to know, and if you can remember the address, the price,
the hours, the phone number, so much the better.

Please send your comments with the subject line
"**Rough Guide Jamaica update**" to mail@uk.roughguides.
com. We'll credit all contributions and send a copy of the
next edition (or any other Rough Guide if you prefer) for
the very best emails.

Reader's updates

Thanks to all the readers who have taken the time to write in with comments and suggestions (and apologies if we've
inadvertently omitted or misspelt anyone's name):

Davor Brkan; Catherine Fawdry; Paul Rhodes; Zach Wagner; and Jackie and Robert at the *Prince Valley Guest House*.

Acknowledgements

Lebawit Lily Girma: My sincere thanks go to Diana
McIntyre-Pike, Keith Wedderburn, Christine Marrett,
Rebecca Wiersma, Winnie Hylton, Omar Lawson, Diana
O'Gilvie, Jacqui Sinclair and My Jamaica Travels.
Sarah Hull: First and foremost, thanks to everyone who
opened their home to me at *The Lion House*, including
Layla, Jaheim, Oli and Kemo. Elizabeth Bentley spent
hours combing through and correcting text, cooked
life-sustaining breakfasts, and time and again, offered
encouragement, sage advice and a smart editorial ear.
I cannot thank you enough. To Mahlon Bentley, I owe
hours of road research, patois decoding, hot meals, *toto*
and sugarcane demos. STEA, led by the generous and

brilliant Hugh Dixon, was a lifesaver. I would like to thank
everyone in Albert Town: Ainsworth Smith and Wayne
Pingue (my Vegas co-conspirators), Violet Donaldson
(Miss Vonnie) and Patsy Stobbs. Leah Schwartz, Chris
Esposito and Becky Hill were Portland gamechangers.
Fabian Cumberbatch saved me many times over in
Montego Bay. It was such a gift having Lily Girma as a
co-writer, and Rachel Mills was an editing powerhouse.
Many thanks to my brother, for forwarding me money in
a moment of math lunacy, and to the sweethearts back
home: Sabrina Canfield, Amanda Hurn and Rachel Hass.
And of course, a huge heartfelt thank you to Brian Coore:
jumpnowthinklater.

ABOUT THE AUTHORS

Lebawit Lily Girma is an award-winning travel writer, photographer and author specializing in the Caribbean region. A former attorney who ditched her Washington DC office for the road, she has resided in multiple countries, including Jamaica, Belize and the Dominican Republic, and explored the Caribbean for the past 13 years. Her work has appeared in numerous publications, including *CNN*, *Sunday Times Travel*, and *Afar*, and in guidebooks on Belize and the Dominican Republic.

Sarah Hull has been a contributor to Rough Guides since 2005, writing about New England, Miami, Canada, Mexico, New York City and the American South. She fell hard for Jamaica in 2017, when she had the good fortune to trade a cold front in Manhattan for the coconut-filled hills of Ocho Rios. When she's not on the road, she's in New York Supreme Court reporting on corporate shenanigans and celebrity lawsuits.

Index

Main references are in **bold** type

Map symbols

The symbols below are used on maps throughout the book.

┄┄ ┄ Parish boundary	✗ Aerodrome	⊥ Gardens
┄ ┄ ┄ Chapter division boundary	★ Transport stop	Reef
Highway	P Parking	▲ Mountain peak
Road	Petrol station	Mountain range
Pedestrian road	Site of interest	Waterfall
┄ ┄ ┄ Path	(i) Tourist office	Cave
River	Post office	Ruin
Ferry	Hospital	Lighthouse
Wall	Golf course	Bird sanctuary
✈ International airport	⊙ Memorial/statue	Farm

Stadium

Building

Church

Cemetery

Park

Marsh/wetland

Beach

Listings key

■ Accommodation
● Eating
■ Drinking/Nightlife
● Shopping